Annie Hutton, G. B. Rinuccini

The Embassy in Ireland of Monsignor G.B. Rinuccini, Archbishop of Fermo, in the years 1645-1649

Annie Hutton, G. B. Rinuccini

The Embassy in Ireland of Monsignor G.B. Rinuccini, Archbishop of Fermo, in the years 1645-1649

ISBN/EAN: 9783743336377

Manufactured in Europe, USA, Canada, Australia, Japa

Cover: Foto ©ninafisch / pixelio.de

Manufactured and distributed by brebook publishing software (www.brebook.com)

Annie Hutton, G. B. Rinuccini

The Embassy in Ireland of Monsignor G.B. Rinuccini, Archbishop of Fermo, in the years 1645-1649

THE EMBASSY IN IRELAND

OF

MONSIGNOR G. B. RINUCCINI,

ARCHBISHOP OF FERMO,

IN THE YEARS 1645-1649.

PUBLISHED FROM THE ORIGINAL MSS. IN THE RINUCCINI LIBRARY,
BY G. AIAZZA, LIBRARIAN.

TRANSLATED FOR THE FIRST TIME INTO ENGLISH,

BY

ANNIE HUTTON.

DUBLIN:
ALEXANDER THOM, PRINTER AND PUBLISHER,
87 & 88, ABBEY-STREET.

1873.

NOTE BY THE EDITOR.

THE translation of this work was commenced many years since at the suggestion of one, who to many distinctions added that of a passionate interest in the history of Ireland. It was carried on during a long illness, and when the MS. at the request of some friends was examined last year, it was found that a large portion had never been revised—that the pen had stopped suddenly some pages before the conclusion. To supply this deficiency and revise the rest has been the duty of the Editor. The first object throughout has been a faithful, not slavish adherence to the text. Except in the case of proper names there has been no attempt to correct errors, or remove inconsistencies—no letter, no sentence it is believed has been omitted—and but few of the redundancies and superlatives in which the Nuncio is prone to indulge have been dispensed with.

The Collection of the Carte Papers published under the direction of Lord Romilly, refer to the same period as the present work, and each may be found to throw light upon the other.*

---

* See final Report by the Rev. Dr. Russell and J. P. Prendergast, Esq., Commissioners for selecting Papers from the Great Carte and Ormonde Collection of State Papers relating to Ireland, in the Bodleian Library, Oxford. Published for the Record Office, February 20th, 1871. Vol I.

CONTENTS.

	PAGE
To the Courteous Reader,	i
Biographical Notice of Monsignor Rinuccini,	v
Letter from Pope Innocent X.,	xiii
Instructions for Monsignor Rinuccini,	xxvii
Secret Instructions,	li
Memoranda for Monsignor Rinuccini,	lvii
Letters written during the Embassy,	1
Report on the Affairs of Ireland,	485
Illustrative Documents,	553

TO THE COURTEOUS READER.

It is a question which still admits of doubt, whether the conflict that for two centuries past has agitated the kingdoms of England and Ireland, is the result of continued provocations on the part of the conqueror, or an effort of self-defence forced upon the conquered. In either case the struggle has entailed misery on *both* countries. Certain it is, however, that in the year 1641, Ireland, weary of her slavish subjection to England (like a wild beast which, having broken the chain which maddens him, rushes to the destruction of the neighbouring flocks), rose suddenly upon the oppressor, and with such fury, that not one town, not one district in the Island escaped its doom—all, without distinction, were bathed in the blood of the English. Then came the avenger. The blood of her children called to England for revenge, even for the utter extermination of the Irish Catholics, who, surrounded in their turn by the legions of their exasperated enemies, paid dearly for their impatience of the detested yoke. Soon they were reduced to a condition more desperate, if possible, than that which had caused the outbreak.* Then it was that these unhappy

---

* Amongst the works which may be consulted with advantage on this subject are the following :—MacGeoghan's "History," Musgrave's "Irish Rebellions," Haumer's "Chronicle," Hardiman's "History of Galway," "Ancient Irish Histories," Leland's "History," Gordon's "History of Ireland," Davies' "Discovery of the Causes why Ireland was never Conquered," Tone's "Memoirs," Lewis' "Irish Disturbances," Hume's "History of England," Lingard's "History of England," lib. x., xi., Moore's "History of Ireland," Hallam's "Constitutional History of England," Thierry "Histoire de la Conquête de l'Angleterre par les Normands," Parnell's "Collection of Penal Laws in Ireland," De Beaumont's "l'Irlande," &c., &c.

islanders, appalled at the prospect of a general massacre, or the harsh alternative offered to them to renounce the religion of their fathers, sought the aid of the Sovereign Pontiff, and entreated him to grant them, at this fearful crisis, succour, both temporal and spiritual. Innocent X., who had been seated on the Pontificial throne for more than a year, lent a paternal ear to their entreaties, and quickly despatched to Ireland, as nuncio extraordinary, Monsignor Rinuccini, Archbishop of Fermo, invested with the highest ecclesiastical powers and privileges, and entrusted to him a large sum of money to facilitate the arrangement of affairs.

The work which is now presented for the first time to the public, contains the letters written by Monsignor Rinuccini to the Court of Rome, and to different distinguished persons during the period of his embassy, from April 7th, 1645, to July 21st, 1649. To these letters is added the report, addressed to the Pontiff, in which he detailed the various steps he had taken to strengthen the Catholic religion in Ireland. It is evident from this correspondence, that if discord and mean jealousy had not existed between the leaders of the Catholics (more zealous for their own selfish aims and personal interests than for the holy cause they were bound to defend), and had the wise counsels of the nuncio been allowed to prevail, Ireland would assuredly have triumphed over her enemies, and possibly Charles I. would not have perished by the axe of the executioner. But it is a long established fact, the common fruit of civil broils, that nations never profit by the salutary lessons to be learnt from their mistakes; and while base passions predominate the counsel of Cassandra herself is despised. Laying aside, however, till a more fitting time, the calculation of political probabilities, it is necessary to acquaint the reader that this correspondence was transcribed near the close of the year 1670, from the original documents, under the supervision of

Cavaliere Tommaso, the brother of Monsignor Rinuccini, in order to be published with the "History of the War from 1641 to 1649."* This good intention, however, was never fulfilled; and, therefore, as the struggle still continues, although with greater moderation, I think it advisable that the first steps of a movement so variously judged should now be published, and light be thrown upon points which are still doubtful. I have thought it convenient to add some letters which were addressed to Rinuccini by the Sacred Congregation, containing his instructions, together with other illustrative documents of great interest. It will probably not be displeasing to the reader to see prefixed to the work a biographical notice of the author, the Papal Bull by which the nuncio was appointed to his arduous office, and the instructions given to guide him in his truly apostolic mission. Further, I must premise that I have intentionally, and not through ignorance or carelessness, admitted into this work many foreign names of cities and persons altered from the original and true manner of writing them, but not so different as to cause any difficulty in recog-

* Among the MSS. in the Rinuccini library this work exists, with the title, " De hæresis Anglicanæ in Hiberniam intrusione et progressu et de bello Catholico ad annum 1641, capto, exindeque per aliquot annos, gesto commentarius." It is in six vols. folio, with pages numbered from 1 to 2,666. Of this History, a copy exists in the library of the Earl of Leicester, at Holkham, in England—see the " Transactions of the Royal Society of Literature," vol. ii., p. ii., page 358, London, 1834, where it is incorrectly attributed to Monsignor Rinuccini. The writer, in fact, towards the end acknowledges that he had compiled it at Florence from authentic documents collected by the nuncio with the intention of writing the history himself, had not death intervened in the year 1653. Some persons believe this commentary, written in good Latin, to be the work of Thomas Coke, the learned editor of Dempster's " Etruria Regale." I cannot prove or disprove this opinion, but this I know, that the Rinuccini MS. is the original autograph; and, from the preface written by Arch. M. Salvini, it is evident that the nuncio intended it for publication. The character of the handwriting of the commentary is assuredly not Italian, and suggests the probability of its being the work of some learned Irish monk.

nising them.* I have done this from my desire to adhere to the text. All students are aware that in the writings of the best men of that day it is rare not to find mistakes in foreign names, which an Italian would naturally desire to soften. Anxious in every way to avoid the imputation of carelessness, and perhaps of ingratitude, I hasten to acknowledge publicly the obligations I am under for the use of historical records to the Noble Marchese Gino Capponi, who proposed the undertaking to me, and I gratefully recall to mind the kindness and politeness of my patron, the Marchese P. Rinuccini, who gave me permission to undertake it, and assistance in carrying it into effect.

GIUSEPPE AIAZZI.

---

* In the present translation these errors have, as far as possible, been corrected. From the original a few specimens may suffice—Lochel for Youghal; Musgri, Muskerry; Trasforth, Stafford; Cestro, Chester; Neutrevil, Netterville, &c., &c.

A SHORT BIOGRAPHICAL NOTICE

OF

RINUCCINI.

GIOVAN BATISTA RINUCCINI was born on September 15th, 1592. His parents were the Senator Cammillo, a Florentine patrician, and Virginia, daughter to Pier Antonio Bandini, and sister to Cardinal Ottavio. If splendor of birth, a brilliant intellect cultivated by great study, and a pure life devoted to public usefulness, suffice to gain esteem and veneration, Rinuccini deserved them in the highest degree. Born in Rome, where his father resided; from his earliest childhood he devoted himself with ardour to his studies, under the superintendence of able preceptors, and on the return of his family to their native city, his zeal in the pursuit of knowledge did not abate, although he was thrown entirely on his own resources. Having expressed to his father his decided wish to take orders, he returned to Rome by the advice of his maternal uncle, the Cardinal, and in the Propaganda (the College of the Jesuits) he commenced a regular course of study, by which he profited even beyond the expectation of his friends. In his eighteenth year he went to the university of Bologna, thence to that of Perugia, to study law; and we may judge of his progress from the public examinations held in the latter city, when his success and literary ardour were no less admired than commended. Pisa had in the mean time honoured him at the age of twenty-two with the doctor's degree, which he received with a laudatory speech from Cavaliere Piero Girolami; and at the same time the Accademia della Crusca elected him a member of one of its colleges. Summoned to Rome by his uncle the Cardinal to fill office for him, he hurried thither, but from his delicate constitution, weakened by immoderate study, he was reduced to so miserable a state of health, that he was soon obliged to abandon the capital and return to breathe the pure air on the banks of the Arno. After this failure in his health, his evil fortune so far prevailed that during his life-time he never recovered the strength or physical energy which make life dear, and sustain the mind in great undertakings. As soon as his strength was in some degree restored, finding the life of idleness which he led at home intolerable, he returned to Rome, and practised at the bar, under Monsignor Buratti, then a celebrated auditor of the Rota. It was at this time that, his fame reaching the ear of Gregory XV., he was named Chamberlain of Honour to the Pontiff, and shortly after Secretary to the Congregation of Ecclesiastical Rites.

On the death of Gregory, Urban VIII., who succeeded in the chair of St. Peter, also entertained a high opinion of Rinuccini, created him Civil Lieutenant of the Cardinal Vicar, and afterwards, on the death of Monsignor Dini, Archbishop of Fermo, the vacant See was bestowed on him in 1625. We may pass over in silence the joy and exultation with which he was greeted by the clergy and the whole diocese on his arrival, as well as his wise and truly charitable government, and the improvement which, more by example than precept, he introduced into ecclesiastical discipline and education; but we cannot so deal with the cordial affection which bound him to his beloved Spouse in Christ—an affection which he proved in the highest degree possible, when, by the death of Monsignor Cosimo de Bardi, the Metropolitan See of Florence falling vacant, the Pope himself in a splendid brief offered it to him, and Ferdinand II. in the most courteous and flattering manner invited him to accept it. But the good Archbishop yielded neither to the Pontifical counsel, to the invitation of the Grand Duke, nor to the persuasions of friends and colleagues, nor, in fine, to the innate love of country which has such a large hold on a good heart. He gave a gentle refusal to this new call, softened by his strong reasons and humble words, and determined to remain faithful to the first church which the Lord God had confided to his guardianship, and for which he maintained through life an unchanging love.*

---

* Letters of excuse from Rinuccini to the Pope, the Grand Duke, and the Grand Duchess:—

HOLY FATHER,—I have devoted my talents to the care of this church with so much affection that it has astonished me to hear from his Eminence Cardinal Barbarini that it has been supposed I should wish to change it for that of Florence. As I cannot sufficiently unfold the truth in a simple letter, I despatch to the feet of your Holiness my Vicar General, with the assurance of my constant and resolute resolve to give up my life in the arms of the Spouse to whom your Holiness has bound me. Your Holiness will honour me so far as to hear him, and be assured that besides the motives which bind bishops, and my unchangeable desire never to leave this diocese, I am strengthened in my determination by the truly paternal discourse your Holiness deigned to hold with me, and by those which I recollect to have heard at the conference held at this Archbishopric. I have already returned thanks to his Serene Highness for the honour he has done me, and I have given him the same reasons which I now communicate to the Vicar of God.

I humbly kiss your Holiness's sacred feet, and pray for a prosperity equal to the wants of the Holy Church.

To His Serene Highness the Grand Duke Ferdinand II.:—MOST NOBLE LORD,—When I consider the greatness of the honour conferred upon me by your Highness' invitation, I must acknowledge that the consciousness of my unworthiness is alone the cause of my refusal. The excuse that, from the time when the Lord God established me here, I have loved my diocese of Fermo with unvarying affection, would not, perhaps, be accepted by anyone who fully comprehended the great kindness of your Highness, who is my rightful Prince, and whose condescension is indeed unprecedented. But that of my failing health has the more weight, when it is remembered that my efforts in the diocese should be so great as to render me worthy of the affection with which your Highness honours me. It will be represented to you by my father and brother, with the reverence which they owe to your person, that I may perhaps have done something for the benefit of this church; and as the best years of my life have now passed away, I could not expect to effect as much in a city so

During twenty years this good pastor had carefully tended his flock, when in 1645 grave and sanguinary disturbances broke out in Ireland against the English on religious grounds. The inhabitants of that country im-

much larger, and, what is of more consequence, I could not equal your Highness's zeal. I shall certainly not fail, when the passes are open,[*] personally to express my gratitude to your Highness, so that the world may see how highly I estimate the honour done me, and that you, by the recognition of my unworthiness, may acknowledge the truth of my excuses.

In the meantime I salute your Highness, and pray for your never-ending prosperity.

To the Grand Duke:—SERENE HIGHNESS,—I have thought it advisable to send to Rome my Vicar General, that he may explain to His Holiness the reasons for my determination not to leave this church; and as I hope and expect that they will be approved by His Holiness, I may also surely hope for the same indulgence from your Serene Highness, as in the whole of this affair you have testified so great kindness to me as leaves me unable to compare it to any other happiness I could enjoy. This people, loved by me with no common love, know that I shall never abandon them, but feel deeply your Highness's compliment to me. Be well assured that they will pray for you as for me at this juncture, which I shall permit and encourage, as a recompense for the infinite kindness received from you.

I ever remain your Highness's humble servant.

To the Grand Duchess:—By nominating me to the vacant Archbishopric in your city, your Highness and the Grand Duke have performed so signal an act of beneficence, that it is evident to everyone your Highnesses have thought only of my advantage, without remembering that many men are to be found much more worthy of such an honour. And I know that the same affection which prompted you to favour me, will cause you to accept the excuses which my brother must before this have conveyed to you from me. I must add that, on account of the infinite obligation I am under to your Highnesses, I shall ever seek to make public manifestation of the homage I owe to your illustrious house, and which I hope you will not value the less on account of my voluntary exile from your dominions; as Sovereign Princes always judge it advisable to extend the exercise of their authority. All this I hope to explain to your Highness some day in person, and in the meantime I ever remain your Highness's humble servant.

---

[*] Florence was also at that time afflicted with a dreadful pestilence.

plored Innocent X. to send them, in his wisdom and paternal love, an Envoy Extraordinary to assist them with advice and help to strengthen them in the Catholic religion, and at the same time to plead for them with the irritated English, and if possible pacify these two nations, or at least obtain for this unhappy Ireland, that as they had only taken up arms in defence of their religion and through fidelity to the Holy See, they should be treated by a neighbouring kingdom with less rigour, and not with the harshness and cruelty of an enemy or a slave. Difficult was the duty, perilous and arduous the enterprise ; but the Pontiff, who saw all its gravity and importance, could think of no one so likely to fulfil its duties as Rinuccini,[*] who seeing a large field opened to him for the exercise of an Apostolic ministry, willingly accepted the office, and, forgetting his advanced age and failing health, immediately prepared for the long and dangerous journey. It is not possible to describe here the fatigues and prolonged exertions, the snares avoided, the privations endured, the bitter persecutions and calumnies with which he was assailed by the enemies of the Catholic faith. Enough it is that he, till now a peaceful labourer in the field of humane and ecclesiastical science, abhorring by nature and education all political intrigues, all revolutions, all the tumult and horrors of war, found himself through zeal for the cause of the Church of Christ, entangled in the civil dissensions of an exasperated people, in religious assemblies, in councils of war, in sieges, in the fury of battle, or wherever else he was called by the duty to which he had consecrated himself, exposing his life more than once to certain peril.[†] If, in the unequal contest, he did not obtain the complete success which the justice of the cause

[*] Luigi Omodei, Chierico di Camera, and afterwards Cardinal, was first chosen, but as a Spanish subject he was superseded, that no suspicion of partiality might be excited, and Rinuccini, a Tuscan subject and a neutral, was substituted.

[†] In proof of this *vide* the letters written during his embassy.

deserved, we must conclude that it pleased the wisdom of Providence to try the faith of this devoted people by yet fiercer trials, which are not even yet brought to a close.

Rinuccini arranged the spiritual affairs of the kingdom to the best of his ability, in the disordered state of the country; he overwhelmed with the thunders of the Vatican all who openly or secretly showed themselves averse to the measures necessary for the re-establishment of the Catholic faith; and then, followed by the regrets and blessings of all good Catholics, departed for France, whence, after a few days of rest, he pursued his way to Rome, to render an account to the Pontiff of his labour in the vineyard of the Lord. *

In the meantime Innocent X. had been informed, both by letters from the Nuncio himself, and also from the bishops and other persons of respectability in Ireland, of his negotia-

---

* See his Report. In the hall of the Archiepiscopal Palace Rinuccini had painted the principal events of his mission to Ireland. These pictures were still extant in the middle of the last century, when, on the nomination of Cardinal Paracciani to the See of Fermo, the latter, through envy or ignorance, had them destroyed.

To give an idea of the amount and importance of the aid sent to the Roman Catholic party in Ireland by the hands of the Nuncio Rinuccini, we give an extract from a document found amongst the papers of the Archbishop of Tuam, when shot by the Protestants. From this it appears that the Nuncio was preceded to Ireland by a vessel laden with 1,000 pairs of pistols, 4,000 cartouche belts, 2,000 sabres, 500 muskets, and 20,000 pounds of powder. Whilst in France he drew on the Holy See bills of exchange for the sum of . . . . . . 150,658 dollars.
Cardinal Antonio Barberini, the friend and protector
of Ireland, assisted him with . . . . 10,000 crowns.
Cardinal Mazarin with . . . . . . 25,000 dollars.

A part of this sum, according to the accounts furnished by Invernizi, was expended in the purchase of the following arms:—

For 2,000 muskets, ...	10,000 dollars.
For 2,000 cartouche belts, ...	1,000 ,,
For 4,000 sabres, ...	4,800 ,,
For 400 pair of pistols, with holsters, . . .	6,800 ,,
For 2,000 pikeheads, ...	3,000 ,,
For barrels, chests, casks, and cordage, to pack the arms,	400 ,,
For the purchase of two frigates, &c., by Invernizi, .	29,000 ,,

tions and continued struggle against the enemies of the Church, and received him with fraternal tenderness, expressed his full satisfaction, and highly commended his prudence, zeal, and Apostolic self-denial. The Pope would have wished to retain him near himself as Pontifical preacher, but Rinuccini respectfully refused the honour, alleging as an excuse his failing health which needed repose; but in reality he desired to return to his See, and to assist in person in the pastoral care of his chosen flock, who longed no less to see again their beloved pastor.

It was in June, 1650 that he made his entry into Fermo. It was a true and moving triumph to witness the solemnity and joy of the preparations to welcome him—the triumphal arches, the fireworks, and public thanksgivings. But human joys are short, and are ever mingled with sorrow and tears ; it was not long before this best of prelates was laid low by an apoplectic stroke, which threatened at an instant to cut short his life. The skill of his physicians saved him from immediate peril, but could not restore him to health, and some months after, in December, 1653, being again attacked by illness, he placidly ceased to live. The public and sincere sorrow and tears of the people of Fermo bear assured testimony to the grief occasioned by such a loss—a grief which

For the frigate bought at Nantes, ...	10,600 dollars.
For furnishing the frigate with sailors, soldiers, and provisions, ...	1,090 ,,
For powder and ball bought at la Rochelle, . .	5,400 ,,
For the transport of arms and baggage from Paris to la Rochelle, for lading, unlading, and storage, .	1,060 ,,
For provisions and wages to the sailors for 3 months, .	1,200 ,,
Repairing the Fort of Duncannon, ...	3,200 ,,
Ready money furnished to P. Scarampi, . . .	8,100 ,,

For the Nuncio's journey, and the maintenance of himself and suite in Paris, he was allowed by the Pope only 3,000 crowns, and 200 crowns a month afterwards. Although in Ireland living was very cheap, he expended the revenues of his Archiepiscopal See of Fermo, and besides 15,800 crowns of his own private income.

was redoubled when it was found that the good shepherd, who in life had fed the flock confided to his care with both spiritual and temporal food, had by his will bequeathed to them his whole large private property.

To nobility of birth and great talents Rinuccini joined gentleness of demeanour, true Christian piety, profound knowledge of sacred and profane literature, prudence and consummate skill in the management of affairs, strength of mind equal to every emergency, and an intellect powerful enough to grasp every subject. The proof that nature and art had enriched his mind with these great gifts is to be found even more in the unedited manuscripts in his private library than in his published works.

His obsequies were celebrated with pomp and splendour in the Cathedral over which he had presided with so much honour for thirty years; and his brother Tommaso caused to be sculptured on his monument the following inscription, composed by Francisco Rondinelli, the familiar common friend of both brothers:—

Christo Mortuorum Primogenito
Joanni Baptistæ Rinuccinio Archiepiscopo et Principi Firmano
Ad Foederatos Catholicos Hiberniae Pontificia Legatione Functo
Vero Spiritu Apostolico Ac Pastorali Vigelantia Praefulgenti
Qui Lumbos Praecinctus Innocentiae et Scientiae
Ardentes Lampadas E Manibus Nunquam Deposuit
Cuius Dextera Et Aperta Et Clausa Fecit Virtutem
Misericordiae Plena Ad Pauperes Semper Extenta
Quos Moriens Dixit Haeredes ex Asse
Contracta Calamo Plurimos Erudivit
Cuius Pedes Pacem Evangelizantis Mire Speciosi
Gregem Irrequieto Labore Circumierunt Atque ultimum Terrae
Perlustravere
Ita Ecclesiae Omnibus Episcopis Forma Virtutum Factus
Totidem quot acceperat superlucratus talenta in Domini gladium
Uti spes est intravit
Id. Decemb. A. S. MDCLIII. Aet. Lx Nondum Expleto
Thomas Rinuccinius Camilli Senat. F. S. Steph Eques
Serenissimae Victoriae Magnae Ducis Etruriae Cubiculo Praefectus
Fratri Optime Merito Moestissim. Posuit.

Venerabili Fratri JOANNI BAPTISTAE Archiepiscopo Firmano, Nostro, et Apostolicae Sedis in Regno Iberniae Nuntio extraordinario.

INNOCENTIUS P.P. X^{mus.}

VENERABILIS Frater, salutem et apostolicam benedictionem. Romanum decet Pontificem suos et Apostolicae Sedis ad remota procul loca Nuntios facultatibus apostolicis cumulate prosequi, ut ipsi illis suffulti possint in functione muneris sui eiusdem Sedis benignitatem erga populos ad quos mittuntur, cum venerit usus, liberaliter impertiri. Cum igitur nos te ob singularem fidem, doctrinam, prudentiam, Catholicae Religionis zelum et in gravibus negotiis tractandis solertiam et dexteritatem, nostrum et Sedis praefatae in Regno Iberniae, cuius pars etiamnum haeresi, proh dolor! infecta est, Nuntium extraordinarium destinaverimus, ut mandatis et consiliis nostris instructus, ea quae ad Catholicam fidem ecclesiasticamque disciplinam in illis partibus conservandam vel restituendam, ac debitum Omnipotenti Deo cultum et honorem exibendum pertinent, sedulo provideas. Idcirco necessarium et peropportunum esse duximus Te nonnullis facultatibus communire, et personam tuam amplius honorantes Tibi nostram et dictae Sedis auctoritatem plenius impertiri, ut mandata nostra commodius et fructuosius exequi valeas, et Christi fideles in illis partibus adeo remotis et longinquis, unde ad Nos et Romanam Curiam propter maris interiecti vastitatem itinerumque et navigationis pericula et incommoda aliaque impedimenta, difficilis patet accessus, ad Te recurrentes in variis casibus pie consolari, ac haereticos et schismaticos aliosque ab erroribus resipiscentes benigne recipere, eisque salutis viam aperire, gratiisque tam spiritualibus quam temporalibus prosequi, et denique cunctis Te utilem et benignum, ut illos in Domino lucrifacias, exibere possis. Itaque motu proprio et ex certa scientia et matura deliberatione nostris, deque Apostolicae potestatis plenitudine Fraternitati tuae ut in praefato Iberniae Regno legatione tua huiusmodi durante et intra illius fines, atque erga eius personas et loca ibi existentia, dumtaxat per Te ipsum vel alium seu alios viros probos et idoneos, patriarchales, primatiales et alias Ecclesias cathedrales, collegiatas, parochiales, monasteria tam virorum quam mulierum, prioratus, praeposituras, loca saecularia et quorumvis Ordinum etiam Mendicantium regularia, hospitalia etiam exempta et sanctae Sedi immediate subiecta, et quocumque alio privilegio suffulta, eorum capitula, conventus, universitates, collegia et personas tam saeculares quam regulares sive subiectas sive exemptas juxta sacros canones et Decreta sacri Concilii Tridentini, toties quoties tibi videbitur apostolica auctoritate visitare; in eorum statum, formam, regulas, instituta, regimen, statuta, consuetudines, ritus, mores et disciplinam coniunctim sive divisim, ac tam in membris quam in capite diligenter inquirere, statuta reformare, mutare, corrigere, et de novo, quatenus opus sit, juxta sacrorum Canonum et Conciliorum generalium decreta condere, sacrisque Canonibus et Concilio Tridentino non repugnantia confirmare, publicare et executioni demandari facere. Abusus quoscumque tollere ac regularem observantiam et ecclesiasticam disciplinam restituere. Decreta Concilii Tridentini proponere et custodiri facere et praecipere, omnes supradictas personas male viventes, relaxatas, ab eorum institutis deviantes, delinquentes corrigere, emendare, punire prout justitia suaserit; nec non contra quoscumque Ecclesiasticos tam saeculares quam regulares etiam exemptos, falsarios, usurarios, raptores, incendiarios, criminosos et delinquentes quoscumque, sive contra eorum fautores et receptores cuiuscumque conditionis et dignitatis fuerint, per viam accusationis, denunciationis ex officio summarie, simpliciter et sine strepitu et figura judicii procedere, eosque ut supra debitis poenis punire juxta canonicas sanctiones vel alias, ut tibi videbitur.

Praeterea praefatorum criminum ut supra expressorum, nec non alias et quascumque criminales, civiles, matrimoniales, meras, mixtas, causas ecclesiasticas, profanas vel alias ad forum ecclesiasticum pertinentes et in prima instantia, quatenus coram locorum ordinariis introduci commode non possint, easdemque causas ut supra per appellationem et irreparabili gravamine sententiae vim diffinitivae habentis, et tam per viam recursus, querelae simplicis, quam etiam quarumcumque appellationum a judicibus ordinariis, delegatis apostolicis, vel alias quomodolibet devolutas cum omnibus annexis, dependentibus, incidentibus, connexis etiam summarie, simpliciter et de plano, sine strepitu et figura judicii sola facti veritate inspecta, terminisque substantialibus unico contentu, vel etiam non servatis sed illorum loco praefixo termino, arbitrio tuo audire cognoscere, et prout juris fuerit terminare, et ad hunc caeterorumque contingentium effectum quoscumque etiam per edictum publicum constito prius etiam summarie et extraiudicialiter de non tuto accessu citare, eisque ac etiam quibusvis judicibus caeterisque personis, quibus et quoties opus fuerit, etiam per simile edictum, ac etiam sub censuris et poenis ecclesiasticis tuo vel delegatorum tuorum arbitrio moderandis et applicandis inhibere, ac contra inobedientes et rebelles, censuras et poenas ipsas etiam iteratis vicibus aggravare, interdictum ecclesiasticum apponere et relaxare, et quatenus opus foret auxilium brachii saecularis invocare; seu causas ipsas alii vel aliis idoneis personis in dignitate ecclesiastica constitutis modo et forma praemissis, ac cum simili vel limitata facultate ut supra pariter audiendas, cognoscendas et terminandas delegare, quascumque personas in integrum prout juris fuerit adversus sententias rei iudicatas et contractus quoscumque restituere; quaecumque juramenta ad effectum agendi tantum, relaxare. Praterea ab haeresi, apostasia a fide, et a schismate quoscumque etiam ecclesiasticos tam saeculares quam regulares (non tamen eos qui ex locis fuerint ubi sanctum officium exercetur, nisi in locis in quibus impune grassantur haereses, deliquerint, nec illos qui judicialiter abiuraverint, nisi isti nati sint ubi impune grassantur haereses, et post judicialem abiurationem illuc reversi in haeresim fuerint relapsi) in utroque foro, nec non omnes et quoscumque delinquentes ab excommunicatione aliisque censuris et poenis ecclesiasticis et temporalibus etiam in utroque foro, iniuncta poenitentia salutari; nec non ab omnibus casis Sedi Apostolicae etiam in Bulla in die Coenae Domini legi solita reservatis, absolvere. Ac cum quibusvis super quacumque irregularitate, per eos ratione etiam homicidii voluntarii occasione bellorum contra haereticos commissi, simoniae realis etiam retentis beneficiis, si sint parochialia et non sint, qui parochiis praefici possint, haeresis, laesae majestatis, bigamiae, indebitae perceptionis fructuum quomodolibet contracta, iniuncta aliqua eleemosyna vel poenitentia salutari etiamsi irregulare censuris sic ligati missas et alia divina officia (non tamen in contemptum clavium) celebraverint, vel alias se divinis immiscuerint, ita ut nondum promoti ad ordines etiam sacros et praesbyteratus, et tam ipsi quam alii in susceptis rite ordinibus etiam in altaris ministerio ministrare, beneficiaque tam cum cura quam sine cura, quaecumque et qualiacumque et quomodolibet qualificata recipere, et alias per eos obtenta retinere, etiamsi plura et incompatibilia sint, libere ac licite valeant. Ac insuper cum quibusvis personis quae invicem tertio ac quarto, simplici vel mixto consanguinitatis vel affinitatis gradibus sint coniunctae, vel sese attinent, et matrimonium contrahere cupiunt in futurum, ut impedimento tertii et quarti graduum huiusmodi nonobstante matrimonium inter se publice, servata forma Concilii Tridentini, contrahere, illudque in facie Ecclesiae solemnizare, et in eo postmodum remanere valeant, dispensare; haereticos vero ad catholicam fidem conversos, qui invicem etiam secundo simplici vel mixto consanguinitatis seu affinitatis gradu sunt coniuncti, vel sese attinent, et matrimonium de facto scienter vel ignoranter de praeterito sive hactenus contraxerunt, ac etiam carnali copula subsecuta, consummarunt, ab incestus reatu et excommunicationis aliisque ecclesiasticis sententiis, censuris ut poenis propterea incursis, iniunctis tamen poenitentiis salutaribus, in utroque foro absolvere, atque cum illis, et impedimento secundi gradus huiusmodi non obstante, in jam contracto matrimonio remanere, vel illud de novo contrahere, et in facie Ecclesiae solemnizare juxta decreta memorati Concilii Tridentini valeant; et simili modo super impedimento publicae honestatis justitiae, ubi sponsalia dumtaxat intercesserint; nec non super impedimento cognationis spiritualis etiam inter levantem et levatum; ac pariter cum aliis qui per fornicationem vel adulterium se polluerint, dummodo alter tantum in mortem defuncti coniugis machinatus fuerit ut matrimonium inter se (ut praefertur) contrahere et in facie Ecclesiae solemnizare; ac cum his qui huiusmodi impedimentis non obstantibus, illud jam scienter vel ignoranter contraxerint, ipsos ab incestus reatu et excommunicationis aliisque censuris ecclesiasticis propterea incursis, in forma Ecclesiae consueta, iniuncta eis pro modo culpae poenitentia salutari, et aliis quas de jure fuerint iniungenda, absolvere et etiam in matrimonio jam contracto remanere, seu illud de novo contrahere, et (ut praefertur) solemnizare, debitumque coniugale exigere libere ac licite valeant, dummodo in singulis casibus praedictis mulieres propterea raptae non fuerint, vel si raptae fuerint, in potestate raptoris non existant, dispensare, prolemque exinde susceptam et suscipiendam legitimam decernere et nunciare. Nec non quaecumque vota simplicia, si alias causa legitima subsistat, in alia pietatis opera commutare, ac cum catholicis super fructibus bonorum ecclesiasticorum male perceptis, et cum eisdem catholicis, ut possint retinere bona ecclesiastica tempore schismatis occupata, et fructus ex illis percipere, accepta ab illis promissione de stando judicio Ecclesiae circa eorum restitutionem, cum fieri poterit, illis interim admonitis, ut de dictus fructibus faciant eleemosynam judicio confessarii in usum Religionis cuius ante haeresim et schisma erant bona, si ibi adsit Religio illa, sin minus, in pauperes catholicos, et memores sint illa bona esse revera Ecclesiae. Nec non cum eisdem catholicis ut supradicta bona ecclesiastica tempore schismatis occupata, vel alias quomodolibet ab illis, seu eorum antecessoribus acquista retinere, illorumque fructus percipere, nec super illis a quovis tam in foro exteriori quam in foro conscientiae molestari possint, assignata tamen per supradictos parochis congrua portione, nec aliter nec alio modo dispensare, et cum praefatis catholicis super praefatis bonis, ut vel ea in emphyteusim ad tertiam generationem vel in perpetuum ab Ecclesia recognoscant, soluto aliquo laudemio, nec non annuo canone, prout tibi magis expedire videbitur, reservato dominio directo bonorum ut supra concessorum Ecclesiae vel Ecclesiis seu monasteriis a quibus occupata fuerunt, concordare. Ac utriusque sexus personis ecclesiasticis et saecularibus, non tamen regularibus, ut proper adversam valetudinem et infirmitatem ovis, butyro, caseo, lacticiniis et carnibus tam quadragesimae quam aliis anni temporibus et diebus, quibus horum usus est prohibitus, secreto tamen et sine scandalo ac de utriusque medici consilio, uti ac vesci possint, indulgere, nec non in omnibus jejuniis de jure vel consuetudine introductis dispensare, illaque in alia opera pia, vel ut tibi in Dominio expedire videbitur, commutare. Praeterea quaecumque beneficia ecclesiastica simplicia, etiam metropolitanis, cathedralibus et collegiatis ecclesiis consistentia, extra romanam Curiam per obitum illorum ultimorum possessorum vacantia, dummodo alias quam ratione mensium apostolicorum reservata non fuerint, et dummodo beneficia praefata consistorialia et dignitates maiores post pontificalem in cathedralibus, et principales in Collegiatis non sint, personis idoneis conferre. Ac ut quis plura beneficia simplicia, etiamsi alterum eorum ad congruam sustentationem sufficiat, ac sub eodem tectu existant, etiamsi uniformia sint, retinere possit. Quo vero ad residentiam requirentia, vel alias curata, vel si necessitas vel utilitas Ecclesiae emerserit tantum, dispensare. Nec non quosvis in aetate legitima constitutos et alias idoneos, qui beneficium vel patrimonium ad congruam sui sustentationem sufficiens, pacifice possederint, etiamsi arctati non sint, ad omnes etiam sacros, usque ad praesbyteratum inclusive, ordines, etiam quoad sacros ordines quibusvis tribus dominicis vel aliis festivis de praecepto diebus continuis vel interpolatis, etiam extra tempora a jure statuta ac anni curriculo non expectato, interstitiisque a praefato Concilio Tridentino praescriptis non servatis, promovere, illisque ut ordines praefatos a quocumque quem maluerint catholico antistite gratiam et communionem sedis Apostolicae habente, in propria diocesi residente, vel in aliena de diocesani loci licentia pontificalia exercente (ut praemittitur) promoveri, et in illis promoti etiam in altaris ministerio ministrare possint, licentiam concedere, ac ob penuriam operariorum cum quibusvis ut si et quando unus annus tantum sibi de aetate ad id a praedicto Concilio Tridentino requisito defuerit, ad sacrum praesbyteratus ordinem servatis alias servandis, et dummodo ad id idonei reperiantur, promoveri possint, dispensare; nec non missam quocumque in loco decenti, etiam sub dio, sub terra una hora ante auroram et alia post meridiem, ac bis in die si necessitas cogat, dummodo tamen in prima missa non sumpserit purificationem nec ablutionem, et super altari portatili, etiam fracto aut laeso, et sine sanctorum reliquiis, ac etiam praesentibus haereticis aliisque excommunicatis, si aliter celebrari non possit, et non sit periculum sacrilegii, dummodo tamen inserviens missae non sit haereticus, vel excommunicatus, celebrare, ac primo conversis ab haeresi atque etiam fidelibus quibuscumque in articulo mortis, saltem contritis, si confiteri non poterunt; nec non orationis quadraginta horarum occasione etiam pluries in anno diebus tibi benevisis instituendae omnibus et singulis utriusque sexus Christifidelibus contritis et confessis, ac sacra communione refectis, qui orationi huiusmodi intervenerint, et ibi pias ad Deum preces pro Christianorum Principum concordia, haereticorum conversione, catholicae fidei propagatione effuderint, quibus diebus ex praefatis id egerint, si tamen ex concursu populi, et expositione sanctissimi Sacramenti nulla probabilis suspicio sit sacrilegii ab haereticis et infidelibus aut magistratum offensum iri, plenariam omnium suorum peccatorum indulgentiam et remissionem misericorditer in Domino concedere; singulis quoque dominicis et aliis festis diebus iis qui tuis concionibus intervenerint, quoties id egerint, decem annos et totidem quadragenas de iniunctis sibi, seu quae merito iniungi debuissent, vel alias quomodolibet debitis poenitentiis in forma Ecclesiae consueta relaxare; et iis qui praevia sacramentali peccatorum suorum confessione, sacram communionem in Nativitatis ac Paschatis Resurrectionis D. N. Jesu Christi et Assumptionis B^{mae} Virginis Mariae festis diebus sumpserit, similiter plenariam omnium peccatorum suorum indulgentiam et remissionem in Domino concedere. Tuque ipse easdem indulgentias et poenitentiarum relaxationes consequi; nec non singulis secundus feriis non impeditis officio novem lectionum, vel iis impediti, die immediate sequenti, missam defunctorum in quocumque altari etiam portatili, pro anima cuiuscumque fidelis quae Deo in charitate coniuncta, ab hac luce migraverit, ita ut ejusdem Domini nostri Jesu Christi ac prafatae B^{mae} Virginis Mariae Sanctorumque omnium meritis sibi suffragantibus e purgatorii poenis liberetur, celebrare; ac sanctissimum Eucharistiae sacramentum occulte ad infirmos sine lumine deferre, illudque sine eodem retinere pro eisdem infirmis, in loco tamen decenti, si ab haereticis aut infidelibus sit periculum sacrilegii. Insuper vestibus saecularibus, si aliter vel transire ad loca curae tuae commissa, vel in eis permanere non possit, indui, illasque palam deferre. Nec non Rosarium ejusdem B^{mae} Virginis Mariae, vel alias preces si Breviarium tuum deferre non poteris, vel divinum officium ob aliquod impedimentum legitimum recitare non valueris, recitare, et per recitationem huiusmodi, obligationi recitandi divinum officium huiusmodi satisfacere. Ad haec etiam simplicibus sacerdotibus potestatem benedicendi paramenta, et alia utensilia ad sacrificium Missae necessaria, ubi non intervenit unctio, et reconciliandi ecclesias pollutas, aqua tamen prius a te vel alio catholico antistite benedicta, et in casu necessitatis etiam aqua non benedicta ab episcopo, delegare; olea cum quinque saltem sacerdotibus, non tamen extra diem Coenae Domini, nisi necessitas aliud urgeat, consecrare; libros prohibitos haereticorum ad effectum eos impugnandi, et alios quomodolibet prohibitos, praeter opera Caroli Molinei, Nicholai Machiavelli et libros de astrologia judiciaria, legere et penes te retinere, ita tamen ut libri ex ipsis provinciis non efferantur; ac quascumque facultates quibusvis archiepiscopis, episcopis, sacerdotibus tam saecularibus quam regularibus, etiam societatis Jesu hactenus a sede Apostolica vel a venerabilibus fratribus nostris S. R. E. Cardinalibus in universa republica christiana adversus haereticam pravitatem, generalibus inquisitoribus a sede praefata specialiter deputatis concessas, in dicto Iberniae regno revocare, et si in posterum concedi contigerit illas suspendere, moderare, limitare, prout in Domino expediri judicaveris; omnibusque supradictis ne absque tua licentia speciali praefatis (ut supra) concessis facultatibus a te non revocatis vel limitatis in dicto regno utantur, prohibere; nec non facultates tibi per praesentes concessas uni vel pluribus sacerdotibus tam saecularibus quam regularibus nec non archiepiscopis, episcopis et aliis in dignitate ecclesiastica constitutis in totum vel in parte, et alias prout tibi videbitur, delegare. Atque in ecclesiis ac monasteriis aliisque locis piis derelictis, administratores ad tempus sive in perpetuam, ubi expedire judicaveris, apponere. Et monasteria quaecumque monialium ac quorumcumque ordinum, non tamen societatis Jesu, in regno praefato existentium, fundare ac erigere, illisque beneficia simplicia tantum, nec residentiam requirentia, applicare ac unire; nec non in usum belli pro catholica religione excitati vel excitandi bona monasteriorum aut ecclesiarum, non tamen cathedralium aut collegiatarum aut curam animarum habentium, usque ad summam scutorum quinquaginta millium una vel pluribus vicibus, uni vel pluribus viris catholicis tantum alienare; Concilium generale nationale convocare, in eoque nostro vel apostolicae Sedis nomine praesidere, ac decreta in eo quaecumque facere, non tamen publicare, nisi a Sede apostolica prius fuerint confirmata. Praeterea archiepiscopis, episcopis aliisque ecclesiasticis qui in Concilio supremo, seu alias in causis criminalibus, etiamsi inde mors vel mutilatio membrorum sequatur, vota dare tenentur, ut id sine ullo irregularitatis incursu facere possint, dummodo per ipsosmet sententiam mortis aut mutilationis membrorum non ferant nec illam subscribant, indulgere. Nec non duodecim viros quos videris sive, nobiles sive gradu et doctrina aliisque virtutum meritis praestantes ac nostri ac dictae Sedis in primis devotos Clericos, in nostros et dictae Sedis notarios, auctoritate nostra apostolica recipere, admittere et creare, ac illos aliorum nostrorum, et dictae Sedis notariorum numero et consortio favorabiliter aggregare; illisque ut etiamsi habitum et rocchettum non non deferant, nihilominus omnibus et singulis favoribus, honoribus, praeeminentiis, indultis, privilegeiis, exemptionibus et praerogativis, quibus alii nostri et ejusdem sedis notarii tam de jure quam de consuetudine utuntur, potiuntur et gaudent, ac uti, potiri et gaudere possunt et poterunt quomodolibet in futurum, absque tamen nostrorum et ejusdem sedis notariorum de numero participantium praejudicio, et citra exemptiones a Concilio Tridentino sublatas; et facultates legitimandi, ad gradus promovendi, ac notarios creando, aliaque similia privilegia eisdem notariis de numero participantium concessa, seu ab eis praetensa, quibus notarii a te creandi nullibi uti valeant; et si secus ab eis fieri contigerit, irritum et inane existat, uti, potiri et gaudere possint et valeant, concedere et indulgere. Ac illos qui enorme duelli crimen commiserint, vel duellis huiusmodi interfuerint, aut quoquomodo auxilium, consilium vel favorem praestiterint ab excommunicationis aliisque sententiis, censuris et ponenis ecclesiasticis propterea incursis, auctoritate nostra absolvere. Et Christifidelibus in articulo mortis constitutis benedictionem pontificiam impartiri, et ut concessiones, gratiae et literae per te vigore praesentium concedendae, sublatis obstaculis, suum sortiantur effectum, quascumque personas ad effectum dumtaxat omnium et singulorem praemissorum consequendum, ab omnibus et quibuscumque excommunicationis, suspensionis, et interdicti, aliisque ecclesiasticis sententiis, censuris et poenis a jure vel ab homine quavis occasione vel causa latis si quibus quomodolibet innodati fuerint, dummodo in eis per annum non insorduerint, absolvere et absolutos fore censere, judicis, assistentes, commissarios executores pro praefatorum et literarum tuarum executione et observatione delegare; mandata, prohibitiones, monitoria etiam sub censuris et aliis poenis praefatis caeterisque bene visis remediis, etiam appellatione postposita, decernere, et omnia et quaecumque alia in praemissis et circa ea necessaria et quomodolibet opportuna facere, decernere et exequi etiam per aliam seu alios possis et valeas, auctoritate nostra apostolica praefata tenore praesentium plenam et liberam licentiam, facultatem et auctoritatem concedimus et impertimur. Decernentes te omnibus facultatibus et concessionibus praefatis, etiam cum derogationibus, suspensionibus, indultis irritantibus, aliisque decretis et clausulis necessariis et opportunis ac in litteris apostolicis concedi et extendi solitis, libere et licite uti posse, ac in concessionibus, dispensationibus, aliisque gratiis per te auctoritate praesentium tuique officii faciendis, soli narrativae tuae, ac etiam solis concessionibus et literis tuis absque praesentium insertione seu exhibitione, aut notarii testiumve adhibitione stari, nec ad id alterius probationis adminiculum requiri, sicque per quoscumque judices ordinarios et delegatos, etiam causarum palatii apostolici auditores ac S. R. E. cardinales in quavis causa et instantia, sublatis eis et eorum cuilibet quavis aliter judicandi et interpretandi facultate et auctoritate, judicare et definiri debere, ac irritum et inane, siquid secus super his a quoquam quavis auctoritate scienter vel ignoranter contigeret, attentari. Non obstantibus literis fel. rec. Sexti papae quarti praedecessoris nostri, quibus inter alia cavetur expresse quod Nuncii dictae Sedis, tam quoad beneficia conferenda, quam dispensationes et alias gratias concedendas, facultatibus uti non possint, nec quaevis clausulae in literis facultatem huiusmodi appositae adversus dictas literas quidquam suffragentur, nec non defectibus et aliis praefatis ac Lateranensis novissime celebrati de certo notariorum numero, etiamsi ad illum nondum deventum sit, cui per hoc alias non intendimus derogare. Nec non piae mem. Bonifacii Papae Octavi similiter praedecessoris nostri de una, et Concilii generalis de duabus dietis ac aliis apostolicis, et in universalibus provincialibusque et synodalibus conciliis editis, generalibus vel specialibus constitutionibus et ordinationibus, etiam specialem et individuam mentionem et expressionem requirentibus ; nec non Cancellariae apostolicae regulis, nullis prorsus exceptis, et quae sigillatim in quaque re exprimi et extendi possint. Statutis quoque et consuetudinibus Ecclesiarum et Monasteriorum, universitatum, collegiorum, civitatum et locorum quorumlibet dicti regni ; nec non ordinum quorumcumque etiam juramento, confirmatione apostolica, vel alia quavis firmitate roboratis, etiamsi de illis servandis, et non impetraudis literis apostolicis contra illa et illis etiam ab alio vel aliis impetratis, seu alias quomodolibet concessis non utendo personae praestiterint eatenus, vel in posterum forsan praestare contigerit juramentum a quibusvis alias privilegiis et indultis apostolicis generalibus vel specialibus quorumcumque, etiam Cisterciensium et Cluniacensium ordinum, quae praemissis quovis modo obstare videantur; per quae praesentibus non expressa vel totaliter non inserta effectus earum impediri valeat, quomodolibet vel differri, et de quibus quorumque totis tenoribus de verbo ad verbum habenda sit in nostris tuisque literis mentio specialis; quae quoad hoc nullatenus cuiquam suffragari volumus; quibus omnibus et singulis caeterisque contrariis quibuscumque, ubi et quando expediet, secundum rei casus, exigentiam in genere vel in specie, ac tamen coniunctim quam divisim, prout tibi placuerit valeas derogare ac super his indulgere; quodque aliqui super provisionibus sibi faciendis de huiusmodi vel aliis beneficiis ecclesiasticis in illis partibus, speciales vel generales, etiamsi per eas ad inhibitionem, reservationem et decretum, vel alias quomodolibet sit processum, quibus omnibus personas in quarum favorem per te de beneficiis praefatis providebitur, et alias disponetur, in eorum assecutione volumus anteferri; sed nullum per hoc eas quoad assecutionem beneficiorum aliorum praejudicium generari; seu si locorum ordinariis et collatoribus vel quibusvis aliis communiter vel divisim ab eadem sit sede indultum, quod ad receptionem vel provisionem alicuius minime teneantur, et ad id compelli, aut quod interdici, suspendi vel excommunicari non possint, quodque de huiusmodi vel aliis beneficiis ecclesiasticis ad illorum collationem, provisionem, praesentationem, electionem seu quamvis aliam dispositionem coniunctim vel separatim spectandam, nulli valeat provideri per literas apostolicas non facientes plenam et expressam, ac de verbo ad verbum, de indulto huiusmodi mentionem, et qualibet alia dictae Sedis indulgentia generali vel speciali cuiuscumque tenoris existat, per quam praesentibus nec non literis per te earumdem vigore concedendis non expressam vel totaliter non insertam, effectus earum impediri valeat, quomodolibet vel differri, et de qua cuiusque toto tenore habenda sit in eisdem literis mentio specialis. Volumus autem ut praesentium transumptis etiam impressis manu regentis cancellariae tuae et sigillo tuo obsignatis, eadem prorsus fides in iudicio et extra adhibeatur, quae praesentibus ipsis adhiberetur, si forent exhibitae vel ostensae. Datum Romae apud Sanctrum Petrum sub annulo Piscatoris die XV. Martii MDCXLV. Pontificatus nostri anno primo.

M. A. MARALDUS.

INSTRUCTIONS

TO

MONSIGNOR RINUCCINI,

ENVOY EXTRAORDINARY TO IRELAND,

FROM

HIS HOLINESS POPE INNOCENT X.

Your Excellency has been called by His Holiness to a great and glorious office—to restore and re-establish the public exercise of the Catholic religion in the island of Ireland; and further, to lead her people, if not as tributaries to the Holy See, such as they were five centuries ago, to subject themselves to the mild yoke of the Pontiff, at least in all spiritual affairs—thus to gain over souls innumerable to the glories of Paradise. It is with good reason the Holy Father has turned his eyes upon you, because in your early years you gave proofs, in the Court of Rome, of an innocent life, and of no common prudence and virtue. When translated to the Church of Fermo you acted there the part of a vigilant pastor, and have left the impress and clear record of your ardent charity and apostolic zeal. His Holiness therefore trusts that, in a wide field of not dissimilar usefulness, you will devote all your talents to bring this noble enterprise to a speedy conclusion, and thus be approved of God and the Apostolic See in as great a degree, as you would have been by a more laborious work of many years duration.

For your Excellency's information as to the present state of affairs in Ireland, I briefly mention four points, referring you for all needful details to Father P. F. Scarampi, who, being sent to that kingdom by Urban VIII. of blessed memory, two years ago, will remain there until joined by you.

First, I shall state the causes of the late movements amongst the Catholics.

Secondly, the form of the political government maintained in the island at the present time.

Thirdly, in what circumstances you will find the exercise of the Catholic religion.

And lastly, in what way your Excellency must direct your activity for the benefit of the said religion.

The kingdom of Ireland, which contains within itself four noble provinces—Munster, Leinster, Connaught, and Ulster—was once an ancient possession of the Apostolic See. It was converted to Christianity during the reign of Celestin I., in the fifth century of our redemption, first by St. Paladius, afterwards by St. Patrick, the disciple of St. Germanus. For a long period the true faith maintained itself, till the country, invaded by the Danes, an idolatrous people, fell for the most part into impious superstition. Those who remained faithful still bowed in obedience to the Holy See, and acknowledged no other supreme Head but the Sovereign Pontiff of Rome.

This state of darkness lasted till the reigns of Adrain IV. and of Henry II., King of England. Henry, desiring to strengthen his empire, and to secure the provinces which he possessed beyond sea in France, wished to subdue the island of Ireland; and, to compass this design, had recourse to Adrian, who, himself an Englishman, with a liberal hand granted all he coveted.

The zeal manifested by Henry to convert all Ireland to the faith moved the soul of Adrian to invest him with the sovereignty of the island. Three important conditions were annexed to the gift. 1st. That the King should do all in his power to propagate the Christian religion throughout

Ireland. 2nd. That each of his subjects should pay an annual tribute of one penny to the Holy See, commonly called Peter's pence. And 3rd. That civil liberty should be guaranteed, and the privileges and immunities of the Church be held inviolate. Henry, having thus become master of Ireland, soon planted colonies of his English subjects through the country, and sought from that hour to reduce the betrayed inhabitants, no less in spiritual than in temporal affairs, to his will.

Shortly afterwards violent disputes arose between Henry and the Blessed Thomas, Archbishop of Canterbury. The veneration in which Henry had hitherto held the Pontiff was greatly impaired by the Holy Father's support of that prelate. The conditions of the gift were violated, the people ill-treated, ecclesiastical affairs so mismanaged and vilified that John, the successor of Adrian, reproached Edward, Henry's son, with his broken faith. In spite of all this the Catholic religion was preserved in its original purity until England was unhappily separated from the Church of Rome owing to the licentious marriages of Henry VIII., and great part of Ireland also was infected by heresy; and although the Irish were not in general ill-treated, and the cruel laws enforced against the English Catholics were not prosecuted in Ireland with much violence, it cannot be denied that many of the ecclesiastical benefices were seized by the heretics, while the churches and monasteries were profaned and passed into the hands of those perfidious agents who, paid and protected by the governors of the Island, found no difficulty in devoting the Church property to their own purposes. But Providence watched over the afflicted people, the ecclesiastical hierarchy still existed, the archbishops and bishops retained their titles and exercised ecclesiastical jurisdiction by means of vicars-general, and vacancies when they occurred were filled up by the Holy See. Some few monasteries and abbeys, miserable remains of the rage of the schismatics, were confided to the care of the secular clergy; others remained under the rule of the monks, who by secretly performing the rites of the Catholic Church succeeded in preserving amongst the people both the ancient faith and obedience to the Sovereign Pontiff. Verily did that miserable nation groan under the harsh yoke of England during the reigns of Henry and Edward, but still more under the tyranny of Elizabeth, who, almost like a fury shaking aloft a flaming torch, seemed bent upon reducing to ashes all that still lived of Catholicism in Ireland. The unhappy people in despair flew to arms, more in defence of their religion than of their worldly goods. But, by the mysterious judgment of God, the Spanish troops sent to their aid were defeated and dispersed, and the true faith lay, as it were, buried under the ruins of their hopes.

On the death of Elizabeth the crown fell to James, King of Scotland, who, at the commencement of his reign, treated the Catholics of the two kingdoms, especially the Irish, with less cruelty, as he wished to unite the country under the name of Great Britain. But the Gunpowder Plot, discovered soon after, and universally attributed to the Jesuits, changed the good intentions of the King. He renewed all the cruel laws of Elizabeth, and persecuted the faithful with all the pains of imprisonment, exile, and death. Colonies of Scotch and English heretics were planted in various parts of Ireland, and nothing was left undone to destroy the Catholic religion throughout the three kingdoms, all the rigours of the law and the fury of eloquence being joined in war against it. Various writers gave to the press works pernicious to the faith. There also appeared an exhortation, in the King's name, addressed to the principal Catholics, to induce them to refuse obedience to the Pope and the Apostolic See. This cruelty happily was not of long continuance, for, desirous of marrying his son to Margaret, the Infanta of Spain, James deemed it politic to abate the severity of his proceedings, and on the marriage of the Prince to Henrietta Maria of Bourbon, sister to Louis XIII. of France, he granted to all the Catholics in his dominions the free and unconditional exercise of their religion. Affairs were in this state when Charles I. succeeded to the throne, and with it to the hatred which James, his father, had borne to that sect of the heretics who, following the pure doctrines of Calvin, under the name of Puritans, separated themselves from other Protestants. These Charles stigmatized as traitors to the religion which he professed, and as pestilent enemies of that absolute monarchy which he desired to establish free from the authority of a Parliament. He determined to inflict signal mortifications upon the Puritans, by forcing them to perform ceremonies not very dissimilar to those of the Catholic Church, and proposed to raise the power of the Crown above that of the Parliament, by imposing taxes and compulsory loans, and by various other irregular proceedings, without the consent of the two Houses. Moreover, in order to reduce the Scotch to conformity in religion, he commanded that the new ceremonies should be introduced into Scotland; but the people, tenacious of the doctrines of Calvin, were enraged at the introduction of the obnoxious liturgy, and broke out into open rebellion. The King hurried thither, but, unable to quell the outbreak by his presence or by his edicts, or even to punish the ringleaders by appointing a High Commissioner (equal in authority to the head of the Catholic Inquisition), he found himself forced to yield to the demands of the rebels. This concession produced no favourable effect, and, instead of quenching the flames of rebellion, seemed rather to augment them, so that it became absolutely necessary to have recourse to arms.

An army was hurriedly raised, chiefly owing to the efforts of the English Catholics, incited no less by inclination to save their Prince than by the good offices of George Conn, a Scotchman, at that time Apostolic Envoy in London. With these troops Charles marched towards Scotland, but by imprudently halting on the confines of the two kingdoms, he enabled the Scotch to obtain aid from France and Holland, whilst, by sending officers to York to treat with the King, they succeeded through artful representations in averting the impending storm. The Scotch had on their side all the English Puritan nobles, and easily induced His Majesty to sign a most disadvantageous treaty, thereby greatly lowering himself not only in the eyes of his own subjects but in those of foreign princes, as they were fully aware that he might have succeeded by a sudden and well-concerted movement of his whole army. He soon repented of this treaty, which, sanctioned neither by the Archbishop of Canterbury nor by the Council of State, was not likely to be of long duration, and he vainly hoped to retrieve his error by again resorting to arms. Having no means of raising money to reassemble an army, he foolishly endeavoured to obtain it from a Parliament hastily summoned for that purpose. Thomas, Lord Strafford, his friend and minister, strongly opposed this measure, as it appeared to that wise and far-sighted nobleman that no time could be more inauspicious for appealing to such a body, when the people were full of discontent, and the King himself without arms, reputation, and resources. The sequel proved the truth of the Earl's predictions, for Parliament showed itself utterly contumacious, and was as hastily dissolved as it had been unwisely assembled.

Meanwhile the Scotch, still under arms, menaced England itself. Under these dangerous circumstances Charles took courage; he raised by some means a second army under the command of Strafford, and dispatched it to the banks of the Tweed (the river which separates Scotland from England), with strict orders at all hazards to guard the Ford. But no sooner had the royal troops arrived within sight of the Scotch than they fled in the most disgraceful manner, not only without striking a blow, but leaving the Ford and the whole country a prey to the invader. Hitherto Ireland had watched in silence the vicissitudes of the royal fortunes, but now, touched by the distress of her Prince, she dispatched to his aid an army of 10,000 infantry, whose assistance would indeed have been most opportune had not the want of money sufficient to support so large a body of troops crippled those whom they came to assist. In proportion to the decline of the royal strength was the increase of boldness amongst the Scotch and English Puritans. While the one presented insolent and exorbitant demands, the others insisted that Parliament should at once be convoked. The unfortunate King was forced to accede to their demands, and on the first day of the session the Scotch deputies rose and proposed that a Committee be appointed of an equal number of English and Scotch members, to discuss amicably, as they said, the best manner of settling their differences. But instead of this they united in a secret league against the King, and agreed that the Scotch army should be maintained and quartered at Newcastle, in England, for the defence of the Parliament. Armed with such power, the House hurriedly framed those cruel resolutions which caused the horrible war now raging in the country. Lord Strafford, who had ever been the most faithful and the ablest minister of the King, was the first victim of their wrath. They feared to see so wise and favoured a subject near the King's person, and they wished also to test the King's temper, which if it yielded to the first blow, would make it easy for them to deal the second.

On this account the gravest accusations were brought against the Earl. So violent were the efforts to make him appear guilty of high treason, and to secure his conviction, that neither his own innocence, the wonderful eloquence with which he for many hours defended himself in Parliament, nor the defence drawn up for him by Lord Digby, could avert the sentence of death which was pronounced by the House of Lords. The King tried every means to save the innocent victim—he entreated, he threatened, he even sent a free pardon by the hands of the prince his eldest son; but his solicitations fell unheeded on the ears of men bent on the destruction of the Earl, and at length, in order to avert from himself the rage of the populace, he was obliged to sign the death-warrant of his last remaining friend.

Strafford having been sacrificed to their wrath, the Parliament rashly thought to overthrow at once both the Royal power and the Catholic religion. They deprived the King of his revenues as well as of the command of the fleet and of the fortresses; they abolished the Star Chamber and the office of Lord High Commissioner, and passed various decrees for the curtailment of the royal prerogative. They bound themselves by a sacrilegious oath to maintain and defend what they called the true reformed Protestant religion against all Popish inventions and innovations, and determined to extinguish every spark of the Catholic religion, by extirpating all who adhered to that faith, not only in England and Scotland but even in Ireland. This dreadful sentence came to the knowledge of the Irish at a time when four thousand men were under arms, who had been levied for the service of the King of Spain, but were then detained in Ireland by order of the Parliament. The most zealous Catholics, mindful of the tyranny exercised by their Puritan and Protestant governors, and fearing from their hatred the strict execution of these horrible decrees, plotted secretly amongst themselves to throw off the heavy yoke of the heretics and to defend their lives and religion by arms. They agreed that no time nor occasion would be more favourable to such an attempt than the present, when England, engaged in her own intestine quarrel, would have no leisure to extinguish the flames in other homes while they burned so fiercely in her own. But all were not of one mind—some feared the issue of so vast a design; others doubted if all the Catholics in the country would come to their aid; many lost courage from poverty and want of arms. At last the plot, to the sorrow of all true men, fell to the ground, and was no longer discussed save in the strictest secrecy.

Some few ardent spirits, however, determined to surprise at once the city and Castle of Dublin, the metropolis of the island, and make themselves masters of these places, where arms and munitions of war were kept by the Royalists; but while one party met with success, the other was entirely defeated, and one unworthy són of Ireland betrayed the whole plan. Some of the leaders were arrested and hurried off as prisoners to London; the rest, more fortunate, escaped by flight. After this catastrophe the whole body of Irish Catholics, forced to take up arms by the ungoverned fury and cruel enactments of the English Parliament, rose in insurrection. The rising, at first doubtful and tumultuous, was gradually organized into a well-arranged movement by the prelates and other clergy, who willingly gave both advice and assistance. But seeing that the army was led without military skill, its movements guided without any knowledge of civil or political government, the bishops convened a council in the city of Kilkenny, in April, 1642. At this national synod they declared, first, that the rising was justified, and that its sole object was the preservation of the Catholic religion, by insuring the public an unrestrained performance of its rites throughout the island; secondly, in order to unite all the disaffected into a strong religious confederacy, they introduced a form of oath which, administered in the first instance to the members of the assembly, was afterwards to be taken by all who desired to join their party before any active measure should be attempted; and, thirdly, a proclamation was issued for the general assembly to meet at Kilkenny in the following May, to decide finally on the form of government they should adopt. When the time arrived all the nobles of the island hurried thither; and as we have now come to the second part of these instructions, intended to assist your Excellency in your important office, I must inform you that from the time when Ireland fell into the hands of the King of England, the country was governed by a Viceroy, nominated by the King, sometimes under the name of Lord Keeper, sometimes of Lord Justiciary, sometimes of Lieutenant, and often under that of Deputy. The authority of this minister was very great—equal in fact to that of the Sovereign. He was empowered to proclaim war, to sign treaties, to appoint inferior magistrates, to take cognizance of treasonable offences of which the King himself is judge, and to punish all the graver crimes. A council composed of nobles and ecclesiastics, of whom the principal officers were the Chancellor and Lord Treasurer, resided with him, but more for appearance sake than for any real assistance they rendered to the Government. Justice was administered by inferior judges, nominated by the Viceroy, from whom an appeal lay to the Council. In addition, the island was divided into four provinces, and subdivided into various counties and districts, each of which was governed by a Commissioner or President, with assessors and judges to assist him; but all were equally subject to the Viceroy and his Council. Two judges were sent from the capital twice a year to try criminal cases, and were invested with unlimited power to decide the causes which came before them, to condemn the guilty, and to acquit the innocent. The laws and customs of England were forced upon the Irish by Henry III., and universally observed until the reign of Henry VII., by whose permission the Parliament of the island made some alterations which have remained in force to the present day. The power of the Viceroy was limited in one respect: he could not decree any *permanent* law without the consent of the General Assembly, composed of two orders—*i.e.*, of peers and commons, and of ecclesiastics of high rank, who sat with the nobles as in the Imperial Parliament. Such was the form of government in all the provinces subject to England until the revolt of the Catholics, when in 1642 a General Assembly, as before mentioned, was convened at Kilkenny. On that occasion a Supreme Council was chosen from amongst its members, and comprising a certain number of prelates and nobles, to whom was confided the power which had before lain in the hands of the Viceroy. In each province a local council was formed, headed by a president, but subordinate to the Supreme Court, all however willingly acknowledging the supremacy of the General Assembly.

The Supreme Council decided on peace and war, and on all civil business; but in order to divide this labour, at the General Parliament of Kilkenny, in 1644, a separate tribunal was erected, over which presides the Chancellor, an ecclesiastic, at this moment the Bishop of Clonfert, who hears and decides upon all disputes in civil and criminal matters, without reference to the Supreme Council. A similar tribunal was erected for the administration of home affairs, consisting of the Lord Treasurer (a layman), aided by other officers, who not only have control over the expenditure in time of peace, but can decree the expenses of war. The army is commanded by four Lieutenants-General, each at the head of a separate body of troops in the several provinces, over the whole of which the Supreme Council is General-in-Chief. The laws remained nearly unchanged, those prejudicial to the Catholic religion and its free exercise alone excepted. We now come to the third part of our subject. It would be impossible to enumerate to your Excellency the cruelties and vexatious prohibitions of the Viceroy against the Catholic religion in Ireland when, on the death of Queen Mary, England was again distracted by schism under Elizabeth, her sister and successor. The unhappy Catholics were forbidden to assemble in their churches; and indeed those churches, which were profaned by the administration of Calvinistic sacraments and rites, they looked upon as temples of abomination rather than houses of God. Masses were performed in private houses in the strictest secrecy, as discovery exposed the assembled few to no less a peril than imprisonment, confiscation of property, and even death. Bishops, priests, and monks, despoiled of their peculiar dress, were no longer to be distinguished from the laity; no congress, no spiritual meeting, could be held without incurring the displeasure of the Queen and her ministers. The children of Catholics, who, after the death of their parents, fell into the wardship of the Crown, were placed under the care of Calvinists, and were perfidiously instructed in the wicked doctrines of that sect. Thus, to the deep grief of the faithful, Protestantism appeared at last triumphant in the island, and the nobility, more exposed than the common people to the influence of the heretic ministers, were the first to be corrupted. In a word, affairs were in a deplorable state from the wickedness of the times, the desolation of the cities, the want of solemnity at the altar and even in the sacrifices themselves. But a happier hour approached. After the revolt of the Catholics and the consequent expulsion of the heretics from nearly all the counties of Munster, Leinster, Connaught, and from many parts of Ulster, to the great joy of all true men the profaned churches were on a sudden thrown open and re-consecrated, the holy images borne aloft, and the sacred offices performed by the four archbishops of Armagh, Dublin, Tuam, and Cashel. The two last named have re-consecrated their churches and regained possession of their property and revenues; those of Armagh and Dublin hope soon to recover theirs, because part of their dioceses are already in their hands, and part of their tithes again received by them.

The suffragan bishops have been almost invariably recognised by the people of their dioceses, and their incomes restored; many secular parishes no longer wished for rectors as formerly, and by degrees consigned to them their tenths, although many enjoyed the whole income. The monks, formerly dispersed in the towns, lodged and supported by private charity, and not to be known by their dress from laymen, have reassembled in the monasteries, and, habited according to their order, are the object no less of astonishment than admiration to the common people, so long unaccustomed to the sight of the religious habit. Among these the reformed Franciscans exceed in number the Dominicans, Augustinians, sandalled and bare-footed Carmelites, Capuchins, and Jesuits, who are all to be found already in Ireland. The orders of Benedictines and Cistercians returned there after the revolt of the regular canons; and the Premonstrantines are now preparing to transport themselves thither, having formerly had monasteries in the island. But, in order to prevent disturbances, they will be prohibited by a special decree from repossessing themselves of the churches and monasteries formerly belonging to their order without express permission from Rome. The nuns, dispersed in various places, have mostly reassembled in private houses, observing the rules and strict seclusion, conformable to the order of St. Clare, which they had formerly professed. There have been processions of the Holy Sacrament in presence of immense multitudes, to the great astonishment of the heretics, provincial chapters held by the Franciscans, Dominicans, and bare-footed Carmelites, for the purpose of public discussions, besides many other pious acts, much to the edification and consolation of the faithful. The ecclesiastical causes, which are at present entertained by the Supreme Council, presided over by the prelates, will by degrees be transferred to their tribunals, where the same archbishops and bishops, again seated in their respective dioceses, will induce the Council to take no part in any censure of which these ecclesiastics are themselves the proper judges. It will, however, be your Excellency's province at the proper time to establish these ecclesiastical tribunals.

Having now arrived almost imperceptibly at the fourth and most important point of these instructions, I must observe that the first and greatest object of your Excellency must be to establish in Ireland an unalterable right to the public exercise of the Catholic religion. To this object all your skill and energy must be assiduously devoted.

On your arrival in Ireland you will consult with the four Archbishops, at Kilkenny, Waterford, or wherever the Council is sitting, and at which your Excellency will preside. You will acquaint them with the object of your mission, the powers vested in you, and the aid to be sent to the country by His Holiness, by the Roman nobles, and by other pious persons, for the service of God and the Catholic religion.

You will, at the same time, learn from them, and also from Father Scarampi, every particular respecting the state of public worship, and all other necessary matters, in order that your authority and skill may be directed in the most efficacious manner to sustain the power and relieve the distress of the Church.

When thoroughly conversant with these matters, you will endeavour to unite the clergy amongst themselves, to animate their zeal, and to employ well the opportunity placed in their hands by the all-blessed God, as from advices received we find that, although the greater number are warmly interested in the enterprise, timid men are not wanting, nor even some who, preferring a private and undisturbed life to the public weal, are unhappily indifferent on the subject, nor think it of importance that a Government under a Catholic head be established in the island, provided the private celebration of mass be not forbidden by the heretical Viceroy. Your Excellency may, perhaps, find some who, much to their shame, fearing a rigid reformation in the observances and discipline of the Church, will strongly oppose all measures taken to re-establish the public exercise of the Catholic religion in Ireland. Towards these you must proceed with consummate skill and prudence, just as in a vineyard which has been allowed to run wild for a century, we cannot all at once clear the ground of suckers and brambles, but must gradually and carefully extirpate these, and bring the land again under cultivation.

By means of this union your Excellency will be enabled to introduce into the Church a strict observance of the decrees of the holy Council of Trent; and to this end you will use the utmost diligence, as on its success will depend the success of the reformation necessary in the present relaxed state of clerical discipline. These decrees, founded on ancient canons and councils, will appear neither new nor more strict than those which prevail among all well-regulated churches and clergy.

Father Scarampi has engaged in this work with great ardour.

The archbishops are, by a special order, obliged to obey these decrees, and to secure the observance of them by their suffragans throughout their dioceses; and though some of the regular clergy have shown themselves averse to it, we hope that your Excellency's skill, prudence, and influence will overcome every obstacle in the establishment of this primary and important point. You will receive much assistance from the archbishops and bishops, who will emulate the zeal shown by yourself, as they are already convinced that if the habits and discipline of the clergy were regulated by these holy decrees, the laity would be induced to respect their pastors, to venerate the jurisdiction of the ecclesiastical tribunals, and to guard the immunities and privileges of the

Church. But your Excellency will do well to pay the closest attention in providing for the latter, as many of the principal benefices in the island are now vacant. It is probable that the Supreme Council may object to all the vacancies being immediately filled up, partly in order to prevent the increase of ecclesiastical votes, and partly that the revenues of the vacant bishoprics may be applied as hitherto to the expenses of war, and for other political purposes. Nevertheless, due provision for these will not fail to be made in Rome, so soon as your Excellency deems it to be really necessary, as we are frequently assured it is. You will, therefore, send us full particulars respecting the character of all who themselves aspire to benefices, or are proposed for them by others; and these promotions will be conferred on the most learned, the most pious, and those most versed in ecclesiastical affairs, so that by a good selection of bishops we may secure that of the parish priests, whose office is so all important in leading the people to the way of truth, and in upholding the practice of divine worship.

The priests must be men of acknowledged merit and exemplary character, and it will be your Excellency's duty to designate such for election, and to induce those of the laity who are in possession of Catholic property to provide sufficient means, not only for their support, but for the proper administration of the Holy Sacraments. And, speaking of ecclesiastical property, I must not omit to inform your Excellency that much of this is in the hands of heretics and of secular Catholics, and that when restored, as we fervently hope it may be, a portion must be applied for the use of the churches and monasteries originally in possession of it, as well as to the poorer parishes, and for other such ecclesiastical requirements. Much of this property may have been secularized by Cardinal Pole, by virtue of a bull of Julius III., of which a copy will be given to your Excellency. The rest will probably be found to be in the hands of Catholics or of heretics, who, converted to our religion with their sons or nephews, have retained possession of these lands without any just title. Now, the first have nothing new to learn on this head, although few of them will of their own accord desire to adjust matters with the Church; the second class must be taught that, if they would live with a safe and untroubled conscience, they must come to proper terms with the Church. Full power is therefore conferred upon your Excellency to treat with the landowners, and you will exercise it with great circumspection, applying to each abuse its fitting remedy. Some you may be obliged to discharge from all liability, while it may be advisable to grant leases to others, either in perpetuity or for terms of lives; in fine, you will vary the conditions according as the various cases may seem to require. But, under all circumstances, your Excellency must insist that a sufficient income, arising either from tithes, annual collections, or assignments of cultivated land, be granted by the secular holders of Church property to all priests and parishes, as in no other way can their possession be secured of what was originally intended *solely* for the support of the clergy and of the churches.

Until now the power of deciding on the retention of these lands has been vested in the missionaries, provided the possessors bound themselves by oath to abide by the judgment of the Church, whenever the whole kingdom of Ireland should again acknowledge the supremacy of the Holy See.

This oath has awakened scruples and fears in the minds of many of these persons, as seeing the kingdom gradually reduced to obedience, they doubt whether they may not soon be obliged, not less in virtue of their oath than by the requirements of justice, to restore the whole or a part of their gains. Hence they are, I do not say merely lukewarm, but actually indifferent to the welfare of the public; and, swayed by self-interest, they neither care nor wish for the establishment of the public exercise of the Catholic religion in the kingdom. With persons such as these you will proceed by gentle means to lead them to a knowledge of the truth and the way of salvation, but not in such a manner as to discourage the faithful and the humble, as self-interest too often leads men to excuse their own shortcomings by the bad example of others. The regular clergy have always been the great support of the true faith, and the island of Ireland in times past felt more than any other country the benefit resulting from their labours. The monastic orders were the first to plant the banner of the faith there; and, to say nothing of the ancient monasteries founded by St. Patrick, St. Columbus, and St. Malachy, not unlike those of the antient Anchorites in more recent times, the Regular Canons, Benedictines, Cistercians, and Premonstrantines have established many new colleges and new monasteries.

Under Honorius III. two new orders arose—the Franciscans and Dominicans—and from time to time other mendicant orders were piously received in the island, where they built houses and convents in which flourished many learned and holy men.

But, at one time, both monks and monasteries were reduced by heresy and schism to the lowest ebb. The monks, deprived of their convents and homes, wandered from house to house, and endeavoured, by assuming various disguises, still to remain in Ireland. Now, however, some of the Franciscans, Dominicans, and Jesuit Fathers, clothed in the habits of their orders, have been restored to their old monasteries, while others propose to found new ones.

Your Excellency will, therefore, enjoin them to reside in their cloisters, and to subject themselves to all the regular observances. For this purpose they must not scatter themselves in many different convents, but should only occupy a few, according to their number, so that considerable bodies may thus be established, which, at a future day, may be again dispersed throughout the kingdom to occupy the monasteries of which they were formerly deprived.

In order to secure good scholars, young men of a proper frame of mind, and clothed in the habit of their order, ought to be placed as novices in the convents, under the care of superiors of known virtue and exemplary conduct so that these new plantations, taking firm root in piety, may, without fear of being overcome by the fierce temptations of Satan, happily fructify in the vineyard of the Lord, and spread abroad by their lives the sweet odour of sanctity.

For the novices there should be introduced into the convents the study of philosophy and of scholastic and moral theology, while good readers and tutors should also be provided, and from time to time public examinations and discussions be held, so that the scholars may, by a holy emulation, ascend to the temple of religion by the steps of knowledge and virtue.

But emulation, however laudable when restrained by modesty and directed to the service and glory of God, is, on the contrary, baneful, when under the mask of religion, it breaks the ties of charity, causing disturbances and dissensions, scandalising and offending all mankind.

Your Excellency must especially put down the shameful exhibitions of rivalry, which so generally occur at the establishment of a new confraternity, on the institution of some particular congregation, or at the solemnities and processions held on the same day and hour by different monks in honour of some particular festival.

You will, with your usual prudence and skill, study to eradicate these disorders, and, at the same time, make public such regulations as may prevent a repetition of them, and maintain the union, charity, and peace, which are so necessary to the settlement of affairs.

From the discipline of the regular clergy I pass to the education of the secular youth, who should properly be educated in colleges and universities; but as these were destroyed by the heretics, permission must be given to the Jesuit Fathers to erect their schools in some principal city; and Father Scarampi has already been in treaty for a church and monastery in Kilkenny, which formerly belonged to the Benedictines, and is now in the possession of the magistrate of that city. It is to be given up to the Fathers, as they have always been willing to instruct the young, when inclined to piety and to the acquisition of knowledge.

This treaty, if not concluded already, must be speedily brought to a termination by your Excellency. You will, however, carefully guard against exciting the opposition of the Benedictines, or of other persons concerned; as much of the success I hope for to the holy cause, from the labours of the society, will depend on the interest taken by the city itself in what is to be done. In furtherance of this end it is proposed to assign also to the Jesuits a parish church in Waterford, if no great difficulty or opposition be made by those whose interests are naturally involved. In this matter also your Excellency will seek in so good a cause to avoid all grounds of dispute.

Some nuns of the order of St. Clare, who were expelled from their convent during the last revolution, have no asylum, but wander about the country, living in private houses, although still endeavouring to observe the regulations and seclusion of the cloister. They must be immediately provided for. Orders were transmitted to Father Scarampi to summon them all to Galway, and to induce the Archbishop of Tuam to provide a habitation and other necessaries for them, so that they may no longer be seen wandering about, to their own great peril and to the scandal of religion. If this has not been found practicable, perhaps your Excellency may deem it advisable to settle them in Kilkenny, Waterford, or some other city, where alms will not be wanting to provide them with needful food and the proper dress of their order.

Nothing will give greater vigour to your Excellency's authority in promoting the free exercise of the Catholic religion than the union of all the Catholics, particularly of those to whom the government of the kingdom is deputed; though, if their ardour is allowed to cool, they may equally incline to peace on disadvantageous conditions, and return (which God forbid) to their former miseries and afflictions.

In the General Parliament, held at Kilkenny shortly after the rising, the Catholics explained their intentions in a petition which they presented to the King, and in which they declared that, not having taken up arms against His Majesty, but against the English Parliament, which had endeavoured to annihilate the Catholic religion and to establish Puritanism in the island, they were entitled, equally with the Scotch, to the free exercise of their religion. They further demanded that the ecclesiastical hierarchy and the religious orders should be maintained in their ancient condition; that the bishops and priests should enjoy the Church property to the exclusion of the heretics; that the Viceroy and other governors and ministers of the island should be Catholics; that all the property taken from the Catholics during the reign of Elizabeth should be restored; that no colonies of English or Scotch should be introduced into the island, unless composed of Catholics, or at least of liberal Protestants; that foreign trade should be permitted; that a Parliament should be held in Ireland, distinct from that of England; and, finally, they declared that they had never refused obedience to the King. They promised to defend with their lives the royal prerogative, and to recognise the King as the legitimate and supreme head in all civil affairs, as they do the Roman Pontiff in all that regards their spiritual welfare. Their laudable anxiety to obtain above all things the free exercise of their religion you will encourage and confirm with unabated zeal, and you will assure them that whatever conditions the King and his ministers may propose, if not founded on this basis, will have no security, and will be a source of disgrace and of shame. To this end Pope Urban, of blessed memory, unceasingly laboured; and to this end now labours His Holiness, through your Excellency's means, with the aid of the money and arms already intrusted to you, and with the hope of further assistance, if required. It is evident that no advantage has accrued from the truce concluded a year ago to last till next May, nor from the proposal which has been made for peace; as the first has only served to cool the ardour of those who prefer a life of idleness and inactivity, and the second has been rendered fruitless by the arts of the Marquis of Ormond, the present Viceroy, a Protestant, who, although Irish, not only will never yield, save by force, to the wishes of the Catholics, but, by gaining time, hopes to create dissensions amongst them, and to wean them from the common cause. They must then be induced to adhere to their first resolution not to enter upon a treaty, truce, or peace of any kind, unless the first and essential point of the free exercise of the Catholic religion in Ireland be secured; and your Excellency will know without my here entering upon the subject, what course to take, what means to employ, to what devices to resort, what correspondence in and out of the island to maintain, whom to trust and whom to distrust, and, in fine, all that ought to be done to complete the glorious enterprise with which you are now intrusted.

I will only observe that, although all the four Archbishops are full of zeal, the one most to be confided in is the Archbishop of Tuam, and, amongst the bishops, Emerie of Clogher. You will on all occasions show yourself frank and friendly to all, and will avoid all appearance of artifice, as the Irish, like all the other Ultramontanes, are full of suspicious doubts; therefore, as there are partisans of France and Spain in the island, your Excellency will do well to maintain a complete neutrality, so that no leaning to one party more than another may be visible or may be commented upon in public.

This will be accomplished by always bearing in mind the chief object of your mission, which is the restoration of the public exercise of the Catholic religion, the reform of the secular and regular clergy, and by not being diverted to any other negotiations, since both Crowns are equally desirous of the propagation of the true faith, and the preservation of Catholicity. And, whether you pass through France, which is the more convenient and agreeable journey to Ireland, and consult with the Queen of England, now residing at Paris, and the French ministers; or, whether you go to Spain or Flanders, and confer with the Spanish King or his ministers, we rest satisfied of your Excellency's prudence, and are convinced that it will guide you in your future communications, which need not extend beyond simple compliments, and a positive assurance that His Holiness has no other object in this mission, than the salvation of souls by means of the public exercise of the Catholic religion in Ireland. You must everywhere exclude the sinister idea of any partiality, so objectionable in a minister of the Church; but as secrecy is the soul of the most important negotiations, your Excellency will recollect to preserve it above all things. For this purpose two forms of cipher will be explained to you—one for the Secretary of State alone, the other in common with the Nuncios of France and Spain, and the Apostolic ministers resident in Flanders, but with whom you will hold only such correspondence as may be necessary for the ends proposed.

I have left to the last to represent to you, that as your Excellency goes to Ireland as the representative of the Holy See, you must carefully uphold its dignity, not only in your own person, but in that of your subordinates, who, according as they show themselves men of letters and of good manners, will gain reputation, and will preserve the good name which Father Scarampi has earned there for the ecclesiastics of Italy. They should, therefore, avoid ladies conversaziones, drinking parties and banquets, guard themselves against speaking too much of passing events and reports, especially of war in England, Germany, Flanders, or Spain, as the evil-minded are apt to judge of the intentions of the masters by the sentiments of their dependents. But this may appear superfluous to your Excellency, whose household has ever been an example to those of all other prelates.

Let your Excellency then depart with good courage, and with the benediction of His Holiness, paternally bestowed upon you. It remains to me only to pray God that all happiness may attend you, and yet more, that success may crown your negotiations, to the glory of His Divine Majesty, of these you will give us constant and minute details, and especially inform us of the exact state in which you find the Catholic religion on your arrival in Ireland, and of all other matters which you may consider deserving of our notice.

SECRET INSTRUCTIONS.

I. It is necessary that the Nuncio should depart as speedily as possible, and not linger on the journey, that he may arrive in Ireland before the new campaign begins, in order to assist the troops with money and advice. By prompt movements his passage will be safer, being made before the sea becomes infested by the hostile fleets of the Parliament of the Dutch and the Turks.

II. In passing through France he must try to remove all the suspicions afloat in that nation; and assure the Queen Regent and Cardinal Mazarin, that his visit is one of friendship only; he may afterwards assure the Queen of England and her powerful favourite Lord Jermyn, of his perfect good will to the kingdom of England, that he has no other object than to sustain and propagate the Catholic faith there, and to endeavour to unite believers in the bond of a single religion which would bear fruit in the greater security of that Crown.

III. He must persuade the Queen of England to see the great advantage of this negotiation to the English Crown, which, being in a minority in Parliament, and hopeless of foreign aid, will, together with the English Catholics, find its only resource in the assistance of the Irish Catholics, as none can be expected from his Majesty's Protestant subjects or from the loyal party in the Island, because their strength is utterly exhausted; on the contrary, the troops of the Puritan Parliament and of the Scotch are powerful and flourishing; but if the Catholics could only defeat them they would afterwards, when strengthened and victorious, willingly turn to the assistance of the King.

IV. The Queen thus convinced, it will be useful to discover dexterously, who has influence and authority over the Marquis of Ormond, and if he is dependent on the Queen, to procure from her some letter, or private paper, or countersign, to the end that, if unwilling or unable to give up Ulster and Dublin which he commands, openly into the hands of the Catholics, he may at least secretly assist them by his connivance and secret counsels. It is to be hoped also that the Marquis, having some hint from the Queen, may defer to her wishes, as he certainly will do if he has the good of his country at heart, for he is not only Irish, and by some thought to be a Catholic in secret, certainly born of Catholic parents, a Catholic till his sixteenth year, and was then sent to England and educated at Court, where he imbibed the Lutheran doctrine, or at least feigns to profess it.

V. These interviews with the Queen must be private and so rare, that her Court may not suspect their object, she being surrounded by heretics, both Protestant and Puritan, who take fright and offence at every little thing, even at a shadow.

VI. He must be on his guard against the many English Catholics at the Court, whose zeal for the faith is not ardent enough to hear with pleasure, of the victories gained in its cause by the Irish; on account of the natural and undying hatred which exists between the two nations, the English always desiring to keep the Irish under their yoke, on account of their being useful in carrying out the decrees, and strengthening the authority of the government.

VII. He must not remain long in Paris, lest the ill-affected should warn the Parliament of the enterprise, and by discovering his place of embarkation, enable them to devise some mischief at sea.

VIII. The most secure means of transport for the specie must be considered; if several ships sail together, it might be well to send it all at once, as the French merchants have no corresponding bankers in Ireland on whom to give bills of exchange. But if the passage is not safe, and if there are no ships of war provided, a part should be deposited in the hands of the Nuncio at Paris, and the remainder forwarded to Ireland to defray all necessary expenses, and to encourage the soldiers by the hope of immediate pay.

IX. In choosing a port for disembarkation, the Nuncio must avoid that of Waterford, defended by the fort of Duncannon, in the hands of the Parliamentarians, unless he hears that it has fallen to the Catholics who are now besieging it. Let him inform the Supreme Council of his arrival, that he may have a speedy answer; and let him cheerfully take up his abode wherever it has been prepared for him, provided it is suitable and at the place of reception.

X. He must fix his residence as near as possible to the said Council, and through private friends gain over its cleverest, most faithful, and zealous men, such as Malachy, Archbishop of Tuam, and Emerie, Bishop of Clogher, but taking good care not to excite a shadow of suspicion in the minds of the other members of the Council devoted to Ormond.

XI. In order to keep up the correspondence between the Papal Nuncio and the Roman Curia, and to facilitate the transmission of despatches and assistance, let him treat with the Council for two light fast ships, to serve as couriers, the experience of the last two years having shown how much communication is interrupted from want of some such arrangement.

XII. Let him use all diligence to urge the Council to storm the fort of Duncannon (if not in their possession previous to his arrival), as it is most injurious to the Catholic interest, its situation giving Parliament the power of landing at its pleasure both troops and stores for the two provinces of Munster and Leinster.

XIII. The city of Limerick, as neutral and isolated, rules itself, apart from the government of the Council, and although it is Catholic and aids the Catholic cause, its separation, caused by private reasons and domestic dissensions, is most injurious to the common cause of the Catholics: wherefore he will employ every possible means, with skill and moderation, to bring it into union with the other Catholic cities.

XIV. Let him promote the interests of the Catholic religion in such a manner as to show he considers it one with the English Crown, and hold firmly to the principle that at no time could he wish its yoke to be thrown off, nor ever hearken to propositions which tend to the contrary.

XV. To stimulate the Catholics to concord and to the prosecution of the enterprise, let him assure all who are in possession of ecclesiastical property that it will not be taken from them, nor will they be molested on account of it, but rather that it will be confirmed to them, as is explained in the other document.

XVI. He will make some reform in the expenses of the provincial magistrates who have large stipends; any of them distinguished by rank, experience, and knowledge of military affairs should be chosen to preside over and direct all warlike preparations, and the governors of the other provinces must submit to these resolutions.

XVII. The achievements of the army in Scotland were of the greatest advantage to Ulster, where the Scotch are more numerous and powerful than elsewhere, and also to the Crown, on which account he will take care to maintain it; and as the best reason for this let him vaunt of the acknowledged allegiance of this army, and thus be able to devote it to the defence of the Crown according to the wise and well-known wishes of the Queen.

XVIII. Let him cultivate secret conferences with her, and for this purpose employ a prudent, faithful, and proved emissary, but not one so conspicuous as to induce suspicion; and impress upon her how truly this negotiation will open the way to greater submissiveness to the throne, and to the restitution of its rights throughout the kingdom.

XIX. Let him exert himself to defeat with subtle industry and vigilance the machinations of certain royalists and others of Paris who are desirous that the Queen shall proceed to Ireland; as such a measure would have an injurious effect on the progress of the Catholics, because the well-affected and the zealous, seeing her constantly surrounded by heretics, would become suspicious and fearful; while the lukewarm and political neutrals would find it easy to disembarrass themselves from the opinions and counsels given by the heretics. Besides, it would be necessary to provide for all her expenses, which would exhaust the treasury of the Catholics, who are in the greatest want of all their funds to carry on the war.

XX. It will be very expedient to find out if the Marquis of Ormond, the chief head of this affair, has any particular predilection of which advantage might be taken. He has a brother in the Catholic party named Richard Butler, an excellent Catholic and an illustrious man; he might also be influenced by Viscount Mountgarret and the Bishop of Ossory, both noble and wise men, most ardent for the party and for the common cause, as Richard Butler has always shown himself also to be.

MEMORANDA

FOR

MONSIGNOR RINUCCINI,

ARCHBISHOP OF FERMO,

AND DESIGNATED NUNCIO TO IRELAND.

In order that your Excellency may be informed of the present state of the English Catholics, you are to know that despite the rigorous penal laws enacted against them, they have never, during this tempest of plots and rebellion, failed in the fealty and obedience due to the person of their King. On the contrary, they have testified so great zeal to his Majesty, that although his enemies have sought by divers means and with much subtlety to corrupt them, and even offered to revoke the said laws (which are of such a nature that if put into execution they would totally ruin them), if they would unite with them in this rebellion, yet they have never listened to these proposals, and piously resolved to sustain with patience the utter ruin of fortune and goods in the provinces governed by the Parliamentarians, rather than abandon their King, and at the peril of their lives, and at the sacrifice of all they possess have ever maintained the rights of the Crown. There is not to be found in the kingdom a single Catholic of any consideration by birth, or wealth, or other distinction, who has served the Parliament against the King; but, on the contrary, many of the most eminent have contributed large sums of money for his Majesty's use, one in particular having advanced 60,000 crowns, and others, who were unable to assist him with money, have done so with personal service, with name and character.

Notwithstanding these striking proofs of loyalty, His Majesty has been guided by the counsels of those who, hostile to the Catholics and envious of their merits, have taken every occasion to misinterpret their actions, suspect their intentions, and throw contempt on their persons; so that, although in all the confusion and treachery towards the King, not a single Catholic was found, who either through incapacity or malice failed to carry out the duty assigned to him with loyal fidelity, it was publicly declared in the royal Council, and in the King's presence, that the Catholics had never served him nor done their duty, and that whilst they held any command in the royal army, the arms of His Majesty would never be successful. Such calumnies were industriously circulated to destroy their credit with the King, and render them suspected by him. Again, when it was hoped that the piety and goodness of the Queen would be a refuge for the Catholics in their desolation, those who influenced her were unfortunately also of the royal council, being persons alienated from the Catholic religion; and thus the Catholics were abandoned even by her; and many noblemen of high rank and talent, whose counsel would have been most important to Her Majesty, were obliged to absent themselves from the court, as she looked coldly on them. And more than this, by the subtle machinations of the heretics, by whom the Queen is entirely guided, she became a powerful instrument for the destruction of the Catholics, and of the Catholic religion.

For these reasons many of the most eminent Catholics have retired into France and Flanders; others are dispersed in various parts of England, where they are treated as prisoners by the Parliamentary party, where it predominates, and by the Royalists where the King rules. From this it follows that whatever their rank and fortune (unless perhaps invited by the King), it will not be possible at present for them to unite in one body, by which means alone they could perform some signal service and regain the favour of the King, in spite of the malice of their enemies.

The most probable means to remedy these evils, and to

enable the Catholics to reap some benefit from the disturbed state of the kingdom, will be to procure an amicable adjustment of the differences between the Irish and the King. This may be done in two ways: the first, that the Irish should include in the articles of accommodation with the King some conditions in favour of the English Catholics. This measure, although undoubtedly the more efficacious, might perhaps not only fail in its object, but make the condition of the English Catholics worse, and perhaps impede the negotiations between the Irish and the King, by making their proceedings suspected of being rather the result of factious combination, than of a real desire to serve His Majesty; besides which, those of his ministers who through hatred of the Catholic religion have thrown obstacles in the way of an accommodation between the Irish and the King, would become more exasperated, and would have a better pretext for opposing it, if conditions were demanded for others besides the nation itself.

A second way would be to insist on terms which would secure the Irish in their own property, and enable them to send a considerable army into England to the assistance of His Majesty; with this army the English Catholics would unite, and thus form together a Catholic army of the two nations, by means of which they might do some signal service, and thus find favour with the King, despite the malice of all their enemies.

To insure success in this negotiation, two points remain to be well considered; first, that the requisite conditions be well weighed, so that the services we hope from this Catholic army be efficacious, the second, to facilitate by every means the agreement between the King and the Irish. The first of these conditions may be reduced to the following articles:—

I. That the Irish army shall never agree to land in England with less than ten or twelve thousand effective men, that they may be able to defend themselves without danger of being cut to pieces by the English, who serve under the King.

II. That two seaports, well fortified, be placed in their hands, to disembark their troops in England, and that these places be under the command of persons in their confidence.

III. That the Generals of the army and all the officers, colonels, captains, &c., besides the governors of the said places, be appointed by the Irish.

IV. That their Generals be not subject to any other commander whatever, nor be obliged to obey any orders except such as come direct from the King.

V. That this army be not dispersed nor divided, but shall remain always in one body, nor be separated, or ordered on any particular service save with the consent of their General and the Council of war.

VI. That permission and authority from the King be accorded to the English Catholics to form themselves into a body of cavalry proportionate in strength to the Irish infantry, to join them when and where appointed by the Irish General, to serve in his army and under his command. This condition is so essential to the Irish Catholics, that the King cannot refuse it, as they are so hated by the English Protestants that they would be in constant danger of treachery, if marching with cavalry, commanded by Protestant officers.

VII. That the Catholic general of this cavalry be a person whom the Irish can entirely trust, and must therefore be first accepted by their own General.

To facilitate the agreement between the King and the Irish, the articles must be so framed that as nothing essential to the full establishment of the Catholic religion in Ireland be omitted, matters of less moment may be remitted, in particular those tending to changes in the political government, as they would, without any doubt, retard the agreement, and force the King to make peace with his Parliament rather than with his Irish subjects, and this step would bring inevitable ruin on the Catholics of both kingdoms, since they never could resist the united forces of England and of Scotland.

And more, if the Irish seek to introduce changes into the government they will commit the same error for which the Parliament has been so much blamed, and whereas till now they have maintained a just war, that is one purely for the sake of religion, they would then become rebels, and justify the war carried on by the King against them.

Again, when the confederated Catholics of Ireland have once obtained from the King an agreement, by which all the offices and fortresses of the kingdom are placed in their hands, opportunities will not be wanting to do away with the taxes, and reform abuses in the political government; these for the most part introduced by heresy, will disappear with it, by the help of a free Parliament, and without disturbing the existing laws. Lastly, His Holiness, sending at this juncture, a Nuncio of eminence with money and other supplies to the Irish, if new protests be made which refer, not to religion, but mainly to the government, every change will be ascribed to his counsels, to the great exultation of the heretics, and to the greatest prejudice of the poor Catholics as it might appear that His Holiness, not content with the establishment of religion, sought to incite the King's subjects to open rebellion against the temporal crown, and to divert them from their legitimate subjection to His Majesty. Therefore, as His Holiness can do nothing more glorious before God, than to strengthen the resolution of the Irish to establish on a permanent foundation the Catholic religion in Ireland, so your Excellency can do nothing more effectual to help them in this work, or more worthy of apostolic zeal, than to seek to hold them firm in loyalty and temporal obedience to their King, and consequently, to cut short any new or political propositions, which might create a shadow of suspicion to the contrary.

It may be that, at present, the confederate Catholics of

Ireland have no other thought than for their religion, still when united into one powerful body, and accustomed to govern themselves, they may readily, and with some prospect of success, become ambitious to throw off the Royal yoke; therefore they will require to be restrained, as we see by experience of the English Parliament, is quite necessary, since at first its members were moderate in their demands, but are now puffed up by the ambition to govern, and by confidence in their own power.

Another means of facilitating the treaty between the King and the Catholics of Ireland would be to induce the Queen to promote the negotiation by using her influence with the King; in this His Holiness can do much, partly by paternal admonition, but more effectually by expressly refusing to grant the supplies she entreats for, when her Ambassador, Sir Kenelm Digby, shall arrive at this Court, unless the King first agrees to concede to the Irish their just demands for their religion. It is evident that His Holiness, if he acted otherwise, would not only lose the fruits of the aid he would send to her Majesty, but would even retard the reconciliation between the King and the Catholics of Ireland, it being certain that His Majesty will never come to this agreement unless forced to it from the want of troops to oppose the Parliament. And moreover, if His Holiness and the principal Catholics should grant to the King all the supplies he requires, it is quite certain that he and his ministers would not fail to accept the first offer made by the rebellious Parliament, provided it did not touch the royal prerogative, even though it might prove the ruin of the Catholics, despite every promise made to them by His Majesty in order to obtain assistance. If, therefore, His Holiness should advance money on promises alone, without other security, the King may perhaps perform what he at present intends, but in such a way as will prove injurious to the Catholics, as the Parliament, so much the more exasperated against them, and unable to show their displeasure otherwise, will wreak their vengeance on them; and the King, bound not only by promises but by oaths many times spontaneously taken and published to the world, and agreeing on this point with his Parliament, will consent to whatever persecutions it may ordain to extirpate the Catholic religion in England. Thus did His Majesty when, notwithstanding his oath to the contrary, he consented to the sentence of death on the Viceroy of Ireland; thus did he when he allowed the bishops to be removed from Parliament, in spite of his solemn oath to protect them; and thus did he when he persecuted the Catholics in the first Parliament, after his marriage with the sister of the King of France, in spite of the stipulations made between the two kings in their favour. Before, therefore, His Holiness agrees to send any considerable assistance for the benefit of the Catholic religion in England, it will be necessary that their Majesties condescend to certain conditions, of which the following are the principal:—

1. The revocation of all penal laws against the Catholics.
2. The abolition of the prescribed oath of supremacy.
3. That Catholics be declared capable of holding governments, offices, dignities, and all honourable situations in the kingdom and Parliament not less than the other subjects of His Majesty.
4. That no treaty shall be concluded between His Majesty and his rebellious Parliament, until they ratify these articles.
5. That in order to secure these conditions, all the fortresses in Ireland be put into the hands of English and Irish Catholics, because without some such pledge, their Majesties' promises can not be depended on.

Lastly. In case His Holiness should vouchsafe to assist the Queen with a considerable sum of money, it will be more safe that the pontifical ministers in Ireland and France shall have the charge of disbursing it, and that it shall not be consigned to the royal ministers, because a great part of it would be applied to the benefit of private persons, and the

King be but ill served. Perhaps it may be better not to send any assistance until a Catholic army is on foot, as it appears the supplies furnished by His Holiness to the Queen cannot be employed in a manner more beneficial to the King and to religion than in properly maintaining this Catholic army; and the more powerful this army is, the more favourable will be the conditions obtained from the King by the Catholics of England.

What I have now stated to your Excellency is the opinion of English Catholics in general. Some there are who, from want of judgment, or from motives of self interest, would desire peace on any terms, allowing themselves to be deceived by the fine words of the Protestants, and perhaps would persuade the Irish to make peace with the King without the conditions necessary to the security of an affair so important. This I have wished to notify to your Excellency, in case you should meet with any of these men who for the most part are of those employed by their Majesties or the royal ministers in this negotiation with Ireland.

In fine, this rebellion in England has already caused so many divisions in religion, and so many disputes among the Protestants themselves, that all who have some belief in a future life are beginning to waver, and would become Catholics if they were not restrained by the fear of losing their property and temporal comforts. If, then, by means of this Catholic army, you can obtain from His Majesty the revocation of the penal laws against the Catholics, the abolition of the proposed oath of fidelity, and freedom *in religion*, *i.e.*, that the Catholics be able to hold all appointments in the kingdom and in Parliament like his other subjects, we may hope in a few years for the conversion of the whole kingdom—a most important step towards the eradication of heresy from the whole north, and without which, the Irish can never hope to enjoy in peace the conditions granted in favour of the true faith in Ireland.

EMBASSY IN IRELAND.

To Cardinal Pamphili.

Florence, April 7, 1645.

In my letter of 28th of last month I informed your Eminence of the approaching return of the Grand Duke and the Court to Florence, which took place yesterday, and all in good health. On the same day His Highness was pleased to send one of his gentlemen to my house to conduct me to the palace, where all those honours were rendered to me, which this Court is accustomed to bestow on the Nuncios of the Apostolic See, and which in my person, being by birth a vassal of this Serene House, have shone with great lustre, and have made me sensible how high the favours of His Holiness can raise the lowly, and cover the imperfections of a subject.

I presented the letters of His Holiness with the expression of his paternal affection towards these Princes, which is now so well known by other tokens to their Highnesses, that even my weak voice could act as its interpreter. The Grand Duke, in particular, is very much edified by His Holiness's watchful care in aiding and protecting the Irish Catholics; and were it not for the present necessities of the other troubled parts of Europe, he would have condescended to offer some assistance for those people. Hence I am not without hope that in the progress of time the vigilance of the Holy See will induce this prince to show some notable proof of his piety. His Highness has shown me, with his usual sincerity, that he was greatly pleased by what I said to him on the part of your Eminence; and I am happy in seeing in the close affection of their Highnesses, the felicity of that union which was so much desired for many years.

At the end I pronounced the benediction from His Holiness to the Serene Prince, who has been brought up in such a spirited lively manner, that of his own accord he made an obeisance, and told me that he humbly kissed the feet of His Holiness for it. I look every hour now for Invernizi, who is to bring me the remainder of the despatches and papers, when I shall immediately depart for Leghorn, where I am still prepared to go, even if he should not arrive within two days. So great is my desire to show my ready obedience to your Eminence's commands, a readiness which with reason increases daily in me from the news received at this Court, lest the ignominious peace between the King of England and his Parliament should be concluded. May it please God that this beginning may second the magnanimous sentiments of His Holiness, and be the foundation of that edifice which the Holy Father with so much merit desires to raise on the traces of the Apostles.

To the Same.

Genoa, April 15, 1645.

As I have already apprized your Eminence on the 7th instant, I determined to leave Florence in any case, and to await at Genoa the arrival of Signor Invernizi, who is to bring me the remaining despatches. I travelled slowly, to give him time to join me, but much to my astonishment, I arrived this evening at Genoa, and have received no intelligence of him whatever. In the meantime I shall celebrate Easter here ; and as soon as he makes his appearance, I shall be ready to proceed on my journey.

Meanwhile I have nothing to add to your Eminence, concerning the short way I have come, except that in Leghorn, as I had foreseen, the English merchants were very curious to learn at what time I should begin my journey, and the road I should take. Amongst these were some of the Parliamentary faction. This new proof of the ill-will of that nation, will make me doubly cautious about my embarkation for France, and this I say, not to induce further measures for my safety, on His Holiness's part, which I am sure are not needed, but that our Blessed Father and your Eminence may be fully assured of my readiness to serve the Holy See, as obstacles raised by an heretical kingdom have no power to frighten me from an enterprise commanded by His Holiness.

I kiss, with fervour, the feet of the Holy Father, through your Eminence, and make my humble reverence.

To the Same.

Genoa, April 15, 1645.

I had scarcely arrived here when I received your Eminence's packet, sent by Signor Invernizi, who still remains in Florence. In it I receive your command to present to Her Most Christian Majesty the Golden Rose, and the Brief from His Holiness which accompanies it.* In this fresh honour conferred on me by His Holiness and your Eminence I find new cause to be abashed, and in weighing my own insufficiency I see in comparison how great is the benignity of His Holiness and of your Eminence. I shall pay my respects to Her Majesty, I shall explain the motives of His Holiness, I shall paint in glowing colours the sublimity of the gift and the high value which Holy Church has set from time immemorial upon it, and the meaning carried with it. I know the effect I should desire as the result of this demonstration from His Holiness, and I pray God, that among my good fortunes, he will grant to me above all, to become worthy of being his minister. And now, rendering most humble thanks to your Eminence for the opinion you continue to hold despite my imperfections, I make my deep reverence.

* See Doc. No. I.

To the Same.

Genoa, April 19, 1645.

On arriving here, Signor Carlo Invernizi brought me the intelligence of the addition which the Holy Father has made to the congregation of Ireland, in the person of your Eminence. Truly an affair undertaken by His Holiness with such apostolic zeal must progress day by day, amid happy auguries. I thank God for the benefits which must accrue to those Catholics, and congratulate myself on the new protection I have acquired by this appointment, and which I pray your Eminence to deign to extend to me, always excusing my imperfections, and condescending to receive at its value the ardour of my will. Meanwhile I assure your Eminence that to be under your guidance will give me a new and greater confidence in a negotiation so arduous, and will impart a new spirit to the joyfulness which supports me.

I now make my most humble reverence.

To the Same.

Genoa, April 21, 1645.

Three days ago Signor Invernizi arrived here and delivered to me the remainder of the despatches for my journey, and the Blessed Rose from His Holiness; of this commission I wrote and returned the thanks due to your Eminence on the 15th instant. Amongst the despatches were three letters to their Serene Highnesses of Tuscany from your Eminence which are still in my possession, as they arrived after my departure from Florence, and the presentation of the Papal briefs to their Highnesses. When so doing I gave His Highness proofs so strong of your Eminence's affection for them, that if ever I had recognised that letters were not necessary, I knew it with certainty when there was such an interchange of sincere and reciprocal professions of affection. The honours I have received from this Republic since I received the briefs from His Holiness deserve now particular mention. Already on my arrival (without any movement on my part) it had been discussed how an Embassy in the person of a Nuncio (which is new to this dominion) should be treated; as it is here customary to make subtle distinctions between Royal and other Embassies. And though perhaps in many minds ingenious considerations arose why it should be separated from Royal ones, nevertheless with much applause and wisdom it was decided not to do so. I heard of this happy result with incredible satisfaction; not from a vain personal ambition, as I have no merit whatsoever, but to see His Holiness's magnanimous intentions towards Ireland exalted so greatly by the public approbation as to deserve no less an epithet than that of a royal thought.

Immediately therefore, six gentlemen were elected by the Senate, who came to visit me, and to signify, in ample terms, the resolution that had passed to treat me as a Nuncio of a Crown. The day following I had an hour appointed for an audience with the Doge, I was escorted from my house by a cortege of almost all the nobility, and having arrived at the palace on foot, I found the whole court-yard filled with files of arquebusiers, who fired a volley, as they also did again on my departure. At the foot of the stairs four Procurators met me, placed me in the middle of them; and conducted me to the presence chamber where the Doge waited. He descended four steps from the raised part of the room, advanced towards me with the rest of the Senators, and conducted me to the canopy on his left-hand, but to a seat a little lower than his own. Here, within sight and hearing of the whole assembly, in presenting the Brief, I unfolded the purpose and most holy views of the Blessed Father in the enterprise in Ireland. The Doge answered with high praise of this intention, and said that this mission was as far above all others as the zeal in the cause of pure apostolic faith transcends that which is tainted with any political purpose. An opinion pronounced so efficiently by the mouth of a Lay Prince, and in a free dominion, with no obligation to flatter, deserves to be esteemed as the conviction of truth. When it became known to him that I should desire to be accommodated with some ships to continue my journey, the Lower Council assembled the morning after, and determined to give me one as far as Cannes; notwithstanding that the Republic requires all their ships at the present moment to carry out expeditions to several places. The resolution passed with such a unanimity of votes, as I understand is not of frequent occurrence here. And so passed this secular compliment.

Cardinal Durazzo has, in equal proportion, done me similar honours, entertained me at dinner, returned my visit, and showed me the various beauties of the city, and although your Eminence will see in his letter, his continued and reverent obsequiousness to the Holy See, and to your Eminence, with all this, I must not omit to represent it myself, that I may not increase my deficiencies in the performance of my duty. To morrow, or the day after at farthest, we shall set off for Marseilles; and inasmuch as in leaving Italy I shall see the distance increase, so much the more do I hope to find my ardour increase to serve the Holy See, proving this marvellous effect of a spiritual charge upon the mind, that in distant countries, and among a strange people, the impulses which emanate from the Holy See, and the influence of the Pontifical authority, are more present and more vivid than ever.

I make my humble reverence.

To the Same.

Marseilles, April 30, 1645.

On the 21st I despatched one ordinary letter and one in cipher to your Eminence. I arrived here to day to resume my journey to-morrow, and have only to say that the Genoese galley conveyed me to Cannes, whence I travelled by land. On my arrival here I found a letter from Antonio and Dominico Mei, dated Lyons, April 26th, in which they say that there had been a report that the Catholics of Ireland had taken possession of all those places in the kingdom which remained in the power of the heretics, who were therefore expelled. These are the precise words of the letter written to Ottavio Cardone, a merchant of this place. Whatever truth there may be in this great news, will be discovered in the letters which are to follow.

In the meantime I cannot but rejoice in the report, which I judge to be founded on the general desire, because hoping that the safety and freedom of that kingdom would be one of the joys of the present Pontificate, one cannot hear without pleasure that the public voice already prepares the way for the splendid successes which will follow. I shall write from Avignon, and in the meanwhile,

With humble reverence to your Eminence, &c., &c.

To THE SAME.

Avignon, May 3, 1645.

Two days ago I wrote to your Eminence from Marseilles an account of the progress of my journey,* and will not omit to do the same from Avignon by the usual monthly messenger, although the place supplies no materials to communicate, save a new profession to your Eminence of my desire to be in a position to begin my services as soon as possible. I shall hasten the remainder of my journey as much as my strength will permit; since some Irish monks whom I met on the way, certify that the new aid from His Holiness, on which hopes of the greatest success are founded, is awaited in that kingdom with indescri-

* See Doc. No. II.

bable satisfaction. And although this news increases my anxiety and timidity on account of my own imperfections; I nevertheless feel they rest on the wisdom of the Blessed Father, and console myself with the opinions of those who know that in ecclesiastical enterprises the instrument however weak, can do all, by the superior hand which guides it.

With reverence, &c., &c.

To the Same.

Lyons, May 10, 1645.

I am now at Lyons, where I have remained a day for necessaries of the journey, and to pay my respects to His Eminence the Cardinal Archbishop. I have had an interview with the Mei, who sent me the news of the Irish successes, of which I informed your Eminence in my letter from Marseilles, of April 30th, and though I suppose you have the Gazette, printed at Genoa or Turin, I send your Eminence part of the letter itself from Rouen, where the others have been faithfully copied also. So large a share of success is hardly credible, but if even a part of it be true, we may reasonably hope that His Holiness's counsel and assistance will effect the rest. I set off to-day on my way to Paris, not so much from any necessity to hasten my arrival, as to have certain news of these successes, so much to be desired at the present conjuncture, when heresy is more triumphant than ever in Germany, and the Holy faith itself grows pale at the threats of the Turk.

&c., &c.

To the Same.

Paris, May 26, 1645.

From Lyons to Paris nothing occurred with which to trouble your Eminence with my letters. I have only to tell you that after having waited in that city on the Cardinal Archbishop of Lyons, His Eminence made no sort of demonstration towards me, although I remained two days after the visit, and although he said that he should call at my inn to offer me anything I might require.

I have been in Paris since Monday, where I was met and received with extreme promptitude and courtesy by Monsignor the Nuncio. I have not been able to begin any of my business hitherto, from a cough which attacked me after a long continuance of stormy weather, from which I hope soon to be free, with a little more of the repose which I have taken till now. I have not ceased, however, to see all the Irish who flock here with a variety of considerations and counsels, as also the English Catholics and other neutrals who come to explain their wishes and wants, and as is usual in important negotiations, making a great mixture of hopes and difficulties, which must be minutely sifted, to give to your Eminence in succeeding despatches as correct a report as possible. Meanwhile, I have learned here the certainty of the Fort of Duncannon being in the power of the Catholics, as I before advised you, but not the rest of the successes hinted at in the letter to Mei from Rouen, and of which I sent your Eminence a copy from Lyons. I have also heard only here, that the Queen of England has sent . . . . to His Holiness, and I shall hope, when in Ireland, to be favoured by hearing the result. I think it probable that this embassy may have some sort of relation with another which the same Queen despatched to Ireland some days ago, in the person of —————— of whom many here believe that he has been sent to forestal my arrival, Her Majesty's counsellors probably thinking that under this truly apostolic mission may be concealed artifices and designs totally alien, not only from the holy thoughts of the Father, but also to the nature of ecclesiastical missions, always and only devoted to the spiritual benefit of the people. I do not despair of being able to eradicate this notion, however strong, in the mind of Her Majesty or the King; since the simple title of my instructions is founded on these two axioms: Fidelity to God first, and then to the King. Count —— who came from Rouen to have an interview with me, told me also that he was apprized that the King of England had sent ———— to Ireland, which if true, must be the effect of a similar conviction. I regret my inability to reach Ireland before the dissolution of the General Assembly, but the respect due to this Court, and the arrangements for the security of my embarkation will occupy many days. I console myself, however, on not having lost a day (after I received the last despatches at Genoa) on the journey, and having hurried on even beyond my strength, makes me hope that His Holiness in his infinite benignity will be satisfied with me.

I have thought of sending, if I can, some person to Ireland to announce my arrival at Paris, and immediate departure thence, as I think this certainty would prevent the Assembly from passing any resolutions either final or contrary to His Holiness's wishes. But I fear that it will not be possible to carry out my wish, as it is said, that without a strong escort the journey and navigation are now dangerous. Yesterday evening the Irish secretary arrived here; he comes from Genoa, and probably we shall cross the ocean together. I have not been able, so soon, to learn any particulars from him, of what he has extracted from the Princes whom he has waited on; but the nature of a negotiation so justifiable and clear, admits of no answer but one, whether the assistance can or cannot be given. May it please God that the circumstances of the times may make this enterprise similar to that of former days in the conquest of the Holy Land, as indeed I esteem it as not very much its inferior. It may be then, that Christian alms will flow largely into that kingdom at once, and the zeal of His Holiness in obtaining and directing them would signalize his name equally with that of many of his ancestors who rendered themselves so famous in that holy expedition. Your Eminence will pardon me if jealousy for the glory of his house, transports me to form a desire so ambitious in this matter, and inasmuch as I am but an imperfect minister of his will so much the more eagerly do I supplicate the goodness and watchful care of His Holiness.

&c. &c.

To THE INTERNUNCIO IN FLANDERS.

Paris, May 31, 1645.

Monsignor the Nuncio has shown me part of a letter from you, Monsignor, in which you are pleased to warn me against allowing my journey to be too much talked of, for fear of the insidious attempts of the enemy. I beg not only to return the thanks due to you for such affectionate courtesy, but would beg of you to apprize me as long as I am here, if anything more touching this matter should come secretly to your ears. I may add that His Holiness and the Court of Rome had foreseen this before I set off; but as it was considered necessary that a person of high position should be deputed, it was impossible that my journey should be kept secret, at least to Paris, where I am commanded by His Holiness to obtain every moral security which can be had for my passage, and with the faith of a good Priest, leave the rest to God, the support and protector of the Irish Catholics, and who inspired His Holiness with the determination to send a prelate to their aid. If I shall be deemed worthy to begin the enterprise, this letter will serve as an introduction to you, Monsignor, for future transactions, and make known to you a servant who professes himself grateful to you in every possible manner.

With deep reverence, I kiss your hand.

To Cardinal Pamphili.

Paris, June 2, 1645.

A week ago I forwarded to your Eminence two ordinary letters, and three in cipher; to-day I have received a packet dated the 8th of last month containing an ordinary letter, and one in cipher, two briefs, and three documents. For to-day I have only to say that in company with Monsignor the Nuncio of France, I paid a visit to the Duke of Orleans, who was on the point of departing to join the army in Flanders. I presented to His Royal Highness the brief from our Holy Father, and your Eminence's letter, with the expression of all that was necessary on the part of both; and so far as we could gather from the usual brevity and medley of French compliments, His Royal Highness showed great compassion for the Irish Catholics, and rejoiced that His Holiness had resolved on consoling them in such a remarkable manner. The Nuncio and I then deemed it befitting to pray that the arms of His Highness might prosper always, when employed however in facilitating the universal peace, so ardently desired by His Holiness. Upon this His Royal Highness replied in a whisper, that the Spaniards did not desire peace, and would not until reduced by force to wish for it. On Sunday morning I had asked permission from the Queen to pay my respects to her, as I had not yet seen Her Majesty; but just as I was setting out I was attacked by a smart fever, which increased after dinner, and continued during the whole of Monday; so that I was obliged by duty to call in a physician; and have been hindered consequently from working to advantage this week. Thanks to God it was not a tertian fever, as they feared, and that with my little strength I have been able to accommodate myself to the French remedies of an incredibly sparing regimen, and taking from me nearly twelve ounces of blood; which fastings and effusion I should have much more willingly reserved, to become meritorious for the Catholic faith in Ireland. But the Lord God will be pleased to accept these sufferings in France also, and will add to them as a merit the grief I feel in losing these few days in continuing the service to which I am destined, but this I hope to atone for by increased zeal in the next week. But as the best means to inform oneself in this great business is to listen, your Eminence may be assured that in this respect I lose no time, not even in the house, where by divers ways I acquire much information and weave many threads together, to fabricate a skilful scheme for the aid of that kingdom, as I shall report to your Eminence daily. I will carry the brief from His Holiness, and your Eminence's letter to Father Scarampi, and I not only rejoice that this good servant of the Holy See will be comforted by the praise of His Holiness for all his fatigues and labours for the benefit of the Irish, but that all other apostolic ministers will see how much benignant gratitude is shown by the Shepherd of Shepherds to all who devote their lives and talents to the exaltation of the Holy Faith.

I make my most humble reverence,

&c., &c., &c.

To THE SAME.

Paris, June 9, 1645.

I sent your Eminence one letter this day week, and by this post you will receive only one more, three in cipher, and a document. Having recovered from my illness, I had an audience yesterday of their Majesties the King and the Queen, and presented to them both the pontifical briefs and your Eminence's letters. The honours I received were the same as those shown to ordinary Nuncios, and the Queen's words showed her well inclined to assist the Irish Catholics, as, indeed, I had heard privately that Her Majesty has very often declared. What she said to me privately your Eminence will find in cipher by this despatch. This morning I visited the Prince of Condé, His Highness having previously sent his physician to make his excuses, as he was prevented by the gout from coming down-stairs to receive me. The affection for the Holy See manifested by this nobleman is so singular, that I have put down in a private letter what he said to me confidentially. He is deeply grateful to His Holiness and to your Eminence for the honour you have done him in the brief and in the letter, and assures me that the confidence placed in him concerning the affairs of the Church must increase both his zeal and reverence towards it. Whilst waiting here to conclude all the necessary compliments, I have been treating for the transmission of letters from Ireland to Paris, by vessels at stated intervals, according to His Holiness's wish; and I am the more anxious on this subject, as I see that more frequent communication with France would be of great importance to the progress of that island, and that every trouble taken, and every obstacle overcome, will be rewarded twofold. Cardinal Vallansè, whom I had met on the journey, was the first to tell me that I should find many persons in this kingdom much disposed to aid this work in Ireland, with both money and personal service; and his opinion was justified, for already it has been mentioned to me, that if they can find some satisfactory security, those well-affected to the Catholic religion would immediately collect as much money as would suffice, with what I have brought from Rome, to bring the enterprise to a happy termination. And if these offers shall be repeated, this will be the first point I must treat of on my arrival. In the meantime, I see no enterprise which more than this requires to be aided by prayer, because a great favour, which will not excite the jealousy of other Princes, demands a sincerity truly apostolic, and one which, by the nature of its important conditions, has a relation to almost all the Governments of Europe, cannot be better promoted than by laying it (through prayer) at the feet of the Father of Mercy, and directing it by means which regard eternity.

To your Eminence I make my humble reverence, and I pray that you may attain to the pinnacle of the most sublime prosperity.

THE PRINCE OF CONDE'S CONVERSATION WITH THE ARCHBISHOP OF FERMO.

Paris, June 9, 1645.

His Highness took me aside and said, with a familiar air of sincerity, that he would lay before me the state of affairs in France, that I might repeat it at length to your Eminence.

He began by describing to me the great power that Cardinal Mazarin holds in the kingdom, being absolute master, as he said, of the Queen's will, and therefore for divers reasons which he gave at length, both he and the Duke of Orleans take care to stand well with him, and consequently the whole Royal Council. From this His Highness inferred that to be able to dispose absolutely of France, it is above all things necessary that the Holy Father and your Eminence should seek to satisfy the Cardinal with whatever demonstrations you may think appropriate; as having done this it will require nothing more to obtain the whole direction of ecclesiastical affairs here. On this last point he enlarged with extraordinary vehemence, expressing his respect for the Holy See, and his constant desire to defend the rights of the Church, glorying not only in being a true Catholic, but, moreover, a Papist, which second word he said, signified a particular reverence for the Pope and the Holy See, and for all the decrees which proceed from that supreme and infallible tribunal. Thence he concluded that with the security of his vote, obligatory on so many accounts, the whole of the Council would depend on the orders of the Holy Father, once that the will of the Cardinal was gained over. He added, that if no way should be found to compass this union, he would not think the Church secure from some extravagance concocted in the brains of the impetuous French, and chiefly on the great occasion of the assembly of the Bishops, among whom, he said, there were some strange heads, naming in particular the Archbishop of Bordeaux and the Bishop of Sens, with some others, who, if they threw off restraint, or became excited, His Highness would not wonder if there ensued some lamentable breach, or some other excesses to which they might be carried by their ambition. In such a case, he added, he did not see how he alone could stem the current of these disorders in the Council, though his zeal and devotion to the Holy See would be unchangeable, whatever might happen. He corroborated all this by showing with what great facility this desired end might be obtained, because with respect to satisfying the Cardinal the wisdom of the Holy Father would know the best means to effect it, without offending decorum; and on the other hand, he observed that this desire of France was a just one, as well as easily granted, because no one would dare to say that Spain was less favoured by His Holiness than formerly, but only that he, the Father of all, distributed its share of his favours to France also. He then turned his discourse in particular to your Eminence, and finished by saying he much desired that now, in your Eminence's youth, a love for this kingdom should be fostered, both for its glory and for the honour of your noble house.

He had told me at the beginning of our interview that he wished to converse with me alone, since it appeared to him that the Nuncio here, who is not yet fully accredited, has as it were only an uncertain authority, and begged of me to request the appointment might be confirmed, that His Highness may be able to confide his opinions to him freely and without reserve. At the last he wished me to promise to write all he had said to His Holiness and your Eminence, and I consented for many reasons to obey him, not only because it is a part of my duty as Apostolic Minister, but because as I hear and see that on all sides there is a uniform desire tending to the same end, I therefore believe that it is of necessity a sign of the will of God, in which I am bound to co-operate, not only by reporting faithfully but where I can do no more, by prayer and offerings. I pray God then that at this moment, so essential to the welfare of Christianity, He will inspire His Holiness with such resolutions as we may hope for from the holy intentions of the Blessed Father, and from the assistance he so constantly receives from Heaven.

And to your Eminence I offer
My most humble duty, &c., &c.

To CARDINAL PAMPHILI.

Paris, 16th June, 1645.

In your Eminence's packet of the 22nd May, I received two ordinary letters, two in cipher, and one letter for Father Scarampi; by this day's courier I have despatched two letters besides those sent last week. Enclosed are also the Prince de Condè's answers to His Holiness and your Eminence, which he sent me with renewed expressions of his fidelity to the Holy See, and his intention of coming immediately to favour me with a visit. I will send Father Scarampi's letter by the first safe opportunity, and if none should occur before my departure, I will myself take it to him.

Your Eminence judged wisely in observing the warning given by the said Father in December last, as, besides the changes which have taken place in affairs, we have here the earliest, and, without comparison, the more ample news. Whilst in my first visit to Cardinal Mazarin, I confined myself to the necessities and desired speed of my embarkation in order not to lengthen out the negotiation; and though I testified to your Eminence's zeal in the service of God, and those good Catholics, with all this it is needful to look to many matters, such as opportunity and convenience, and not to hazard anything without advice. I will lose no time since this delay, and my lengthened stay in Paris may be prejudicial to me in many ways, and perhaps cause some inconvenience in the arrangements of the enterprise. It is certain that in these ports there are to be found vessels ready to sail, and if by interest they can assure themselves of the protection of the King, I shall require no other satisfaction. The character of this negotiation considered sacred by all men, and the zeal of His Holiness towards that long-abandoned kingdom will, I hope, be as a magnet to guide me through every peril, and a restraint on every tempest. With humble reverence and prayers to Heaven for the continued prosperity of your Eminence,

&c.,   &c.

To the Same.

Paris, June 16, 1645.

I feel it my duty to inform your Eminence of what the Prince de Condè said, and at great length, when he favoured me with his visit, after my letters had been despatched. His Highness repeated forcibly to me what I reported to your Eminence in the past week, of the necessity for the good of the holy Church, that His Holiness should show a particular desire to favour Cardinal Mazarin, and with many and strong reasons he proved that the authority of his Eminence cannot now transgress the rule against excessive favours in France, or as he said, offend the susceptibilities of the Spaniards. Granting therefore the union and correspondence of the Holy See with this minister, the Prince always repeating that no one desires in any way to prejudice the Spaniards, nor obstruct the favours which His Holiness wishes to bestow on them; his Highness then passed on to say, that under the Government of a minor as now, great effects for the benefit of the Holy See might be looked for, and an increase of spiritual jurisdiction such as perhaps had never been heard of before. He named for example the revival of the rules of the Council of Trent, an exemplary reform of the lists of exemptions now running over into irremediable disorder, and such a weakening of the heretics that they might not be able readily to raise their heads again, or greatly infect the kingdom with their heresy. His Highness offers to introduce and carry on this affair in the Council, and whenever needed, to use his own fervent and unalterable zeal to further it, a zeal which when employed to advance the greatness of the Church, he glories in far more than in his royal blood, or in the other splendours of his family. These are in substance the opinions of the Prince, and were expressed to me with so much affection for the Holy Father, and for your Eminence, that they deserve to be acknowledged, not only on private but on public grounds. I willingly repeat them as this conversation touches His Holiness solely in what he has so long desired, that is, to be the father and shepherd of all; on the other hand, I see that not only it would be an incomparable glory for the Pontificate, if one only of these things should be obtained, but that even if not one of them should be so, the same glory would attend the attempt, having been made through prayer and all those lawful means which are suggested by the prudence of the Holy Father. I therefore lay all at the feet of His Holiness, and make my most humble reverence to your Eminence.

To the Same.

Paris, June 23, 1645.

By this day's post I have received from your Eminence one letter and one in cipher, and I reply with one letter and two ciphers, reminding you that I had previously sent an ordinary one in cipher the answer from the Prince de Condè, and in a separate packet, another letter partly in cipher and partly plain, which the lateness of the hour prevented me from finishing in cipher. Cardinal Mazarin is so much occupied with the various expeditions for the war, that though I have frequently solicited an interview, I have been unable to see or conclude with him the last arrangements about my departure, though I have urgently pressed for it, nevertheless I hope that it may take place very soon. The latest news from Ireland is that several places have been taken between Carlow and Youghal, thus cutting off the communication between these two towns and increasing the hope that they will both be speedily reduced. It is said that negotiations for peace with the King are however going on in Dublin, and that his Majesty through his Deputy offers more favourable terms than he has ever done before. Particulars are however so scantily given in the letter that I cannot at all judge what may follow. If the treaty includes the conditions demanded for the Catholic religion, and with the assurance of its being maintained in good faith, I have no doubt my negotiation will be prosperously shortened, and we may reasonably hope for still greater progress, but if not, I am resolved that wherever I shall be, to await the commands of His Holiness and of your Eminence, in order that his favours and supplies may not be employed without a certainty of profit; therefore should such advices reach me on my journey, or on my immediately landing, I pray God to inspire me to act as will be most useful and befitting to the Holy See, and make to shine forth the promptitude which His Holiness has manifested in relieving the distress of Catholic Christianity.

With humble reverence, I am, &c., &c.

To the Same.

Paris, June 30, 1645.

I have received only one ordinary letter by this day's post from your Eminence, and you will have had from me one letter and two ciphers. This week we have at last had letters from Ireland, some written in the month of April, others in the beginning of May. The contents of them all show that the news before received was merely conjectural. First, the reported taking by assault of Youghal was false, as we hear now that the Irish troops were then only preparing to besiege it, and that in the meantime they were taking possession of the small towns and villages near it, in order to facilitate their purpose and which possibly may by this time be accomplished. As to the peace with the King, there is nothing certain at present, although negotiations are still going on. Some private letters openly repeat that the Catholic Confederation is more resolved than ever not to conclude anything unless on the conditions so many times agreed on for the security of religion. At least in this they all agree that nothing will be done till the return of the Secretary, who is still here, and who will not set off I believe without me. The Supreme Council and Father Scarampi both write, that although men and provisions are not wanting, nevertheless the supply of ammunition was nearly exhausted, and without it they do not know how the campaign could be carried on. This had determined me, in order to facilitate operations during the summer, to invest some 1,000 crowns in providing arms and powder, which I will take with me, as the safest way to convey them. This measure will, I hope, produce good results. First, it will be an encouragement to the people to see me arrive with a supply of what they most particularly require, and if I succeed in sending any one beforehand to notify my arrival, this subsidy will, I hope, be considered in the light of assistance from Heaven. Second, I hope to prevent the necessity of further disbursement for the present campaign, as the armies will be supplied with what they most need, and, perhaps, least expected. Third, I shall thus know how the supplies are administered, as the arms will not be given except in cases of great necessity; whereas if the money were employed to pay the soldiers or sent to different or distant places, I should not be able to keep an account of it. I am confirmed in these opinions and intentions by the Nuncio, as well as by the best informed of the Irish, such as Father O'Hartigan, and also by Signor Invernizi. Yesterday a report was spread that the royal vessels which were sent to Ireland four months ago, to bring over troops for this kingdom had returned to La Rochelle. If this be true, they will take me to Ireland, as Cardinal Mazarin assured me that if they arrived in time, they should be at my disposal. If the report be unfounded, I must be contented to sail with others, which I hope will have the royal protection in appearance, if wanting it in reality. Many persons here have no hesitation in alarming me by strange stories of the dangers of the sea. At all events I have the strongest desire to go on, for the reason which your Eminence will read in the cipher. Nothing of importance has occurred in Paris, except that I presented the Papal brief and your Eminence's letter to my Lord the Cardinal of Lyons, who has come here to preside at the assembly of Bishops, and I have taken this opportunity to charge him strictly to keep peace at the Congress, that no dissensions amongst the prelates may increase the bitterness felt by people of all conditions against them. I will inform you how his Eminence meets the demonstrations made by His Holiness, and I trust that the example of the Cardinal, if he performs all he has promised, will be followed by others, and that the paternal affection testified by His Holiness will be rewarded in this kingdom as it has always been in others.*

To the Grand Duke of Tuscany.

Paris, June 29, 1645.

I consider it to be my duty to pay my respects to your Highness previous to my departure for Ireland, and the great benignity and noble zeal shown by your Highness for the welfare of Christianity, encourages me to acquaint you with all I have heard in Paris. Before I left Rome I was aware that some difficulty had arisen between His Holiness and this Crown on the subject of the promotion. But on my arrival here, I found it so much increased by the retention of Count de Beaupuis,† that M. C. de Brienne came at once to the Nuncio and to me on the part of the Queen, to make complaints and strong protestations against it. A few days after, the Queen, in a private interview confirmed this, and charged me to write on the subject as a point most essential to the peace of the kingdom. Not only did the Prince de Condè speak of it twice at great length, but everyone well disposed to the Holy See, said how necessary it is for His Holiness to give satisfaction to Cardinal Mazarin, the ruler at this moment of France, and placed in this position by the favour of persons who, according to the customs of the country ought never to have consented to it. It is particularly insisted on that as they have here every right to the person of the prisoner, His Holiness may be assured that by

---

* See Doc. No. III.

† M. de Beaupuis was engaged in the conspiracy said to have originated with the Duc de Beaufort, for the assassination of Cardinal Mazarin in 1643. It was called La Conspiration de Chalais, from the name of one of the parties to it, executed in that year.
See Sismondi's "Hist. de France," vol. xxiv.

finding some means of sending him back to them either in justice or in mercy, he will allay former suspicions, and by a mutual understanding open the way to a great advance in all ecclesiastical affairs. They told me boldly, that if, on the contrary, satisfaction on this point be not given, other perhaps pretended offences will be taken into account, and what is worse, there is a risk of acts being done and declarations made to be afterwards deeply lamented by everyone, besides the danger of inconvenient disclosures in books and writings. In short, all confidence in the mediator would be destroyed, and the negotiations for peace, at a period when it is more necessary than ever, be either altogether stopped, or concluded without credit or reputation to the Holy See. Cardinal Mazarin, who is modestly unwilling to touch upon what only concerns his own person and interest, converses chiefly on other subjects, but does not hesitate, like others, and with equal gravity to insist on the imminence of these dangers. As a palliative to all this, they add that nevertheless the Queen and her Council have not the slightest wish to alienate the Pope from Spain, nor to stand in the way of the favours he wishes to grant to that country. They desire only that France may share in the favours of their common Father; believing that the Spaniards themselves would, for the benefit of the Church, be desirous to forward this concord between the Pope and the French; and more, they say that for an example to other sovereigns, the King of Spain ought to be anxious to procure that the prisoner Beaupuis should be handed over, so that in cases of such atrocity, and in all affairs of state, all Crowns may be assured that no one will ever hinder justice being done to them.

All these feelings of resentment, and all these threatenings have been aggravated by the Count of . . in addition to which the Queen before the answers to the letters could possibly have arrived, had heard through her ministers and dependents, that His Holiness had refused to give up the prisoner, alleging as a reason the resistance of the common law, and there being no precedent for a similar step. Because too in *secreto juris* they all here think of course that they are in the right, the delinquent being a layman, and that he was arrested at Rome solely at the Queen's instance. They laugh at the notion that such a very unusual case of assassination should be brought forward as any example; but it does not occur to them that the Nuncio can neither give nor receive satisfaction on the matter, except in succeeding to delay to the utmost the absolute negative, and in this way diminish the displeasure which exists so generally.

I am of opinion that the accumulation of past offences will oblige us to come to some unforeseen resolutions, and perhaps the first symptoms may already be observed at Munster. This, your Highness may believe is a source of the deepest regret to me, and I am hurrying my departure for Ireland, as His Holiness' minister cannot I see honorably remain here. That you may be aware of all the circumstances, I add that the Blessed Rose, sent to me by His Holiness to present to the Queen, is still in my hands, as I waited to see if these differences could be adjusted, I have resolved to retain it, unless some great change in affairs takes place, as, under present circumstances, I feel assured, it would be refused.

In all these perhaps unexampled circumstances your Highness can imagine the uneasiness with which I regard the determination to which we are constrained to adhere, and the slights I receive. Either on account of my slight experience in deep negotiations, or from my anxiety to see peace reign in the Christian world, or from the high ecclesiastical dignity I hold, I must confess to your Highness that I am more afraid of the effects of this alienation than of the warlike threats of the Turks, or the triumphs of heresy in Germany.

Unwilling to leave any part of my duty unperformed

before my departure for Ireland, I send these particulars to your Highness, as my last and most powerful resource, to urge the most zealous efforts on your part, consistent with your accustomed prudence, and in accordance with what you have already done, to stimulate the wisdom of His Holiness to arrive at some means to settle this affair, as upon this rock all the other grievances will probably be accumulated. My hope in you is founded on the universal recognition of your Highness' pious zeal for religion, and that not content alone to imitate your great ancestors in preserving union amongst princes, you increase their glory by your personal virtues. If I should hear when in Ireland that a remedy for all these evils has been found by the noble house of Medici, I shall rejoice as a vassal in the glory of his Prince, and as a Priest in the exaltation of the Apostolic See.

Praying that your Highness may extend to me, even in foreign countries your accustomed favour and protection, I make my most humble reverence.

&c., &c., &c.

To Father Pier Francesco Scarampi.

Paris, July 3, 1645.

If I had had a safe opportunity, I should immediately have informed you of my arrival in Paris, Most Rev. Father, and I trust you will be pleased to accept this letter, and I pray you not to ascribe its tardiness to any neglect. You will, I am sure, believe me, when I tell you that every hour appears to me a year, not only till I begin my labours, but till I have the necessary instructions from you towards conducting this great enterprise, hoping in some degree to participate also in your spirit. With faithful sincerity, I say, that if the Holy Father had not himself elected me to this office, I should, with so weak a judgment and infirm a body have feared to be the successor of one who has shown such great diligence, and who thereby has gained the favour of God, and has greatly edified the Court of Rome. May God bless all your endeavours, and, if I am worthy, shed some of His Grace upon me. I send to your Reverence a letter from Cardinal Pamphili, but reserve the Papal Brief, that I may present it to you myself, as it is the reward so well merited by your truly apostolic zeal. I leave to Father O'Hartigan to inform you of everything besides, and I assure you that as soon as my departure can be arranged, I will be with you. Meanwhile I kiss your hand, and pray that every happiness may attend you.

To Cardinal Pamphili.

Paris, July 4, 1645.

By the return of the courier who arrived here at the beginning of the month, I have only to inform your Eminence as before, that the question of the embarkation is still pending, as Cardinal Mazarin assures me he has written to the proper place, but has not as yet heard whether the royal vessels had really arrived from Ireland, as was reported. Meanwhile I am collecting provisions and ammunition, as letters arriving since from Ireland bring the same report as before, of the great want of these things amongst the people, and from what I hear, I believe that all their successes are owing to their resolute courage, as I doubt not I shall find as great a want of discipline and military skill as of supplies. I am not without hope, if my designs succeed, of animating the people by the help I shall take to them.

I have already informed your Eminence, I believe, that the taking of Youghal was not true, as reported in letters from Flanders and England; the fact is that the siege is going on at this hour.

The Queen of England was to have gone to St. Germain's yesterday for the whole summer; her confessor, a Scotch priest, when visiting me, spoke of the regret felt by Her Majesty at being unable to receive me in due state, alleging the reasons already mentioned, and adding a new one, namely, that by the laws of the kingdom the ministers of foreign princes cannot be received without the permission of the King. I heard much the same from a French Capuchin, who in a secular dress officiates as chaplain to Her Majesty. Three things I have certainly done in this matter. First, I have purposely shown the displeasure I feel that no opportunity has been given to me to assure the Queen personally of the real intentions of the blessed Father, and this I make clear to all who give me the opportunity to speak on the subject.

Secondly, I have answered with all due modesty to all the reasons alleged by Her Majesty for not receiving my visit, showing how insufficient they were for the purpose.

Thirdly, not taking any notice, neither making any remonstrance, nor showing any desire to do so, and I acted thus for the reasons already known by your Eminence.

I have heard that at all events the Queen has spoken honorably of me, and also that she is obliged by what she is told of my readiness to serve her. There is great joy here in the late success of the armies; La Motte has capitulated, and in Flanders, Mardyk is besieged. In Catalonia, after the passage of the Segre, a skirmish took place, in which the Spaniards sustained great loss—Cantelmo flying from the field, and Mortara having been taken prisoner. It is expected that the Duke d'Enghien's success in Germany will be no less striking. Everyone speaks of these events according as their interests or inclinations lead them, but Apostolic ministers cannot and ought not to view them in any other light than as facilitating a holy peace throughout the Christian world, and increasing the general respect towards the Holy See throughout this kingdom. For this end I never cease to pray God, well knowing that by this faith alone tranquillity can be hoped for; and among my other numerous obligations, I feel it ever my duty to pray that it may rest on the house and person of your Eminence.

To the Same.

July 7, 1645.

By this post I have received no letters from your Eminence, but I wrote by the courier who should by this time be with you. I have nothing to mention save the defeat of the King of England, which happened on St. John's day. I enclose a paper containing all the particulars that have reached us. The surrender of so large a body gives rise, in the minds of the best informed to a suspicion of treachery, and it may well be believed, as the King stands between two sects, neither of which know what true faith is, and would willingly unite after abandoning their God, to put aside their King also. What effect this defeat may have on Irish affairs I dare not venture to say. If peace be concluded between the King and Parliament, we shall be placed in a difficult position, but if, on the contrary, his Majesty, distrusting his friends, should turn to the Catholics, the whole aspect of affairs would be changed; something new may occur any day. Meanwhile the poor Queen of England had scarcely enjoyed the delights of St. Germains for three days before she found there were more thorns than flowers there. If Cardinal Mazarin does not soon arrange, as I entreat, for my embarkation, and if the King be reconciled to his Parliament, under the harsh and iniquitous conditions already named, I must beg your Eminence to inform me what His Holiness wishes me to do, as I am always ready, without fear and at whatever cost, to obey the commands of the Holy See. I am inclined, in order to make my good will known in Ireland, to send forward Signor Invernizi, who, would besides, comfort the people with the news of the provisions and arms I am taking to them. Meanwhile all the Irish letters agree in saying that peace has not and will not be made. I believe the King's defeat will ensure this, and prove that Divine Providence has by unexpected means assisted the Irish, at once chastising their enemies, and giving them confidence and support in their extremity.

To the Same.

Paris, July 10, 1645.

As the courier by whom I wrote four days ago has not yet set off, I add to my last a few particulars, and at the same time acknowledge the receipt of a packet from your Eminence, containing one ordinary letter and one in cipher, to which I now answer in the same way.

Yesterday evening Cardinal Mazarin sent me word by Father O'Hartigan, that the four vessels at La Rochelle are at my disposal whenever I wish to embark. I shall at once visit the Cardinal to return thanks and obtain all the information possible of the precautions taken for the safety of the money and supplies which I am to take with me. Meanwhile everyone approves of my intention of taking the arms and ammunition myself, for besides other reasons, it is well that I should come with some effective assistance; and I shall therefore wait here till the various articles are on board, which will be about the end of the month. My letters to the Supreme Council and Father Scarampi will precede me, as also perhaps Signor Invernizi, if the Irish who are here approve of this plan, and if a safe passage can be secured for him.

The royal party are trying to diminish the importance of the defeat of the King in England, mentioned in my last of the 7th; and it is believed that His Majesty will soon take the field again, as his cavalry has been saved.

The more equally balanced events are, the better it will be for Ireland, where from the information received by the last letters, the people are more than ever determined to accept of no peace unless the free exercise of religion be guaranteed. I devoutly rejoice that this resolution is so evidently rewarded by the blessed God, since the misfortunes of others evidently result in benefits to Ireland, whilst those who might oppose them are too deeply occupied with their own troubles to disquiet them.

I pray that your Eminence may enjoy all prosperity, and am
With humble reverence, &c., &c., &c.

To THE SAME.

Paris, July 14, 1645.

The assembled Bishops sent two days ago to me, M. d'Agliè, Theologian of the Sorbonne, a man deeply versed in Church affairs, and elected by them to be first proponent of the matters for consultation during the present meeting. He brought excuses from the Prelates for not deputing two or three of their number to wait upon me, as is customary to the ministers of the Apostolic See; but they cannot see how to do so, on this occasion, as I have no public ministry in France. To this I replied, commending their prudence, and thanking them fully for their courtesy, in desiring to pay me respect, though not officially due to me.

Their deputy then said that the Prelates wished to inform me that they had begun to discuss some controversial points between the Regulars and the Bishops, concerning which, for the peace of the Church, they were most anxious to come to a conclusion. He went into many particulars of the cases, and concluded by saying that they would be perfectly satisfied with a just decision, such as would be given by the Synods, and by the customs observed in Italy, excepting indeed two privileges customary in this kingdom, and which must be inviolate, these are that the people must have parochial Mass celebrated at festivals, and that the Regulars may not hear the Easter confession without the permission of the Curates. I had already conjectured that some one in the assembly had proposed to refer these things to the arbitration of His Holiness, and to abide by the decision of his Supreme Tribunâl; I also remembered that Agliè had himself once told me that he agreed in this opinion, and at the same time assured me of his unwavering reverence and fidelity to the Holy See; it seemed, therefore, just the time to insist more than ever on this point, and to urge him to use all his influence to procure the proposed reference, assuring him and the Prelates that they would receive from the paternal affection of His Holiness all the satisfaction to be expected from the prudent use of that power which God has given him to supply the wants of the Church. He left me with the full intention to act in conformity with my advice, and I am impatient to hear if the Prelates will concur, as I hope they may, because I am desirous that the Government, from observing the conduct of the ecclesiastical party (which ought to be the guide of all others), may form their own conclusions as to what ought to be done at the present conjuncture by the secular party which requires to be enlightened.

To the Same.

July 14, 1645.

Mons. d'Agliè first proponent of the assembly of Bishops of whom I have spoken in the accompanying letter, was, during the reign of Urban VIII. of holy memory, twice proposed for the church of Tulle. The first time, however, being out of favour with Cardinal Richelieu for his too great partiality to the Holy See, he thought it better to withdraw his claim, to avoid increasing the dislike of the Cardinal. His second nomination was not confirmed, owing to the death of Pope Urban having occurred soon after. All this Agliè himself related to me on my first arrival in Paris, to convince me of his devotion to the Holy See, and of the danger he had incurred in defending its right of jurisdiction. Two days ago, when he came to me on the part of the Prelates, I remembered suddenly that the church of Tulle was again vacant; and while repeating to you all that he said, I do not think I exceed the limits of my duty in proposing him with all humility for His Holiness' consideration.

I have had ample opportunity of hearing of him from the Nuncio in France, as your Eminence may do from Cardinal Grimaldi; I find that he is a man of no common literary attainments, of truly ecclesiastical habits, and ardently devoted to the rights of the Church. At this period, when he is in such high repute amongst the Prelates that many, I am told, are entirely guided by his opinions, and that they were unanimous in making him first proponent, an office of no little importance amongst them, they would no doubt be particularly pleased by such an election, and would receive it as a favour and grace to themselves.

At the present juncture this could not fail of being a great advantage by uniting the Gallican Church by a voluntary bond to the Holy See, as she has seemed of late not fully to recollect the ties which bind her to it. If I take too much upon myself in matters belonging to higher authority, I shall not so much ask your Eminence's pardon as pray to God to lessen my ardent desire to see the Pontificate of His Holiness great and reverenced, as this alone is the cause of my venturing to take this liberty.

I submit myself humbly to your Eminence, &c., &c.

To the Same.

Paris, July 14, 1645.

A number of persons piously inclined, now in Paris, are engaged not only in administering the Holy Sacraments, but in many other acts of great edification. Amongst those who thus employ themselves is the Duc de Ventadour, one of the first French nobles, who is a marvellous example of piety. By mutual consent he and his wife have been divorced; he has taken the vows of a priest by a dispensation from the Holy See, while she has professed in a convent at Chambery.

This nobleman, who lives at present in his ecclesiastical duties, has also with some others of his confraternity told me that they have for some time had it in consideration to assist the Irish Catholics with a large sum of money, so that by freeing that country from the Puritans, it may be able with all its strength to aid the King of England against the Parliament. This subsidy, amounting to 100,000 crowns, subscribed by the greater number of the order, is by their desire to be spent solely in the way most useful for carrying on the war. They also ask to what place of security the persons they send to assist in the outlay, can retire in case of defeat or any unexpected revolution.

Having heard from persons well informed on Irish affairs, that such a sum added to what I have brought from Rome, would secure the complete liberation of the Island from the enemy, I have greatly encouraged these ecclesiastics in their good work. I have urgently tried to persuade them that on no account should such an action (no less meritorious in a worldly point of view than admirable in the sight of God) be left incomplete; but as to the security they seek for, neither I nor anyone here can promise it, without consulting the Supreme Council of Ireland. I have, therefore, advised them at all events to send a person to that kingdom with me, and as soon as I arrive I shall at once arrange it in some way or other, and I trust that this great additional assistance will incline the Council to act in all respects reasonably. They agreed to this, and everything was settled, even to the person to accompany me, who unites much military knowledge to holiness of life, when news of the King's defeat, greatly exaggerated by the Parliamentarians, arrived here, and cooled a little the ardor of the congregation, who, viewing the victories of Ireland not as an end but as a step to those of England, hoping thereby to draw the King to the true religion, now fear that his losses will cut the thread of this work, and prevent the execution of their great design. I do all in my power to convince the Duke and his companions that this casualty is not irretrievable, more especially as we hear that His Majesty is again about to take the field, and that success will, no doubt, be evenly balanced as heretofore, but further, that even should the King be worsted, the work in Ireland ought not to be abandoned, as it is meritorious in itself, and if at this moment it do not lead to any great ends, it may do so at a future day, if such be the will of Providence, to which our desires can prescribe neither rules nor laws.

As I do not know what will now be done by this confraternity, I thought it right in the meantime to communicate with your Eminence in order that you may know what I have done in support of this enterprise, and in anticipation to express my sorrow if the reverses of the King should cause its abandonment, as those who do not acquiesce in the dispensations of Providence, will deem it a mystery that the King, who if victorious would do us harm, should when defeated do the same indirectly.

To THE SAME.

Paris, July 14, 1645.

Three days ago Lord Jermyn, Chief Counsellor of the Queen of England, came from St. Germains to entreat Cardinal Mazarin on the part of the Queen, to interpose his authority, to bring about a peace between the Irish and the King, alleging that she was empowered to do so by her husband. His Eminence informed the Irish Secretary and Father O'Hartigan of this application, and desired them to put upon paper what they believed were the wishes of the kingdom on this head. I am of opinion that there is every desire shown by this party to make peace with His Majesty, in order to be able afterwards to unite with him against the common enemy, and my advice has been offered and accepted that the conditions should be arranged under as few heads as possible, instead of being lengthened out as formerly, that no suspicion may be excited by the apparent extent of the demands, and the meaning obscured by the number of clauses. O'Hartigan and the Secretary also offered to discuss the whole with Lord Jermyn in presence of the Cardinal, and to endeavour by every means in their power to convince the King of the real subjection of the people to him, second only to that which is due to their religion. This seems a new artifice to delay my departure, together with the aids promised to me from different quarters, and also to defer reaping the advantages which some think must follow from the defeat of the King.

While this is pending, I do not omit to use the same diligence, or intermit my urgent solicitation to have my departure hastened, hoping that in a short time I shall have the arms conveyed to the port, and have finally adjusted with the Cardinal concerning the time, and the ships for the passage. God grant that this delay may, however, end favourably, as if Ireland be at peace with the King before my departure, I shall have one more safeguard, and one enemy the less. And on my arrival I should hope also, with the aid of the Divine Majesty to advance more successfully in my ecclesiastical administration, being entirely free from the political idea of holding the people in subjection to their prince, without injury to the cause of religion.

Your Eminence shall be made acquainted with everything which occurs, and any success we may obtain will be much more the result of His Holiness' labours than of ours.

With humble reverence, &c., &c.

To the Same.

Paris, July 16, 1645.

The courier who has so often said he was ready, appears really to intend to depart now. I therefore having to-day received from your Eminence two letters, with two in cipher, and a document dated June 26, will add what occurs to me in this short time. To the memorial presented by Digby to His Holiness I shall pay due attention, and at the first opportunity, I shall say what my little experience of the negotiation dictates, in obedience to your Eminence's command. This morning I returned thanks to Cardinal Mazarin, as I shall soon do to the Queen, for the vessels granted for my embarkation, and considering the manner in which His Eminence spoke of his desire for my safety, I trust that every thing will end happily, with the protection of God and of the King. With the blessing of His Holiness, I trust, within a fortnight to be on my way to La Rochelle, from whence I hear it is easier to get out to sea.

By the next post I shall write further particulars, and assuring your Eminence of my devotion, only fearing that distance may increase to my prejudice the sense of my demerits, and with profound respect

I bow before your Eminence.

To the Same.

July 21, 1645.

On the 19th of this month the courier was despatched from this court, and by him your Eminence will receive three packets of letters from me, dated the 4th, 11th, and 16th, in each of which is a note of the contents. By the same I informed your Eminence of having received the document from the Counsellor of the Queen of England, and in compliance with your Eminence's command to give my opinion on the subject, I have written the enclosed as briefly as possible, and have given you likewise the opinions of others who are most versed in English negotiations. This much is certain, that the English Catholics are of so different an opinion from Digby, that I have been privately informed that many of them had determined to protest against the representations he had made in Rome, and they believe that he speaks more with regard to his private interest than in that of the Queen or the cause. I have returned thanks to her Majesty the Queen Regent for the accommodation of the vessels preparing for me, and at the same time, entreated her to grant some assistance to the Irish, proportionate to the greatness of this Crown, and also permission to request subsidies from several noblemen here who are piously inclined. This permission I have obtained, and have had some fair promises for the other. Before I set off, I shall endeavour to perform my duty by speaking to many of these gentlemen, who on my application will, I trust, be induced to act generously, and I rejoice to have been allowed to share in the exceeding glory of begging for the Faith. The arms, &c., have already been sent to the port for embarkation, and I, spreading my sail to this favouring wind, am about to set off myself under the protection of heaven, of which I have satisfactory auguries in the blessing of the Holy Father.

ANSWER TO THE MEMORIAL PRESENTED BY DIGBY.

Paris, July 21, 1645.

To send assistance at the same time to the King of England and to the Irish, and consequently to divide the money and supplies destined by His Holiness to the benefit of the Catholic religion alone, seems not only likely to fail of the effect explained by Digby in his memorial, but also to create both difficulties and embarrassments, because the King could not possibly regain his power with the moderate assistance which would fall to his share, if the Pontifical aid were divided, not only because his need is great, but also from the bad management of the Protestants by whom he is surrounded, who spend the money foolishly and without restraint; as I have been assured by Cardinal Mazarin was the case, when the King of France assisted him repeatedly by sending him 100,000 crowns at a time, which His Eminence says melted away without producing any good fruits. The same would probably happen with the Holy Father's supplies and neither the King nor the Irish derive any benefit from them. Further, the English Catholics cannot hope that the King is either able or willing to favour them more than formerly, being surrounded by heretics, who if they cannot dictate to him can prevent any manifestation of his feeling towards them or maintaining any promise afterwards. On this account the Catholics themselves are of opinion, that to gain their end Ireland must first be completely pacified in order to be able to send a considerable army to England, which, united with the Catholics of that country, would be sufficiently powerful to serve the King, and at the same time to keep him in check, and oblige him to make those concessions which, if left to himself, he would neither have the will nor power to grant. This appears clear from the document (of which I send your Eminence a copy) drawn up by the English Catholics at my request, on my first arrival in Paris, after they had frequently given me their opinions on the matter. Your Eminence will see that they look to the conclusion of a favourable peace as the foundation of all good to Ireland, and if in these articles they make some remarks respecting the political superiority of the English, they at least acknowledge that the well being of their country depends entirely on the assistance to be expected from the Irish, when their own island is at peace. If this be true, the Queen, who has assured His Holiness of her deep anxiety for the good of religion in England, cannot oppose those who are still more deeply interested in its advancement. Moreover, everyone must see that of the two enterprises it is better to prosecute one only at a time, and bring it to a successful conclusion (as it is hoped that the first may almost be happily concluded in one more campaign) than to attempt both, at the manifest risk of spending all without benefit to either kingdom, and if, as the Irish constantly affirm, the sum of 100,000 crowns will secure the whole of that kingdom, it is without doubt better to place it where it will afterwards be the foundation of future success in England, rather than send it where it will be utterly wasted.

For these reasons it is superfluous to enter now on the good intentions of the King and Queen, so much exaggerated by Digby, which, if even they are real, would not avail in the present difficulty. As however every point should be considered, I must add that I see no particular inclination in the mind of the King towards the Catholics, except that having received proofs of their fidelity, he speaks as truth compels him to do more favourably of them; all the wise and experienced men with whom I have conversed during my residence in Paris concur in my opinion as to the Queen, even if she has done all that is averred in the kingdom, still I see nothing to corroborate her alleged affection for the Catholics, for not only is she surrounded by heretical counsellors, but she has spoken hardly of the Irish in this late rising, stigmatising them as rebels, and declaring that she would not acknowledge or receive me as Nuncio, because my mission is to a rebellious people. All this will confirm the Irish still more in their determination to secure themselves at home first, and then generously to assist their Sovereign, rather than without due securities trust to him, and doubtless draw upon themselves an implacable persecution. It is a matter to be considered, however, that if the Parliament should make peace with the King it will be the ruin of Ireland, as the united parties would conspire against her. But to this it suffices to answer, that the assistance asked from His Holiness not being sufficient to restore the King to power, nor avert the above mentioned danger, the subsidies would be thrown away, and things would remain exactly in the same state as before. The Irish add, moreover, that their country once freed they would have no fear of the united force, and cite as an example of what they can do (besides many ancient proofs) the skill of the Earl of Tyrone, as with Ulster alone, he sustained a war for sixteen years against Queen Elizabeth, at a time when Great Britain was in its most powerful and flourishing state. But without going into particulars, if His Holiness should agree to grant assistance directly to the King of England, a heretic, although really for the benefit of the English Catholics, would it not be advisable for His Holiness first to see some certain manifestation of the King's good-will to the Catholic religion, such as may be depended upon for the future?

To THE SAME.

Paris, July 28, 1645.

Since I returned my thanks to the Queen for the ships which have been placed at my service, I have never been able to see Cardinal Mazarin, to whom I must notify my departure, along with some other matters of minor importance. His Eminence has constantly expressed an intention of coming to visit me, which I hear he is about to do this evening, and therefore I fear I shall be unable to inform you of what may be the result of this and another matter. The Nuncio of France sent his auditor to St. Germains, to communicate to the Queen of England the contents of some letters received from Rome, one of them being an attestation from your Eminence on the part of His Holiness that the zeal of the Holy Father and my mission tend to naught but the spiritual weal of the people, without any relation whatsoever to temporal affairs. Her Majesty would have learnt this from His Holiness' brief, had she condescended to receive me. The Auditor informs me that on hearing it, the Queen said she would send by a messenger her answer to the Nuncio, but none has as yet appeared. The supplies of arms are already at Orleans, and I now only await the passport promised by the Cardinal, to empower me to take them out of the country. I also expect to receive a large sum, not only from private persons but also from the Crown in aid of the kingdom; and although it is impossible to foresee what may occur after the dissolution of the Assembly, at all events it is certain that they do not lose heart, and are expecting the subsidies. We are still ignorant as to what effect may have been produced in the kingdom by the change in the aspect of affairs in England, since the unfortunate difficulty in transmitting letters safely, or in a definite time, still exists. I hope, however, immediately on my arrival, to remedy this inconvenience, as this was one of the earliest commands given me by His Holiness; and I well know that the Holy Father, in this as well as in all else, is inspired by God and guided by wisdom.

I take leave of your Eminence with humble reverence, &c., &c.

To the Internuncio in Flanders.

Paris, August 4, 1645.

The Secretary of the Confederated Catholics in Ireland is about to visit Flanders, in the interests of that kingdom. It is superfluous to recommend him to the protection of your Excellency, since you yield to none in desiring and promoting the good of our religion. Nevertheless, I write these few lines to assure you that every favour you are pleased to show him I shall consider a personal obligation.

I have seen a letter from Flanders, in which it is said that the two frigates prepared for me are too small for winter navigation; therefore it was necessary to order two of a larger size, for which a passport has been sent from this kingdom. In this matter, also, I shall be under deep obligations to your Excellency if the Secretary should find it necessary to apply to you for your interference. News from England comes scantily. The King must find his position very perilous, and it seems as though God were preparing some great change in that kingdom, which, if it should tend to the profit of the Catholic religion, will be a matter of great rejoicing.

With every respect for your Excellency,

I kiss your hand.

To Cardinal Pamphili.

Paris, August 4, 1645.

This week I have received from your Eminence two ordinary letters and two in cipher, dated July 10th, and I must now report what has happened during the present week.

On Friday last Cardinal Mazarin did me the honour to call at my house, which I think I mentioned to your Eminence, as in this and on other occasions, he has distinguished me from ordinary Nuncios. He was accompanied by four Marshals of France, and his cortège consisted of five carriages. His visit was short, so as not to inconvenience the noblemen in attendance. All, however, that I desired to confer upon with His Eminence was arranged in an audience two days later, of which I have elsewhere written the particulars. Your Eminence will receive with this letter three in cipher, and also the usual packet and note of advice from Ireland.

I now make my most humble reverence.

To the Same.

August 4, 1645.

This week, the French Minister received a letter from Father Scarampi who wrote that he was not certain if I had arrived in Paris, and if arrived, whether I was still here. In it he informs him that the General Assembly was about to break up, and that the members were more eager than ever to conclude a peace with the King, having more than once sent deputies to Dublin to that effect; and he further says that the council not having consulted him in any way in this matter, he had absented himself from Kilkenny so as not to be present during the negotiations which, he is convinced, must be disadvantageous to the Catholic religion. His words are *that the peace, if concluded, would be fatal.* The contents of this letter incline me to fear that the constant assurances given me by the Irish that no peace would be accepted, may have been an artifice to hurry me to the country, so as through me to receive without delay the honour conferred on them by the Holy See. I also fear evil results from the efforts unceasingly made by the Protestants, and by the King through his agents, of which I informed your Eminence at the beginning of July; still it is possible that Father Scarampi, desirous of fulfilling his duty in every respect, and anxious not to have the holy fabric he has raised with so much zeal, dashed to the ground, may be more fearful than is warranted by events, at least so the Irish wish me to believe.

And although the Father in his modesty adds in this letter that my arrival would have lessened the danger, I dare not hope that my presence would have had an effect which his long residence, and profound knowledge of the state of affairs in the country has failed to produce. Besides, if the embassy from His Holiness, and the promptitude with which he has sent it, as explained in my letters to the Council, my arrival in Paris, my speedy embarkation, and my joy in undertaking this enterprise, if all this does not prevent the conclusion of the peace, I do not believe that my presence could have restrained them. I therefore fervently thank God that although I arrived here at the end of May, I have been so detained by illness, and then by preparations (which have been so protracted that they are still incomplete) to enable me to leave Paris, that when I would have hurried on matters I could not in any case have reached the port before the meeting of the Assembly was over. I have avoided hearing this news at the moment of embarking, or what would have been worse, immediately on my arrival, so that I have been saved the painful uncertainty as to what measures it would be right for me to take.

I think of now sending Signor Carl Invernizi to Ireland as I intended to do a month ago, but was dissuaded by some of the Irish here. He will take care to inform me of the real state of affairs, that I may know whether to proceed or not, and I shall be prepared so as to depart instantly on the receipt of his information. If, however, no certain news should arrive to the contrary, touching English affairs, I should, without consulting anyone, depart on the moment.

In the middle of all this uncertainty, I received a letter three days ago, from a merchant of Nantes, dated July 19th, stating that a vessel had arrived from Ireland with news of the capture of Youghal, and the setting out for the siege of Cork, which the Irish are convinced is true, especially as it confirms the report of Father Scarampi.

The latter further asserts that no peace whatsoever had been concluded with anyone. We shall soon know the truth, and if the information is such as I desire, we may hope the future course of affairs will be favourable. Meanwhile the indications of good-will I received from the Queen in the enclosed letter, may not only raise our hopes, but open a vast field of future enterprise, as the paternal zeal of His Holiness well deserves.

With deep reverence, &c., &c.

To the Same.

August 4, 1645.

Since my interview with the Chaplain of the Queen of England, of which I give your Eminence an account, I have had many proofs that Her Majesty was well pleased with what I said to that priest, and in signifying her satisfaction, added many praises of myself. Of this I was first assured by the English Catholic Chancellor, whom, when leaving Paris three days ago for St. Germains, I requested to offer my humble respects to Her Majesty, because in bringing me her reply, he assured me that Her Majesty expressed herself convinced of my good intentions, and of my anxiety to serve her, and was rejoiced I had been chosen to go to Ireland, as she hoped that besides the good I should do for the Catholic religion, I should forward and aid the interests of the King. This was confirmed by the above mentioned Chaplain when he signified Her Majesty's approbation of my reasons for not waiting upon her, unless in a manner suitable to the dignity of the Sovereign who had sent me. They both added that the Queen had commanded an English gentleman, just arrived from England, to wait upon and inform me of the King's present position, which he did yesterday morning. This gentleman had been sent with all speed by His Majesty to the Queen after the conflict of June 24th, which ended so favourably for the Parliamentarians.

His name is Edmund Dudley Wyat, and it is not known whether he is Protestant or Puritan; he however appears very discreet, of excellent manners, and is about thirty-two years of age. He enlarged upon the high opinion entertained of me by the Queen, and Her Majesty hopes that in this emergency, when the royal cause so much needs assistance, I shall effect a firm peace between the King and the Irish. He showed however a great desire that the negotiation should be carried on here, and offered in the Queen's name, to send for the necessary powers from the King, provided the Irish would obtain the same from the Supreme Council. He spoke at great length of the necessity of the two parties coming to this conclusion; on that of the King, because his position is perilous, being every day in greater need, and wishing more than ever to be assisted by his own subjects; on that of the Irish, because if they are rigorous in their demands, the King will be constrained to come to an agreement with the Parliament, when the Irish would find themselves confronted by the united forces of both England and Scotland, and without hope of being able to resist so many. On this point Sir Dudley Wyat laid great stress, as it might induce the Irish to moderate their pretensions, and not stand out for all at once. Finally he entreated me on the part of the Queen to remain here until this negotiation be concluded, hoping that in obedience to the precepts of His Holiness, I should assist in the success of a project so much to be desired by the Princes of Europe, who, with reason, dread that with the fall of the King of England they would see the growth of a hydra so powerful as would be the Parliamentarians of England, the Dutch and the Huguenots of France, who would unite in one body against all Monarchical Government.

If I did not know how the King has been situated since his last defeat, I should suspect that all this negotiation was a device to delay my departure, for fear that it may produce some great benefit to Ireland. But, even if this be the case, it was well to listen to these proposals; and, therefore, after expressing my gratitude for Her Majesty's praises and favours, I replied that His Holiness desired nothing more (after the interests of the Catholic religion) than to see a favourable peace concluded with the King, that he would be greatly pleased if it could receive more attention from the Court of France, and that if there was any hope of the success of the negotiation, I knew His

Holiness would not be displeased at the delay in my journey. And, concerning the pretentions and articles advanced by Ireland, I said that, except those touching religion, they might be quietly discussed, and probably both the King and the Irish would be satisfied to yield in some points—the former from necessity, and the latter from anxiety to preserve the name of faithful subjects.

This concluded the interview of which I doubt not an account will be given to Cardinal Mazarin, in order that the design may be forwarded by his authority. In the meantime, I will send one of my gentlemen to St. Germains to testify my gratitude to the Queen for this benign demonstration; and certainly, if there is no concealed deception, it will be a great honour to this mission, if, before I leave Paris, the greatest hindrance to the success of Irish affairs shall have been overcome, and I arrive in the island bearing the olive branch of peace; and not only be able to occupy myself wholly in the re-establishment of ecclesiastical affairs without distraction (having only a single war in common with the King), instead of being obliged to wait for an opportunity to undertake one for the benefit of His Majesty and the Catholics of England, besides having the good fortune to be able at once to send supplies to England. If the Lord God will vouchsafe to reward with this consolation the piety of His Holiness, and his zeal in the cause of this people, I, as the most deeply interested of all, will be the first to feel the happiness that so glorious an idea merits, &c., &c.

To the Marquis of Castel-Rodrigo.

Paris, August 5, 1645.

Although on many accounts it was determined that I should begin my journey to Ireland by the way of France, still I always hoped that some occasion might offer to ask a favour at the hands of your Excellency. I now beg you to grant me one, for which I shall be personally grateful. It is for your protection to the Secretary of the Confederated Catholics, who is about to visit you, and to pray you to aid him in the interests of the Holy Faith in Ireland. I shall esteem it a happy commencement of my embassy, and one I shall keep in my memory as a stimulus to the reverence and affection which I conceived for your Excellency first in Rome.

I offer you my most humble respects.

To the Duke of Amalfi.

Paris, August 5, 1645.

My respect and former connexion with your Excellency encourages me to recall myself to your memory through the Secretary of the Irish Confederates, who is about to visit you on some affairs connected with the Catholic religion in Ireland.

I have been appointed by His Holiness his Nuncio to that country, and until I have a more immediate opportunity to recur to your Excellency's patronage and assistance, I cannot commence my labour more worthily than by recommending to your protection this cause, and the negotiations by which it is to be promoted. I entreat your Excellency to accept from my deputy the assurances of my respect, and to believe that any assistance is well directed which is given to a people who in the midst of such conflicts, have maintained with so much constancy their fidelity to God.

With humble reverence, &c., &c.

To Cardinal Pamphili.

Paris, August 11, 1645.

I informed your Eminence of my intention to return thanks to the Queen of England for the attentions paid me, and I therefore despatched to St. Germains Signor Domenico

Spinola, who belongs to my party, to assure Her Majesty anew not only of my sentiments towards the royal service, but much more that of His Holiness, shown in so many ways, but particularly in the commands given me on the subject of my mission. Spinola was received with benign and kindly condescension, and the Queen, after expressing abundantly her trust in my intentions, and her knowledge of my good qualities, as she said, complained loudly of the Irish, and among them of O'Hartigan, and the Secretary, who from the first made use of the Catholic religion in general as a pretext to throw off their allegiance to the King, that they did not wish to make peace with him unless they saw it to be an absolute necessity, and were always adding new petitions, and more exorbitant than the last: on these two particulars she insisted with vehemence, and that they had dared to tell her that they would fight against the King to the last drop of their blood, if they did not obtain what they desired, and similar complaints. She added her hope that I, knowing the disposition of the people, should be able to restrain them within the bounds of religion, but not beyond those of obedience to their sovereign. She then turned to her wish to have seen me in private, declaring herself, however, satisfied with the reasons assigned by me for declining this honour; and after questioning Spinola on the subject of my departure and other particulars, at length dismissed him. The following day she sent her thanks to me by the same English gentleman who had come to me the week before, and informed me that Her Majesty proposed to send to the King for full powers to treat of this peace, giving as security the word of the Queen of France, upon which I offered to procure the same from the Irish immediately on my arrival, in order that no delay shall impede the good results to be hoped for from this agreement. Since then, having received your Eminence's letter containing some more considerations upon this negotiation, I determined the day before yesterday to send the same Signor Spinola to see Her Majesty again, and after rendering thanks for the continued demonstrations she has made towards me, to assure her that His Holiness had never desired in any way that Her Majesty should put herself to any trouble whatever to receive the Nuncio; so that he trusted she had taken in good part what had been done on the matter; but that he desired she should be convinced of His Holiness' sincere wish that not in the smallest thing should the matter of religion interfere in the obedience of the kingdom, and begging her to observe in the Brief which had been given to me to present to her, how constant he had been to this determination from the beginning. After this I desired Spinola to ask permission for me to depart, and to repeat the usual compliments of obligation and devotion.

The Queen, at this second interview, received Spinola standing, perhaps because she knew she would have to receive the Brief which I had previously intimated my intention of sending; she received the message with her accustomed courtesy—took it, together with your Eminence's letter, and after repeating what she had said before, ended by her usual expressions of confidence in my good offices, and wished me a good journey. Your Eminence will see, therefore, how easily I succeeded, not only that the letters should reach the Queen, as you desired, but also in leaving her satisfied with me, that I truly desired to convince her of my upright intentions, without incurring the danger of pledging myself (in a private interview) to what might afterwards prove to be prejudicial to the ecclesiastical cause, or what I might find it impossible to maintain when in Ireland; so that, without seeking any other means or ways, I think what has been done is quite sufficiently successful. From all that has passed, I see the necessity of enlightening the Irish on many points concerning Her Majesty, as many things, both public and private, have been misrepresented, no doubt owing to the mistakes of the mediators, or the effect of those clouds which usually intervene between two parties in a negotiation, and hinder them from understanding one another. On the other hand, it will be my care, if I see the Irish misuse the name of religion to cover some other interests, to restrain and direct them to the needful end, so that the desired successes once gained, considerable aid may be sent to assist the poor King, and consequently the English Catholics, but not till religion in Ireland is established securely. On this point, having discovered that many in France are anxious to assist the King of England (but would rather it should be by the help of others, and consequently they would greatly like he should be aided by the Irish), I have consulted with Cardinal Mazarin, and received a promise from him of every assistance from this kingdom whenever the Irish require it, either on account of extra expense, diminution of strength, or continuance of war in the country itself.

The Cardinal highly approved of all I had done from the beginning up to the final arrangements with the Queen of England.

I see clearly that although the various changes and perils which result from the disturbances in Great Britain may occasion much anxiety and uncertainty in my negotiations, they will also open a wide field to the benefit of religion. Under all circumstances, I trust that God will enable me to act in a manner worthy of a chosen minister of His Holiness, zealous in prosperity, constant in misfortune.

And I offer my humble reverence, &c.

To THE SAME.

Paris, August 11, 1645.

After writing the two accompanying letters to your Eminence, advices arrived from an Irish merchant of La Rochelle, with news of a considerable success of the Scotch in Ulster.

They had taken three towns, and threatened to besiege Galway—a city, as everyone knows, of considerable importance. Besides this, the King of England, perceiving how perilous was his position after the two defeats, had sent a Protestant deputy to the Marquis of Ormond, commanding him to conclude at once a peace with the Confederates of Ireland. This news makes me fear, with Scarampi, that a disadvantageous treaty will be entered into, and that to await the certainty of this will cause much loss of time, on account of the French campaign, without profit to anyone. There is still one hope left me from not having seen the original letter, and the frequent danger, in time of war, of exaggerated reports with no foundation in truth.

I shall ascertain the facts as soon as possible. In the mean time, I pray that God may lighten the darkness, and enable us to see our proper course.

With humble reverence.

To the Same.

August 11, 1645.

In order to quit Paris with as little parade as possible, I think of going with some of my suite to Chartres to celebrate the Feast of the Assumption near that miraculous Virgin.

I have been counselled by some to feign setting off by one road, and then to go incognito by another, but I shall not do so, as my health is not sufficiently good to travel privately, without necessary attendance. I have always laughed at the idea of trying to deceive those who might wish to do me harm, as there is an agent here of the English Parliament, who I believe to have had no other occupation than to watch and ascertain my movements.

Cardinal Mazarin has, in the King's name, placed at my disposal four vessels with His Majesty's flag, and added that I shall be served in them exactly as if it were he himself.

He does not however guarantee me against attempts of the enemy, but gives me this not very consoling assurance, that in case they do me any injury they will be obliged to make full restitution. I find that to go by Flanders would be still more perilous, as having to sail down the English Channel and to land in Spain would be attended with great loss of time and expense. I shall therefore embark from La Rochelle, from which port we can stand out well to sea, and avoid the Channel, trusting to the blessed God to direct and watch over an enterprise devoted to His holy service, and in which every step I take in danger will be reckoned to me as a merit in His sight. I must add that I have provided two frigates to carry the despatches when in Ireland, and as they are now at Dunkirk, I shall also be accompanied by them, as in any case their swiftness will make them useful and perhaps more, a safeguard; and Cardinal Mazarin quite approves of my having them. I am not without hopes that this same Cardinal will present me with some thousand crowns beyond what he promised eight months ago. I think the Queen will do the same, and perhaps the Prince de Condé may contribute also; and the Crown has taken off the duty levied on arms exported from the kingdom, besides some other dues. Besides this, I hear that a donation of three or four cannon will be made to me. I have not been able to apply as I intended to several private persons, as the hurry of departure has taken up all my time; from the same cause I leave incomplete the project arranged with the Duc de Ventadour, but leave it in the hands of a person capable of forwarding it. I leave Paris, having received satisfaction and honours from all orders of people; everyone has favoured me with visits and professions of esteem, with the exception of the Cardinal of Lyons, who has continued in Paris the same line of conduct as when I passed through Lyons. If my conduct also has given satisfaction to others, and in particular, if my remaining here has in any way served His Holiness and your Eminence, it will be the most fortunate omen for my future success which I could have on my departure from this city.

Recommending myself more than ever at this increasing distance, to the grace and protection of your Eminence, I kiss through your good office the feet of His Holiness, and make my faithful reverence.

To the Same.

Paris, August 18, 1645.

I received from your Eminence one letter and one in cipher by the last courier, and answer now with one plain and two in cipher to report what has occurred since. I have been detained some days longer than I expected, as a sudden opening has been made by which I can do a signal service to the Confederates in Ireland; I shall send you an account of it this evening in the Irish despatches, if Cardinal Mazarin, on whom the affair depends, has decided on it, otherwise I shall send a full report by a gentleman who will set off in two days to overtake Cardinal Valansé, and who may possibly arrive before the courier. By the same opportunity I shall send a detailed account of all that we may have heard up to this day of the peace which is in treaty in Ireland, and on it alone depends my immediate embarkation or its delay.

Yesterday the "Te Deum" was chaunted for the taking of Bourburg in Flanders, which surrendered at discretion to the Duke of Orleans, and for the battle between the Duke d'Enghien and the Bavarians, of which the following account has reached us.

After the departure of Königsmark the Duke d'Enghien drew the Bavarians on to battle and fought for two days. On the first, the French were at a disadvantage, many being killed, their right wing broken, and Marshal Guise taken prisoner. On the second, the Bavarians had the worst of the day, and victory inclined to the French. Mersy, the

Bavarian general, was killed, Glen taken prisoner, but at once exchanged for Marshal Guise, and General de Vert fled with 3,000 of the cavalry. Of the Bavarians, 4,000 were left dead on the field, and there are 2,000 prisoners; the loss of the French is diminished at each account, but many say it cannot be less than 4,000, nearly all of whom were Italians, and most of them killed on the first day.

Turenne was wounded, and the Duke d'Enghien also had two slight wounds, one on the arm, and one in the side. The Duke has written for reinforcements as he wishes to penetrate into Bavaria; and we hear that the city of Nordingen remains in his hands. Here they magnify the victory greatly, and hope rises higher and higher.

The Cardinal of Lyons has since done me the honour to visit me, and enclosed is a recapitulation of our conversation. Hoping for some signal success on the part of His Holiness against the forces of the Turks to reanimate the hopes of afflicted Christianity,

I am, &c., &c.

To the Same.

Paris, August 19, 1645.

On Thursday letters arrived from Father Scarampi to the Nuncio of France and to Father O'Hartigan, and we gather from them that my three despatches, sent in the month of June, have not yet been received, which shows how uncertain is the passage, and how much it needs improvement.

These letters confirm the account of the Scotch irruption into Connaught, and their intention to besiege Galway, as I mentioned in my last; besides this, we hear that Sligo has been taken, and that the enemy conduct their warfare most barbarously, killing all, and sparing neither age nor sex. As to the peace, the same letters assure us that the hostile deputies had been called to Dublin, but a postcript, written on the last day of July, says that they had returned without coming to any conclusion, and that it was believed no further steps would be taken before the new convocation of the Assembly which will be during the present month. The Archbishops of the kingdom, and two of the Bishops, wrote to me on the 5th July, saying that they had heard of my departure having been delayed by a fear of finding the peace concluded without the articles in favour of religion, which, however, they repeatedly assure me will not be the case. I must, however, await more certain information.

I wish here to send your Eminence four articles presented some days ago by the Secretary and O'Hartigan to Cardinal Mazarin, when it was believed the treaty would be brought to Paris, and in the margin I have noted down where they appear to me to differ now from the demands which were made in Ireland during the same negotiation, according to Father Scarampi's account; wherefore the congregation at Rome will take into consideration, if the peace should be concluded in the manner demanded by the kingdom, and whether it can be considered consistent with the free exercise of religion as His Holiness piously desires. I think your Eminence will be surprised to hear that the Queen offers far more ample conditions than the Irish demand; and the Protestants, as Father Scarampi writes, refuse almost everything, and are more unyielding than the King himself, although they have neither soldiers nor supplies, and His Majesty is losing ground every day with little hope of retrieving it.

It seems to me that the position of this poor King foretells some great change, unless he obtains assistance from this kingdom; and therefore the time is come to pray to God, so to dispose events that the Irish Confederates may take those measures most likely to benefit both religious and temporal affairs.

With much reverence, &c., &c.

To the Same.

Paris, August 25, 1645.

I should not have delayed my departure beyond the conclusion of the Feast of the Holy Madonna, had not I been unexpectedly employed about the negotiation of which I informed your Eminence, and of which I had hoped to give you a full account by the present post, believing that it must certainly be concluded; but, owing to the usual delays in this country, there remains something still to be finished. The matter is this: O'Hartigan was speaking to me of the vessels destined for my convoy, when he told me that Cardinal Mazarin was to pay some thousands of crowns for their hire, which surprised me; and I expressed the wish that the money had rather been laid out in buying two good frigates to give to the Irish. O'Hartigan, delighted with this idea, declared it would be impossible for me to do a greater service to that kingdom. I spoke of it, therefore, to Cardinal Bichè, who came to me the same evening, and he, having consulted with Cardinal Mazarin, sent me word on the following morning that His Eminence agreed to the proposal. I then took courage to entreat His Eminence to add the 24,000 crowns promised to the Irish many months before, but which had never been paid, and God willed that he agreed to this also; and after ten days' anxious delay the whole sum, amounting to 25,000 crowns, was yesterday paid—that is, according to his reckoning, 5,000 for the ships, and 20,000 as a donation, although I saw that the two sums should have amounted to 29,000.

With this money Signor Invernizi will set off to-morrow for Dunkirk, and, I hope, will procure three, if not four frigates of the best quality, which will be of great use to protect the coast of Ireland, to annoy the enemy, and serve other useful purposes. And in these frigates, which he will bring to Nantes or La Rochelle at once, with all the necessary passports, I shall make my sea passage, with the same security as to safe conduct, protection, and royal ensign; but as to speed, the use of oars, &c., perhaps with greater than the other vessels. In the meantime, seeing that this negotiation and the collecting of the money—all of which I have resolved to carry with me—would cause some delay, I resolved to send Signor Domenico Spinola before me to the ports, with orders, if he could find men and means of embarkation, to proceed to Ireland, to give notice that I am on the way, and to ascertain from Father Scarampi what the Confederates have really done, and whether there are still hopes that the peace may be advantageous to the free exercise of the Catholic religion, so that I could be informed before I sail.

I chose this young man because, since he has been with me, he has shown extraordinary ardour in the cause of religion, and had begged of me several times, through other people also, to allow him to go before me and make this discovery, offering, if need be, to travel incognito through England without the least fear.

I also send him because a month ago I had determined on sending Signor Invernizi on the same mission, but was dissuaded by the Irish and by Invernizi himself, who all agreed that if I sent anyone before me, it would be generally believed throughout that kingdom that I did not intend to go. I see also that had I despatched him, God knows if he would have arrived in time, as Scarampi wrote on the 28th of July that during the space of more than a month contrary winds had blown so violently that no vessels had sailed from France in that direction, and this is proved by my having received no answers to the letters sent at the end of June. As to Secretary Belling, I succeeded by various means and incitements in keeping him in Paris, and when he informed me of his determination to set off, we agreed to induce him to go first to Flanders to execute his commissions, and there he still remains. If he return here, as he intended to do, he will certainly not set out before me; but if he should choose to cross the Channel from Flanders, I hope that with all the devices he may put in practice during the few days before my arrival, the said Spinola, who is already fully master of the whole negotiation, and not suspected by any party, may, by the assurance of my coming, and by proclaiming my intentions, be able to make a successful opposition to him. I have to inform your Eminence that, in order to keep back the peace with the King, Father O'Hartigan has collected some letters of His Majesty's, which were printed by the Parliamentarians when his secretary was in their hands, from which, as you will see by the copy of the one which I send, faithfully translated from the English, it appears that the King feigns to be favourable to the Irish until his circumstances change. O'Hartigan has therefore endeavoured to impress on that people not to trust him without extraordinary securities. Whether this effort has been for good or for evil I shall soon hear—perhaps, indeed, before my arrival.

Cardinal Mazarin, when giving the order for the money of which I have spoken, sent word that he wished to see me again, and this only may perhaps cause my departure to be delayed to-morrow. So much it is my duty to make known to your Eminence in the hope that from henceforward as I approach nearer the scene of my labours, my reports will become more important, and tend to the greater consolation of His Holiness and your Eminence.

With humble reverence.

To the Same.

Chartres, August 30, 1645.

I have received by this post three letters in ordinary character, and eight printed pastorals to distribute during my embassy, to exhort the faithful to prayer in this crisis of Christianity. I hope by making public at once this proof of His Holiness' paternal remembrance, to give more importance to my arrival in Ireland, as for more than a century there has not been seen or heard any similar demonstration from the Apostolic See in that country, and how greatly will the people rejoice in their souls to be in a manner united by public prayer with the remaining body of the Church, and so much the more shall I rejoice in being its first minister. As therefore I desire to carry out punctually the wish and command of His Holiness respecting my departure, I am glad that your Eminence's letter found me at the moment of setting out in a carriage of Cardinal Mazarin's for Chartres, to give a day to my attendants to follow me to Orleans with the rest of the baggage and the money, which after much trouble and more loss than I expected in the exchange, has been placed as much as possible in safety until I embark, but at sea it must run the same risk as ourselves.

The Queen of England is ill with a tertian fever, very slight at certain hours, but nevertheless business is not suspended by it, and Cardinal Mazarin, who went to see her the day before yesterday, told me he had consulted with her how the peace between the King and the Irish might be debated and concluded here in France, as was agreed upon a month ago, or at least that in any case the word of the Queen Regent should be given as a security to both parties. I fully approved of this, and offered to assist him if I shall arrive in time, as I hope to do, since Invernizi must already be at Dunkirk, and provided that he shall have the frigates, will send them at once to La Rochelle, while he, with the same promptitude and with post horses, will overtake me on the road. I had the whole 25,000 crowns from Cardinal Mazarin besides all the passports necessary for the other matters, and as everyone expects that great things will be done with this money, it is one satisfaction the more to have obtained it at the moment of my departure, in addition to that of beginning to devote myself more directly to the service of the Holy See in an enterprise equal to any other in the Church, for which the vigilance of His Holiness is implored. One thing alone grieves me, that for the future as there will be no regular couriers nor posts as heretofore, my letters and reports will go and come without order or regularity, their due course be disturbed, and it will be needful that your Eminence shall magnanimously suppose with your usual benignity, that I do not fail on my part in due diligence, although the difficulties of the passage do not allow the evidence of it to be seen. I invoke the same magnanimity most humbly to make amends from your memory for all the mischances and silence which may result from the distance between us.

I am, with profound reverence, &c., &c.

To the Same.

Chartres, September 3, 1645.

I came to Chartres on Wednesday, as I informed your Eminence, in order to await in a place so famous for its holiness the arrival of the rest of my suite. I have represented in my poor prayers to this blessed Virgin the present necessities of Christianity, and the prosperous course of His Holiness' life, hoping that she will grant the assistance and grace so desired by all good men. I have not been able to preserve my incognito even for the short time I have to be here, as besides some friends I have met also the Capitular of the Cathedral, which by an ancient privilege granted by the Holy See is in direct subjection to His Holiness, who on hearing the name of Apostolic Nuncio at once came with five Canons to visit me, and to attest their said dependence on the Pontiff of which they are so justly proud. I had then an opportunity of commending their zeal and to animate them to show before all eyes, this immediate subjection by particular affection and reverence towards the Holy See, assuring them that they would receive from it at all times every rightful gratification of their just demands in the hope that they would be distinguished above others by gratitude, as they are, and profess to be by dependence.

This morning, Sunday, they begged me to be present in the choir at High Mass, where all sorts of honours were paid to me, and I observed many ancient rites and ceremonies, one of which I must not omit to mention, it was presenting me with bread and wine in the name of the Chapter; they tell me it is done to all priests in token of communion in the true faith, as recalling the eulogies and symbols of the Primitive Church.

The more frequently I find, in the rest of my journey, churches like this, acknowledging that their prerogatives are held from the Holy See, so much the more shall I rejoice to see practically, how widely spread is the dominion of the Church, and also in what esteem the humblest minister dependent on her is held. From this I infer that if I shall succeed in Ireland in imprinting these sentiments, and inducing that people to maintain a filial reverence to the Supreme Chair, it will appear that I shall have done a great work in bringing affairs to this perfect state, and restoring to order the true union of the members to its Head.

In the matter of my charge I have nothing new to add, but if I should receive favourable news at Orleans I shall send a report of it. I will only add that an hour before I left Paris, the letters from Flanders were opened, and Father O'Hartigan had at last, after six weeks, the news that the two prime frigates I had bespoken in the beginning are now being put in order, which makes me happy to believe that Signor Invernizi will find at once all ready convenience to prepare them, and to provide others at the same time. The news from Brussels tell that the usual story had come from London of peace with the Irish, and that therefore 10,000 of them were about to cross over to take service with the King. Thank God I am nearer than ever to clear up this report since, even now, Spinola may know the truth of it, and I cannot be in suspense longer than till I arrive at La Rochelle.

I pray that every happiness may attend your Eminence, and that a prosperous commencement of the second year of the Holy Father's pontificate may be a precursor of many to come.

Reverendissimis d.d. Capitule et Canonisis Ecclesiæ Carnotensis.

Icunculam auream Beatissimae Virginis, quam vos Reverendissimi D.D. ex ipsa Deiparae theca, ut mihi dono mitteretis, avulsistis, habebo (ita sincere profiteor) non tam munus, quam munimentum. Scilicet non sine Divinitatis afflatu suscepisse me hoc iter intelligo: nempe ut provisis, quae iam in longissimum iter humanitus poteram, coelestia superadderem. Rogo vos igitur D.D. ut existimetis sacro hoc amuleto praesidium mihi in adversis, solatium in prosperis contulisse. Stella duce haud difficile cavebuntur insidiae. At vos, qui Romanae Sedi immediatam profitemini subjectionem, existimate non levem eidem operam rependisse, dum eiusdem Sedis Nuntium in dissitas longe terras proficiscentem, ideo sincere, quia coelesti ope deducitis. Estuent Oceani fluctus, vis ingruat hostilium armorum, abeant in minas elementa omnia, Carnotensi imagine fultus nihil expaveseam. Refert illa merito indusium Beatissimae Virginis, ut discam, illius opem non ut extimum vestimentum, sed ut intimum, ac primum velut animae amictum, aestimare. Habui quo vobis in egressu plurimas agerem gratias, Reverendissimi D.D., habebo quo maiores referam in reditu, et eadem Deipara (ita opto, voveoque) quae me nunc aspicit gratias impetrantem, videbit aliquando eadem genuum inflexione sincere reddentem.

Valete, Domo, 4 Septembris, 1645.

To Cardinal Pamphili.

Orleans, September 10, 1645.

By the last post I wrote to your Eminence from Chartres. By the present I write from Orleans,* where I arrived the day before yesterday, and met all my company and the baggage. Immediately on my arrival I went by the river to inspect the armed boats provided for me, and this morning I have sent by the same way a part of my retinue and the money with all the precautions and care which appeared to me necessary. Your Eminence cannot imagine how many days and how many vexations it has cost my attendants to obtain the passports, exemptions, licences, and other necessary forms from the hands of the royal ministers, with prayers, commands, and delays, such as can only be conceived by those who have experienced them. Two days hence I shall myself go by the same river with those attendants who remain with me, and we shall all reach Nantes at the same time. O'Hartigan writes that since my departure from Paris he has received several favourable accounts from Ireland, and in particular, that the Scotch had been obliged to retire from Connaught, and that our troops closely besiege Youghal; on the same day, in a second letter, he tells me he has heard that the Confederates had finally concluded a truce for three months more with the Protestants; if this be true, I ought to arrive before the commencement of any treaty, to have a better opening to make known the true sentiments of His Holiness.

Signor Spinola, whom I sent on before me, has executed all the instructions I gave him for La Rochelle, with diligence and much judgment; and having fortunately found there some merchant vessels bound for Ireland, he wrote to me on the first of this month, that they only waited to sail for a change of wind, which they hoped to have soon, as already

* See Doc. No. IV.

the weather had become rainy; hence I may reasonably believe that he has by this time arrived in Ireland, and not only assured the people of my coming, but gone even farther and confirmed them in faithfulness to the Catholic Church, should the negotiation be arranged, as I mentioned before. Secretary Belling kept his promise of returning from Paris, and having written to me directly on his arrival, I expect him here every moment, in order to take him with me, and thus your Eminence's uneasiness will be allayed. The accounts from Signor Invernizi from Flanders are not satisfactory, as he heard on the way that there were not many frigates on sale at Dunkirk, and that they would cost a much larger sum than the merchant believed and named in his letters to O'Hartigan. Invernizi, therefore, has written to ask my opinion before he takes any further steps. Fearing that this difficulty might detain me on the coast longer than I wish, I have begged Cardinal Mazarin to give new orders for one large vessel at least, of which I will pay the freight, and which, with two other frigates, will be a sufficiently safe escort. Meanwhile Signor Invernizi will have time to decide on the best plan; and in any case, the money given me by the Cardinal will be laid out in some other way for the benefit of the Catholics. Your Eminence has given me infinite consolation in my very humble service by assuring me in the cipher of the 14th of August, that His Holiness condescended to bless my voyage paternally; because recollecting that the hand of the Holy Father has no less power and authority than that of all his predecessors, it does not appear to me that I rashly exalt myself when I hope, that from this mission will follow effects not inferior to those which in former days were witnessed in the same parts of the world to which I am now destined. May the Blessed God pour on His Holiness a multiplicity of Heaven's favours in exchange for all that he has given me, and praying for a long course of uninterrupted felicity for your Eminence.

I am, &c., &c.

To the Same.

Tours, September 17, 1645.

I waited at Orleans for Secretary Belling to join me, and in his company I set off immediately by water, a mode of travelling I greatly enjoy at this moment while I write. At Blois I received the letter of August 21st from your Eminence, with one in cipher annexed, which, being an answer to one of mine, I do not know that I have anything to add now. Cardinal Mazarin immediately gave orders to prepare another vessel at La Rochelle, in case the frigates I expect from Flanders should delay too long in making their appearance. In this vessel, and with two more for escort, as I have apprized you, I intend to embark as soon as possible; but the time for sailing is beyond belief uncertain, and Spinola, whom I sent on so long in advance, and who is most desirous by all means to arrive in Ireland before me, writes on 4th September, that he is still detained on the coast at La Rochelle awaiting a fair wind, with all the weariness that enforced idleness and solitude occasion to an ardent spirit like his. I nevertheless can reckon among the other happy auguries for this my sacred mission, that I celebrated before my departure from Orleans the anniversary of the elevation of His Holiness, and prayed that God would continue in this second year to give to the Blessed Father means to make immortal through all posterity the glory of his Pontificate.

And now to your Eminence I make
My most humble reverence.

Illust.^{mis} et Rev.^{mis} DD. Supremi Consilii Confederatorum Catholicorum Hyberniae.

Ea fuit Illust. ac Rev. DD. de iniuncta mihi a summo D.N. in istud Regnum legatione gratulatio, ut cum primum

Parisios advenerim, nihil ardentius exoptarim, quam citissimam reliqui itineris expeditionem. Sed ut prudenter Apostolicae Sedis negotium tractarem opus fuit, et plura in hac civitate curare, et tutam quantum fieri posset, maris transvectionem opperiri. Interim vero dum necessaria parantur, existimavi muneris mei esse hanc epistolam Illustr. DD. Vestris, testem videlicet paternae in vos Summi Pontificis benevolentiae, atque insimul animi erga vos mei velut imagine praemittere. Ex illa siquidem die, qua inspirante caelitus Deo, Summus D. N. imbecillitatem meam ad onus hoc evangelicum destinavit, mirum dictu est, qua ratione ex Italo in Hibernum repente mutatus, res vestras, ecclesiam vestram, istum ipsum erga fidem Catholicam animorum vestrorum ardorem, et ipse non minus ardens sim amplexatus; adeo ut, si pro asserenda inter vos quam adeo suspiratis Religione, non labores tantum, animique vires, sed vitam etiam ipsam profundere contingeret, nihil tamen pro iustissima causa impendisse putarem; unde enim homini corporis infirmitatibus iam diu obnoxio, ac praematuri senii nuncios iam sentienti tanta innascatur alacritas, ut posthabita Ecclesiae firmanae gubernatione ac peramoenis Italiae littoribus, ignotas istic sedes, bellicos tumultus, ac furentes oceani fluctus non expavescat. Sed tanti est Illust. DD. viro sacris infulis mancipato Sedis Apostolicae classicum atque in Romano Pontifice Petrum audire! Vobis vero, ut plurimum gratuler facit eiusdem summi D. Nostri in istud Regnum propensio, qua spero omnibus tandem Christiani orbis partibus declaratum iri eos populos, qui magis ab Apostolica Sede distant longinquitate terrarum, eidem esse sollicitudine, ac benevolentia proximiores. Plane si quidem Romanus Pontifex Innocentius gloriosius sibi futurum ducit Christi nomen apud dissitas disseminare regiones, quam undecumque terreni fines imperii prolatare, ut qui scilicet intelligat; cuicumque terrarum parti suos praefiniri terminos, animarum vero ditionem nullis limitibus coerceri. Ultinam Illust. DD. quemadmodum indignus tanti Pontificis auctoritatem, ita erga vos amorem digne possem referre, quem tamen si non corporis viribus, ex summo mentis conatu repraesentare conabor. Vos interim Deum Opt. Max. precari decet, ut ingressum meum, progressumque custodiat, dum vobis omnibus, caeterisque totius Regni Proceribus, ac populis delegatam mihi ab eodem Summo benedictionem ex animo impertior, etc.

Parisiis, 1645.

To THE SAME.

Nantes, September 22, 1645.

The last letters which I received from your Eminence were in answer to mine dated July 20th, from Paris. By the last post I wrote from Tours, and by this I beg to inform your Eminence of my safe arrival at Nantes in company with the Secretary, and all in good health. I found here many Irish waiting for a passage in my vessel, and have learnt that Spinola sailed at last on 13th, with a fair wind, accompanied by the coadjutor of Limerick, who had been waiting on these coasts six weeks for an opportunity to embark. The arrival in Ireland of these two persons will give the greatest comfort and assurance to the people, as the uncertainty respecting letters still continues to be so great that I have never yet received answers to the first letters I sent to Ireland, and only duplicates and even triplicates have reached me of some of those which were written to me by the Bishops on 5th July. Such casualties, if I had not hoped to have found a remedy for them, would make me feel with the greatest grief the distance from Rome, and would prepare me, with incredible difficulty however, to be separated more in intelligence than even in space. For to-day I do not enter further on the subject of my departure and its circumstances, as I shall write fully by the next post, contenting myself in the meantime by assuring your Eminence of the solicitude caused by your admonitions which, if successful, will be so much the more meritorious as I have neither heard nor received any conclusive news from Ireland to give me greater light or raise my spirit for the enterprise in this near approach to it, since the news is all old, and we have only the usual hope that Youghal may have been taken. I find that with all this baggage, attendants, and chattels, I cannot move so secretly as not to be discovered in places where there are good Catholics, and with the name of Apostolic Nuncio which is in some sort adored. At Tours, in the Church of St. Martin, where I celebrated Mass because that Chapter is in immediate subjection to the Holy See, they paid me every honour that was possible impromptu, at the moment. In other places the Clergy and the people flocked to my lodging for the benediction; and here at Nantes the Mayor and Sheriffs of the city came at once to visit me with offers of a residence, and to present me with some wines. Every one joins in lauding the piety of His Holiness towards the necessities of Ireland, and in desire to show their dependence on the Holy See, in a manner which one sees is no new feeling, but a desire written in their hearts from old times and by religion; glorifying themselves here in Brittany particularly, that this Province has always had the name of being the most obedient to the Church of Rome. From whence I judge that if the Nuncios of France *pro tempore* took more particular account of the universities, colleges, places and persons scattered through the kingdom who profess these sentiments, they might give notable assistance to the ecclesiastical cause in the emergencies which are continually occurring, by keeping alive the affection of adherents such as these. I shall reserve the remainder for the next post, and recommending myself more than ever to the protection of your Eminence, from whose benignity I am certain neither sea nor land can ever separate me.

I am, &c., &c.

To the Same.

Nantes, September 28, 1645.

At this moment the packet arrives from your Eminence with the four letters in cipher of 20 August.* I shall send answers to all that require it immediately on my arrival at La Rochelle, whither I shall travel in a litter with a part of my people. Yesterday I sent forward Secretary Belling to secure in my name an Irish frigate of known speed, which has just arrived in that port, in order that it may go before and serve me as a scout. Here at Nantes I have found a larger one which will carry the people and the supplies, and with these two, I hope to have no other favour to ask from royalty, than permission to hoist the royal standard.

The news brought by these frigates is too uncertain to be worthy of report. It hints that General Preston had approached Dublin, to give colour to the prolongation of the truce as though he intended to besiege the city, if it were not concluded: and yet former letters told us that this was an accomplished fact. All agree that the siege of Youghal still continues. I should esteem it great good fortune if the news of this victory were to be the first which I had to send your Eminence after my arrival. I have wished to give these details to prove to your Eminence the pains I always take to lose no time, and that my efforts have succeeded and have given satisfaction, as Secretary Belling assures me in the name of the whole kingdom.

With reverence.

* See Doc. No. V.

On the 22nd May I arrived in Paris, and had hardly presented the Papal Brief to the Duke of Orleans, who was on the point of departing for Flanders, when I was taken ill with fever and cold which kept me in the house for nine days. I had my first audience of the King and Queen on the 5th June, and up to 13th was occupied in paying my necessary visits, accompanied always by the Nuncio of France. In my first interview with Cardinal Mazarin he informed me that there were at that time no royal vessels in port; but that he would write to see if they could be had in some other way. I returned a second time to His Eminence on 24th, and through the press of his own affairs he seemed entirely to have forgotten mine, as he spoke very coldly of them, wherefore at the end of the month I went twice to Cardinal Bichi entreating him to hurry the expedition since I found it impossible to obtain an audience of Cardinal Mazarin without waiting for it at least five or six days, although sending Signor Invernizi morning and evening to request it. On the evening of 8th of July Father O'Hartigan assured me that on the same day His Eminence had told him that the vessels were then at La Rochelle, and were at my disposal. On the following day therefore I went to return thanks to the Queen and Council, intimating to all that the next interview would be to take my leave. I then gave my people orders to prepare everything necessary, the arms and the money to be taken with me. By the end of the month I had taken my leave of every one and was on the point of setting off. But two things determined me to fix my departure at the end of the Madonna of August. The first was the journey of Secretary Belling to Flanders; therefore as I knew His Holiness particularly desired that he should not arrive in Ireland without me, I made him promise to return to Paris and gave him hopes that I should wait for him. The second was to receive from Cardinal Mazarin those 8,000 crowns which he had promised some time before, and which every one assured me, if not paid then I should never receive. I can truly say that if I could have conceived the time, fatigue, and trouble this money was to cost me, I should have laid it aside, but it is impossible to foresee everything. Add to this that when the money was paid the Cardinal desired to speak with me again, which audience involved the usual days of waiting as before. Nevertheless I set off on 29th of the month, on the receipt of His Holiness' command notwithstanding that the negotiation about the money was not concluded; for this purpose therefore I left the Dean of Fermo, and also before the Secretary had returned from Flanders but he afterwards joined me at Orleans.

To the Same.
La Rochelle, October 5, 1645.

I arrived at La Rochelle two days ago, and am residing at the College of the Jesuits as privately as possible, waiting only a favourable wind as everything else is ready; the frigate which I hired at Nantes is expected every hour with my baggage, attendants, and many Irishmen who were awaiting this opportunity of returning to Ireland. Here also I have found six Irish merchant vessels ready to set sail, which will keep me company all the way to that kingdom—an occurrence certainly ordained for me by Divine Providence, as I am told that a long time often elapses without such an event. I therefore thank the Blessed God fervently for having thus caused me to arrive at this moment without my having any previous knowledge of the circumstance. I therefore reply to your Eminence that I shall need no help or further royal favour than permission to hoist the ensign, to let it be known that I sail under the protection of the Court. The evening before my arrival Mr. Galfrid Barron, treasurer of the kingdom, reached this city in four days from Ireland, on his way to

Paris by order of the Supreme Council, to attend as I hear, for some time to the affairs of the Confederates, while perhaps Father O'Hartigan may retire to his religious duties. This cavalier has an excellent countenance, a very affable manner, and has informed me that he is a relative of Father Luke Wadding. He has brought me several letters from Ireland, some of them answers to my first from Paris, others complimentary, expressing a desire to see me there very soon; amongst these was one from Father Scarampi who, as I hear from your Eminence also awaits my coming to be able to return to Rome. He begs me to pay to this Mr. Barron a sum of about 200 crowns advanced by him, and this I have at once done. This same gentleman tells me that in the General Assembly nothing had been concluded about a peace; the truce only was tacitly continued, and that no more will be done before my arrival. In proof of this he brought me a letter from the Earl of Glamorgan, an Englishman and most excellent Catholic, who has been sent to Ireland by the King with some secret instructions, in order to see if he can facilitate an agreement between him and the Irish. He writes that he wishes first to have an interview with me, and is expecting me with the greatest impatience. As to news Mr. Barron brings none save that the siege of Youghal is still proceeding. It is hoped that it may soon surrender, but he adds that there is so great a want of ammunition that what was provided at La Rochelle will arrive very opportunely. The King, as I also saw in a gazette at Paris is gone to the north of England, perhaps to join Montrose who is making successful progress in Scotland; and as there are a great many Irish in that army the King will now learn from experience the fidelity and bravery of his Irish subjects. Mr. Barron did not meet Signor Domenico Spinola whom I had sent on before me because, having to disembark at Limerick while Mr. Barron sailed from Waterford, it is probable that while the one was going on board ship, the other was on the point of leaving it, and would arrive at Kilkenny a few days after. To the letters of 28th August, which were the last I received from your Eminence, I have nothing to say but what you will see in the subjoined ciphers and paper, since for the particulars which suppose me to be still in Paris, I do not wait now for many reasons, but pray continually that God will not only prosper the holy sentiments of the Blessed Father, but also that the whole Christian world may know and profess them, as does already a great part of it. I conclude with my humble reverence, hoping to write next from Ireland.

To the Same. (In Cipher).
La Rochelle, October 12, 1645.

When Cardinal Mazarin spoke to me of the change of Nuncio, I certainly did not remind him that M. de Gramonville had been the principal cause of my taking the way of France, having already in paying my first compliments, and at other times afterwards signified it sufficiently to him; but as to His Holiness I did say that he had commanded that route, to carry on the negotiation for Ireland to more advantage, and to give no umbrage to this Court, or to the Queen of England. When Cardinal Mazarin told me that he had received advices from Rome, I was certain that the blow would soon fall upon me and that I was accused of ambition, I therefore showed at some length that it was God himself and His Holiness of his own motion, who had called me to this office the most meritorious and the most glorious of our day, and therefore that I should show little judgment in preferring any other to it. Besides it is an office to which my bodily strength is equal, as it does not require like many others to be sustained with a pomp and show, which I could not possibly maintain. My motive in reporting this conversation to your Eminence is that I think it right to let you know that Cardinal Mazarin speaks of the change of Nuncio in a very different manner from many others of the Court; and above all from Cardinal Bichi, who has said several times that at this juncture no other Nuncio however faithful would have been accepted. This is my only motive in advising you of the whole matter, for as far as I myself am concerned I feel certain that some few days after my departure Cardinal Mazarin would be satisfied that his intelligence had been false, &c. Thus much I have thought right to add to the cipher of 28th August, &c., &c.

To the Same.

La Rochelle, October 15, 1645.

The delay here is occasioned not so much by the wind as by the broken promises of the merchants, which I should endure with greater impatience if I did not see that the Secretary and the other Irishmen who are equally desirous to embark, nevertheless bear the delay with patience, being more accustomed to the uncertainty of sea affairs. I have received here one ordinary letter from your Eminence, of September 11th; but as according to my reckoning there are wanting some others of 14th of the same month (if your Eminence did favour me by that post), I hope that by some means the letters may overtake me, as they have probably been redirected to various places. The weather is most beautiful and the heat greater than usual not without sorrow to the sailors, who for the greater security and swiftness of the passage would like to have more wind. The only consolation in the weariness of waiting is, that I willingly consecrate myself to the enterprise to which I am appointed, and to the prompt execution of the commands of His Holiness.

With humble reverence, &c., &c.

To Cardinal Pamphili.

Ardtully, October 16, 1645.

Now that I have safely arrived in Ireland, it appears to be the time to explain exactly to your Eminence how the negotiation for the embarkation under the royal protection of France was conducted, to which so much importance has been attached, which lengthened out into so many journeys, but which after all God decreed should be unnecessary, in fact to be of no use. Even before my departure from Rome, Father O'Hartigan had written that he had arranged with Cardinal Mazarin for the security of my voyage; and perhaps this was one of the motives which induced His Holiness to command me to take the route of France. Immediately on my arrival in Paris, the said Father pompously confirmed this assurance and the Nuncio asserted positively that it was true; at the same time O'Hartigan begged of me in thanking the Cardinal, not to mention the number of vessels but to leave it to him as he had determined to ask for six, in order to secure at least four. As I placed full confidence in him, I always spoke of them in the plural to the Cardinal without naming any number. On the evening of the 8th of July O'Hartigan came to me on the part of the Cardinal, told me that the vessels would be all ready, and explicitly said that four was to be the number, and I know that I wrote this to your Eminence, as I firmly believed it during the whole month that I waited to pay my visits and to make my preparations. But at the beginning of August, in an audience which Signor Invernizi had on my part with the Cardinal he mentioned by chance the four vessels; whereupon the Cardinal said he had given orders for no more than one, and that O'Hartigan had asked for one only. Invernizi was so much astonished that he came instantly to tell me this news and I confess I was much perplexed, because O'Hartigan still insisting that four had been promised to him, I did not know how to decide between him and the Cardinal; on the other hand I believed that my safety depended upon the number of vessels, and I felt ashamed to have made a false statement to your Eminence even upon the word of others. I thought the best way out of the difficulty would be to draw upon Cardinal Mazarin for the 8,000 crowns, and to send to Dunkirk to provide vessels which would make up the number I had mentioned to you. But I feared as indeed has happened, that to procure them at Dunkirk would take some time and as I did not wish to wait or make any delay, I obtained a letter from the Duc de Brezè, Admiral of the fleet, to the minister at La Rochelle to equip at my request a vessel for my transport to Ireland. This letter was of no avail because having sent it forward by one of my attendants, the answer was received that there was only one vessel at La Rochelle, the repairs of which would require an outlay of 1,000 crowns and could not be ready in less than six weeks. Disappointed on all sides I threw myself into the frigate the "San Pietro" which was lying at Nantes, on board of which I experienced those blessings and miracles which I relate in the first accompanying letter. And so, all these interviews, delays, and journeys, in order to sail under the protection of France have borne no fruit except to put the King's flag on my frigate, a privilege denied to no one but however of no great use, because in the event of our being chased by pirates (this is private) all here laugh at the idea of their respecting the French lilies, as Cardinal Mazarin tried to convince me they would, but it is concluded that at the worst we should all be taken to London, where there would be a dispute whether the flag should have been respected or not. However I think I was not far wrong when I wrote to your Eminence some months ago, that my successors would bless me for my poor labours and efforts in these transactions, since they will find everything easy and the issue made clear, whereas I am obliged to fight my way between uncertainties and doubts as to what resolution to take, and with endless threats of danger conveyed to me every day by all sorts of persons, without my being able to gainsay them except by putting on an appearance of ease and security and with much waste of words.

And I am, &c., &c.

To His Holiness Pope Innocent X.

Ardtully, October 16, 1645.

From what I have written at great length to Cardinal Pamphili, your Holiness will deign to understand through what dangers and by means of what miracles it has pleased the Blessed God to signalise my journey and voyage to Ireland. I should not have presumed to approach so soon before your Holiness but that having at an eventful moment felt myself ready to sacrifice my life for the Holy Faith, I know that I have acquired the true character of Bishop, and therefore my desire is increased to throw myself at the feet of your Holiness, and to pray more than ever for your paternal protection. Already I see that among this people so devoted to the Holy See; I may scatter the seed of your Holiness' commands and instructions successfully, as all those have done who have been sent to this kingdom by the Holy See, but I hope that in one respect my admonitions will stand alone, because I shall be able to show that in order to avoid the greatest of dangers, there is no safeguard so powerful as the Apostolic Benediction. The fervent prayer of this kingdom is that God may long preserve the life of your Holiness.

I humbly bow and kiss your blessed feet.

To Cardinal Pamphili.

Limerick, October 25 (new style).

After various impediments, and after having (according to the usual ways of these merchants) lost every hope of the vessels which were to accompany me, Divine Providence favoured in a miraculous manner, as your Eminence shall hear, my most ardent desire to reach Ireland. In proof of this I must first inform your Eminence that I put to sea much indisposed; my illness began in Paris at the end of the month of July, and greatly increased on my departure from that city. Hence I was obliged to take many remedies; blood was often taken from me during the journey, but it seemed only to increase the evil and I had several accessions of fever. I did not inform your Eminence of this indisposition, as I did not wish to offer any excuse however legitimate, for deferring my departure and the execution of His Holiness' commands. Obliged then to depart with the one frigate which I had provided and had laden at Nantes, I set sail from the Island of San Martino on Monday the 18th instant, in company with Secretary Belling and several other Irishmen who had been waiting for this passage, and having with me all the money, arms, and other necessary stores. All Tuesday and part of the Wednesday following, the wind was so favourable that we made sure of arriving at Waterford on the Thursday, nor had we any adventure till we saw seven English vessels, two of which gave us chase for four hours, but the superior speed of our vessel soon made them resolve to turn back. On Thursday the air was dark and owing to its being full moon, the sea was so rough that it was thought better not to approach Waterford, but to keep out to sea, as we might have easily mistaken one port for another, and so fall into the mouth of the Parliamentarians who have possession of the surrounding places, without hope of escape.

On Friday morning, after having been tossed about during the night, there were seen at break of day at the distance of about two leagues, a large vessel in full sail together with a small frigate in chase of us. The Irishmen on board and the sailors concluded that these were the vessels commanded by one Plunket an Irishman who, having now become a Puritan, had been ordered by the Parliament to keep watch over these seas. The nearness of the danger and knowledge of the man they had to deal with, suddenly caused a great commotion in our little vessel. The Irishmen and Secretary Belling in particular, who knew into whose hands they would fall and how they would be treated, immediately armed and resolved to defend themselves to the death. All superfluous articles were thrown into the sea, the deck cleared, the cannon prepared, the unarmed placed securely at the prow, and no precautions omitted which could be taken in so short a time. On the other hand, all my family and attendants perhaps thinking on a greater evil than that which had come upon us, much to my edification commended themselves to God, preparing themselves to submit wholly to whatever the Divine Goodness willed. I was in bed, my illness very greatly aggravated, and already for two whole days without any attendance whatever from my servants, as they were prostrated by sea-sickness and as little able to hear as to obey my orders. Nevertheless, even in this pass I felt my courage rise to a greater height than ever in my life before, and confident in the protection of the saints who guided me, in the blessing of the Holy Father, and in the holy ends of the work for which we were then braving the sea, I endeavoured to encourage those around me, assuring them continually that I had no doubt of the Divine aid. Nevertheless I prepared in my own heart (to avoid presumption), to give up life and liberty in whatever way God should dispose of me, even if it seemed to him necessary that both I and those whom he had given to my care should be left in the city of London.

It was noted when I ordered the frigate at Nantes, that the vessel was dedicated to St. Peter, whose gilded image was placed at the poop, and as she had come from the Loire to offer herself to me as it were, I hailed it as an omen that the Head of the Church on whom all missions depend, and who had inspired His Holiness to arrange and undertake my present one, would please also to conduct it to the end, and would show on every occasion how feeble are the forces of hell compared with the authority of the Keys; and truly I see the hand of the Saint in the miraculous issue of this pursuit, because notwithstanding all the advantages possessed by the enemy's ship in size, wherewith to weather the storm, and its superiority in numbers of men and of ordnance twice as large as ours; it remained from the first far behind the little frigate, and after chasing us for a hundred miles or more, gaining scarcely any advantage on us, at last, an hour before the daylight failed, the great ship suddenly changed its course and sailed away in another direction. We all sung the hymn of thanksgiving with incredible devotion, and I recognised the protection of Saint Peter, not only in the issue, but that I had maintained the greatest confidence in it, even to the end.

This confidence only increased with my horror at the idea of seeing the passengers and the sailors slaughtered, the ship stained with their blood, and my friends with all the rest committed to my care lying dead before my eyes. Rather than this, I should have been inclined to yield magnanimously where I could not resist, recalling to mind the words of the great English Martyrs, "Ecclesia Dei non est custodienda more Castrorum." The general opinion concerning this event, from some circumstances which afterwards became known, and especially that Plunket had been seen to watch this sea for more than two months, is that I was known to be in Paris, that intelligence of my movements had probably been forwarded to London by the Parliamentary agent who resides there, and as it was thought that this pirate could easily intercept my passage, he was ordered to do so in every way possible, besides which, other vessels were stationed at different parts of the channel and in the harbours of Ireland for the same purpose for upwards of a month. If this be true as I believe it is, we may conclude that the safety of the whole affair has been the result of my boldness in having sailed with one vessel only, and thus what seemed to begin in misfortune has ended by the grace of God in great good fortune. As it was known publicly that I had ordered several frigates from Flanders, and had made arrangements to be accompanied from La Rochelle by a large number of vessels, the enemy no doubt never imagined that I should put to sea with one only, and therefore did not on that night, follow us as long as they intended, lest by the appearance of my convoy in another quarter they should, through chasing this single frigate, lose the chance of securing a greater prey. Thus I am convinced that in spite of the incredible trouble I took to have a strong escort, Saint Peter willed that I should sail with his vessel alone, to be my only protector and deliverer from all perils. But to proceed; on Friday night as we did not know on what part of the coast we might be, we still kept out at sea, but on the following morning when from the chart and compass we expected to see Ireland, we could only ascertain that we must have passed Cape Clear and be on some part of the western coast. Here arose another difficulty as great as that of the preceding day, and some, fearing we should not find it easy to return, began to count the provisions lest they should not hold out many days, in order to be prepared for a long pilgrimage on the ocean. Thinking on the uncertainty of human affairs I marvelled to have set out to seek a kingdom which could not be found, and could not help saying jestingly, that my embassy had changed the earth into water if I might not rather say, that having lost the earth, I should soon vanish into air. At last, carefully following the course pointed out by the chart, we first saw some land birds, and towards evening descried Ireland, and found ourselves in a bay which, from a little river that flows into it is called the Bay of Kenmare. That evening we cast anchor in a secure place, and on the following day, with little wind and very slow sailing, we arrived at some poor little huts on *terra firma*. And here I may give your Eminence another proof of the Divine providence towards me, in having discovered and touched land on 21st and 22nd of the present month, which seem to be consecrated to an Archbishop of Fermo, as on the 21st my Church celebrates the feast of Saint Mabel, one of the 11,000 virgins, whose head we have at Fermo, and whom we believe on no slight grounds to have been of Irish birth ; while on the 22nd we also celebrate the martyrdom of Saint Philip, Bishop of Fermo, therefore I confidently believe that this my great predecessor, wished to conduct me himself to the place to which I have been destined by the Vicar of God. My first lodging was in a shepherd's hut in which animals also took shelter, and there I remained two days not so much to repose after our trials as to return thanks for our safety. The Secretary and others regretted much that we had not been able to land at Waterford, where, they said, I should have been received with prepared demonstrations, and firing of cannon. I however rejoiced greatly that fortune had brought me to a sterile and unknown part of the country where no Apostolic minister had ever been before, as it thus appears to me that God desired to signalise this new embassy by some similitude to the great work of the Redemption; which by His permission was first announced to the shepherds, and His Apostolic work begun within the walls of a stable. I went slowly towards Kilkenny stopping on account of my indisposition, at the villages belonging to Catholic Barons well affected to the Holy See. People now began to join me from all quarters, hastening to offer welcome and to testify their respect for my person, and showing by their joyful aspect the satisfaction which I expected to find amongst them. This letter, which does not pretend to do more than to announce my arrival and to assure your Eminence of the joy which I felt in all my perils that I could willingly lay down my life for the Holy See, as its grandeur merits from all bishops in acccordance with the oath which we take at our consecration, but which I am more particularly called upon to do, since by the grace and goodness of His Holiness, I have been considered not unworthy of this great mission.

The remainder I send in the other letters,

I am, &c., &c.

To the Same.

Limerick, October 31, 1645.

In my first letter I described the perils which I passed through by sea, in this I shall briefly relate those that were to be feared by land, because having landed in Munster not very far from Cork which is now in the hands of the Parliamentarians, every day brought new accounts of vessels stationed on the coast to take me, and it was reasonable to think that similar attempts would be made by land. I therefore travelled with great circumspection, often times leaving the high roads, posting sentinels about at night, sending spies on before, and taking in fact all the precautions necessary in war. Besides the people who gradually joined me from the neighbouring counties and many volunteers who came of themselves to guard my person, the

Supreme Council having heard of my arrival, sent Mr. Richard Butler brother to the Marquis of Ormonde, and two other officers with some troops of horse to accompany me through all the dangerous places. It would be impossible to give your Eminence an idea of the ruggedness of the roads, and the steepness of the mountains and passes over which this escort conveyed us and our baggage. My mind was not completely at ease until we had left the hostile country behind us, because in spite of the good-will of these people aided by the said military escort, I am perfectly certain that if the enemy had had resolution we should have had something to do to escape. Of the arms which I brought from Paris I had a part landed and deposited in the Castle of Ardtully, a strong post and approved of in the public name by Secretary Belling; the rest remained in the frigate. I had given orders that the vessel should go round to Waterford, but as it left the coast it was driven by contrary winds to the port of Dingle. As numberless reports were flying that the enemy enraged at having missed the party, would plunder the vessel, I considered it advisable to carry the stores by land to Limerick where I arrived yesterday evening, and shall leave the vessel in that port until the weather improves and other dangers have diminished. I trust that Saint Peter who has favoured us so far, will finish the good work by protecting what is so needful for its success. I came to Limerick, because having heard that at last a few days ago it had declared for the Confederates to the great joy of the whole kingdom; I thought it well by my presence to cement this union and assure myself that there should be no other change. Here I found Father Scarampi in good health; I delivered to him the letter which your Eminence had sent by me but I have not yet had time to confer with him, and therefore cannot inform you of the state of affairs as my duty requires. Your Eminence may be assured that the inhabitants of this city as indeed the people everywhere have done as much to honour my coming, and have testified as deep a devotion to the Holy See as if His Holiness himself had arrived in Ireland; they have done all but sacrifice themselves for the holy cause, nor will this be wanting if we may judge by the demonstrations of affection that have been now made.

I conclude with my humble salutation, &c., &c.

To the Same.

Kilkenny, November 20, 1645.

During the few days of my stay in Limerick there came news so sorrowful for Ireland of the unfortunate death of the Archbishop of Tuam, before I had had time to know or even to confer with him as your Eminence's instructions command. This worthy prelate after the loss of Sligo left Kilkenny and repaired to Connaught, in order to put an end to the disorders of that province. I understand that on quitting Kilkenny he carried with him all his property, took leave of many persons as if he never should return, alleging as a reason some prophecy concerning the pastors of his Church. I find this people much given to believe in these vain predictions.

While besieging the above-mentioned castle he received notice that the enemy, greatly increased in numbers were advancing towards him; either he did not believe the news or for some other reason, he did not take the steps that were necessary, was charged by the enemy and completely routed. Two monks and some officers who were with him were killed, and his own life was suddenly terminated by a pistol shot. It is well known that before his death he had used all his strength in defence of the Catholic religion, that he willingly gave up his life to the same purpose and he has worthily closed all his earthly labours; receiving in heaven a reward equal to the greatness of his merit.

It is well known that the Scotch lament greatly that they did not know his person, that they might have taken him alive and wreaked a greater vengeance upon him. Not more than forty of the Catholic army were killed, and the defeat would have been of little consequence but for the irreparable loss of the Archbishop. I proposed that his funeral should be a public one, not only on account of his rank but because he died in actual defence of the Faith, and it will take place on Monday next. By his death from all I hear Connaught is incredibly destitute of persons with either power or resolution to direct the operations of the war for the people of that province are not brave, nor is there order or true union amongst those who are more capable. The ecclesiastical party more than any other is disheartened by this event, as amongst them both in council and in public assemblies the late Archbishop had great influence from his knowledge and eloquence; and therefore, in order that the Church party may not entirely lose ground (for your Eminence is aware that many churches in the kingdom are not yet provided with pastors) I have employed by Father Scarampi's desire the arguments which he tells me he has already often brought forward, and which he entreats me to repeat on this occasion. From Limerick I wrote to the Supreme Council and to some of the Deputies sent to treat of peace in Dublin, begging them, on this my first arrival, to conduct the treaty with a constant reference to religion, in order that the first reports I send to His Holiness may be worthy of the cause and of the Sovereign who awaits them. It is impossible at present to know the effect of these letters, for we are not yet acquainted with the state of the negotiation. Two days after my arrival at Kilkenny five of the Deputies returned declaring that nothing had been concluded; but from their having left two of their number behind, we judged that some new discussion must have taken place, their return however two days ago shows clearly that it is from here all future resolutions must emanate, but I will report in a separate sheet all that I hear. This evening also the Earl of Glamorgan returned from Dublin, he has secret powers from the King respecting the religious conditions in the treaty, as Father Scarampi tells me he has been informed. I arrived in Kilkenny a week ago and have to-day for the first time attended the meeting of the Council to present the brief from His Holiness and your Eminence's letter. The particulars of my reception I have put in a separate paper that they may be deliberated upon for the instruction of future Nuncios, and in case you may deem that any of the observances should have been amplified as may well be, I thought it above all things necessary at first to win love and good-will towards my office, and did not think it advisable therefore to dispute some things to which this people have not perhaps been accustomed, and which probably would only have been obtained with great repugnance. One of my first acts was to pay to Father Scarampi the sum of 1,760 crowns, expended by him for various necessary purposes and of which as he wrote to me several times to Paris he says he has given you an account.

I have found a tolerably good residence ready for me here, and in so far as my means will allow I shall conduct my mission with all the propriety and dignity in my power, and I shall hope to supply all deficiencies by the edification of the work and the example of those who have accompanied me. If my health which at present makes me feel every change of this extraordinary climate does not give way entirely, I shall consecrate it as I have already done in words, and now do in acts, to the service of His Holiness as long as life lasts and I continue to be favoured by the commands of the Blessed Father.

With humble reverence, &c., &c.

ACCOUNT OF THE RECEPTION OF THE NUNCIO BY THE INHABITANTS OF IRELAND.

The members of the Supreme Council hearing from Secretary Belling of my arrival previous to the receipt of my letters, sent three deputies with two companies of horse to congratulate me on my safe arrival, and to escort me as long as danger was to be apprehended from the vicinity of the enemy. These officers were Mr. Richard Butler, brother to the Marquis of Ormonde but a Catholic; Lord Netterville and Nicholas di Teglier a priest, who met me at Dromsecane twelve miles from Macroom. By them I was escorted to Limerick, whence as all danger was at an end the cavalry returned to their quarters, but the gentlemen remained with me. The evening before my arrival at Kilkenny I stopped at a villa three miles from the town, to give time for all the preparations for my reception. Here I was visited by four noblemen on the part of the Council accompanied by Mr. Belling who came to welcome me again, and one of them a man of letters pronounced a short oration. As soon as I was in my litter we set out, and in the space of those three miles I was met by all the nobility and all the young men of Kilkenny, besides crowds of other persons in different detachments the leaders of each dismounting to compliment me. The first to come was a band of fifty scholars, all however armed with pistols who after caracoling round me conveyed their compliments to me through one of their number, a youth crowned with laurel and in a richer habit than the rest, and who recited some verses to me.

Outside the doors of the Church of Saint Patrick were assembled the secular and regular clergy, who immediately started the procession. At the gate the Magistrates of the city were waiting and amongst them the Vicar-General who handed me the cross to kiss. I then mounted on horseback wearing the pontifical cape and hat; the poles of my canopy were carried by some of the citizens who walked uncovered though it was raining. All the way to the Cathedral, a distance perhaps not less than the length of the Via Lungara in Rome, was lined with soldiers on foot carrying muskets. In the middle of the city and at the foot of a high Cross, where a crowd was also assembled we all stopped and a youth pronounced an oration, after which we moved on till we reached the Church. Here, at the door the Bishop of Ossory, the Ordinary of this place, although of great age met me in the Cope, offered me the aspersorium and incense, and conducting me to the High Altar delivered an address suitable to the ceremony, after which I gave a solemn benediction and granted the indulgences, and then another oration was pronounced in honour of my arrival.

My first visit to the Supreme Council passed in the following manner :—General Preston and Lord Muskerry brother-in-law to Ormonde, waited upon me on the part of the Council, upon which I set off on foot accompanied by all the nobility and armed soldiers towards the castle, to which out of compliment to me, the Council had transferred for that day their sitting and had prepared the reception in a beautiful hall. At the foot of the stairs I was greeted by four other Councillors, two of whom were the Archbishops of Dublin and of Cashel. At the head of the hall was seated Lord Mountgarret President of the Council, who rose as I approached but received me without moving at all from his place. My seat of red damask enriched with gold and handsomer than that of the President was placed on his right hand, but so turned that it principally faced the left side and indeed both appeared to be in the centre. I made a forcible speech in Latin, explaining the feelings, resolutions, and aims of His Holiness. I then had the Papal brief and the letter of Cardinal Pamphili read, and concluded with a few more words after which I pronounced upon them all the Apostolic Benediction, which was mentioned in the brief. I was answered by the Bishop of Clogher standing, and in a short habit, and having taken leave of the President who did not move from his place, the four gentlemen already mentioned accompanied me to the east gate of the castle, and Preston and Muskerry with the same guards escorted me to the threshold of my house. All this has been done because as a formal visit must necessarily pass between the president and me, I thought it well to pay him the first visit, he being the head of those to whom I am accredited, and we have been treated alike in everything. The whole course of this reception was arranged by Secretary Belling, to whom, as lately come from Italy and cognizant of Italian customs the direction of these affairs was given.

To CARDINAL PAMPHILI.

Kilkenny, November 22, 1645.

By the last despatch I received your Eminence's letter of the 30th of September, in which you are pleased to favour me with the latest news of the Christian army received that day by way of Naples. I cannot express the joy I feel in the hopes which may be fairly entertained from this victory gained over the Ottomans. The public prayers commanded by His Holiness in his pastoral letter, had already commenced throughout this kingdom; but I shall now insist the more on their being fervently continued that we may obtain the confirmation of so signal an acquisition for the glory of the Holy Faith, for the Pontificate of His Holiness, and for the meritorious labour of His Excellency the Prince Piombino. Your Eminence may be assured that we shall pray with all earnestness, both pastors and people, knowing that if His Holiness be delivered from the thoughts of this fierce enemy, he will be able to turn his magnanimous thoughts more fully to the condition of this poor kingdom, which can look only to His Holiness for its safety and peace.

With much reverence, &c., &c.

To THE SAME.

Kilkenny, November 28, 1645.

I have now passed a fortnight in Kilkenny. All the Commissioners sent to Dublin since September to treat of peace have returned, and the answers and resolutions of the Marquis of Ormonde and his Council have also been transmitted. The Council here in their morning and evening meetings are engaged in examining all these papers, and when they have decided in their own minds on the question of peace or war, they will consult me on the subject. Great differences of opinion appear every day, weariness, self-interest, want of money, and respect for the King incline many to peace, and dispose them to listen to the proposals of Glamorgan under his private commission; concerning which Father Scarampi has written to you. The greater part of the clergy, those who have no confidence in the King and those who are convinced that if the dissensions among the commanders could be allayed, it would be easy to expel the enemy from the whole kingdom, incline to war. And such as these would not object to give assistance to the King without concluding peace or even insisting on conditions from him; but they would carefully guard their own possessions in Ireland and gain as many more as possible, believing that if they were united with the English Catholics, the Parliament would be so terrified as to be unable to think of interfering in the affairs of this country, and further, that more could be obtained and with greater security from the King when restored to power, than he could give now for fear of the Protestants. I cannot this evening inform you what will be the final determination as it is yet very uncertain, but I will write at length when affairs are arranged; in the meantime, by prayers and warnings I endeavour to dispose the minds of all to do what will be most to the glory of God and the Catholic religion. It was said at first, that many were inclined to make a peace satisfactory enough on political grounds (with the condition of retaining their possessions) but would keep silence on ecclesiastical affairs; I do not know however, if this will be acted on. We understand to-day that Lord Digby, Chief Secretary of State to the King has arrived in Dublin from Scotland; it is believed that he has not come to negotiate, but has merely taken this route to join the King as being the safest way to escape the enemy.

Father Scarampi is gone to Wexford, to preside at the consecration of a bishop, and I must send this packet to him that he may enclose his own, and forward it by a vessel bound for Rouen but I shall send the usual duplicate by Flanders.

&c., &c.

To the Same.

Kilkenny, December 23, 1645.

The Supreme Council have drawn up and sent to me after a delay of twenty days, various papers under the pretext of wishing to hear my opinion before coming to any determination; and I have at once discovered the aim of the negotiations now pending for so many months, and the ardent longing of most of the Council for peace with the King on any terms. In one of the documents they take occasion greatly to exaggerate the benefit derived from the past truces and cessation of arms. In another, they expatiate upon the resources and power of the enemy, confounding together the Puritans and Protestants in order to strike greater terror into those who are inclined to war.

In other places they enumerate the advantages to be derived by the kingdom from free communication with the

Marquis of Ormonde and the Protestants of Dublin; and in others they endeavour to influence me by showing the present great necessity of the King for aid, and his sorrow in not being able to confirm at present the concessions he had promised to the Irish. They then conclude by asserting that no assistance can be sent to His Majesty unless peace be made, that to leave him unaided would be the gravest violation of fidelity, and would draw down inevitable ruin on the country by the increased power of the enemy.

From all this I cannot doubt that the peace has long been fully determined on, that its publication has only been deferred on account of those who are not perfectly satisfied with the conditions, and under various other pretexts, one, that of consulting me on my arrival. I send to your Eminence copies of all the papers of importance, retaining those which are unnecessary. But these articles for peace are to be divided under two heads: those which concern the political Government, possession of property, distribution of offices, abolition of certain magistracies, and the new concessions respecting the tribunals, are to be treated of and concluded with the Marquis of Ormonde, by virtue of the powers given him by the King, passing over in silence nearly all the conditions which belong to religion, and concerning which, in Ormonde's articles nothing more is mentioned than that the public exercise of the Catholic faith must be left to the benignity of the King. The other part wholly ecclesiastical, is to be concluded with the Earl of Glamorgan in virtue of two most ample but secret powers, confirmed under the King's private seal and given by His Majesty to the Earl. These articles are really good, but to have them ratified by the King it will be necessary that 10,000 Irish infantry shall cross to England under this same Earl, there to be joined by as many or fewer English Catholics, and the King strengthened by this force without fear of losing the Protestants, will be in a position to ratify the concessions now made through Glamorgan. The Earl is bound by an oath taken before the Supreme Council, not to take these soldiers into any engagement until the articles are first ratified, and if His Majesty refuses, the Earl is either to insist upon it at the head of these forces, or faithfully to send the whole 10,000 men at once back to Ireland. The Council therefore are anxious that the concessions made through Glamorgan shall be kept secret until confirmed by the King, but that those of Ormonde shall at once be published and put in force, and of these written articles I also send your Eminence a copy. As to the substance of the political articles I left the determination of them almost entirely to the Supreme Council, and as to those of Glamorgan I pressed him to give me a separate undertaking by virtue of the powers conferred on him, to add several particulars which appeared to me absolutely necessary viz.: That the Viceroy of Ireland after Ormonde's retirement shall always be a Catholic; that the Catholic bishops shall sit in the first Parliament, or if this be not possible at least in the second and all succeeding ones. These two points perhaps the gravest as regards the Catholic religion, had been entirely overlooked by the Council in the negotiations in Dublin with Glamorgan, though they carefully remembered to limit the duration of the Viceroy's government and jurisdiction in many things. But how they could frame the political treaty so carefully and leave the affairs of the Church in such uncertainty, I can neither understand nor approve, and in a Latin speech delivered in Council, and subsequently by a document of which a copy is enclosed, I showed them what scandal and astonishment would be created amongst Christian princes, in the Court of Rome, and in the heart of His Holiness, on hearing that in this treaty there was not one word on the most important point of all, and for which the whole world believes Ireland to have taken up arms in the beginning. And I have shown them that they could expect nothing less than to be the derision of the Scotch and of their other adversaries, and that if so great an affair as the transmission of soldiers to England were followed by any disaster, such as the shipwreck of the men, or the failure of the English to join them, the death of Glamorgan, or want of will or power on the part of the King, the Catholics would unite with the Protestants in saying that the Irish had known well how to adjust all that touched their political and private affairs; but all that concerned their religion they had left to chance and uncertainty. And more, for as soon as the articles of the Ormonde Treaty are published the abolition of the Supreme Council is to follow, and a mixed Government of Protestants and Catholics to be established, and thus there will not be left to the Apostolic Nuncio even the title of the Confederation to which his mission is directed. Besides this, the armies of the Marquis of Ormonde and of the Catholics are to combine against the Puritans; and whereas in past and present times if for example Cork or Youghal had been taken, they would at once have received a Catholic Bishop, and the public exercise of religion have been established; in this case, because peace will be made the Protestant worship will prevail, and that of the Catholics be exercised only in secret though by this union of the armies the Confederates will have to bear the greatest share of the expense and most of the fatigue. To these absurdities many others might be added which I commented on in my address; and I told them openly that they must take care what they do, lest they cool the zeal or lose the protection of the Pope, especially at this juncture when His Holiness has testified so much affection towards them, for in this manner they would not only prejudice the cause of Ireland but that of England, which are one, and in consequence, while intent on serving the King, they would on the other hand only do him harm by such a peace. But the truth is, that the King's interest would in nowise be affected by the Ormonde Treaty remaining secret like Glamorgan's, or if they were both put into execution before being ratified by His Majesty; but the sole aim of the Council is to please the Marquis and invest the property of the Catholics in him, so as to entitle them to rewards and favours hereafter as they are mostly relations, friends, clients, or dependants of his House. Some audaciously declare that the Catholic interest could not fail to prosper under the government of a nobleman so warmly attached to the cause of Ireland as the Marquis of Ormond; others are not ashamed to say that it is sufficient to perform the Catholic service in secret, provided it can be done in safety, and that to expect more than this from the King, restricted as he is at the present moment in his liberty would be open injustice; and finally, that it is not lawful to contend with him in this cause. No one holds forth more loudly in favour of this doctrine than that priest Leyburn sent here six months ago by the Queen, and whose words almost amount to sedition. I use all possible diligence in private in remonstrating with every one, and have drawn to my side here in Kilkenny nine Bishops, who have in my presence subscribed their names to a protest to be presented to the Council if we see matters drawing near to a conclusion; and I use similar diligence in many other ways. But although many here have great faith in the effect of my coming and of my offices I confess that I have little hope of arresting the progress of events which have been so long meditated, or of curbing their course, which is something like rushing towards a precipice. I do not deny that the Ecclesiastical party, the Nobles who have been discarded by the Council, and the populace who are dissatisfied with this most perilous peace would willingly go to war in the belief that it would please the Nuncio, and that they could effect a great deal by themselves with the supplies which I brought to the kingdom with me. Many have therefore come from all the four provinces to offer men, arms, and other subsidies; some for a longer some for a shorter period; but I have explained to them that His Holiness would not approve that his minister should ever be an instrument of division in the Kingdom, but desires rather that he should be a promoter of peace and union as befits all good Catholics; but that if the peace should not give universal satisfaction, then with the assistance of God and the blessing of His Holiness, means shall be found to remedy everything. Nevertheless, despite of all my remonstrances, there are many sensible men who are of opinion that in whatever way peace be proclaimed it will produce some breach or rupture. For my part, its course is so complicated I cannot even imagine what will happen in the event of its being published. As it is impossible to go against the current, I have induced the Earl of Glamorgan to promise me all the conditions which your Eminence will see in the enclosed papers signed by him, in which I have included all that I thought necessary for the security of religion, explaining to him at the same time that in the affairs of England in which he is also engaged, nothing displeasing to His Holiness should be published in this peace now that he is so much interested in the religion of that country also. And as your Eminence will see the Earl not only promised most readily, but declared that if he did not succeed he would abandon the negotiation altogether; and so he set out immediately for Dublin to treat with the Viceroy. Two Commissioners of this Council have gone with him, summoned thither by Lord Digby Chief Secretary of State who had arrived there as I wrote to you, and wished to learn in what state of preparation are the aids promised to the King. In the meantime as the Earl will attend to this, the Council have answered my letter by another, a copy of which I send, where it may be seen that although they try to avoid giving offence to His Holiness and other Princes, and therefore represent and disguise everything in their own fashion, yet in the matter of the peace no human persuasion will avail to turn them from it. Meanwhile, of the King no certain intelligence is to be had. Some days ago the Marquis of Clanricarde wrote here that His Majesty had gained a victory in the taking of the Port of Plymouth, as your Eminence will see from the enclosed copy; but as the victory now confirmed, cost Fairfax 2,000 of his men the acquisition of the port is mere vain glory. On the other hand the Parliamentarians were closing on Chester, and to assist in its defence Glamorgan has begged that 3,000 infantry out of the 10,000 promised should embark at once, and this the Council have granted without consideration, though they may by unforeseen circumstances, be prevented from joining the other troops. Having now said all for the present, I send finally a deposition made before me by George Geraldine, who was a prisoner in Plunket's ship when he gave chase to my frigate, by which His Holiness will see further proof how the blessed God and St. Peter favoured my voyage, and also the obedience I consecrate to the commands of the Holy See.

With humble reverence,

&c., &c.

To THE SAME.

Kilkenny, December 26, 1645.

Whether there be peace or no peace as I have written to your Eminence, at all events the war between this Kingdom, the Parliament and the Scotch, must go on. These last hold almost the whole of Ulster, and are only kept within that province by a few troops in garrison, but are thus prevented from ravaging Leinster.

In Connaught they have taken Sligo, a seaport though in itself not of much importance, still very convenient for them in receiving assistance from Scotland and Ulster by sea. Finally, in Munster they have three principal ports which are the keys to that part of the Kingdom. But if it could have been resolved here to send an expedition against them, the three Provinces might easily have been freed from the invaders in one campaign, before the English Parliament had become powerful enough to attend to the affairs of this Kingdom; but on the other hand, if the Council continue to think so little about providing for the future or collecting money, they run the risk of having no time to repair the evils which may occur. I have deposited the greater part of the arms at my house in Kilkenny, and in the distribution of these as well as of the money I shall take care not only to have security for their faithful delivery, but also that the Catholic cause shall derive some signal advantage by not spending the money without good profit. It is however very true that the assistance and succours should be proportioned to so great and glorious an enterprise; I therefore do not hesitate through your Eminence to entreat His Holiness to look upon the necessities of this people, and with a liberal and zealous hand to favour them so as to give them spirit to look to the end, and to work out willingly and steadily their complete liberation. It only remains to consider one difference suggested to me between making and not making peace. If the treaty be not concluded matters will go on as at present, and it cannot be doubted that all the money furnished by the Holy See will be employed for religious purposes, the great cause for which there has been the present recourse to arms. But if peace be made, and the confederated troops unite with the Protestants as I explained before, I do not see with what propriety the pontifical subsidies can be used to give help and stimulus to an army which full of heretics, will everywhere enforce the celebration of the Protestant worship, and scarcely permit even the secret exercise of the Catholic faith. If however, with these same subsidies there were chosen for instance 2,000 men depending on and marching under the banner of His Holiness, they might be ordered from place to place as they were required, and by giving an impetus to the enterprise secure the free exercise of their religion in all parts of the country. This militia might also be equally useful if peace were not concluded, because we should always have ready, vigorous and faithful assistance in every enterprise, and also to put down the dissensions and disorders which are constantly arising between these leaders to the great prejudice of the common cause. If this were done the Bishops and Clergy would willingly contribute to this flying column two parts of the revenues which are now assigned to the Supreme Council, about which they complain of two things: namely that not only the property is not left in the hands of the Bishops themselves to be improved and made more useful, but is under the control of persons appointed by the public. It is never known to what purpose these revenues are applied, as they pass through the hands of collectors and ministers, who render no account of them, while all the time the soldiers remain unpaid. Meanwhile, I have supplied the important fort of Dungannon with some arms, as owing to the negligence of its governor it had been left even without swords. I must do the same for those on the borders of Ulster, so that the two forts of the island on which the safety of the whole Kingdom depends, may be strengthened; knowing as I do that on the report of the state of the country, made in obedience to your Eminence's instructions will depend the resolution you will take on the two points submitted to you. I shall endeavour to send it as soon as possible and thus fulfil one part of my duty.

Hoping that my continued illness from fever, occasioned by the unaccustomed influence of this north-east wind and northern climate, will plead my excuse to His Holiness and your Eminence for having allowed a month to elapse without sending the report,

I remain, &c., &c.

To THE SAME (in Cipher).

Kilkenny, December 27, 1645.

The Earl of Glamorgan, after having showed me two patents in which the King gives him secret but full powers to conclude a peace with the Irish, on whatsoever terms he thinks advisable, allowed me to see a letter from the King consisting of a quarter of a sheet, folded in the smallest possible compass and directed to His Holiness thus, "Beattissimo Patri Innocentio Decimo," but he neither explained its contents nor when it was to be sent. At last he presented to me a letter directed to myself from His Majesty, in the ordinary form sealed with a small seal in two places with the superscription in French, and dated 30th of April last. Great doubts passed through my mind whether I ought to receive a letter from a heretic Prince without permission from His Holiness, but after much consideration I thought it better to accept it, remembering the full powers intrusted to me to treat with all heretics; and also that at this present time His Holiness rather wishes to treat with the King on the subject of religion. I thought therefore that a refusal would be ill advised in the present state of affairs, but I resolved not to give any reply without first having His Holiness's permission, and I write for precise orders as to the terms in which I am to express myself. The letter is confined to explaining to me the authority he has given to Glamorgan, and entreats me to respond to it by showing a desire to take everything into account, and assuring me that it is the first letter His Majesty has ever written to a Minister of the Pope.

The following is its tenor, and as I have written it in French cipher like the original, I think that for its better understanding, it might be well that your Eminence should employ a French subject to translate it.

A Monsieur Monsieur l'Archevesque de Fermo.

Monsieur, entendant de vostre resolution pour l'Irlande, nous nous doubtons point que les choses n'yront bien, et que les bonnes intentions commencées par effect du dernier Pape ne s'accomplisseront par celuy icy, et par vos moyens en notre royaume d'Irlande et d'Angleterre joignissant avec nostre cher cousin le Comte de Glamorgan : avec qui ce que vous resolvez, nous nous y tiendrons obligéz, et l'acheverons a son retour. Ses grandes merites nous obligent a la confidence que sur tous nous avons en luy, nostre cognoissance estant de plus de vingt années. Pendant quel temps il s'est tousiours signallement avancé dans nostre bonne estime, et par toute sorte de moyens a emporté le prix par dessus tous nos subjects. Le quel joint a son sang, vous pourrez bien juger la passion que mesmement nous avons en son endroit, et que rien ne manquera de nostre costé a perfectioner ce que a quoy il s'obligera en nostre nom, au prix des faveurs receues par vos moyens. Fiez vous doncques a luy ; mais cependant selon le commandement que nous luy avons donné; combien il iomporte que se tient secret, il n'y a pas besoign de vous persuader, ny plus de recommander, que vous ne voyez que la necessité mesme requiert, celle cy estant la premiere ques nous avons jamais immediatement escrite a quelconque ministre d'estat du pape, esperant que celle ne sera pas la derniere ; mais qui apertement (apres que le dit Comte et vous avez faicts vos effects) de nous monstrer, comme nous luy avons asseuré.

Vostre Amis,
Charles R.

De nostre Cour d'Oxford,
　　　Le 30^{esme} d'Avril, 1645.

This letter has raised a variety of doubts in my mind, as I cannot understand why in the month of April, when the King was as yet not much cast down, he should have shown such a desire for peace and assistance from Ireland, or why he should have given such full powers to Glamorgan. Neither do I understand why that little letter to His Holiness was not sent. This coil will however unrol itself more and more every day, and we shall then see what God will bring out from so strange a beginning.

Kilkenny, 27th December, 1645.

To the Same.

Kilkenny, December 31, 1645.

When I least expected it, the Supreme Council sent me the enclosed recommendations of persons for all the vacant churches in this kingdom; I have altered the word into *recommendation* although presented to me under that of *election*, but I explained to the Secretary the absolute insufficiency of this latter term. I can imagine no reason for these gentlemen making such a provision at this time, when they were before so strongly opposed to it, save that one member in Council may have proposed a friend, and the rest not willing to be considered of less importance have each brought forward some one of his own choice. The number nominated is thirteen, of whom three are proposed as coadjutors; these perhaps should be elected under a different provision being more difficult to agree upon. Six of those named are Regulars, to whom I see many persons are inclined, as they interest themselves greatly in public affairs and have much experience, having been living until now very much out of their convents. All the information I have received of each of them I will in a few words impart to your Eminence. To begin with the first on the list—the Bishop of Clonfert is a man of mature judgment and of upright intentions but a little slow in debate, and at present has a bad attack in his eyes which may injure his sight. I was acquainted in Paris with his brother Father Francis Hugh, who appeared to me a cleverer and more efficient man, and to recommend him, in case the present Bishop is translated to the Church of Tuam, would I think be much to the honour of the brother already consecrated. Abbè Patrick Plunket is worthy of all honour on his own account, but even more through the merit of his brother, who is one of our most honoured members of Council, and perhaps the man of all others best affected to the Catholic religion to be found at present in the kingdom. Edward Tyrrel studied and officiated in Paris where I met him, and I have never heard anything against him but that in public affairs he may have sometimes spoken too favourably of the party of the King. Concerning him the difficulty will be that he has been proposed as coadjutor to the Archbishop of Dublin, who has really no ailment but that of being exceedingly corpulent, and as we are to our misfortune not in possession of Dublin, the Archbishop only exercises jurisdiction in a small part of his diocese. Andrew Lynch has been for a long time Vicar Apostolic in the same bishopric for which he is recommended and it is reported that he is an excellent man, although his temperament is more inclined to Christian simplicity than to ardour. Friar Terence, Provincial of the Dominicans is a man of prudence and sagacity, has been in Italy, and is so expert in the management of Church affairs that happy results might be expected from his care. I know that the Bishop who desires him as his coadjutor is in the worst possible state of health. Robert Barry has laboured greatly for the faith in England, in Dublin, and in other missions, and is a man of such great knowledge that he is fully equal to the charge of which he is universally esteemed so worthy. Friar Oliver Darcy has consulted with me several times during this month, and has likewise laboured much in the Catholic cause in Dublin. He is a great preacher and adorned with many noble qualities, of which the greatest perhaps is, that in this matter he is neither ambitious nor self-seeking, as I have been assured by many. Terence O'Kelly I am told has been nominated by His Holiness, and awaits the Papal bull; therefore I do not know why his name is placed in this list. Of Terence O'Neill I need say nothing, as he is at present in Spain in attendance upon the former Earl of Tyrone. Of George Dillon also I have made but little inquiry, being the coadjutor of the Bishop of Ferns who does not appear to have any reason for asking assistance except that he suffers from sciatica and rides with great difficulty; but in other respects his age and strength appear to me to be quite equal to his work. Friar Joseph Everhard is now guardian here at Kilkenny, and his life is a great edification to every one; his father suffered signally for the faith in the late persecutions, but I have already written of him to your Eminence at the request of those by whom he is proposed. James Farrell has long been the Vicar-General of this Church, and the people who are greatly attached to him earnestly desire him for their pastor. This is all I have been able to discover in this short time, in pursuance of the duties of my office. The blessed God who has placed the supreme authority in the hands of His Holiness, will inspire him now, not only to supply the necessities of so many people but also to elect those who are the most worthy of the spiritual office. I shall faithfully obey the commands of His Holiness, and glory in being his minister in a country so far removed from all the rest of the world.

&c., &c.

To the Same.

January 1, 1646.

After writing the above to your Eminence, a change took place in the whole aspect of affairs in this kingdom, owing to an unexpected occurrence. It had been suspected that the Marquis of Ormonde and Secretary Digby were plotting to deprive the Earl of Glamorgan of the command of the army about to depart for England, either through jealousy or perhaps because as heretics, they wished to prevent the possibility of a union between these troops and the English Catholics. This suspicion was confirmed last Friday, St. Stephen's Day by an atrocious act, for having arrived in Dublin a day and a half before, the Earl was arrested that morning at the dinner hour by order of Ormonde and conducted to the Castle, where after being deprived of his arms, he was confined so strictly that not even a servant was left to attend him. The gates of the city were quickly shut and from that hour to this no one has been permitted to depart thence, except the two Deputies from the Supreme Council, who had been invited there by Digby as I advised you before. To give a colour to this proceeding the Earl is accused of high-treason, and Digby, who perhaps does not wish to deny being the author of it, told our Commissioners that on the Monday previous to the arrest, a paper had fallen into his hands containing the articles in favour of the Catholic religion concerted between Glamorgan and this Council since last August, which paper was found by the Scotch in the baggage of the Archbishop of Tuam killed at the siege of Sligo two months ago, and that the document was signed by the Archbishop of Cashel who certifies that it agrees with the original. This last assertion is quite true because the Archbishop of Cashel told me that he drew it up, and gave it to the Archbishop of Tuam by order of the Council, who thought that every Ecclesiastic should have a copy, in order to be able to consider it. Lord Digby subsequently added, that for the Earl to have endeavoured to induce the King to make concessions to the Catholics which His Majesty absolutely could not and ought not to do, was so great a crime that the Marquis and he had determined to seize his person before taking counsel with the King, as they knew His Majesty could not but entirely approve the course they had taken in this most important affair. Then turning to our Commissioners he added that they might congratulate themselves on this arrest, as they might be quite sure that the King would never have conceded what Glamorgan had promised; and that consequently they would have sent the troops and expended their money in vain, but that now they might by other means obtain more secure and reasonable concessions. For himself he asserted that he would rather imperil the lives of his wife and his sons than advise the King to yield more than was just; knowing that if the Protestants who serve His Majesty found him at all inclined to confirm Glamorgan's articles, they would have taken him by the neck and thrown him out of the window; and so this poor Earl after labouring long and earnestly for the Catholic religion, finds himself in prison in the hands of his enemies—all in consequence of a paper not even signed by him—which contained no absolute promise but left everything to the will of the King under whose express and full powers he had acted; and now he is accused of High Treason, and it is hard to tell what may befall him. On the receipt of the news in this city there was great perturbation. Nearly all the principal members of the Council were in the country to spend Christmas with their relations and friends; nevertheless as a sufficient number of members still remained for the first and second Council, I dexterously contrived to assemble them, in order to discover how their first opinions would incline. The truth is that on learning the wrong done to the Earl the insult offered to this Council by the imprisonment of their acknowledged General, and one empowered by the King to treat with them, their first idea was to declare war and attack Dublin at once. By degrees however, when the relations and partisans of Ormonde appeared, they so far calmed the rest as only to resolve to summon the General Council to deliberate on what conditions war should be declared if it were possible to carry it on. In pursuance of this resolution five of the members came to me yesterday morning, to beg me to inform them on what sum of money they might depend out of the subsidies I had brought here from Rome; to which I replied that it would not be proper that the contributions of the Apostolic See and of the Court should be thrown in a mass with other sums, as they were given by grace and not as a debt; but I proposed they should lay before me the wants of the provinces in case of war, and I should then take upon myself some particular and useful enterprise for which I should send money through persons dependent on me, to greater advantage than through the hands of the public functionaries. They appeared highly satisfied with this answer; and even if I had wished to name the precise amount of the money, I could not have done so until Signor Inverizzi returns from Flanders, and renders me an account of what he has expended on the frigates. We are now therefore as your Eminence will see full of thoughts of war, whereas at first we were for precipitating ourselves into peace. I see clearly and have also informed myself diligently on the subject, that this would be the best time and opportunity to make ourselves masters of Dublin, and I endeavour to insinuate this to the well-affected with all necessary caution; but from the partiality of many to the Ormonde party, and especially from the ill will they bear to the Ecclesiastics who voluntarily depend on me, I am obliged to proceed with infinite circumspection. I already see that they make the truce which is to last till the 17th instant an excuse, and allege as a ground for fear that the Marquis would unite with the Puritans; and, finally, for the sake of delay that they will propose to convoke the Assembly; yet it is true that with the soldiers now dispersed through Leinster, Dublin might be besieged in eight days, the city which is almost open taken, and in three days more the Castle, in which there is not even bread to eat. To encourage the people to this great undertaking public orations are constantly delivered, and prayers offered up to God that this poor Kingdom may be inspired to pursue the path that will most easily lead to the much desired peace; so as to show forth the true religion in splendour and security.

With humble reverence,

&c., &c.

To the Queen of England.

Kilkenny, January 2, 1646.

Madam—The Great God has conducted me to this Kingdom with many wonderful signs of His protection, of which I had proof in being delivered from the persecutions of those enemies who did not spare your Majesty. On my arrival here I found a general desire for peace with His Majesty the King by negotiations carried on through the Earl of Glamorgan, at which being a minister of peace and anxious that the Irish should testify some particular act of fidelity towards their Prince I greatly rejoiced; but, unexpectedly and to the great astonishment of everyone the Earl himself was arrested in the Castle of Dublin, everything was suspended, and our designs have been greatly disarranged. The ever blessed God may deign to open a way for this Kingdom to obtain the holy offices of religion, and the people will then prove by their services how faithful they are to the King and to your Majesty, in accordance with the instructions given through me by His Holiness. Praying that Heaven may grant to your Majesty infinite consolations, I remain with profound respect.

To Cardinal Mazarin.

Kilkenny, January 2, 1646.

The perils and persecutions with which I was threatened at sea, prove that assuredly the flag borne by my frigate would not have been respected if Divine Providence had not aided me. Arrived in this kingdom I found everything tending to peace with the King as I had informed your Eminence; but about a week ago owing to the imprisonment of the Earl of Glamorgan in the Castle of Dublin, the treaty which was under his management fell to the ground, and the kingdom is in greater uncertainty than ever. The comfort of these poor Catholics is in the hopes they cherish of aid from all Christian Princes and Crowns, particularly of that for whose peace and welfare they continually pray as the source of blessing to the whole world. I constantly assure them of the holy and efficient desires of your Eminence for the good of religion, and animate them to prove their entire fidelity to the King with every aid possible, when once they have obtained the privilege of the free exercise of their faith, as had been agreed upon with the Earl of Glamorgan. I beg to recall to your Eminence my humble services, and beg of you to allow them to suffice to obtain honour in my person for the office I sustain.

With humble reverence, &c., &c.

To Cardinal Pamphili (in Cipher).

The members of Council now see clearly that failing the assistance of Glamorgan, they cannot hope for peace from Ormonde except on ignominious and infamous terms, as nothing more will be obtained from him than the remission of penalties and the celebration of the Catholic religion in secret; and thus the labours of five years will vanish in smoke. Compelled therefore to obtain it by war, they are met by two obstacles : the doubt of being able to maintain it, and the hatred which it would excite in the Parliamentarians whether the King lose, or whether he accommodate matters with them. I will seek to reassure the Confederates on both these points, that no time may be lost, and that we may thus defeat the wishes of Ormonde's partisans; he has even sent deputies here to apologise for the imprisonment of Glamorgan, and to allay the anger it may have excited. Meantime, I do not cease to assure everyone that if resolutions be taken in conformity with the first oath, and if fidelity to religion be maintained, His Holiness will not fail to give further aid, and will benignly induce other Princes to do likewise. It may be that His Holiness has already concluded something in this way with Digby, according to what Father Luke has written to Father Scarampi, though the weakness of the King gives reason to believe that all treaties for peace concluded how they may, will be vain because he is not free, is sorely oppressed by the Protestants, and is completely surrounded by them and the Puritans.

To the Same.

Kilkenny, February 10, 1646.

Among many things which I had determined to do on coming to this mission, one was to have the business of the Chancellorship of the Embassy done *gratis*, without any tax on the people.

It seemed to me that in a new undertaking much good and edification might result from this step, and I believed that it would put an end to a calumny which I have read in the works of some historians, that no little evil had been wrought in England by the rapacity of some of the ecclesiastics. I was confirmed in this opinion when I found that my power was limited to the collocation of simple benefices and canonries; because for these, being totally abandoned and without revenue the provision is very scanty, as the few Catholics who feel any remorse, are not willing to make restitution to those Churches from which as it appears to them, they receive no spiritual aid, but are induced to do it solely to the parish churches in return for spiritual care, and for the administration of the sacraments. I have therefore appointed a Priest of my own household to be Chancellor, and have ordered that he shall do all that is required without payment, except about eight jiuli for the labour of copying. I shall follow out this plan until I receive the commands of your Eminence, and till His Holiness has declared his opinion if it would be well as a rule to my successors to institute a tax and to declare it, though as yet, no criminal causes nor party controversies have been brought before him. I shall therefore expect the commands of your Eminence with the satisfaction which it will give me when from the Holy See will emanate the laws for every part of the earth.

With most humble reverence, &c., &c.

To THE SAME.

Kilkenny, February 13, 1646.

The return of the Prince of Piombino at the termination of his voyage, need not cause the overthrow of our hopes for Christianity, as in the next summer under the auspices of His Excellency, I doubt not that with the assistance of the other Princes we shall recover Candia and repulse the rash ardour of the Turks. Prayers are daily offered up here for this object since the news arrived which your Eminence graciously sent me, because the successes or reverses of Christianity not only touch this kingdom though so far distant, but affect the people in their own interests; inasmuch as when His Holiness is freed from other cares, they know his thoughts will be more promptly bestowed on the concerns of this part of the world.

With these desires and prayers,

        I humbly salute your Eminence.

To the Same.

Kilkenny, February 13, 1646.

The change of affairs and thoughts of war lasted but a short time in this kingdom; as on the Supreme Council insisting for its own honour, that the Marquis of Ormonde should liberate the Earl of Glamorgan, protesting that otherwise they would never treat of peace, he was on a sudden set at liberty on the twenty-eighth day of his incarceration, on condition of his appearing before the King or his representatives within thirty days of being summoned, under a penalty of £40,000 sterling. Glamorgan instantly fled to Kilkenny, much to the astonishment of those who think this second event a greater miracle than the first, since to set at liberty a prisoner arrested on a charge of high treason, without the knowledge and commands of the King, is an unheard of proceeding.

This unexpected event plunges affairs into still deeper confusion than before, because those who entertain the desire for peace, and have been detained here in the matter a month against their will, are bent on rushing on now with an impetuosity which I can only compare to a river, which breaking through its banks precipitates itself over the country without restraint or impediment. Not only they have begun to publish the terms, as though all were concluded,* but doubting that the General Assembly

* See Doc. VI.

on its convocation might raise obstacles to their wishes, they endeavoured to prevent its assembling; as for this, however there is not time, they have resorted to the most underhand practices to secure the election to the Confederation of those who belong to their faction. For the corporations as they are called, which are in the hands of the heretics, they have made the Council appoint *ex officio* persons from other counties, and consequently all adherents of their party. In opposition to their great violence, I began by showing them that the security of the peace had completely vanished with the imprisonment of the Earl, not only because he had irritated the King by making public the powers secretly intrusted to him, but also because Lord Digby had in Dublin shamefully protested against the concessions themselves, and against all who had counselled the King to grant them. Besides this, as the Earl is even yet only liberated on parole, the Confederates can never be sure that he may not be summoned by the King's orders in the very execution of the preliminaries, or while conducting the soldiers to England, and thus leave the whole affair in more confusion than ever. Whilst I was still arguing with great anxiety, your Eminence's despatches of the 2nd, 11th, 12th, and 27th of November arrived, containing the two signed papers in cipher and the copies of the three documents; finding that amongst them were the articles agreed upon by His Holiness and the resident minister of the Queen, I instantly proposed their consideration, and took the opportunity of the opening of the General Assembly to present the briefs and your Eminence's letter, and urged upon them the importance of the favour shown to this country by His Holiness, who has given so much thought to its affairs. In a second speech when entering into closer particulars, I restricted myself to asking them to wait for the originals, as your Eminence will see by the abstract which I send. But not for this did the members who are bent on peace abate their clamour, nor did they show any sign of gratitude for the great benignity of His Holiness, but at once sent off two commissioners to Dublin to put the last stroke to the negotiations with Ormonde. Nor is this the worst, as on receipt of letters from their agent in Paris containing the same news of the articles concerted in Rome, the Council, having received the letter, no more communicated its contents to me than if it had been a treaty with the Indies! Upon this I convoked an assembly of all the bishops and vicars representing the clergy, with whose assistance I drew up a protest against assenting to any other peace than that subscribed in Rome. I am also endeavouring to obtain a few votes in the assembly, in which if I had not feared to create divisions I might have drawn over to myself besides the ecclesiastical party, all the members belonging to the old Irish families, and the opponents (who are not a few) of the Ormonde faction. But to proceed with gentleness, the best plan I could think of was to persuade Glamorgan to accept the Roman treaty and to withdraw his own entirely. For the reasons given in the enclosed paper (though the Earl at first excited much indignation among his friends and relations who strongly opposed him) he in the end frankly made his choice and submitted himself to my wishes. This done, I resolved to apply with great urgency to the Assembly to give me time, being convinced that the votes would be in my favour. Meanwhile, through Glamorgan's influence he and seven other noblemen had been deputed by the Assembly to consult with me about some measures, and on this occasion it came out that the Supreme Council, which has power to conclude peace, had not (nor have they even yet) made known its conditions to the Assembly; in general perhaps it is well not to reveal important deliberations to the whole of their number, but on this particular occasion the Assembly are not pleased that they should seem to approve a treaty of which they know none of the conditions, and thus be led by the nose by a minority. Then I understood that this deputation was sent lest I should return to the Assembly, and make public all the facts of the case. In Council we debated the question with incredible heat and prolixity for several days; when the deputies offered as your Eminence will see in their report, that the Ormonde peace should not be published without ours, while I insisted that no peace at all should be concluded, as my replies will show you. From this resolution I would not depart, so they yielded at last, and an additional document was framed which contains two articles the substance of which is a new truce to last till the 1st of May, at which time, if His Holiness' treaty be not concluded, we shall go back to Glamorgan's, and in the meantime neither the one nor the other shall be concluded or published. When this agreement became known to those who are clamorous in their desire for peace, an apparent reconciliation took place between the clergy and laity, as if everything had been finally arranged, and that this small beginning was the happy completion of the whole matter, though in fact this notion is a mere bubble in the air. When I went to the Council this morning to exhort the members to provide for the efficient government of both war and peace, I was received with general acclamation and the first noblemen of the kingdom were deputed to thank me for all I had done. In truth, I may congratulate myself on having succeeded in restraining them from the precipice to which since last September they were tending; and I recognise as a special Providence that this negotiation has been guided through such various impediments to succeed in the way appointed by His holy will. Two days ago I received your packet with the three letters of the 10th and 17th of December and the four in cipher, containing the proposals of the English Catholics and the second copy of the articles concerted with Sir Kenelm Digby, and signed by your Eminence. If the safe transmission of the originals had not been hindered by the perils of the sea they would have been of great importance. May God, who makes all earthly affairs uncertain, permit at least that the winds shall prosper the arrival of Digby and of the others he brings with him, so that we may conclude a peace honourable, because it cannot be arranged by nobler hands, and holy because no object can be more sacred.

With deep reverence, &c., &c.

To the Same (in cipher).

Kilkenny, February 21, 1646.

At the head of the opposite faction is Viscount Muskerry a brother-in-law of Ormonde, supported by the Mountgarret and Butler families with their adherents and followers. To all appearance Ormonde, despite the great depression of the King's affairs, has vast expectations for this Kingdom; so at least his artifices lead one to infer, as well as the assertion of Muskerry and others that religion in Ireland never could be in a better position than under the guidance of Ormonde, that is to say of a heretic! The priest Leyburn, sent here by the Queen has created much discord amongst the people, alleging that His Holiness is deceiving the Queen and Ireland, and that I propose mere chimeras to disturb the peace of the country and ruin the King.

In order to put a restraint on him I have drawn up a process against him declaring that I will send it to His Holiness. The truth is that it is through his great affection for Ormonde that he spreads these impertinent reports.

The articles proposed by the English Catholics I shall proceed with according to your Eminence's commands; and as Glamorgan has already bound himself that if the originals of the papers do not come from Rome on the 1st of May, he will ratify all that I desire by virtue of his patent, we have now only to see how far we may trust to his promises; but I hope they will arrive by that time. Meanwhile 3,000 soldiers are to be sent to the King for the relief of Chester, and I have thought it well to make no opposition, in order to show that the Pope really wishes to assist His Majesty, a necessary point to keep constantly in view. Father Scarampi from his own experience has always approved of what I have done.

Advice of the Nuncio to the Earl of Glamorgan.

The Earl must on every account desist from prosecuting the peace concerted by him some months past, and adhere in all respects to the one agreed upon by His Holiness and Sir Kenelm Digby. First, because if he has at heart the welfare of the Irish Catholics, he must desire that they should have the greatest possible security for the free exercise of their religion. He will therefore consider that if previous to his imprisonment he could give no greater security than an uncertain promise, he cannot now that he is at liberty promise even this, because in Dublin he openly spoke of his negotiations and promises here, and besides made public the concessions which by order of the King should have been kept secret; and as Lord Digby declared that the Protestants would rather throw the King out of the window than permit His Majesty to confirm them, it is manifest that all security has vanished and all his promises have melted into air. Hence, by every debt of conscience he is bound to accede to the peace concluded in Rome, by which owing to the interposition of His Holiness, the Irish will in return for the money granted to the King, receive all the security possible under the present circumstances. Secondly, because in regard to the fidelity which the Earl protesses to his King and the love he bears to his country, he ought to uphold that peace, which will give the most powerful assistance to His Majesty, as will be the case in this Pontifical peace, in which are stipulations for the same aid in soldiers which are promised in the other by the Earl; and moreover, an annual sum of money with the exercise of the Catholic religion also in England—two things which the Earl could never promise. Therefore he must advise the Irish to unite with him in showing this loyalty to their King, and this charity towards their neighbours of England. Thirdly, because by this Roman peace the Earl will lose none of his rights or prerogatives, but on the contrary be freed from two great responsibilities. He will in the first place have the honour before all others of conferring large benefits on religion; he will be confirmed in the command of the Irish army bestowed upon him with the great applause of the whole kingdom; and, although it was decided in Rome that the troops should march always under Irish officers, I shall, by virtue of the authority I hold from His Holiness to add, to alter, or to diminish, confirm the Earl in his command pursuant to the general desire. In the second place, whoever has heard the Earl promise that the Irish army shall be employed to force His Majesty to sign the concessions will think he has been released from an ungrateful task; and to say nothing of the safety of the transaction and the authority of His Holiness, he will no longer be bound by a promise so unworthy of a vassal towards the person of his Prince. Besides, by the conclusion of the Roman peace the Earl will be freed from the appearance of vanity and presumption in the eyes of His Holiness and other Sovereigns, who may have thought that his object in forcing on his own peace was to do honour to himself and to promote his own interests. Fourthly, because its acceptance after the Pontifical articles have been declared, would be a virtual refusal of them, and would be so great a disrespect to the person of the Pontiff and to the Supremacy of the Holy See, as would oblige His Holiness to testify his displeasure by the removal of the Papal Ministers from Ireland, and would excite the disgust of all other Sovereigns. In this case the fate of this unfortunate Kingdom may be easily foreseen. The Earl therefore as a good Catholic, and thereby owing obedience to the Holy See, must avert such a misfortune by awaiting the original documents from Rome. To this end he must grant time and a truce, and yielding to the authority of the Pontiff, allow this country to feel the happy effects of his paternal care and foresight.

Abstract of the Second Speech Delivered in the General Assembly by the Nuncio.

He recapitulated what he had told them that the treaty of peace negotiated with the Earl of Glamorgan was neither honourable nor safe, because its terms were to be concealed until confirmed by the King, which would have been a great scandal to Christianity ; and also because the Earl's promises had no certain foundation, but depended on the will of another. That on the contrary, the treaty proposed by His Holiness was in every way most honourable and trustworthy, both from the known benignity of His Holiness, and on account of the money promised by him, which otherwise would have been given as a subsidy in Ireland. He reiterated how much more full and better is this treaty, as it stipulates for the public exercise of religion and that all the churches and their properties shall be restored. It moreover stipulates for a Parliament distinct from that of England, for Catholics to hold the various offices of the kingdom, and for the absolute authority of the Nuncio in all ways. He thought it wiser to be silent on the subject of Dublin, lest the Ormonde faction should grow suspicious; but when speaking of the Churches he took occasion to say that, as to the monasteries now in possession of the laity, he had ample powers from the Pope to decide according to circumstances. He added that this peace would also be most advantageous to the King on account of the yearly aid promised to him, as well as to the English Catholics for whom the free exercise of their religion is insisted upon; hence everyone who is really loyal to the King, will try to secure the acceptance of this peace. There is reason to believe that it will also please the Marquis of Ormonde and Lord Digby, as the latter when the Earl was in prison took occasion to inform the Nuncio through the priest Leyburn, that if he would promise some annual subsidy to the King on the part of His Holiness, he would bind himself to obtain from His Majesty the free exercise of their religion for the English Catholics; and he will see that what he wished is already accomplished. Further the Nuncio insisted that such a peace would be most beneficial to the Earl of Glamorgan, for the reasons already given in the report. After this he showed that on the completion of the peace the war with the Parliament would be the only one on their hands; and for this he thought it fit to mention all the supplies he had brought, namely the frigates he expects, the quantity of arms in his possession, and the sum of money which would supply a considerable part of the provinces for the future campaign. He spoke of the hope of fresh assistance from the benignity of the Pope, whenever he had good accounts of concord being established amongst themselves; but if on the contrary he heard of any want of ardour in the cause of religion or any other falling off from their duty, he would be constrained to show his displeasure by removing his ministers, and they might easily imagine the consequences of such a disgrace. Lastly he adverted at the end to two objections which had been spread about; first that Ormonde would not grant a longer truce, and therefore while awaiting the original Papal documents, they would be immersed in a new and perilous war; against this the Nuncio offered to guard the frontier of Leinster and hold it safely at his own expense till the articles should arrive. Secondly, that having to send as soon as possible a subsidy of 3,000 infantry to relieve Chester, the men would not trust themselves in England unless peace was concluded, lest they should be treated as rebels. To this the Nuncio said that, besides the Earl's known intention to select the troops himself, it was not very likely that the King who expected 7,000 more men from Ireland, would ill-treat these 3,000 on their coming to serve him.

The Nuncio then restricted himself to an entreaty to give as much time as was required for the arrival of the original documents so that the truth of his declarations might be proved, and the advantage to be derived by the kingdom from the paternal care of His Holiness publicly acknowledged, adding that if the papers could be sent by land a time for their arrival might have been specified, but coming by sea and exposed to contrary winds their arrival must be uncertain. There was a hope however that the King might by that time have received all the information, and have signed the concessions and that the news might arrive at any moment. He concluded by declaring to the assembly that it rested with themselves to draw upon the country either the inevitable evils which would follow the adoption of any other treaty, or eternal salvation by obeying His Holiness, a course which would also secure aid for the King, conciliate the powers of Europe, and obtain new favour from the Apostolic See.

REASONS ASSIGNED BY THE DEPUTIES FOR THE CONCLUSION OF PEACE WITH THE MARQUIS OF ORMONDE, BEFORE THE ARRIVAL OF HIS HOLINESS'S ARTICLES.

First, the Marquis of Ormonde has been empowered by the King to treat for peace with the Irish till the 1st of April only, and in the event of this being revoked, the kingdom will be deprived of all the advantages they hoped to gain by the conference with him. These advantages include besides the political articles, the union of the two armies against the Puritans, the assistance of the Marquis of Clanricarde with that of several other noblemen now neutral, but who would then unite with the Confederates. Secondly, if a truce merely and not a peace be concluded, the soldiers intended for the King's service will not embark lest they be treated in England as rebels. Ormonde himself will not approve of their departure without such conclusion of peace; and the King will consequently be deprived of assistance at the moment when any delay must be fatal to him, and perhaps be forced to make terms with the Parliament much to the detriment of Irish interests. Thirdly, the conclusion of this peace will greatly serve the Pontifical treaty—as amongst the Ormonde articles is one declaring that all the King promises to the Catholics through any deputy whatever in matters of religion shall be made good; and this article, already approved by the Dublin Parliament and granted under the King's great seal, is absolutely essential to the Pontifical treaty—since if it be wanting, the King will have to ratify it by some other means; and these means will be opposed to the utmost by the Protestants, who have already grown suspicious of the facility with which the King grants these concessions.

Fourthly, if the Earl of Glamorgan offers to treat anew with the Nuncio touching ecclesiastical matters in case His Holiness' peace should not be concluded, the Council will bind itself to observe their wishes provided the Ormonde treaty be now accepted; thus there will be no division between the laity and the clergy, nor will either have to suffer any uncertainty whatever. Fifthly, to conclude it finally but without publication should be sufficient, since till the promulgation of the clerical articles it is certain that the political will not avail, and both treaties as the Nuncio desires may advance side by side.

REASONS BROUGHT FORWARD BY THE NUNCIO AGAINST THE CONCLUSION OF THE ORMONDE PEACE BEFORE THE ARRIVAL OF THE PONTIFICAL ARTICLES.

First, that the necessity to prolong the present truce should be no obstacle, as the Council (to the misfortune of the country) have been only too ready hitherto to seek pretexts for a cessation, and it may be asked if it would not be a scandal if it were denied on the demand for a treaty between His Holiness and the Queen, upon which turn nearly the whole fortunes and well-being of Ireland.

Secondly, by concluding this peace we come back to a matter condemned by the Nuncio from the first, viz., that a political peace is promulgated, whilst the religious one is kept in the back ground. A promise not to publish either is perfectly useless, as such matters when concluded are readily divulged; and this more especially as it will be necessary to inform the troops destined for England, since they refuse to cross without being certain of the result of the treaty.

Thirdly, if this peace be concluded the Nuncio can have no security that the Marquis with perseverance, strength, and free communication, may not be in a position when the Pontifical articles do arrive to oppose either the whole or a part of them, and thus hazard the loss to the country of the favour and authority of the Pope. It is better therefore to insist upon the truce (in which course there is no risk but that of a most improbable negative result) than, by concluding a political peace involve the whole affair in further confusion and entanglements.

Fourthly, by carrying on both treaties together, we shall more easily maintain peace in this kingdom, not only between the clergy and laity but amongst the laity themselves, as the old Irish oppressed by the newer race have joined the clerical party; therefore it is the duty of an Apostolic minister to propose means which more directly lead to so desirable an end, in conformity to the duties of his ecclesiastical mission and to the express command of His Holiness.

The Nuncio observes in answer to the first of the opposing arguments, that it would be easy to obtain a renewal of the Marquis's patent, supposing that what is said concerning it be true; and that there is no preponderating benefit to the Confederate union which may not equally result from preferring one peace to the other.

To the second, the Earl of Glamorgan assures us that it is sufficient now for the 3,000 infantry to pass over quickly to England, it being most improbable that they should be illtreated when the King is hoping for a further body of 7,000— that the Earl takes upon himself to raise a body of volunteers —and that there are ports enough whence the troops may set sail without any possible hindrance from Ormonde.

To the third, when the articles do arrive, the means of supply will come with them, so that no foreign assistance will be required.

To the fourth, that the offer of the Earl comes as a suggestion; that is to say, in case by any accident the Pontifical peace has not taken place and that it is not possible to compare the two together, the laity would inevitably separate from the clergy, the one side asking for the delay required for the arrival of the articles, the other refusing to allow it.

To the fifth, for this no security can be given that would not endanger the arrival of the articles, as was before said.

To Cardinal Pamphili.

Kilkenny, March 5, 1646.

Yesterday at last the general committees of the Assembly broke up. Only two notable resolutions have been passed. The first, that in consequence of the confusion attendant on the meeting of so great a number of members (as I mentioned before to your Eminence), the Council has been reduced to nine, two for each province and one Secretary. The second, that a decision respecting Church property has been arrived at, that it should no longer be managed by laymen in order to keep back two-thirds for the necessary expenses of war; but it is to be left in the hands of the clergy who will then be obliged themselves to pay a fixed rate into the public exchequer. This may open the way to other consequences of great moment. The Assembly were unable to pass some other important resolutions as to the negotiation for peace, because the old Supreme Council was obstinate to the last in not yielding up the absolute power vested in them by past committees, and therefore did not choose to refer or remit the whole question to the general meeting. In the meantime letters from Paris of the 1st of February have been received, stating that Sir Kenelm Digby the Queen's agent was at Nantes, awaiting despatches from England on his way hither. There is no mention of this in my private letters, but I am glad to believe it, not only because of the account such a journey may be turned to, but from the hope I entertain of hastening by his presence the conclusion of this great treaty, on which depends the future progress and good government of the kingdom. The Earl of Glamorgan has entreated that 4,000 of the promised troops may be sent to England immediately according to agreement; but we do not see clearly what end this can answer as all our despatches announce the fall of Chester, and if the news be true we do not know how so small a body of men could be sure of reaching a place of safety, so as to succour the King without suffering defeat.

I have prepared a report on Irish affairs, the completion of which I delayed till the General Assembly should be dissolved. But I do not venture to confide it to this first opportunity, lest it should fall into the hands of the enemy, being a document of such length that it could not be put into cipher. I have shown what assistance the kingdom will require in order to expel the common enemy; much discussion has taken place as to what province the Papal succours shall be given; as they will be the principal means for this year of carrying on the war with vigour. If the goodness of His Holiness deign to supply some more money for other parts, so that the succours may last for six months longer, I believe with the help of God some notable success may ensue, which would spread throughout the whole Christian world the knowledge of His Holiness' zeal and paternal care for his people.

With humble reverence, &c.

To the Same (in cipher).

I have already conveyed to your Eminence my doubts whether, even if the King accepted the peace concerted at Rome the Marquis of Ormonde would be contented to do so, as it is opposed to his ends in more than one of its articles. I may now add that my doubts have increased as the Ormonde faction speak openly on the subject; I am therefore dying to see Digby to sound him on the matter, though I have strong suspicions that we shall have to resort to force, and in such a case it is difficult to avoid a form of civil war, since where His Holiness and the Queen have arranged it, no change can possibly be made, and there is also the Dublin article, which will be the most difficult, and yet of such importance that it can neither be abandoned nor moderated in any way.

To the Same.

Kilkenny, March 7, 1646.

To the letter I wrote to your Eminence the 31st of December concerning the vacant churches, I must now add some considerations to be submitted to the wisdom and prudence of His Holiness. Firstly—I see that in general both Bishops and laymen are disappointed that so many of the Regulars are raised to the Episcopal dignity, as they are considered here as in Italy and elsewhere, to be more of Theologians than Canonists, and consequently have not had much practice in the external jurisdiction of the churches now perhaps more necessary than ever, as in the next National Synod I must insist on the formal recognition of the Council of Trent, the doctrines of which require administrators well versed in canonical rights as your Eminence well knows. It also appears to the Secular Clergy that the monks, accustomed as they have been to live as chaplains in the houses of the Barons, may be in many important matters and particularly in this of the peace, too intimately united with the laity, and too ready to admit differences of opinion, which has already done much harm. The Metropolitans again, and particularly the Prelate of Armagh, are indignant with the Supreme Council for having given me a list of persons nominated without their consent, and this Bishop of Armagh has frequently both by word of mouth and by letter, entreated me not to nominate anyone without his approval. I wished to inform you of this, but as for the rest I answered that His Holiness is not bound except through his benignity, to grant him this satisfaction, and that having a Nuncio here, His Holiness will receive from him all the necessary notices; but in no one thing is there a more unanimous desire than that the Bishops may be natives of the province to which they are appointed, and if possible of the same diocese. This has been the practice for some time past, and the opinion that it is not well to admit foreigners seems to be deeply rooted. In proof of this it is stated that the late Bishop of Tuam who was not a native of Connaught, only gained after a considerable time by his talents and liberality the love and respect of the people. This has induced the clergy as well as the nobility of the Diocese of Ardagh, to send me a memorial numerously signed, declaring that the Abbé Plunket recommended by the Council, being of Leinster and never having been in these parts, would never be accepted ; and they propose in his place Friar Francis O'Farrell, a Franciscan theologian originally from this part of the country, or Cornelius Gaffney, now Vicar-General of the Diocese.

I must remind your Eminence that if His Holiness resolves to yield this point, Plunket deserves to be presented to some other See, as he is brother to the most able member of Council in the Catholic cause, and who after the recent reform carried in the Council, has still continued to be member for his province by ninety-two votes. The people of Clonmacnoise show in the enclosed supplication that Queen Elizabeth united that church to the Bishopric of Meath, and therefore, being governed by Protestants it has suffered the greatest spiritual wrongs, they entreat that their ancient liberty and their own Bishop may be restored. They recommend for it Father Francis Anthony Geoghegan a Franciscan, a person of good character and now guardian of Kilkenny. This church is one of the poorest in the kingdom, but by good fortune a gentleman moved by some scruples in keeping possession of church property, has resolved to restore it, and this addition will I hope be of some advantage to the prelate elected.

For the church of Kildare, besides the Father recommended by the Council, the people and several Bishops of Leinster highly recommend and desire James Dempsy, now for several years Vicar-General of the Diocese, to whom they are much more inclined than to Friar Everhard, whose name I once mentioned.

Concerning the Coadjutors, I have only to inform your Eminence that being every day more convinced of the evil disposition of the Bishop of Emly, I have thought it advisable to send you a petition signed by several Bishops, who, for the good of the diocese supplicate His Holiness to name as Coadjutor, Burkitt the present Vicar-General, who, having attended the Assembly I know to be a man quite equal to the office. Generally speaking, the old Bishops are lax in their attention to passing events, those only lately appointed have vigour enough to understand them. I can therefore, positively assure your Eminence that it is most necessary to make new appointments and to increase the number of them, so that the Ecclesiastical resolutions which are needed for the direction and advancement of the holy faith, may be well carried out.

With profound reverence, &c., &c.

Report on the State of Ireland.

March 1, 1646.

I beg to submit to your Eminence a report of the state of Ireland at the time of my arrival in the island. I shall divide the subject under three heads, viz., Ecclesiastical, Military, and Political. I begin with the last, as on it depends the well-being and order of the other two.

Concerning politics then, I must inform you that at the commencement of the last war, the confederated Irish bound by their oath of association, formed a court of all the provinces named the "Supreme Council," in which were enrolled twenty-four nobles, *i.e.*, six for each province, but who from various causes seldom assembled in greater number than twelve or fourteen. In progress of time when peace with the King was proposed, and particularly when

Commissioners were sent to Oxford to treat of it, they added to the deputation some who were not of the twenty-four members of Council, whose office was to hear and examine the conditions of peace, and report on them to the public. This practice continued on several other occasions, especially when Commissioners were sent to Dublin, and by degrees those deputies began to sit in Council under the name of supernumeraries, and thus the number increased almost imperceptibly to forty. This increase gave rise to three disorders in the government, one patent, the other two less apparent. The first was the confusion and difficulty of passing resolutions, since as every vote must be taken on every decree, none could be passed without much time lost in vain disputes. As every affair trivial or grave was brought before this same Council, contrary to the forms of all well regulated Republics, it followed that time was lost and affairs of importance were not properly examined by the wearied Council, who had to sit for many hours together, both in the morning and evening.

But the two less apparent evils became beyond comparison the most grave. The first, that the Commissioners having to treat for the peace of Dublin and of England with the Marquis of Ormonde, it was so managed under the pretext of sending deputies agreeable to him, that members were always chosen who were well affected to his party, and the consequence was to fill the Irish Council with the favourites of that faction, the prime cause now and perhaps for the future, of all the turbulence and misery of this kingdom. The second was having increased the disunion between the old and the new Irish, which will always be the greatest obstacle to the progress of religion; the old, perceiving that the Council to please Ormonde, was by degrees becoming entirely composed of their adversaries, expecting to be oppressed, deprived of their share in the government, and abandoned in their poverty, are alienated in heart, and wish for disturbances in the hope of recovering some of their power. This wide division has been the origin of the great diversity of opinion which prevails in the island. Now the old nobility to increase their power have contrived to draw to their side the clergy, and with these have declared that if they cannot obtain a glorious peace, they would much rather go to war. Their opponents on the contrary are suspicious of the clergy and wish for peace on any terms, not being ashamed to declare that if they obtain the free exercise of the Catholic rites at home, they would consider it superfluous and unjust to ask for more. The old Irish awaited with the utmost impatience the arrival of a Nuncio, supposing that he would have orders to exclude all idea of peace and to think solely of war. I have had no little trouble in persuading them to the contrary, and ridding myself of the importunities of those who persist in believing that I brought money to raise a Pontifical army, not so much to fight against the Puritans, as to put an end at once to any treaty or agreement with the King. The opposite party by no means welcomed my arrival, as they knew I should not be disposed to purchase a peace such as they desired, and would accept none unless favourable to religion; hence in order to diminish the credit of my authority, they have actually spread the report that I am come to take temporal possession of Ireland for His Holiness, and that Father Scarampi had been sent on before to see if such an attempt would be practicable. Finally, the principal desire of the old Irish is for the splendour of religion and the equality of the nobles, whilst for the others, the satisfaction and advancement of Ormonde constitute their great aim.

This therefore is the place to speak of him, and I must inform your Eminence that this man since he abandoned the Catholic faith under the teaching of the Archbishop of Canterbury in England, has always exercised some military authority under the King, and lately that of Viceroy of Ireland, with considerable address and to the satisfaction of all. By nature he is endowed with attractive and courteous manners, under which he dexterously conceals the ambitious thoughts which he nourishes, which are probably more ambitious than they appear outwardly, but which may be disclosed if the King's affairs approach nearer to the precipice. It makes one believe in the greatness of these designs, to hear of the insinuations he dropped after accepting the Viceroyalty, the promises he makes to his partisans, and the arts he employs to ingratiate himself with every one. It is greatly to be feared that if the King be not assisted in his present reverses, Ormonde, in spite of the fealty he owes His Majesty, will use his utmost efforts to oppose any peace or any treaty not concluded by himself, although ratified by the King, and thus foster sedition throughout the country. After deliberating on the course he is likely to pursue in case the King be entirely ruined, I have taken care to show to all who are likely to report my words to him, how much more useful and glorious it would be for him to declare himself a Catholic, than to pass over to the Puritans as it is reported he is about to do. I added that if he should take such a step he could not possibly escape the infamy which follows a betrayer of religion, and if he shows himself to the world as the friend of His Majesty's enemies he will prove that he had never at heart been faithful in his allegiance; whereas by declaring himself a Catholic he would not only have the merit of coming into the true faith, and obtain the favour of His Holiness and all other Princes, but would gain the support of this kingdom in his designs with a legitimate and honourable title. Nor let your Eminence wonder that I should propose to the Marquis a holy resolution founded on motives of self-interest, because I am sure that except through a special interposition of Providence, he will never be gained over by other means; nor do I find that the hope of his conversion entertained at Rome and mentioned in my instructions has any foundation, as the dogmas taught by the Archbishop of Canterbury are firmly implanted in his mind, and I know that he has several times declared in private the impossibility of believing two articles in the Catholic creed, viz. :—the presence of Christ in the sacraments, and the authority of the Roman Pontiff.

The persons nominated by your Eminence in my instructions as qualified to assist in his conversion are quite unequal to the task, since the Bishop of Ossory reduced to extreme old age, rarely leaves his house and Viscount Mountgarret also much aged, has besides no talents for such an office; and Richard Butler is of so gentle a nature that he would rather mourn over his brother and entreat our common Mother to pray for him, than have sufficient resolution to advise or gain him over.

On this man then and on the hopes nourished and divulged by him, depend at present all the weight and direction of this government. It is reported that he intends to employ the peace to be concluded by him between the King and the Irish, as a stepping-stone to his own advancement, and has therefore heaped promise on promise to his adherents; and as he knows the tenacity with which the Irish hold to their religion, it is said that he has granted every facility to its exercise, not only by words and declarations of tolerance, but by a general clause introduced into the articles of his peace, which declares that with respect to the Catholic religion he consents to all the conditions which may be approved by the King in favour of every one. His faction deluded by such promises, and deceived by his manner, protest that no event could be more favourable to religion than a union with the Marquis, and that it would be better to rely on him even in ecclesiastical matters, rather than stipulate for them one by one, and that in short the kingdom could not be in a more secure or more enviable position than under his care and providence, and in trusting to magnanimity of the Marquis. At the head of this faction is Viscount Muskerry, brother-in-law to Ormonde, and he is followed by all the Butler family, the Moungarrets and many others, not to speak of the neutrals such as Clanricarde and as was Thomond their adherents, and many private gentlemen of Leinster principally dependent on the house of Butler, and who may rather be called clients than factionists.

Many believed that the Assembly convoked in the past month would find some remedy for all these disorders, being filled with members well acquainted with the breaking-up of the government, and partizans of the Marquis.

But although the Council was by a great effort reduced to nine members only, and made many rules for the receipt and administration of the revenue, the root of the evil has not been reached, not alone because of the difficulties in the way, but still more because the old Council, with pertinacious resolution would never consent to despoil themselves of the authority about the peace given them by the late Assembly; and thus, in spite of all attempts to the contrary, the matter has remained at their disposition; it is therefore of no small moment that all the old Council and supernumeraries have been summoned to a meeting on the 20th of April, to examine and approve of the convention concluded with Ormonde. This is all that can be said concerning the political condition of Ireland without entering into the minor disorders of justice, of penalties, and of the magistracy, which if many and of no small importance (as no one is ever punished or rewarded on the merits of the case), do not at all events touch the main question, which is nothing more nor less than to place the Marquis in such authority as to rule at will over all the provinces; and in flagrant violation of the oath taken by the entire kingdom at the beginning, to subject to his discretion alone, the exercise and public celebration of the Catholic religion.

Secondly. From this statement the present condition of military affairs may easily be conjectured, being governed by the same influences as the political. It is evident that if at the beginning of the war the Irish had steadily continued to take possession of all the fortresses of the kingdom, and principally of Dublin, they would now be masters of the whole country and by professing in virtue of their oath to hold all for the King, in effect excluding the Puritans, from whom no concessions could be hoped for religion, they would have served their cause better than by truces and treaties which have not even saved them from being called rebels by His Majesty and all England.

It was the Ormonde faction who partly under the pretence of neutrality and partly to please the Marquis, introduced, by little and little the cessations with the Protestants, much to the injury of the common cause, as they have interrupted the course of victory, checked the first ardour of the people, and wasted the means which might have been employed against the Puritans; since during the three years of truce it has been calculated that a large part of the revenue has found its way into the coffers of the Marquis, which would otherwise have passed into the hands of the Irish, and might have absolutely terminated the war.

The military negotiation then, tends chiefly to the conclusion of the long-desired Ormonde peace, to be followed by the appointment of the Marquis as general of the whole army, and thus give him all the glory and all the fruits of the whole enterprise. Besides this there are abuses in the conduct of military affairs which make our prospects infinitely worse; one of them is that all resolutions are passed by the votes of the Council most of whom are quite inexperienced in military tactics; in spite of my repeated solicitations no council of war in which useful resolutions might be quietly carried out has ever been appointed, and in consequence preparations are never made in time, fortresses are unprovided, wants are not anticipated and are supplied only when letters become urgent or the necessity becomes stringent. The money which is the very nerve of the army, is not only badly administered by a useless number of collectors, but the pay of the soldiers is always in arrear, and no account of expenses has ever been rendered. What is worse, it has never been taken into consideration how money might be raised on an emergency, and there are probably no merchants in the island who would be willing to trust to an assignment of the taxes as a security as I have myself tried; therefore being obliged to arrange everything according to the time these payments become due; to our shame either the occasion is let slip or what is more intolerable it has passed away. As to the distribution of the army in the provinces, it is most unfortunate that the Council neither have nor desire to have, the power of ordering the generals to any place they deem advisable; each general having the charge of his native province can on no pretext whatever be sent elsewhere, commanding more as masters than as officers and invested with absolute authority. They use all the force under their command to serve their own private passions; of which proof sufficient was seen in the unfortunate expedition against Youghal last year; to the conduct of which the two generals Preston and Castlehaven were most unadvisedly deputed, for they soon quarrelled. Castlehaven, one of the most devoted of Ormonde's adherents, imagining that the failure to reduce the town would excite the desire for peace, did not scruple to say that he would have guided the negotiation in such a manner that peace would have been concluded without the other General. Although this occurring in the most conspicuous part of the kingdom caused deep and general disquiet, it is still more to be lamented that in Ulster, where the irreconcilable enmity of

Owen and Phelim O'Neill, both aspirants (failing heirs) to the Earldom of Tyrone, and from other private causes, have caused a total suspension of affairs for two years past, and their dissensions have served no other purpose than to permit the enemy to advance, and, excepting in two counties to lord it over the whole province.

In Connaught, while the Archbishop of Tuam lived he was obliged in a manner to be captain-general; because the Council believed for the reasons already mentioned, that the conduct of the army could devolve on no other than the Marquis of Clanricarde a native of the province; and he maintaining a strict neutrality, no one in fact had dared to send any other person; and therefore there is not a single officer in command who has had a semblance of success. Finally, in Leinster, where we have no other enemy than the Marquis and the Protestants, it is easy to conjecture that the soldiers and the garrisons serve only to supply our adversaries with food, to collect the revenue for the Marquis, and thus to our cost we are doubly exhausted between contributions and quarters. And there is all the greater reason to be displeased by these things because, not only the soldiers of this kingdom by long rest and present vigour are quite equal for active service, but the captains themselves are of tried valour, as O'Neill showed in his many years' service in Flanders; and Preston by his defence of Louvain, confided to him against the French; and conducted in such a manner as to merit an encomium in the learned descriptions of Henri Van der Putte. On this account I cannot cease to commend the prudence of His Holiness, in refusing permission to Pallavicini and others to accompany me to Ireland; as although their advice might perhaps have been sometimes taken, they would certainly not have been chosen to execute any design, and their coming would have most surely given rise to envy and suspicion.

Thirdly. I now pass to the consideration of Ecclesiastical

affairs, the principal object of my mission, and to which the efforts and the cares of the other two should always be directed; and of these neither, can I speak without lamenting to have found the Church infected with the contagion which has poisoned both political and military affairs; because the old Bishops accustomed to celebrate their few functions in secret without trouble or interference, make little account of the splendour and grandeur of religion; foreseeing that it would put them to great expense, and always doubting if they could maintain it, either from the new resolutions framed for the kingdom, or from the necessary diversion of the revenues to the necessities of the war. Hence, one sees nothing less than abhorrence in them of being subjected to any forms either in dress or ceremonial, almost all of them officiating as ordinary priests; and administer for example the sacrament of Confirmation, not only without stole or mitre, but what is little else than a secular dress; and therefore they would be alienated, and would be content to receive from the King and the Marquis permission for the free though secret exercise of religion, which would they think, save the substance of the faith without drawing down any difficulties upon them. As I have said, these opinions are chiefly held by the old Bishops who lived at the time of suppressions and alarms, but the young, ordained in better times, show more resolution and spirit. Such, for example, are the Bishops of Clogher and Ferns, and the Coadjutor of Limerick; with this difference however, that the first is entirely swayed by political rules and motives, the third by the practice and example of Rome; and the Bishop of Ferns, by his affection for the Church, which he maintains with so much prudence in his outward relation with the people, and his inward service to God, that he must be esteemed of all men in this kingdom the most likely to promote ardently and judiciously, the cause and the splendour of religion. But if the Bishops are for the most part lukewarm in the cause, I can assure your Eminence that the Regulars are without comparison much more so. Accustomed to live out of their convents, and acting as chaplains with good stipends to the Barons of the island, not constrained by the discipline of the monastery to wear the religious habit, with difficulty they accommodate themselves to a peace which restores ecclesiastical vigour, and takes from them all these exemptions from duty. They therefore attempted, first in private meetings, and *tête-à-tête*, to persuade the ignorant of the injustice of trying to force more from the distressed King on matters of religion than he ought to concede; but now they dare to preach this almost seditious doctrine from the pulpit, whence some of them have impudently gone on to prove that it is not necessary to the support of the faith to have churches, since in the Old Testament we are told that the Hebrews were for centuries without a Temple; and in the New that Christ instituted the Eucharist in a private house. If those who felt differently had not advanced reasons to prove how false was this teaching, the lower orders would have been easily impressed by it, as none who have had Mass in their own room appear to care for any other mode of worship, and the convenience is so much esteemed that it has been found impossible to introduce the practice of carrying the Holy Sacrament from the church to the infirm, which would be of the greatest edification, nor yet to keep the consecrated Host in the Tabernacles, as even the lowest artisan wishes in sickness to hear Mass at his bedside; but often, to our great scandal, on the very table from which the altar cloth has been but just removed, playing cards or glasses of beer together with the food for dinner are at once laid. Perhaps the ample power vested till now in the Regulars, under the title of Missionaries, which equals and in some respects exceeds that of Apostolic Nuncio, has been the cause of these disgraceful proceedings because, besides enjoying with full liberty all their privileges while not restricted to their convents and to formal obedience, they foresee that in the event of a peace favourable to religion their patents will be restricted, and all things be put under the rule of the Ecclesiastical Hierarchy. I experience every day how unwillingly they assume their proper habit, even in places where they are living secure from all danger, availing themselves of every sort of excuse, such as not yet having houses formed, or being employed in some negotiation, or having soon to visit some other place, or like the Jesuits, scattered about in such small numbers, it would be impossible to observe the precept never to leave the convent alone; all most frivolous considerations which hinder the people from witnessing to their edification, the due decorum and obedience of their guides. It may be noted above all, that this nation, perhaps more than any other in Europe, are negligent by nature of all that might with industry and activity improve and mature them, but content themselves with great tranquillity of mind to what nature has given to them with their earliest ideas, whence we find neither in ecclesiastical nor in secular affairs any solicitude or extraordinary diligence, still less any ardour to promote the interests of the Church as there ought to be, and as little of anger when any attempt fails. The cause of this defect, besides the climate and coldness of blood, may be found in the length of time the Irish have lived under the oppression of England in such bonds of vassalage, that not only were they prohibited from every industrial occupation, and from embarking in commerce, but in a still more miserable slavery were prevented from receiving education, or perfecting themselves in any science. They have thus come to content themselves with a Mass in their cabins, and to feed only on what the earth produces without labour or trouble, they have thus imbibed a coldness of spirit, and quietly accommodate themselves to the misery of the times. On this account to worship in church, to all ceremonies, to ecclesiastical decorations, and to every secular occupation that requires the stimulus of application, they scarcely lend a thought, or have a desire that goes beyond their ordinary condition. But this does not prevent them when instructed and placed in some post under strict rule from the first, from liking and maintaining the course they have adopted. Thus it is that the seclusion, discipline, and habit of the nuns have continued even to this day in their original strictness; and the same might be hoped of the bishops, parish priests, and monks when admonished and put into a path of diligence in their ecclesiastical office. It is certain that from having seen me this year perform the ceremony of the washing of the feet on Holy Thursday, the people have felt such compunction that I have been told it will be a sufficient stimulus for them to have seen this spectacle once, to make them cling to the Catholic religion and defend it for ever. I am for these reasons inclined to believe that in the first National Council, not only will the Council of Trent be accepted, though it presents many difficulties, but that still stronger foundations will be laid for a church worthy of the approbation of His Holiness. I am also of opinion that when undisturbed by the impediments of war, the clergy will be restored to the choir and to all other ecclesiastical functions, and that the Regulars now so far from obedient, will submit themselves in all things to the direction of the Nuncio and the Holy See.

From all that has been said, it will appear most eminent Lord, that the remedy for all the evils which have penetrated into every branch of this government will be very difficult to find; particularly under circumstances such as the present, when the kingdom is distracted by wars, and the King has no longer force nor courage to restore the peace of the island. But as all the disturbances take their origin from one source only, that is the faction of the Marquis of Ormonde, it is manifest that this once remedied whatever disorders there are in the three estates might be repaired at one moment, because if the Supreme Council had wished, or would wish to secure Dublin, and have the Marquis as their colleague but not as their superior; one could have formed at once, and could even now form a union between them and the nobility of the kingdom, from which the political government would acquire sufficient strength, and resolutions would be promulgated with common consent and approval. Likewise, as all matters concerning the war against the Parliamentarians would be managed without respect or hope of obtaining from the Marquis any sort of advantage, it would advance with all the ardour due to the greatness and merit of the cause, and in conformity with the first and fundamental oath of the Confederates when they took up arms.

Finally, the ecclesiastics having no other care on their hands but to contribute to the army, and freed from the thought of having to consult with the Viceroy day by day on the condition of religion, would defend it everywhere and strengthen themselves so that they should never lose ground, assured that when the King was in a state to make concessions, he would do so with the good faith due to an armed people resolved to obtain them by every means in their power. But as there is no human force that can either destroy or weaken this Ormonde League, it has often occurred to me to question whether it would be better for this country that the King of England should regain his power, or that the Parliament by his ruin should become masters of Ireland. On the one hand I think with respect to the Faith, it would be more secure to treat with a Prince not unwilling perhaps in this matter to yield all in his power convinced of the fidelity of the Irish; with a Catholic wife, and on a friendly footing with all the other Christian princes. But, on the other hand, I am alarmed by the general opinion of His Majesty's inconstancy and bad faith, which creates a doubt

P

that whatever concessions he may make, he will never ratify them unless it pleases him, or, not having appointed a Catholic Viceroy, whether he might not be induced by his Protestant ministers to avenge himself on the noblest heads in Ireland, and renew more fearfully than ever the terrors of heresy.

Therefore I am disposed to believe that in considering the subject of religion, which grows and is purified by opposition, the destruction of the King would be more useful to the Irish. In this case a union of the whole people to resist the forces of Parliament would immediately follow, and by choosing a Catholic Chief or Viceroy from among themselves, they would establish according to their own views all ecclesiastical affairs, without danger of being molested in the execution of their designs by the pretensions of the Protestants or their adherents. Nor am I daunted by the apprehension generally entertained of a sanguinary war waged against Ireland by the King and Parliament united, inasmuch as if money be supplied from abroad, the kingdom is not so destitute of men but that it could defend itself against very large armies. In this case also it would so move the compassion of His Holiness and of other princes, that as Christianity could not have an enterprise more important or meritorious than this, so the people would live in the assured belief that they would never be abandoned by the goodness of the Holy See, and the piety of Christians. And why may we not hope to see in the present century results similar to those we read of in the past? It is certain that the people of Scotland have ever been enemies of the English, and have often had bloody conflicts with them; and why, when their common interest in the downfall of the King has ceased, may not a war break out between them on matters of dominion, bitter as such struggles always are between rivals who are neighbours? And cannot we imagine that the two Crowns, though disagreeing on one point might easily unite not to suffer the loss of this kingdom, or to allow it to go into the hands of a growing and heretical republic, which besides, having feelings in common with a faithless aristocracy, may some day league with the Huguenots to humble France, and supported by the Dutch, end by destroying Flanders? And finally, who can believe that the Holy See already the patron of this kingdom, can suffer that at this extreme boundary of Europe it shall lose a glory so great as to sustain in the face of ocean a new world, and amidst so many accidents the Holy Catholic Faith, and not employ a force here to maintain it for ever? In these circumstances everyone can see that Ireland would remain almost certainly within her ecclesiastical boundaries for a long time; but in the end with assistance could force the Parliament to yield to her demands and leave her in peace to her Catholic vocation. This is all I can write now, affirming nothing but waiting on future events, which depending on a variety of circumstances may change every hour. But subjecting much more than I can say to the lofty wisdom of His Holiness, whose directions inspired by God exclude all inferior reasoning, and show the self-deception of those who are guided only by the suggestions of an ordinary intellect.

With humble reverence, &c., &c.

To THE SAME (IN CIPHER).

March 12, 1646.

New Commissioners have gone to Dublin, and amongst them Viscount Muskerry, whence we cannot doubt that their object is to arrange finally the articles of a peace with the Marquis of Ormonde, to be made public in the beginning of May. In the meantime it is disputed here every day, how the supplies brought over by me are to be applied, but seeing these long delays many suspect that there is really nothing to be undertaken though with peril to the provinces before Ormonde by virtue of the peace becomes general of all the armies, and reaps all the fruits and glory of the negotiation. I am impatient for the arrival of Sir Kenelm Digby, who I hear from Paris is at Nantes, and this is the only news received. His arrival will clear up what is to be done about the peace and the league with the English Catholics, and I will determine with him what is to be done in case the peace meets with opposition from the Ormonde faction.

To the Same.

We are on the point of deciding to what part of the kingdom the supplies which I brought with me from Rome are to be sent, and I believe that it will be to the two provinces of Ulster and Connaught, with a separate army to each. I have always inclined to these more than to the province of Munster, because, although there, by taking towns and seaports more might appear to be gained, yet the province of Ulster being almost entirely lost, and lying so near to Scotland as to be constantly open to new enemies, is therefore more in need of assistance; and Connaught too, inundated by the Scotch, who overran Ulster, is in equal danger. Besides Ulster, being more Catholic than the others, and professing singular reverence for the Holy Pontiff, deserves to be the first to share in the Pontifical succours. This Council never would enter upon the subject of these expeditions notwithstanding my urgent representations, until now that accounts begin to arrive from Connaught of new incursions and losses, and that the Ulster soldiery in want of their pay and much reduced have entered the friendly country to make demands for money. Such is the want of foresight they show in everything, and imagine that His Holiness is at once to take thought of all their wants; and when I press them to say what they will do on their part for Munster, the only answer I receive is, that if peace be concluded, they will be assisted by the Marquis of Ormonde.

God inspired me to send my auditor to inspect the fortress of Duncannon; he found everything wanting, not one thing having been done to put it in a state of defence since the day it was retaken from the enemy. I therefore gave a large sum of money and sent Captain Preston to set the necessary works on foot, thanking God in my heart that the enemy was not aware of its defenceless state, for it would have been lost in a few days and the kingdom in a more calamitous state than ever. And still the wonder continues that we have heard nothing from Digby since the 1st of February, nor from Invernizi since the 6th of January, yet on that day the Nuncio of France wrote to me that he was about to set off immediately. The time being now come for requiring the ships, I begin to fear some sinister accident, as I am sure he would not willingly lose any time. I add these particulars to the letter I wrote on the 7th of this month, so that your Eminence may be acquainted with every move in the commencement of this campaign, which I pray to God may succeed to the exaltation of the Holy Faith and the depression of its enemies.

I humbly salute your Eminence.

ADDED TO THE LETTER OF 7TH MARCH.

Kilkenny, March 12.

The Nuncio has lent a large sum of money for the restoration of the fort of Duncannon, which, owing to the negligence of the commander is in want of every kind of supply, and he hopes that in a few days the defence of the place will be complete. The Parliamentarians in Ulster have sacked the town of Coleraine on the western coast; the Scotch also have taken some places in Connaught, and we think of despatching some regiments now to each place to attack and to recover them. Our army in Scotland on the contrary, has routed 400 of the enemy's cavalry, and has sent here for reinforcements of men, which the Marquis of Antrim has urgently done more than once. If this can be effected it will be a good diversion for Ulster. Meanwhile, in order to introduce into this country the observance of the Fridays of March, unusual in this country, the Nuncio has a service on those days accompanied with music, after which he delivers a sermon on the Passion.

To the Same (in cipher).

March 13, 1646.

The Earl of Glamorgan when made prisoner by the Marquis of Ormonde, wrote to the King; and I send a copy of the reply to your Eminence, as it appears to me that His Majesty still continues to have a favourable inclination towards the Catholics, and consequently will not dispute the articles of the Roman treaty, and this I am very impatient to ascertain. We are in great anxiety here on account of news received from Limerick, that the Parliamentary army has entered the mouth of the river, and is attempting to raise a fort on a spot which would prevent the entrance of our vessels; we have also heard within the hour that the Earl of Thomond, hitherto neutral, has joined them. The Supreme Council have done, and will do nothing, refusing even to nominate a Council of War to superintend military affairs. I imagine that this attack has been made to prevent the promised assistance from reaching the King, and perhaps will show more clearly what the kingdom requires.

To the Same (in cipher).

March 15, 1646.

If, owing to the defeat of the King or any other cause, the peace drawn up by His Holiness should not be accepted, it will be impossible to defer the publication of the Ormonde peace beyond the beginning of May, so as to secure the

Marquis's assistance for the remainder of the war. If the Roman peace be concluded in order to be able to do without the Marquis's aid, a few thousand crowns more will be needed to assist Munster, and enable us to introduce the public exercise of the Catholic religion in the newly-acquired towns, without opposition from the Protestants. I represent this necessity to the goodness of His Holiness through your Eminence, because if he favour the undertaking, it will be my object not to make use of the subsidies unless matters are arranged for the benefit of religion.

To THE SAME (IN CIPHER).

March 21, 1646.

Immediately after the defection of the Earl of Thomond, of which I informed your Eminence in my letter of the 13th instant, was known here, letters from his wife who is in England were intercepted, advising him to withdraw from the Parliament, notwithstanding the King's total overthrow. At the same time there has appeared here, through various channels from London, a declaration made by the King, a copy of which I enclose, in which he denies having ever given directions to the Earl of Glamorgan to treat for peace, and in substance leaves Ireland totally at the disposal of the Parliament. If this declaration be authentic, and not forged by the Puritans, we must infer that the letter written by the King to the Earl, which I sent to your Eminence in my despatch of the 15th, was either altogether false or meant to deceive; in accordance with the King's well known instability of character. I imagine that Digby, of whom no news has even yet arrived, may have been arrested in France by his command, since if His Majesty desire to make peace with the Parliament, he will not care for the supplies from His Holiness or for aid from Ireland. The news has caused great fear every one dreading concealed enemies about him, and seeing no remedy they have at once despatched to Dublin Dr. Ffennel a physician, and entirely dependent on the Marquis, to induce him to join with them as he has often declared himself hostile to the Parliament, and to bring with him all the neutrals; but there may be also some other ends in this secret commission.

I do my best to give encouragement by showing that my being in the same peril, ought to increase their courage, and I have represented how much should be done in this emergency to prevent our being taken by surprise; such as sending succour to the towns which most need it, erecting forts in exposed places, making known the state of the island to both crowns, and meanwhile detaining for our own defence, the soldiers who were to have been sent to England. I give them hopes also, that His Holiness will send still further assistance, or devote to the service of Ireland what he had destined for the King in case peace had been concluded. I also propose, in case Digby should not appear, to consider amongst ourselves the propositions of the English Catholics sent to me by your Eminence, and when our resolution is taken, to inform the Nuncio of France, who will communicate with them. As to the Marquis, he has said that the ecclesiastical peace will not be concluded, since the King no longer wishes for peace with the Irish, and that as the Confederates will be masters over religion and its exercise, his assistance and supplies may then be acceptable. I have given orders to Ffennell on my own part to communicate to Ormonde the reasons why it appears to me that on this proof of the King's inconstancy he ought to become a Catholic. But above all I insist to the Council upon the necessity of our securing Dublin, lest it fall into the hands of the Puritans either through Ormonde or in any other way, and lastly, I endeavour to convince them that acting thus they will reap a reward without incurring danger, but by pursuing a contrary course they will deserve to be abandoned by the whole world. But the incredible lukewarmness of all these men, or their fear of offending Ormonde, make me despair of obtaining my object. Your Eminence is now fully acquainted with our position, preparations, and the peril in which we stand, and if His Holiness thinks that in case of the treaty with the King being concluded, or of the complete success of the Parliament, it would be necessary for this kingdom to adopt other resolutions, or pursue other measures, you will doubtless favour me with information. It is possible a union may be effected, and in that case it will be my care that the Apostolic See shall be the arbiter, and His Holiness' advice followed; already it is felt that our principal if not only hope is in the aid granted by His Holiness, to whom, more than to any other prince it is of importance that the Holy Faith be upheld in this remote corner of the world, and that this poor country shall not fall into the hands of a vindictive heresy such as that of the Calvinism of the Parliamentarians.

To the Same (in cipher).

March 22, 1646.

If the decree published by the King against Glamorgan, and if the necessity which forces him to make peace with the Parliament be true, all our treaties for peace go for nothing, as well as the articles proposed by the English Catholics; which, based on the aid and authority of the King, will have no foundation unless reformed by other means, such as the separate Confederation which is to be attempted here between them and the Irish. The whole matter it appears to me is this, that we must come to the point whence we started, that the Confederates must first of all recover possession of this kingdom, and then do the best they can to aid the cause of religion in England. Perhaps it has pleased God to show how shamefully we have erred from the right course by that long truce for the sake of the Marquis, and by listening to his flattering words and also of those about him, who think much less of the interest and grandeur of religion than of the conveniences of daily life.

And I trust that if His Holiness does not abandon us, but sends us the necessary aid, and continues his favourable interposition for us with the other Princes, that the enterprise will succeed to the glory of God and the exaltation of the Holy Faith.

To the Same (in cipher).

March 28, 1646.

Not only has Digby not appeared but we have heard no news of him, on which account I am more convinced than ever that the treaty on this side will be hurried on; but as to concluding it with the Earl of Glamorgan, as your Eminence commands in the cipher of January 28th, I fear it would be not only a great risk but all in vain, as his promises are not to be depended on if it be true that the King did make that declaration, and that his treaty with the Parliament is a fact.

Meanwhile, on the 21st of this month, the city and Castle of Dublin were nearly taken by the Parliament, as your Eminence shall hear separately. You may be sure that I availed myself of the occasion, and declared it was the voice of God to teach the Irish what they must do if they did not desire to lose that city and the whole kingdom; more particularly as I had by the inspiration of God attended at Council that very morning to speak on the subject. The Council answered that my reasons were very cogent, but that they did not wish to make any resolution until their commissioners had returned from Dublin; and as amongst them is Lord Muskerry, brother-in-law to Ormonde, he will doubtless endeavour to prevent any final decision until he hears the opinion of the Supreme Director.

In fine, the Commissioners have not even now concluded anything with the Marquis, whose pretensions I hear are more lofty than ever, in spite of the reverses of the Royal party: whence it is evident he entertains no idea of peace but is solely bent on war.

To the Same (in cipher).

March 28, 1646.

The Earl of Glamorgan, who went to Limerick to punish the defection of the Earl of Thomond, has we hear already besieged the palace into which the Earl had admitted the Parliamentarians, and is seeking means to sink or damage the enemy's ships in the river. If the Council carry out this enterprise and recover that important seaport, I will assist them with His Holiness' supplies; and if they determine to attempt Dublin, I will advance all the money I possibly can, trusting to the goodness of His Holiness to supply the rest, as success would in itself be equal to a gain of half the kingdom. Meanwhile I continue to reinforce Ulster; and if success attend our endeavours, the Scotch will be obliged to retire from Connaught also.

To the Same.

Kilkenny, March 28, 1646.

As usual in the uncertain deliveries of this miserable sea passage, I have received five packets from your Eminence at the same time—those of the 7th, 21st, and 28th of January and 18th of February, together with the two ciphered despatches of the 28th of January and 18th of February. I am greatly astonished that Signor Invernizi has not appeared, as your Eminence writes that he was on the eve of departure at the end of December; nor can I understand why, after so many months, he has provided only one frigate, though I left 9,000 crowns or more with him of your money; but of all this, however, I can write with more certainty when he arrives. To Father Scarampi I have paid all those debts for which he asked for money as I have advised you; and I will provide him with money for his living and other necessities as your Eminence commands in two of your letters. I have sent him copies of the two ciphers to Waterford as you desired. I write by every opportunity that presents itself; and Father Scarampi assures me that he has received all; therefore my despatches will I believe arrive though tardily at Rome; and it appears to me that I have not omitted anything of consequence, and have done my duty in working and writing. But the boldness of the Parliamentarians is increasing, navigation will be more uncertain and less secure; and truly when I think of the remote situation of this island, my hope increases that God will extend His protection to us all the more as we seem to be abandoned by commerce, and every other accustomed aid.

&c., &c.

To the Same (in cipher).

April 6, 1646.

The Marquis of Ormonde finding the King's affairs in a desperate condition, seems to incline to a union with the Catholics against the common enemy and is therefore anxious for peace; and it is certain that the Commissioners of the Confederates last sent to Dublin have adjusted all the articles, leaving what belongs to religious affairs to the Earl of Glamorgan. I do my best to persuade people that in the present state of uncertainty as to what the King will do, and on account of the declaration lately made by His Majesty, no peace ought to be concluded and no negotiations be carried on with the Marquis as though he had authority and the King was in the field, but merely join with him as a Baron of the kingdom against the Puritans, the Confederates reserving the power of establishing the Catholic religion everywhere without opposition from the Marquis; especially since the authority of Glamorgan is annulled, and even if Digby makes his appearance, the religious conditions can only be established by arms and by ourselves. But I am not sure of obtaining my wish as a union with the Marquis is esteemed absolutely necessary, and his adherents do all they can by a thousand inventions to make it appear so; on the other hand he, for reputation sake desires peace, since it might be thought he had joined this party from mere fickleness; but whatever happens I will do all I can for the best in the cause of religion and according to your Eminence's instructions.

To the Same (in cipher).

April 6, 1646.

Having heard that the Prince of Wales had fled to the Island of Scilly, I immediately guessed that he intended to take refuge in Ireland, and at last I have found out that this is the case, and the Marquis is urging it on the Council. They rather incline to countenance his coming, as there seems to be no reason, nor would it be becoming to prevent it, and they hope some good may come of it. I know not how to judge, as its success depends on so many different circumstances, the youth being no friend to the Catholic religion, but if he were, he would be the hope and the glory of the kingdom. I must consider how best to act in the matter, and will inform you with all the diligence which the uncertainty of communication from this place will allow.

To the Same (in cipher).

April 6, 1646.

Ormonde proposes to yield to the Council possession of the Island of Scilly where the Prince of Wales has taken refuge, on condition that they send an Irish garrison there.

They think of accepting his offer, and to send a Catholic commander as I advised, in order to secure the place, already strong enough but necessary as a safe passage from France to Ireland, and from England to Ireland also.

To the Same.

April 10, 1646.

It is now decided what provinces are to receive the money which I brought over; and although I wished that the whole should be devoted to Ulster on account of its greater wants and danger, the Council has decided that half should be sent to Connaught, where the enemy are making great ravages. There will then be two armies of 3,000 infantry each, and 500 horse, and we hope before three months are over to have further supplies from His Holiness, so that the campaign may be finished successfully; and if the Parliament does not send over many more troops as it is feared, we may be able to liberate these provinces soon.

In Ulster, Owen Roe O'Neill will command as he has done for a long time; he is a strange and grasping man but it would be impossible to remove him.

It is said the Marquis of Ormonde himself will proceed to another part of Ulster, his troops joining in this emergency with those of the Confederates against the common enemy.

In Connaught will be stationed the Marquis of Clanricarde, who seeing the inclinations of the royal party and feeling the necessities of his household in Connaught, has at last resolved to abandon his neutrality and join us, and under him Preston will command; who by being content to serve under Clanricarde has edified us all, and gives me the best hope of good service from him. I have taken upon myself to say, that if His Holiness does not send large supplies to this province he will at least deign to contribute some part of the necessary expenses of these armies, which will amount to 12 or 15,000 crowns. The arms have been distributed to all the soldiers, and seeing how greatly they were needed, I repine less at the great expense of their transport.

If Signor Invernizi's frigate arrives, as we hourly expect, it will be joined by two others to coast along the island, and carry aid when it is required. I do not yet know what is projected in Munster, all thoughts being turned to the danger which menaces Limerick, and to repair the mischief of Thomond's rebellion; but the slowness with which measures are taken is perfectly inexplicable to me, for the enemy are allowed to establish themselves everywhere before a thought is given or a measure taken to oppose them.

This is all that will be done in the war for this year.

To the Same.

April 11, 1646

Although I have not been able to obtain a regular council of war, as I have informed you, I have at least induced the Supreme Council to depute four of their number to consult with me on military affairs, with the power of calling also the captains-general and other persons of experience to hear their opinion, as your Eminence will see in the articles laid down, and of which I enclose a copy. This congress, if matters be well considered, may be of some use because if the Council does not remove to a distance I shall constantly convoke it, and at all events it will provide for many things beforehand, and consider many others which at present are never even spoken of.

To the Same (in cipher).

April 15, 1646.

The Marquis of Ormonde has promised certainly that immediately on the receipt of some money, which is to be sent to him from here, he will set off at once for the eastern part of Ulster against the Scotch, but in a different direction to that of the army of O'Neill, who with his people will proceed to the west. I shall try to prevail as I wrote on the 6th, that the subject of peace shall not be mentioned at present, because either the King will regain his power completely, in which case he will confirm the articles brought forward by the Queen and His Holiness, or he will be entirely overwhelmed, when it will be better to have made no peace, but to establish by the sword and with authority a proper state of affairs. I do not therefore oppose this league with the Marquis, on which such a stress is laid that one cannot say a word against it.

To the Same (in cipher).

April 15, 1646.

On the subject of the Prince of Wales, I put before everything the consideration of the evils and expense which his coming here would entail upon the kingdom, and the Supreme Council apparently having no power to prohibit it, have at least resolved not to further his coming or to invite him but to leave the affair to chance. Of the soldiers destined for the Island of Scilly a part will remain there in the fortress, and should the Prince come here he will be accompanied by the remainder. I wished that a person of consideration and a Catholic should have been sent from here, so that the Prince might be under this obligation to the Confederates, and to contradict a report much spread abroad that Secretary Digby a Protestant, is to have the conduct of this negotiation with the soldiers and also of the kingdom as he boasts in Waterford; where he is waiting at present to make use of the vessels which are to be sent to the island. But, as I have said, the Council will not take on any positive step, lest they seem to have a part in the coming of the Prince, nor indeed can they be persuaded to form any ideas, save those suggested by the Marquis, or Muskerry his brother-in-law.

To the Same.

April 29, 1646.

On this occasion of a vacancy in the see of Cork, I consider that it would be very desirable and proper to bestow it upon Robert Barry, once recommended to His Holiness for the Bishopric of Ross, and if no other has as yet been sent or appointed, I think your Eminence would do well for Cork to appoint this person, who has good manners, is much attached to the Ecclesiastical party, and universally esteemed.

I make this proposal in performance of my duty, and in obedience to the commands of your Eminence.

To the Same.

May 3rd, 1646.

After I had written to your Eminence on the 7th of April one ordinary letter three in cipher and a folio of despatches, I received your Eminence's two letters of the 31st of December written before those of the 18th February which I had already received. I have nothing to add here, having answered at length in my last. I have only further to inform your Eminence that with your letters I received a memorial from the Regular Canons of St. Augustine; and to assure you that I shall closely observe the instructions with which you have favoured me. I have not given away any of their monasteries save one, St. John of Kilkenny to the Jesuit Fathers for a college or seminary which had been all but made over to them before my arrival; and the object being one of such importance as a good education for the whole kingdom, the proposal had been willingly and warmly acceded to by all parties. Such a decision in a newly established church and directed wholly to the benefit of the people, cannot be displeasing to the enlightened and holy mind of our Blessed Father, &c., &c.

To the Same (in cipher).

The Prince of Wales has quitted Scilly and it is believed has sailed towards France; and has thereby freed this Kingdom from a great dilemma, the soldiers who went to take possession of the Island found it occupied by Parliamentary troops; and being unable to effect anything the greater number returned home, while the remainder with Secretary Digby in another ship, went I know not where. If Digby has employed for his own purposes the money intrusted to him by the Confederates for the benefit of the Island; I was a true prophet when I warned them against having any dealings with the heretic. The Marquis of Ormonde also, after having accepted the money sent to him by the Council, takes his time in going to Ulster and perhaps he too will deceive these good people; I therefore make use of these doings to prove how necessary is the close union amongst the Catholics, which is so much desired by His Holiness. At Limerick too our troops are doing nothing against Thomond; in Connaught, Clanricarde had routed the Scotch, but they had immediately after received fresh assistance and he fearing some reverse begs that Preston may be despatched with troops to his aid.

To the Same (in cipher).

Sir Kenelm Digby never sent me your Eminence's despatch with the original articles; and now, Monsignor, the French Nuncio writes to me that as soon as he has the King's ratification he will return at once to Rome. For three months I have employed arguments and entreaties having nothing else at command, in order to prevent the proposed publication on the 1st of May. I have taken advantage both of the reverses of the King and of Glamorgan's having been discredited by the edict of London, to insist that instead of treating of peace we should go out against the common enemy. I tell your Eminence freely that if I had another sum of money sufficient to finish the campaign, I should obtain all that I desire. I send you a report of the state of the Kingdom drawn up in March, but as many changes have since taken place I must make some additions to it.*

To Monsignor the Nuncio of France.

Kilkenny, May 3.

I take a safe opportunity of informing your Excellency that yesterday evening on the return of my frigate I received your letter with the three large packages and the Gazettes, so courteously sent on the 10th of April. I should have taken some steps before now to remedy this uncertain transmission of letters had Signor Invernizi arrived with his vessels: his delay causes me much inconvenience both in public and private affairs. I have undergone incredible toil to delay the publication of the peace which was to have taken place on the 1st of May, but is now put off till June; it is impossible to tell you how prejudicial it has been to me that Sir Kenelm Digby has never forwarded the packet containing the signed articles of the Pontifical Treaty intrusted to him by Cardinal Pamphili; as evil-disposed persons declare, that I have acted without authority and have delayed the peace for purposes of my own. I especially regret to hear from your Excellency that Sir Kenelm Digby intends returning to Rome after receiving the Royal confirmation of the articles instead of coming here, as new charges will infallibly be made against me, but with the aid of God I hope to keep up my courage. The campaign has already begun here, and the London Parliamentarians threaten to overwhelm us but this news is very uncertain, and all I can do at present is to keep up the courage of those around me; and the truth is that if His Holiness could favour this kingdom with a fresh and

* See page 132.

considerable assistance, I should be able to do great things. Under all circumstances however while thus surrounded by perils, I entreat your Excellency to remember me in your prayers and to obtain for me the signal protection and aid of the Blessed God. Meanwhile if the English Catholics notwithstanding the King's loss of power, still wish to unite with us, I will assist them vigorously and as I wrote lately try to make them one with our party. It is true that if we are not assisted by them or others to free this kingdom, we can scarcely hope to do much good. For this reason I have adroitly prevented the 10,000 infantry from being sent to the King's aid, although on other accounts I should have much wished to do it—but to despoil this country, without being certain of relieving England, appeared to me a step fraught with danger.

The affairs of the Barberini family could not fail to turn out as they have done, from the beginning they seemed so irretrievable. I await with the greatest curiosity to hear what course they will pursue after the publication of His Holiness's bull, because here in my judgment lies the great danger of a rupture; and although I am grieved that your Excellency should be placed in so embarrassing a position, your courage so often proved, gives me assurance that you will act with all your accustomed prudence. I render my thanks to your Excellency for the delivery of the letters which must have given you so much trouble; also for the news of Signor Guadagni, and of the satisfaction you express with the captain of my frigate; and lastly, I regret that in return for your full notices of so many interesting matters, I have only these reports as dry and meagre as the smoked herrings of this sea to send you. But so it is that the poor must return the favours of the rich.

    I humbly kiss your Excellency's hands.

To Cardinal Pamphili.

Limerick, May 21st, 1646.

The last despatch brought me three letters from your Eminence, dated the 4th, 5th, and 18th of March, and two besides in cipher of the same dates. From what Monsignor the Nuncio of France writes I gather that all my letters have been received, notwithstanding the loss of the dispatches of the 20th, 22nd, and 28th of November which may have been thrown into the sea, since no account of the frigate which carried them has been received. Signor Invernizi has never arrived, nor any news of him, therefore the same uncertainty in forwarding and receiving letters still continues to my great vexation, as I had fully provided against it by the two frigates he was to have bought. The difficulty will be increased if I am obliged to remain at Limerick where I arrived last week; because on account of the conflict at Bunratty, the river is now blocked up by the enemy and our vessels are unable to enter freely; opportunities to Waterford are not generally known in time here, whence it may happen that Father Scarampi who resides there constantly can perhaps often write before me, as I find he did in particular on the imprisonment of Glamorgan. I am grateful for what your Eminence says of my indisposition. I cannot deny that besides the disturbance in my blood, this air has induced twenty or more attacks of fever lasting for twenty-four hours at a time, but as they have been outwardly mitigated I have not troubled myself much about them, and have borne them with the greatest patience. Your Eminence may rest assured that in having condescended to write even once on this subject, you have abundantly satisfied me of your infinite goodness towards me; and as since the day in which I consecrated myself to the service of His Holiness and the Apostolic See I have taken no thought for my life, I am still prepared to lay it down here in Ireland at the command of His Holiness, provided that I do not seal it with the character of an unworthy minister of the Catholic religion. I have received another order perhaps a duplicate, to pay Father Scarampi what he has disbursed or will have to disburse, and I shall punctually obey the commands of His Holiness and of your Eminence, who are the representative of his authority.

TO THE SAME (IN CIPHER).

Limerick, May 21st, 1646.

The verification of the caution which I gave to the Council, that Secretary Digby would deceive them in the negotiation between the Prince and this island, leads me to think that what I have said many times, that in the end they will be deceived by the Marquis also, may prove equally true. Not only does he delay his long promised visit to Ulster, but having received a packet of letters by two Parliamentary ships, he for seven days following assembled the Secret Council. From this and many other doubtful matters it is believed that he will be drawn over to the other party; or even if he should join us, we must understand at least that we can never trust him. Nevertheless, they are bent on concluding peace with him, and on publishing along with the treaty the ecclesiastical parts of Glamorgan's instructions; although he is disallowed, and his authority revoked by the King, who is in no position, even if willing, to ratify them unless the 10,000 infantry were sent to England, this being one of the most important conditions. Resolved not to become entirely dispirited, as I see Father Scarampi is, I have always seconded the idea of uniting with the Marquis against the common enemy, and approved of his joining the campaign, but have always protested against any treaty of peace being entertained now, since at present he represents no authority, still more

I protest against his having the supreme command of the army, because this would prejudice the Catholic religion, cut off all hope of a Catholic Viceroy, and subject our faith to the arbitration of his arms.

This opinion was expressed by me first, *currenti calamo*, in a letter written after the return of Plunket from Dublin, and then in a document relating entirely to the Marquis, of which I sent your Eminence a copy. I have on this account transferred my residence now to Limerick, and to see the state of the war. I intend to consult the clergy here, and afterwards to try if it be possible to convoke the Assembly again; should this fail I shall follow the command given in your Eminence's first cipher—to stand aloof, to give neither consent nor denial, to let things pass, and perhaps retire to Waterford, or some other place, and there await the further commands of His Holiness.

To THE SAME (IN CIPHER).

May 24th.

To your Eminence's cipher of March 18th I can only reply that after the king's declaration, Glamorgan fell so much in credit and esteem that he is now treated with scarcely any consideration, and it is wonderful how the Supreme Council, who were so enamoured of concluding peace with him, should have so completely abandoned him that he has lost credit with everyone, the merchants in particular; so that he has really not enough to live upon. Of Father Scarampi I do not deny that he has often written for his licence to depart, but my answer has always been that it was not for me to anticipate the commands of His Holiness, who would be the best judge when it would be the proper time to grant him leave to return.

To the Same (in Cipher).

May 25th, 1646.

Plunket who has returned from Dublin, brings news that the king has made peace with the Scotch, and I think that we shall have another cessation till July. Before then many things may change, because Digby may resume his negotiations, and the king be in a position to confirm them; and a good peace might then be concluded as every one greatly desires. We may also hope for success in Ulster, and to be able to liberate Munster and the sea coasts, and if I had money this certainly might be effected during the disturbances in England.

To Monsignor the Internuncio of Flanders.

Limerick, May 29th.

Mr. Plunket's request that you should have a quota of Irish soldiers, has met with so much opposition that with all my efforts I have not succeeded in effecting it. An agent from the most Christian King is here, and at every moment renews his solicitations for troops, and it is not deemed proper to grant to one party what is denied to another. But besides this, I assure you that the miserable condition of all the provinces in this kingdom is such, that instead of sending our troops away we require additional aid ourselves. I hope you will not only accept these urgent reasons, but believe that on any other occasion I should serve you with infinite pleasure and zeal.

I affectionately kiss your Excellency's hand.

To the Duke of Lorraine.

Limerick, May 29th, 1646.

I greatly wish that the letter with which you honoured me through Mr. Plunket could have given me the good fortune to serve you, but the necessities of this kingdom are so great that no troops can be sent away without danger to it, nor indeed without failing in respect to the other sovereigns who have asked, and been refused similar assistance. I have availed myself of all the means pointed out by Mr. Plunket and many others suggested by my own judgment; but the current of popular opinion here is too strong to be withstood, and I hope that the benignity of your Highness will be convinced by the weighty reasons brought forward by the Supreme Council, and not the less maintain the friendly correspondence which has ever existed between the two countries. I entreat that your Highness will favour me at all times with your commands that I may prove how truly

I am your humble and devoted servant.

To Mr. Thomas Plunket.

Limerick, May 29th, 1646.

Not content with introducing the subject to the Supreme Council only, I have spoken separately to each of the Council concerning the levy of troops of which you have written, and I find all are agreed that we have no means of granting your request. Because, not only has a similar demand for soldiers been made by two Crowns, but it is absolutely necessary to prepare for future campaigns which cannot fail except from want of soldiers. Seeing therefore the impossibility of assisting the Duke of Lorraine, I have not hesitated to write to His Highness, convinced that a Prince of his great judgment will be satisfied with our excuses, and will not interrupt the friendly intercourse subsisting between the two kingdoms. By this opportunity I write to the same effect to the Internuncio in Flanders, and must request of you to deliver my letter into his hands, and thanking you both for the confidence you have reposed in me, and deeply regretting my inability to serve you better on this occasion.

I kiss your hands, &c., &c.

To Cardinal Pamphili in cipher.

June 1st, 1646.

I hear that at Lord Muskerry's solicitation, the Supreme Council have recommended Dr. O'Callaghan to the See of Cork without consulting me. I therefore think it necessary to repeat to Your Eminence that no better choice can be made for that church than Robert Barry who was before named for the See of Ross; a man of the highest qualities, beloved by all, and devoted to the Catholic cause; and having been in constant communication with him I am thoroughly acquainted with his character. O'Callaghan is a Doctor of the Sorbonne and an excellent man, but at this crisis it would not be wise to promote one so dependent on the Marquis of Ormonde, and frequently with him in Dublin; since those who are independent, and owe no deference to any superior, will have more courage to aid both religion and the common cause. Always, however, submitting my own opinion to that of His Holiness.

I am, with humble reverence, &c., &c.

To Monsignor the Internuncio in Flanders.

Limerick, June 3rd.

After eight months of expectation, during which time we have suffered great anxiety concerning Signor Invernizi, I have at length heard from Dunkirk that he had sent the large frigate laden with arms and stores to Ostend, and had set sail himself in the small one on the 9th of April; but not having received any account of him since then I fear he may have met with some serious accident, such as shipwreck or imprisonment. I entreat of you to give orders that the large frigate bought with the money of the Apostolic See, may be well taken care of, and either kept in repair or sold with as little loss as possible, this I ask in case no other directions have been transmitted from Rome by His

Holiness or by Cardinal Pamphili, to whom the news was, I am sure, transmitted sooner than to this country. It is quite unnecessary to add any stimulus to you in the service of His Holiness and in aid of religion, but fervently praying for your happiness.

I am, &c., &c.

To Cardinal Pamphili.

June 3, 1646.

Whilst I was looking for the arrival of Signor Invernizi with more anxiety than ever, a letter arrived from the merchant Everard to his uncle in Waterford, dated April 18th, saying that the frigate laden with stores having sprung a leak had returned to Ostend, and that Signor Invernizi had embarked in the small frigate on the 9th of April, since then we have heard nothing of him, and I greatly fear he has suffered either shipwreck or imprisonment, but I trust in God that there is no foundation for a report spread abroad last week of the loss of the small frigate. I hope my fears may prove groundless, but a delay of so many months makes me dread some great misfortune, because the loss of the money to come from France would be fatal to this kingdom. I have written to the Internuncio in Flanders to take care of the frigate and stores or to sell them, as in his prudence he may think best, unless Your Eminence had otherwise commanded, and I hope that if time bring misfortune on our side that the pain of this news will at least be mitigated by the appearance of Signor Invernizi in safety and prosperity.

To the Same.

Limerick, June 14, 1646.

Glory be to God and to the Holy thoughts of the Blessed Father, the Divine Majesty has condescended to accept my efforts to bring about a reconciliation between the two Generals O'Neill in Ulster, and to prosper my fixed resolution to make that province the first to be assisted by the Pontifical subsidies. The fruit has been the victory obtained by the Catholics against the entire Scotch army on the 5th of June; a victory so signal, that in the memory of man no greater has been known here, since with scarce 4,000 infantry and 400 horse; they routed ten regiments of the enemy's infantry and fifteen companies of horse.

Of the hostile infantry almost all are dead, and but few of the cavalry escaped. Twenty-one officers were taken prisoners; all the baggage and munitions, &c. have fallen into our hands, as I have written more at length in the accompanying report. In this city I have offered up public thanksgivings and do all that I can to ensure the course of victory going on uninterruptedly in order that this poor part of the kingdom under the happy auspices of His Holiness, may see the end of its miseries, and be received into the bosom of the Catholic Church. And truly the constancy of this people in retaining their religion and their ancient reverence towards the Holy See, may have merited the aid of God, and therefore that His Omnipotent arm was miraculously stretched forth to aid them in this fortunate conflict. I fervently rejoice that since your Eminence shares the most arduous cares of the Holy See, you will now participate in all its triumphs and glories.

To His Holiness Pope Innocent.

June 16, 1646.

At the moment when great perils menaced this poor kingdom, the arms and aids sent by your Holiness occasioned the destruction of almost the whole Puritan army in Ulster. I cannot in the midst of such triumphant rejoicings refrain from prostrating myself at the feet of your Holiness, to lay before you the forty flags and the great standard taken from the enemies of Christ. Permit me while humbly kneeling before you, to triumph in being a minister of your

Holiness, and that even these extreme confines of Christianity should now resound with applauses at your blessed name.

Permit me likewise to give utterance to my ardent desire that the trophies of your Pontificate may be even greater at the other extreme of the world, in your warfare against the forces of the Ottomans. I humbly kiss your holy feet and pray that the Divine Goodness may long spare the life of your Holiness, and with this constant prayer I am, &c., &c.

ACCOUNT OF THE BATTLE IN ULSTER BETWEEN THE CATHOLICS AND THE SCOTCH.

Limerick, June 16th.

When the two Generals, Owen Roe and Phelim O'Neill, had been reconciled by the good offices of the Nuncio, they joined their forces and encamped on the confines of Leinster. Owen O'Neill hearing that the Scotch under Colonel Monroe were in the county of Tyrone, determined to advance towards them; and having given orders that every soldier should carry provisions for sixteen days he marched forward, and advanced sixty miles into Ulster.

The enemy hearing of the intention of the Catholics to move towards the city of Armagh, wasted the country through which they were to pass, and at last arrived within a mile of their outposts at a place called Benburb, on Friday the 5th of the present month, when both armies took up their positions with great skill. The Scotch had ten regiments of infantry and fifteen companies of horse, followed by 1,500 carts carrying ammunition and baggage, and five pieces of cannon for each company. Our forces consisted of nearly 5,000 infantry and eight troops of horse only, which enhances the valour and skill of the generals, the courage of the soldiers and the miracle of the victory. The first preparations on the part of the Catholics deserve notice. The whole army confessed, and Owen O'Neill with the other generals piously partook of the holy sacrament; the testimonials of their confession were given by the hands of O'Neill to one of the generals of the Observantines deputed by the Nuncio to the spiritual care of the army, who after a short exhortation pronounced the Apostolic benediction, and instantly calling on the name of His Holiness, they rushed to the conflict.

The Scotch cannon opened the battle, but after many rounds only one Catholic soldier was killed. Hand to hand they fought for four hours with such valour that it was impossible to know which side had the advantage, although the Catholics besides being fewer in number, had the disadvantage of the sun and wind in their faces; this last however, as if by a miracle, began to fall soon after the commencement of the battle. At length the general perceiving that the Scotch were about to retire, and assuring his troops that retreat must be fatal to the enemy he gave the order to charge, promising them certain victory. "I," he exclaimed, "aided by God, and the good augury of the benediction which we have just received, will go before you all; and let the man who refuses to follow me remember that here he deserted his leader." At these words a universal cheer rose from the army, and the colonels all dismounting in order to cut off their return, the whole body rushed forward with incredible ferocity.

The Catholic horse broke the opposing squadron, and having come to pikes and swords the Puritans began to give way disordered and confounded, so that at last they were dispersed or remained dead on the field; even every common soldier on our side being satiated with blood and plunder. Those killed on the field have been counted to the number of 3,243.

It is impossible to know how many were killed in flight, but as the slaughter continued for two days after the battle it is certain that of the infantry not one escaped; of the cavalry but few remain, and baggage, cannon, stores, tents, all were taken; General Monroe fled wounded, and his hat sword and cloak were found upon the field; twenty-one officers only are prisoners all the rest were killed.

Of our troops seventy only were killed, amongst them an Ulster gentleman who served as a volunteer; only one hundred are wounded, among whom is Colonel Farrell, who was struck on the shoulder while signalizing himself by incredible bravery.

The whole army recognises this victory as from God, every voice declares that not they, but the Apostolic money and provisions have brought forth such great fruits. Every one slaughtered his adversary, and Sir Phelim O'Neill, who bore himself most bravely when asked by the colonels for a list of his prisoners, swore that his regiment had not one, as he had ordered his men to kill them all without distinction. The annals of the history of this Island show that at no period has a greater defeat and loss of life been sustained by any enemy; and that 400 years ago, only one equally crushing had been sustained by the Scotch. On reviewing the whole affair from the beginning to the end, one can see nothing to find fault with in its management, either in judgment or foresight; and even envy can impute no failure or imprudence either to officers or men. The enemy's army was to have been joined by Tyrconnel's Horse and 2,500 Infantry, (which however did not arrive in time) and to have marched immediately upon Kilkenny; a resolution which we discovered from letters found upon Viscount Montgomery, General of the cavalry one of our prisoners, who has since confessed to the whole and has shown where the troops were to have been quartered. This, more than all the rest makes the goodness of Providence more wonderfully apparent towards the followers of its Holy Faith.

On the evening of Saturday the 13th news and confirmation of the victory arrived in Limerick and Father O'Hartigan conveyed to the Nuncio thirty-two ensigns and the great standard of the cavalry : Monsignor then ordered that public thanks should be offered up in the following manner :—

The succeeding day at 4 o'clock P.M. the trophies were brought in procession from the Church of St. Francis where they had been deposited, preceded by all the militia of Limerick armed with muskets; next came the Ensigns, borne by the nobles of the city. The Nuncio followed with the Archbishop of Cashel and the Bishops of Limerick, Clonfert and Ardfert, and after them came the Supreme Council with the Prelates and Magistrates in their robes of State. The people were collected in the streets and at the windows and as soon as the trophy arrived at the Cathedral, the Te Deum was sung from the music of the Nuncio, who after the customary prayers gave a solemn benediction. The morning after high mass was performed *pro gratiarum actione*, sung by the Dean of Fermo in presence of the same Bishops and Magistrates. These prayers it is hoped will procure from Divine Goodness a happy sequel to this victory as it is said that General O'Neill is marching towards Tyrconnell's army, and all true Catholics wait on the will of the all-perfect God, knowing that He will listen when they implore Him with faithful hearts and guided by the Supreme Pastor and Director of Souls, &c., &c.

To CARDINAL PAMPHILI.
                    Limerick, June 20th, 1646.

No one here doubts that considering the circumstances and the time the victory gained was miraculous, and that therefore, according to the decrees of God our joy will surely be tempered by some trial—this trial comes in the new and apparent danger that the Supreme Council will conclude a peace more disgraceful and more doubtful than ever, and of which I now proceed to give your Eminence some particulars.

You must know then that after the 1st of May the period

assigned for the publication of both the political and ecclesiastical peace. The Ormonde faction, despite the complete change in the King's affairs and not less in those of the Earl of Glamorgan, and also the hope of the arrival of Sir Kenelm Digby, have never ceased to press on the conclusion and publication of the articles drawn up by the Marquis, and (as since discovered) signed on the 28th of March by our Commissioners, who went at that time to Dublin. Under pretext of the present miserable state of the country they palliate this conduct, and the affair has been patched up under the name of a private league with the Marquis to draw him over to resist the common enemy; suppressing or tacitly assuming the clause by which he was to be made generalissimo of the kingdom, his adherents to hold all the principal offices, the Marquis of Clanricarde for example, the lieutenancy, Castlehaven to be general of the cavalry, and so on through the others. We saw indications of this promised authority particularly in Connaught, where Clanricarde who had joined us has done nothing, and will not move without a commission from the Marquis. Disgusted with such a mode of proceeding, I wrote the two letters from Kilkenny of which I sent your Eminence copies, one on the 27th April, the other on the 5th of May, and made two speeches in which I laboured to convince the Council that even if Ormonde did wish to unite with the Confederates against the Scotch, no league should have been made under the name of a peace when the King's power had so much declined as to render uncertain even the authority of the Viceroy; nor when His Majesty had published a declaration against Glamorgan which rendered his promised concessions impossible. In another speech I showed them how they might have treated with the Marquis without incurring any risk for the Catholic religion, which is the principal object of all our negotiations. Even after t is I was not satisfied that I had done my whole duty; and suspecting

R

that my letters would not meet with much attention, as is always the case with this Supreme Council when they contain matter displeasing to them, I resolved although at much personal inconvenience, to come to Limerick and hasten the preparations which I trust Divine Providence will not suffer to be made in vain. On the arrival of Colonel Barry and of George Hamilton, Ormonde's Commissioners, it was precipitately determined to publish the old political articles, and in order to give some colour to them amongst the Church party, also the concessions made through Glamorgan without the smallest regard to their invalidity. I therefore sent the paper (marked A) to the Council, including the protest (signed B) which was drawn up and subscribed by me and all the other ecclesiastics in February; insisting that they should wait for the originals of the treaty concluded between His Holiness and the Queen of England; this document I had kept by me, determined not to bring it forward except in case of absolute necessity, notwithstanding the accusations and subterfuges which were resorted to then.

This protest put the whole Council and Committee into the greatest confusion, and a violent altercation arose with two of the bishops who were present. They immediately determined however to give me satisfaction in writing, and it was publicly announced and by every one of them, that nothing should be done without the advice of the Nuncio. Nevertheless on the evening of the 13th the very day I received this answer, Nicholas Plunket and Geoffry Brown came to me to take leave and kiss my hand; saying that they were going to Dublin to take the answer to the proposals brought by the Marquis's commissioners. At this announcement I confess it appeared to me necessary to change the courteous tone and bearing I had hitherto maintained in all my proceedings. I therefore replied that since they had acted without any consideration for my opinion, and had sent me their reply too late even to read it, I should have nothing to do with the treaty, nor even give them my blessing on their journey; adding that I should take the steps which the dignity of my office demanded, and hoping that they would at last see to their cost, that they had not treated with the accustomed deference the minister of His Holiness, towards whom all Christian sovereigns testify the utmost respect; and hereupon I dismissed them. They departed in evident confusion, and the same evening Plunket had to go to his bed and still keeps it, attacked as I hear by fever; the other reported my words to the Council who on being made acquainted with my opinion, and also by the letter marked "C" which I sent the following morning, acknowledged the error of which they had been guilty. Then came eight of the Council with Secretary Belling to explain to me the necessity they imagine themselves to be under to publish this peace. Many reasons were brought forward; most of them based on fears of the King's future proceedings, and the danger of his uniting with the Scotch and the Parliament to the detriment of Ireland. They then attempted to mask the nature of the treaty showing by many arguments that it was not a true peace but merely the semblance of one, which they called a union for the common benefit; they likewise magnified to the utmost the Ecclesiastical conditions, declaring that if only one of them was touched they would all be ready again to take up arms against the Marquis. It seemed to me however that my replies silenced them completely; since I showed them without hesitation and with the greatest freedom, that our present necessities were not by any means so great as they imagined; that treaties with England were uncertain and perhaps far from being concluded, and that the union with the Marquis even if it succeeded could avail them nothing. Finally I assured them that it was the merest vanity to boast that after having raised the Marquis above their own heads, they could ever turn their arms against him in case of his failing to observe the Catholic conditions, since they trembled before him now, though he could exercise no authority and was actually in want of their money. All this your Eminence will find expressed at greater length in my reply to their address, which I send with their proposal and with some marginal notes to it where it appears to me to touch some points with but little judgment. The effect of my opposition was this, that Brown's instructions were entirely changed, that he has been sent to Dublin to find out the intentions of the Marquis and to inform him that until we are made acquainted with the King's wishes and determinations, it will be impossible to come to any conclusion. A deputation was sent to inform me of this proceeding and I only hope they are not deceiving me. The Earl of Glamorgan having repeatedly declared that he does not wish his articles brought forward without a new and legal authority from the King; it is intolerable that this faction contrary to the wish of their own leader should insist on publishing the articles; and under a subtle pretext too of the law of England, which forbids the King to revoke a concession once made, hoping thereby to throw dust in the eyes of His Holiness and the other Sovereigns, and make them believe that the interest of religion was not neglected when the political articles were published without those concerning the Faith. On the 13th July (old style) the truce will be at an end, and if the commissioner now in Dublin cannot procure a prolongation of it, we shall soon be in the same difficulties as before. I confess that I have with all possible devices delayed this peace for eight months, but now that the hope of seeing Digby has vanished and the time assigned by His Holiness in the articles having expired, my powers of invention fail me and I have no spirit left for further opposition. Nevertheless as in the cause of our holy religion, the more human strength fails, the more does hope in the Divine increase, so I, with confidence equal to our wants await some immediate and unlooked for aid from the Blessed God. I am certain that if I could obtain a considerable sum of money, I could reduce the greater part of the country to obedience to the will of His Holiness, and this I say, not to do violence to the prudent determination of the Holy Father, but merely to represent the pure truth according to my duty as his faithful minister.

With humble respects to your Eminence,

&c., &c.

To THE SAME (IN CIPHER).

Limerick, June 20th.

The union between the King and the Scotch suffices for Ormonde's last excuse for not proceeding against them, and also for applying to his own use the money granted him by the Council. But worse than this, it is more than suspected that he is actually in league with the Scotch, and was either an accomplice or consented to their design of marching on Kilkenny, which, if it be true, proves that his hatred to religion and to me personally still exists, although he dissembles both the one and the other. I have sent my Auditor into Ulster to congratulate the General for me, to make presents to the officers, succour the wounded, and animate the army to go through the remainder of the enterprise. I also desired him privately to inform himself fully if there are grounds to believe what is said, and I suspect, that the soldiers from one of the Ormonde's fortresses were at the battle in the enemy's ranks, that he sent surgeons to tend the wounded, and many similar acts which if they be not false, will greatly tend as Your Eminence will judge, to perfect a union amongst the Confederates by taking away every excuse for fawning any longer on this man.

To the Queen of England.

Limerick, June 20th, 1646.

The departure of the new agent whom the Confederates are despatching to the most Christian Court reminds me to allow no longer time to pass without recalling to Your Majesty's remembrance my deep devotion to your person. He is so well aware of my devotion to the Catholic religion and obedience to the King, that he can assure Your Majesty of my diligence in trying to secure the well-being of both. I shall consider myself the most fortunate minister the Holy See has ever had, if God permits me to combine these two objects, and to foster amongst this people a greater love of religion, and an absolute fidelity to their Sovereign.

I am Your Majesty's faithful and humble servant,

&c., &c.

From the Camp at Bunratty to Cardinal Pamphili.

July 3rd, 1646.

Commissioner Brown, who was lately in Dublin, writes from Kilkenny that the Council of Dublin wish to make no peace at present with the Catholics, until the will and pleasure of the King be known; but however, that Ormonde is of a different opinion, and that he will sign a new truce till the 13th August. He adds that after the victory at Benburb many Puritans left Dublin; some because they feared for their lives, and others to see if they could return with fresh aid against Ireland. Every day proves more strongly that this peace is impossible, and that the question must be decided by arms. Great alarm is testified at this prospect, because many believe that the King is as it were imprisoned and unable to dispose of himself, and they are convinced too that the Scotch have united with the English to the great detriment of Ireland, and believe our affairs to be irretrievable.

The necessity for a Protector is already spoken of, and there is no doubt that His Holiness is uppermost in men's minds, but they fear that his aid is too far off, and that their needs are too great for the Holy See to supply.

After him they would incline to France rather than to Spain, with the assent however of His Holiness, and this not from natural inclination which leans towards Spain, but from policy, as France has always assisted the King, while the Parliament party stand better with Spain.

It will be necessary for me to be able to signify clearly His Holiness's intentions on this subject, and what aid we may hope from the Holy See; I have as yet merely said generally without going into particulars that if they continue the war for the sake of religion, they shall have further assistance. I hope that all the Confederates will at last confess how they have been entrapped by Ormonde. Some do confess it already, and since this may bring about a closer union amongst themselves I do all I can to insinuate it. Fearing that the siege of Bunratty would be abandoned by the troops owing to their want of pay, I have come to the camp and brought all the money I had left and some of my own also to lend to them, and I will not leave the place until I see a certainty of success or else that victory is despaired of.

To Cardinal Mazarin.

July 3rd, 1646.

The uncertainties and decline of the Royal party keeps this Catholic island without hope of making peace with His Majesty, and the threats of the Parliament fill us with fear. I tell the people how much they may hope from the powerful protection of the Most Christian King, and from your Eminence's benign disposition towards the interests of religion. I feel moved therefore to address myself to you in the name of every one here, and beseech of your Eminence to look upon this kingdom with the pious love of a Cardinal of the Holy Church, and free it from the imminent danger with which it is menaced, especially from Scotland. And most Eminent Lord I do not see in the whole earth to-day a work more useful to the Church, or one more illustrious for you than to strengthen these Catholics in their determination never to turn away from their God; and therefore it seems only my duty to propose to your Eminence a work no less holy than great. I will add no more, as I am certain that you already see all that can be suggested by this prayer, and that to protect the Holy Faith you will do more even than I can desire.

To the Grand Duke of Tuscany.

Bunratty, July 4th, 1646.

Your Highness still continues to favour my brother, and to honour him by placing him in so important an office as that in the service of Her Serene Highness the Princess of Inspruck; hence my great and constant desire that he should prove himself worthy of so much goodness is needless, as the favours he receives far surpass any that he can possibly merit.

The great distance at which I am, has obliged me to offer my thanks to your Highness thus tardily; and I should fear to appear wanting in respect did I not know that your Highness would be assured how deeply my obligations to you would be felt, and that the favour shown to my brother is as profoundly acknowledged as though I had been thus honoured in my own person. May the blessed God grant your Highness long life and tranquillity, and prosper all you undertake for the benefit of your subjects, and I remain

Your Highness's most humble servant.

&c., &c.

To Cardinal Pamphili (in cipher A).

July 7, 1646.

Knowing that the King had sent a confidant of Glamorgan's to Dublin with friendly letters for the Earl, and that he had been detained there more than two months by the Marquis of Ormonde to prevent him (such is the belief) from delivering them in person according to his orders; I took the opportunity to persuade the Earl to send his brother to the King with a copy of the treaty signed by the Pope and the Queen, that for once I might know clearly his Majesty's real intentions, whether the treaty had ever been laid before him, and what is his real opinion on the matter, and thus arrive at an understanding of the artifices and evasions of those two Digbys.

We were just deciding on this mission when the bearer of the said letter arrived, having gone first to Waterford to meet Digby the Protestant, and thence to Limerick, where he delivered it. Here is a copy of the letter— " Glamorgan, time does not suffice nor do you require that I should repeat here what I have so often said to you. Therefore in referring you to Digby about the negotiations, I give you the faithful assurance of my friendship for you, which appears to me all the more necessary in this alienation so common amongst us, so that *let what will happen, you cannot doubt but that I shall keep to all the instructions and promises made to you and to the Nuncio.* Undoubtedly and constantly your friend.

" CHARLES REX."

The under lined words were in cipher. This letter would give me courage to prosecute Glamorgan's mission, if what I write in the added cipher (B), did not make me irresolute in the fear that His Majesty is playing a double part, or is forming some unworthy resolutions, &c.

TO THE SAME (IN CIPHER B.)
7th July, 1646.

The heretic Lord Digby has made it understood in France, that a peace has been concluded here with the King, or that it is in his power to bring it to a conclusion to the satisfaction of all parties, and as this information must be pleasing to the Queen, who perhaps does not care to carry on the negotiation through a Catholic, she has induced Cardinal Mazarin to advance freely 10,000 pistoles in order that Ormonde may be able to fight against the Parliamentarians and on the condition as I understand, that peace is to be made if not already concluded. Hence Digby is expected immediately from Dublin to give an account of his commission.

It is much complained of here, that France has given more money to a heretic on false grounds than she has ever done to this Catholic kingdom in all these years of their real want. I much fear that Digby, owing to the money which he has brought will do what he likes: as money governs more here than the Supreme Council. At all events we must be prepared for every emergency, &c., &c.

To the Same (in Cipher C.)

From the Camp, July 7, 1646.

A friend of Glamorgan's writes a great deal of news from France, amongst it he gives one article which he says is translated *ad verbum*, from the original which he has seen· "Mr. Digby has had two interviews with the Papal Nuncio in the monastery of the Carthusians, by means of which he hopes to induce the Nuncio who is with you in Ireland, to give up the treaty and is endeavouring by all the means in his power to alienate the Queen from the Irish Nuncio; though it is believed that the Pope will conclude nothing except through this Irish Nuncio." Here ends the letter. This news makes me sure of the intentions of the two Digbys, the heretic Lord Digby having asserted that the Catholic, Sir Kenelm Digby says that the articles of which I told you I had a copy, were not the same as those signed in Rome, and it may be that the Queen will be deceived by this invention; but if it be true as it is said that she has sent Digby back to moderate some of the articles, I do not see why on this account she should turn from me, who have ever laboured most faithfully for her honour and the interests of the King. The greater confidence which they place in the Nuncio of France proceeds perhaps from the hope of obtaining better conditions from one not so well informed; and I must not on this occasion withhold from you my suspicion that the Supreme Council have had a similar idea; since I had frequently pressed on them the necessity of rendering thanks in a particular letter to His Holiness for these articles; this they delayed to do under various pretexts, and now I find they have done it through your Eminence some days ago; on the occasion of the victory in Ulster in a letter to the French Nuncio sent without consulting me. Father Scarampi excited their displeasure by speaking out with great freedom, and as I am constrained by their own conduct to do the same, it is no wonder that this same council and faction have begun to feel equal displeasure against me.

To the Same (in Cipher D).

February 8, 1646.

To the preceding cipher I now add that a monk, who arrived in Digby's vessel says that Digby tells him he had received from Monsignor the Nuncio of France a copy of a letter of mine in which I spoke of having delayed the peace; that the Queen had sent to Rome to complain of my having done so, and that she had induced Cardinal Mazarin not to write to me by this opportunity of Digby's coming, nor had she written herself. Supposing all this to be true, though as yet I have no certainty, merely reports, I do not understand by what right Monsignor the Nuncio had shown my letters, or gave a copy of them on so grave a matter; or when he did give it, why he had not explained my reasons for delaying every peace other than that of which I awaited the articles arranged by His Holiness and the Queen so that

I might the better serve her Majesty and the King. This seems perfectly clear from the tenor of the letter of which I enclose a copy to your Eminence, although I suppose Monsignor the Nuncio will have done so himself.

As all this was not explained to the Queen, and she only heard of the delay of the peace, she may have imagined a thousand things which have no foundation. The resident French Envoy has been here at the camp to-day to present letters and to explain his orders to the Supreme Council, and his having brought none for me confirms what I have told you about the letters; in a long conversation with me he did not say one word either of the Nuncio's letter, or of any impediment on my part to the peace, neither did he touch on the Queen's opinion. It is true we stopped at two propositions relating to the peace, one, the necessary removal of all those persons who desire that religious rites here should appear in the same splendour as in Rome, because these things cannot be obtained all at once; the other that the Marquis of Ormonde deserves to be held in the greatest consideration and esteem; and here I recognise that these are the sentiments of France, and of those who already begin to domineer and to make changes in everything. So soon as the most Christian King begins to act, I shall proceed advisedly, and perhaps there may be time for me to receive more particular instructions from your Eminence, while I can occupy myself without loss of time with other matters spiritual and temporal.

To the Same (in cipher).

July 17, 1646.

The substance of Digby's accusations against me may be classed under the three following heads, so far at least as I can learn from a conversation between him and Nicholas Plunket. First, that I have disobeyed the Pope in delaying the peace by bringing forward articles falsely alleged to have been drawn up at Rome; and thereby have injured the Queen by publicly declaring that these articles are more favourable than all others to the Catholic religion. Second, that I have done all this to favour the Spaniards, and to give them possesion of this kingdom. Third, that if I continue to act in this manner, I shall be recalled at once by the Holy See. This is such a deep mass of falsehood without any imaginable foundation, that I have resolved unless your Eminence otherwise commands, to pass it by in silence. This same Digby contrived that his Secretary, an English Catholic, under pretext of a visit, should try to find out if I would receive him; I replied that the ministers of His Holiness receive and listen to every one; and therefore if he should come and touch on these topics, I shall answer him as seems best at the time. I cannot but suspect that the other Digby, the Catholic, has been the cause of all this by not forwarding the articles in his hands, and that it is all for the better that he returned to Rome. I have besides heard that Digby says the Queen instantly rejected the conditions subscribed by your Eminence, and was displeased that I had named her. Every day this error, to call it no worse, becomes more glaring, since if Digby had but condescended to write me one line I should neither have spoken of the articles nor hinted at their existence as your Eminence commanded, &c., &c.

To THE SAME (IN CIPHER).

July 17.

I must not omit to inform your Eminence that Owen O'Neill as well as Preston after their victories in the different provinces secretly offered to march on Dublin if I wished it; I was greatly tempted to encourage them to do it, but as His Most Christian Majesty had begun to take a part in the negotiations I thought it better to decline the proposal, lest it should be said that I had superseded

Ormonde without the consent of the Supreme Council; and also lest I should cause any new disagreement between His Holiness and that Crown. It will be a great favour to let me know your Eminence's opinion because, even if I have done wrong now, I shall have your advice to guide me in the future.

To the Same (in cipher).

July 17th.

I do not see that I have anything to answer in the ciphers from your Eminence of the 25th of March, 1st and 23rd of April, and 6th of May, since affairs have taken altogether a different direction as you will have seen from my despatches.

The King is treated as a prisoner, therefore no one can negotiate with him, nor can he keep any of the promises he made to Rome. Glamorgan has no more authority than credit; so that we can only wait to see whether the King of France will interfere in earnest, and favour the cause of religion as he did last year; but on this point I cannot say more than I have done, because the Commissioners have not returned from Dublin, nor have I seen Digby who it appears manages everything.

To the Same.

July 19th.

The success in Connaught obtained by the supplies of His Holiness, consists in the taking of the strong castle of Roscommon which the enemy gave up on favourable conditions, and the defeat of their cavalry while storming the castle, where 350 horses were killed and but a very few of ours. In the province there is no place of any consideration but Sligo, it is near the sea and was taken by the enemy last year, when I was in Paris. This, with several towns of minor importance, we expect to have in our possession before many days, if we can only find money with which to keep the soldiers quiet and united.

The taking of Bunratty is of no small consideration to Munster and to the City of Limerick; and although the money employed was not sent direct from Rome, I had at all events lent some of my own, and having given in person and otherwise constant assistance during the siege, the people recognise it as an Apostolic undertaking of the same kind as all the rest. Ten standards have been taken from the English, and will be carried in triumph when the Te Deum is sung, as was done on the former occasions. Your Eminence may be assured that the safety of the kingdom and the success of the campaign are to be attributed solely to His Holiness' aid and protection, without which the war could not have been begun this year, and we should at the present moment have been involved in endless misery, since it would have been impossible for us to have prevented the Scotch army from pouring into Leinster. Whence you may perceive what money well spent can do in this country, and that if more were sent us, not less than the complete liberation of the whole country might be expected. I pray the Blessed God that our future success may equal the present, and that the glory of His Holiness may serve as a constant stimulus to these people to cling to their religion, and after it to their Prince, now so much in need of help.

To THE SAME.

Limerick, July 19th.

To-day, in the full Senate of Limerick I presented His Holiness' Brief addressed to the magistrates of the city. It was received with all due consideration and reverence, and I consider it most providential to have received it at this moment, since from the long siege of Bunratty and for other reasons, some symptoms of alienation between the city and Council were beginning to show themselves; but I hope that

His Holiness' paternal remembrance and favour will now unite them more closely than ever as I insisted it should do. I took the opportunity of entreating the citizens as I had done the Supreme Council, to forbid the public preaching of heretical ministers in this city within certain ancient ruins of a monastery of St. Augustine; a desecration I have always felt bitterly, and of which there is not another example in any of these Confederate towns. For this purpose I have availed myself of the late victory and of the Brief, assuring them that they could offer no thanks more meritorious to God for the one, or more grateful to his Holiness for the other, than the removal of this scandal. There will be many difficulties to be overcome on account of the number of heretical professors who reside in the city; yet God will perhaps reveal some way to obtain our desire. I reserve till another time writing of the second Brief sent to me by your Eminence; having met with some difficulty in delivering it, upon which I must first ponder from the respect due to so signal a favour. Meanwhile I make my humble reverence to your Eminence,

&c.

To the Same.

Waterford, August 3rd, 1646.

Having found on my arrival at Waterford a vessel ready to sail for France, I send your Eminence duplicates of the two last despatches, and have only to add that I have convoked for this week a meeting of the clergy to deliberate upon the pending treaty, and to acquaint myself with the general opinion upon the subject. When the meeting is over, I will give your Eminence an account of the whole state of affairs, some great change being I am convinced at hand.

To the Same (in cipher).

August 3rd, 1646.

When the peace was proposed in Dublin the Heretics would not consent to it; it was twice rejected by two-thirds of the meeting who protested against it. But when Ormonde declared that he would publish it in spite of all opposition, they were forced against their will to sign it, and it was to be proclaimed last Saturday. The beginning is all confusion: may God help us with His Holy hand.

Further Report of the Churches in this Kingdom.

August 11th, 1646.

I have nothing to add concerning the church of Tuam, as the Bishop of Clonfert from my six months experience, appears to me quite worthy of his elevation to it.

In case that His Holiness approves of this change, I am of opinion that it will be for the advantage of the province to give the church of Clonfert to Dr. Walter Lynch, Chief Vicar of Tuam; a learned man, an eminent preacher, and possessed of much authority in the country, most ardent for the Catholic cause, and supported by many of the clergy and laity. I do not see any reason for removing Dr. Plunket from the See of Ardagh, because of the one alleged that he is not a native of the province, as perhaps it will be well for His Holiness to begin to break through this custom, since it will give him more freedom of choice in his elections. And on the other hand Dr. Plunket's brother must be considered more than ever, since he has sustained to the utmost, the Catholic party in the Supreme Council.

I am of opinion that no provision should be made at present for the Coadjutorship of Dublin; as Tyrrel shows himself every day more lukewarm towards the church, and his friendship with the Marquis of Ormonde has given rise to many suspicions; besides this we may learn something of his qualifications from France where he is at present. At all events it is plain that *that* church should be filled by the first subject in the kingdom.

For the Bishopric of Finbar, I can suggest no one better than Andrew Lynch, of whom I have good reports from everyone.

The Bishop of Emly lies insensible in his bed and must therefore have a Coadjutor; and of this office no one can be more worthy than Terence O'Brien, who besides has a claim for some remuneration from the Catholic cause as the mandate of the clergy will testify. For the church of Cork, as I before wrote, there cannot be a better choice than Robert Barry.

I must have a little more time to think before I propose anyone for the church of Dromore, as Oliver Darcy does not show the constancy I could desire and I must seek for information concerning him from others.

I am confirmed in my opinion that the Bishop of Elphin does not require a Coadjutor, because he appeared at the last Council in perfect health and good spirits, therefore an assistant is unnecessary.

Father Anthony Geoghegan, has the good will of the whole kingdom in a wonderful degree, and will therefore be necessarily chosen for the church of Clonmacnoise; and for the church of Kildare, I can confirm all I have written concerning Father Everhard.

If Barry is nominated to Cork, I should propose Father Boethius Egan, General of the Franciscans for the See of Ross. He has served me as Vicar-General of the Exercises to my great satisfaction, and has served the Holy See with great merit.

I do not speak of the dismemberment of the Church of Cloyne, as I mentioned it before, because perhaps His Holiness will not at present come to any decision on the subject.

I do not think that in these nominations the proportion

of Regulars is too great; and indeed we cannot make it less as the nobles join the Regulars more frequently than any other Order.

The Bishop of Meath a very old prelate, asks for his Coadjutor, his nephew, a man of every good qualification; I think the Bishop's death may soon be expected, therefore his merits will I am sure be held in the greatest consideration by His Holiness.

Report of the Peace Concluded.

Waterford, 16th August, 1646.

The peace lately proclaimed between the Confederates and the Marquis of Ormonde, was in reality concluded by the Ormonde faction in August of last year; when the clergy declared themselves satisfied with the concessions of Glamorgan to the Catholic religion. Its publication was deferred at that time on account of the expected arrival of the Nuncio; each party ashamed that he should find it already published, or else hoping to secure his interest. After his arrival it appears that the agreement was dissolved, partly because of his objections to it, but still more on account of the imprisonment of Glamorgan in Dublin, which greatly changed the opinions of the Confederates. The Earl's liberation taking place about a month after; the treaty would have been then concluded but for the unanimous decision of the Council which had been summoned on the Earl's sudden imprisonment, and but for the Nuncio's announcement that conditions had been already subscribed in Rome; on this, it was agreed to suspend all further negotiations until the following May. From that time to this, the originals of those articles have never arrived, new impediments have arisen, such as the fall of the King, and his passing into the hands of the Scotch; the irresolution of the Marquis in these great changes; and his doubts which side he should join, since it is well known that more than once he thought of joining the Puritans. In the month of June however, he at last determined to join the Catholics; and announced his intentions by two Commissioners whom he sent to Limerick; but again this measure was delayed by the arrival of letters from the King, commanding the Marquis to make no terms with his rebellious Irish subjects. Whilst these letters seemed to quench every spark of hope, the unexpected return of Lord Digby from France with money and assurances from the Queen of England that no faith was to be placed in orders purporting to come from the King, whilst he was detained in the hands of his enemies, determined the Marquis to satisfy the impatience of his faction by publishing the treaty on the 1st of August in Dublin.

These vacillations and intrigues whilst they bind his partisans more closely, have on the contrary, always excited the suspicion of all the rest of the kingdom; so that since the publication of the negotiation two classes in particular have evidently changed their minds—these are the clergy and the more ancient nobles of the island, who, differing on some points, unite in a common devotion to the Catholic religion. The nobles believe that the power which the Marquis acquires over the forces by the authority of the articles, will act prejudicially on all who do not hold to his party; and if they had a leader they would without a doubt combine to kindle a civil war. The clergy finding no mention made of religious affairs, fear that the dominant Protestants will soon deprive them again of the churches and of the public exercise of their religion; and with these ecclesiastics are united the most zealous towns of the kingdom. Further, the whole province of Ulster, and many of the Barons of Munster, consider themselves especially aggrieved, because, although by the terms of the peace the adherents of the Marquis are all to be reinstated in their possessions; no mention whatever is made of them. It is generally believed that this so-called peace will probably be the cause of even greater tumults than ever, and, instead of extinguishing war, will give rise to one perhaps even fiercer than the last.

The clergy when assembled at Waterford to consult on some affairs relative to the National Council, began also to debate on this peace, and on receiving from the Supreme Council the original articles, not seen till then by the greater number of them, or even by Monsignor the Nuncio, determined to write instantly to the Council and to all the corporations, begging of them to suspend its publication for a few days till they could maturely deliberate and weigh the securities held out for their religion. After this, Nicholas Plunket and Patrick Darcy, two members of the Supreme Council sent by that body, were heard at the same meeting. They came to talk over the clergy, but after all did nothing, and only said that the Council intended to include under a general article all the concessions made by the Earl of Glamorgan relative to religion, as well as all that the King would grant of his favour to any other Prince whatsoever; that even if the confederation were dissolved, the Government changed, and that the Marquis of Ormonde should have power over this army, the Confederates would nevertheless remain bound by a secret article giving them power to summon the General Assembly, and to take up arms if the above conditions respecting religion should ever be violated. This is the substance of an English document presented to the Nuncio on his departure for Limerick, and of which a copy translated into Latin is enclosed.

The clergy seeing that no express mention was made of the churches or their property, and that they had no security for their future maintenance except empty words and promises, or the useless alternative of convoking the General Assembly, and taking up arms against the Marquis when he would be powerful enough to direct everything at his pleasure, came to the conclusion that the Catholic religion was in greater danger than ever. They also unanimously agreed, that in virtue of the first oath taken by the Confederates, a copy of which is herewith sent, all those who had concluded this peace or adhered to it in the future will have committed perjury, and will be considered to have done so because they had sworn to uphold with all their strength the True Faith, and to do nothing directly or indirectly to injure it. Before coming to this conclusion, however, they wrote a second letter to the Council, of which a copy is also enclosed, in which they fully expressed the sentiments of all, and proposed two alternatives by which a rupture might be avoided. First, to suspend the publication of the treaty till an answer should be received from His Holiness, and for this a courier should be expressly despatched; or second, to convoke the Assembly when they might be able to say that all that had been done was with the consent of the whole kingdom.

It appears that the Council either were offended by these two letters or despised them, since they delayed their reply for several days; and in the meantime as the herald who came from the Marquis to proclaim the peace at Waterford had been sent back, and there were some disturbances in Kilkenny, the son of Viscount Mountgarret collected some mounted soldiers from the neighbourhood to strike terror into the city; on the other hand the Bishop summoned the clergy, exposed the holy sacrament, and calling together the few members of the Council then in the city, made in their presence a strong protest against any disturbances in the cause of religion, but recommending zeal for the Holy Faith to all who heard him; two of the Council replied by renewing their oath, and protesting they were more than ever in favour of the Catholic religion. But not the less was the peace actually proclaimed the very next day in the presence of the Mayor and the magistrates only, the people not choosing to appear whereupon the Bishop threatened an interdict, but there was not time to publish it. From all this it may be gathered that affairs are in a desperate condition, and that the treaty has been promulgated more in the fashion of war than of peace.

Monsignor the Nuncio read to the congregation all the notes, letters, documents, and protests that had passed between him and the Council since March, in order that every one might see how much he disapproved of such a peace, how many alterations he had proposed that no injury might accrue to religion; copies of three only of these are again transmitted, viz.: of the 3rd May, and of 10th and 25th June, as in these three, almost all the others are included.

It has likewise highly displeased the clergy to observe that the peace was concluded immediately after the supplies of His Holiness were exhausted; and that after the declaration of the Council and Commissioners, that they would do nothing without the approbation and consent of the Nuncio, they have done everything against his advice, and what they consider still worse, that after signing the peace of the 28th March, they persisted in saying it had never been concluded.

The Council passed a sudden resolution which has not yet been carried out, to send some one to Rome to justify their measures. The clergy will do the same, to explain their reasons for not consenting to the peace, and to entreat of His Holiness not to abandon the Catholic party. From the first messenger you will hear the motives which the Council pretend have swayed them; from the second, all that the clergy have done up to this period, and how they intend to proceed for the future, as they are resolved never to acknowledge this peace, from which they apprehend much danger and violence on the part of the Protestants. It is believed that a large number of the nobles will join them, and several even of this Council, who already feel some remorse; we have yet to see what many of the cities will do, and also the two Captains O'Neill and Preston with their armies, who might be a great addition to our party if they should declare for a safe peace. Therefore it is thought that a new Catholic Confederation may now spring up, more resolute and more powerful than the first, and therefore worthy of the protection of His Holiness and the other Catholic princes.

To His Holiness.

Waterford, August 16th, 1646.

Notwithstanding the happy course of the victories obtained by the supplies and protection of your Holiness, the Supreme Council have chosen to publish under the pretext of want of aid, the peace signed and concluded some time ago. The clergy finding in it no security for the Catholic religion, despatch with all haste to the feet of your Holiness the Dean of Fermo, my auditor, to notify their resolution not to countenance it in any way, and to implore more than ever the patronage and protection of the Holy See. For what touches my own office, I humbly supplicate your Holiness not to think so much of the evil that a few may work in the island, as of the undying resolution of the many and greater part, to sustain with their life and blood the free and secure exercise of the Catholic religion. With me they prostrate themselves before your Holiness, and kissing your sacred feet, pray unceasingly for long life and prosperity to your Holiness.

To Cardinal Pamphili.

September 12th, 1646.

Since the departure of the Dean of Fermo, the state of the country has daily become more and more disturbed. The clergy, for whom Generals O'Neill and Preston have declared, and who have been, or will be joined by an immense party, will soon be in a position to form a new government, and a new Catholic Confederation. This will probably include the greater number of the nobility, and will suffice to curb the Viceroy and his adherents, who already stand nearly alone. The Marquis came to Kilkenny, and thence proceeded to hold a general convocation at Cashel, but all the towns on his route shut their gates; and Cashel itself, supported by the captain of the Munster cavalry, declared for the clergy. No one knows what steps the Marquis of Ormonde will now take, as the regiments, composed of his relations and dependents are all flying. The old Council and the Ormonde faction are in despair; they are preparing documents and appeals against the declaration of the clergy, promise large remuneration to every one, threaten the rebellious with punishment, and have even gone so far as to calumniate me. If the clergy however had money, your Eminence may be assured they would soon put down this faction, and purge the kingdom of heresy. Their object is to defend the Catholic religion, and to aid their King and country by a secure peace. The clergy have not failed to propose new arrangements and conditions, and the opposite party have sent commissioners here to declare themselves willing to admit all that is demanded; but for this they can give no security, since not only the Marquis acknowledges that he has no power, but the Council itself is already dissolved; yet they would have the clergy trust to the word of a Protestant, hence there appears little hope of any adjustment. Father Scarampi is now at Limerick, sent there by the clergy, but he is at a loss what to do, in consequence of the dissensions amongst the citizens who are of Ormonde's party. I send this short account of the present state of affairs by a French vessel about to sail. The Marquis thought of retiring to Kilkenny and fortifying himself there, but the people would not allow it, and yesterday he fled with only six horsemen to Dublin, whence he had set out powerful and triumphant, not fifteen days ago. His flight has raised the spirits of the Catholic party, and many will now declare themselves for the clergy, who unceasingly think in conjunction with me, on the best means of advancing the holy faith. The Council is dispersed here and there, and the Commissioners who came here to treat with the clergy do not insist so much now on an answer.

To the Same.

September 12th, '46.

Your Eminence's two letters of the 2nd and 24th of June, with two in cipher have arrived, and I will answer them by a more safe opportunity.

My letters written in March and April, and consigned to the same ship which carried those of Father Scarampi, have I know been received by the Nuncio in France. I cannot therefore understand how neither they nor the duplicates have reached you. Your Eminence will also receive an additional letter in cipher from which you will know the state of affairs, and I feel pretty sure you will have heard that Digby had not then left Paris, nor had he been desired to leave it by any one.

With respect, your Eminence's humble servant.

To the Pope.

Kilkenny, September 21st.

It is many months since the Earl of Glamorgan intended to throw himself at your Holiness's feet, and to inform you not only of the state of this kingdom, but of the means by which your Holiness could at once advance the cause of religion and alleviate the miseries of the King. He was to have set out on his journey at this time, but when the great changes occurred in the affairs of the kingdom, it was thought better that he should remain to give an impetus to the progress we hope for in religious matters. He has therefore sent his brother the Viscount Somerset, in his place, and he will explain to your Holiness all that he would have said, and assure you of his never-failing fidelity to the Apostolic See, a fidelity which has ever been the glory and inheritance of this family. I hope that your Holiness will welcome the Viscount with paternal warmth, and permit him when speaking for his brother, to assure you also of my deep and everlasting gratitude. Kissing your holy feet, I pray that never-ending prosperity may attend you.

To Cardinal Pamphili.

Kilkenny, September 21st, 1646.

This autumn the Earl of Glamorgan was to have prostrated himself before His Holiness, and to have paid his respects to your Eminence. For many months he has been anxious to explain to the Court of Rome the affairs of these kingdoms, and to show how a union might be effected in religious affairs between England and Ireland, by means of the assistance which the King still hopes to obtain. But after the great changes in affairs here, of which your Eminence will have first heard from the Dean of Fermo, the ecclesiastical congregation thought it better to keep the Earl at home to assist the measures in progress for the safety of religion.

The Viscount Somerset, his brother, will therefore undertake the journey in his place; he holds the same opinions as the Earl, and can assure your Eminence better than any one else of the great fidelity of their house to the Apostolic See, which they have shown in the sufferings and losses they have sustained for the Catholic religion. I therefore humbly entreat your Eminence to grant a friendly audience to this nobleman, that you may hear all that is going on in this kingdom; and you will hear at the same time how grateful I am to your Eminence, for devoting me to a service, at once so noble and meritorious as this in which I am now engaged.

Praying for every happiness for your Eminence,

I am, &c., &c.

To the Same (in Cipher).

September 21, 1646.

On the 12th inst. I wrote of all the changes that had taken place in affairs up to that period. After the Marquis had retired to Dublin, he fortified many parts of the city, joined the Parliamentary party, and sent to England for assistance. This step clearly shows the nature of this man's motives in the past; and will prove to the Council on what sort of foundation their peace was built; and this I think will so materially strengthen the Catholic Union, that all his adherents will by degrees be alienated from him.

Negotiations are at an end and we are at open war, while the documents and appeals against the Clergy are seen no more. I did all in my power to have the Ulster army sent at once against Dublin before the Marquis had returned there; but want of cannon and other pretexts brought the General first to Kilkenny, where I came ·four days ago at the request of the citizens. This opportunity lost, we are about to bring the two Generals together and they are to make a combined attempt before assistance can arrive from England; to accomplish this and other matters we only want money, the scarcity of which we do all we can to remedy and I hope soon to have some notable success to report. The old Council, together with the greater number of their adherents have been shut up in this castle of Kilkenny by the Generals, who will I believe send them to different parts of the kingdom. The Bishops and Clergy, now the dominant party, were but one month ago the most despised and depressed. We have made no delay in appointing a new Council which will have power to summon a general Assembly, to carry on the government for the benefit of religion, and to lighten the calamities of the King; neither do I fail in this new state of affairs, to pursue the ends so ardently desired by His Holiness—the establishment of the Faith and the extermination of heresy, which may God grant.

Reasons for accepting the Earl of Glamorgan as Viceroy of Ireland.

To the Dean of Fermo.

Kilkenny, September 25, 1646.

In the present revolution in affairs, the Clergy have in a manner constituted themselves arbiters of affairs in Ireland, and it does not appear to them possible to make any other choice than the Earl of Glamorgan for the office of Viceroy.

1st. Because the attempts to have a Catholic Viceroy appointed, have hitherto been unavailing, and if this succeed it will be the greatest stimulus to religion, which can never perish under a Catholic chief, and it is believed that this one point gained, the rest will follow; while without it, all would have been uncertain and perhaps unattainable. The affection felt for the Earl throughout the country, increases our confidence in him, and our hopes that he will have the approval of His Holiness and the Court of Rome.

2nd. Because the Clergy in the present crisis profess their desire not to injure the King; therefore, not only to show their good faith, but also to silence those who do not credit it; there seems no better choice than the Earl, since it was from His Majesty himself, that he received his powers to treat with the Clergy; and they may therefore be certain that he will be acceptable to the King, who a prisoner in the hands of the Scotch is unable to make any appointment himself. It does not appear that the small private seal attached to the above mentioned powers need present any obstacle, as it is enough that the Clergy and the country have reason to believe it valid, especially in the present state of confusion in government affairs, when small matters are less curiously examined into than when the country is at peace.

3rd. Because all our efforts being directed to introduce a Catholic army into England and Scotland in order to succour the King; no one could be more suitable than Glamorgan who is a staunch Catholic, has correspondence with both countries, and was originally appointed by His Majesty to command the 10,000 infantry promised for his aid in England; and which if God permit will soon be carried out. All these advantages are more than a sufficient answer to those who oppose the Earl simply because he is an Englishman; a nation the Irish have never yet been able to trust; but at this moment and when treating of the security of religion, it is better to choose a man well known to be inclined to peace, rather than an Irishman of whom his countrymen would soon become jealous, and thus throw the whole kingdom again into confusion.

To Cardinal Pamphili (in Cipher).

September 25, 1646.

The aspect of affairs having completely changed; I answer only those questions in your Eminence's cipher of the 20th of May which touch upon points still at issue.

Your Eminence will have seen from my letters, that the light troops were not raised with the money which I brought, and that I have avoided as much as possible exciting any jealousy in these matters; a caution all the more necessary now, since all authority has passed into the hands of the Clergy of whom I am the head. It is evident also that the late Council never had any intention of surprising Dublin; an enterprise which perhaps God has reserved for the present time, that it may be done with a sole aim to His Glory and the propagation of religion.

The priest Leyburn, left this kingdom in great haste for France, where it is probable he has done us many bad offices with the Queen of England and others; because the reports and slanders which Digby the Protestant brought from France of which I advised you, appear very similar to those of Leyburn.

I shall implicitly obey in this matter as in every other,

your commands to await the minutes of the reply I am to make to the King. His Majesty is more strongly guarded, and more looked down upon than ever by the Scotch; but he has just written in most affectionate terms to the Earl of Glamorgan, and always speaks of me; in a preceding letter written in cipher, he said that if God should relieve him from his miseries he would throw himself into our arms, adding that the princes had all deceived him. I believe that the letter itself will be presented to His Holiness by Glamorgan's brother, who is going to Rome as I mentioned before.

I shall with all haste despatch *gratis ubique*, the other documents according to your Eminence's commands; and you may have observed that I was inclined to do this from the first, for the reasons I then explained. On this point Father Scarampi was of a different opinion; he thinks that it will injure my successors if I do not put on a tax, and says that the same sum as that paid in Rome was offered here spontaneously. I thought it better, however, not to delay putting into execution the plan proposed by your Eminence, and I have begun it accordingly.

I render my best thanks to your Eminence for your warning touching the expressions in my first document which seemed to approve of the fidelity of this people to the King; and I shall have greater reason than ever in the present revolution to avail myself of such a record. I am certain that neither the Council nor anyone else observed the words, and if I had made any other excuse than that which I have done, I should only have directed attention to them, when otherwise they would never have been thought of; so under pretext that I had lost the copy of the document, I dexterously obtained the original from the hands of the Secretary, and substituted a copy in which I entirely changed that sentence, I can therefore, positively assure your Eminence that all danger is over.

Should the arms of this new Confederation prosper, it will be more than ever necessary to provide for the Churches since God has so greatly increased the power of the Ecclesiastics. I send to your Eminence by the Dean of Fermo, a new report on the subject, drawn up after deep consideration, and which quite satisfies my conscience that I have done the best for the kingdom. Of Invernizi, we have heard nothing, and it only remains for us to lament his fate. Father Scarampi is going to Waterford to write by a vessel ready to sail, and I shall send these letters in his despatch. Should many letters fail in coming to hand, your Eminence may be assured that the complaints of the French and Spanish agents are much louder; their despatches meeting with many more misfortunes than ours.

To the Grand Duke.

September 25, 1646.

The Viscount Somerset, one of the first noblemen of England, is about to visit the Court of Rome; he is brother to the Earl of Glamorgan, who after materially serving the King of England, is now in Ireland assisting those who have at heart the interests of His Majesty and of the Catholic religion. Your Highness may, I think, like to see this nobleman, who besides high qualities of his own, possesses those of his family; he will inform your Highness of the great changes which have taken place in the affairs of this kingdom during the nine months of my mission. And as I have begged of him to assure your Highness of my never failing devotion to your person, I beseech you to receive him graciously, that he may have greater courage to express this truth which I consider one of my greatest glories.

To CARDINAL MAZARIN.

September 28th, 1646.

I have never ceased the whole time of my embassy to protest by word and by writing to the Supreme Council, that if the peace which is generally believed to have been concluded last year with the Marquis of Ormonde be published, it will meet with the greatest opposition from the whole kingdom, most especially from the clergy. My opinion was founded on the discovery that no security is given in the said peace for the Catholic religion, though the very cause of the commotion in this kingdom, nor yet for the lives and property of the nobles, an omission which would displease as many if not more than the first. I was induced to redouble my exertions when I found that several of the concerted articles as well as the pending negotiations were concealed from me; for instance, although the peace was signed on the 28th March, in July they tried to blind me and to lead me to believe that even then it was not decided upon. My reasonable expostulations met with no attention from the Supreme Council; and on the 1st August the treaty was published in Dublin, but since then there have been greater changes than were ever before seen in Ireland. The ecclesiastical party with many of the nobility, for the reasons just mentioned, openly opposed the peace, and the clergy proceeding to threats of excommunication against all who should take the oaths, the cities joined them and refused to receive the Marquis of Ormonde when he came to enforce it; on seeing this bold opposition he returned immediately to Dublin, and now an open war between the Catholic armies and the new Confederation, which is in rapid progress, seems to be inevitable. Being well assured that in this great revolution the clergy and their adherents have no other end than the security of the Catholic religion, and after this the liberty of the King, I deem it well to reassure your Eminence on this head, and likewise to lay before you the explanation of the Ecclesiastical Congregation. This explanation the clergy think due as a proof of the respect they owe to his most Christian Majesty, and to obtain the protection they hope from so great a power; and also from the fear that this new union may be falsely represented to His Majesty and to your Eminence, since the peace was published only on the arrival of Digby from Rome, and it is supposed that he with the Marquis of Ormonde acted by authority brought from France. But I humbly entreat your Eminence to believe that, the interests of religion once provided for, the greatest anxiety of this people will be to assist the King with large supplies, and thus to render to their Prince the debt due to him from them, second only to that they owe to their God. But in truth if your Eminence had seen, during the first few days after the publication of the peace, the consternation of all good Catholics at having no security for the exercise of their religion; and on the other hand, with what a proud air the Protestants went about using threats and presuming on the restitution of the churches to themselves; I am sure that your Eminence as Grand Cardinal of the Church would have sought to obtain the authority of the most Christian King in favour of their cause and to mortify the pride of their opponents. What I was unable to ask at the beginning, owing to the irregularity of communication caused by the uncertainty of the sea, I now hope to obtain for the clergy; namely, the benignant protection of your Eminence, to whom I earnestly recommend them with my most fervent prayers. This opportunity of writing to your Eminence is given me by one who has been an eyewitness of all these events; and I was unwilling to lose it, lest I should lose at the same time the very great confidence which I am bound to place in the uprightness of your Eminence's intentions. Hoping that the Lord God may shower blessings on your head,

I am with humble reverence, &c., &c., &c.

To Cardinal Pamphili (in Cipher).

Kilkenny, September 29th, 1646.

Amongst the powers brought from England by the Earl of Glamorgan, signed and sealed by the King, was one appointing him to the Viceroyalty of Ireland at the expiration of the Marquis of Ormonde's term, or in case that nobleman should commit any crime which would merit deposition. I was therefore of opinion that the Earl, although about to depart for Rome, should remain in Ireland in case any opening should occur for his succeeding to office. And in fact it seems as though the opportunity were about to present itself, since the Marquis is publicly treating with the Parliament, and consequently is to be considered as joining the King's enemies. The Earl, who is desirous of advancement, has begun to canvass for the approval of the kingdom; he thinks he has already gained over the two generals of the armies and almost all the new Confederation and Council. I have thought it advisable to forward his views since, in case Dublin should be taken, the Kingdom must immediately provide itself with a Viceroy; and to appoint a Catholic, and one beloved by the King and country to that office, is of no small importance at the present crisis. It is to be considered also that we thus consult the wishes of the King himself, who conferred the authority under his private seal; the Irish have therefore just cause to consider his nomination legitimate, and if the Confederation carry the war of the Holy Faith into England, no one is more fit to be at the head of the army than the Earl, being as faithful to the King as to the Catholic religion. Besides he was to have led the promised 10,000 infantry to England last winter. Some make an objection that the Earl is English, of a very gentle nature, and may not be as favourable or as constant to Ireland as she needs in this emergency. But it is my opinion that in the present state of affairs no better provision can be made; and to have a

Catholic Viceroy bound to the Holy See in so many ways as the Earl, is sufficient to banish every doubt. I look forward to have occasion to write soon again to your Eminence, and meanwhile should the affair prosper I am considering in what manner I should communicate with Glamorgan, which I must do constantly; that is, whether I am to give him precedence, as I believe the Nuncio does to the Viceroy at Naples, or to treat him as an equal. The first appears proper, supposing that His Holiness does not wish to treat the two Kings differently, although one of them is a heretic; but on the other hand, since I am not accredited to the Viceroy as the Nuncio at Naples is, but to the Catholic Confederates, it might be said he ought to treat with me as with a foreign prince.

To Monsignor the Nuncio of France.

Kilkenny, September 30th, 1646.

A person is about to set off for France, who has been an eye-witness of all the changes which have taken place in this kingdom since the publication of the peace by the Marquis of Ormonde. On the 16th of August I sent to His Eminence Cardinal Pamphili a short account of the occurrences; and I now enclose a copy of it for the inspection of your Excellency, that you may be fully informed of these affairs, of which you will doubtless hear from many both by letter and word of mouth. I must however add that, since the occurrences mentioned in the report, the Marquis on travelling through the kingdom to publish the peace, found the gates of many cities closed against him; whereupon he instantly returned to Dublin, where we now intend to besiege him with the Catholic armies, whose Generals have declared for the ecclesiastical party. We hear further that the Marquis has joined the Parliamentarians and sent for aid to England; showing what sort of regard he has had for the Catholics in this peace, and what fidelity to the King.

Your Excellency will hear other particulars from the bearer of this; but since it is generally believed that Lord Digby, the author of all these evils, has written disadvantageously and malignantly of the intentions and aims of the Clergy and the new Confederation, I most solemnly assure your Excellency, and entreat of you to make known if necessary, that in all its proceedings this new government has only in view the good of religion, and after that to assist the King; which objects must be the same as those of the Queen of England, if she knows her own interest, and are identical with those professed by the most Christian King. I also assure your Excellency that the kingdom and clergy of Ireland are convinced they can look for no patronage or assistance more certain nor any more efficacious than that of the French Crown, as they testify by the letters which will reach you through this same opportunity.

I am your most devoted, &c.

To Cardinal Pamphili (in Cipher.)

October 2nd, 1646.

This Ecclesiastical Congregation formed a Council to govern the kingdom to sit as long as the first assembly; electing for each province one Bishop and two laymen besides the three Generals of the armies. They were anxious to nominate me President, and to hold all the meetings in my presence. For a short time I refused, in order to avoid giving offence by interfering in temporal affairs; but at length I consented, the better to superintend the war; and the office will not be of long duration; I also hope that the moderation with which I treat all matters which do not concern me may be still more conspicuous on this occasion, from my refraining from doing all that would be in my power to do.

With the blessing of God therefore I intend to go immediately in the direction of the armies which are marching to Dublin in order to smooth the difficulties that every day arise, especially from the want of money; but this I hope God will inspire the piety of His Holiness to grant us. These great changes give us some hope of gaining over the Marquis of Clanricarde, and if so this will be the time to present to him the Papal Brief, for which I have not as yet seen a proper opportunity on account of the close union between him and Ormonde.

To the Queen of England.

Kilkenny, October 4th, 1646.

I have had on two occasions to assure your Majesty by letter that the efforts of the Catholic confederacy of this kingdom were solely directed to obtain a secure peace with all due consideration for the person and authority of the King. This I again desire to bring before your Majesty, because of the changes which have taken place in Ireland; changes of which I can confidently affirm the object, since they have been brought about principally by the Clergy and the Ecclesiastical party. The person who will present this letter to your Majesty was with us all through, and can with perfect truth declare that he heard me exhort and thank the Clergy, because, by rejecting a peace so disastrous for religion and the King as that published in Dublin, they had done their very utmost to promote a new union which will further the interests of both.

I impatiently await the result of this movement in hope that it may restore all which of right belongs to God, and that your Majesty may see clearly that the heart of this people is faithfully inclined to your service,

With reverence and respect,

&c., &c.

To Cardinal Pamphili (in Cipher.)

In answer to the cipher of June 24th I can only say that I have never treated of, nor concluded any weighty negotiation in this kingdom without the counsel and assistance of Father Scarampi. When therefore within a few days of my arrival he retired to Waterford, I wished him to return to Kilkenny, and to remain with me always till the end of the Assembly. As he wished however to keep Easter at Waterford and to retain his apartments there, I invited him to Limerick; but he excused himself, although I wished him to be present during the threatened danger of that peace. Finally, after its publication I fixed on the city of Waterford to hold the congregation of the Clergy, that he might be present at all the proceedings without inconvenience. Since I have acted thus in the past, your Eminence may believe I shall do so still more in the future when affairs will be of so much greater importance; and my desire to acquaint your Eminence with every thing that occurs will consequently be thus greatly increased. The Father has already been present at all the meetings between me and the Council, a privilege for which he never could obtain permission from the previous government.

To the Same (in Cipher).

Kilkenny, November 27th, 1646.

The campaign against Dublin did not succeed as was hoped by all good subjects; for the armies, after having advanced almost to the gates of the city, retired on the approach of the winter season. This is explained partly by the want of money and provisions, but still more by the disunion of the two generals, whose ancient jealousies have been more manifest than ever during this enterprise.

Preston especially has conducted himself in such a manner that he has given rise to suspicions of an understanding between him and the enemy to hold back and to do his utmost to force on the peace of August. I wished to be constantly with the armies, undeterred by danger or inconvenience, because I foresaw a serious rupture; and if I have prevented a greater evil I shall be most grateful to the Lord God.

On the approach of the army the Marquis of Clanricarde met us offering to arbitrate between us; after proposing to the Council some articles which were instantly rejected, he, after their departure, brought a second and a third proposal to me alone (I having determined to remain in the camp); and gave as a reason the absolute necessity in which the Marquis of Ormonde stood either to take part with the Confederates or to admit the Parliamentary troops, which with fifteen ships had already arrived in Dublin. I referred the entire decision to the Council, but made some remarks on the second and third articles which I send to your Eminence (marked A and B), together with the answer which he made in English, and which I have had translated into Latin (marked C), by which your Eminence will see the pride of this man, and the little hope there is of bringing about a union between him and our party; believing as he does that he alone understands how to negotiate, and putting faith in no one but the Protestant Digby and a few others like him. The Council has determined to print the articles with the reply to each, and to despatch them throughout the kingdom; so that no faith may be placed in the reports spread everywhere that the Council will not hearken to any overtures of peace, and that religion is but a pretext to cover other designs. Till yesterday it was believed that Preston had made a separate compact with Ormonde, and had accepted the above mentioned articles, as he had advised the measure, and had written to the cities to recommend it; for which he was near being proclaimed a traitor; but yesterday, letters from him were received, in which he shows a disposition to come back and act under the orders of the Council; and at this very point of uncertainty as to what may happen I am now writing. The whole affair is an artifice of Digby's, who, in an interview with me in Kildare last month, advanced some arguments which I wrote down the same evening in Latin and enclose to your Eminence (marked D); from which you will gather much that I said of him in July, and likewise some not obscure indications of this plot of Clanricarde and Preston. This negotiation is full of subjects for consideration, and therefore I reserve for the first opportunity a detailed and minute relation of them. Entreating your Eminence to accept for the present this short report.

I am, &c., &c.

D. Digbeus tria in substantia dicit. 1° Incipiendo excusationem de iis, quae locutus est contra Nuncium, fassus est libere se diminuisse quantum potuit auctoritatem Nuncii apud suos ut melius causam Regis promoveret, addendo quod politica ratione existimet hoc fuisse sibi licitum. Insuper fateter dixisse Reginam male sentire de Nuncio, eo quod impedierit pacem Ormonicam. Item dixisse quod S. M. obtinebat a Summo Pontifice illius remotionem ab hoc Regno, et quod hoc ipse existimet futurum, et quod certo sciat S. Suam aegre laturam quid quid actum est hic a Nuncio et a Clero post reiectionem pacis. Praeterea fatetur vidisse litteras in Gallia, quod Nuncius iactaret se pacem impedivisse, sed illas non fuisse eiusdem Nuncii sed unius dependentis ab ipso, quem noluit nominare. Negat tum se unquam dixisse quod Nuncius sit Hispanus, et quod venerit ad tradendum Regnum Regi Hispaniae, sed tantum fatetur dixisse, quod Regina Angliae ob impedimentum paci praestitum a Nuncio, venerit in hanc suspicionem, et addidisse, quod si Nuncius perseveraret in tali impedimento faceret hoc verisimile, cum notum sit

Regum Catholicum esse bene affectum Parliamento, et quod e re ipsius sit hanc pacem non concludi, maxime cum apud omnes sit manifestum, et praecipue apud Gallos, summum Pontificem inclinare in partes hispanas.

2° Dicit Reginam Angliae aegerrime tulisse quod Nuncius in Assemblea generali promulgaverit quaedam capitula, asserendo fuisse conclusa inter summum Pontificem et M. Suam addens quod non displicuisset Reginae si fuisset dictum quod illa capitula essent tractata, sed solum fuisse dictum quod essent conclusa; ex hoc enim dicit satis acriter quod maxima fuit facta iniuria Regi et procuratum illius exterminium, nam omnes Protestantes et Puritani ceperunt hinc occasionem M. S. deserendi ac demum perdendi. Quod magis urget ponderando, quod ex ista reiectione pacis fuerit inflictus ictus securitati ipsius Regis, quia inde consequitur quod nullam spem habere amplius possit in suppetiis hibernicis, quibus reservabatur gloria ferendi auxilium M. S. prout iam inter Marchionem Ormoniae et Confoederatos fuerat conventum. Atque in hoc proposito magnifice profitetur intelligere se quod Rex a nullis iuvari potest melius, immo quod unice tantum a Catholicis huius regni, nec ignorare se quod iidem Catholici fideliores sint omnibus aliis subditis.

3° Narrat D. Marchionem Ormoniae iam esse iunctum Parliamento ac proinde se protestatum apud illum fuisse, et postea exivisse Dublino. Nihilominus ex caritate erga Regem proponit posse iterum, si Confoederati velint, haberi declarationem sufficientem pro omnibus rebus quas desiderant Catholici, nec non securitatem pro iis obtinendis, ac tandem revocandi eumdem Marchionem ad bonam frugem. Addit itaque optare se ut Confoederati ponant in aliquo libello quid quid desiderant in materia Religionis, atque ipse vice versa offert dare pro securitate litteras Regis, Reginae, ac Principis Angliae, ac insuper alias a Rege Christianissimo qui obliget verbum suum etiam de inferendo bello Regi Angliae si promissis non maneat. Sed tantum vult hoc esse secretum, asserens mullo alio modo posse fieri citra periculum Regis; atque ideo proponit conscium fore de hac re interim summum tantummodo Pontificem, et hunc Nuncium cum aliquibus Episcopis; aliocumsque modo publice pernegat rem fieri posse. Tandem suadet haec omnia debere amplecti Confoederatos, quia vi neque Dublinum neque aliam partem obtinebunt, et contra se demum Scotos et Anglos excitabunt, quibus simul irruentibus nulla unquam ratione pares esse poterunt, ut per se patet ec.

To the Same.

November 28th, 1646.

The present opportunity of a vessel about to set sail induces me to send your Eminence seven letters and despatches, which I confide to the care of Father Scarampi at Waterford, who will forward them by Flanders or France as he thinks best, and your Eminence will receive them with his letters.

It is now three months since letters have arrived from Rome, and as we have heard meanwhile from Paris and Florence that in September His Holiness was raising a remittance for this kingdom, I am in the greatest anxiety to know if it has been sent or gone astray, to the great prejudice of the war now on our hands, in which even a small assistance would be quite sufficient for some enterprise of importance. If I had some of that money I could give orders to set afloat the unfortunate frigate which Invernizi left at Ostend, concerning which Father Scarampi and I have frequently written to the Internuncio of Flanders; and as we have had no decisive answer from him, I fear we shall lose this vessel without the power of remedy.

The General Assembly is announced for the 10th of January next, when we shall take into consideration the best manner of rejecting the peace if not secure, or the prosecution of the war if necessary.

I am, &c., &c.

To Cardinal Mazarin.

November 29th, 1646.

I cannot refuse a testimony which is due to truth, and I trust the justice and wisdom of your Eminence will not deny me credence.

Don Diego della Torre, who is here by order of the Catholic King, requested the clerical congregation on the change of Government here to permit him not only to conclude the levy of a regiment promised to him by the late Council, and of which he had already sent a part to Spain, but to raise other troops for the same purpose. The deliberations upon this subject lasted many days, and at last the new Council agreed that they could not and ought not refuse to ratify the obligations incurred by their predecessors; but they referred the question of a second and similar concession to the future General Assembly. M. du Moulins has confidentially complained to me of this determination of the Council for two reasons. First, because they had permitted soldiers to be sent to the King of Spain whilst he is actually at war with the most Christian King; and secondly, because the Council did not speak to him on the subject before they passed the decree. I, having been present at the deliberations of that day, assured him that as to the first point, the Council would never believe that his most Christian Majesty could be offended by their fulfilling an engagement made by their predecessors, since his own wisdom would recognise the necessity of keeping a promise made to any person whatsoever; and it seems to me sufficient to point out the difference between granting the contingent of the first levy, and refusing the application for a second; and it is ·in this only, and not in the first, that they could fear to have shewn any want of respect to the French Crown.

For the second point I did not deny that it would have been better if they had first imparted to Du Moulins Don Diego's request, since for the above reasons I am convinced that he would not have made any opposition to the Council; nevertheless I thought the members were to be excused, as the deliberations took place twenty miles from Kilkenny where Du Moulins had remained, and being we may say on their way to the army and urged by Don Diego who had come there in person not to defer their answer; hence there was neither time nor opportunity to consult with Du Moulins, though as minister of the King of France he was fully entitled to expect it. If the Irish nobles do fail sometimes in any of the forms which are observed by friendly courts, it will not be deemed inexcusable by your Eminence who is so well aware of the hardships and cruelty with which these poor people have been governed by the Protestants for so many years; and if I have not succeeded in satisfying Du Moulins, who is naturally warm on any subject concerning His Majesty, I entreat of your Eminence to give me credit for earnestly desiring it. As I know the intentions of the Council and the manner in which the affair has been conducted, I can assure your Eminence that everything has occurred exactly as I tell you, and I leave the judgment of the whole to your Eminence's wisdom and goodness. And I must here assure your Eminence that this nation never has made and never will make any demonstration to the Catholic King on account of the old or the new ties with that Crown, that can in any way diminish by one point the devotion professed to the most Christian King ; since I know positively that the greater part of the nobility are fully sensible of the obligations they owe to His Majesty, and not less of the need in which they stand of the commerce and assistance of France. I was anxious that Du Moulins should be satisfied with this strong attestation of the truth, as His Majesty's service would be thus carried on more smoothly ; and the Irish with the protection of the most Christian King would prosecute more ardently the cause of religion and of their own King.

Entreating your Eminence to forgive my troubling you with this letter, and with prayers to God that every happiness may attend you.

I am, &c., &c.

To CARDINAL PAMPHILI.

Kilkenny, December 20th, 1646.

Four months have now elapsed since I received any letters from Rome; wherefore I am without the commands of your Eminence, which are the soul of our proceedings and the glory of my mission. Besides this, we have but uncertain news by vessels coming here from France, because ever since August nearly all of them have been weather bound in the port of Waterford awaiting a favourable wind which has never come; and many of them have ventured out to sea four times, and been driven back by contrary winds. This makes me the less regret the unfortunate issue of Signor Invernizi's purchase, as the frigates would have been useless when the wind is against them. I send this by the Provincial of the Barefooted Carmelites, who is about to visit Rome for the General Chapter; but after Christmas I hope by a safer opportunity to send you an exact report of all the success of the expedition against Dublin, which, since it has laid open the principal defects of the Catholic Union in this kingdom, will enable His Holiness in his infinite wisdom to devise and make known to me the remedies which he considers most advisable. The opportunity I speak of will be through Flanders; whither I have thought it well to send a person who, with the assistance of the Internuncio, will liberate, set afloat, and bring over the frigate bought by Invernizi in Ostend. I have promised to repay him all he may disburse; depending on the truth of the news received from Florence that His Holiness was in September on the point of sending a remittance of money to Ireland, of which however not having received any further account, I am not certain. The orders above given are to be followed only in case no other commands have been received from your Eminence concerning the disposal of the frigate.

In a few days the assembly will meet, when it will be finally decided whether or not to conclude a peace with the Marquis of Ormonde, and how to place religious affairs on an advantageous footing. I trust that I shall not fail in the duty I owe to the Apostolic See and to His Holiness, even if I am not successful in my actions, since hitherto I have shown my desire to serve them in intention only.

I am, &c., &c.

To the Same.

Kilkenny, December 23rd, 1646.

Viscount Costello of the Dillon family, who held the Presidency of Connaught some years ago under the King, has for some months past shown signs of returning to the Catholic Faith, in which he was educated up to his fifteenth year.

I have always used my influence to guide him in this direction, and I had the greatest satisfaction in receiving him into the Catholic Church last week to the great joy of an immense crowd in this city. He abjured Protestantism before me in one of the Churches; and after receiving the Sacrament with much devotion, he took the oath of the Catholic Confederates, and has given me hopes that not only his sons but also his wife will soon follow his example. I send your Eminence his profession with his signature; and if His Holiness deems it advisable to honour him with some special mark of favour, I think it would serve as a great example to the other Protestants in the kingdom; particularly in the province of Connaught, where the Marquis of Clanricarde has always by his neutrality done more harm than good to the Holy Faith.

With humble reverence.

To the Same.

Dec. 28th, 1646.

After having written the accompanying letters to your Eminence expressing my regret at not hearing from you for so long a time, I received with the greatest satisfaction seven packets of letters from your Eminence with the ciphers and documents mentioned in the enclosed sheet: I shall carefully answer them all, and send them perhaps by Father Scarampi, who, having received permission to return to Rome, wishes to accelerate his departure. I rejoice also that the orders given by me to the Internuncio in Flanders concerning the frigate were to be subject to your commands, as I find that you have wisely ordered it to be sold.

I am, &c., &c.

Report of the proceedings of the Catholic Armies against Dublin.

Kilkenny, Dec. 29th, 1646.

It will not be inopportune to write a little more diffusely to your Eminence on the subject of the successes of our arms during the preceding autumn, as, if I am not mistaken, you will recognise the three sources of those disorders which are the ruin of this kingdom, and of which I spoke in my report of last March. First and greatest—the want of money, second—the jealousy of the Generals, and third—the immoderate affection of his faction for the Marquis of Ormonde.

I must begin a little way back and inform your Eminence that, when the congregation of the clergy had determined upon turning their arms against Dublin, and had given the necessary orders to General O'Neill who was then on his march from Ulster, a controversy directly arose whether General Preston then occupied in Connaught should be called upon to assist in the enterprise.

It was represented by many that, to the misfortune of the kingdom, the two captains never could come together without something untoward occurring; and this was more to be feared now than ever, when their former jealousy would be exasperated by the mutual hatred of the people of their respective provinces, who never can agree. The opinion however prevailed of those who deemed it impolitic to introduce another General into Preston's province without giving him a share in the enterprise; at the risk of inducing him to unite with the factious and dissatisfied members of government, and thus divide the opinion and strength of the kingdom. As to the fear of jealousy between the Generals, it was said that the goodness and conscientiousness of O'Neill, who has always been most faithful to the Catholic religion, would suffice to insure perfect safety.

Preston was consequently summoned by the Council, but in many ways speedily showed how grievously mistaken were those who supported him. During the summer, to my great displeasure, he had consigned all the castles taken by him to the Marquis of Clanricarde, a neutral; whether at the command of the former Council is not yet known. He had also shortly before received from Clanricarde a sum of 6,000 crowns to reinforce his army for the campaign in Connaught; this was part of the sum brought over by Digby, and distributed to several persons, not so much to forward the enterprise as to buy their acceptance of the peace then on the eve of publication. Preston had it proclaimed in his camp with every appearance of satisfaction; and although he soon after excused himself to the clergy for this act, saying that he had not been aware of the determination of the ecclesiastics, still it transpired afterwards that he and his friends also thought that the peace was good for the cause of religion; that he had agreed with the Marquis of Clanricarde to promote it as far as he could in honour, and (although bound to serve the ecclesiastical party) to contrive

U

either that Dublin should not be taken or at least to give no offence to the Marquis of Ormonde. To this was added the subtle and malignant assertion that this dissimulation was allowable, because O'Neill's march with so powerful an army into Leinster proved that the pretext of religion given by him and others was utterly futile; that the clergy were in fact bent upon making him master of that province for other purposes; and therefore that, to avert such a danger, every stratagem of war should be made use of. With this sophistry they succeeded in persuading the facile General to raise on his own authority as many soldiers as would render his army equal in number to that of O'Neill, in order to remove all fear of him; thus losing sight of religion and acting on a miserable policy. On his arrival in Kilkenny and receiving increased powers from the newly elected Council, he marched out to join O'Neill; and soon began to act in a manner which left no doubt of his intentions. On the route, by virtue of a truce concluded without permission of the Council, he left unmolested the fort of Carlow where there were thirty soldiers only, all the rest having fled to Dublin: and although he excused himself under the plea that a rapid advance towards the principal object of the enterprise was necessary (and which he declared would have been retarded by the loss of four days before that fortress), still under various pretexts he lingered at a place in the neighbourhood for more than twenty days.

He complained bitterly that O'Neill placed garrisons of his own soldiers in the towns which he took in various parts of Leinster: threw out hints that he did not know with what justice they were sent against Dublin: and was once or twice heard to say plainly that without greater justification he would not fight against the Marquis. Upon this the Council decided that it was necessary to draw up and adminster an oath to the two generals, by which they would be bound to acts of hostility against the Marquis. Preston refused to take it unless these words were added, "after the summons to give up Dublin should be made known to him, and in case he should not offer favourable conditions;" hoping by these reservations to attain his own ends even while taking the oath. From Kilcock, where these difficulties first presented themselves, the armies nearly united marched first to Harristown, thence to Naas, and afterwards to Lucan, only five miles distant from Dublin. In this place where the captains first met, the poison of suspicion infused itself into all their dealings, so that each began to regard the other as an enemy, and it was impossible to reconcile them since what one proposed the other objected to. At this time also a want of food began to be felt, for a supply of which they had made no proper provision; money too was scarce, and in consequence of the rising of the river Liffey every place was flooded and supplies of every kind were hindered from coming in for ten days,—no one having thought of repairing a bridge which could have been done without any difficulty. All this operated so that each general went his own way without concert or design; the Leinster men began to doubt if O'Neill had any other aim than to overpower them: the Ulster, that Preston had already made a compact with the Marquis to place him between the two armies and put them to flight.

In all these irreconcilable differences, which at once showed that the Dublin campaign could not succeed, and that the arms at first devoted to religion were about to minister to private passions alone, I was of opinion that the Council should as often as possible follow the armies; and for my own part I determined never to leave them at what danger soever to person or health, since if I can prevent some great outbreak or effusion of blood I consider it my duty as an Apostolic Nuncio to avert so terrible a calamity, recollecting the Catholic title of the war and the displeasure which such an occurrence would cause to His Holiness. I therefore travelled to Lucan and had interviews with both generals;

and whether in this business I fulfilled my duty, your Eminence will judge when you hear the report of all that happened and the perils that I incurred.

The Marquis of Clanricarde very quickly came to Lucan escorted by some of Preston's soldiers, whence I doubt not the whole affair had been concerted, since it had been remarked that on the route Preston delayed or accelerated his march as his letters gave him hope of a speedy meeting or the contrary. Clanricarde brought news that sixteen Parliamentary ships had arrived at Dublin with 1,500 infantry to assist in making terms with the Marquis of Ormonde, adding that he must not be allowed to join the enemy, and then proposed to the Council some alterations in the August peace which were rejected the same evening, since in reality little or nothing was added and no security was given save the word of Clanricarde himself, who promised in case of the violation of the articles to join the Confederates, as if the gain of his sole person would outweigh all the dangers which might follow. But the same evening an event occurred which disturbed the course of affairs. Whilst the Council were sitting, secret intelligence came to Preston that the Parliamentary troops, having made a compact with the Marquis of Ormonde, had landed. Upon this the Ulster general was the first to propose retiring from Lucan as an unsafe place, and that very night the cannon were transported across the river. The Council agreed as to the wisdom of this measure, and on the following morning everyone departed in terror and with great celerity into safe quarters. I was considering how to depart with the greatest dignity possible, as I saw I was completely in the hands of Preston and must needs trust myself to him, when letters arrived from Clanricarde alleging that the report concerning the disembarkation of the English was not true, and proposing new articles of peace specifying that Ormonde would receive garrisons of Catholics into all the places held by him, and entreating me to give my opinion thereupon as soon as possible. This news determined me to remain, to show that our party would never refuse to enter into terms for a fair peace. But I put down in writing the considerations which I enclose to your Eminence, referring the rest to the decision of the Council, whom I sent to recall; but in this I was not successful, as they had proceeded too far on their journey. I therefore set off myself to propose the negotiations to them, but was overtaken in two places by gentlemen with new letters and conditions from Preston, declaring, under pretence of the danger of delay, that my approval would be quite sufficient for them apart from that of the Council. I saw clearly that some deceit had been already practised, and that all this haste was made to accumulate excuses for some rashness or to cover some error he had committed, and here actually is the whole business as it happened.

Lord Digby, the Protestant and author of all these plots, had drawn up at Clanricarde's suggestion a protest and promise of consent, a copy of which I send your Eminence, and which he induced Preston with all the others to sign; the substance of it being that, besides introducing Catholic garrisons into Dublin, the Leinster army was to join that of the Viceroy and force the Council to accept Clanricarde's second peace. This document was kept a profound secret amongst them; they endeavoured by the means above mentioned to influence me and the Council; but, finding that we intended to make our opposition public, they resolved to act without further delay. The General therefore moved his army within a mile of Dublin, but some difference arising concerning the allotment of the garrisons, Preston, highly indignant, retired first to Lucan and then beyond the Liffey, the opposition of the Council having already in some degree induced a change in his opinions; yet though when encamped near Kilkenny he had twice visited the city and declared his unwillingness to act in any way prejudicial to the interests of the kingdom, we understood that on his return to the camp, he continued to correspond with the enemy and determined to unite his army with that of the Marquis: and already all the Butlers with those of the Ormonde faction who were dispersed in the neighbouring districts showed a disposition to unite with him. This uncertain and vacillating mode of proceeding, being most perilous to the kingdom, determined me to interfere; and knowing that Preston's conscience was delicate on some points I wrote to him in a pastoral tone and entreated him to tell me openly how he was bound to the Marquis, that I might find means to free him honourably; showing him that by concealing the truth he was plunging his country into danger, and exciting jealousies at a time when its energies ought to be solely directed to make the Catholic religion respected.

The reply was that my words had caused a change in his opinions, and that he would come to Kilkenny on the following day and make a complete confession. He accordingly came, and after informing the Council of everything, said that he had signed the protest believing it to be advantageous to religion and to the country; but that he had withdrawn from it not only because the Council and Clergy would not recognize it, but because the Viceroy, by refusing to admit the garrisons agreed upon, had been the first to break his word, whence he (Preston) believed himself absolved from his oaths and promises. After this he wrote to Clanricarde, and began forthwith to distribute his soldiers in their quarters, which under various pretexts he had till then delayed to do, contrary to the command of the Council. His letters were received by Clanricarde, who had marched from Dublin with the vanguard beyond the river, at the very place where Preston had appointed to meet him; and the Marquis, having read them and vented his anger in curses, immediately returned to Dublin. I then set myself to persuade Preston that, as he had acted with so much duplicity, his honour could only be saved by a public declaration of his present opinions. I earnestly desired that the truth should be known through the Assembly, and the breach between him and the Ormonde faction be made irreconcilable. It was easy to persuade him, and we drew up the enclosed document, which to make it more public was put into print. The two Marquises, Ormonde and Clanricarde having at the same time marched into Wexford to entice all whom they thought they had inveigled into the above-mentioned peace; and I, expecting that our armies might speedily have to recommence the campaign was anxious before the Assembly sat, to reconcile the Generals as much as possible; I therefore drew up a form of mutual reconciliation (of which I send your Eminence a copy) to be signed by both, by which they are bound to fight either separately or together for the benefit of the Catholic religion. And at this moment such is the present state of affairs in the kingdom.

Your Eminence will be able to judge how great is the disunion amongst this people, and how great is the affection of the Ormonde faction to their leader. But as I find that every one makes a pretext of the want of money, I believe that this is the greatest evil of all. Preston in all his evasions and turnings, excused himself on the plea of being unable to find provisions for his soldiers; the nobles, who have accepted the peace, plead the devastation of their property and consequent poverty. All who desire the treaty are influenced solely by want of supplies, and amongst the Ormondes I am certain that for money the greater number would willingly sell their adherence to the party. From this it may be concluded that the occasional display of money and the power of distributing it liberally would have secured, so far as we can judge, the completion in this year of our victories and the taking of Dublin; so also, whenever the necessities of the Apostolic See will permit further aid, the result will be greater than could be hoped for, seeing the present condition of this kingdom.

To the Grand Duke of Tuscany.

Kilkenny, December 29th, 1646.

I have received by way of Germany your Highness' condescending recommendations of Father Nicholas Donnelly, an Irishman, for the Church of Tuam. I must however inform you that, immediately after the death of the Archbishop, the Supreme Council as well as myself proposed to His Holiness more than one subject for the vacant See; and from what I have heard I conclude that His Holiness has already declared his nomination. Nevertheless, by the first opportunity which occurs I will obey your Highness' commands and write on the subject to Rome; and, if my letter should arrive too late, I shall not fail to take advantage of any other occasion which may present itself during my embassy; in saying which I am not so much actuated by a desire to reward the good qualities of the person you recommend, as by my anxiety to prove to your Highness, who honours by thus commanding me, my faithful and unchangeable devotion.

I am, &c., &c.

To Cardinal Spada.

December 29th, 1646.

May the Blessed Lord God reward your Eminence a thousand fold for the comfort contained in your Eminence's letter of the 26th of August. The kindness of your Eminence is well understood by a poor minister who, while under so many obligations to the Apostolic See, cannot refrain from desiring to see that his services give satisfaction elsewhere. The approval of my labours contained in this letter will be an incitement to me to continue them in such a way that your Eminence may never have to repent of having thus honoured me; and while my obligation to you must be eternal for having expressed it in a letter, it is increased, as your Eminence will believe, by your having deigned to express it to His Holiness also. This kingdom may be called a primitive and persecuted Church, for which reason we may always hope for devotion and reformation; but on the other hand time only can bring about the necessary changes, since the constant disturbances prevent any rapid improvement.

I grieve that the state of the country, and the experience I have of its great need, constrain me constantly to mention the necessity for money when I see that the Holy See is so much straitened. But I trust that, by zeal and courage, especially on your Eminence's part, this want will be supplied by some extraordinary means; and praying that your life may be long preserved for the benefit of the Holy Church.

I am, &c., &c.

To Cardinal Pamphili (in Cipher).

December 29th, 1646.

The regulars, as your Eminence will also hear from Father Scarampi, have had a great share in the ruin of this kingdom, by spreading strange opinions and defending them without regard to consequences, quite in opposition to public sentiment. The accompanying sheet contains the answers made by the regulars in Dublin to the Marquis, and will show how they acted during the late proceedings, naming the King "their supreme Lord" without it being required of them and against the wishes of the clergy. In the other sheet your Eminence will see their opinion upon the second peace proposed by Clanricarde, although we do not yet know whether their opinion has been asked. The example of England, where the clergy so readily fell into apostacy, makes me proceed cautiously; but up to the present time, without much recourse to authority, I am endeavouring to gain them over and cajole them. Nevertheless, as this is a point which always troubles the country and will be hastily concluded, I request your Eminence to inform me of His Holiness's opinion on the subject, by which I may regulate my conduct for the future, and in the meantime I shall endeavour to act for the best.

To the Same (in Cipher).

December 30th, 1646.

The Marquis of Clanricarde shows more and more every day his estrangement from the Confederates and his desertion of the Marquis of Ormonde. Your Eminence will hear from Father Scarampi how he has acted of late, making himself the arbiter and head of a new peace drawn up by himself, and which he has induced Preston and others to sign, as I have informed your Eminence at length in the accompanying report.

But I have further to inform you that when I cited two monks to appear before me in Kilkenny for grave offences, Clanricarde who was then in Dublin, fearing that perhaps I might do the same to all the friars in that city, published on the part of the Viceroy another citation to all the parish priests and monks forbidding them on pain of being considered rebels to leave the city. One of those I had summoned however obeyed me, and made the enclosed confession; but the other by name Father Dominic Burke, a Dominican, and the confessor of Clanricarde, remained in Dublin fearless of excommunication;. he is a proud man and arrogant in doctrine.

The Papal Brief which your Eminence sent for the Marquis, will therefore remain in my hands, since I find him every day more unworthy of so great an honour.

To the Same.

Kilkenny, December 30th, 1646.

Father Scarampi, having obtained from your Eminence permission to depart, writes to me from Waterford that he will come here to-day to take leave of me, and will avail himself of the opportunity of some vessels about to set sail. I urged him to delay his departure in order to be present at the approaching Assembly, by which he would be enabled to inform His Holiness and your Eminence of the exact state of affairs which are at present very doubtful; but as he is not inclined to take my advice, I am hastily preparing a despatch, that he may not return to Rome without proof that my duty has been fulfilled.

The Father, amongst other good qualities, has the name of perfect fearlessness in publishing the wishes and opinions of His Holiness and unceasingly forwarding them by writing and word of mouth; but the former Council, by their pertinacious adherence to the Ormonde peace, showed themselves most ungrateful to him. I pray the Lord God that I may be able to imitate Father Scarampi in all that relates to his mission, that like him I may be worthy of the protection and grace of your Eminence.

I am, &c.

TO THE SAME.

Kilkenny, Dec. 30th, 1646.

Notwithstanding the changes in affairs, I can in one letter briefly answer the seven in cipher which your Eminence has sent me with the last despatches, because Father Scarampi will soon be with you to give a fuller report. Although I have not yet been advised from France if the 15,000 crowns have arrived, or in what bank they will be placed, I nevertheless return to your Eminence the thanks of this whole country, in which this favour is felt as much as its need. Your Eminence will not repent of your intimation of further aid, when you hear that this autumn we have recovered all the country between Dublin and Kilkenny, so long in the hands of the heretics; although we were obliged to abandon the enterprise against the city from want of money. All the reports which reached us concerning the imprisonment of Invernizi have turned out to be without foundation, no certain news having been received of him by anyone; but it seems most extraordinary that nine months should have elapsed without some account reaching us. I wrote to London six weeks ago, but have had no reply; and as to the frigate, your Eminence will see by my letters that I have made great and constant efforts to save it: since its loss to my great regret, will be equal to that of 15,000 crowns to my embassy.

I shall send to Rome as soon as possible the ensigns taken in battle last summer, and which were hung up in different cathedrals. I shall have them taken off the banner staffs, although many were so torn in the rage of battle as to leave little else; but I trust that the blessed God may deliver into our hands many more.

Your Eminence will in the meantime receive from Father Scarampi the great standard of the cavalry which I promised some time ago.

With all the authority and commands which the Council and others have committed to me in military affairs, there has been no cause to fear that the people expect as they previously did that the expenses of the war were to be defrayed by the Apostolic See; I think they were much more inclined to believe it on my first arrival, than they are now: perhaps this is due to Secretary Belling, whose good offices have always been directed to this end. We shall hear the opinion of the next Assembly, when I intend at once to resign the place given me in the Council, until it is partly composed of the clergy, and confine myself to my accustomed office of giving good advice and letting things take their course as your Eminence prudently admonishes. I am most impatient for the return of the Dean of Fermo, as he will inform me of what has been determined upon with Sir Kenelm Digby; for we have had news from London of a great victory obtained by the Scotch over the Parliamentary party, and as our Catholic Marquis of Antrim was engaged in it with a considerable force, it is to be hoped that the aid thus given to the King will be an advantage to religion according to the sacred desire of His Holiness. I have the good news from Paris that that Court will never countenance any peace in this kingdom unless it be perfectly satisfactory to the Catholics: this is contrary to all that the heretic Digby continues to asseverate. The reply from the Queen of England to my letter of the 27th of August could not be more friendly.

Finally, I entreat your Eminence not to allow my report to make you despair of the reformation of this people, because you will see that I speak also of their docility and submissiveness when authority is properly exerted. This is a primitive and persecuted Church; therefore the more difficulties are overcome, the brighter will shine the glories of the Apostolic mission. And I may venture to promise that when His Holiness has nominated the new Bishops I shall be able if we have even a short peace to form them so much to my wishes, that they will accept and persevere in the Roman ordinances, to the eternal obligation of the Island to the Holy Father.

CONSIDERATIONS UPON THE FUTURE ASSEMBLY.

December 30th, 1646.

We have heard from France that the Court will never assist in forwarding any peace in this kingdom, unless it be favourable to religion and quite satisfactory to the Catholics. We know also the benignant favour of His Holiness, the renewed assistance he has given us, and his satisfaction at the victories gained; and many now recognise the cunning of the Marquis of Ormonde, who has always endeavoured to ingratiate himself with the people for the sole purpose of deceiving them afterwards.

For these reasons it is plain the assembly should determine not to accept any adjustment except one giving advantage and security to religion. They should also intrust to the Clergy the preparation of the terms, in conformity with what has been embodied in so many articles up to the present time. And in case peace cannot be concluded, then the war should be prosecuted against Dublin, which would be the most promising course; for I still retain my former opinion, that so long as the King is not at liberty there can be no sufficient security to induce us to conclude peace.

But to lead the assembly to arrive at such a resolution and prevent them from flinging themselves into this last peace of Clanricarde's, there are three very great difficulties—

1st. The dislike and abhorrence of all classes to the extortions and billettings of the soldiery: in fact the people, and many nobles too, care very little how much injury is done to religion, provided they may (so to say) eat their mouthful in peace.

2nd. The discord between the two generals, especially on Preston's part, in whom it appears no one has any confidence, inasmuch as they believe that he only desires the company of O'Neill to make war in his province.

3rd. The bent of the factions to the Marquis of Ormonde and Clanricarde, whom they desire to be powerful, both from attachment, and in order also to serve their own private interests. The remedy for this last point will not be difficult to find if the Assembly be well attended; as the greater number of the members are inimical to the Marquis, and by the last resolutions his adherents were kept sufficiently in check. As to the second point, besides the temporary reconciliation I effected between the two generals, I am endeavouring to induce them to propose in the Assembly as good Catholics that no peace should be accepted which is not good and approved by the ecclesiastics. But if the war is to be prosecuted I do not despair of so dividing the armies as to take away all cause of jealousy between them.

The first however is the greatest difficulty of all, because it touches the poor, and cannot be remedied without complete order being established in the militia, which up to the present time has never been found possible; and it must be added that a large sum of money is required to keep the soldiers contented, and in this our great need our poverty becomes every day more evident.

To Cardinal Pamphili.
Kilkenny, February 1st, 1647.

Conformably to what I wrote in my letter of December 30, Father Scarampi came to Kilkenny to take leave of me previous to his embarkation, and after parting conditionally on account of the weather, such contrary winds began to blow that after several days I advised him to return hither and assist us in our present need; and though on a slight indication of favourable weather he went again to Waterford, with all that he returned for the third time and remained here till to-day. He set off hoping that a day might be favourable, which is considered critical by the sailors; but I did not fail to embrace him with the usual proviso, as the south wind has blown during the whole season almost without intermission, and every vessel has returned to port two or three times. He will give your Eminence an account of all that has occurred up to this period in this factious Assembly, and will relate it with more vivacity than I can do in my despatches.

I beg to inform your Eminence that I have received your packets of the 4th and 11th of November with the additional ciphers, to which I have nothing to reply, except with respect to the confidence which is placed in Rome in Mr. Digby's assertion that the Dublin peace entirely fulfilled the wishes of His Holiness; concerning which I hope that if a general declaration now in progress throughout the whole kingdom should succeed, which may happen at any moment, it will serve as a sufficient answer to all his asseverations.

With humble reverence, I am, &c.

To the Same.

Kilkenny, February 1st, 1647.

During this month I have received letters from the Internuncio of Flanders and the pastor of Ostend, who as an Irishman has had the care of Invernizi's unfortunate frigate. Your Eminence will see by the copies of these letters that the frigate was finally sold for 3,000 florins in Flanders money; of which sum the said pastor writes that, the expenses being deducted, 600 alone will remain. There are besides 15 cannon of iron and three of bronze, but it is not certain whether these last are ours. I shall write to both dignitaries to send me the money by a Wexford captain who is about to set sail, and as Father Scarampi is to go with him the affair will be as favourably conducted as possible. Thus ends poor Invernizi's unfortunate enterprise; of himself we have heard nothing, therefore I can but fear the worst for him.

I am, &c.

To the Same.

Kilkenny, Feb. 1st, 1647.

I received by way of Germany about a month ago a letter from His Serene Highness the Grand Duke of Tuscany, in which he recommended for the See of Tuam Father M. Nicholas Donnelly, an Augustine and native of Connaught. Accompanying the letter was a paper on his qualifications for the office; he is at present reader to a convent in Vienna, after having fulfilled much to his credit the office of Provincial of Austria. I replied to His Serene Highness that I should represent what he said to the Holy Father and to your Eminence, in accordance with my duty; but that as several persons had been proposed and recommended for the vacant See, I feared the nomination had already taken place. The Grand Duke had probably communicated with your Eminence previous to writing to me; but I must not on that account omit to mention that the person spoken of is brother to an agent or perhaps master of the household to the Marquis of Clanricarde, so that under present circumstances the confederation would hardly be benefited by his nomination; I shall however be strictly guided by the advice and commands of His Holiness and of your Eminence.

I am, &c.

Report of the Speech delivered by the Nuncio in the Assembly.

He reminded the members that he had already been a year in the island endeavouring to obey the instructions of His Holiness; which were to exhort all men to union, and not to accept any peace unless it promised to be efficacious and secure.

On this account he said he had opposed from the first Glamorgan's peace as disgraceful, and offering no security for religion; for this reason also he had induced the Supreme Council to wait for the articles proposed in Rome by Cardinal Pamphili, and which were in the hands of Sir Kenelm Digby: upon which point a promise had been publicly given that the originals of the articles should be waited for till the month of May, and that then no peace should be concluded or published save that agreed upon by the Nuncio and Glamorgan. He left it to the judgment of the assembly, whether or not the public faith had or had not been compromised, when another was promulgated without the consent of either Glamorgan or the Nuncio, and without their having been in any way consulted. He then said that, having heard towards the end of April of the King's discomfiture and imprisonment by the Scotch, which changed the whole aspect of affairs, he had written to the Supreme Council saying, that in consequence of the King's loss of liberty and authority he saw no means of concluding a peace with His Majesty's Ministers; and again, when he thought the kingdom might be benefited by a union with the Marquis of Ormonde, he had written a letter on the 3rd of May on this subject alone, showing how it might be brought about without prejudice to the Catholic religion. To which letter, as well as to many others written from Limerick, he complained that no replies had been sent, and alleged this as his reason for permitting the publication of three of them by a priest who had written against the last peace; because he wished the whole kingdom to be aware of their contents, that every one might know the sentiments of His Holiness expressed through him.

He added that, in spite of this and other protestations and declarations made by him in his own name and that of the clergy, the peace had been proclaimed; upon which he was constrained to convene the clergy at Waterford, where upon an examination of the articles in question (which he had never been permitted to see before) they were by common consent rejected as deficient and offering no security to religion. This done, that he had proposed various modes of adjustment, one of which was to suspend the publication until the Assembly had met, or until the whole question should be submitted to His Holiness; that after this the clergy had published some of his propositions, none of which were accepted by the Council. The Nuncio further said that he had much to his astonishment seen a letter signed by them, in which they declared that they recognised no power equal to their own in determining the matter of the peace; he enlarged upon the falsity of this notion, which denied the supremacy of ecclesiastical over temporal power, and showed how such ignorance of the true source of power had ruined the neighbouring kingdom, asking at the same time what the Assembly thought would be said in Rome if it were known there that such an opinion had been broached. He added that the clergy had assumed the Government, nominated the

Council, and organized the militia, from the necessity alone of not leaving the kingdom without a head, and not because they considered that temporal things belonged to their jurisdiction. When the Assembly met, which had been convened by them, they laid down their authority, as the Nuncio himself had resigned that given to him in the Council for the three months in which it had been partly composed of the clergy.

He then passed on to exhortations on the part of His Holiness concerning present emergencies, and first enlarged upon the advantages of a new union; the necessity of which was proved by the unfortunate issue of their enterprises, the cost and the insolence of the soldiers, and the factions and parties into which the armies were divided: insisting that no union could be so advantageous or durable as one founded on the Catholic Faith. Further, as to concluding a peace, seeing that all agreed in the end, but none in the means, he proposed that after taking every needful precaution for security, the Assembly together with the clergy should make choice amongst the articles that had been at different times proposed, added, and withdrawn, of some that would be good and glorious for the Catholic Faith; and then swearing to uphold them should leave the issue to the Lord God, who by permitting them to succeed would grant them tranquillity, or by reverses would teach them constancy and valour.

He said they were bound to this by knowledge founded on past experience, and likewise by gratitude to the Holy Pontiff, of whose paternal love he would mention three instances.

1st. That His Holiness had heard with the greatest joy of the victories obtained over the Puritans, for which he not only returned thanks to the Lord God, but desired that the ensigns taken from the enemy might be sent to Rome, there to be hung in one of the Basilicas as a perpetual memorial and incitement to assist the cause of Ireland.

2ndly. That the Holy Father had now sent additional supplies which he believed had already arrived in France, and that even more might be confidently expected. The Nuncio thought this the place to censure a document given to him last July in Limerick, in which those supplies were depreciated as much below the needs of the times. He therefore mentioned the different sums of money that had been furnished to Ulster, Connaught, and other places, enlarging on the advantages resulting therefrom, of which the principal had been the repulse of the Scotch just when preparing unopposed to march upon Kilkenny. The Nuncio asked what, if this had taken place, would then have become of the city? how profaned the churches! how dispersed the priests! and in fine what might not have been done in the very hall in which they were at that moment assembled?

3rdly. He said that His Holiness manifested the above sentiments in a letter of reply to the Council at the time when the happy news reached him; this letter together with that from Cardinal Pamphili, although directed to the Council, he presented to the Assembly, all power being now vested in that body in consequence of the dissolution of the General Council.

The Nuncio concluded by enumerating the advantages that would result from following his counsel, and the evils from despising it. And, after speaking of the authority delegated to him for the benefit of the kingdom, he gave the Apostolic Benediction to all present, who received it kneeling.

REPORT OF THE PUBLIC REJECTION OF THE PEACE OF AUGUST BY THE GENERAL ASSEMBLY.

Kilkenny, February 4th, 1647.

The Assembly commenced its session with all those signs of discord and intrigues which generally reign in such meetings, and consequently there was great danger of an open rupture between the two parties. On the one side were the clergy with their adherents, on the other the Ormondists and all who promoted or treated of peace. These last had two objects in view: one common to the whole faction, to force upon the kingdom the acceptance of the peace in spite of the declarations of the clergy: the other touching those alone who had taken part in it, who wished to clear themselves from the charge of perjury laid against them by the clergy in their edict, and to show that they had throughout acted honourably and with good faith.

The aim of the ecclesiastics was to procure the total rejection of the peace by the entire kingdom and the establishment of a closer union; but there was a division of opinion as to the condemnation of the Commissioners, many insisting that for the honour of the clergy, this should take place before proceeding further: others declaring that it would be more suitable to an ecclesiastical body not to show such urgent desire for revenge. It soon became evident that in the end it would be nearly impossible to reconcile the two parties; and the question was debated in the Assembly for three weeks with so much acrimony in public, and such underhand doings, such intrigues, such malignity in private, that on some days it appeared as if the Ormonde party were on the point of gaining their object. A decree was then issued appointing a stated number of each party to meet and see whether they could not come to some satisfactory agreement.

It soon appeared at this Congress that all the uproar had been created by the Commissioners in their anxiety to ensure their own justification; all the rest being willing to condemn the peace, and offering to pass a resolution which should embrace the two points, namely, to annul the peace and pardon the contumacious.

In the private meetings of the clergy I forthwith gave it as my opinion that we ought to listen to this party and see how the resolution might be amended; since the rejection of the peace was necessary for the honour of our decrees, for security of conscience, and in order to obtain my signature: every other consideration being of less importance than this, since on it rested the honour and conscience of the ecclesiastics.

The document then after many replies and changes of opinion was modified into the form now published; a copy of which I enclose, in which your Eminence will see that the peace is rejected in sufficiently significant terms, after declaring the condemnation which was pronounced upon it by the clergy. As to the justification of the Commissioners, it is expressed in such a manner as appears to me to touch neither the honour or judgment of the clergy; though the ecclesiastical decree being founded upon the thirty articles published in Dublin, the Commissioners allege that it is not founded on these alone but on some secret ones, Glamorgan's for example, and on others arranged and managed privately. This induced me to countenance the declaration of the assembly that they had acted with good faith and had not violated the powers intrusted to them. But those who know how the negotiation was really carried on by these deputies, and what confusion and disorders they caused in their anxiety to aggrandize the Marquis of Ormonde, can plainly see that what is said in the manifesto bears a double face, and that the words well considered carry far more of accusation than justification in them. Those men can never deny having known from the first of the revocation of Ormonde's authority with regard to the peace, nor yet the denial by the King in London of Glamorgan's power. Setting apart many other considerations, how could they in honour proceed under secret powers which they knew to be annulled?

In this affair Father Scarampi held a contrary opinion, and communicated it in writing to the Bishops and the congregation: he considered that the matter of the peace and the setting at liberty of the contumacious should on no account be in any way connected, but that the first should be definitively settled, and the last left to the arbitration of the assembly; since the union of the two proceedings would give the impression that the clergy had yielded the second point, because they could not secure the first. He added that the Commissioners were anxious for the liberation clause not for any good purpose, but in order to reinstate themselves in the government of the kingdom, and so place affairs on their old footing, or perhaps with a worse intention to accept the very peace already condemned. He therefore advised that first of all the peace should be annulled by the assembly, and if this were refused, that the Bishops should quit the Committee and declare all further proceedings null and void, a threat which he was sure would secure the adoption of all necessary measures.

The Prelates one and all were of a contrary opinion, and I confess that I was inclined this time to agree with them, because they assured me nothing but discord could be expected in the present bad humour of the Assembly; and it appeared to me that, if the Bishops should leave it, they would seem the very cause of disunion among those who profess to have no other desire than to promote union. I believe therefore that, if a division must come, it had better take place when new proposals in favour of the Catholic faith are brought forward, when the disgrace would fall on our opponents who refused, and not on the clergy who proposed them as both necessary and useful. Besides, the included declaration being an act not of the clergy but of the Assembly, I was not displeased that it combined both propositions, as nothing more or less could have been done if the clergy had not consented; and if the justification had been separated from the peace, it might have been so extended and modified as to be but little honoured by the clergy, and on the part of the Assembly all sorts of evil reports might have been raised against the Ecclesiastics.

Seeing the Bishops inclined to this opinion, and being fearful of a schism and anxious to avoid giving our opponents any occasion for a rupture, I authorized them to act as they desired. The sequel of the affair has produced these three notable effects. The first that, at the publication of the manifesto, twelve only out of 300 showed themselves openly averse to it. Secondly that on the arrival of Viscount Taaffe and Colonel Barry with a safe conduct on the part of the Marquis of Ormonde to treat among other matters of the confirmation of his peace and summoned perhaps by the faction which hoped to obtain it, the declaration was made as it were in spite of them after they arrived in Kilkenny and before they could gain admittance into the assembly. To the third I devote the accompanying cipher.

(IN CIPHER).

Kilkenny, February 4th, 1647.

At the beginning of the disturbances I frequently assured Father Scarampi, that nothing would cause me so much regret as that France should interfere in the matter of the peace, as I could not then so strenuously oppose it; remembering that the sentiments of the French Envoy (of which I informed your Eminence in a letter written on the 8th of July from the camp before Bunratty) were but little favourable to religion, and showed a strong inclination to aggrandize the Marquis of Ormonde.

This man has since then shown great interest in the said Marquis and made constant efforts to smooth all obstacles to the peace, blaming the Clergy who rejected it, and always making use of the King's name. On the first day of the assembly he presented credentials from His Majesty signed October 18th and expressed himself in almost threatening terms. Seeing that this had no effect, and that the assembly evidently inclined to condemn the peace, he wrote a very angry expostulation of which I enclose a copy. On that very day however, the rejection took place accompanied by the conditions of which I wrote. During these proceedings I laid before some few of the members the letter written to me on the subject by Monsignor the Nuncio of France, dated November 20th (that is, a month later than the Envoy's letters), and giving an opinion quite contrary to what he had asserted; I could not therefore hesitate to communicate this also, without bringing the word of the minister into disrepute.

I do not know what part the King will take in this affair, but if it appears that he really does wish to interfere, I cannot see how we can act without trenching upon the government of Ormonde, to which indeed all these movements tend.

To Cardinal Pamphili.

February 5th, 1647.

I send to your Eminence by Father Scarampi, three reports and one in cipher, which will comprise all that has taken place in the General Assembly; and likewise inform you of a sally made into the quarters of the Marquis by General O'Neill, in which he was completely successful and sustained scarcely any loss. I hope by the next vessel to send you further accounts.

I am, &c., &c.

To the Same (in Cipher).

February 15th, 1647.

In the Assembly, after the written condemnation of the peace was read, the proposals made by the Clergy were examined one by one with the most scrupulous care in order that they might be sworn to by all the members, and that no peace could possibly be made without their consent. By degrees all obstacles will be overcome, but a secret plot has been discovered including many who have thus sworn; the members of which bind themselves by oath not to enter into any agreement until some adjustment of affairs has been come to with Ormonde. Here then we encounter our greatest difficulty—the general compact is refused by none, but the manner and the conditions are understood by every one according to his own view, and to further his own ends.

If few are engaged in this plot they will have to yield; if many, either a division will take place amongst the Confederates, or the Marquis will obtain all that he desires.

I am, &c.

To the Same (in Cipher).

February 15th, 1647.

The Dean of Fermo* wrote to me on the 4th of December to send two frigates to La Rochelle for the safe transport of the money. On the 13th of January I had a letter from the Nuncio of France, advising me that he had not yet been able to obtain an order from the Court for its exportation from the kingdom. By different opportunities I wrote to the Dean that there were no frigates here, and that even if there were I should be doubtful what course to pursue, as in consequence of the above-mentioned advice I did not know what was best to do. At the same time I entreated him not to be in too great a hurry: assuring him that I did not want the money until the end of March, and before then there may be vessels to send him.

I am, &c.

To the Same.

On the very day on which Father Scarampi set sail from Waterford, Mr. Geoffry Barron landed at the same port a few hours later on his return from his embassy in France. He rejoiced the kingdom by assuring us that the most

* See Doc. VII.

Christian Court would not countenance any but an advantageous peace in Ireland, and that the rejection of the one lately published in Dublin had been highly applauded.

He also brought me two despatches from your Eminence dated the 10th and 17th of December, to which I shall not now reply, having scarcely opened the letters when an unexpected opportunity presents itself of writing by a vessel about to sail. Herewith I send two duplicates of the letters sent on the 1st and 5th of February, together with one letter and two in cipher.

To the Same (in Cipher).

February 23rd, 1647.

Richard Belling when justifying himself to the assembly for his share in the rejected peace alleged the following, besides other reasons: That when in Rome two years ago the Holy Father had said to him in presence of Father Luke Wadding that, considering the King's position, it would be well for the Irish to obtain all they could from the peace, and if unable to procure public security to be content with a secret one. He added that this above everything else had induced him to approve and conclude the treaty. I was anxious to hear if this excuse had made any impression; as I was in that case prepared to refute it publicly, and to justify my opposition as conformable to the wishes of His Holiness. But as the assembly were not influenced by it, I merely summoned him, explained his error, and showed him how little it would have served his cause; because, granting that His Holiness had said these words in consequence of his report (and God knows what that was), he could not deny having heard from me both in speaking, writing, and many other ways, that His Holiness had given me totally opposite instructions as soon as he had learned the true state of affairs from Father Scarampi in 1645; and that therefore either his excuse was false, or he accused me of being a minister who did not obey the commands of my superiors.

He could only say in reply that, having made a report of it to the Supreme Council on his return from Rome, it had been registered in the archives and could not be subsequently revoked: promising at the same time to let me see it, which he has never yet done. This conduct shows what sort of man he is, and with what sort of faith he acted at Rome; since now, in treating of an adjustment with the Marquis of Ormonde, no one speaks or writes more discreditably than he does: wishing to bestow the government on Ormonde contrary to all sense and reason, after he had many times said to me that there would be no safety for the kingdom but in a Catholic Viceroy: which Father Scarampi who is well aware of the fact can testify.

To the Same.

Kilkenny, February 23rd, 1647.

An unexpected opportunity enables me to send your Eminence a duplicate of the dispatch forwarded on the 15th of February, and in addition some papers in cipher, that you may have constant news of our proceedings.

I have now only to say that after passing the condemnation of the peace, the form of which I send, the Assembly after much discussion agreed to accept the propositions made by the clergy concerning religion, and are bound by oath to conclude no peace without them. After this the form of oath to be taken was considered and approved, but its administration deferred until it is seen whether an accommodation can be effected with the Marquis of Ormonde, as is greatly desired. Of all this I shall send your Eminence a full and particular account, hoping that the true ends are attained, although difficulties and incredible disputes are not wanting, which must delay the issue of resolutions so important.

I do not fail to supply all possible arguments in favour of a strict union amongst the Confederates for the benefit of religion, availing myself of the hope entertained of supplies from His Holiness, the arrival of which at this juncture would be the most fortunate circumstance that could occur. I pray God that they may arrive in safety, and that every happiness may attend your Eminence.

To the Same.

March 1st, 1647.

Whilst the congregation of the clergy were drawing up the propositions which were to be sworn to for the establishment of the Catholic faith, some Bishops read, as already decided on, a paper to a similar effect, that so long as the King was a Protestant, the election of the Bishops and the other beneficed clergy in this kingdom should be vested in the Supreme Council the Metropolitans and the Chapters, according to a settled form. This struck me as something quite new, and I immediately asked why any change should be made in what I had found established and considered most just, viz. that the election depended on the free choice of His Holiness. I was answered by almost all that this was a necessary article, which if not granted would impede the conclusion of all others ; and they gave me two reasons in particular for this assertion.

First, that the whole kingdom wished and had sworn to preserve the King's prerogatives, one of which consisted in the nomination of the Bishops. Secondly, that there would be no way of preventing the King from filling the vacant bishoprics with Protestants unless a particular provision was made for them, and that the provision could not be made except by vesting the real privilege in the Supreme Council and the kingdom. To refer the nomination to the Pope, they said, would be to destroy all hope of obtaining further concessions from the Protestants. With regard to this second reason it was not difficult to prove to them that by swearing to the other propositions, of which I shall speak immediately, the Confederates would be bound to unite their whole forces if necessary, to dismiss from their benefices not the Bishops alone, but all heretics, and at the same time to restore the ritual and splendour of the Catholic religion; and therefore it was not to be feared either that the King would send such persons, or that they would be allowed to set foot amongst the Catholics. With respect to the first point, I was obliged to put forth all my strength, as I never had met with such opposition before. Many things were alleged either utterly false, or founded on false assumptions of which we have no certain knowledge. For example, that the King had the privilege of nominating the Bishops, and that the bishoprics are in the patronage of the Crown; that His Majesty has this privilege not only in England but also in Ireland; and that he always exercised it before heresy crept into the kingdom. And when I, in order to avoid a long disquisition on the truth of these facts, replied that whether the privilege had been granted or not, certain it was that on account of the King's heresy it had returned to the giver, *i.e.*, the Holy See, and that it was ridiculous to say the Confederates had sworn to preserve intact a prerogative which the King no longer possessed, they replied that their doctrines were different from those of Rome. I then said that it would be the safest way to leave the matter as it was, and that when the Lord God granted the conversion of the King they could act as might be agreed upon between him and the Apostolic See, but no one approved of this addition to the article. Four of the best informed lawyers were deputed by the Assembly to try to convince me, and I was obliged to listen to all the crude maxims which hold good in temporal courts, as for example that the King has *ipso jure* the nomination of the prelates,—that this patronage of the Crown is not lost by a heretic, but that it passes to those who hold in deposit the kingdom and other royal prerogatives,—and that at all events the English law nominates lay judges, who are competent to decide upon the validity of appointments. These fancies being beyond removal by any remedies I could apply, I only answered that it was not for them to discuss questions of doctrine with me, which must I knew be decided on different principles; and seeing that we should never agree, I proposed to leave the matter undecided, and that they should acquaint me with what they desired to obtain from the great bounty of His Holiness, to whom I would faithfully report it; at the same time informing them that I was determined not to allow any change whilst I remained in the kingdom, and that I should therefore oppose any such measures by all the means in my power. They reported my words to the Assembly, and returned to me very much softened, saying they were satisfied I should write, and that the affair should remain as at present. They then expressed their fears, which I perceived were at the bottom of all this turmoil, that the churches might be bestowed against their wishes on strangers, and especially on the English, and that the benefices of Catholic patrons might be conferred without presentations, that is to say, as if free; adding that the Council desired to propose candidates as before, and prayed that such might be preferred. I replied that as to foreigners and the inviolability of the rights of lay patrons I could assure them of their requests being granted, knowing that His Holiness' wishes are solely directed to the well-being and tranquillity of the kingdom. I assured them also that His Holiness would willingly attend to the recommendations of the Council as he had hitherto done; but I could not promise that all whom they proposed for benefices should receive them, as the power of the Apostolic See was not to be restricted by anyone, but having already received such satisfaction on this head from it they might very well judge what was likely to happen in the future, especially if they fulfilled their part as might be expected from obedient sons of the Holy Church. Thus ended the controversy. I was convinced from the first that it would bring out some extravagant proposal, as the tenacity with which this people insist on their demands is extraordinary; however as it has been silenced, I think that the crisis may be considered to have passed with as little peril as could be expected.

To the Same (in Cipher).

March 2nd, 1647.

The Earl of Glamorgan, now Marquis of Worcester, has received letters from France from the Earl of Crawford a Scotchman and a great friend of his, saying that the Queen of England is most anxious to come to Ireland with the Prince, being but little satisfied with the proceedings of the Court of France; and adding that Her Majesty wished him to induce the clergy and nobility to invite her by letter. The Marquis has not as yet spoken of this to anyone but me, and I do not think that the invitation will be given, both for the old reasons and also to avoid having a Protestant prince here. I also think that the Queen made the proposal under the impression that Dublin was in the hands of the Catholics, as Geoffrey Barron on his return from France mentioned that Her Majesty had hinted it to him, and had said that she would be satisfied if one church were kept for the prince and his religion. We cannot therefore be certain whether she is still of the same mind; but if it be true (as is believed) that the King has fled to Scotland to Antrim's army, he may come over here some day unexpectedly. In this case the others might come too, and I should wish your Eminence to inform me how to act under the circumstances. I shall in any case wait to know what determination the Confederates will come to on the subject.

Richard Butler, brother to the Marquis of Ormonde, is

gone to France, accompanied only by Lord Digby without warning to his wife or his friends; some say that he went on the part of Ormonde to invite the Prince of Wales to Ireland.

To THE SAME (IN CIPHER).

March 4th, 1647.

The first business done in the Assembly was the proposition made by the clergy of the measures necessary for our religion, so that, when an oath to observe them and to conclude no peace without them has been taken by every one, there may be no room for further vaccillation. The articles after much trouble and dispute were drawn up to the number of four—these comprehend all that concern the public exercise of the Catholic religion in splendour. The demand for a Catholic Viceroy is not included, but I do not permit the clergy to fail in this resolution, and among the nobility there are many to support it; but as the Ormonde faction will not hear of it, it is better to defer urging this point until in treating of peace we demand securities, of which this will be the first. Your Eminence will find enclosed the said proposals, to which I have appended some marginal notes. They were sworn to by all the members in the form of oath which I also enclose: but this only took place after much discussion and incessant difference of opinion, the evil disposed wishing to reserve the power of reconstructing every resolution as they pleased; it was however finally agreed in a separate declaration that with the Assembly alone should rest the power of declaring the kingdom unable to carry out these proposals. This did not entirely please me; for although in a full assembly there is no fear of the well-disposed not prevailing, still this inability might be asserted and without any foundation if but few members, and those our opponents, should be present, and so bring us to inferior conditions. However, as the clergy are to frame the oath, we may hope that things will turn out favourably. And it is certain that for six years no advantage equal to this has been gained; and considering the disunion existing in the country, it is no slight thing to have done so much.*

To THE SAME (IN CIPHER).

March 6th.

Although your Eminence will have seen from my letters that something has been done for religion in this Assembly, still in the fundamental point of forming a close union in the country, we are completely at a stand still,—dissensions raging more bitterly than ever, and the Ormonde faction more than ever bent upon depressing the clergy, Owen O'Neill, and his army, and on aggrandizing the Marquis. This unwearied faction constantly meet in secret and turn every thing to their own ends. Yet of public affairs no one seems to think; although the enemy is advancing, and in Munster they are at Cappoquin where one Cellis† has been sent as Lord Lieutenant by the Parliament, and it is thought that this year they will make a great effort in that quarter.

The Scotch also are gathering in great force on the confines of Ulster, while the Confederates have neither union, money, nor provisions of any kind, and are occupied with their private quarrels; at which the Ormondists rejoice greatly, since they will be able now to reproach the clergy for not having concluded that peace with the Marquis. Your Eminence can imagine our condition; and I can say nothing of the supplies sent by His Holiness, as I have heard nothing, and can only pray for their safe arrival.

Yesterday some resolutions were passed in the Assembly (which I will send to your Eminence) which will lessen the

* See Doc. No. VIII.   † *Qu.* Lord Lisle ?

force of the oath, and prove how anxious the faction is to deprive the clergy of power and vest it wholly in the Marquis.

To the Same (in Cipher).

March 7th, 1647

Your Eminence will see that the first clause of the oath taken in this Assembly is fealty to the King, and this all the Bishops took without hesitation. This point is so warmly insisted upon by every one, the Clergy included, that a Nuncio could not in anywise oppose it without giving rise to a suspicion that his object here was not simply that of his embassy; which the ill affected have frequently, without even this reason, insinuated in my case. Therefore I took care from the first in nowise to oppose their professions of loyalty; and as I found the proposal still pending for sending the 10,000 soldiers to the King, I put in a few words to urge them to do so: saying that they should uphold and assist the King, prove themselves good subjects, &c., &c.

The error which I acknowledge in reference to the alleged perjury, I committed also last year in the document drawn up by the Bishops and Clergy against Glamorgan's peace and sent to Rome in which they protested against the injury done to religion and the King, and which I was the first to sign. But when I learnt that the promised assistance was only to be sent in the event of an advantageous peace, I confess that a similar feeling induced me to agree to the decree, knowing that in the former oath it was clearly understood that the King was to be assisted against the Parliament; and if an opportunity should present itself, I should have had a great field upon which to explain myself on the subject. It may be that a similar idea passed through the mind of Father Scarampi; because although accustomed to give me his opinion on all occasions, he said nothing concerning either the protest or the perjury. This I say, not to excuse what

I have done, as I see clearly I should not have signed it; although, as being the first decree of the newly assembled Council, I was warmly entreated to do so. My aim is solely to induce your Eminence to believe that this is and will be for some time to come a point of the greatest difficulty to ministers; since nothing is treated of, nothing concluded and nothing demanded, without introducing this question of fealty to the King. On many occasions it is absolutely necessary to avoid the subject, on others to dissemble, and to live in perpetual watchfulness, which with the aid of God I hope to use more and more through the gracious advice and admonitions of your Eminence.

To the Same.

March 7th, 1647.

Father Oliver Walsh, an Irish Carmelite who is going to Rome to attend a Chapter of his order, gives me an opportunity to inform your Eminence of what has up to this period occurred in the Assembly. I send by him four ciphers, two papers half in cipher, and four ordinary documents. The Father promised to forward the despatches carefully, in case he should take any other route; I therefore hope they will arrive in safety.

I send back a letter to Father Scarampi received in the last despatch, which arrived after he had set out. I rejoice to think that he must have had a good passage to Flanders, as for four or five days after his departure the wind was most favourable.

To the Same (in Cipher).

March 17th, 1647.

Letters have been read in the Assembly from one of our agents at the most Christian Court, which confirm all that Geoffry Barron said on his return, of which I wrote to your Eminence on the 2nd of this month; viz. that the Queen of

England would highly approve of the Confederates having in their possession all the churches and fortresses in the kingdom, and a Catholic Viceroy,—that Cardinal Mazarin was of the same opinion—and that the Queen was about to send some one to Dublin on purpose to explain her sentiments to the Marquis. The agent who wrote added as if from his own idea what your Eminence will see in the enclosed letter, in regard to which much discussion has taken place; since many believe that the proposal comes direct from the Queen and Prince who are in great want; others think that the Dean of Fermo and His Holiness' money are detained in France with this design; which I should consider a most disgraceful proceeding on the part of that kingdom; since in the present emergency, we cannot be certain of obtaining anything from the astute Marquis of Ormonde, and we should lose on every side; whereas on the contrary, if we had to treat with a man of even common honesty, I should think it not unadvisable to devote part of the money to buying the churches and fortresses now in the King's districts. The person sent by the Queen has not yet arrived; and God knows what orders he may bear, since the changes in the King's position may alter her intentions. The Marquis is in treaty with commissioners from the Parliament and is trifling with the Catholics; and having received no letter from the Dean of Fermo, we are in the greatest state of perplexity.

To Cardinal Mazarin.

March 23rd, 1647.

As I deeply regretted the contumacy of the Barberini family towards the Holy Father, principally on account of the differences that might thence arise between His Holiness and the most Christian Crown; so on hearing from your Eminence of their restitution in the favour of His Holiness with demonstrations of affection on both sides, I was exceedingly comforted, and returned fervent thanks to God for the happy conclusion of the affair. Hearing likewise that His most Christian Majesty had met this favour by acting with great generosity towards the Prince of Piombino, in consequence of his relationship to His Holiness, I am quite convinced that this will be the foundation of an affectionate intercourse between the two Sovereigns, from which must result the greatest advantages to Christianity; and I beg to offer my sincere congratulations. Concerning the levies of which Monsieur de la Monière spoke to me, I freely confess that I do not quite understand the business. The Council and congregation who now govern, far from having any intention of refusing the remainder of the soldiers formerly promised to the most Christian kingdom when they conceded the same permission to Spain, have always resolved to serve that Crown also and to show no preference or difference between them. I can also bear this further testimony that Monsieur de Molins was judiciously advised by some one to make the same request, and was assured it would be immediately granted; but he apparently had reasons for refraining then from doing so. The promise has not been as yet fulfilled, since it appeared to the Assembly that the present necessities of this kingdom did not admit of such a concession; and if it be refused, I do not know whether those who are anxious to maintain a friendly understanding with the most Christian kingdom will be pleased, for the greater number are averse to granting to one country what is refused to another. For my own part I do not deny having had some authority with the members, while the clergy of whom I am the head had a share in the government: but after the convocation of the General Assembly, which took place at my suggestion, and the formation of a new government, I voluntarily laid down my temporal authority, so as to devote myself, if God permit, to spiritual cares alone; for in this country where the Church is but slowly reviving, matters which require to be reformed daily suggest themselves and require the constant exercise of pastoral vigilance. Nevertheless whatever I may be, my principal desire will be to use my best endeavours to obey the commands of your Eminence.

As to the peace with the King of Great Britain, the Confederates have never wavered in their wish for it, always taking for granted the free and public exercise of the Catholic religion; in proof of this, the present Assembly sent two Commissioners to signify the same to the Marquis of Ormonde and to entreat him to open a communication with them on the religious articles, but it appears that while apparently eager to negotiate with us he has throughout preserved an understanding with the Parliament; and now, after pledging his word to us has joined entirely with that party, and the departure of one of his sons to London has raised a suspicion that he expects some men of authority in order to give Dublin over into the hands of the Parliament. Thus the underhand proceedings of this man are at last unveiled, after plunging the country and this kingdom into a state of the greatest distress; it only remains for us to entreat for assistance from all Catholic Princes, who I firmly believe will never allow a country so devoted to the true faith to fall into the hands of an enemy so powerful, and moreover so entirely bent on overthrowing the monarchy. Your Eminence will be informed by others as well as myself of the great confidence placed by this Assembly in the kindness and magnanimity of His most Christian Majesty, and in the assistance and favour of your Eminence, to which I willingly add a word to strengthen all I have many times written of their deference towards you, to pray you not to give credence to what has been said to the contrary, and to believe that I have no greater ambition than to write and explain the whole truth.

I am, &c.

To Cardinal Pamphili (in Cipher).

March 24th, 1647.

After many and extraordinary efforts by both factions in the kingdom, the Assembly have at last decided to elect twenty-four members of Council for the future government; viz. twelve resident and twelve to move from place to place, of all of whom I enclose a list. Except four they are all adherents of the clergy, so that the body elected is publicly called the Council of the Clergy; and from this, it may be seen how much the ecclesiastical party has increased in authority and how much it preponderates over the other. The Ormonde faction are extremely mortified; and it is evident that if they meditate a new effort, they must submit at last. I am perfectly satisfied, since I see more confidence may be placed in the present Council than in that of last year; and even if things turn out differently from what I write in the subjoined ciphers, still this must be considered as a good beginning. During the whole session of the Council, the Bishops of Clogher and Ferns above all others have supported our plan with great constancy, and have fully confirmed the hopes I expressed of them in my first report.

To the Same (in Cipher).

March 24th, 1647.

While I awaited a reply from the Marquis of Ormonde concerning the agreement which he had sent a messenger to solicit, he had finally made terms with the Parliament and despatched to London as hostages, one of his sons and the Earl of Roscommon, and is now awaiting troops to take possession of Dublin and other places. There is much variety of opinion as to what he will himself do; some say he will cross to Holland, and others to the most Christian kingdom: while many believe that he will remain as Viceroy for the Parliament and remain so during his whole life, and thus be the fatal instrument of Ireland's ruin. In his reply, although as usual ambiguous, he informs the Assembly of his determination, and endeavours to prove that he has been driven to it by the want of confidence in him shown by the Catholics; which indeed is insisted on by his obstinate faction, who are not ashamed to say that the clergy by rejecting the peace have forced him to this step, and that the Catholic religion will never flourish as it might have done under his administration. The news however has had an astonishing effect on the greater number and even on many of his most intimate friends, who not only call him traitor but are disposed to join our party. From the large body of evidence now accumulated we are of opinion that a year previous to my arrival in the Island the Marquis was already leagued with the Puritans, and had determined to conquer the Catholics, thereby opening the way to his partial or complete government of the kingdom. I cannot tell your Eminence what alarm and confusion the news has caused. None believe it possible to resist so many enemies; Munster is in arms, the remembrance of last year is strong in Ulster, and what with the loss of Dublin and the arrival of more enemies, it seems as if hope had utterly abandoned us. We have no means of raising money, or obtaining provisions, and since the 10th of December last I have had no news of the Dean of Fermo; so that unless God aids us, we cannot doubt that this year misfortune will overwhelm us and that our only safety will be in flight. I shall not fail in my duty as apostolic minister devoted to the will of the Lord God and His Holiness; I encourage this people by all means in my power, showing them that their cause must now be left in the hands of God and the Princes, who will never allow the Holy Faith to be expelled from this part of the world or the power of the Parliament to be increased by such an acquisition.

To the Same (in Cipher).

March 25th, 1647.

Monsieur de la Monière, sent by the Court of France, arrived here last week. He brought with him five vessels, showing that the principal object of his embassy is to levy soldiers, in which on account of the distresses in the kingdom he will experience considerable difficulty; since the Spanish Court has asked the same favour, and both declare that promises to this effect were made to them more than three years ago. La Monière informed me that he had orders to propose a peace between the King of Great Britain and the Catholics, insuring to them the free and public exercise of their religion. In all this his account did not vary from the advices already received from France (of which I have informed you) that not only the Court but the Queen of England wished the Confederates to receive every satisfaction. He further assured me that the Queen had sent a messenger to signify this to the Marquis of Ormonde, but that nobleman having in the meantime taken the unworthy step before mentioned, La Monière immediately sailed to Waterford to consult with Lord Digby, who is still there waiting for a passage to France; and, the meetings having been secret, it is not well known whether they have determined to give up the negotiations or to employ some secret means.

Many think that their attempt will be to place this kingdom under the protection of France, since the Confederates, in consequence of Ormonde's infamous conduct, have again begun to discuss the subject of a Protector, as they did last year when this same Ormonde seemed averse to peace. The fact of the King having fallen into the hands of the Parliament will be a most powerful incentive to this resolution; but I will have nothing to do with it, partly because no commands have reached me from your Eminence, and partly because as the question treats of one of the Crowns I must preserve a strict neutrality. It is quite plain that the choice will lie between His Holiness and the King of France. Those who are in favour of the King allege in support of their opinion his near neighbourhood, the better supply of money, and the interest that he has in preventing the conquest of this country by the Parliament. Others say however that no other Christian prince can lose anything by the choice of His Holiness, and that we may therefore count upon the assistance of all, because we shall give offence to none,—that the Holy See has more means of raising money than any sovereign whatsoever,—that none can honour Ireland with ministers of higher rank and authority than the Pope,—and that to none can it be of more importance than to the Roman Church that the Catholic Faith should be preserved in this remote part of Europe. This is all that has yet been brought forward on the subject.

I am, &c.

To the Same (in Cipher).

March 25th, 1647.

The desertion of the Marquis of Ormonde to the Parliament has begun to show some of the results for which well judging men have all along hoped. A stricter union has already become visible between the different parties, but every one allows that necessity alone can cement it entirely.

Dissatisfaction however is still evident, and the evil disposed do not fail to declare that there is still hope of an accommodation with the Marquis; good resolutions therefore are tardy in being passed. Enclosed are the articles proposed in the Assembly as the ground-work of a reconciliation with Ormonde, to which I made the clergy add those which are particularly marked, the others appearing to me to be more to his advantage and honour than to that of the Confederates. As he has refused to accept them, the pride and the objects of this man may easily be conceived.

The kingdom is in great distress and misery. In Munster a plot has been discovered, headed by Viscount Muskerry, against the Marquis of Worcester who is general there, and prosecuted with so much ardour that it may cause the loss of the whole province this year. Preston is still under the shadow of his treaty in Dublin, and he is consequently more exasperated than ever against O'Neill, as is O'Neill against him. In Ulster the Scotch are reinforcing themselves, and if Dublin be taken we shall be hemmed in on all sides. Nevertheless I keep up my courage, and trust in God and the counsel of His Holiness for the salvation of this island.

Since I wrote the above we have heard of the arrival of sixteen Parliamentary vessels in the river Shannon under Bunratty, perhaps with the intention of retaking that place. God grant that such be not the fruits of the dissensions now rife in that province.

To the Same.

March 27th, 1647.

All that has occurred in this Assembly in addition to the other proceedings in the kingdom is related at length in the five accompanying sheets in cipher. But I must further inform your Eminence that the said Assembly has in a public decree declared the Capuchins and Jesuits to be entitled to all the prerogatives enjoyed by the other religious communities of the kingdom; and they are not to be considered for the future mere missionaries as they were formerly.

If the Lord God grants a short interval of tranquillity to this kingdom, this concession will be productive of the most important results in the salvation of souls. I must also inform you that the Bishop of Raphoe, taken prisoner by the Scotch some three years ago, has been at last liberated in exchange for the prisoners taken last year in Ulster; this is a great consolation to me, as I always thought it disgraceful that the clergy here did not ransom their brother in the church, even though it involved much expense. If the vessel by which I write be detained as usual by contrary winds, I will add anything that happens, since every day some event of importance may be expected to take place.

To THE SAME (IN CIPHER).

Kilkenny, March 31st, 1647.

Lord Digby, who had waited several days on the coast for fair weather, after two interviews with Monsieur Tallon (who came a few days since from France) suddenly set sail without waiting for a certainty of fair weather.

This occurrence, taking place immediately on hearing of Ormonde's defection, has given rise to the suspicion that he is gone to France to bring over, if not the Queen, at all events the Prince. There is no doubt that this was proposed by France, which perhaps is anxious to be rid of the expense; the agents are of course in favour of the project, and perhaps many of the nobles of the Ormonde faction know and will uphold it for their own ends; indeed I have some hints that the Prince had been invited before by public and private letters. This will be an addition to the other troubles of this kingdom; because if Dublin is in the hands of the Parliament, the Prince must disembark at Waterford or some other Catholic port, necessarily creating expense and confusion. I am earnestly considering how I shall act in this matter as I have no time to receive your Eminence's commands nor to know the will of His Holiness.

To CARDINAL PANZIROLO.

April 7th, 1647.

The resolution taken by His Excellency Don Cammillo Pamphili to divest himself of his Cardinalship is doubtless worthy of the highest praise, since His Holiness has accepted his resignation, and as he himself thought long and anxiously before laying down his dignity. To me, who am one of the humblest and most devoted servants of His Excellency, it remains but to hope that the results of his marriage will be as fortunate as he can desire, and that by thus providing for the succession of his family the life and happiness of His Holiness may be secured.

I return fervent thanks to your Eminence for this news, of which a report had already reached me; but it was so vague that until the receipt of the last despatch, I did not dare to change the superscription of the letters, which on account of the distance to Rome will be the last received by His Excellency under the title of Cardinal.

To Don Cammillo Pamphili.

April 7th, 1647.

During the time that your Excellency held the rank of Cardinal you were so condescending a protector of my person and office that, although you have now judged it advisable to lay down your dignity, I trust you will still be equally gracious to me; and I, who up to this period have constantly prayed the Divine goodness to crown with success all your efforts to lighten the cares of His Holiness, shall henceforward pray that by perpetuating his house the life of His Holiness may be prolonged and his happiness permanently increased. The extraordinary obligations I am under to His Holiness and your Excellency I entreat may be considered as the strongest testimony of the truth of my prayers.

In Cipher.

April 7th, 1647.

The discord between the two Generals threatened at one time to bring the Assembly to a tragical termination. The bishops and clergy, suspicious of Preston from his conduct in Dublin and from what he has since said, drew up a protest against him in order that he might be deprived of his military command. Upon this, a large part of the laity were convinced that the clergy sought only to aggrandize O'Neill, and such disputes and recriminations arose as nearly to occasion a personal struggle in the public Assembly. I was requested to interpose, and the affair was easily managed, as the bishops seeing the danger immediately withdrew their protest, and a hearty reconciliation took place; after which, Preston having given every possible security to the clergy by public promises, submissions, and expressions of fidelity, everything returned to its former position. Confidence is even greater than ever, and the danger has brought about a still closer union, which I only hope may last. The danger incurred through O'Neill is more to be feared, as he is inflexible by nature and very different in character from his rival. I shall write another letter in cipher upon the subject, but I am not without hope that the dispute may be amicably arranged, as I shall employ all the means in my power to prevent its continuance.

I am, &c., &c.

IN CIPHER.

April 7th, 1647.

Although many here besides these French agents still throw doubt on the declaration of the Marquis of Ormonde in favour of the Parliament, the Council continue their preparations as if it had been completely authenticated. I cannot mention without high praise the readiness testified by the Assembly in devoting to the expenses of the war, besides their usual contributions, the tenth of all their property in lands &c. This induced the clergy and bishops to offer an eighth, and the monks the same even down to their chalices. Every one fears that the enemy will this year seize the whole island, and that the Catholics will be in a more miserable condition than ever.

Troops are being raised and expeditions laid out, and we

shall begin in the direction of Dublin to take possession of all that is not already in the hands of the enemy and to prepare for greater enterprises. I give all the encouragement I can in words, since I can do little by acts, as I find that even in February the Dean of Fermo had not yet set out from Rome.

To Monsignor the Nuncio of France.

April 18th, 1647.

Your letter, written in recommendation of Bartholomew Archer, enables me to give you in answer a short account of all that has happened up to this period in regard to the benefice to which he aspires. The rectory of Callan being vacant, and I, hearing that Archer declared it to be in the gift of the Marquis of Ormonde or one of his tenants, and also that the presentation had been made before his bishop, I determined, in order to preserve the rights of the Holy See and the freedom of benefices, to bestow it as a free living without prejudice to the asserted power of patronage, in order that by means of a legal refusal it might be better seen how the Marquis as a heretic could have a right of patronage, and how being forfeited it could pass to his tenant.

Archer, without informing me, obtained from His Holiness the said rectory, as if free: but this nomination being subsequent to mine did not stand; upon which he had again recourse to the patron, and without obtaining either judgment or process and with his mere presentation went to take possession, although his rival was already established there. His priors, unused to ecclesiastical affairs, think that they will thus conquer *de facto*, and do not perceive that, where I have no interest in the affair except to see that justice be done, I must take care for their sake that the Apostolic authority be upheld. Finally, I have arranged that two bishops shall be chosen, to whom I shall delegate my power, and who will pronounce sentence, which is as much as I can do to serve you who have recommended him to me, or ought to do to serve Archer. But I wish he could hear from your Excellency that his friends in this country by not trusting me, greatly perplex the affair; so that I am afraid it will at last have to be referred to Rome, where such matters are better understood, and therefore I do not see any certainty that he will be able to overcome the obstacles in his way. Meanwhile as the Duke of Orleans has written to me on the same subject, and as I do not wish to interrupt by my letters the course of His Royal Highness' more important business, I shall beg of your Excellency to show the enclosed to one of his ministers, that he may be made acquainted with all my proceedings.

To the Grand Duke I have replied as you will see by the enclosed copy, hoping that His Highness, Archer, and all others will be satisfied that I can do no more; but if more be desired which will not prejudice the authority and nature of the benefice, I entreat you to inform me of it, and in the meantime

I kiss your hand, and am, &c.

To the Duke of Orleans.

April 19th, 1647.

The honour done me by your Royal Highness in recommending the interests of Bartholomew Archer to my care, would induce me to give you a full account of all that has occurred concerning him, and of what I myself did on the receipt of your Royal Highness' letter; but as I am unwilling to trespass upon your time I have requested the Nuncio to inform you of the whole from a document which I have sent to him. I entreat your Royal Highness to believe that I am particularly anxious to fulfil your wishes in this as in every other respect, and I desire nothing less than that the justice of Archer's cause may permit him to urge successfully the claims which he puts forward.

I am, &c., &c.

To Monsignor the Nuncio of Spain.

April 26th, 1647.

Your Excellency's two letters of October and March together with that for Father Scarampi arrived safely, the last according to your command shall be sent to Rome; the Father having gone there at the end of February, sailing to Ostend, thence by way of Paris, and I hear that he had continued his journey in good health. The people of this kingdom as well as I, are under many obligations for the kind terms in which your Excellency speaks of our late alarm on the publication of a peace with so little security for religion.

After that event the Assembly was convoked, and in consequence of the importance of the subjects and the variety of interests discussed, it lasted three months; the Clergy notwithstanding the great difficulties thrown in their way having prevailed that the terms of that peace should be rejected by the whole country; they then called a new Council from which we may hope better things than from the last. I cannot conceal from your Excellency my satisfaction in the midst of these labours in seeing the ecclesiastical party whom I found much depressed, in such a position that for three months from the rejection of the peace, they governed the country and the Assembly; overcame all opposition in that Assembly, and regulated at their own will the greater part of political affairs. This increase of power His Holiness has still further assisted by his election of eleven new Bishops for the vacant benefices; a step which I always represented as absolutely necessary for the well-being of religion, and I congratulate myself that Father Hugh Burke was amongst those promoted.

If your Excellency obtains the grant of money of which you speak, it will be a new proof to the Confederates of the piety of His Catholic Majesty. It shall be devoted solely to the advancement of the Faith; which increases in strength daily, principally because the overthrow of the King of England has caused the depression of the royal party in Ireland, and consequently diminished the dissensions between the nobility and gentry. Efforts, more than I thought advisable, were made to induce the Marquis of Ormonde to join this party against the Puritans without prejudice to the Catholic religion; but he, not content with moderate conditions, all at once began to treat with the Parliament; the French agents however are still in hopes of breaking off the treaty and of conciliating him by concessions. I have no greater desire than to see an end put at once and for ever to these negotiations; since they keep the whole Island in suspense; and I am convinced that the truces which have been made from time to time, have been the ruin of the whole affair. The levy requested by Don Diego della Torre was finally confirmed by the Assembly; whence your Excellency who condescended to inform His Majesty of the determination of the Clergy, will favour me now by adding the report of what has been done to overcome the difficulties raised in the Council by private interests and animosities. That your Excellency may be induced to communicate with me in cipher, I send you an example of a few lines; and entreating you to remember me and my perils in your prayers, and to represent the necessities of this unfortunate kingdom to the worthy religious people of your country,

I am, &c., &c.

To the Nuncio of France.

April 27th, 1647.

Mr. Winter Grant who brought me your letter came first to Kilkenny, and then went twice to Dublin to propose terms of peace, which it appears is earnestly desired by the most Christian Court and the Queen of England.

I am of opinion that if the Marquis of Ormonde had not hastened his compact with the Parliament, to which he was always inclined, we should have concluded a treaty to the satisfaction of all parties and especially to that of the Courts which recommended it; because the Confederated Catholics were most anxious in the last Assembly to come to an amicable understanding with him on any terms; provided it was not to the prejudice of religion. The General Council sat for more than ten weeks, hoping to obtain from him some decision, which decision never came; but on the very day he had promised to send his Commissioners with his answer, to the astonishment of everyone he dispatched his son with the Earl of Roscommon to London, as hostages for his good faith with the Parliament.

When therefore Mr. Winter Grant and M. Tallon entreated the Supreme Council to agree to a cessation of arms that they might induce the Marquis to break with the Parliament and unite with us, the Confederates refused, unless security were given that during the truce the Parliamentary troops should not be allowed to disembark and quarter themselves in Dublin; and unless they should be made acquainted with the proposed conditions for the reconciliation. As Messrs. Winter Grant and Tallon could not give this security, the Confederates finally proposed a cessation of seven months duration under the same condition of not giving a hearing to the Parliamentarians; to this proposal a deaf ear being turned, the affair is at a stand, and war more probable than ever. During the holy days in which all this passed, I went to visit the Church of Wexford; and consequently was not present when the proposals were made. But I can assure your Excellency that if my advice had been asked I should have recommended the very course that has been taken; as previous to my departure from Rome, I was made acquainted with the opinions of His Holiness and all his Court, that these truces with the Viceroy have been the destruction of the kingdom and of religion; the only result of them having been to enable the Marquis to maintain and increase his forces while proportionately weakening those of the Catholics; who if they had been in possession of Dublin and the other fortresses as they might have been from the first, (as I believe Father Scarampi frequently informed your Excellency); not only would the rights of the Church have been secured but also those of the King; whom none could serve with greater fidelity than the Catholics. Further I am sure that if it had been possible to convince the Queen of this, she would have been as anxious for her own sake as for that of the Prince to preserve the Confederates from a third faction such as Ormonde's which has been the cause of constant disunion; and to keep them united in the one great object of overcoming the party so hostile to God and their King. M. Tallon is about to return and acquaint the most Christian King with all that has occurred; and I have now informed your Excellency of all that is doing in this kingdom for the Holy Faith. Winter Grant has acted with the wisdom and good sense to be expected from what you said of him in your letter; although the Catholics are of opinion that he brought letters to some of the cities and nobles but not to the Supreme Council, and also that his mission was really directed to the Marquis, and not to them.

I affectionately kiss your Excellency's hands.

To CARDINAL MAZARIN.

Kilkenny, April 27th, 1647.

During the holy days which I spent in visiting the church of Wexford, the terms of a treaty between the Confederates and the Marquis of Ormonde were again brought forward by Messrs. Tallon and Winter Grant, who went twice to Dublin for this purpose. But as I informed your Eminence in my last letter, the Marquis having bound himself to the Parliament, they could come to no satisfactory conclusion. When the Commissioners proposed a truce for the purpose of negotiation, the Confederates deemed it prudent to refuse it unless a promise should be given that during the truce the Parliamentary troops should not be admitted into the quarters of the Viceroy; and unless there was some probability of a union taking place; as otherwise the Catholics are well aware that a cessation of arms would be productive of the greatest advantage to the Marquis who has a footing in so many places; and equally of the greatest disadvantage to our party which has but one object in view. Such complete changes occur daily that, considering the present uncertainty I could not desire anything better for this people than that the most Christian King, and the Queen of Great Britain should be convinced of the benefit to the King himself, if he would secure to his subjects in this kingdom the free exercise of their religion; since in that case their Majesties would find everything left to their arbitration. M. Tallon will be the bearer of this to your Eminence, as I hear he is about to return and report all that has occurred to His Majesty; and I wished to add these few lines to assure your Eminence anew of my real intentions when religion shall have received its due honour, in accordance with the wise sentiments of your Eminence communicated to me in Paris and in your gracious letter.

A few days after I had written my last to your Eminence, it was determined in Council to grant the levy requested by the most Christian Crown; and the same favour was conceded to Spain as I informed you. Previous to my departure for Wexford M. de la Monière told me that the articles were yet to be drawn up, which I hope was done to his satisfaction.

Assuring your Eminence now as ever of my deep and constant reverence.

I am, &c.

To CARDINAL PANZIROLO (IN CIPHER).

April 28th, 1647.

It was not true that Lord Digby had set off as I reported, for after an interview with Winter Grant who was sent over by the Queen of England, he went to Dublin with him to be present at the negotiations. Winter Grant came first to Kilkenny, and in a visit to me said that he was directed by Her Majesty to go first to Dublin, but that contrary winds had driven him out of his course; adding that he had letters for me from the Queen, but also orders not to deliver them until he had communicated with the Marquis. He assured me of his intention to obtain every satisfaction for the Catholics, provided they agreed to a composition with Ormonde, and when I mentioned the Marquis's league with the Parliament, he replied that it might be easily annulled. Exactly the same was said by the French agents, one of whom went twice with Winter Grant to Dublin, but did not bring back any new propositions except an entreaty for a truce, which the Council have up to this time steadily refused, except under the condition that in the meanwhile the Parliamentary soldiers shall not be received in any of the King's quarters, or that some articles are brought forward which offer a hope of accommodation. These agents however being unable to give such security the affair remains unconcluded; things incline to war, and the Council begin to suspect that all the negotiations have been undertaken to induce Ormonde to pass over to France, with all his force for the King's service; that a truce is demanded to give the Parliament time to send troops to Dublin to prevent its falling into the hands of the Catholics, and that the whole is done with the consent of the Queen, who is anxious to please the Parliament hoping to secure good treatment for her husband; and thus the intrigues of the Marquis go on and religion makes no progress. Winter Grant has not yet delivered the letters to me, but the French agents, one of whom is ready to set sail, expatiated with me upon the obstinacy of the Council about the truce, condemned the Irish as the true criminals, and said they were rebels who cared nothing for the King nor considered themselves his subjects because he was a heretic, &c. M. Tallon who has been in Rome, and is known to the Marchese del Buffalo, told me he knew that this was the opinion held there, also that the Pope had pretensions to this kingdom, and for that reason these sentiments were set afloat. I very frankly replied that no one knew better than myself the opinions of His Holiness; that I neither had nor professed to have any instructions save to aid and protect religion; and that I was astonished at any one daring to attribute other aims to me; he then retracted and made a formal apology, saying that it was not to me he had referred, and there the conversation ended. In a word, their opinion is that the Catholics ought to throw themselves on Ormonde's generosity, and that neither religion nor the kingdom could be more secure than under his jurisdiction; as to his having entered into a compact with the Parliament and sent hostages for his good faith, they said that the conditions were not yet signed, that nothing was concluded, but that he had been driven to the measure by the violence of the Catholics, against whom he only sought to defend himself. In contradiction to this, letters have been received from the Duchess of Buckingham at Brussels, saying she had heard from London that as long ago as the 15th of February he had concluded with the Parliament. Last July when before Bunratty, I wrote to Rome that if France interfered insuperable difficulties would arise, and that if the Faith so much favoured by God was not upheld I should be fearful of the results. It was fortunate that I happened to be at Wexford when the proposal for a truce was deliberated upon here, since the Council followed the course I should have recommended, and I was not obliged to come forward. In the meantime there is no fighting at Carlow, and if Owen O'Neill were not so insubordinate, and the Dean of Fermo had but arrived, God might grant us even more glorious victories than we obtained last October.

When I had written thus far Winter Grant came to present the Queen's letter to me, of which I enclose a copy, with another to the ecclesiastical congregation. Her Majesty is anxious for us to be reconciled to the Marquis, believing it would be beneficial to the King. The answer made here is that Ormonde's league against us precludes any further intercourse with him, but as Winter Grant declares the compact incomplete, I have requested the bishops to discuss with him any means likely to serve Her Majesty, in order to convince her that it is not the fault of the Catholics that no peace has been brought about. May God grant a decision one way or other, as uncertainty injures the cause and the people, and makes us who are labouring for religion unpopular, because it appears as though we wished to injure the country.

REPORT OF THE PROCEEDINGS OF OWEN O'NEILL.

Immediately after the victories in Ulster, Owen O'Neill began to show that he wished to make use of his good fortune, (under cover of religion) for his own advancement above every one else. He gradually increased his army without permission from the Council; and hearing soon after of the rejection of the peace by the Clergy, declared himself the champion of that party and endeavoured by magnificent promises to secure the name of Promoter of the Faith. But no sooner did the congregation of the Clergy assembled at Waterford command him to march upon Dublin, than he declared it absolutely necessary first to secure Kilkenny; this was however considered a proof of his avarice, which induced him to wish under pretext of religion to despoil that opulent city, and revenge himself on his enemies the Butlers. This intention was strongly disapproved by the Clergy and by me, and if I had not sent my Confessor to dissuade him from so unjust a resolution, the city would have been sacked and much innocent blood shed. Then followed the undertaking against Dublin of which I sent you a full account; during which O'Neill had reasonable cause for suspecting that Preston intended to oppress and weaken him by favour and aid from the Marquis; but still it is well known that had he not given proofs of his high pretensions and determination to restore the old Irish faction, Preston would not have entered into a league so prejudicial to the cause and to his own reputation. After this step which so greatly imperilled Preston's honour, and the good opinion of all men, one would have supposed that O'Neill would take the opportunity of reconciling the factions and securing to himself the affection of all parties; and thus easily obtain the advantage he had so long sought over his rival. But to my great astonishment and with little regard for my advice he acted in a totally contrary manner.

The Castle of Athlone being on the boundary of Connaught and Leinster is one of the most important fortresses in the kingdom; it was taken last September by stratagem from Vicount Costello, who had held it for the King; but on his abjuring heresy before me, the Council and congregation restored the command to him. The Commander however refused obedience to the order, and as his contumacy increased in proportion to the penalties threatened, it was at last suspected as indeed turned out to be the case, that O'Neill held, and wished to keep possession of it for his own purposes. And although the General Assembly confirmed the decree of restitution under all imaginable penalties, and the present Council reiterated the same, the matter remains in the very same state, and God only knows what will be the end. Besides this, when the Assembly summoned O'Neill like any other delinquent, he being surrounded by a considerable part of his men refused to appear, alleging that he did not feel it safe; in a word all his actions prove that he recognises no superior. One thing I cannot pardon; either through gratitude for the money given last year, or for the glory of his country, or for some other purpose, he allowed his soldiers to call themselves the army of the Pope and the Church. The result is that whenever the Ulster soldiers (barbarous enough by nature although good Catholics) perform any act of cruelty or robbery, the sufferers execrate His Holiness and me, and curse the clergy whom they consider the patrons of this army. Nor has it availed that I make public declarations that His Holiness has no special soldiers and loves equally all the provinces, and is willing to aid them according to their necessities in all that concerns religion. But O'Neill has lately done what his most partial friends blame him for, in sending two regiments without any orders to quarter themselves in the county of Kilkenny; where defying the Council, they have devastated the country and perpetrated the atrocities to be expected from an unrestrained soldiery. I was at Wexford, but the Council sent to inform me, and entreated my return that we might deliberate upon some remedy for this delinquency. I immediately came, and had scarcely arrived in Kilkenny when O'Neill foolishly imagining that we intended to imprison him; suddenly set off before I could have an interview with him, and at the same time Viscount Mountgarret whose lands had been plundered, collecting a party of women from the devastated country insolently directed them to the city and to the very door of the Council room as I am told, whence he brought them to my house, where they made a dreadful uproar with howls and lamentations, thus giving it to be understood that I countenanced the cruelties perpetrated by the Ulster men. Yesterday O'Neill hanged seven of his soldiers and officers, pretending by this demonstration to satisfy all parties. The Council and I hope to bring him to order, since from his popularity in the province, and having the whole army at command, his aid is only too necessary to the Republic. The truth is, that if he will firmly join with us, be obedient, and act as his duty dictates, every advantage may be hoped to result this year to religion; since England we hear is not sending over more troops, and will perhaps from her internal dissensions be unable to send any: but if O'Neill cannot be induced to act as he should do, I shall greatly fear for the kingdom, and it will be a grief to me to see such an unhappy result from the assistance of His Holiness, and from my unceasing endeavours to keep a Chief of this description well affected to us. I feel assured the real object of the war is religion, because I see that opposition is preparing in those places where it can only be the work of the enemy of our Faith; who must every day see that the field is more and more open to its success and to the sacred intentions of His Holiness.

With profound respect, &c., &c.

To Cardinal Panzirolo.

April 30th, 1647.

Your Eminence's letter and cipher of the 18th of February* have been received, it is unnecessary however to answer them as from the annexed despatches you will see that I

* See Doc. No. IX.

continue to follow as far as lies in my power, the course which you graciously point out in your cipher. We hear that in all the Provinces the enemy is greatly increasing in number without receiving external aid; and as the Confederates are in great want of provisions and money we much need the aid of God and the protection of His Holiness whose blessed feet I kiss.

To the Same.

May 3rd, 1647.

Although I have already sent my despatch of the 30th of April to the vessel bound for France, I hope to have still time to send a separate letter informing your Eminence that after a siege of fifteen days General Preston much to his credit has taken the fort of Carlow, the only one not in our possession between Dublin and Kilkenny; and a town that has been for more than 100 years the hotbed of heresy. The Te Deum is to be sung here to-day, which will give us some comfort under the dangers threatening from other quarters and especially Ulster; where I do not see how to avert the storm that threatens, unless the Dean of Fermo arrive soon with some aid, there being no means in the kingdom wherewith to make a stand. There is however no relaxation in these negotiations with the Marquis, as Winter Grant the envoy of the Queen of England, of whom I made mention in former letters is constantly urging them on.

I am, &c., &c.

To the Queen of Great Britain.

May 3rd, 1647.

Every testimony which can convince your Majesty of my unalterable desire to benefit this kingdom, will be considered by me as a happy result of the negotiations in which I am engaged. The Earl of Crawford is about to pay his respects to your Majesty to inform you of our designs and intentions concerning Scotland; and I have requested him when he has concluded the subject of public affairs, to assure your Majesty of my continued reverence for your person, and my determination to fulfil all the duties of my charge and of a good Catholic. Your Majesty in believing these assurances will honour me as well as him, and I trust you will believe I am not less anxious to act upon this truth than to proclaim it.

May God grant your Majesty many years of health.

With deep reverence, &c., &c.

To Cardinal Mazarin.

May 3rd, 1647.

The interests of the kingdoms of Ireland and Scotland are so closely united, that if the Supreme Council had means of supplying the wants of both, the progress of the cause of religion and of the King of Great Britain would be twofold. The Earl of Crawford is about to visit Paris for the purpose of explaining this to Her Majesty and your Eminence, and of receiving through the favour of one or the other, the assistance expected from His most Christian Majesty. I recommend the Earl to your Eminence not less on account of the importance of his mission, than of his own merits: he is so well affected to the Catholic faith that I have the greatest hopes of seeing him one day in possession of this best and highest of all perfections.

I am, &c., &c.

To Cardinal Panzirolo (in Cipher).

May 12th, 1647.

As there was imminent danger of a rupture between the Council and O'Neill, I thought it well to go and visit him in company with the Bishops of Clogher and Ferns. The meeting was not entirely useless, since with respect to the Castle of Athlone which was the principal point at issue,

I made him promise to refer the question to the arbitration of the Council after satisfying himself by making known his own views; and I did the same with other points of disagreement. I then spoke to him about marching suddenly upon Dublin before reinforcements could arrive for the enemy; he assured me of his willingness to do so in fifteen days provided he should receive provisions and money during that time; but the Council have never been able to raise money rapidly, and are besides afraid that Preston and the Leinster soldiery will never allow O'Neill to advance into that Province.

I must then reconcile myself to seeing this enterprise slip from our hands a second time for want of money, the fatal misfortune of this country. We have lost Dungarvan a seaport, owing to the disunion in Munster, and because the soldiers mutiny for want of pay. If the 15,000 crowns of which I was informed in November by Don Cammillo Pamphili had arrived, they would suffice to repair in one Province at least, the unfortunate commencement of the campaign. Here at Kilkenny we shall be by no means safe and I do not know what we shall do, but I have written this hoping to send it by some vessel about to sail. From our unaccountable losses in Munster, it is suspected that the Marquis of Ormonde and his faction are in league with Inchiquin and the Ulster Scotch to surround the Confederates. I do not believe this as yet; and the inference is founded only on suspicion.

I am, &c.

To THE SAME.
May 12th, 1647.

Having found it necessary to add the enclosed cipher to the despatches already sent, I forward to your Eminence by the same opportunity some letters written by the Marquises of Ormonde and Clanricarde, which the Council have intercepted and had printed, to prove to the whole kingdom how closely the Marquis is leagued with the Parliament. Winter Grant the Queen's agent, is however gone to Dublin to see if there be still any opening for a reconciliation; of the result of his journey I will inform you by the first opportunity that presents itself.

To Monsignor the Nuncio of France.

May 12th, 1647.

On the 30th of March Father Scarampi sent me from Rome copies of two treaties, drawn up he informs me in your Excellency's presence by the Queen's secretary, confessor, and two other English priests. One of these was to stand in case the Marquis remained faithful to the King; the other, if he were already in league with the Parliament; that he is so now, is considered certain from letters written to the Marquis of Clanricarde intercepted by the Confederates, and printed by the Council, of which copies are enclosed. The packet from Father Scarampi was detained at Waterford by the bearer, which greatly displeased me; especially as in the meantime Winter Grant, the Queen's agent had gone to Dublin to find out if there was still any probability of a reconciliation with the Marquis, and I do not know whether or not he also had received copies of the articles in question, which Father Scarampi assures me have most probably been sent to him by the Queen. I however beg to assure your Excellency confidently, that the Council had demanded through Winter Grant conditions far more advantageous than these; some of which will I am sure neither satisfy nor be accepted. I should be greatly relieved could I but know the opinions and wishes of His Holiness concerning these treaties, since surrounded as we are by enemies, to act under His Holiness' commands would exonerate me from all blame in the issue of this most doubtful and arduous negotiation. We lost Dungarvan, a seaport, entirely through the negligence and disunion of the whole province, superiors and inferiors; this makes me still more fearful of the power of the enemy, because internal diseases are far more dangerous and difficult of cure than any others. Your Excellency will doubtless inform Father Scarampi of what I have written, as I shall not have time to write to him at length, though I will do so when the negotiations are concluded.

To CARDINAL PANZIROLO (IN CIPHER).

As June has now nearly arrived, and no news has been heard of the Dean of Fermo* since his departure from Rome, it is thought that he has been detained on the way, or that His Holiness has withdrawn his paternal affection from this kingdom; hence I can no longer hope by means of his assistance to ward off the perils I foresee.

I have already informed your Eminence that the Ormonde faction secretly proposed to return to the August peace, in spite of the previous rejection of it and the oaths taken in the Assembly. Their motives for this were their anxiety to restore the Marquis to his former power, of which they think more than of their religion, or of the disgrace they cast on the clergy, who rejected the above mentioned peace. Indications of this secret plot appear in the dissensions in Munster, where it is certain that the two cities taken by the enemy were gained by treason; the guilty persons were not only not imprisoned, but were publicly defended in Council by Viscount Muskerry; and the Council took the opportunity of proposing a truce with the Marquis for six months, as I was informed by a letter which your Eminence will see in the annexed dispatch. This truce will inevitably produce the effect I prophesied before, since the Marquis will take the opportunity of making himself more powerful than ever, and by his artifices will deceive all around

* See Doc. No. X.

him, while I know full well that he will never yield more than he has done already. In my immediate reply to the Council I laid before them the evils that must accrue from this cessation of arms; to which they replied (as your Eminence will see from their second letter) that they were willing to summon a council of bishops and laymen at Limerick, where I shall also be; but I am convinced that the general timidity and hostility of the laity to the clergy will outweigh my opinion, and cause the acceptance of the truce.

Remedies are difficult to find; since it is impossible without money to constrain the Marquis to march towards Dublin, and His Holiness' supplies cannot possibly arrive in time; a short time ago they would have prevented all that has occurred. To keep up the power and authority of O'Neill would be equally perilous, as his harsh proceedings and the insolence of his soldiers have produced an indescribable hatred towards him still more towards the clergy, he being considered their champion. We are therefore in a position which renders it marvellous that the enemy has not made greater progress; and if God does not aid us we shall soon have to throw ourselves into the arms of Ormonde. I shall fulfil the duties of my office and let things proceed as they will, according to your Eminence's instructions.

To the Same (in Cipher).

May 29th, 1647.

I received from Father Scarampi the two sets of terms drawn up in presence of the French Nuncio for a treaty between the Confederates and the Marquis according to the Queen's desire. Your Eminence will see by those which I send,* that we had thought here of everything contained in them (and perhaps even more) for the advantage of the Confederates and the Catholic religion.

* See Doc. No. XI.

Besides, if the Council do not change their opinion, as they often do however, there are some articles in the French treaty to which they would never consent; for example to that giving the Queen and Prince the power of appointing any of the members of the Council; and still less that which vests the appointment of Bishops in the Queen; therefore after I assured them that His Holiness would never give the Churches to the English, they agreed to avoid the risk of trusting Her Majesty. But the fact remains, that Winter Grant and the French Envoy have made it perfectly clear that the Marquis will not, nay, cannot grant the smallest concession to religion without a new commission from the King, that given by the Queen not being sufficient. In plain language this means that no treaty can be made save the one already rejected, or unless the Marquis be recognized as supreme head; and that we take his word or perhaps that of the King of France that no interference shall be attempted in the affairs of the Confederates. Thus you see everyone is working to establish Ormonde in his former position and to give him even greater power; and the French if I am not mistaken want to send the Prince over here, and the Queen likewise, whom they do not fail to hint we ought to invite. These two letters in cipher will inform you of our affairs, and prove how necessary are the aid of God and the wise counsels of His Holiness.

To Monsignor dei Bagni, Nuncio of France.

Kilkenny, May 29th, 1647.

I take the opportunity of sending to your Excellency the accompanying packet for Rome, which I trust you will forward with your accustomed kindness.

The Catholic arms here meet with very indifferent success; our troops in Munster owing to discord amongst themselves allow the enemy to advance with great rapidity; in the other provinces however we gain more than we lose. Winter

Grant and the French deputies assure me that the Marquis of Ormonde is not so bound to the Parliament as to preclude the hope of detaching him from it, and are most anxious to effect a reconciliation. Some resolution will speedily be taken on the subject, and I shall wait till then to give an account of the whole affair to your Excellency, since I believe that M. Tallon must on his arrival have informed you thus far. I am, &c., &c.

To the Same (in Cipher).

Kilkenny, May 29th, 1647.

Although some of the articles sent by Father Scarampi do not satisfy us, we are ready to take them into consideration; but Winter Grant says plainly that the Marquis of Ormonde will not yield anything on religious points until he receives further powers from the King, those given by the Queen not sufficing. From this we conclude that the truce proposed by Winter Grant is not an opening to a reconciliation, but merely desired as a means of increasing the power of Ormonde, and perhaps of returning to the condemned peace, so that we are in a more perilous position than ever, with nothing but war before us. I shall write at length after the convocation has met.

To Cardinal Panzirolo.

May 29th, 1647.

All that has taken place since the last despatch sent on the 3rd of May, is contained in the accompanying ciphers. The envoys of the most Christian King and those of the Queen of England have constantly assured me that the Marquis of Ormonde is not by any means permanently leagued with the Parliament, but can free himself whenever he chooses; the Council have therefore willingly recommenced their negotiations of which I will give an account as soon as possible. I have received letters dated the 11th of April dated Lyons from Father Scarampi, but no news from the Dean of Fermo.

To the Same (in Cipher).

Clonmel, June 11th, 1647.

Father O'Hartigan has perhaps informed you of what he wrote from Bordeaux on the 15th of April to the Confederates. He had he said received certain news from Paris that the Queen and Prince of England aided by France, have formed a design of coming to Ireland; that their intention is to land at Waterford and surprise the city by disembarking men and arms, under pretext of arming the troops levied for France in this country. For this purpose, all the Irish and English in France and Flanders are to be summoned under pretence that their assistance is required for the King; all this is done to prevent a rupture with the Parliament, with whom the Queen is anxious to be on good terms on the King's account, as I informed you some months ago. He adds that money and commissions to begin the enterprise have already been sent to Ireland; and that in this kingdom a thousand have already joined the plot, who will easily be recognized by the Council when they hold back from serving the public cause.

At first I considered this a false report, as I had received letters from Scarampi and the Nuncio of France, dated the end of March, and who must necessarily I thought have heard something of the matter; but they say not a word of it. On the other hand, there are so many signs of such a plot that I can hardly believe it is wholly without foundation. Ormonde's faction by their mode of proceeding have evidently some secret intentions; and the French Deputies frequently hint and prepare for the arrival of the Queen and Prince. What is more important still, is that a few days ago it was discovered that a heretic had attempted to induce the Commandant of Wexford Castle by a gift of 1,000 crowns to give up the fort to the Prince as a place of landing.

The Bishop of Ferns, then in the city, examined him, and took his confession with that of ———, an English Jesuit, a man most pernicious in his influence upon the affairs of this kingdom. It is a strange thing that Winter Grant the Queen's agent, has never made any mention of the articles drawn up, as I was informed by Father Scarampi, in Paris. He denies that Ormonde can grant anything to religion without further powers from the King; and seeks either to reinstate him in the Viceroyalty, or to bring forward the August peace, which, without regard to his oath he brought before the Council; as your Eminence will see in the enclosed propositions.

I cannot understand how the Marquis could have entered into a league or semi league with the Parliament and sent his son to London as a hostage, without offending the Queen, unless she countenances his proceedings and agrees with him to keep down the Catholics and gratify the Parliament. When this affair is likely to happen (if it be true) I cannot imagine, I shall deem myself fortunate if some hint of it should reach Rome in time for me to receive His Holiness' instructions as to the manner in which I should conduct myself in such a case: for as the Queen did not recognize me as Nuncio in Paris, I presume she would not here, for the same reason which moved her then, and I should therefore be obliged to retire to some remote quarter with little honour, or power of being useful; at present I do not see how anything else can happen, unless affairs undergo some change.*

* See. Doc. No. XII.

To the Same (in Cipher).

Clonmel, June 18th, 1647.

As I said in my letter of the 28th of May, a meeting of Bishops took place here to deliberate on the truce with the Marquis proposed by Mr. Winter Grant; and after much difference of opinion, the clergy resolved to leave the whole decision to the Council without offering either assent or dissent. As we hear accounts every day from Dublin of the arrival of fresh Parliamentary troops, I do not see how any reconciliation can ever be effected with one who daily becomes weaker and holds more and more aloof. It is said that on some difference with the Parliament, the Marquis had sent for O'Neill who was approaching Dublin; the Parliamentarians, on the contrary, show a disposition to advance against Preston; from which we cannot but conclude that the Marquis, according to his custom is deceiving everyone. Meanwhile Muskerry under pretext of arming himself against the enemy, and increasing the power of the Council, has made himself master of more than half the Munster army; we cannot fathom his intentions, since fear for his life is so frivolous a pretext and his ambitious views have so long been known that I conclude he is leagued with Ormonde and the French, to secure for the Prince the power to come here, to prepare forces and support for him, and subsequently to establish any peace he may choose. I do not relax in my efforts to preserve unanimity in this Province, insisting to all parties that if they are united, we may accomplish great things this year since the hostile army is mutinous, weakened by disease, and a part it is said about to be recalled to England in consequence of disturbances there. The Lord God must do the rest, as the men do not come when we want them. I am writing to the Dean at Paris not to set out this summer as the sea is infested with parliamentary ships; but to keep the money safe, as Providence did not permit it to arrive at a time when it certainly would have had important results. I deeply grieve over the delay both for the glory of God and of His Holiness.

To the Nuncio of France.

Clonmel, June 18th, 1647.

If the Dean of Fermo has arrived in Paris, or any other place in France I beg of your Excellency to give him the enclosed letter, and furnish him with what advice and assistance for his journey your prudence and goodness may suggest. I am now waiting an opportunity to bring forward the articles agreed upon between your Excellency and Father Scarampi; but as Mr. Winter Grant seems ignorant on the subject I think Her Majesty the Queen ought to give him orders to propose them; the Council being of opinion that if the Queen's envoy does not open the negotiation, neither can they. If in the meantime we could be informed of the wishes of His Holiness on this matter it would be of the greatest assistance to me in the midst of these uncertainties. The continued introduction of Parliamentary troops into Dublin by the Marquis of Ormonde, will disconcert everything and make everyone suspicious. This year although without money, the Catholic arms may make some progress if the quarrels of the Confederates do not frustrate their attempts; but we must determine to leave all to the Lord God who protects His cause in spite of our faults and imperfections.

With all respect I am, &c.

To Cardinal Panzirolo (in Cipher).

Galway, June 30th, 1647.

The disturbances in Ulster, of which I spoke in my letter of the 18th, ended entirely to the satisfaction of Lord Muskerry; although the Council sent two bishops and one nobleman with power to declare him in rebellion against the Confederation, if he did not quit the army and retire to his own property. The weakness shown by the Council in yielding to this man makes me suspect that many of them are on his side, and that this is the first step of the plot laid by the French agents, Ormonde and his faction. I did not fail to explain that two great errors had been committed; the first, in treating with Muskerry at all before making him obey the Council and retire; the members have lost both credit and power by this weakness, and their authority is no longer respected. The second, in having deposed General the Marquis of Worcester without first reinstating him for a few days in his position in the army, his return being opposed with great violence by the Viscount, and people say that treatment so ignominious to a man of his rank is enough to create even worse disturbances. However it cannot be undone, and we must wait the end to see clearly who are the deceived. I have meanwhile come to Galway, whither I was invited some months ago and where I shall have constant employment in attending to spiritual matters, and besides be for a time free from the opposition of those who meet all my propositions by insisting on the delay of the Papal supplies, which they say would have prevented all our misfortunes. I left the Council on the verge of a truce with the Marquis for two months, granted at the instance of the Queen's agent in order to leave time for negotiations.

To THE QUEEN OF ENGLAND.

Galway, August 12th, 1647.

Since Mr. Winter Grant brought me your Majesty's condescending letter I have taken the greatest pains to discover how, through the Marquis of Ormonde, a treaty might be made with His Majesty the King in conformity with the wishes and obligations of the Catholics of this country. Of this I had great hopes when I found in the last Assembly a unanimous desire for it in all ranks in the country, and I should have tried to sketch out the articles concerning the Catholic religion, but that the compact which the Marquis had entered into with the Parliament, although considered by Mr. Winter Grant and others to admit of being easily dissolved, has held the treaty in suspense, so that uncertainty increases every day and the hopes of an accommodation diminish. Finally, the fact that he has given into the hands of your Majesty's enemies the Castle of Dublin and the ensigns of his office, and subsequently departed for England (an act of which your Majesty and the world must judge), seem to me to cut off every hope of a reconciliation.

I represent this to your Majesty with the deep concern natural to a minister of His Holiness, who is anxious both for the peace of these kingdoms, and for the well-being of your Majesty. I am at present in Connaught on some ecclesiastical business, but am ready to return at any moment to the Confederation whenever I see a chance of further negotiation which I desire most earnestly. Hoping that God will long bless and preserve your Majesty,

I am, &c., &c.

To Monsignor the Nuncio of France.

August 14th, 1647.

For six weeks now we have been treating with Mr. Winter Grant and the agents of the most Christian King for the conclusion of the often begun and much desired peace with the King, through the Marquis of Ormonde. But as the latter has openly and to the horror of the Catholics leagued with the Parliament and given up his quarters to them, we have been unable to conclude it honourably or profitably to the Catholic religion; although the envoys have always defended him and given various interpretations in excuse for his disgraceful proceedings. The end has shown where his inclinations lay, since to his eternal dishonour he embarked for England on the 28th of last month, after giving up to the Parliament the city and castle of Dublin together with all the royal ensigns. I leave to the most Christian Court, and to the King of Great Britain the judgment to be passed on this act, by which His Majesty is believed in this country to have been, and for the second time, sold to his enemies by his politic vassal. In the enclosed letter which I send open to your Excellency, I have given an account to the Queen of England of the whole affair, to whom (or if you deem it better to her ministers) I beg you will say in addition that as we have now no adversaries in this kingdom but those of the King of England himself, it will be easy for her to obtain from this people all that she desires for His Majesty; and I can assure your Excellency that if she will now appoint a Catholic Viceroy, it will greatly facilitate a good understanding, and I shall myself be ready to receive him with all due reverence and honour.

The Marquis, like all pestilent beings has left the kingdom in the greatest confusion, and God in His unfathomable wisdom permitted the Catholic army, numbering 7,000 infantry and 1,200 horse under the command of General Preston, to be entirely routed on the 8th of this month, by the Parliamentary troops of about equal numbers in a campaign against Dublin; on which occasion we lost 4,000 men exclusive of thirty officers taken prisoners, and all our baggage. The enemy left 3,000 dead on the field; but of this I shall write more minutely in my despatches. In the other provinces but particularly in Munster, all has been laid waste by the enemy, who profit by the old dissensions amongst the nobility, now raging more violently than ever. I think the delay of the Papal supplies concerning which I am more in the dark than ever, is the only cause that during this year defeat and not victory has attended our arms. According to the Roman reckoning this is the 24th of August, and to this day I do not know whether the

Dean of Fermo has reached France, or whether he is alive or dead. I can then give neither hope nor promise of the money to this people, and have not myself a *giulio* left in the world to make a blind man sing. It has been my singular lot to be a Nuncio to an island, and among enemies; therefore I am in a position to congratulate all Nuncios on terra ferma, on their extreme felicity. I am not sure whether this letter will go by Flanders or directly through France, but I shall send it by the first opportunity, and hope soon to hear from my Superiors and your Excellency, since many months have passed without your accustomed favours and communications. I am devotedly, &c., &c.

To Cardinal Panzirolo (in Cipher).

Galway, August 14th, 1647.

On the 28th of last month the Marquis of Ormonde set sail for England from Dublin with his wife and sons; after giving up to the Parliament not only the city and castle, but his royal ensign, as stipulated in the articles of his treaty. This proves indisputably that the assurances of Winter Grant and the agents of France that the Marquis was quite free, were utterly false and were given solely to serve their own purposes, showing how much more they value the friendship of the Marquis than that of the Catholics. The plans however of the Marquis's partizans seem now to be greatly disconcerted if not entirely overturned by his abrupt departure; their aim throughout having been to reinstate him in power, and restore affairs to the same state as when the peace was published last year. Among these Viscount Muskerry, who placed himself at the head of the Munster army in the violent manner mentioned in my despatch of the 18th of June, alleging as his reason for so doing the fears he entertained for his life; laid down the command a week ago (after shamefully suffering the enemy to ravage the whole province with fire and sword), and as he has done this without any reconciliation, it proves that he never had any real fears, but had other ends in view which have been frustrated by the departure of the Marquis. Viscount Taaffe, the intimate companion of Ormonde, remained neutral till the Marquis left Ireland, when he at once took the oath of the Confederation, and the Council immediately elected him Lieutenant-General of Munster. The Marquis of Clanricarde on the contrary, opposed now by all his friends for having joined the enemy, inveighs with his usual arrogance, and blames more than ever the Catholic government, declaring there is no remedy for the ills of the country but in submission to a single head. It is very evident, from the frequent and secret meetings which are held, that he wishes to bring about the arrival of the Crown Prince of England, or the return of Ormonde himself; and in speaking to the Bishop of Killala, who spoke to him on some business of mine a few days ago, he declared openly that he could not confer with me, without the Marquis of Ormonde. That nobleman on his departure, which may be considered as one of the greatest blessings granted to the kingdom since the commencement of the war, left the country a prey to such confusion and misery that, as your Eminence will collect from the account I have given separately of the great defeat of the Catholic army, we have been unable to feel the joy we ought to do at having but one enemy in the kingdom; and since the war is now justified in the eyes of all men, as undertaken for religion and in order to preserve Ireland for the King, we may now hope also that many will unite together who were formerly kept apart by Ormonde's promises and professions. Our misfortunes, I cannot but think, are chiefly due to the delay of the Pontifical supplies, concerning which I am more in the dark than ever. I have stated my opinions on the subject in a separate paper, to show what would have been undertaken and what evils averted if even a small sum of money had been received some time ago, and this, not to incite His Holiness to further exertions, but merely to fulfil my duty of representing events as they occur. I hope that securing foreign aid for religion, and facilitating a peace with the King, will be the immediate results of Ormonde's departure; because the implacability of the enemy will necessitate union; the Catholic Sovereigns will be interested to prevent the seizure of the kingdom by the Parliament; and as to the King, when he sees that his subjects here are fighting against his enemies, he will be more favourably disposed towards them; and if, as we hear, he has regained his liberty, he will perhaps nominate a Catholic Viceroy, a vast step towards securing the welfare of Ireland.

To THE SAME (IN CIPHER).

Galway, August 22nd, 1647.

In the month of February we heard that His Holiness proposed to send considerable assistance in money to the Catholics by the hands of the Dean of Fermo. At that time the state of affairs was as follows.

The Deputies from the Assembly to negotiate for Munster were evidently so opposed to each other, that it was impossible to reconcile them; one part were adherents of Viscount Muskerry, the implacable enemy of the Marquis of Worcester, who was at the head of the other party and General of the Province.

The new Council, to whom the Assembly remitted the whole regulation of affairs, took as usual a middle course, which is always pernicious in state affairs; and thought to satisfy both parties by continuing Worcester in his command, giving him some of his own friends as officers; but at the same time so fettering him that he could not even write a letter without reference to the Council of Commissioners and others, all dependents of Muskerry. The Marquis of Worcester, by the Nuncio's advice, was more than once about to throw up his command, but the persuasions of others or his poverty prevented his following it.

In the meantime it was discovered that the enemy had determined to seize Cappoquin (probably upon some understanding with those in the city) in order to open the way to Dungarvan or Waterford.

The Marquis requested supplies for the city; the Council gave all necessary orders to the Commissioners, who frankly replied that since the 15th of April they had not been able to raise a farthing, nor to assemble any troops. This caused a great outcry among the Marquis's adherents, they declared that the Commissioners were in league with Inchiquin; and either to distress the Marquis, or please the Viscount had purposely neglected to levy the taxes. Thus, Cappoquin being left undefended and Dungarvan without aid; suspicions and quarrels increased to such a degree that three Dominicans, chaplains to the army, began to insinuate that it would be allowable to murder the Commissioners and Muskerry, and to refuse obedience to the Supreme Council who seemed to favour the traitors; such propositions, theologically defended, and audaciously promulgated, made the impression to be expected on these idiots. Here was the origin of the dissensions, of the Viscount's suspicions, and of his seizure of the Generalship; of the dismissal of the Marquis, and in fact of all the disturbances mentioned in my letters from Clonmel; and finally of the devastation of the Province, the defeat of the Catholic army, and all the misfortunes from which we now suffer. Hence it appears, that had the Dean of Fermo arrived in Ireland at the beginning of April with but 6,000 crowns, the army would have been assembled, sent to the aid of the cities, and no suspicion of the Commissioners having arisen, the campaign would have been undertaken, and even at the very worst, the enemy would now have been in only the same position as last year.

The measures taken by the Council in Connaught have been productive of similar disorders in that Province.

The Connaught army had chosen for their general Owen O'Neill, and to him were deputed Commissioners not only suspicious of him but supposed to belong to a rival faction; and consequently, according to the custom of the country, suspected of wishing to embarrass rather than to assist him. They soon quarrelled about the provisions, which were dealt out so sparingly that the general said he never had enough at one time to enable him to march anywhere. By these disputes, suspicions and delays, 20,000 crowns were completely thrown away, and what is of greater importance the season passed without any occurrence of note save the devastation of the Catholic country and quarters by a friendly army! Had then the Nuncio been able to send 8,000 crowns at once to O'Neill for the recovery of Sligo, which he had promised the Nuncio to effect, the whole Province of Connaught would have been in the power of the Catholics; the army would have marched into Ulster to reduce the fort of Enniskillen, and to take possession of the Holy Place of St. Patrick's Purgatory, now about 100 years in the hands of the heretics.

As to the battle followed by such loss in Leinster, it does not appear that the arrival of the money would have altered the state of affairs, except that it would have thrown the campaign forward by a month and given less time to the enemy, though the fact is that Preston's army was in a very flourishing state without that money and sufficiently numerous—but some great error must have been made in the conduct of the battle which Papal assistance could not have averted. Indirectly however it would have made a great difference, as the irresistible courage of the enemy arose from a reinforcement of 2,000 Scotch and 300 horse, who arrived from Ulster the evening before the battle; and who could not have quitted that Province had they been wanting to defend Sligo against O'Neill, who would have marched to attack that place if he had had but the necessary funds. Thus a little money from His Holiness would have saved all the three provinces.

To the Same (in Cipher).

Galway, August 23rd, 1647.

The vexation manifested by Clanricarde, Digby, and their partisans at Preston's defeat has brought still more to light their secret intentions. I believe it certain that Clanricarde proposed to seize the government from the Council of the Confederates, and to vest it in the Prince Royal, who was to be invited to Ireland; meanwhile he himself was to hold the office of governor or lieutenant by letters or patents from the Queen, which are now in possession of the French agents, but containing a clause to the effect that it was with the consent of the Supreme Council. I doubt not that the General had agreed to all this, as he hates the present government to the full as much as Clanricarde, and as his portfolio was carried off amongst the booty taken by the enemy, some further information with regard to this matter may perhaps be published. Their only hope now is in the coming of the Prince, concerning which Digby is gone to consult the Council at Kilkenny, spreading a report that he is about to declare himself a Catholic, and has already been to mass, which I do not believe to be improbable since he told me last year that to serve his purposes he would think it quite allowable to simulate, and also to tell lies. As I have had no commands from His Holiness on this matter I shall keep myself aloof from the Council unless summoned thither, in which case I shall deem it right to attend, but to keep myself as neutral as possible.

Account of the Battle of Trim between the Catholic and English Armies.

Galway, August 29th, 1647.

General Preston's army had been increased in number to about 7,000 infantry and 1,000 horse, so well armed and appointed, as to be considered the finest troops ever seen in the country.

With these, the General first approached the city of Trim with the intention of besieging it; but in two or three days fell back either to obtain provisions, or because he heard that the enemy was marching towards him. But after two Councils of war had been held, it was determined not to accept battle at the risk of so many lives against so desperate an enemy. It was thought that the enemy would not advance, and perhaps it would have been so, had they not received on the evening of the 7th of August a reinforcement from Ulster of at least 2,000 Scotch with 300 horse. On the morning of the 8th they marched boldly towards us offering battle; whilst the Catholic army was led with so little decision they did not know what they were to do.

Necessity, and great confidence in themselves finally induced the Catholics to face the enemy, but not in good order, nor even as I am told to their full number; and the cavalry was so badly placed as to be utterly useless: but this I shall explain more fully later. The conflict began with great courage, but the cavalry were the first to give way, although their Colonels remained in the thickest of the battle when unable to prevent the flight of their men.

The infantry, on the contrary, charged so courageously that at first many more of the enemy fell; but seeing themselves abandoned by the cavalry and entirely surrounded without hope of aid, they resolved to die bravely. Amongst these 400 Irish-Scots particularly distinguished themselves: they had shortly before arrived from their Island, under the command of Colonel Alexander Macdonnell, and did not fall till satiated with blood; Macdonnell refused the quarter offered to him, saying he would not accept life from men faithless to their God and their King, and killed three or four more before he was cut down.

Accounts vary so much that it is difficult to know the extent of our loss. The common opinion is that 3,000 Catholics and 1,500 heretics were left upon the field. Our officers were made prisoners to the number of 106; all our banners were taken, all the baggage seized. The spoil, in which were several barrels of powder, cannot be put down at less than 50,000 crowns; Preston's baggage also fell into the hands of the enemy, as also his portfolio containing letters which may prove the ruin of many, and it is said will do little credit to the Marquis of Ormonde. All this booty, together with the ensigns, was carried to Dublin with the greatest triumph and greeted with unheard of rejoicings, the Catholics of the city being forced to make the same demonstrations and to illuminate like the Protestants; the Catholic party never remember to have received so great a blow as this.

The Council, the General and their party throughout the kingdom have not however lost heart and are making great preparations, hoping with the aid of God, to recover all that has been lost; and in all these misfortunes, good men rejoice with true Catholic feeling that so many soldiers and nobles were ready to lay down their lives for God and religion.

To CARDINAL PANZIROLO.

Galway, August 29th, 1647.

I send your Eminence a letter written to me in Madrid on the 9th of March by Father Hugh Burke who is promoted by His Holiness as we understand, to the Church of Down. This Ecclesiastic aspired to the Bishopric of Clonfert, vacated by his brother when promoted to the Archbishopric of Tuam; and as you will see, he complains of my having recommended another to His Holiness; and not satisfied with vilifying the nominee; blames me, and what is worse reflects upon the wisdom of His Holiness. As to Lynch whom the Holy Father translated to Clonfert, the testimony borne by Father Scarampi who has long known him will suffice, and I thank God that this appointment has been made, as the prelate proves himself every day more worthy of this dignity. Since I came to Galway I have found him more than all the rest exact and diligent in his holy office, exercising the functions both of Preacher and Judge, and so beloved in his diocese that none speak ill of him save those who envy him. No one can give better proof than I that he obtained this dignity by no unworthy means, for I was solely influenced by the report of Father Scarampi and others; and I also soon formed the opinion that it would not be advisable for the two highest Prelacies in the Province to be held by two brothers, both considered not a little ambitious, and bent upon governing according to their own opinions; and I have found that one of them the new Archbishop of Tuam is more intractable and adverse to the recognition of my authority, than any other among the Bishops. As to His Holiness, it seems to me that Burke should be made both by word and in writing, to submit to the Majesty which he is not worthy to name except in the humblest and most reverent terms. I write this to your Eminence in the cause of truth and to justify the resolution which has been taken by His Holiness.

To the Same (in Cipher).

August 29th, 1647.

I believe I have at last discovered the precise designs of Preston if his army had been victorious, which are at the root of all the machinations and plots which were talked of. He intended to wrest from the hands of O'Neill and the Ulster people all the places in Leinster and Connaught recovered last year by that general, and under pretext of enforcing obedience weaken him to such an extent that he should no longer be a cause of fear to him. To this all Muskerry's movements in Munster tended, and to this also the difficulties thrown in O'Neill's way by the Connaught Commissioners, who hoped by doling out the provisions in small quantities to fetter him and prevent his moving. I can see that hatred of these Ulster troops is the cause of all the dissensions, and that all future events will be influenced by it. Meanwhile, in consequence of Preston's defeat in Leinster, Muskerry has been obliged to invite O'Neill, and to throw himself on his protection; almost all the nobles are joining him also, and thus the aspect of affairs has undergone a sudden change.

To the Same (in Cipher).

August 29th, 1647.

Digby and his partisans with the French have proposed a new peace with the King, and some of his friends have been heard to say that the Supreme Council are well inclined to accept it, and that the conditions in general are to refer all religious points to the Pope, and leave the political as they are. The departure of the Nuncio from Ireland is to be made a primary stipulation. I doubt not that this is the work of Lord Digby, both to please the Queen and to suit his own inclination. Of this negotiation we shall of course hear more, and I shall carefully report its progress.

To the Pope.

August 29th, 1647.

I lay at the feet of your Holiness not only the triumphs but the losses of the Catholic Confederates; the supreme wisdom of your Holiness will doubtless find matter of consolation in both cases. In the campaign against Dublin our whole army except the cavalry was entirely defeated, through either too great confidence in human strength, or some mistake or irresolution at the time. It is impossible to think without tears of the courage shown by the infantry, amongst whom a regiment of Scotch Islanders met their death fighting for their religion and their God; and we know that they did not fall without making a great slaughter of the enemy. I find that courage is again rising and union increasing so rapidly on all sides, that I doubt not to write very soon of some great recompense according to the accustomed course in the dispensations of God, and the progress of the Faith. Since as I believe this was the first battle fought solely for religion, I trust that in this fact the wisdom of your Holiness will discover some compensation for our misfortune. Hoping for your Holiness long life and the greatest prosperity, it only remains that I humbly kiss the holy feet, &c.

To Cardinal Panzirolo.

August 30th, 1647.

It is probable that the Puritans, who made extraordinary rejoicings in Dublin after the victory obtained over our army in Leinster, may have published at once reports of that success, I therefore take the earliest opportunity of sending your Eminence a separate account of all that we have heard, nor have I abstained from writing directly to His Holiness, because although the news was sad, still a defeat in the cause of religion may be considered rather as a victory than a loss. I thank God that I was at a distance at the time, as I would not have refrained from being on the spot even with personal danger, and sharing the discomfiture of the Council. The Catholics are not discouraged, and perhaps necessity will draw them together since all other means have failed.

To the Nuncio of Spain.

September 1st, 1647.

From this port of Galway in which city I am at present residing, a vessel is about to sail for Spain, and I must not lose the opportunity of paying my respects to your Excellency. I have none but fatal news to send you, since the Marquis of Ormonde previous to his departure for London gave up the city of Dublin to the Parliamentarians instead of to the Catholics, and these met with a great defeat from their enemies on the 8th of last month with the loss of 3,000 men, besides 100 of General Preston's officers being taken prisoners. In the other Provinces also discord amongst our troops has been the cause of many misfortunes; insomuch that if (which God forbid) the two hostile parties were to unite and surround the Catholics, the whole kingdom would be in the greatest peril. I believe that had the Papal supplies arrived in time we should not have had less good fortune than last year, when we received money to be devoted to the advancement of religion. This much is certain, that now more than ever the Irish war is solely a war of religion, as in consequence of the Marquis of Ormonde's departure all other interests and anxieties have merged into this one great object. I can assure your Excellency that you can do nothing more glorious in the sight of God, or more meritorious in that of His Holiness, than to induce His Catholic Majesty to assist this people, who are remarkable for their constant and unshaken determination to give up their lives rather than their religion. As a part of my duty I suggest this to your Excellency as a means by which you may obtain a crown far more glorious than that which could be obtained by any other labour whatsoever.

I am your Excellency's devoted servant.

To Cardinal Capponi.

Galway, September 6th, 1647.

The events of the war so different from those of last year, I cannot but believe are mainly attributable to the delay of the Papal supplies; the money has not yet arrived, nor have I even heard if it is on the way. Of this I wrote to Cardinal Panzirolo, and he has doubtless communicated to your Eminence and the other Cardinals in conclave, what I considered it my duty as a faithful minister to represent of the state of affairs previous to the campaign; and of the advantages that must have accrued had the supplies then arrived. And truly, as His Holiness did condescendingly determine to aid the Catholic cause, it is fervently to be desired that his liberality had arrived in time to secure those victories which I anticipated, and in which the public voice agreed with me. It will now be necessary to employ the subsidy next year, it will hardly be sufficient to regain what we have lost in this, and to restore matters to the state in which they were before when we hoped for the complete liberation of at least one Province. But we must remember that all events are disposed by God, who justly afflicts me also, who am not worthy to assist in obtaining for His Holiness a glory proportionate to the wise care he has bestowed on our affairs. Since our losses I see that the people here are more than ever anxious to be again on foot, and the enemy more than ever divided into factions by the dissensions now raging in England; they have in consequence withdrawn to the fortresses in their power without attempting to follow up their victory, and seem to have no intention of moving this year. There is no doubt that this country must derive the greatest benefit from the dissensions in London if they should become more violent, nor less perhaps from the necessity of union among the formerly disunited Catholics;—owing mainly to the absence of the Marquis of Ormonde the plots and machinations formerly carried on under cover of religion have cooled down, and it is certain that his defection may be looked upon as a great boon to the inhabitants of Ireland; since the name of the Catholic Faith is now supreme in this kingdom, and therefore this cause is more than ever worthy of assistance from the magnanimity of all Christian princes. To have made these things known to your Eminence is I am confident, the same as to have procured great support for this people; since I know the prudence and constant zeal of your Eminence, and I trust soon to be able to send good news to verify my hopes, and revive those who rely always on the patronage of their Eminences of the congregation.

To Cardinal Spada.

Galway, September 6th, 1647.

From the report which I forwarded a few days ago to Cardinal Panzirolo, your Eminence will learn the defeat sustained by one of our armies on their march towards Dublin. Every day that passes however brings diminished accounts of the number of dead on our side, but increases our knowledge of the errors and folly of the general in command. We can do nothing without His Holiness's money, and its non-arrival, added to our uncertainty of its safety, is the greatest misfortune to Ireland, and the deepest mortification of my embassy. The advantage which could be hoped for from this subsidy will be diminished in value by a full half, though it ought to suffice to recover what has been lost this year: whereas had it arrived in time it is certain that the attack on one of the Provinces would have been successful. On the other hand, your Eminence will find comfort in the fact that the disaffection caused by the Marquis of Ormonde's practices has entirely disappeared; and the undisguised and irreconcilable hatred borne us by the enemy has been the cause of a strict union amongst the Catholics, making this a war for religion, and therefore worthy of the assistance of all Christian princes. Armies of some strength are already on foot, and we hope that the discord in England will not only enable us to defend what we have, but to get possession of part of the enemy's territory. Winter is however approaching, during which we must endeavour to find an opening for a treaty with the King; and then prepare for fresh campaigns in the spring. It is not necessary for me to recommend to your Eminence's care this great work, as I know how great are your zeal and anxiety for the advancement of the Faith, and the glory of His Holiness's Pontificate.

I am, &c., &c.

To the Nuncio of Spain.

September 8th, 1647.

Although the high rank of the Marquis of Worcester's family must be well known to your Excellency, as also the extraordinary services rendered by him to the King of England, I am acquainted with so many particulars concerning him, not known to others, that I consider it right to inform your Excellency of them previous to his intended visit to Spain. This nobleman, as good a Catholic as he is jealous for the prerogative of his King, acted first for His Majesty in England, and then hoping to assist in the pacification of Ireland, came over to negotiate a peace not less favourable to the interest of religion than to those of the King. He was unable to effect his purpose, because amongst many other obstacles the Marquis of Ormonde, moved by envy, brought his powerful opposition to bear. But by remaining here, and devoting himself to the advancement of religion both in his public office and private capacity, he has gained the approbation of all Apostolic ministers, and the right to demand assistance from them in every possible way.

I therefore entreat your Excellency to forward his views

in everything concerning religion, since he has undertaken the journey in the hope of communicating with England and the King more easily from Spain than from any other country. And if he requires introductions or to be presented at court, I beg of you to extend your favour to him on this point also, hoping at the same time that the pious inclinations of His Catholic Majesty and his affection for Ireland, may induce him to grant an audience to the Marquis, and to listen favourably to his propositions. I will leave your Excellency to make acquaintance with this nobleman's character by personal communication, rather than by what I could say, since his high qualities and virtue must be apparent to your discerning judgment. The Marquis will assure you of my reverence for your person, and I promise myself that you will show no less goodness in believing it, than in attending to the wishes of the Marquis himself.

To Monsignor the Patriarch of the Indies.

September 8th, 1647.

The Marquis of Worcester, of the well known English nobility, has shown so great zeal for the Catholic religion both in the wars for his King in England, and in the treaties for peace commenced in this kingdom, that all ecclesiastics are bound to serve and show him all possible honour. I, who for two years have never acted otherwise than according to the desire of the Apostolic See, know not how better to repay the obligations I am under to him than by writing to secure him your Excellency's protection and favour during his contemplated visit to Spain. The high qualities of this nobleman will speak for themselves, and the aims he has in view deserve that your Excellency should recommend him to the favour of His Catholic Majesty, and procure for him the condescension of so great a sovereign. I esteem myself fortunate in having an opportunity of expressing my reverence for your Excellency, and of informing you that I should prosecute my laborious duties with redoubled ardour if I thought you would be pleased to signify your satisfaction by any favours shown to me through the Marquis.

To Cardinal Panzirolo (in Cipher).

Galway, September 14th, 1647.

I wrote to your Eminence on the 28th of May that the articles concerted in presence of Father Scarampi in Paris had been approved, and that others more favourable had been drawn up by the Assembly. Mr. Winter Grant never mentioned them, as might have been expected from one who placed all his hopes in the Marquis of Ormonde, hence I had not much difficulty in preventing their discussion; and this is all I need to send in answer to your Eminence's cipher of the 13th of May.

To the Same (in Cipher).

September 14th, 1647.

Lord Digby, before setting out for France, made two proposals at Kilkenny to the Council. The first was to place in his hands a new treaty of peace, and he would then bind himself to induce the King to grant the religious conditions desired by the Pope, pretending thereby to know the sentiments of His Holiness. The Council replied that they had always determined to refer all religious affairs to His Holiness, and that therefore they would adhere to this by whomsoever proposed. His second proposal was that the Council should grant a passport for some place on the sea, where 2,000 of the enemy might disembark, when he was confident he could draw them to his side, and induce them to follow him elsewhere. It was immediately evident that the first offer was made to pave the way for the second; and I doubt not that Digby intended to lead these troops against some port, surprise it, and then invite over the Prince of Wales, which is his sole aim and that of his faction, as I have frequently advised your Eminence. He received a direct refusal, upon which he set off for France, where during the winter he will plot with the rest of them to secure his object in some other way, advancing more or less according as the King succeeds.

To the Same (in Cipher).

September 14th, 1647.

The Dean of Fermo writes to me that the brother of the Marquis of Ormonde and two other Irishmen are as much as they can, spreading false reports of me in Paris. The same or worse will be done by Digby and those who go with him, and also by those of their faction who remain here. I should have been ill prepared for this, had I not known before setting out from Rome, that a spiritual and important office like mine has always for its reward a thousand hard words. Father Scarampi can bear witness that when the peace was unanimously rejected by the Bishops and Clergy in the Congregation of Waterford, I said jestingly that I was quite prepared to bear the weight which would be laid on my shoulders of all the blame and all the maledictions for the damage which would ensue in a new war. I tell your Eminence this once for all, as I am sure that His Holiness will not believe any reports of the kind without hearing me, and I trust that he and your Eminence will know that I shall not be thereby discouraged, nor induced to devote myself with less earnestness than before to my sacred labours.

To the Same (in Cipher).

September 14th, 1647.

The Dean of Fermo will not be here before winter as he writes from St. Malo that I must send an order for the 3,000 crowns, which are only payable to me, adding that he had written before on the subject. By the same opportunity which enables me to send this to your Eminence, I am sending the order and writing to tell him I had received no letters from him. This year, at all events the money will be of no use to us, but your Eminence can imagine our joy at hearing of its safe arrival even in France. It may be that God has destined it for a time of greater need, as will be the case if the King makes peace with the Parliament and both unite against us; this is the rock on which both Religion and this Kingdom may yet be wrecked, but may God forbid it!

To the Same.

September 16th, 1647.

After a delay of many months, I have at length received from your Eminence a package of letters dated May 13th, to which I now send answers. At the same time I received letters from the Dean of Fermo from St. Malo, Paris, and Amiens, mentioning that he was waiting in France for instructions and for an order from me in order to be able to receive part of the money. He also spoke of having written to me some months ago, but I have never received any letters from him except those which were brought by the person who had also charge of the others. This extraordinary uncertainty is owing to the dangerous navigation in the Irish seas and the great danger of being captured by the enemy. With this I send partly in reply to you, and partly as a report of all that has happened four letters in cipher and two sheets of advices.

I am, &c., &c.

To the Pope.

Galway, September 21st, 1647.

The Marquis of Worcester is about to set out for France after having done much in this country for the Catholic Religion and obtained but little reward. The great desire which he has always testified to assure your Holiness of his filial and reverend affection, inclines me to believe that he will take this opportunity of fulfilling so holy a wish. I think it then a part of my duty to furnish him with a letter of introduction, although I have nothing to add to what I wrote before, save that up to this moment he has laboured in the good work with as much zeal as at first. Of the reward for which he may hope from Heaven, he can receive no greater certainty than words of approval from your Holiness, on whose supreme protection he has ever had a sincere and Catholic reliance. Prostrating myself, through him, at your holy feet, I pray that Heaven may send your Holiness the highest consolations.

To Cardinal Mazarin.

September 21st, 1647.

It is not easy to say how much the Catholic Religion owes to the unremitting labours of the Marquis of Worcester, nor yet how zealously he has united his interests with those of his King. I can assure your Eminence that had the treaties proposed by this nobleman been happily concluded, the affairs of this country would now be in a very different position. He is going to France anxious to make known his views to your Eminence, and also the esteem in which he holds that powerful court. I send this letter not because he is in need of an introduction, but to honour myself by speaking to your Eminence of one so great and worthy. Remembering the great obligations I am under to your Eminence,

I am, &c., &c.

To Cardinal Panzirolo.

September 24th, 1647.

The Marquis of Worcester is about to set off for France with his wife, his object as far as I hear is solely to please the Queen, and find out how to obtain the Viceroyalty of Ireland from the King. I consider his object most difficult of attainment, whilst the King is it is thought utterly powerless, to say nothing of the Marquis's usual ill-fortune and that he is not gifted with the needful prudence; besides which, Digby and his party who are also in France, are his most determined enemies: at the same time the Catholic Religion could not have a warmer advocate, nor the Apostolic See a more devoted servant.

To the Nuncio in France.

September 24th, 1647.

I should consider it quite superfluous to give the Marquis of Worcester my testimony of his unwavering affection for the Catholic Religion, did I not know that many of his enemies had gone to France from this country because they could not obtain their political aims, which were fraught with peril to Religion and contempt for the Church. I do not send my letter as a recommendation, for a person of his quality requires no favour nor assistance, but merely to represent to your Excellency your obligation as an Apostolic Minister to do all in your power for one who has sworn in my presence to obey punctually all the commands of his Holiness. You will know best how to assist the Marquis, whose first wish is to place the people in quiet security in the exercise of their Religion, and then to serve the interests of his King, and I have found him so unfailingly constant in both, that as the Catholics are under great obligations to him so the Royalists have always behaved badly when they have suspected him. Your Excellency will hear of our proceedings from him.

To Cardinal Panzirolo (in Cipher).

September 29th, 1647.

Since I wrote last the enemy have taken Cashel in Munster, and killed all who had taken refuge at the altar of the Church of St. Patrick! but their loss in men is as great as ours. Clonmel and then Kilkenny may expect to be attacked by the Dublin troops; in which case we shall be in a perilous position, and I shall be cut off and unable to communicate with the Council. I trust however that the attack will not succeed, since the Catholic armies are in high vigour; that of Munster has ravaged the county of Cork, by which the enemy is said to have suffered greater injury than they have done us. Your Eminence may be assured that we are not discouraged, and that I shall continue my arduous duties until my last breath. May God assist me to fulfil them!

To-day (the 2nd of October) I have received news from the Council that in Munster the enemy has retired, and now holds only the castle of Cahir in our districts; Kilkenny therefore is safe, and probably nothing further will be attempted this autumn.

To the Same (in Cipher).

Galway, October 1st, 1647.

A book with the title "An Apologetic Discussion" has appeared in this country, printed in Frankfort, but written in Portugal, perhaps by an Irishman named Constantius Marlow, believed here to be an assumed name. The first copy was brought from France, and others have since come from Portugal. It is directed against the English and the King, to prove that they have forfeited all rights over Ireland, both as heretics and having violated all the conditions laid down by Adrian IV. It ends with an exhortation to the Irish to drive out the English and to elect a king, a native of the country and of ancient blood! A great outcry has been raised on all sides, as these it is said are matters of high treason. I hear that at Kilkenny the book was publicly burned, while here in Galway a rigorous search is made to seize it. The ill affected and the Ormonde faction make use of it to serve their own purposes, to increase the general hatred against the ecclesiastics and the people of Ulster; asserting the book to be their manufacture in order to bring round men's minds to make a king of O'Neill, in whom the two conditions, to be a native of the country and of ancient blood are combined. I can see that the greatest outcry is raised by the judges and lawyers, who abhor the proposition that the heretical King is not a legitimate sovereign, because this would bring overwhelming ruin on all who hold ecclesiastical property from him, as they infer that their titles also would be illegitimate, and that they would be forced to make restitution. This, the real and perilous stumbling block in this country, will at all times give rise to suspicion and dissension, and will open the way to its enemies to punish their avarice. Hence it is that so few care to obtain dispensations from me to retain their property, believing that such dispensation could only be a fresh indication of illegitimate possession, and being incredulous that the ecclesiastics will not take every means to reinstate themselves. And on this point, though I speak, promise, and preach to the contrary, not one of them believes me.

To the Same (in cipher).

Galway, October 2nd, 1647.

I agreed with many others in thinking that the Marquis of Clanricarde's residence in this city would open some way of drawing him over to the Catholic Confederation. I therefore endeavoured to obtain his confidence by paying him every possible honour, and even invited him and his wife to pass the anniversary of His Holiness' elevation to the Papal throne with me. I do not see much hope of attaining my object, as this man trusts no one but himself; and far from recognising the authority of the Supreme Council does not think it worthy to treat with him; on the other hand, on account of his property in England and here he desires to stand well both with the King and the Parliament; and pretending to despair of this country he sometimes says that he is determined to go to France and sometimes to England, according as his interest in the one, or anger against the other predominates. He has carefully avoided paying the slightest attention to me even after having received my friendly advances, and keeps the more aloof as he knows that the Council do not wish me to pay him the £1,000 which he lent last year for the Connaught campaign, because they discovered that it was part of the money which Digby had brought over, and which should have been given to the Confederates and not to the Marquis of Ormonde, consequently, if on the arrival of the Dean of Fermo the matter is not otherwise arranged, I shall be obliged to make it a public deposit. All these considerations have prevented me from presenting to the Marquis the Papal Brief sent to me many months ago by Prince Pamphili, since I cannot be certain in his present humour that he would be glad to receive it or would treat it with the respect due to so great an honour. Father Scarampi can tell you that when in the reign of Pope Urban a dispensation was sent to this Marquis, which his wife had solicited, he said that he had never asked for such a thing, and showed how little account he made of it. I am not rash then in thinking that whether he accepted or refused this Brief, he would treat it with some disrespect.

THOUGHTS OF THE NUNCIO ON THE FUTURE ASSEMBLY.
TO THE SAME.

Galway, October 6th, 1647.

I have to-day received notice that the General Assembly will meet on the 12th of November, and in anticipation I lay my opinions before your Eminence; although the distance I am at will prevent my offering more than conjectures.

I fear that this Congress will not only be tumultuous on account of difference of opinion, but that perhaps violence may be resorted to by those who are bent on forwarding their own interests. On account of the disasters of this year, the greater number will declare against war from inability to sustain the expense, and these will be divided into two classes. One for the mere longing for quiet will desire peace with the enemy on any terms whatsoever, without caring if they should lose the Churches or see the splendours of Religion obscured, and will submit to contributions, to compacts and government of any kind.

The more malignant will not desire a treaty only, but will endeavour to make it such as to throw discredit upon the resolution passed by the clergy and disgrace on O'Neill and his Ulster men, whom we know are the objects of their especial hatred; the first because they rejected the Ormonde peace, and the last because they favour the Clergy and are the irreconcilable enemies of the English. But it is evident that both parties will find many difficulties in attaining their respective ends; as those who desire above all things to enjoy quiet once more, can scarce hope to do so now when their only enemy the Puritan party daily exhibit their implacable hatred of the Catholics, observe neither laws nor compacts, and threaten to exterminate every Irishman. Certainly in Dublin where the General is English all this is true; in Munster only, where the hostile Commander is an Irishman, such a treaty might be adjusted, and it appears that one is in contemplation in those counties where the nobles are so ready to help the enemy. But even they will soon find to their cost where the ambition of that most ambitious of Heretics the Marquis of Ormonde will lead, who thinks only of aggrandizing himself as he always did while he was Viceroy.

Those again who desire to revenge themselves against the Clergy and O'Neill, feel that they must take some strong measures to secure the success of their designs. There are many who swear to the truth of a plot to invite over the Prince of Wales and suppress the Supreme Council. For this purpose two Catholics, Richard Butler, a brother of Ormonde, and the Earl of Castlehaven are to be sent to France in addition to Digby and Daniel O'Neill heretics, already gone; it is also said that ever since May Baron Inchiquin is in the plot, and that when Viscount Muskerry pretended that his life was endangered by the dissensions of the Munster officers and assumed the command of the army, he arranged with the said Baron to take a good opportunity of declaring that he was not inimical to the King, of joining others in inviting the Prince to come over and in changing the Government. Further it is said that Viscount Taaffe, the General appointed to command in Munster, at the moment that he took the oath to the Confederation after many years of neutrality shared Muskerry's views; and therefore during the last days of the campaign, though he had manœuvred a good deal had increased the strength of the army and had marched to the gates of Cork, nevertheless always kept at a distance from the enemy; allowed Cashel, Callan, and Fethard to be sacked and other places to be taken, and permitted Inchiquin to return home; who thus encountering no opposition, received one might say a welcome in the midst of his enemies. But, as I said, this party will find themselves in great perplexity when they come to conclude a treaty. The first thing will be the maintenance of the Prince, who will require a large sum of money for his appanage, and in any case there will remain in all the other provinces the war with the Parliament and the Scotch; for even if a truce be granted to Munster out of respect for Inchiquin, there will be no hope of foreign assistance to the rest of the Kingdom, since the Catholic Princes will furnish no more money when a Protestant Prince has been brought over and the army is no longer fighting in the cause of religion. Secondly, if the provinces, and Ulster in particular do not approve of the Prince's residence here, a new cause of disunion will exist and a civil war doubtless be kindled. Again it seems to me very unlikely that Inchiquin would enter into any such league, as I hear from the Marquis of Clanricarde that all hopes of recalling Ormonde are not even yet given up; but as he was an old rival of Inchiquin, how could they be a party to the same design? Again, if Inchiquin be in the plot, why so ill-treat those people of Munster who are on that side also? How too could General Taaffe deceive his whole army which in this point would certainly not agree with him? I do not consider these people great masters of finesse, and therefore until I hear positively to the contrary, I shall believe that in Munster there is good faith kept; that our party owing to its customary bad management is now depressed, and that the Ormonde faction alone think of inviting the Prince, though I am not certain of this since I know the attempt has been made more than once. Whatever the plot may be, those engaged in it were greatly disconcerted by Preston's defeat, and O'Neill's recall to Leinster, since they are certain that if Preston had taken Dublin he would have permitted the Prince to disembark there, to which they know well that O'Neill would never have consented.

In this uncertain state of affairs, in a country not only divided but full of suspicion of treachery, without a chief ruler capable of cutting the knot of difficulty—the Assembly begins its labours. My endeavours, which must at all times be to effect a union amongst the parties will I fear avail little at this crisis. First, because having no commands from your Eminence on the subject I cannot directly oppose the invitation to the Prince; being desirous to avoid every appearance of alienating this people from the King and his sons. Secondly, because the delay in the arrival of the Dean of Fermo which has surpassed all expectation; and my inability to show any part of the money so often promised, have weakened my influence at least with many who do not hesitate to reproach me with want of good faith, and are anxious to have it believed that the supplies are all a pretence and would be inconsiderable even if forthcoming. But not the less do I fulfil my duty and rejoice with those who believe that some portion of the money has already arrived in France, and may yet avail us much if applied at once to the purposes for which it is sent. I take every opportunity of reminding the Council that when the Kingdom is once united and the true Religion supreme, His Holiness and the other Christian Princes will take this Kingdom under their especial care and protection.

To the Same.

Galway, November 3rd, 1647.

During my absence from Kilkenny, the Supreme Council published the edict of which I send your Eminence a copy, inviting as you will see the men of the hostile forces to join us, with promises of receiving the same military rank and honours which they enjoy with the heretics, and perfect liberty in the exercise of their religion. I expressed to the Council my disapprobation of the edict and my regret at seeing the signatures of the Bishops of Clonfert and Ferns affixed to it, entreating that it might be revoked or suppressed in some way or other. But I have dug in the sand, for all orders of persons here consider free communication with the heretics for any purpose whatsoever, to be perfectly allowable. The Bishop of Ferns answered me in the name of all—you will see his arguments stated in the enclosed paper and opposite to them my replies, upon which your Eminence and the sacred assembly will honour me with your opinion, that I may know for the future what to say and do in such cases, since in this Kingdom they are of daily recurrence. I cannot possibly tell what resolutions may be brought forward in the next Assembly by a people so disunited and unwilling to take good advice; and it may happen that all the trouble I have taken will be thrown away. But if with the aid of God affairs take a better direction, it will be of infinite importance to me to have the opinion of your Eminence upon this point, that I may be able to raise from the eyes of the Irish the cloud which prevents them from seeing the direct path in the matter of religion. As I am not bent on carrying out my own opinions, I refer everything to the decision of your Eminence and the Sacred Conclave.

To the Same (in cipher).

Galway, November 5th, 1647.

I am now fully informed of the intended proceedings of the malcontents in the next meeting of the Assembly. They are to propose an invitation to the Prince on pretext of having one sole governor, since the Council of the Confederates is unable or unwilling to enforce obedience. Then they are determined on peace with the Puritans on any terms whatsoever, and whether the churches be lost, the bishops displaced, the Nuncio dismissed, it matters not to them; and through all these propositions there are some who defend and inherit the doctrines of Digby. Their pretext for this peace is the devastation of the country from which we have suffered this year, and fear of O'Neill who they industriously insinuate aims himself at the sovereignty. It is said that the Catholic army in Munster now very powerful, remains inactive that it may serve as a counterpoise to that of Ulster, and force the Assembly to pass the resolutions. This has all been arranged by Muskerry and his followers who intend afterwards to recall the Marquis of Ormonde, and perhaps revive the rejected peace. I am going to Kilkenny to be present at the deliberations, but have given orders that public prayers for Divine aid may be offered up everywhere in this great difficulty. I am invited to two places on the road by Clanricarde, from whom I will obtain if possible some confirmation of this news. I will help the well disposed who are numerous; and as far as a man of my weak powers can, will strive to avert civil war though it appears almost inevitable if the dissensions in England oblige our enemies to leave us to ourselves. Meanwhile I do not see any reason to despair, because despite the machinations of hell, the Catholic religion is openly professed in this city as in Italy; and this summer I have performed my functions and processions in Galway as I should have done in Fermo, whence it may be that God wills that religion shall be strengthened by arms, and provided the end be attained the means signify but little. But if the Assembly come to any unworthy resolution I shall obey the command given by Prince Pamphili, in November, '45, to give neither assent or dissent, and keeping myself aloof use the power granted to me by His Holiness at the time of Ormonde's peace to remain or to retire from the island. In this I shall act according to circumstances.

To the Same (in Cipher).

Kilkenny, November 21st, 1647.

Before I set off from Galway Mr. Winter Grant, the Queen of England's agent, came to inquire from me what course I should take in the Assembly as to the pending negotiations and the new form of government. On my reply that my office was not to lead, but to hear and advise, he frankly proposed to me to accept a Viceroy of the Queen's or Prince's nomination, and obtain from him all the concessions needful for religion. I answered that if the Viceroy were a Catholic, and the Confederates had security that not in a single point should the public exercise of religion as practised now be diminished, I should not oppose such a measure; but added that a heretic Viceroy must not be thought of, as the glory reaped by the clergy in expelling the Marquis of Ormonde would prevent their bearing any such state of uncertainty again; and I suggested that he should write to the Queen that there are no other means of saving the kingdom. Winter Grant is a sincere man enough, he gave me his hand and confessed that these two measures were absolutely necessary to prevent the Prince from losing all. I see that Clanricarde and his adherents are of the same opinion, perhaps because he aspires to the Viceroyalty; or is eager to suppress the Confederate Council with whom he is always at strife. If affairs take this ground, the great difficulty of a Catholic Viceroy will be at an end, and this would be the beginning of security for religion. I fear however as your Eminence will see from the enclosed cipher, that they will take another direction, for the Assembly seem inclined to choose a Protector, a subject which I have more than once mentioned to you.

To the Same (in Cipher).

Kilkenny, November 21st, 1647.

La Monerie, the newly appointed agent from the Most Christian King came yesterday to tell me that in his first instructions he had orders from Cardinal Mazarin to treat me with every confidence; and to communicate to me everything respecting the Kingdom. He restricted himself to two points; the first that the Cardinal wishes that I should represent by letter and by means of chosen persons to His Holiness, how useful it would be that he should treat paternally with the Queen of England, impress upon her what she should do and what concessions she should make for the security of religion; since it would avert so many of the miseries of war if peace could be confirmed on this point at least. In the second place he said that if this treaty were delayed or came to nothing; and if the state of the Kingdom required the stronger remedy of a protector, he would wish that I should recommend such a measure in general terms to the Clergy and others, without leaning more to the King of France than to the King of Spain; professing to know well that I, the Minister of His Holiness who is the father of all, could not properly act otherwise. But not the less did he in the heat of his discourse hint at the reasons why Ireland should rather incline to the King of France, amongst these reasons that Spain had already in some degree countenanced the Parliament which the King of France would never do; having always for reasons which every one knows shown his doubts of them; and would on the contrary aid the Irish at all times against them with all his heart. My reply was that as His Holiness had already condescended to consult with the Queen's deputy in Rome, he would probably not refuse to do so again for the benefit of Religion in this Kingdom; and that as soon as Her Majesty gave me permission I would open the subject by letter. As to remaining neutral in the choice of a Protector, I could not give any better security than my conduct hitherto and the conditions of my office; although on this point Secretary Digby had calumniated me at the Most Christian Court for no other reason than that I had refused a peace injurious to Religion, which Cardinal Mazarin as he knew had confessed. I was pleased when he replied that it was all true and that your Eminence had written to M. de Moulin his predecessor, blaming him as the principal cause of all the evils that have ensued, and it is generally believed that he was recalled on this account. This was the substance of our conversation from which your Eminence will see that whether the plan of the Queen or Prince be adopted, His Holiness will be the arbiter of the religious conditions, and from the manner in which I have treated the matter without pledging His Holiness in the absence of his instructions, so he will be if a Protector be chosen.

To the Same (in Cipher).

Kilkenny, November 23rd, 1647.

The last battle in Munster, of which I wrote your Eminence a separate account, inclined this country to have recourse to external aid and to choose a Protector; this is now in course of deliberation in the private committee in order to report to the General Assembly. As this may become a matter of the greatest importance to this kingdom, I think it necessary to send a statement by anticipation to His Holiness. It is for certain proposed to send an envoy to the Holy Father to entreat him to take upon himself the protection of Ireland now in such straits from the victorious heretics; and in case of his refusal to receive his advice and assistance in conjunction with one of the two Kings. It is easy to see however, that all are inclined to France, as I said more than a year ago, because not only they hope for more assistance but because they perceive that the King of France has shown himself through his agents more willing than the King of Spain. The Holy Father will doubtless send at once his commands to the Nuncio of France to apprize the Court of his approval, if indeed he does approve of this negotiation. I have acted throughout without involving His Holiness in any way, and have always said that the affection of this people cannot but be acceptable to the Holy Father; but that on the other hand he is already constituted by God protector of all Christendom, especially of Ireland which he so paternally loves and compassionates. As I see that the Assembly will be disposed to apply where there is most money, I do not fail to represent the want of it in the Holy See, the heavy and continual expenses incurred in the war against the Turks, and in putting down disturbances in Italy. In all respects the affair will be so entirely at the disposition of His Holiness, that he will be able to decide it as he thinks best. I must not fail to add that it has been proposed by some few to apply to the Grand Duke of Tuscany, always of course subject to His Holiness' commands. They are greatly mistaken if they imagine that the Grand Duke has much money; but it has occurred to me that if we could succeed in having one of his brothers, not only to serve His Holiness in the present juncture if he decides on adhering to this plan, but also to have a chance of winning the whole kingdom if the King's sons in any manner failed; I believe in such a case the different classes would willingly elect him, and probably without exciting the jealousy of any of the crowned heads, who ought to be agreed that this country must not fall into the hands of the Parliament, and should be governed by a neutral prince too far removed from supplies to become powerful. This however is my opinion alone, and consequently subject to His Holiness' correction and commands.

To the Same (in Cipher).

November 24th, 1647.

Five members of the Assembly were deputed to-day to give me an account of their deliberations upon the subject of a Protector. They protest to have merely consulted among themselves and decided on nothing in public; that they wished to begin by sending a courier to His Holiness, and promised to show me all the letters and instructions. I find however that they desire first of all to offer the government to the Queen and Prince, with all the religious conditions desired by His Holiness; and failing this to treat of a Protector. It seems to me that influenced as they are in these resolutions by the question of money, they do wrong to take the part of the Prince who cannot give them a farthing, nor put an end to any of the wars now on their hands; whence I doubt they will not only lose time, but find themselves more embroiled than ever. I shall not fail to bring forward all that occurs to me but without direct opposition, as I have often told your Eminence.

To the Same.

November 25, 1647.

In the four accompanying ciphers your Eminence will see most of the deliberations of the Assembly which I have taken every opportunity of writing down, that His Holiness may take them into consideration and forward instructions to me. I shall reserve some things for the next despatch, and in particular an account of the battle in Munster, the accounts of which still vary. Although the number of killed was greater on the side of the enemy, we lost all our arms, and camp, and many officers were taken prisoners. I could have wished to see this people more terrified by the defeat than they are, since it is evident to me that on account of their dissensions and sins, God has for some time past withdrawn His aid from the cause. May He console us with the arm of His power, as He has punished us with the arm of His justice! Your Eminence will find enclosed duplicates of the despatches sent on the 3rd and 5th of November.

To the Same.

Kilkenny, November 26th, 1647.

In the last general Chapter held by the Franciscans in Spain, this province of Ireland demanded and obtained permission to divide itself into two portions, at whatever time the Provincial Chapter of the Kingdom should judge it expedient. The reasons for this were considered sufficient because the faithful having so greatly increased in number, and extended over the whole island, one Chief Provincial was unable to govern it with the strictness demanded by the rule. In the Chapter held this September, it was eagerly desired that this division should be carried out, but as I have told you, even in religion there are here as many factions as there are amongst the nobles themselves, and it has been observed that all the monks who desired the division then, were either of the party or relations of the party who wished last year for the Ormonde peace, and still perhaps persist in the same desire. A great suspicion was excited in the other party that under this persistence lay hidden some perilous design whence a division was imminent in the Chapter. It did not suffice that I exhorted them to concord and prayed them to suspend the resolution; since both sides wished to appeal to His Holiness, to the Cardinal Protector, and to the General of the Order. I have thought it my duty to apprize your Eminence that it will be advisable not to give just now any precise answer, but to put them off with fair words, until the Government of the country is placed on a different and more durable footing. In this course there will be no risk, while in sanctioning the division, there will be the great danger of carrying into the cloister (to our grave scandal) all the partisanship of the outer world. If this suggestion approves itself to the unfailing prudence of His Holiness, your Eminence can easily prevent the General or others from coming to any declaration, and insist that every thing shall be submitted as also this my opinion to the command of the Holy Father. With humble reverence, &c., &c.

ACCOUNT OF THE BATTLE OF KNOCKMONESS * IN MUNSTER.

The scene of this battle is in the county of Cork. The two hostile armies approached each other on the 13th November. The Catholic army consisted of 6,000 infantry, and 1,200 horse, and the English of 5,000 infantry and 1,300 horse. under the command of Baron Inchiquin, while our forces were led by Viscount Taaffe, with General Alexander Macdonnell of Ulster as his Lieutenant.

The Catholics were drawn up in the following manner. In front of the right wing, was Macdonnell with 3,000 infantry composed of Ulster and Connaught men and the Irish Islanders supported by Colonel Purcell with two regiments of cavalry. On the left wing was Lord Taaffe, with nine Munster legions to the number of 4,000 infantry and two regiments of horse. In this order the battle was begun.

Inchiquin had placed the best part of his troops opposite to Macdonnell whom he greatly feared, and not without

* Commonly called Knock-na-gaoll or Englishman's Hill. See " The Confederation of Kilkenny," by the Rev. C. P. Mahon. Page 202.

reason, as his soldiers after firing one or two volleys threw away the musket, and seizing the sword, rushed upon the enemy with such fury that they pursued for three miles killing them as they fled to the number of 2,000, without losing more than five men, after which they took cannon, carts and baggage of which they retained possession for a whole hour. Meantime on the other wing the one regiment commanded by Lord Castleconnell fired but one volley, and then with all the Munster troops fled in the most disgraceful manner, throwing away their arms in their flight, and though the General cut down some of the cowards with his own hand, he was unable to keep them back ! Hence the cavalry also of the right wing, which under Purcell had made their way bravely, on hearing and seeing the flight of the infantry, abandoned their colonel and fled. Their flight was so ignominious and so rapid that Lord Inchiquin, after pursuing them a short way and killing many returned, and with the rest of his army charged the victorious Catholic party, who believing that victory was on their side and were standing carelessly around the enemy's cannon when suddenly attacked, could only defend themselves in a disorderly manner, and fell to the number of 700; after a great slaughter of the enemy 3,000 escaped, but with the loss of the cannon they had just captured.

General Alexander Macdonnell who had separated himself a little from his troops to see after a messenger whom he had sent with an account of his proceedings to the other wing, met on his return fourteen of the enemy's horse, refusing quarter he killed four of them, and while parleying with their captain was treacherously stabbed from behind by a soldier and at once fell dead.

The enemy lost 2,500 men, but got possession of our arms and the camp. It is believed that the slain on our side do not amount to 1,500 in all, amongst whom were Macdonnell, his lieutenant-colonel, and nine captains. Amongst those killed on the opposite side were the Sergeant-General, the Commander of the Artillery, six colonels and other officers. Among those who fled thirty-two Catholic officers were taken prisoners, but of the right wing there was nothing but slaughter.

This battle is rendered memorable by the ignominious flight of the Catholics and the loss of Macdonnell, who had fought thirty battles in Scotland, victorious always in defence of religion and the King, and he would have been so now had not the Munster troops basely abandoned their brethren.

To CARDINAL PANZIROLO (IN CIPHER).

December 4th, 1647.

Several of the new Bishops having received from Rome and elsewhere letters speaking openly of their respective appointments, I resolved two months ago to make them known to the Supreme Council, since it was sufficient for me to have had notice from your Eminence of the preconization on the 23rd of February referring to the list sent by the Dean of Fermo, who mentioned in a letter from Paris that he was in possession of the necessary Bulls; and it appeared to me that they referred to the same appointments. I determined upon this because last year as soon as I mentioned the intentions of His Holiness towards the Bishop of Down, he was immediately admitted into the Assembly although not absolutely preconized, and they hope that the same may be the case now with those already elected, which in the present state of affairs would be very useful. Nor was I disappointed, for no sooner had the Council received my communication than they summoned the candidates to the Assembly without the least hesitation. But the lawyers and malignants opposed their entrance, alleging many English laws, amongst which was one declaring that unconsecrated Bishops have no temporal possessions, and consequently are not Barons of the kingdom, which is the title by which they take their seats in Parliament. Muskerry added that, even if the others were admitted the Bishop of Ross must be excluded, as he had been elected by His Holiness without being nominated by the Council. I was however of opinion that they ought to enter without showing any doubt, which they did, and I have left the points of the law and of their consecration almost to themselves, making it understood more to intimidate than for anything else, that with my certainty about the Bulls they might even act in their dioceses. But as to the second, that of excluding one appointed *proprio moto*, I was and am prepared to use all the strength of my authority to prevent their arrogating to themselves the power of making so haughty a declaration. I hold that if no positive decree has passed there will not be much difficulty in proceeding; all the bishops being at present admitted and sitting like the other members, and perhaps the thought of the protection of His Holiness and reference to him has prevented further action, and certainly the addition of these ecclesiastics has averted many other evils and put some fear into the hearts of the factious, as I have told your Eminence before.

To the Same (in Cipher).

Dec. 8th, 1647.

An unexpected opportunity enables me to inform your Eminence that there being but few well-disposed members from the provinces in the Assembly, the malignants have a great majority of votes and are beginning to do all that I prophesied in my letters throughout the summer. All thoughts of a Protector are at an end, and the latest project is to ask peace from the Prince of Wales and perhaps invite him over; the greater number persuading themselves that such a step must be the salvation of the kingdom; and hoping that the enemy will declare in favour of the Prince; while no one bestows a thought on religion. O'Neill sees that all this is done to oppress him and the clergy, and fearing for his life has refused to attend the Assembly, and as menaces are not wanting some grave scandal is to be feared.

A Bishop however will be sent to His Holiness and indeed no less could be done, and they will refer to him the entire adjustment of the religious articles, and entreat of him to be the mediator in a peace with the Queen and Prince. In order that this may not be a seeming mission only, and to prevent the previous conclusion of the treaty in France, I insist that they shall send first to Rome and the reply of His Holiness be received before any further steps are taken: the French agent fully agrees with me, which proves that his King will not act in this affair of Ireland without the advice and prayers of the Holy Father. If a Protector be proposed His Holiness will find himself perfectly free, since I have never involved him in anywise, as your Eminence advises in the cipher of July 15th just now received; but the others, in which your Eminence mentions having written more fully upon this subject have not yet arrived. Everything is in confusion; I see no possibility of doing good and can but endeavour to avert greater evil: this however will prove to your Eminence that the mission of a Nuncio with some authority has not been thrown away.

May God assist His own cause.

ACCOUNT OF WHAT HAPPENED TO THE BISHOP OF CLOGHER.

Kilkenny, December 18th, 1647.

In the separate Committee where affairs are discussed before being reported in the Assembly, it was proposed to send to France Viscount Muskerry, the Bishop of Clogher and Geoffry Brown. The Bishop excused himself in a long speech, adducing many reasons for his refusal, of which the principal were; first, that he spoke neither English nor French, and would therefore be useless at court; second, that he was hated by the Queen, who not only believed that he had been amongst those who first kindled the war but that last year the rejection of the peace had been his doing; third, that having been threatened by Lord Jermyn, the Queen's favourite and by Secretary Digby, he would have just cause to fear for his life if he should go to France. These excuses were neither listened to nor admitted, upon which the Bishop perceiving that these demonstrations were made not to do him honour but to get him out of the kingdom, came that same evening to the congregation of Bishops then sitting in presence of the Nuncio, where it was decided that when the subject was again discussed in the Assembly he was to state his reasons firmly and modestly, that the other Bishops should support him, and then wait to see which party would have a majority. Without delay therefore the question was brought before the Assembly the following day; and although the Bishop reasoned and disputed for several hours assisted by many others, he could not even obtain the suspension of the decision for one day, as his opponents with unheard of precipitation began to cry out for a division; and he was defeated by a majority. He then rose and with much displeasure uttered the following words: "You, sirs, have gained your victory, but I say that under no circumstances will I go to France." Upon this more than fifty members jumped up, and exclaiming that the union of the Confederation was at an end left the hall. Many more would have done so, had not a Bishop remarked that he saw no reason why the disaffection of one should dissolve the union of the rest; they then returned and showed a desire to punish the Bishop.

The Assembly broke up tumultuously; Muskerry with Taaffe and Preston went to entreat the Mayor of the city to imprison the Bishop of Clogher and one or two of his particular friends; but the Mayor replied that he did not recognise them as his superiors, and immediately sent to the Bishop to offer him every security for his person. The gates of the city were however shut to prevent accident; and troops paraded the streets as in time of war, many fearing that perhaps O'Neill, who with his army was but a few miles distant, would hasten to the assistance of his friend; and Preston quitted the city to assemble his Munster troops to prove his alacrity in defending the city against the Ulster army. On the following day the Assembly again met, and the Bishop attended as usual, but the members crying out that he was the subject of deliberation, drove rather than dismissed him from the hall. What was subsequently said by the lawyers concerning the punishment of a Bishop would be difficult to repeat; but no extravagance was omitted.

Custom and the decrees of the King who was represented by the Assembly would countenance they said the incarceration of a Bishop. But the other ecclesiastics protesting against the legality of this, they issued a precept to prevent his leaving the city. This being also objected to by the Bishops, and in fear lest the Bishop of Clogher would call in O'Neill to his assistance, the Council contented themselves with cancelling the decree and signifying to him through the Speaker on the part of the committee that he was not to quit the city.

Many attempts were made to effect a reconciliation since it was evident that the affair would be productive of the worst results; men of judgment perceiving that the Assembly had never thought of the consequences of grievously insulting O'Neill's best friend at the moment when they were entreating the General to take up his quarters in the city, the better to unite the people. On the other hand the Nuncio, not understanding by what authority the verbal command had been laid on the Bishop, insisted for the due recognition of ecclesiastical immunity. The agent of the most Christian

King fearing that his negotiations would be delayed by these disturbances, resolved to go in person to O'Neill, not only to conduct him to the city but to pacify him with respect to the Bishop. His journey was however fruitless, as O'Neill refused to set foot in the city or even to approach it, until he saw that the Bishop of Clogher was completely and courteously freed from the charge of contumacy.

It may be supposed that the report of the agent alarmed the Assembly, since on the following day five members were deputed to examine whether the Bishop's speech had contained actual contempt; and on its being represented that for various reasons such could not be considered the case, it was decided that he had not offended the committee, and another Bishop was deputed to recall and conduct him from his house to the hall, where being made to declare that he had not intended to insult the Assembly but solely to allege his reasons for refusal, he was absolved and forbidden to renew the controversy for the future.

The Nuncio had yet to be satisfied, and owing to the different accounts brought to him by persons influenced by various passions and interests, he could not discover whether the message sent to the Bishop was a command or not, he had therefore recourse to the Speaker, who assured him that it was simply a request, and that the Assembly had not intended to exercise any jurisdiction over a Bishop. Not content with this, he caused them to be interrogated in open court, and all the members of the Assembly unanimously agreed that they had not attempted to lay any commands on a prelate, nor would they wish to do so; this satisfaction received, the affair ended by the substitution of the Marquis of Antrim for the Bishop in the deputation.

To Cardinal Panzirolo (in Cipher).

December 24th, 1647.

At the commencement of this Assembly I was in hopes that affairs might not turn out so unfavourably; but afterwards discovered that the suspicions of which I informed you were but too well founded.

The evil disposed in concert with France, undoubtedly plotted to bring over the Prince with some semblance of a peace, and by change of government to introduce the protection of the most Christian King; thus far the plan is not objectionable, but the hidden evil of it is, that many efforts will be made to restore Ormonde, while there is little thought for religion, and the Bishops are set aside.

The deliberations were now to begin, when it was discovered to our great ill-fortune that the Province of Ulster, either from poverty or some other cause had not sent its seventy-three members, and the Assembly would not admit nine of them with proxies for the whole number; and it happened that with the exception of Leinster the members of the other provinces owing to the obstacles thrown in their way by the enemy were also very few in number, so that the Assembly seemed made up solely of the mob of Leinster, many of them the minions of Muskerry.

The first proposal, to give colour to the rest was to seek the protection of a foreign prince; they therefore appointed three embassies: the first to His Holiness, consisting of the Bishop of Ferns and Mr. Nicholas Plunket; the second to France to the Queen and Prince of England of three persons, Viscount Muskerry, the Bishop of Clogher, and Geoffrey Brown a jurisconsult, the last more especially to the Queen and Court of France; the third to Spain, of one only, who is not yet named. The simplest could see through the artifice of this choice; Muskerry and Brown the two great protectors of the Ormonde peace, open enemies of the clergy, are certainly not sent to France to take the air. The two destined to Rome, well-known supporters of the clergy and of the Bishop of Clogher were exiled under colour of doing them honour, principally because a new Supreme Council was appointed to remain here, composed (as I shall explain hereafter) of those who were imprisoned for their conduct about the peace, or have declared themselves adverse to the ecclesiastics for various causes. On the Bishop of Clogher's refusal to leave home as I have related, the Marquis of Antrim was appointed to take his place.

The Bishops, in order to counteract these plots meet day and night in consultation at my house, and fearing with them that the reference to His Holiness of all the religious articles is a pretence, that a peace may be concluded against our wishes, and the Prince or some heretic be brought here as Viceroy, I have bound the Bishops in writing, not to sign any of the articles there set down in case they are proposed in the Assembly. I have impressed on them that the Assembly should send first and alone to His Holiness, to obtain his views on all religious matters and to retain the other Envoys until his answer be received, so that His Holiness may have no reason to think that his holy resolutions shall be made in vain or not carried out in time. I have urged too that the Commissioners to Rome should set out before the others, but the Council desire that the others should await the answer in France, alleging divers excuses, reasons, &c., &c., for this step.

On the point of despatching the embassy to Rome before the others, I am supported not only by the French resident, but even more by the Spanish, who complains aside of the preference shown for France and of the larger number of Commissioners sent there, though in public he offers no opposition.

As the instructions to the embassies must be signed by all the Bishops, to whom they were not submitted till the last day of session, they have not spared themselves any labour in examining them, and I have wished to make a separate report that your Eminence may see that both of their own accord and at my entreaty they have done everything they could to show their reverence for the Holy See; and at least have used their best endeavours that an embassy shall be sent first to Rome to entreat His Holiness to assume the protection of the kingdom, and that negotiations be suspended till his wishes are known. They have besides declared that had not the instructions been changed at their express desire, they would never have subscribed them. The greatest difficulty we met with was in nominating the Council, since persons hostile to the clergy were invariably proposed, and the Bishops resolved not to recognise the Council unless constituted more fairly; and as the malignants founded all their hopes on it, both parties were so obstinate in maintaining their respective resolutions, that for two days we were in imminent danger of an open and sanguinary quarrel. At last a new nomination was agreed to, and as but one of these was objectionable, I was unwilling to disturb the peace of a whole kingdom for so small a cause, and said that we might be satisfied with the list of names enclosed. All seemed arranged when at the last hour the General Committees tried to substitute a Grand Council of 48 persons who would be permanent, and among these were all of their own party who were not of the Council. Although some satisfaction was accorded to the Ecclesiastics on this matter also, nevertheless their feeling was embittered by the abruptness of the measure and the suspicions it excited. It is certain that had there not been a determination to keep the Bishops united and watchful, and if the powerful Ulster army had not been close to Kilkenny, Ecclesiastical affairs would have gone to the ground. But the Lord God aided us by putting into the hearts of our adversaries a desire for the immediate arrival of the O'Neill in order to induce him to agree to their resolutions, seeing that without him they could do nothing. Hence he seized on the occasion of the insult offered to the Bishop of Clogher, came accompanied by his army, and had in some degree curbed the licence of these gentry. You see then we are still alive and in better heart than ever, and it appears to me that without money and with little authority I could not have done more.

To the Same (in Cipher).

December 24th, 1647.

I must intimate to your Eminence the intentions of the clergy in case a rupture of this union had taken place; so that if ever the misfortunes of this country lead to such a result, His Holiness may know in what state affairs will be. It was expected that O'Neill with his army of 10,000 infantry and 1,500 horse would declare for the Church and for a new union, whose object would be to restore religion to her ancient power and splendour, and to preserve the kingdom for the King. Of Preston's and Taaffe's armies we were certain of more than half, and even had a part united with our opponents it would have been but of little consequence, since the Ulster army could have been increased to any number. For the support of these forces we had the two-thirds of the Church income, His Holiness' supplies, various sums contributed by the nobility, and assistance in money secretly promised by the Spanish agent to O'Neill. Besides all this, we had great hopes of being joined by the Ulster Scotch who proposed it some time ago and who would have supported the Catholic army in their quarters. All who approved of the rejection of the peace last year by the clergy were so certain of success that they seemed almost to wish for a quarrel; this however I always deprecated for two reasons; first, because in so important a subject it appeared to me that we ought to wait for a better opportunity of throwing the blame on our adversaries; secondly, because I was not sure what cities and corporations would join us, for being composed of merchants and others devoted to the acquisition of money and to repose, they would I feared listen more willingly to those who promised them peace by the coming of the Prince however chimerical it might be, than to the clergy and Ulster men who are disposed for war. I was unable to judge from last year as the hatred of the Ulster army has so greatly increased that it might possibly change the feelings of the half-hearted. But your Eminence must be aware from this that should an open quarrel ever ensue, religion will still have many defenders, more in number perhaps and more devoted to her than ever, and who will be worthy of the assistance of His Holiness; such as Clement VIII. bestowed on the Earl of Tyrone, who when left alone sustained for so many years a war against Queen Elizabeth, and all that part of the kingdom which acknowledged her supremacy.

I am your Eminence's humble and devoted servant.

To THE SAME (IN CIPHER).

24th December, 1647.

The Bishop of Ferns and Nicholas Plunket are going to Rome as ambassadors to His Holiness, the former one of the best among the ecclesiastics and the latter among the laymen. But nevertheless both one and the other have such a kindly nature that they have occasionally done great mischief with the best intentions. It was principally owing to Plunket that those who lent a hand to the peace were released last year from prison; and then, though I strongly advised him to the contrary, he assisted Viscount Muskerry to become a member of the Council; which two things have been the cause of all the misfortunes of this year as may be gathered from my letters. Nevertheless they will give great satisfaction in Rome their manners and their behaviour are sure to please, and I am certain their first desire is to have His

Holiness for their father and protector. I have always been on good terms with them, the Bishop has always supported me from inclination, and Plunket was still further moved by gratitude when his brother was promoted to the church of Ardagh. Both of them are very eloquent in English and the Bishop speaks Latin also fluently, and this is all that at present seems necessary from me.

To the Same (in Cipher).

24th December, 1647.

When the choice of the orators to be sent to Rome was discussed in the Assembly—Belling, formerly secretary, was of opinion that no Bishops should be sent, alleging that all Bishops are flatterers, and that when the Sovereign Pontiff speaks, they have neither the will nor the power to reply. His opinion was laughed at, but he showed very plainly how much he loves our Church. I have had no dealings with this man since the day when he spoke of His Holiness with reference to the peace, and when it has been absolutely necessary to see him, I have stated I was constrained to do so in virtue of my office: I shall therefore esteem it a favour if His Holiness, in his great kindness should signify his approval of my conduct in the manner which seems to his infinite wisdom most fitting.

During those five days in which the affair of the Bishop of Clogher was discussed with so much violence the Assembly never deputed anyone to report to me on this matter or to tender an excuse, not even after I had sent up a remonstrance though the Convocation was held in the very house which I occupy. The wisdom of His Holiness will decide whether it be well to pass over this matter as the natural result of the rudeness and barbarity of this people which is manifest in everything they do, or whether he will speak to the ambassadors who are going to Rome, in order that they, seeing the favours which the Apostolic See has it in its power to bestow, may learn how they ought to behave, even if they were sovereigns and not subjects; since, even independent monarchs if I do not deceive myself, act very differently towards the ministers of His Holiness in these matters of courtesy.

To Cardinal Mazarin.

Kilkenny, 27th December, 1647.

These Irish gentlemen, discouraged by the reverses of this summer, have called together the General Assembly in order to provide the necessary remedies. I, believing them to be sincere and their object to be reasonable, have earnestly desired and used my best endeavour, that they may come to the discussion of the necessary measures with united hearts and honest purpose, so that all may agree in opinion, as all seek a common good which concerns the whole kingdom. But my success has not been so great as I had hoped, because it turns out that all those who took part in the peace of the Marquis of Ormonde, or are in any way attached to him, though they are well aware that in their end and in all essentials the clergy are in perfect accord with them, yet when they come to consider the means and modes of action, always treat us as if they wished to deceive and to oppress us, and continually throw upon us new doubts and new suspicions. Taking advantage therefore of the long experience gained in the course of a whole year, and of an Assembly in which, owing to various accidents the Church had a scarcity of votes, they have decided on certain embassies, and have chosen as ambassadors to Rome, France, and the Queen and Prince of England, the Viscount Muskerry and Godfrey Brown, the very men who have most openly shown their distrust both of the clerical party and of the army which support it; and what is a still more serious matter they have set up a permanent Council, which is entirely composed of men who are one and all hostile to the Church.

Your Eminence can imagine what a task it has been to guide four-and-twenty Bishops through all these hot discussions, for having approved of these embassies and the objects they were intended to accomplish, they cannot endure that our common interests should be committed to the care of unbelievers; and they have made, on fit occasion, such opposition to the formation of the Council, that it is reduced, as far as possible, to members who are at best indifferent; so much, however, were our minds disturbed, that we were on the very point of breaking up the Union of the Confederates and causing on the spot a very serious rupture. This is the way, as your Eminence will observe, in which they discuss the remedies required for this unhappy island. The clergy have no other object than to establish and secure the articles concerning the Catholic religion which are now submitted to the judgment of His Holiness; and, although it is determined to send two ambassadors to Rome, they fear from their mode of proceeding, that our adversaries are about to start some new project, either to recall Ormonde, or to propose a peace upon the same terms as those rejected before, so that no provision would be made for the safety of the Catholic religion, the embassy to His Holiness would prove to be a mere cloak to save appearances, and a heretical viceroy would be re-established in the Government, a concession to which they will never consent. I rejoice to find that the Count de la Monerie is of precisely the same opinion as myself, inasmuch as he has twice declared in the Assembly that before everything else His Holiness should be acknowledged as supreme in all matters pertaining to the Church, and that if the clergy were not satisfied all other arrangements would be useless; hence I cannot see without astonishment that opinions are still entertained which differ so much from my own. I have ventured to trouble your Eminence with this narrative, because the wisdom and energy you have shown in governing a kingdom make it easy to believe that you will always be willing to give your assistance to one who stands in need of it. When the persons who have been chosen arrive in Rome, it will be easy for your Eminence to persuade them to refrain from reviling a party which only desires the security of religion, and can justly claim their sympathy and assistance in furthering this object. When the end in view is a good one, I feel assured the clergy will vie with each other in giving every satisfaction even to those who do not deserve such a return. But, if the clergy are ill-treated, I should be unwilling to promise anything on their behalf, but can only pray God to dispose things according to his holy will.

To CARDINAL PANZIROLO (IN CIPHER).

The agent of the most Christian King, fearing possibly that the clergy, in spite of the resolutions which have been passed, might have determined to oppose the mission of the ambassadors to France, came to me to-day to make complaint. I told him frankly that the clergy had never intended to offer opposition to this Embassy, but that they certainly do suspect, from the character of the persons chosen, that it is in contemplation to pass certain resolutions at the Court of the Queen of England prejudicial to the Catholic religion, without waiting for, or possibly without regarding the proposals which His Holiness is about to make. He spoke at great length, made large promises, and gave me his word that they would not decide on anything, that neither the Prince nor the Marquis of Ormonde nor anyone else, should be sent thither till they had heard what should be determined in Rome. He then endeavoured to convince me that this mission to the Prince would be highly advantageous even to the clergy, since, even if no other benefit should accrue from it, they would at least have given to the people the satisfaction they so eagerly desired: and he added that, even if the Prince should come, it would be stipulated that the Nuncio and two Frenchmen, on the part of the King, should always be present in the Council, so that no resolutions could be taken either against religion or against the words of the Pope and the King of France.* I answered, that as to this matter I must await precise directions from His Holiness, not being able to decide on it myself. I added that although the clergy would not oppose the Embassy to France, he need not attempt to persuade us it was necessary, because there were many who believe it to be utterly useless. It is certain that France wishes the Prince were in Ireland, if it could be managed at the present opportunity privately and with the sanction of His Holiness. So France hopes little by little to gain a footing in this country.

To the Same (in Cipher).

December 28th, 1647.

As the Bishop of Ferns and Mr. Nicholas Plunket are just the kind of men who would desire to stand well with everybody, they may make many statements in Rome which are literally true, but nevertheless may not assign the real reasons. If they say that this people have lost courage owing to the defeats they have this year sustained, and that they believe they are no longer able to defend themselves, they will tell the strict truth; but the real cause is not the weakness of the country but the divisions and the envy of the rival parties; this fact was so manifest that, last year when I led 16,000 infantry to Dublin; if the Leinster men had not then envied the army of Ulster, and Preston had not thought more of Ormonde and Clanricare, than of the clergy, the Confederates would at this moment be masters of almost the whole kingdom, and religion would be everywhere re-established; moreover, the defeat of Leinster this year was entirely produced by the mistakes of the Generals as the two ambassadors

* See Doc. xiii.

are able to inform you, both of them having been present. And in this last defeat in Munster so disgraceful a flight was never heard of as that of the left wing, where the Munster men were. Moreover when O'Neill lately offered to quarter 4,000 of his men in the districts under the command of Inchiquin, in order to harass the enemy while he spared the Confederates, the Munster men refused their consent and preferred to look on while the enemy inflicted new damage every day. For these reasons we are bound to confess that the state to which we are reduced is the consequence of our own errors and of no other cause.

They will say that the country is ruined by its poverty and that everyone in it is a beggar. Nevertheless it is a fact that this very autumn, when the Baron Inchiquin was scouring two counties of Munster, he levied contributions of more than 100,000 scudi. Hence it is evident that the bad government of the Catholics is the real cause why money is not to be found; I am even told that there are many commissaries whose accounts have never been examined, especially in Munster, where they are all of them dependents of Viscount Muskerry

They will say that the people are determined to make peace on any terms and to submit to the King, and that this is the object of the Embassy which is now sent to France. But the truth is that the people in this matter, as in all others, does not know what it wants, and allows itself to be persuaded by others. It is the Ormonde faction who are bent on this Embassy not to please the people, but to forward their own objects, as I have repeatedly said.

They will say that the hatred against the Ulster men has reached such a pitch, that many of the nobles are determined rather to join the enemy than to tolerate these fellows any longer in their province, and that therefore it is necessary to devise some other remedies. I told the Bishop that it would not be wise to employ this argument in Rome, as His Holiness and the court might be disgusted, and their generosity might be checked if they discovered that their protection was sought for a people who would rather embrace the heretics than try to find some mode of uniting with their brethren. Of a truth the damage the Ulster men have done is not to be denied, and the overbearing temper of O'Neill has increased the resentment which is felt. Moreover as O'Neill sides with the Church all the hatred he has drawn upon himself recoils upon the Bishops, and still more upon me. The malcontents do not scruple to give out that it is I who direct the movements of the army; they also strive to irritate the lower class against me, and abuse me to the utmost of their power.

The real cause of all our losses is want of money, want of quarters, and the failure of all O'Neill's schemes, which are always disconcerted by his adversaries. It is not true that this hatred has been the cause of the new resolutions; on the contrary, it is those most in favour of these resolutions who use this hatred as a pretext, and labour every day to make it more virulent, as they see that every day this army is more zealous in the cause of religion and the clergy; then too, a rumour has been spread abroad by our adversaries that O'Neill has higher aims, which so far as I know, is an arrant falsehood. All this I have stated that these gentlemen in Rome may not give a false colour to the truth. This kingdom suffers from no other evils than the bad feeling which is cherished towards the men of Ulster, and the suspicion on their part that they are not treated as equals, and these two evils form as it were a circle, so that it is impossible to discover where the beginning really is. Though I have said this much it is not because I no longer desire that His Holiness should protect this poor island, on the contrary, I desire it more than ever, and I believe that whatever be the success, whatever the extravagance of these parties, that party which shows the most regard for religion will always merit this protection and that it ought not to suffer for the faults of others. Such a party I trust, whether great or small, will never be wanting in this kingdom.

To THE SAME (IN CIPHER).

December 31st, 1647.

The instructions drawn up for the ambassadors to Rome have been laid before me; amongst them I see one, commanding them to represent the state of the kingdom as desperate; hoping thereby to induce His Holiness to accede at once to the nomination of a heretic Viceroy and the other measures approved by the Ormonde faction.

They will not at once entreat His Holiness to take the protectorate upon himself, because they agree that without seeking all other means of procuring assistance, this would be treason towards His Majesty. But they will resort to it, when the two embassies to Rome and France agree that there is no other hope; therefore the negotiation will be much protracted.

They will supplicate His Holiness to act as mediator with the Queen and Prince for a peace, and to prescribe all he desires for religion; and having included in the instructions the demand for a Catholic Viceroy and the other proposals of the clergy, they have added the words "if all this is agreeable to your Holiness" with the hope I have stated above.

Finally assistance in money is to be requested; and this is in truth the only want of the kingdom. This is the only means which can keep united the discordant parties, reconcile O'Neill with the others and consequently ensure the safety of religion. It cannot be denied that these instructions contain not the slightest reference to any of the proceedings in France, whence I cannot divest myself of a suspicion that some plan may already be put into execution there. I must freely confess that if the French are anxious to get rid of the Prince and he to come, I am surprised that he has not done so ere this, and I look for him daily, since those who desire his presence number more than half the kingdom, and none would dare to oppose him.

More than all I am astonished that the Assembly, when nominating these embassies, should have entirely overlooked the wants of the present year; the war will recommence in ten weeks, and I strongly suspect that while looking for aid from abroad we shall be taken by surprise at home.

To the Same (in Cipher).

January 5th, 1648.

I have now likewise seen the instructions for the ambassadors to France, and find strong reason to suspect that in spite of all our efforts and opposition, some secret agreement has been made between that country and the Ormonde faction here. Because although the instructions expressly declare that no final measures can be taken until after the decision of the Court of Rome; and that the question of the Protectorate is to be referred first to His Holiness (in which the Roman and French instructions agree), nevertheless as in case of a peace the promise of the most Christian King is to be obtained, and as no mention is made of an ambassador to Spain, the Bishops fear that the protection of France and the invitation to the Prince have been already decided upon. And this fear is strengthened by the fact, that although the mission to His Holiness was to have set off first, the other ambassadors announced a day or two ago their intention of departing immediately, for the purpose they say of raising money for the approaching campaign, which they hope to do in France.

The Bishops therefore have resolved not to sign the French instructions if the ambassadors set off before those to Rome. I hear also that O'Neill will not sign at all if Geoffry Brown be sent to France. Hence you will see that suspicion and dissatisfaction are rife amongst us.

I agree with the clergy in wishing the first Embassy to be to His Holiness, because this is both right and advisable; and the agents of both crowns are of my opinion as to a Protector. I always declare that he ought to be elected by the whole kingdom, and not by a few individuals; that His Holiness will assuredly favour whoever is thus elected, and that the Holy Father is well aware that if the entire kingdom does not concur in the choice, a division amongst the Confederates will inevitably ensue. Perhaps God has willed this either for our advantage or chastisment, and that no human endeavours can change the result.

I am, &c.

To THE SAME (IN CIPHER).

January 5th, 1648.

Since the increase of hostilities between England and Scotland, the general of the Ulster Scotch has shown an inclination to join the Catholics against the English. The O'Neills are zealously pursuing the negotiation, and I hear will make the Supreme Council give their assent. I have always thought that it would be the better fortune for our party; since besides fomenting the dissensions between England and Scotland, the Ulster men now so hated in the other provinces, would return to their own crowned with honour and profit; and perhaps afterwards pass over to Scotland and carry the Catholic religion with them to that country. Certain it is that Ireland will never be at peace until the war be carried into the homes of others; and it will be my task in that case to secure articles as advantageous to religion as can be obtained under the circumstances of the times.

To the Pope.

The Supreme Council once before recommended to your Holiness Dr. Edward Tyrrell as coadjutor of the Archbishop of Dublin. I have been requested to renew my humble offices with your Holiness to assure you that he has always given great satisfaction to the ecclesiastical party in the conduct of the negotiations intrusted to him while agent at the most Christian court from this kingdom; and I have no doubt that the Nuncio of France will be able to confirm my report of his excellent qualities.

To Cardinal Panzirolo (in Cipher).

January 7th, 1648.

That part of the instructions given to the ambassadors who go to Rome, which represented to His Holiness the state of this kingdom as desperate has been expunged, and is left to the discretion of the ambassadors, because I told them how prejudicial a false statement would be. I therefore wish to give your Eminence a separate and plain report of the state of the kingdom according to my view, and in which all the Bishops concur. They wish me to pray His Holiness to be a mediator for a peace between the Prince, Queen, and Confederates, but I have left this point in silence and to His Holiness's opinion, since he may consider such a peace useless and disgraceful as many here believe, inasmuch as the King and the Prince are not at war with us, nor could they give us any assistance in the world. I also think that if, as is suspected, this peace and other matters are already concluded in France, His Holiness might himself in some degree be imposed on. These Roman instructions are very passable, and if those who go to France are faithful, both may effect much good.

REPORT ON THE STATE OF THE KINGDOM IN THE YEAR 1647.

The affairs of this kingdom having been in the last year most prosperous, and being now considered by many to be desperate, it is needful to investigate the causes of so great a change.

I find that in four things there is a great change: 1st, the scarcity of money; 2nd, the great increase of disunion; 3rd, the loss of several towns in Munster; 4th, the devastation of the country by the enemy, and even by the marches and halts of our own troops. In other points the affairs of the Provinces are much in the same state, or perhaps in some a little better.

It is certain that these four evils combined have been together cause and effect, since the want of money has increased the hatred of one party to the other, from this hatred come our losses; and from all together our poverty; whence if a way can be found by which Ireland can obtain sufficient assistance, the remedy for all four evils would be easy and all be reduced to one only.

It is evident the want of money is owing to the expenses of the war without any foreign aid, to the exactions of the enemy in three counties, and to the injuries to the land by the constant passage to and fro of the soldiery.

On the score of the hatreds and dissensions the evidence is still stronger, since all who wished for the peace seeing the events of this year, revenged themselves on the clergy who rejected it; representing them as the cause of all the evils which followed, and since they know that the Ulster men approved of the rejection add to their old dislike of that province this new one. But it must be owned that the ravages committed by this army, and the increase of their numbers beyond that of the other provinces, have greatly contributed to alienate friends and exasperate enemies, and in truth this state of things is truly miserable, and O'Neill has great reason to believe that the other party have done, and are doing all in their power to ensure the coming of the Prince and to oppress him and his army; while this other party on the contrary being day by day worse treated by the Ulster soldiery and observing the conduct of O'Neill, are in their turn persuaded that he wishes to impoverish them, and make himself master of the whole kingdom. Neither can the clergy do anything to remove this suspicion, because they favour O'Neill who always stands by them, and are therefore considered partisans and not judges.

I come now to the Provinces, and of what is to be hoped from them if they are in the miserable state alleged.

In Ulster where at the beginning of the war scarcely any Irish were to be found, part of it even being full of heretics, the Catholics have now recovered a considerable portion. The Scotch since our victory in '46 have rarely shown themselves, nor done anything material. They still retain the seaports on the coast opposite to Scotland; but if we had money to lead an army there we might easily recover them. Nor must I omit to say that if the quarrel between the other two kingdoms continue, it is perhaps probable that these Scotch may unite with the Catholics, to the great loss of the English.

In Connaught, although much devastated by our own and the enemy's troops, there is no place of any importance to recover except Sligo, the capture of which might be easily effected, and would give an opening through Ulster to the North and to the acquisition of Enniskillen, the strongest fort in that quarter. In Leinster, the only change in the past year was that Dublin passed into the hands of the Parliament from those of the Marquis of Ormonde; persons who understand the matter consider this an advantage, because Ormonde, with his relations and adherents did much more harm than the open and implacable enmity of those who are now in possession. As to our forces, Preston's defeat might go far to make one believe that they had deteriorated; but those who saw the errors that were committed on our side in that battle, are of a contrary opinion. It is true that the enemy had 600 horse better armed than ours, while we had to supply the deficiency with infantry and pikemen. But on the other hand, the Catholics retain all the quarters they gained last year and which are of the greatest importance. In Munster, besides the sack of Cashel and other misfortunes we have lost Cappoquin, Dungarvan, and Cahir, now in the hands of the enemy. Baron Inchiquin however has at present but little money, and is in want of men unless reinforced by England; and in this province more than in any other, it is evident that were not the Catholics divided into two parties, they might easily recover all the places they have lost. It may therefore be gathered that if money were not wanting, the Confederates might not only make a successful resistance this year but carry on an offensive war and recover their losses, because in Munster, Taaffe's army will be superior to Inchiquin's. In Connaught and Ulster, O'Neill's troops would be more than sufficient even if divided into two parts; and in Leinster he would have another army which could defend it; or reinforced by troops from Ulster might accompany the other, if the Dublin enterprise should be attempted.

If, by the grace of God, the Dean of Fermo should soon arrive with the Papal subsidy, this year's campaign may be thus arranged:—1st. To see if the enterprise against Dublin can be attempted, and if not, with the sum we shall have in hands we must be content with our possessions in Leinster, and prevent the advance of the enemy. 2nd. To reconstruct in Munster the army which Taaffe had before the last battle, to attack Inchiquin, and recover all that he has gained from us this year. To push the army of O'Neill through Connaught into Ulster to recover the places lost, as the Nuncio proposed this summer when he went for this purpose to Galway, when having borrowed 10,000 crowns this plan would have been carried out had not the Supreme Council urgently recalled O'Neill to Leinster after Preston's defeat. But if His Holiness sends us further supplies for this year, still the attempt on Dublin may be brought to a successful termination.

From all this it may be seen that the affairs of this kingdom are in a perilous state and subject to change at any moment, but they are by no means desperate as many pretend, and it is certain that if what the Nuncio has proposed be carried out, that His Holiness and the other princes grant their aid, and the dissensions in England continue, we may hope in two or three years to gain over the whole kingdom to the Catholic faith, pass over into England or Scotland, and carrying the war thither introduce the true religion to the glory of Ireland, and thus insure her tranquillity for many a year.

To the Pope.

January 9, 1648.

The General Assembly of this kingdom have deputed the Bishop of Ferns and Mr. Nicholas Plunket to represent the present position of the Confederation to your Holiness. The desire shown by all orders that in the first instance we should obtain your Holiness' paternal councils and assistance, authorized me to promise a gracious audience to these ambassadors, and every other favour necessary for the benefit of the Catholic religion. I trust also that these gentlemen will merit favour on their own account, being two of the most honoured and well affected men in the island, as they have proved by their labours continued through many years for the welfare of this disunited Republic, and to maintain the original purpose of the war. Referring your Holiness to them for a full account of this kingdom, I prostrate myself at your feet and pray, &c., &c.

To the Same.

January 9th, 1648.

The ambassadors from this kingdom will in my name, present to your Holiness twenty-five ensigns taken by the Catholics in the battles of this year. They were taken from the Scotch in Ulster, and from the Parliamentary armies in the other provinces, under the auspices of your Holiness, and the greater part by the aid of your supplies. The blessed God knows how ardently I long to lead all the rest of this country before your sacred throne, in order that the heresy which prevails in these kingdoms should be trampled out as well by your most holy feet as by the authority which you hold. If I am permitted to receive this favour no servant of the Holy See will ever have been more blessed, as this will be one of the most signal conquests of your Holiness' reign. Kissing your holy feet, &c., &c.

To the Nuncio of France (in common Cipher).

January 9th, 1648.

This kingdom is about to despatch the Bishop of Ferns and Mr. Nicholas Plunket to Rome, and Viscount Muskerry, the Marquis of Antrim, and Geoffry Brown to France. They have instructions to propose a reconciliation with the Queen and Prince of England, the Pope acting between them, and to his arbitration it is left to decide on the articles of religion. If the arrangements for the peace do not succeed they will demand a Protector; and the first proposed will be His Holiness; as I insisted on introducing into the instructions a proviso that those who are sent to France can neither begin nor conclude anything, nor accept a peace or a change in the government, until the terms have been proposed in Rome and approved of by His Holiness. But as Muskerry and Brown are much suspected by the clergy, whose avowed enemies they are, it is feared by many that in spite of their instructions they may come to some resolution, and perhaps conduct the Prince to this country before anything is decided in Rome. I inform your Excellency of these matters in order that you may remind those who need it, that anything done without the consent of Rome will be in danger of rejection; and I entreat your Excellency to inform His Holiness at once of any such attempt. Your Excellency may perhaps already be aware of all this, from an open letter which I sent to Cardinal Mazarin on the 29th of last month, but of which I enclose a duplicate lest the first should have gone astray.

To Cardinal Panzirolo (in Cipher).

Kilkenny, January 16th, 1648.

As Muskerry under pretence of travelling more safely, insists on setting off with the ambassadors to Rome, I have induced the Council to write and apologize for it to His Holiness and assure him that neither Muskerry nor his colleagues will arrange or conclude anything in France without first having the opinion of His Holiness; and in truth they are so strictly bound by the instructions, that it will be at their peril to do otherwise.

The French agent has written to the Queen of England to recommend her to appoint a Catholic Viceroy, as otherwise affairs will not go well for this country. The said agent professes himself perfectly satisfied with my conduct in the matter, saying that I have always been neutral between the two Crowns; but since he has had the best of it, it is no such great matter that he should be satisfied.

The Ulster soldiery being now all in quarters enemies are not wanting who boast of their intentions to disarm them in one night and that they have many accomplices. But since the troops are forewarned, things may turn out very differently.

As the ecclesiastical articles are to be negotiated in Rome I send your Eminence a copy of those subscribed two years ago in case the originals have been lost. Two letters will be presented to His Holiness from me recommending Tyrrel, who wishes to be Coadjutor in Dublin; and Archer who applies for the same office in Kilkenny, both of them are in France. Of their worth and habits the Nuncio dei Bagni is better informed than I am; but I must add that the Bishop of Kilkenny is very old and rarely leaves his chamber. The Bishop of Dublin is incapacitated by extreme corpulency, and if we ever regain possession of that city, it will deserve one of the best qualified ecclesiastics as his successor.

To THE POPE.

January 18th, 1648.

The Supreme Council as well as the whole city of Kilkenny unite their humble prayers to your Holiness that you will be pleased to nominate Dr. Bartholomew Archer to be Coadjutor of the Church of Ossory. I can testify to your Holiness the extreme old age and inefficiency of the Bishop, who is no longer able to fulfil any of his duties, and also desires to be favoured with an assistant. As to Archer being the Almoner of Mademoiselle d'Orleans, I can say nothing now of him beyond his honorable descent and the consideration in which he is held by well-informed persons as a theologian; but the Nuncio of France can supply all necessary information. Awaiting any commands which the wise vigilance of your Holiness may prescribe, I kiss your holy feet and pray for the long continuance and prosperity of your reign.

To CARDINAL PANZIROLO (IN CIPHER).

January 21st, 1648.

The Marquis of Antrim when taking leave of me before setting out for France, confided to me that the Prince of Wales has no intention of coming to Ireland as long as I remain here. This makes me believe there was some foundation for the scheme attributed to Digby last summer to come to an agreement provided they got rid of the Nuncio; and of which I spoke in my letters from Galway. The Dean of Fermo writes to me that the two Digbys are endeavouring by all sorts of falsehoods to compass my ruin, and I can see no other object than this; but their judgment is at fault, as it would be only too great a glory for me to have frightened away an heretical Prince.

It is said that the Scotch, moved by the French, have declared for the King against the Parliament. This has long been my wish and is the only way in which Ireland can be benefited. God grant that it be so!

To the Grand Duke of Tuscany.

Waterford, January 29th, 1648.

To the misfortune of this country the supplies of arms granted by the piety of your Highness have been delayed. But not on this account must I delay the thanks due for them, and the hope that so liberal a gift may produce proportionate results to the benefit of our Holy Religion. The members of the Confederation acknowledge their deep obligations to your Highness, and with me desire that you may enjoy the many years of felicity which your devotion to the Catholic faith so well merits.

I am, &c., &c.

To Cardinal Panzirolo (in Cipher).

January 29th, 1648.

The Dean of Fermo sent me an account of his interview with the Queen of England, but not of that with the Marquis of Montrose, unless indeed his letters have miscarried. I was particularly glad to hear of it from your Eminence, as I have always thought that for the tranquillity and security of religion no means could be so effectual as to divert the war into Scotland. I shall therefore avail myself of this information as affairs have not changed on this point, and we shall have no great difficulty as far as I can see except the want of money, because these Scotch have always fought here. From the Queen we must hope nothing, except propositions hurtful to religion since she is entirely in the hands of Jermyn, Digby, and other heretics. I know but too well that her wish to send the Marquis of Ormonde hither will be embraced with avidity by Muskerry and Brown who desire nothing better, although the Marquis of Antrim, the third Commissioner does not agree with them, and moreover their instructions expressly prohibit it. With all this, the two set off with the determination to carry out the scheme by every means in their power. If they do succeed, your Eminence will hear of the sudden end of the Confederation; and the affairs of the country will be ruined between them.

I have seen the speech delivered in London on 25th July, which, as it merely shows a new change in the affairs of the King now a fugitive in the Isle of Wight, is only of general importance; and as the same speech says, time will clear up many things, and the prospect of any revolution in England is cheering to us. I have come to Waterford to be able to write till the last moment before the departure of the Commissioners.

The Council have adjourned to Clonmel, to intervene in the great dissensions in the Munster Assembly; where Baron Inchiquin with a handful of men is allowed to override and alarm everyone without our side knowing how to keep order or restrain him in any way. These are the fruits of the proceedings of Muskerry and the Ormonde faction, who foment the disorders to make the people believe that a peace is all they want, and that the clergy have been the cause of all their misfortunes. Besides this they have spread reports that His Holiness is going to remove me because he is ill satisfied with me, and other absurdities which would not deserve a thought but that they alarm and weaken the clergy.

To the Same.

Waterford, January 29th, 1648.

At the moment of the Commissioners' departure I received a large package from the Dean of Fermo, containing four letters and four in cipher from your Eminence, dated 2nd and 6th September. From them I hear of the first audience granted by His Holiness to the Marquis de Fontaine, the ambassador from the most Christian King, to the satisfaction of both parties, at which I especially rejoiced having been the first to propose this mission to Cardinal Mazarin, and have constantly desired to see it carried into effect. I trust in the Blessed God that the condescending kindness of His Holiness will show to all other kingdoms how much it is for their interest to stand well with the Church. When the Dean wrote he was making renewed efforts to obtain a frigate, as he has doubtless informed your Eminence, and in the meantime he has sent over a part of the money in letters of credit with the wise desire to place it beyond the reach of danger. But every'delay is fatal because this kingdom is beginning to know its misery and to value those who favour it.

To the Nuncio of France (in common Cipher).

February 5th, 1648.

The account sent to Rome by your Excellency of the interview desired and subsequently obtained by the Marquis of Montrose with the Dean of Fermo, has been forwarded to me, and I have communicated with the Marquis of Antrim upon the offer of Montrose, to form an alliance with him; and since I found him well inclined to it, I told him to wait upon your Excellency immediately on his arrival in Paris about this negotiation, and to let his conditions be such that they may be carried into effect.

Your Excellency might also communicate with the Abbé Crelly, who goes with the Marquis, as he is a safe and faithful person, and the Marquis, who is easy and tractable, confides very much in him. If God favours this negotiation Ireland may yet be saved. I have often written to Rome that a diversion on the side of Scotland would be the true way to benefit Ireland. Your Excellency will do me the favour to report all that occurs to the notaries.

And I salute your Excellency.

To Cardinal Panzirolo (in Cipher).

Waterford, February 5th, 1648.

I communicated to the Marquis of Antrim, who is on the eve of his departure for France, all that the Nuncio of France wrote to your Eminence of the interview between the Marquis of Montrose and the Dean of Fermo. I found the Marquis well inclined to the alliance proposed by Montrose; and I therefore wrote to the Nuncio that the Marquis would wait upon him at once, and entreated that the affair might be settled as soon as possible, because I have always believed that a diversion of the war into Scotland will be most useful to Ireland. I also informed Monsignor that the Marquis will be accompanied by a Cistercian, the Abbé Crelly, and as he is a trustworthy man and of great authority with the Marquis, is one to whom everything may be confided. I obtained permission for him to join the Embassy, in order that he might restrain the too great facility of the Marquis, and strengthen him against the wiles of his two colleagues, who will endeavour to deceive him on all occasions. A report has been spread, I do not know on what foundation, that the Queen and the Prince are to delegate their authority in this country to two Lords Justices, according to ancient usage when there was no Viceroy, one to be Catholic and the other heretic, in order to satisfy all parties. If this be true, the consequence would be more fatal than the severest measures because the heretics will always be the strongest party, at least if they come to arms and divide into separate parties. It is however a great matter seeing manifestly that a Catholic Viceroy is the only means of putting things right, that they should try every other measure before coming to that which is the easiest of all.

These agents to Rome and to France have been unable to find vessels in which to sail, and those to Spain are so seldom spoken of that I doubt when they will be ready. So God confounds the opinion of those who expected to return by the month of March, and to bring back a large store of blessings and a peace.

To the Same (in Cipher).

Waterford, February 13th, 1648.

When all our soldiers were in quarters, and the Congress of Munster yet sitting in Clonmel, Inchiquin surprised Carrick and approached Waterford, but afterwards turned towards Kilkenny. At the same time Colonel Jones left Dublin and has taken the Castle of Kildare, whence we suppose that they are still, as in September, endeavouring to unite their forces. Their troops are however few in number and badly disciplined, except the cavalry of which the greater part is good.

The Council immediately gave orders for the armies of all the three Generals to unite to prevent the accomplishment of the enemy's design; but it is expected that some amongst the Catholics have both invited and advised them, and many conjectures are afloat. The truth is, if we had but a little money and that unanimity prevailed this would be the time to cut off both enemies, since they have been driven out by a scarcity of all kinds of food. All communication is cut off from Kilkenny where I left my baggage and a part of my household, but I trust in God that I shall soon see them again.

To the Same.

February 13th, 1648.

When I thought that the Roman agents must have arrived in France, they had been driven back to Duncannon by contrary winds. I therefore send to them an addition of two letters in cipher, in which I have written all that has occurred within the last few days worthy of your Eminence's notice.

To Monsignor the Nuncio of France (in common Cipher).

February 17th, 1648.

The danger of the Marquis of Ormonde being recalled, of which I wrote to your Excellency and Cardinal Mazarin, may be freely discussed with the Abbé Crelly who is perfectly trustworthy. Your Excellency will do well to warn all who need it that it will be the ruin of the kingdom; and to represent to the Cardinal that it will give rise to such dissensions that if it takes place the King will never again receive any good out of this kingdom.

To the Cardinal Panzirolo (in Cipher).

February 18th, 1648.

After much reflexion, I see nothing so perilous in all the affairs which may be treated of by these envoys to France as the return of the Marquis of Ormonde; because this would open the way to the revival of the old peace. Most persons of judgment are of this opinion, and at the taking of Carrick Inchiquin let fall some words which tended to show that he too agrees on this point. Great revolutions may be expected, and I am one of those who dread the idea of a heretic viceroy, and the consequent danger to religion.

The Bishop of Ferns will probably inform your Eminence that previous to his departure he advised me to retire to the Castle of Duncannon, as he holds that all around me are corrupted by the malignants. But your Eminence knows that I will never leave any place or any Catholic city unless it is necessary for my safety; nor can I imagine that any Catholic would do me an injury. I trust that the Lord God will be pleased to accept my devotion to the Holy Faith and to the Apostolic See.

To the Same (in Cipher).

February 18th, 1648.

The Duchess of Buckingham now the wife of the Marquis of Antrim, who formerly testified the liveliest zeal for the Catholic religion, has absolutely no means of support save 600 livres granted her by the Supreme Council. As it is very difficult to get in this sum, the poor lady on the departure of her husband for France, was reduced to ask a loan from me of 200 crowns which I immediately advanced to her. But as I much doubt its being repaid, and perhaps shall be obliged to assist her again, I think it advisable to acquaint your Eminence, and I trust that the disposal in this charitable act of a part of the Papal subsidy will be approved by His Holiness, of whose benevolence this lady is truly worthy, and I shall endeavour to act in the case so that no trouble or difficulty shall accrue to His Holiness.

To the Same (in Cipher).

Waterford, February 23rd, 1648.

I received from Owen O'Neill the letter of which I enclose a copy, as also of the answer which I returned at once. I do not know of anyone in Rome who could have seen my letters and made their contents known in this country, and therefore I believe it to be the malicious work of O'Neill's enemies; and especially as your Eminence has not mentioned the words which His Holiness is supposed to have used and which I should certainly have heard; I have advised him to write to His Holiness on the subject, and declare himself more openly than ever for the Catholic religion; a gracious reply which the wisdom of your Eminence would know how to frame, might assure him that no one had ever used his name to His Holiness in the matters on which he writes; because in fact despite of all his defects, if he and his army were alienated from us religion would be completely struck down to the ground. My duty as a good minister is to inform your Eminence as I have done, of all that occurs, and even of all that is reprehensible in O'Neill's conduct; had I always defended him I should have lost many friends and much credit with the other party, exposed myself to some insult, and been unable to avert many passing troubles. All my letters however since May have uniformly shown that he and his army are of the greatest consequence to us.

To the Same.

Waterford, February 24th, 1648.

I take the opportunity of writing by the vessel which takes the two agents to France to inform your Eminence that Baron Inchiquin, after spreading great alarm in Kilkenny and raising a contribution of 12,000 crowns from the county has returned to his quarters, as also has Jones, who from the opposition of the Ulster troops and the intervention of a river was unable to join him. The Supreme Council were resolute not to leave Kilkenny, which otherwise would have been taken. I am now here in safety, but for several nights we were under arms fearing a sudden attack; however as our army is assembled I trust that there is nothing to fear for the present. Your Eminence will find the particulars of what occurred in the enclosed dispatches.

To the Same (in Cipher).

Duncannon, March 10th, 1648.

Notwithstanding all that has been written and said by the agents, we might do great things this year in Ireland if we had but money and unanimity. England is so disturbed that the Parliament has sent for aid from Dublin. I do not see how Inchiquin can receive any reinforcements, and the Ulster Scotch are about to declare for us against the English; this I shall endeavour to turn to the great profit and honour of religion. The well affected still fear however that the agents sent to France will do some great mischief, as the latest news is that Ormonde has arrived there, although it is said flying from the Parliament, and accompanied by two persons only. It is vain to hope for stability in this kingdom, since affairs are never the same for two days together, and many of these changes are not pleasing in the sight of God. I came to Duncannon to see if the Dean had possibly arrived, but he has not done so yet. God grant that this last affair about the frigate may not bring trouble with it from the many claims made, of which I shall write on his arrival. Inichiquin did not obtain the money from the county Kilkenny of which I spoke in my letter of February. The Council disallowed it, and imprisoned the man who carried the first payment.

To the Same (in Cipher).

Waterford, April 6th, 1648.

In this letter I will answer all that is necessary in your Eminence's letters brought over by the Dean of Fermo. First, in the matter of further remittances, I must propose three ways of sending them in order to avoid the delays and inconveniences which have occurred this time. One, to send two frigates to Leghorn or Civita Vecchia to bring the money direct, since there would be no greater risk to run, not even of shipwreck in this passage than in coming from France. The second plan would be to send the money by way of Spain, where I believe they would make no difficulty about its exportation, as they do in France; lastly, to raise the money here, and make it payable in France where the exchange is good and there would be no trouble. Your

Eminence's desire that I should be careful of myself during these disturbances is full of wisdom and benevolence. I confess that up to this period I have certainly thought more of what would benefit the work, but for the future I will be more circumspect, and provide as much as I can against contingencies.

When I wrote of O'Neill's fear that he had fallen into disgrace with His Holiness, he had been very much comforted by some letters I had written to him, and by other considerations which I had conveyed to him through a good priest. This General is now secured to the Catholic religion, and if he has assistance from the Church, he will never show himself lukewarm in promoting its success for many reasons, one especially, hatred to the Ormonde faction will keep him steadfast. Would that I could say as much for General Preston, but he is a most unsteady man, unfit to take council with, easily dictated to by the evil minded, and I greatly fear he may have been drawn into the league of which I speak in the accompanying letter in cipher; and for no other reason than to be able to make head against O'Neill, rivalship with him being firmly rooted in his heart.

Of the protectorship I have written fully in former despatches, and the Envoys who must have arrived at Rome, can tell you that I have carefully refrained from giving any promises on His Holiness' part to either side. On one point alone I have insisted, it is that if they appeal to any Prince His Holiness should be first consulted and his instructions obtained, this being simply the reverence due to the Apostolic See above all the Princes in the world.

The purchase of the frigate by the Dean of Fermo cannot but be most useful, as this kingdom has no greater need than that of vessels for defence against attacks by sea, and in any case can be resold with little loss. The booty taken at La Rochelle has given me much anxious thought. On the one hand I thought that we ought to keep as much as would cover the expenses which have been incurred in the assignments of the subsidies now come, in order that the sum appropriated for the expenses which may ensue might remain free; but when I heard that the booty would be retained in France by the avidity of the ministers who hold all the saleable offices, I should have been better pleased that the Dean had not had even the part which he took secretly from the Governor of La Rochelle, because the Irish who were on board the victorious frigate, told the Spanish agent, through hatred I believe of the captain, that they took for granted the capture money would go to Ostend; and though the Dean besides having brought with him the process, has prudently also brought the captain and all the officers present at the assault in order to make them witnesses, and to make the Supreme Council Judge, I should still wish that the fact of our having received even a single crown of the money should never be known. Monsignor the Nuncio of France wrote plainly to me in February that if the King's affairs became desperate the Prince would be sent hither. In this event I think I cannot do better than retire to some distant part of the kingdom and await the commands of His Holiness, in case the Prince should show any real desire to consult the Holy Father on religious affairs. But if a despotic government without check or respect for others be established, it will be advisable for me to quit the island, and remain wherever the winds carry me, trusting that His Holiness will approve of this as he has honoured me by commending what I have done hitherto.

To the Same (in Cipher).

April 8th, 1648.

After the retreat of Inchiquin, the Ulster troops who had more than once offered to march into Munster and live in the enemy's quarters, not being able to obtain permission from the Council, and weary of the jealousies and persecutions of the other party, resolved to return to Ulster, and wrote to inform me of their intention; of this, however, I could not approve while the other provinces are in such imminent danger. The Council granted them quarters till the 20th April, the nobility and clergy of Munster seeming inclined to call in their aid, but were still opposed by the Council. In this state of affairs, Colonel John Barry who had fled from the Parliament together with the Marquis of Ormonde disembarked at Cork. He negotiated with Inchiquin, and under safe conduct from both parties has treated several times with the Supreme Council. The sum of his negotiations is to persuade them that Ormonde is in high favour with the King, that His Majesty has given him his signet, or cipher, and intimated to the Scotch that whoever shows this signet has full power to treat with them. Further he would prove that there is no way to pacify this country with satisfaction to the King but to invest the Marquis of Ormonde with the dignity of Viceroy, because the Scotch now defending the royal party, would thus be in league with us. He added that on these terms Inchiquin also would join us, and that our only enemy would then be the English in Dublin who could never resist our combined forces. This negotiation therefore, tends to the restoration of the Marquis so ardently desired by his party. I have found out that the Council, at Barry's suggestion, has written to Inchiquin proposing a truce and that he should come to deliberate on these matters. Inchiquin, to show that he does not recognise the Supreme Council as his superiors, has sent an answer to Dr. Fennell alone who is one of the Council, demanding the most impertinent terms for a truce, and amongst them the payment of 4,000 crowns a week, a sum which distributed amongst our own soldiers would suffice to recover the whole province. The Council however, sent two deputies to treat with him, unable to dissimulate their anxiety to attain the blessed end of Ormonde's return. And

in truth that everything they do is to this one end is
evident; besides other proofs two months ago when the
province had determined at Clonmel to raise an army of
7,000 infantry and 1,500 horse at their own expense, and
sent four Commissioners to the Council to obtain the
necessary confirmation, they not only would give no reply,
but have now summoned a meeting of these same persons
at Kilkenny, for the 20th of April, in order to take these
proposals into consideration, which will be when the enemy
is again on foot, and when they should have already acted
on the above resolution. This is all done to make the truce
appear a necessity, and to make way for the often named
return of Ormonde, or at least for the coming of the Prince.
I have written several times to the Council showing them
the danger of this truce, as much to religion as to the honour
of the kingdom and of the approbation of His Holiness. I
send herewith copies of the letters, and in answer they tell me
that nothing shall be done without my approbation. I
shall go next week to Kilkenny in obedience to duty, but
without much hope of any good fruits resulting, as besides
that the faction which desires to be again under the heretical government daily increases in numbers, it is clear that
without introducing some of the Ulster party into these two
provinces it will be impossible to carry on any useful
measures; to this introduction, however, the Council will
never consent except by force. Such is the present state of
affairs; a superficial policy promises us a grand peace, whilst
the Protestants are united with us against the Puritans,
Independents or Freethinkers; but when one looks deeper
the imminent danger to religion is apparent, oppressed as
it will be by both parties till it gradually becomes weaker,
and perhaps be extinguished altogether, which may God
forbid! The Bishop of Ferns on arriving in France, sent
me the news that Ormonde and Digby have joined the army
of the Prince of Condé; I wrote to warn the Nuncio of

France of the dangers of this man's return here, and I have done the same to Cardinal Mazarin; I submit to your Eminence's prudence whether any further orders should be transmitted to Monsignor. Another report is that the Prince will come, but I have no other news from France than what Monsignor dei Bagni writes that this is whispered at Court. May God direct all events according to His Holy Will.

To the Same.

April 9th, 1648.

Immediately on the arrival of the Dean of Fermo I wrote to your Eminence by a vessel which was said to be ready to sail for Flanders, but as I hear she was driven out of her course, I fear the letter may not have reached you. The Dean disembarked on the 23rd of March (new style) in the port of Waterford, when I, as if with some presage of his arrival, was watching from a window in the fort of Duncannon and saw the sails of his ship afar off. And Satan, who as your Eminence says has impeded his voyage for so many months, continued to persecute him to the last; but Providence was on his side now, and enabled him to enter the port though the wind was contrary and he was chased by the Parliament's ships. He found too that if he had not left La Rochelle and arrived at Waterford the very day he did, he would have been delayed another month, and even before my eyes he was exposed to a slight danger in which I could neither assist him nor let him know that I was here. He was quite willing to yield the palm to me when recounting all his sufferings in coming to me, when I summed up all mine in expecting him, and if our misfortunes end here I shall be perfectly satisfied. He brought me your Eminence's letters, which I now answer. The Bishops have at last had the Bull, all receiving consecration from me with renewed obligations to His Holiness who has deigned to promote them. The Dean and I deliberate daily how best to carry on the negotiation for this kingdom and to dispose of the supplies; and I shall report the result from time to time at greater length. I pray for your Eminence's prosperity.

To the Same.

April 9th, 1648.

When I first heard the news from the Dean of Fermo in order to fulfil my obligations I wrote to congratulate your Eminence on the elevation of the Cardinals. The letter written on the same subject by your Eminence and now received with others, demands also a grateful reply. When I see how great is the glory of His Holiness in his most wise elections, I feel every day more bound to pray that the Lord God may grant him long life for the benefit of the holy Church, and to be the ornament of his College.

To the Same (in Cipher).

Waterford, April 10th, 1648.

The Supreme Council wrote to me to-day in haste to tell me that Baron Inchiquin had declared for the King against Fairfax and the Parliament, and that they therefore hoped to obtain good conditions to make a truce for five months, and begged of me to consent to come to Kilkenny as soon as possible to effect this purpose. With my reply I have sent them my reasons of which I enclose a copy, and which are now strengthened, because Inchiquin by declaring himself an enemy of the Parliament, is in such a position that if we marched with an army at once we might obtain what conditions we desired for religion. But as it is very probable that the Council have some other scheme afloat, I do not think this will bear any fruit. This will be the first time I shall have obeyed your Eminence's instructions to allow matters to take their course when I have used all due diligence. The Dean has seen O'Neill and writes me word that hopes prevail everywhere of a union with the Scotch; but I do not yet understand if this negotiation will succeed either with public approval or without it, but you shall have the earliest certain intelligence.

Since writing the above, I have heard that the Council wishes all the Bishops of Munster and some others to come to Kilkenny to consult upon the negotiation for the truce; I must go also since they will not treat without taking all opinions upon it.

In reply to your Eminence I think it will be well for His Holiness to defer nominating coadjutors for Dublin and Kilkenny, concerning which I was obliged to write two letters, as it daily becomes a matter of more importance, since the persons proposed, who live in France are not spoken of as I should wish.

To the Same (in Cipher).

Kilkenny, May 3rd, 1648.

I came to Kilkenny being every day solicited to do so by the Supreme Council, that I might be present at the conclusion of the truce with Inchiquin, of which I have already written, but found that as usual these gentlemen had all but completed it although they had written they should do nothing without me. In proof of this I was met on the way by a reply to my first letter, of which I sent a copy in my April despatch; this I answered, and received another reply from them. .I thought it well to draw up a short general abstract of the whole affair, which is here enclosed, as all their arguments tend to this only, that as it was not possible to maintain two wars owing to the poverty of the people and of the exchequer, and being constrained to make a truce with one, it was better that one should be the Baron, who had declared for the King, rather than with the Dublin people, followers of the Parliament. All this you will see at greater length in the abstract. On the arrival of the Bishops of

Munster they were summoned by the Council together with the nobles of the same province; and I, with those Bishops and some others who were here, held a congregation of sixteen Prelates who having heard my reasons against the truce, and read some of the articles between the Council and Inchiquin which the Council wished to communicate to the ecclesiastics, resolved that in the present circumstances and considering the dangers which threaten religion, the truce would not be secure in the matter of conscience, and sent the annexed declaration to the Council, signed by fourteen Bishops who were all present. It is to be noted that the Bishops of Tuam and Limerick, who were the first to subscribe the instructions given by the Council to the Commissioners sent to treat with Inchiquin, could not do less than subscribe to this contrary declaration; in this matter however it is only the conduct of the Bishop of Tuam which excites our wonder, since with regard to him of Limerick it is now eighteen months since to my great astonishment, and the astonishment of everyone, he joined the Ormonde faction, and every time that an English law comes into conflict with the laws of Rome, he shows but little gratitude for the benefits he has received from the Holy See. And he has reaped the reward of his conduct, since he has incurred the universal hatred of the other party and is looked upon as eccentric, and as separated from the rest of the clergy. When the declaration was published a violent tumult arose in the two provinces of Munster and Leinster, mingled with so many threats that at last some monks came to tell me that a plot against my life had been revealed to them in confession; but I determined as usual to have no fear as long as I shall be among Catholics only, though nevertheless I take all needful precaution, knowing that all this rage comes from the people of Munster; because they have placed their felicity in having six months of peace to breathe in; and from the Leinster men who would have had all the strength of the kingdom employed against Dublin in order to recover their property. It is very true the more sagacious believe that the truce is for no other purpose than with all the forces of the Ormondes to drive the Ulster men out of Leinster, to crush them or force them to return home; but up to this time I have no certain knowledge of such a misfortune. The gentlemen of the Council however, after having seen the declaration of the clergy have behaved differently, because by coming to me several times they have shown a desire to think of every satisfaction to the clergy in order to remove their scruples about the truce; and have desired the Commissioner already sent by them to Dungarvan to postpone concluding it by two days at a time; however to-day it is understood that they may return at any hour because Inchiquin is holding himself high and is demanding larger conditions. On the other hand, seeing the weakness of the Catholics who have no army in the province, he writes to all the cities and to everyone as if the truce were already granted, invites the Catholics to return to their quarters, and in fact the people in Munster act as though everything were adjusted. I report the state of affairs in this first cipher to continue it in following ones, because at this moment I do not know where or how things may turn out. The Council is confused and perhaps divided, and in one respect have acted most imprudently in not having summoned the nobles and the Bishops till after things were all but concluded; whence everyone complains, and only the populace who are led blindfolded are content. O'Neill is not far from this and is collecting a large army, declaring that it is to defend the clergy and their resolutions. Inchiquin has already declared against me, and O'Neill and his adherents, as your Eminence will see in a copy of one of his letters written to a gentleman here, so it appears that everything tends to a rupture and war between us. May God assist us, and cut this Gordian knot with the sword of His justice.

&c., &c.

To the Same (in Cipher).

Kilkenny, May 3rd, 1648.

If this letter from Inchiquin had been written without any communication with the Catholics, I should have esteemed it a boast or still better one of the chief glories of my position to have incurred this open hatred of the heretics; but because I am certain he would never have had this thought without it having been suggested to him by one of our party, it does not appear to me a thing to be despised. The Council persist in saying that the letter is a forgery because they have not had the original, though I have the testimony of my own eyes, but having written to their Commissioners who are with the Baron, they replied that Inchiquin does not deny though he says he does not recollect it, and that he does not repent having written it if he did write it for the reasons which your Eminence will see in the abovementioned copy; and now they begin to say that it is not a thing of any importance and that nothing else could be expected from a heretic. Neither does this sentiment please me, because if the Catholics have taken part in this affair as is most probable and as this same Council confesses, I do not see why towards a minister of the rank I represent, they should not show more respect or better consideration of the matter. I hope I shall know how to guard my person, but I have grave thoughts and anxieties about the safety of the baggage and the money, since the Dean of Fermo having landed between Leinster and Munster which are the two provinces hostile to us, I find at this crisis all that is valuable is in those places, and to transport it into Connaught will be all but impossible; whence if with the help of the Catholics and against the public faith the Baron should chose to act as an enemy, I shall have the greatest anxiety. I will immediately distribute the money secretly in different places and commending myself to God who only can deliver me from so many difficulties.

I am, &c., &c.

To the Same (in Cipher).

Kilkenny, May 4th, 1648.

I thought it well at all events to give His Holiness' Brief sent by the Dean of Fermo, also to General Preston, although he keeps up his rivalry with O'Neill more than ever; nevertheless he has always professed to wish to stand well with me and to listen to my advice. But it is quite true, that as soon as the Dean made public that he had brought the sword of the Earl of Tyrone to O'Neill with the benediction of His Holiness, Preston with his adherents fabricated such malignant reports on this head, that nothing else is talked of throughout the kingdom; they spread about everywhere that the sword is the emblem of royalty, and that at some future time His Holiness will send the crown. I am urged to explain the matter unreservedly as far as possible, but by their nature this people are incapable of being persuaded. At present Preston is in little favour in consequence of his defeat last summer, and his friends support him not because they have faith in him in military affairs, but solely to uphold a rival to O'Neill; and I know to a certainty that the present Council think of removing him from the command; if they succeed it will be nothing but good for the kingdom.

I do not intend at present to consign the Brief to Viscount Costello, because since his quarrel with O'Neill about the Castle of Athlone, he has shown some mistrust of me, whence I wish to wait till he returns to a more healthy tone of mind.

O'Neill received his Brief with so much humility and joy that he will express it in a letter to His Holiness himself, as he has done to me. The Congregation of Bishops has received their Brief, and I will send his to Mr. Terence Coghlan as soon as possible, &c., &c.

To the Same.

Kilkenny, 4th May, 1648.

Of the Briefs from His Holiness brought by the Dean of Fermo, directed to different persons, I have written to your Eminence in one of the accompanying ciphers. With this I must render thanks to your Eminence for your despatch and the Bulls which you have sent me for these new Bishops, and for the increased powers granted me in the service of the Embassy. Concerning all these, I must signify to your Eminence that the power of dispensing marriage in the second degree has been demanded of me, because here every minim priest holds it with the powers of a missionary from time immemorial. Hence, as His Holiness in his wisdom has not conceded it to me, I am on this point inferior to all other ecclesiastics whatsoever in the kingdom; and therefore if their Eminences so judge, perhaps it will be well that I should revoke it to all, and that they should refer themselves directly for it to the Holy See.

Apparently it will be difficult to exercise the power added to me of conferring parishes by means of competitions and synodical examiners, because here there is no preparation for anything of a similar kind, no competitions held, and no examiners appointed, and to wait till every Bishop has created his synod is little less than impossible amidst all the present disturbances. Notwithstanding all this I render infinite thanks for the great goodness of His Holiness, who has deigned to signalize my humble services by increasing my authority, for which I feel daily more constrained to go beyond all my former efforts in his service and in that of the Holy See. These Bishops have all wished to be consecrated by me, and although each of them will return for himself the thanks due to the benignity of His Holiness, along with his oath and profession of faith, it does not the less become me to accompany this offering with my most humble thanks, seeing that the multiplying of these prelates has produced those effects in the resolutions of the kingdom, which your Eminence in the excellence of your judgment, will have gathered from my constant reports; and I now make my humble reverence, &c.

ABSTRACT OF THE REASONS OF THE COUNCIL FOR AND AGAINST THE TRUCE.

First. They infer first the absolute necessity—asserting it to be impossible to carry on the war in Leinster and in Munster together, from the want of all necessary supplies.

Answer 1.—It is not proper that the Council should alone decide on this necessity without taking the Exchequer into account and summoning the Generals to know if there are arms and soldiers sufficient to carry on the two wars; since many hold a contrary opinion, and it is certain that the Ulster army was sufficient to make war in Munster against Inchiquin, and that no part of his army remained for the defence of Leinster.

Second. This necessity granted they conclude easily that it is more useful to make a truce in Munster than in Leinster, since the Baron has declared for the King, and therefore ought to be embraced by the Confederates, in order to be able also to obtain more advantageous conditions from the Queen and Prince in the peace now treated for. And they say they are certain that His Holiness will approve of it, because they suppose he does not desire to deprive the King of anything.

Answer 2.—Inchiquin has already three times declared for the King and has always broken faith; and this may be much more expected to be the case now that His Majesty is in such an unhappy position; and there are grave tokens, and it is spoken of in letters from France, that he and Ormonde are Parliamentarians, and only feign to be Royalists; or in truth because this has been concerted with the Parliament; or probably, because they have seen that those who held in England to the King have obtained good conditions from the same Parliament. If this be true, what certainty can there be that the Queen will wish that the Catholics should treat the Baron as a friend? and also what hope is there that Her Majesty will improve the conditions while she sees that the Catholics are weak; and in order the better to confess their weakness, go with a truce to meet half way one who four days ago despoiled all the provinces, ruined the churches, and has done as much evil as possible to everyone? As to His Holiness it is answered that he always believes it to be of greater service to the King that the lands and districts should be in the hands of Catholics rather than of Protestants, and has in consequence always desired that Dublin should be taken although the Marquis was there; and that therefore they could not hope His Holiness would approve of this truce for such an end, if it were not to the advantage of religion. Again, be it observed that if the armies moved towards Dublin with the aid of Inchiquin as the Confederates wished, and that the Englishman within declared at that moment for the King, what then would have to be done? perhaps he would put himself on our side like Inchiquin and then would not the Catholics be between two enemies, and religion be in more danger than ever? a consideration which has become the more probable since it is seen that one of the articles proposed by Inchiquin for the truce is this: that if Jones declare for the King the Catholics should be bound to do the same themselves.

Third. That if this truce were concluded the two provinces could unite to make an attack on Dublin, and by occupying the metropolis of the kingdom entirely free themselves from the Parliament.

Answer 3.—It may be doubted whether when Dublin was not seized by the same party when there was an opportunity, God will permit it now when they desire it. If the attempt be made by O'Neill and Preston together it will be exactly as before—if by one only, there will be neither means nor hope of success. And if Inchiquin, besides the union of so many Catholics who now favour him, is in accord with Jones as it is said what benefit would it be to religion? If the taking of Dublin serves to bring back Ormonde as so many believe, would not the ecclesiastical party be entirely ruined? What wisdom then in running so many risks whilst we can oppose an enemy who excites such suspicions and defend ourselves from another until God graciously improves the condition of the kingdom.

Fourth. They add, if the truce be not made and that they take up arms against the Baron, he may resolve to sell all his districts to the Parliament, and in desperation do it to the great injury of the kingdom.

Answer 4.—It does not follow that therefore we must fling ourselves into the arms of one whom we have reason to suppose will prove a traitor. But this argument does not weigh with the many who excused Ormonde for having given up Dublin to the Parliament on the plea that the Catholics themselves had driven him to desperation. The most judicious therefore will think it a greater advantage to have the Parliament a declared enemy in these districts than a man of an astute nature like the Baron, who has hitherto never done anything but deceive the country.

Fifth. Finally they conclude that the conditions made with Inchiquin being favourable to religion, so much the more will the negotiation be carried on easily and with satisfaction to the Pope.

Answer 5.—As to the stipulations for religion in this truce, it appears there is only one for its secret exercise, which exists even now in the enemy's districts. But of this more will be said in the paper which touches on the satisfaction of the clergy. It may well be said that if we had cared to make a truce with advantage to religion, it must be treated for with an army in good order; if not greater at least equal to that of Inchiquin, whereby the negotiation would be carried on with decorum, and as is the custom amongst all the Princes of the world; and not ignominiously as will be the case now. And because it is notorious that O'Neill could have marched with such an army to create terror and perhaps defeat the enemy, and since the Council did not choose to send him and that many in the province declared they would resist him if he should go; I cannot see how His Holiness can like to hear of such a state of affairs as that many are more ready to give way to an intense hatred of their countrymen and brothers, and to caress, so to speak, a heretic, rather than use the forces of the country to extend religion and overthrow heresy. Perhaps the agents who are now in Rome, may be better able to express the wishes of His Holiness.

&c., &c.

Abstract of the Reasons brought forward by the Clergy against the Truce in respect of Religion.

First. They lay great stress on the constant disloyalty of this man towards our religion. Cork and Youghal after having a promise from him for the exercise of religion; were at the end of a year deprived in one day of all their Catholic inhabitants, who were driven out by the Baron in spite of that promise, and for no other cause than this very stipulated exercise. Last March he assured those who were in Carrick that they should not be molested by his soldiers, yet in face of this guarantee he plundered all the inhabitants under the plea that he could not restrain the soldiery. In the cathedral of Cloyne a few days ago, the Canons were dismissed and heretic ministers put in their place, it is believed in order that the truce should find Protestants in possession. With the authority then and adherence of the Catholics, what can be expected from this man? Inasmuch as it is known that the clergy feared to put the Marquis of Ormonde in authority on account of the danger to religion, the same feeling should much more militate against the Baron.

Second. The Queen and Prince have never offered favourable conditions for religion, except when the clergy were in high authority and the Catholics united. Therefore in this peace or accommodation which they hope for from Her Majesty, the more weak the Catholics appear in comparison with Inchiquin, and the more the clergy is depressed, the more unfavourable will be the conditions for religion.

Third. As Inchiquin has mentioned in several letters the necessity of humbling the Nuncio, O'Neill, and his adherents, this is a manifest sign of the peril threatening religion, because the Nuncio and the clergy have no other aim than it; and the Ulster army declaring that they will stand by them, consequently it has also the same object. What might not then be expected if to a man so disposed were given forces, adherents, and authority to act? But what does away entirely with the argument which is advanced *ex adverso*, viz., that as the Baron has declared for the King he deserves to be received with open arms, is that as he has declared against religion, he ought to be rejected in accordance with the form of oath of the Confederates, which places religion above the King, and this they have shown since the beginning of the war.

To CARDINAL PANZIROLO.

Maryborough, May 11th, 1648.

Divine Providence which constantly rules the thoughts of His Holiness, has sent here a plenary indulgence in compassion to the great need which this unhappy kingdom has felt for many centuries past. I shall have it published by means of the Bishops, and it shall be received with the greatest unction and devotion which is possible. Perhaps the prayers of the people will make weak the strength of the devil, who has now let loose all hell to restore heresy by little and little. Since by the secret judgment of God this scandal has been allowed to prevail, it will be among the glories of His Holiness to have at least provided in every manner possible that it shall not continue. Nevertheless I trust that God will be reconciled by the prayers of the good, and that the blessed spirit of the Holy Father will not have less satisfaction than merit from this liberal indulgence

To the Same (in Cipher).

Maryborough, May 11th, 1648.

We are at present on the eve of the greatest trials, since we are about to see whether the Catholic religion will be firmly established in this kingdom or not. After receiving the protest of the clergy against the Munster peace the Supreme Council seemed anxious to come to some conclusion that would satisfy all parties; and we were most ardently desiring some result of these deliberations when I learnt that in spite of what had taken place on Monday they had sent deputies to Inchiquin, with the powers and signatures necessary for concluding the treaty. This trick determined me to withdraw secretly the next day to Connaught, leaving a letter for the Supreme Council to explain my reasons for so doing, protesting against the truce and adding that I could now only pray to God since religious affairs had turned out so differently from what I had expected.

I write from a city in possession of O'Neill, where I have stopped one night to find out what course he intended to take, and I find him resolved upon defending the honour of the clergy and providing for my safety unless an honorable reconciliation can be brought about. I therefore must apply the money in my possession to his wants, and entreat God to favour his designs, as the Council are summoning the malcontents and Ormonde factions from all quarters to unite with Inchiquin against the Ulster army and the clergy. This great experiment was unavoidable, but if we once succeed we may expect great progress for the Faith; if we fail, the hand of God and the prayers of His Holiness can alone support it.

To the Same (in Cipher).

Athlone, June 13th, 1648.

The Council bent on mischief have finally concluded the truce with Inchiquin upon much worse conditions than when the clergy protested against it; and at the same time Preston, at the head of 3,000 infantry, proposed to join Inchiquin and Taaffe to the detriment of O'Neill. Upon this I have published the strictest form of excommunication against him, and by the first opportunity to Rome I shall send all the necessary documents relating to the subject, and especially my reasons for coming to this determination rather than allow affairs to take their course. Hell is working with all its powers—some Bishops and many monks have declared against me chiefly amongst the Jesuits who insist that the censure as resting on temporal affairs is null and void, and that it can be suspended by an appeal made by the Council; although this power of suspension is not admitted by me; some even go so far as to say that by the English law I have no authority to exercise jurisdiction. How the Council have endeavoured to rob me of my linen, money, papers, and even my authority demands a separate letter which I shall write soon; but I hardly know whither to go. The Dean is at Kilkenny and cannot come to me, since he is even forbidden to leave the city, so that I suffer nearly as much as an ecclesiastic can do. O'Neill has a good army and is resolved to defend the Church, and if God favour his arms, it is possible that the present occasion may serve at the same time to establish the true Faith, the Roman jurisdiction: and to confound the evil intentions of our opponents who, as your Eminence will see by the articles of the truce, would have given up the kingdom to the Presbyterian Parliament under pretext of showing their fidelity to the King; but I hope it may please God to confound them.

Statement of the Reasons which induced the Nuncio to pass Sentence of Excommunication.

June 15th, 1648.

1st. The iniquitous nature of the articles of the truce which, as stated in a separate paper, was concluded most unnecessarily with a perfidious heretic, to the great and manifest peril of the Catholic religion; and this sin openly committed, the excommunication must necessarily follow, since no other remedy was apparent which could sufficiently mark an evil of such magnitude.

2nd. The censures passed by the clergy on the Ormonde peace having been approved, it was supposed that measures taken to defeat a truce which tended to the same end, would also be approved, because from the following notes it appears most clearly that this truce is a consequence of that peace. I received the first intimation of this last year from Bordeaux in a letter from Father O'Hartigan who, as I wrote on June 10, 1647, said he had heard it from Paris. Colonel Fitzmaurice on his return from France four months ago plainly told me that Ormonde and Inchiquin had pretended to be for the King, and under this pretext would have united with the Catholics, and that Ormonde previous to his return had invited Colonel Barry to negotiate the treaty, as indeed happened—the truce having been concluded under his auspices, as it is known that he went to and fro between the Catholics and Inchiquin. The Nuncio of France writes that Ormonde was leaving no stone unturned to return here as Viceroy. Finally, the Council knowing that the clergy were suspicious of this, drew up for their satisfaction a declaration to the effect that they would not receive the peace unless the Assembly insisted on it; which last they evidently intend shall happen, since it being in their power to summon the Assembly at will, and they have nominated all the members from amongst their partisans in the Provinces, it follows that they have the power to conclude the peace on their own terms. A perusal of the articles in addition to many small indications proves this to be their prime object, as I have so often said.

3rd. On account of the resolution made by the Ormonde faction to humble the clergy, the Ulster army, and perhaps even the Nuncio himself. Of this we had full proof when after their last Assembly the factionists vowed to put the whole Ulster army to the sword in one day, as soon as they were established in their quarters; for which purpose the Council assigned them some so far apart that in the event of an attack they would have been entirely unable to assist each other. A letter of Inchiquin's was intercepted which I forward to your Eminence, in which he said openly that as the kingdom united in desiring a peace, it would be necessary to humble the Nuncio his adherents, and O'Neill also, as they alone opposed it. Finally, it is evident from an article inscribed in the truce, by which all parties are bound to put down those who oppose it, which article was signed fifteen days after the Bishops had made and published a condemnation of it,—that all the Bishops were included in it, and the Nuncio would have been constrained to see them persecuted, oppressed, and perhaps exiled before his very eyes, without being able to stretch out his hand in their aid.

4th. The same may be said of O'Neill and of his army, who having always favoured the Church, could not have been abandoned to the swords of his enemies, who as a proof of their malignant intentions framed an accusation of rebellion against him which, if it had not been crushed at once by the excommunication, would have caused the destruction of an innocent man, without any regard to the benefits he has conferred on the Church.

5th. The probability that on fulminating the excommunication many would declare for the Church; such has indeed been the case, since more than 1,000 infantry and 200 horse have already joined the Catholic army from the hostile ranks, and 500 more only wait an opportunity of following their example; besides which, the levies from Munster and Connaught to the number of 5,000, are about to be embodied; all this, notwithstanding that till now the Church has made no efforts in her own behalf, and that our party has been persecuted and despised by the Council.

6th. Through compassion for some of the noblest families in Munster, such as the O'Sullivans and Macarthys, who have always been found on the side of the Church, and whose estates are now by the articles of the peace assigned as quarters to Inchiquin's troops; and these gentlemen have more than once prayed that I would not abandon them.

7th. Since one of the articles plainly shows that the kingdom was to be filled with heretics and that they were to bear rule everywhere, so that things would be in a worse state than before. Inasmuch moreover as rewards are freely promised to all who declare for the King and the Parliament as Inchiquin has done, it is certain that Jones, Monk, and probably the Ulster Scotch in order to gain this advantage would immediately have declared themselves for the King and Parliament, then all the provinces would have been in the power of the heretics; and the Catholic religion would never have been able again to raise its head. Hence, whatever may happen, I thought it better to leave the remembrance in the kingdom of having done all in my power to avert so great a misfortune, rather than stand aloof beholding all these miseries and then be obliged to leave the country in disgrace.

8th. Besides, amongst other attempts against my authority,

my enemies declare my inability as a foreign power to excommunicate in this kingdom, by virtue of I know not what, English laws; consequently had I spared the censure, the people ran the risk of being confirmed in this belief and the English laws which the Holy See has always opposed would have taken root by my tacit consent. For these reasons I was induced to come to this important resolution, trusting to God to accept my endeavours and to His Holiness to approve their results.

REPORT OF THE WRONGS OFFERED TO THE AUTHORITY AND PERSON OF THE NUNCIO BY THE COUNCIL.

June 16th, 1648.

The Nuncio, at the request of the Council, gave orders that the 4,800 crowns which he expected from Italy for his personal expenses, should be paid at Florence to the Roman agents, and at Paris to the Marquis of Antrim; and although the Council bound themselves to its repayment, so many delays and excuses have been made since his declaration against the truce, that it is evident they will never be refunded.

During the march against Dublin, the Nuncio at the instance of the Council and Congregation who were then at the head of the Government, bound himself for some sums of money borrowed from different cities which refused to furnish it on the security of the Council alone. Among these was a sum of 2,500 crowns to the city of Kilkenny and 1,000 to Waterford, and the Council desired that application should be made to the Nuncio for these two sums although the cities had already given orders to distribute these debts among their revenues, as will be explained at Rome by the Bishop of Ferns and Nicholas Plunket, who were the first to induce the Nuncio to pledge himself, and who, to the day of their departure, assured him that he should suffer no inconvenience of any kind from so doing. His Holiness will therefore doubtless speak to the agents on the subject.

The province of Munster was incited to demand from the Nuncio 12,000 crowns furnished to the Ulster army when it marched against Dublin at the command of the Council and Congregation; which command the Nuncio as head of the said Congregation subscribed. This is told not because any one member could be held responsible, a thing never heard of, but that the spirit which animates the Council may be seen by these unjust and preposterous attempts. Again, when the Spanish agent most unreasonably laid claim to what was left in France, the Council at first refused his demands, but after the rejection of the peace by the Nuncio, fomented the quarrel to such a degree that the frigates were seized, the sailors put to flight, much expense incurred, and the matter still stands in the same danger, notwithstanding the protests and the threats of the Dean, who insists that the vessels are the property of His Holiness.

It is believed that they intimidated a Limerick merchant who came to offer an excellent price for the frigate St. Ursula, in order that this money might not come into the hands of the Nuncio.

They have published an edict declaring that the Nuncio was seconded by but few of the Bishops, either in his first declaration against the truce or in the fulmination of his censure, and that they prohibit all subject to their jurisdiction from obeying him or his excommunication.

They likewise drew up and published a form of oath, forcing everyone to swear to observe the truce in spite of all excommunication past, present, or to come, and menacing with condign punishment all the monks who dared to obey the interdict. All this of course is done under the pretext of serving the King and the kingdom; whether or not it is the case may be gathered from my letters, and the unfortunate King will know it but too soon.

To Cardinal Panzirolo (in Cipher).

Athlone, June 16th, 1648.

As soon as I discovered the object of the Ormonde faction in proposing the truce, and the dangers by which religion was surrounded, I was deeply perplexed whether to quit the kingdom or oppose their efforts to the utmost of my power; since to remain inactive in the country would have been disgraceful. I would willingly have pursued the first plan, but that the thought of leaving the good Bishops and other ecclesiastics a prey to the wolves, deterred me from it. At last, for the reasons mentioned in a separate letter, I determined on following the second, and proceeded to excommunicate and interdict, excluding the power of appeal, according to the enclosed form. I shall be excused if informalities are discovered, as I was obliged to write the whole on my journey without books, without doctors, and with but few Bishops near me, these had however been armed with authority sufficient for the purpose by the others who had rejected the peace. I confess that the results of the interdict have as yet been various in consequence of the threats and horrible activity of the Council. Up to this time Wexford, Dungannon and Galway have not acknowledged the peace while some other towns have been forced to do so. The Jesuits have been the authors of the assertion which they have defended with the utmost arrogance—that the excommunication cannot take effect; and have induced the Bishop of Kilkenny not to promulgate the interdict. Some of the Bishops who signed it have been intimidated; some have declared for the enemy, the Regulars generally obey, but most go with the faction which supports them. The Dean is two days' journey from me; the Council sent him an order through their secretary to depart from Kilkenny but he refused to do so; alleging his disbelief of the order until it should be given in writing. O'Neill has so greatly increased his army that he may yet do great things, and remedy all the evils that have befallen us if the Lord God favours him, and in this case, the kingdom will be so entirely re-established that the Holy See will have to do nothing but assist this party to secure the establishment of the Catholic religion; but if he should be overwhelmed or retires and the factionists keep their ground, there will be no redress. Certain it is that the disturbers of the public peace do not amount to ten, and therefore their extinction may be hoped for. If the Council send long reports of their proceedings to Rome, I entreat of your Eminence to keep an ear open for me that I may be able to reply. Meanwhile I send this short account of late occurrences with some important documents, not knowing however whether they will be suffered to reach you, as every effort is made to obstruct me. I am now in the centre of the island, and unable to find a resting place, surrounded as I am by hostile armies. How my baggage and money have been seized so as to prevent my assisting O'Neill, your Eminence will learn from one of the accompanying ciphers, but I am prepared for everything, and do not forget the duty I owe to the office I sustain.

To the Nuncio of France.

Galway, July 2nd, 1648.

I have received your Eminence's letter of the 22nd May with those which accompanied it from the Palace, but not those which you inform me were sent before from La Rochelle. The proposal to restore the Marquis of Ormonde to his office in this country has occasioned the disturbances of which I wrote to Cardinal Mazarin and to your Eminence, as the Catholics are now at open war amongst themselves. The Marquis's plot is to return to the rejected peace, invest the Presbyterians with the Government, and work out the ruin of the clergy and the Ulster army. This is sufficiently proved by the conclusion of the truce two months ago with Baron Inchiquin, inasmuch as the articles all tend to this end, as your Excellency will gather from the considerations enclosed, and from their rejection in my presence by fourteen Bishops. This plot is no less proved by the disgraceful haste with which the Council concurred in the truce, because it is evident that all the conditions were drawn up with a view to the aggrandizement of an enemy, who ten days before had sallied from his quarters in order to obtain food for his troops; advanced to the very gates of Kilkenny, insulted the Council themselves, and what is worse, might have been easily repulsed, if through hatred of the Ulster troops and the determination not to suffer them in Munster, they had not preferred the friendship of a heretic to a union with their Catholic brethren, who by at least appearing in arms might have gained honourable conditions instead of those so disgraceful now agreed upon. But the plot to restore the former state of affairs was well laid, and upon the declaration of the Bishops against the truce, the Council, in spite of promises to the contrary, concluded their iniquitous stipulations, placed Preston at the head of a hastily raised army, and sent him against General Owen O'Neill, the supporter of the clergy. I was in despair, believing that I must either fly the kingdom or witness the overthrow of the Catholic army, the desolation of the Church, and the triumph of the last year's rejected peace. No remedy was to be found for these evils, and at last I took courage to publish an interdict against all who should acknowledge or favour the truce, or unite with the heretics against those who opposed it. The sentence of excommunication was acknowledged by all the well-affected and neutral, although the interested testified the greatest contempt, as might be expected in a kingdom where heresy is deeply rooted. The Government, besides appealing against it, has made sacrilegious demonstrations against it, has gained over by violence and intimidation a few monks and Bishops, who, either through fear or pride endeavour to lessen my authority, to give force to the appeal, and to throw discredit, if possible, on the validity of my sentence. But still all this coupled as it was with insults offered to my person, and the seizure of my baggage together with the Papal supplies, have only tended to the saving of religion, and re-establishing the exercise of its rites, which has already taken place; the arms of the clergy, in spite of the efforts of hell, being more powerful than ever. I wished to explain the whole matter to your Excellency, as I am aware that this exercise of my power will be discussed in France, and to enable you to assure the well-affected that such a measure was the only one capable of securing the salvation of the kingdom. If God crown my efforts with success the results will last for ever, but if the hidden justice of His Providence permit the reverse, I shall be consoled by the remembrance of having done all that I could. Nevertheless, it will be a subject of wonder to posterity, why when the whole Confederation could have been secured to the King by the appointment of a Catholic Viceroy, the Queen should have persisted in an opposite course, by which the King will obtain nothing but a country weakened by intestine quarrels, and divided into so many factions that it will be impossible to know whom to trust.

I am, &c., &c.

To Cardinal Panzirolo (in Cipher).

Galway, July 4, 1648.

The Bishop of Meath has just died at the age of 80 years, to the great blessing of the country since he held opinions so deeply heretical as to oblige me to threaten him with a citation to Rome in spite of his advanced age. The translation of the Bishop of Ardagh, brother to Plunket, now at Rome, will I fear be urged upon His Holiness, but as he has not conducted himself well in the late events, I beg of your Eminence to refuse the nomination, since it is necessary at present to promote none but men on whom we can rely. The O'Farrells, one of whom was proposed for the Church of

Ardagh, are in high repute amongst the Catholics in consequence of Lieutenant O'Farrell who commands in this province having declared for the clergy; I propose two Regulars of worth and firmness; Brother Francis Farrell one of the Chief Councillors of the Franciscan order and Brother Gregory Farrell, Provincial of the Dominicans; to whom I incline more than to the first. The diocese in question is the largest in the kingdom, so that the choice of its spiritual guardian should be well considered.

TO THE SAME.

Galway, July 4, 1648.

From the duplicate of your Eminence's letter in recommendation of Felice Cecchi to the Penitentiary of Fermo, I find how many letters have miscarried, as even the news of the vacancy had not reached me. Your Eminence who is absolute master of all the offices in my gift, can dispose of that canonry with full authority. I therefore resign it totally and with the greatest sense of obligation to your disposition, hoping that Sig. Cecchi will do honour to your choice by devoting himself to this See with the ardour to be expected from his excellent qualities. I do not recollect if the prebendary has a pension attached to it, if it has, I submit also to the benignant consideration of your Eminence whether you would be disposed to bestow it on some one of my followers who so earnestly labour for the public cause in this country.

I am, &c.

TO THE SAME (IN CIPHER).

Galway, July 4, 1648.

The news from France of the secret plot to restore Ormonde and his peace, prove the truth of what I said respecting the truce, the articles of which I send to your Eminence together with some reflections thereupon. My determination to resort to the interdict may appear a bold one, and I know that the Council will represent it at Rome as unjust; but before God and His Holiness I can prove it to have been absolutely necessary, as the last and only means of averting the downfall of religion inasmuch as it has caused the increase of the Ulster army instead of its destruction, induced many to declare for our party and secured a continuance of the present state of affairs. The future must be uncertain, but at any rate I shall leave the country with the consciousness of having done all in my power to save the kingdom from the heretics, into whose hands it will assuredly fall if the Catholics are overwhelmed.

The Jesuits, as usual devoted to their own interests, have declared against us and induced several Bishops and monks to do the same; and the devil, seeing that nearly all united in rejecting the truce, has now sown discord in every direction. The Council are doing their worst against me, and I fully expect a blind and most unjust decision on their part in favour of the Spanish agent with regard to the seizure he has made in spite of a very plain and severe letter which I wrote to him, informing him that in these times such questions should not be agitated but be left to the arbitration of His Holiness and his Majesty, and that I would not recognise the decision of the Council.

I have only received the letter dated the 1st May, together with the cipher to which I have no answer to send, since everything depends on the present disturbances, the results of which will decide the events of the next few years. I pity the agents at Rome when they shall hear of these proceedings, although they had some intimation of them before they left.

I write by a vessel which unexpectedly sets sail to-night, and must therefore close my letter at once. The Dean of Fermo is at Kilkenny, and I think he has written by Waterford; he has been unable hitherto to undertake the journey to join me with safety.

To the Same (in Cipher).

Galway, July 11, 1648.

I understand that the Council will propose for the See of Meath, the Bishops of Dromore and of Ardagh. The latter, I have already informed you, is utterly unworthy of it.

The former also should be rather deposed from his present church than promoted to another, having been the principal supporter of Preston against O'Neill, and the most open contemner of my authority. I shall shortly propose candidates for all the vacant churches, since it is now of more importance than ever to choose men on whom we can depend to maintain our religion in splendour.

I also hear that the Council have sent an ecclesiastic to Rome; I entreat your Eminence to wait for a month, when I will send another to set the matter before you in its true light and prevent the faction from gaining the victory by clamour.

I am trying to summon a national Synod to unite the clergy in one mind, but I fear that the malignity of this evil-minded Council will raise innumerable obstacles; but more than we ever hoped for have declared for O'Neill, whose army daily increases. If God favour him, the time may have come for a general change and for securing the safety of religion. This I send in addition to the despatch of the 4th of this month.

To the Same (in Cipher).

Galway, August 3rd, 1648.

The three Commissioners have already returned from Paris without awaiting any communication from Rome, or even hearing of the arrival of ours, which is just what I expected. They quitted Paris it is said, at the command of the Queen, and report that Ormonde will be here immediately. They have published a report of the Queen's answer to them in May, which I herewith enclose, that your Eminence may be convinced of Her Majesty's ardent desire to revive the peace, and that they by publishing her replies are paving the way for its re-establishment. It is also evident that Her Majesty wishes to decide upon the religious question without any reference to His Holiness, and lastly, that the Marquis will himself come over to negotiate. I hear that the Council instantly appointed an Assembly for the 4th September, at which it is believed the Marquis will be recognised as Viceroy, and this peace promulgated. As I had named a previous day for the meeting of the national Synod, they are endeavouring by means of threats, and most insulting letters to me, to the Bishops, and to this city, to prevent the Synod by all means in their power, lest they should come to some resolution expressive of disapprobation of their design; or confirmation of what has been done hitherto. The devil is doing his utmost, and the alienation of the Bishops and the Jesuits is producing a great effect upon the people. If God in His hidden wisdom does not strengthen O'Neill and enable him to root out his enemies, we are irremediably lost, and the satisfaction only will remain to me of having done all that I could to avert these misfortunes. I am in the greatest distress, having neither the Dean nor any other secretary to assist me in writing, as they are far distant and are unable to come to me. I expect that amongst other insults and injuries the Council will condemn me with respect to the effects now in France; since the Spanish agent thinks it an excellent time to appropriate a considerable sum, now that the Council have declared against me. And although I wrote to the said agent telling him that I should not submit to this tribunal, that everything which is there belongs to His Holiness, that I should lodge a complaint with His Majesty and request His Holiness to do the same; and that finally I recommended him to defer the matter to another time, or allow that His Holiness with the Ambassador and through the Nuncio should settle it now, I have received only impertinent answers. Hell I see is armed against the servants, the property and the favours of the Holy See. O'Neill has a large army divided between two different places, and his enemies are doing their utmost against both.

I deem it a great misfortune that the castle of Athlone was sold by its traitorous commandant to the Marquis of Clanricarde. Many on the contrary rejoice at it, believing that O'Neill, deprived of this place of refuge will be obliged to march forward, but events are most uncertain, and we must only place our trust in God. What course I shall pursue, it is impossible to inform your Eminence since all must depend on future events. The last despatch from Rome was detained three weeks at Limerick, and I have since heard that there were two packets, that one of them was forwarded to the Council, but which I have never seen, so your Eminence may judge how I am situated. The Bishop of Meath did not die but has remained on earth to be a trial to all good men.

To THE SAME (IN CIPHER).

August 12, 1648.

I must add to the above that O'Neill, having taken all the principal intermediate towns, advanced to the walls of Kilkenny, and sent a trumpeter to inform the Mayor that if he would detain the Council the city should be uninjured, but if he suffered them to escape, it should be sacked. If this be true, religion is saved, nay, I believe even the kingdom itself, and I am in hopes it is true, because a week ago Preston was completely defeated by Maguire, himself wounded, and his cavalry dispersed. I have received no letters, as the Dean of Fermo is a prisoner in a house in Kilkenny. In this province Clanricarde is acting the bravo, preventing the clergy from coming to the Synod; and in a manifesto threatens to imprison me and thrust me out of the kingdom. May God protect me as He has ever done!

To the Same (in Cipher).

Galway, August 21.

Since I wrote on the 12th of this month O'Neill has made himself master of all the country round Kilkenny, dispersing the remains of Preston's army, and apparently marching with perfect impunity. Inchiquin is preparing to send troops against him, but seems inclined to remain himself in Cork. I am regularly besieged here, Clanricarde's troops occupying all the adjacent country, and my letters are sent to, and forwarded from Kilkenny with the utmost difficulty, the Dean being a prisoner there, and I have had no letters from Rome. Religion, however, is daily gaining ground, and since one well directed blow may save all, my hopes are rising. I do not know whether the Assembly will meet while O'Neill's army continues so near Kilkenny, however I am endeavouring to prevent the Bishops going thither, that it may not be said that they have ever consented to anything until the Commissioners return from Rome, when we shall be informed of His Holiness's will and pleasure; meanwhile we fail not to implore the mercy of God by prayers and supplications.

Report of the Truce concluded by the Council of Ireland with Lord Inchiquin.

Since the rejection of the Ormonde peace by the Congregation of Waterford, supported by the Ulster army, the Marquis, and his adherents have plotted to but one end, the revival of the said peace, his own re-establishment in the Viceroyalty, and the oppression of the clergy and the Ulster army, by which means he would secure himself for ever against further opposition. This vengeance, as it might be termed, is founded upon a general and ancient aversion conceived for the Ulster men and the clergy by all the Irish who had at any time received grants of church property from the King; since they feared that the clergy, once re-established in their former power, might resume this property, and that the Ulster men never having desired similar favours, would assist them to deprive all the other provinces of what they themselves did not enjoy.

It would be impossible in a small space to explain all that the Ormonde faction have done to attain their object. Many reports of their proceedings have been received from France, all proving that in Munster the way is opened for the return of Ormonde by means of General Taaffe; and if it is found impossible to destroy the Ulster men directly, they are to be sent back to their own province under various pretexts, and there attacked at all points. For this purpose in the last Assembly they nominated a Council of twelve of their own partisans, and even when the clergy, with great forbearance allowed the larger part of these to stand on the last day of session, they were by no means satisfied, but most artfully chose forty-eight supernumeraries to be elected to fill up the vacancies, foreseeing, as it were, what would happen; and although the Bishops resigned, nevertheless, in the confusion which ever attends the breaking up of these meetings, the vote was passed and all the vacancies were filled with the most fiery factionists. When the persons were chosen they proceeded to deeds. Baron Inchiquin, well aware of the whole state of affairs, sallied out in February from his quarters, ravaged the counties of Waterford and Kilkenny, advanced to the walls of the latter city and then returned back. The Council to all appearance were not alarmed, but it is believed the whole thing was concerted, so that the Commissioners then about to depart for Rome and France, might speak as eyewitnesses of the miseries of the kingdom, and thereby induce His Holiness and the Queen to propose a peace as little advantageous as possible to religion, similar consequently to that of Ormonde. Scarcely had Inchiquin returned to Cork than the truce was negotiated by means of Colonel Barry who had been sent to Ireland by Ormonde. The Nuncio, not aware of the machinations of the Council, wrote to them to say that the truce did not strike him as necessary, but on the contrary, would be perilous to religion, and little likely to satisfy His Holiness; he also demanded why when it had been arranged two or three days previous to send 3,000 Ulster men against Inchiquin, the intention was not carried out, and what they could expect for religion from a heretic who had always persecuted the faith most sacrilegiously? At all events he insisted that during the negotiations an army should be kept on the ground after the manner of all independent powers, and finally that the opinion of His Holiness as delivered to the Bishop of Ferns and Nicholas Plunket ought to be waited for.

The Council frequently entreated the presence of the Nuncio at Kilkenny, and by letter announced their determination to conclude nothing without his consent; but it soon appeared that their course had long been decided on, and for this they excused themselves by saying that as it was utterly impossible for the Confederation to carry on two wars, one in Munster, and one with Dublin, it was necessary to make a truce with one of their enemies, and that Inchiquin having declared for the King and a free Parliament, was the most to be relied on; this, be it observed, had been agreed upon between them and the Ormonde Catholics in order to facilitate the attainment of their designs. As God suffers no treachery to remain long concealed, a letter was intercepted from Inchiquin to Ambrose Plunket in the county Kerry, exhorting him to place a garrison in a castle belonging to him for this reason, that as the whole kingdom was well disposed to a peace except O'Neill, the Nuncio, and their adherents, they must be completely humbled before any further step could be taken. The sentiment of this letter was corroborated by one of the articles of the truce, which bound all parties to unite against those who should object to their proceedings, and the truth of the suspicion became evident when the Council endeavoured to pass the letter off as a forgery; although when it was reported by the deputies that Inchiquin did not deny it, they laughed contemptuously, and asked what else could be expected from a heretic.

Sixteen Bishops were at that time in Kilkenny, fourteen of whom having assembled, examined the articles of the truce in presence of the Nuncio, and recognising their iniquity and the danger to religion decided that they could not conscientiously countenance the truce; and sent up to the Council a protest against it, signed by the whole number.

This was the first rock on which the designs struck that had so long been cherished. The whole faction rose, and proceeded to such extremities that some declared it would be allowable to kill the Nuncio as they were advised by some Carmelite monks.

The Council however to avoid direct opposition to the Church, proposed various modes of reconciliation, and there were daily meetings of members of both parties. The hopes thus raised were nevertheless soon destroyed, for the Nuncio was assured by the Bishop of Limerick that in spite of the fair speeches of the Council, Commissioners had been sent to Inchiquin to conclude the truce; whereupon the Nuncio perceiving that he had been deceived, determined to remain no longer in Kilkenny and departed on the following day, stopping two days at Maryborough, then the head-quarters of General O'Neill.

During those two days, three Commissioners arrived from the Council to the Nuncio and O'Neill, bearing messages expressive of the anxiety of that body to be on good terms with them. The Bishops then present and O'Neill drew up some propositions which the Nuncio as mediator forwarded to the Council. For ten days a reply was expected, which, when it arrived besides being most unsatisfactory, contained the news of two events which finally caused the rupture.

First, that Inchiquin having insisted on the satisfaction of all his claims, the truce had been concluded on conditions much more unfavourable than those at first agreed upon. Second, that Preston having hastily armed 3,000 infantry and 400 horse, went immediately after these answers to Roscrea on the confines of Munster, with the design of attacking O'Neill, thus proving the truth of what had long been suspected. The fact that a rumour had been previously circulated that the Council had declared O'Neill to be a rebel, the march of his rival against him, and the risk incurred of shedding Catholic blood, for no other reason than because O'Neill defended the resolutions of the clergy, all clearly proved that the object of all the negotiation had been, not a truce with Inchiquin, but a conspiracy against O'Neill. The Nuncio, unwilling to witness these disgraceful proceedings without an effort to oppose them, at last determined to resort to excommunication of all who had signed the treaty and who should take up arms for, or unite with the heretics; at the same time assuring the Council that had not Preston taken up arms against the Catholics, he would never have proceeded to such extremities. The grounds of the censure will be found in a separate document, and as to the names of the Bishops who subscribed it, they are shown in the delegation and subdelegation of the fourteen abovementioned when the Congregation separated. The effects of this measure both good and evil have been very considerable. All the well affected took advantage of it either to defend themselves against the others, or to avoid all interference in the designs of the Council. The city of Wexford, the fort of Duncannon, the castle of Athlone, and the city of Galway never accepted the truce; others declared that their acceptance of it was forced through fear of Inchiquin's army, and before they knew of the fulmination of the censure; Preston's army mutinied, and 1,500 infantry and 400 horse joined O'Neill at once; while the desertions are still so frequent, that Preston's army is almost dispersed. Strong indications have been given that the same will occur in the Munster army assembled by Clanricarde in Connaught in favour of the truce. Five even of the Supreme Council abandoned the others, refusing to take any further part in their designs; no Bishop has remained in it. Their places however have been filled up from the forty-eight supernumeraries nominated for such a crisis, as I mentioned before. From all which it appears that the censure has in a measure arrested the movement which was about to throw the kingdom into the hands of Ormonde and Inchiquin, has saved the Ulster army from destruction, the clergy from oppression, maintained religion in its former glory, and that therefore we may say that God is on our side. As to the opposite party, it is very evident that the devil is the author of all their nefarious designs. The Council assailed the authority and property of the Nuncio, and even went so far as to attack his honour. Previous to the excommunication they had reported that the Papal delegates, as ministers of a foreign power had not the right of passing censures, and this by virtue of some English laws, as may be gathered from certain questions proposed by them to theologians and Bishops for the purpose of obtaining their signatures; while in order to prevent the commands of the Nuncio from taking effect, they seized the printing press at Kilkenny, pretending to have bought it from the Jesuits, so that the ecclesiastical party have been obliged to make copies of their proceedings in writing. Further, they published an edict forbidding all under their jurisdiction to pay obedience to the Nuncio or his censures, and finally drew up a sacrilegious oath binding them to accept the truce in spite of future excommunication, imprisoning all who refused to take it. With respect to his property they were not ashamed to resort to vengeance as unjust as dishonourable. They retained 4,800 crowns which at their request he had ordered to be paid at Paris and Florence to their agents. Some cities which had lent money to the Council and Congregation at the time of the campaign against Dublin, and which refused to accept any security but that of the Nuncio, were incited to apply to him for payment, although he was assured by all the Council, especially the two now at Rome, that no inconvenience should result to him in any way. The Council have also recommended the Spanish agent to lay claim to the property which he asserts was taken by the frigate *San Pietro*, and they intend to sequestrate and condemn the frigate. The object of all this is to reduce the Nuncio to such straits as to prevent him from assisting O'Neill in any way, thinking that the army is solely kept on foot by means of his aid.

I said that they had tried to sully his honour because by menaces, deception, nay even violence offered to the Bishops and imprisonment of the well affected monks and nobles, many were induced to declare in favour of the peace, to preach against the censure, to celebrate mass in spite of the interdict, and even to draw up manifestoes against the Apostolic authority. Of these disorders none have had worse effects than the inconstancy of the prelates, and divisions amongst them, some of them, though they had signed the first condemnation of the peace having changed their opinion, and seek by subtle reasonings and inventions to cover their disgraceful vacillation. The greatest evil has been wrought by the three Bishops of Connaught, viz. : of Tuam, Aghada, and Finbar, who under pretext of following a middle course, signed a document without consulting any of the other Bishops, assuring the Marquis of Clanricarde that in order to avert the war from the province it would be allowable to make war even against O'Neill if he tried to enter it. Immediately upon the receipt of this opinion the Marquis declared against the clergy, introduced heretic troops into Connaught, and instead of keeping the war at a distance brought it himself into the province, where it will probably rage for a considerable time.

In order to put an end if possible to this schism, the Nuncio had summoned a national Synod for 15th August, although he is not certain that the Council will not prevent it from meeting as it has shown many signs of an intention to do so, and appears to have great apprehension lest the Bishops should be united in their determination to approve all that has been done up to this time. In any case it would satisfy the people, the nobles, and many of the Bishops, who are all most anxious for it in the hope that a permanent reconciliation might result.

Meanwhile success seems to attend O'Neill's arms. He has now two armies; one marching towards Kilkenny under Colonel Maguire, who has been joined by the two counties of Wexford and Wicklow besides many of the principal nobility of Leinster; this army is estimated at 4,000 men. The other, composed of Ulster and Connaught troops, is said to number 6,000. Preston with merely a handful of troops has returned to Kilkenny to defend himself against Maguire; Clanricarde, with the Munster troops and Inchiquin's heretics had intended to attack O'Neill, but will probably not do so, as his men are considerably inferior in number, skill, and courage. If O'Neill could or would unite with Maguire no one could prevent him from pouring down upon Munster and overwhelming Inchiquin. If God favours our side, religion may be established in its former splendour, and peace be restored to the kingdom, at least as far as the factions of the Catholics are concerned.

The last letters from France prove how fortunate was the opposition to the truce in spite of the consequent outbreaks, for they not only confirm the reports of Ormonde's return, but tell us that his rancour against the clergy and Ulster army is by no means abated, and that he had plotted with Digby, the two Commissioners sent to Paris, and perhaps others more powerful, to unite the Puritans now in Ireland under Taaffe and Inchiquin to expel the Ulster men; to force the clergy to acknowledge him as Viceroy, and accept whatever peace he might choose to dictate. None but the most violent factionists could look upon such a prospect without horror. How blessed therefore are the efforts which have delayed an event with results so fatal as the desolation of the churches, the exile of the Bishops, and the return of those times when religious rites were performed in caves! not to speak of the ignominy that must have fallen upon the nation, if after carrying on a religious war for eight years it had plunged the kingdom into greater misery than at first. Aware of what would be the result of the truce, the Nuncio believed that there were only three courses which he might pursue:—1st. To depart the kingdom as a country in which he had no hope of doing good. 2nd. To withdraw after making a protest, and as a spectator await the commands of His Holiness. 3rd. To proceed to excommunication. Of these he must own that his inclination would have led him to adopt the first, as to leave the kingdom when he found his labours of no avail would have been to save himself infinite anxiety and peril, and he trusted moreover that the sanction of His Holiness would not have been withheld. But the tears and prayers of the prelates and all the well affected, who in the event of his departure would have lost their only protection against the rage of the multitude, restrained him. O'Neill likewise, who had served the Church so long, remonstrated against being left without supplies, to the mercy of his opponents, when the Dean of Fermo had so lately brought money from Rome. Lastly, reason suggested that for an Apostolic minister to abandon his duty in the hour of danger would be disgraceful, and give occasion for a belief that he despaired of Divine aid.

The Nuncio never could bring himself to determine on the second course, he had already been proscribed by Inchiquin and declared his enemy in his letters, and had this nobleman become master of Munster and Leinster, he would have insulted the Legate in his own house; and made him the laughing-stock of the Council and the sport of the heretics. And whither could he have retired that these two arrows would not have reached him? Ought he to stand aside to behold the extermination of O'Neill and the re-establishment of the heretical ministers in their churches and parishes; and to have submitted to be despised by all the magistrates who depended on Ormonde and Inchiquin, and to confer with a few priests in secret without any kind of authority?

There remained therefore only the third course—to try the effect of an interdict; which has already produced the most important results to religion and the kingdom, whence it may be hoped that His Holiness and all men of mature judgment will acknowledge the expediency, if not the necessity of the measure, in spite of all the prognostics to the contrary of the evil disposed, and the subtle opposition of the envious and the proud.

To Cardinal Panzirolo.

Galway, September 15th, 1648.

The Marquis of Clanricarde and the Commissaries of this Province continue to suppress all my letters, which prevents my answering any questions which your Eminence may have asked. Scarcely had the Marquis dismissed his troops after apparently triumphing over the city and forcing it to accept the truce, when he was obliged to set off for his own territory, where it was said Maguire with his army had seized all the strong places on the river which divides the province, terrifying everybody on his march and forcing even the Marquis's adherents to declare for O'Neill; the Marquis, we hear, is almost deserted, and has entreated assistance from the disbanded heretics and the Scotch in possession of Sligo.

There is a strong presumption that this man, triumphant only six days ago, will serve as a memorable example to all who oppose the Roman Church; and make use of religion to cloak their own designs. O'Neill is master of nearly all the important positions and fortresses of the three provinces, whence he can issue and return at will; since no army remains of sufficient strength to harass him save that of Inchiquin, who has still a considerable number of troops. My siege is at an end, but as the Dean is still a prisoner, and my other attendants at a distance; I am nearly helpless. Still I comfort myself with the remembrance that this movement is so great and noble, that if God continues to favour O'Neill the results will be more important to religion than even those of the war carried on by the Earl of Tyrone; and the glorious re-establishment of religion will be an event worthy of the fifth year of His Holiness' Pontificate. May it please God to support me in my sufferings and grant your Eminence never-failing prosperity.

To the Same.

Five times during my mission has General O'Neill saved religion from destruction. 1st. In the year '46 by the victory of Benburb in Ulster, when the Scotch at the instance of Ormonde were to advance upon Kilkenny, at which time the Confederates could only muster 2,000 strong.

2nd. In the same year, when he alone declared for the clergy and the rejection of the Ormonde peace; since without his aid, we must have succumbed to Preston and Ormonde and been forced to accept the peace.

3rd. In the year '47 when after Preston's defeat he was summoned by the Council to descend from Connaught into Leinster to restrain the victorious Puritans; which he did so successfully that while quartered himself in a secure post, he kept at bay for four months an enemy who never had the courage to issue forth and march against him.

4th. In the same year and at the same time when Inchiquin marched upon Kilkenny from one side and Jones from the other in the hope of surrounding the Council, O'Neill, on receiving a summons to the rescue, advanced so rapidly and with so large an army that Inchiquin was obliged to retire hastily and give up all thought of a union with Jones.

5th. In this last matter of the rejected truce, when he had at the beginning but 2,000 soldiers under his command and seven generals to oppose, he managed so skilfully as not only to save his Ulster army from the attacks of their opponents, but increased it by degrees to the number of 8,000, and made a descent upon Leinster. He then raised the army in Munster to 12,000 and more; made himself master of all the strong places, defeated all the generals except Inchiquin, and as far as we can judge at present, may force the enemies of the Church to relinquish their idea of restoring the Marquis of Ormonde or reviving his peace; one of the principal articles of which, stipulated for the expulsion of the Nuncio. The freedom and splendour of religion is consequently, under God, to be ascribed entirely to him.

To the Same (in Cipher).

The objects of the plot become every day more apparent; the Council have at last made Inchiquin General of the Province in lieu of Preston thereby allowing the supremacy of the Puritans. O'Neill has marched into Munster and news arrived yesterday that he had routed Inchiquin near Cashel, had made himself master of all the passes and the strongest castles of the Province, forcing every one to take the oath for religion according to the commands of the clergy, in conjunction with the forces of the Marquis of Antrim. His army numbers 12,000 in all, and is an object of terror to the evil disposed but of confidence to the well affected. I am as it were besieged in Galway by Clanricarde, who has detained three packets of letters which came for me from

Limerick, doubtless coming from Rome, imprisoning the bearer, and your Eminence may judge of my position.

For six weeks I have not known whether the Dean is alive or dead, as neither letters nor messengers can reach me. Two others of my assistants write me word that they have never been able to get hither from Waterford, where it was sought to imprison them, probably with a view to force them to reveal where the rest of the money is secreted; they have now taken refuge at Duncannon. The Marquis had the truce proclaimed here, but the inhabitants only permitted it to be done in secret. The Archbishop of Tuam and the Bishop of Aghadoe preach openly against my authority and the interdict, and are supported by two of the barefooted Carmelites, the only order which has declared against me and my congregation. I hear that their Provincial has been despatched by the Council to Rome, and therefore renew my prayers to your Eminence to delay giving judgment until I send some one well informed with my reply, and in the meantime to compassionate my sufferings. I am quite prepared to find myself expelled the kingdom if it pleases the Marquis, since I am every day more convinced that such was one of the articles of the conspiracy.

I have added the above to the despatch forwarded a few days ago by a vessel setting sail for Flanders, and thank God that now truly am I worthy the name of Apostolic Nuncio, being overwhelmed by all the persecutions attendant on labours to propagate the Faith, and increase the splendour of religion, which has been saved from destruction a second time with the assistance of the Ulster army, the champion of our cause.

To the Same (in Cipher).

October 3rd, 1648, Galway.

The Spanish agent, in pursuance of his claim to the property, and in spite of my protests (of which I send copies to your Eminence), has availed himself of the Dean's imprisonment and the hostility of the Council to me, to extort a sentence from them, condemnatory not only of the captain of the frigate but also of the Dean, who was not present; and lastly, I am held responsible to the amount of 5,000 crowns, although not there nor even cognizant of the event. What steps have been taken in this affair will be seen from the enclosed answer to my letter; the principal motive was undoubtedly avarice, excited by the Council, who are anxious to deprive me of every farthing I possess, that I may leave the country a beggar; the money advanced to the Marquis of Antrim and the other Commissaries never having been refunded: I could not meet the sentence otherwise than by a declaration that I had represented the whole matter to His Holiness and to His Majesty through the Nuncio, and that I wished the cause to be decided there, whither I shall send all the proofs, and if necessary some one to represent me. Meanwhile, all that I can do to turn the current of his violence shall be put in practice, since he intends evidently to lay hands on the frigate, and I am convinced will seize all my property and that of His Holiness without scruple of conscience or respect of persons. The transmission of commands from the Ambassador at Rome, if there is one, or if not from His Catholic Majesty himself to his agent to desist, and to restore all he may have seized, would greatly facilitate the execution of justice, so that such a proceeding on the part of a minister of so great a sovereign may not be made a precedent, and that such a condemnation, pronounced as it was by incompetent judges and without legal forms, may incur the odium it deserves, inasmuch as we are all ready to prove wherever His Holiness and His Majesty may command that the money is at Paris, and that the Parliament acknowledges the legitimacy of the capture, and the Nuncio of France can bear witness to the truth of all I have stated.

To the Same (in Cipher).

October 10th, 1648.

Several days ago the Marquis of Ormonde, with Secretary Digby and his other followers, landed at Cork. He has carefully kept to the time agreed upon with the Council, that is, during the session of the Assembly which was summoned for the purpose three months earlier than usual. This coming has been the aim and object of the factionists from the first, as I have frequently mentioned, and after it, will come the re-establishment of the peace, to the great misfortune of the clergy and of all who upheld them. I hear that the Marquis's patent only gives him the title of Justiciary of the Kingdom, so as to keep in the background the title of Viceroy for the present. However this may be the position of the Ulster army and its declaration in favour of the Church and against the peace will give him some trouble to attain his ends.

The assembly wants half its usual number; no true adherent of the Church party having attended it; some provinces have sent no representatives at all, and but seven Bishops have taken their seats, four of whom came from a distance, and three were already in Kilkenny; all seven are acting in defiance of public opinion. I not only disapproved their proceedings but forbade their attending, by virtue of the oath taken by the assembly, binding them to conclude nothing until the return of the commissioners from Rome, when the decision of His Holiness on the subject of religion would be known. As the worst members of the Assembly meet therefore with little opposition, it is supposed they will do nothing but mischief, but nevertheless that their resolutions will have no lasting effect.

O'Neill's army is large and powerful; it seems that he has determined to harass and destroy all who oppose him, and of the six Generals who were against him three are defeated and Preston severely handled. Inchiquin and Clanricarde still remain; against the latter it appears that O'Neill is now collecting all his forces in this province of Connaught. The Marquis of Antrim has declared for us, and is now in Wexford with 2,000 Scotch-Irish, good Catholics, and expects to be joined by others; the Council are making unheard of efforts to gain him over to their side. It appears to be a true blessing of God that up to this moment in these armies which fight for the Church, not one heretic is to be found, while those of the enemy are a mixed multitude and full of the most pestilent Puritans that exist. I am patiently awaiting future events, but the Dean is still a prisoner, and my attendants are at Duncannon, while I have been unable to recover the letters which were taken from me. I have no means of communication except by this port, whence by the first opportunity I will despatch my confessor to Rome who was present at all the events and assemblies in the late commotions. I hear that the Council have sent the provincial of the Carmelites to Rome, but I entreat your Eminence to await the arrival of my messenger, who will answer all the accusations brought forward by him. Perhaps my sufferings and labours in the cause may induce your Eminence to grant this delay, but I submit myself as always to you.

Since I wrote the above, I find that the Assembly have declared me a rebel against the Crown of England, and are determined to expel me the kingdom. I am quite ready to bear this, and esteem it a glory although they have taken from me all that I have.

To the Same (in Cipher).

Galway, October 31st, 1648.

My confessor is ready to embark for Rome in a vessel now lading at this port. I have no doubt however that we shall depart together, if I can procure a better vessel, or obtain possession of the frigate *San Pietro* now at Duncannon, so often menaced, nay seized by the Spanish agent. I expect a printed declaration against me, containing nineteen distinct charges, with a letter commanding me to prepare to go to Rome in order to defend myself against them. Amongst the charges are those preferred to His Holiness by Digby, so it is plain that the whole work has been planned and executed by him and the Marquis of Ormonde, and are published at the moment of their arrival. Your Eminence will hear from my confessor the difficulties into which I have been brought by the seizure of my property, and the close imprisonment of the Dean, who I cannot hope will be able to accompany me. For eight months I have seen none of my attendants, and am reduced to such a point, that however bad the vessel, the sea is almost safer for me than the land. If I obtain the vessel I propose to land in Flanders and await in some place, remote from court, the commands of your Eminence. The publication of the peace is hourly expected although O'Neill and Antrim oppose it more strongly than ever, and there is a chance of their uniting with the Independents, and steeping the kingdom in blood. Finally one of the two Parliaments must have the direction of affairs, now that the ill affected have attacked religion. I am deeply grateful to God for preserving me in health and courage, trusting that in heaven I shall receive the reward of my sufferings on earth.

I am, &c., &c.

To His Holiness Pope Innocent X.

Galway, November 7th, 1648.

Your Holiness, by the great actions and the great cares of your Pontificate, has made it the privilege of the Church of Rome more than ever was the case under the Empire, to do and to suffer greatly. Hence I, who, in the beginning of my career, had the good-fortune to convey to your magnanimity some of the triumphs of victory, must now with the same frankness report to your fortitude some of the glories of persecution. In my name Father D. G. Arcamoni, a Theatine, and my confessor, will lay at your Holiness' feet an account of all recent events in this kingdom, will narrate faithfully the machinations and doings of the factions united with the heretics, and on the other hand the designs, strength, and hopes of the well intentioned Catholics. As to myself, I know that all I suffer and have suffered, is from the sacredness of the cause and the dignity of the service, the highest honour to myself and to my family; but it will be a never-ending grief to me that your Holiness, whom God has commanded we should adore and serve even to the shedding of our blood, should be so greatly disturbed by these events. I pray to the Divine Majesty which has in its just judgment permitted many times great reverses of fortune against the holy faith may deign whilst your Holiness reigns to send them once for all against infidelity and heresy. And supplicating your favour and protection to the said father,

I kiss your most holy feet, &c., &c.

To Cardinal Panzirolo (in Cipher).

Galway, 9th November, 1648.

As my confessor, Father Giuseppe, is going to Rome, and is well informed of all events here, my report on this occasion may be brief; he leaves everything here in a doubtful state. The Assembly, their faction, and the Marquis, are endeavouring to arrive at this blessed peace, and promise every sort of satisfaction to the clergy. But they are greatly in fear of O'Neill and the Marquis of Antrim, and therefore make them large offers; but, on the other hand, the Parliamentarians offer still more to O'Neill and the Marquis, so that we shall see how they carry out their bargain. We may rest satisfied that all the mischief which may be averted is owing to the supplies of His Holiness enabling the Ulster army to be kept on foot; and if so small an amount has done such good service in such critical times, your Eminence may imagine the good a large sum would have effected. We may at least be thankful that these small grants were not in the hands of the Council, as they would have given them now to support the Marquis of Ormonde. I have not yet seen in print the charges against me, nor do I see that they are willing to release the Dean or restore my letters. I have resolved to leave the country, particularly if the *San Pietro*, a frigate now in Duncannon can be brought here, but as I have no advices, have received no answers to letters sent a month ago; I do not know what to think; but I do know that anxieties multiply day by day, and I recognise that it is all by the will of God.

To THE SAME.

Galway, 11th November, 1648.

You will hear at large from Father Giuseppe, how important it was in checking the progress of evil that His Holiness had nominated new Bishops for this kingdom; since between the violence and the dissensions of the evil-intentioned, the few faithful among the older Bishops could not come to me, and but for the five new ones who always follow me I should have been alone. It is my duty, therefore, to represent humbly that it would be well to provide for three more vacant churches, in order to increase the number of those who follow the Holy See; and to confound the powerful magistracy who with unheard of temerity in a public declaration have called those Bishops appointed by His Holiness without their sanction, " pretenders," and have placed it among the crimes of high treason imputed to me. I have, therefore, given in another sheet the names of those who are undoubtedly eligible, and of whom I have more than a moral certainty that they will be always faithful to the Holy See in matters of religion.

To the Same (in Cipher).

Galway, November 13th, 1648.

To-day my confessor, Father Giuseppe, has sailed in a vessel bound to St. Malo, and if the Lord God prosper the voyage and journey he will be with you the beginning of February. Two hours later arrived the frigate *San Pietro*, which had only been rescued from the Spanish agent with infinite trouble and expense; he has I hear made money by selling the cannon of the frigate *St. Ursula*; the horses and baggage of the Dean, with some of my property which he found here and there. Besides this, the frigate itself was adjudged to him, and he has seized upon more than a million of crowns, which were secreted in Waterford. This is not a single example of the audacity of this minister, and it appears to me that some notice should be taken of it, that he may not boast of having seized with impunity on the property of His Holiness and that of a delegated minister of the Holy See. It appears to me that it would be advisable for your Eminence, besides reporting the matter to Spain, to send a letter to the Archduke at Brussels ordering the Internuncio to present it, and to force this agent to give an account of all he has so unjustly taken, or at least be made to feel the mortification which is his due. If I reach Flanders, and still more if I can meet the Dean there, we can give some assistance, as I intend to assure the Archduke through the Internuncio that this was my sole object in coming, and that I have brought the frigate that His Highness may himself judge of the truth of the facts. I am still determined to leave this country, although two days ago O'Neill gave me to understand that I ought not to think of it, as the well affected will lose heart and the cause will be placed in great danger; but I think when I again give him my reasons for it he will be convinced, because even if as I hope he should be victorious negotiations for peace will be very tedious; and I cannot consistently with dignity remain while the other party hold the government at command; and though we exceed them in numbers our party will not combine as they did formerly, and therefore cannot make head against them successfully. Besides this, being despoiled of everything I possessed under various and unjust pretexts, I find it difficult to support myself. The two envoys sent to Rome might have assisted me in some manner, as they know that the 5,000 crowns claimed by the cities of Kilkenny and Waterford were not taken to repay His Holiness, and so of many other debts, but among the afflictions laid on me by the Lord God there is this in addition, that these envoys have not arrived nor do I know where they are. As to the peace, nothing certain is known, though I feel sure it was concluded some time ago. Some say things will remain as they are till the meeting of the first Parliament, which is arranged so as to include the same members as two years ago; and that under the rule of the Marquis of Ormonde the true Faith will by degrees be exterminated, and with arms in his hand and the command of affairs, he will soon adjust them to his own satisfaction. O'Neill has opened a passage into Connaught but at the cost of much bloodshed, and has great hopes of making himself master of the whole Province. We shall see, and I assist him with my prayers, as his aim is a glorious though a difficult one.

Instructions to Father Giuseppe Arcamoni.

If your Reverence succeeds, as I hope, in persuading the Court of Rome of the iniquity of the treaty, and the obligation I was under to oppose its being concluded, it will be easy with the help of God to demonstrate that I could neither leave the kingdom nor remain as a passive spectator of events, as would have been the case if I had not proceeded to pass the censure.

Had I remained, I must have made up my mind to see every day before my eyes Lord Inchiquin and the heretical ministers exercising jurisdiction, oppressing the Catholics, restoring churches to the Puritans as promised in the printed edict; and to the shame of the Apostolic See I must have borne it all without a word, or knowing how to remedy the evil, being of no authority whatever in the kingdom. And not even in this way should I have avoided being driven away, as Inchiquin had declared I should be, and a resolution to carry it out was not only introduced last year by Lord Digby and the other conspirators (as I was then warned), but at the end of March was determined on in Paris between the Queen and the two Commissioners, before the consideration of the treaty had commenced. This we know from trustworthy letters sent from France to Ireland.

There remains then only the alternative of my departure, and this might be used in favour of it, that while it would free me from many troubles it would in some degree repay this people in a coin they deserve for all their ingratitude.

It will be allowed, that in my position nothing could be more agreeable and advantageous to me than to leave the country; the more as His Holiness, while approving of my conduct throughout, had left the decision whether to go or stay entirely to myself. I hope the venerable fathers, knowing that I had not earlier taken a resolution so grateful to myself, will believe that the motives which have now decided me are dictated by honour and still more by conscience.

Although the kingdom is now governed by those alone who were the framers of the last peace, and were imprisoned for three months for their work, still our cause is not so wholly lost, but that three-fourths of the confederated Catholics are still openly on the side of the Church and its decrees. Although some of the Bishops, after the condemnation of the treaty, changed sides, either through envy or some other base motive, as your reverence will clearly explain, seventeen remained faithful to me, and so also are the Vicars Apostolic with one exception. There is not one dissentient among the Dominicans; of the Franciscans, though so numerous, there are only seven or eight opposed to me, and not more than four among the St. Augustines. The Capuchins are all for us, and even of the Jesuits we have some, though the greater number are opponents, as also most of the Barefooted Carmelites, although it is the Provincials of these two last orders opposed to us, who have strongly influenced their subordinates. When the people came into the towns to sign memorials to moderate the Interdict; in Wexford every one signed, in Galway 300 citizens, and the same is hoped for in Limerick. If now we add to these the whole of Ulster and all the adherents of Ulster in the other provinces, the result will no doubt be the number I have given. All these, on hearing me speak of my departure, protest with tears, that this would be the ruin of religion, would leave the clergy a prey to their persecutors, and on this head your reverence knows and can describe the lamentations of the Archbishop of Dublin and many others. Precisely the same is said by O'Neill with his whole army and adherents, and they declare that they, and not their adversaries the Ormondists, had begun the war for the sake of religion and always followed the Church party, to the great danger of drawing down upon themselves the persecutions of all the other parties. On my departure they say they would be a prey to them, and that a powerful army would be entirely lost, one on which would rest the hopes for religion in the future, and without which they forebode its complete ruin. Finally, I submitted these and many other reasons to faithful and eminent theologians, whose judgment was that I could not with a safe conscience, cease to make every effort not to abandon religion in the present peril. I therefore resolved to hold fast to this decision, since it appears to me a greater weight to bear the blame of desertion from two-thirds of the kingdom, than the persecution which I expected from the hands of the other party. I recollected that this embassy with all its difficulties might be compared in some measure with those in other times in the Church, when the apostolic ministers never lost courage, and knowing that the exercise of public worship is one of the objects of the Holy See in the present time, I felt more ready to bear personal mortifications of every kind, than to give grounds for complaints against the Holy See, such as might be feared would follow my departure. Your reverence will then explain that all other efforts having failed, if I had not proceeded to the censure, nothing that I could have done would have been of any avail. This appears evident from the course of a negotiation between me and the Council. First they wrote to me at Waterford of their intention to make this truce with Inchiquin, as he had declared for the King and promised them good conditions; and when I answered that this truce seemed to me to imperil religion, they replied by inviting me to Kilkenny under a promise to do nothing without my approval, and in the end I did return. Afterwards in a conference of fourteen Bishops, the truce was unanimously condemned; and as they knew the Council was hurrying it on, they authorized me and four others when we should deem it necessary to have recourse to the censure. Meanwhile, the Council endeavoured to make an agreement with the clergy, but at the same moment sent deputies to conclude with the Baron; and as they appeared to me to be making a mockery of the Church, I left Kilkenny without a minute's delay, at which the Council showed a spirit of such bitterness that it was currently believed they wished to have me in Kilkenny only for some ends of their own, perhaps to give me into the hands of the Marquis of Ormonde, whom they expected to arrive, or to chase me out of the kingdom with the greater ignominy. At Maryborough where I wished to stay a night and a day on my way to Galway, I was overtaken by two of their Commissioners with new terms to me, intended to lull O'Neill to sleep, while Preston was collecting his army in hot haste, had joined Taaffe and the heretics under Inchiquin, and were coming against us proclaiming death to O'Neill. In these circumstances, perceiving that all the previous offers were mere mockery, and that if I remained silent the Ulster army would be overthrown, and the heretic triumph over our religion, I felt the time was come to avail myself of the authority given to me and the Bishops, and I pronounced sentence of excommunication, since no other remedy remained to me. And your reverence will assure the fathers that were it not for this rash step of Preston's, I had resolved to abstain from passing the censure, and I had so written to the Council, whence it appears that the Blessed God permitted the first in order that the second might follow. It is quite certain that this resolution has hindered or deferred the ascendancy of the heretics, saved our holy religion, and set on foot a considerable army resolute to defend it, and from which, if it be the good pleasure of God, we may yet hope to see the best results.

However the excommunication did not trouble our adversaries so much as the refusal of the appeal *ad effectum suspensiorum* because being not familiar with these terms, and advised by persons more ill-intentioned than learned, they thought that any appeal would suffice to elude judgment and even prepared to this effect beforehand for they had publicly boasted that even if it came to excommunication they had the appeal ready to send to His Holiness; holding it for certain that in a cause concerning religion, he would decide against those whom they accused; and ridiculed the judge *ad quem* as much as the judge *a quo*. This matter was the beginning of all the disputes which followed, of the pertinacity of the priests, of the schism among the Bishops, and of the insults offered to me. They felt that this act of mine frustrated all the designs the success of which they believed to be in their own hands, such as the destruction of the Ulster army, the depression of the clergy, and the restoration of the peace with the Marquis.

Besides this, it was a strong argument in favour of our taking this step that it was only repeating what had been done in Waterford on the first rejection of the peace ; when moreover all the Council were declared perjured which has not been the case now. As to the rest, there, the members of the Council if they joined themselves to Ormonde were excommunicated, now not only they, but all who combine with heretics. There, the censure was fulminated against those who received the Ecclesiastical tithes, and here the same—there, all the soldiers were exhorted to come into the army of the Church and here likewise. As that measure was received with so much applause in Rome and in all the courts and kingdoms where the news reached, I cannot imagine but that a similar feeling will prevail now; since it may be boldly asserted that this truce is no other than that peace resuscitated and must therefore be disposed of in the same way. But the difference between the first and second is, that then the Bishops were united and the Council was not armed ; therefore everyone readily took the Ecclesiastical side; now, seven Bishops have withdrawn on the most frivolous pretexts drawing after them all their adherents, and the Council is provided with such an array of troops, that six Generals are included in their army, all sworn to act against the O'Neill.

I do not deny that, on my first coming to Ireland, I had the commands of His Holiness if peace should be concluded as Father Scarampi had foreseen, that I was neither by act or word to approve or disapprove of it, leaving me at liberty to stay or not to stay in the island : on other occasions also I know I had been told in general terms that when I had done all that could be done on my part, I should allow things to take their course. But my excuse on the first point, as I tell your Reverence in confidence, is that when peace was concluded I came to Waterford animated with the desire to follow my instructions and to do nothing for or against it ; and this my intention I confided to the Bishop of Clogher a few days before, who approved and will bear witness to my truth. I then found that all the Bishops and Father Scarampi *nemine discrepante*, were agreed that they must positively reject the peace. I therefore thought it better to defer to the general opinion, supposing this would be a quite sufficient excuse for exceeding the commands I had received, as had been the case before. Perceiving then that in the present truce, matters were just as they had been in the treaty, with this exception that the Holy See and the clergy were more injuriously treated, I had no difficulty in believing that the same reasons would have equal weight now, and our diligence meet with the same approbation from the wisdom of the Fathers, as was the case before. Reflecting then on the second general orders given to me, I freely confess I considered them as entirely dependent on the first, and besides the present circumstances, the danger to the faith and the opinions of the Theologians, it appeared to me that I should not have done my duty unless I had taken the means which only could protect us from the precipice so often mentioned.

These are in substance the reasons and the motives on which I leaned and the Bishops with me, in forming our resolution. The results show how well the factions knew that the censure would overturn all their plans, since with little respect to the Apostolic See and its jurisdiction, they have poured out such venomous decrees, proclamations, violations of clerical immunities &c., the past few months, as were never heard of before. The Council and Assembly themselves have not abstained from propositions little short of heretical, declaring the Bishops guilty of the crime of rebellion in having obeyed the Nuncio, whom they said was a foreign power, calling those who were not nominated by the Council or were promoted to other Churches than they desired pretended Bishops; and despoiling the Nuncio of his authority, title &c., &c., in short, things of such a nature as perhaps had never happened except in the time of any but an heretical King.

Perhaps it is well that the factions and the Anglo-Irish of this kingdom have shown their perverse inclinations at the present time, as the Holy See may take into consideration whether any future aid given to them by it may not serve to the increase of heresy and the overthrow of the ecclesiastical jurisdiction; and on the other hand whether it would not be advisable to bestow it on the other party, the old Irish; who never in the memory of anyone has deserted the Catholic faith, or come to any terms with the heretics.

And not less useful was it to discover at once, the ill-will of these people towards His Holiness and the Nuncio, because though it has not been manifested till now, it is perfectly certain the same spirit has been at work among the governing faction since the first day that the Pope put his hand to these negotiations. When Father Scarampi carried the news to the Council that the Pope had appointed a Nuncio to Ireland, he was answered that it was not for a Nuncio they had asked but for money, and that they cared nothing for the one but a great deal for the other. The Bishop of Cork, who was at that time in Dublin with three other Commissioners to treat with the Marquis, testifies that when the report reached them, his companions were all disconcerted. Sir Richard Belling, on his way to Rome, hearing the news at Florence was speechless for two days, and when in Rome showed how bitter was his dislike to the measure. A few days after my arrival in Kilkenny some lawyers inquired from Father Scarampi if I were going to erect a tribunal, when he said yes, they replied that they would not put up with it by any means; and this is the reason I have always acted with extreme caution in this matter, and have wished my authority to be more real than apparent. In the public Assembly Viscount Muskerry said that the day of my arrival was a fatal one for the country; in short, they have shown in every action that they cannot endure the authority of the Pope; they are even not ashamed to say in private and in print that his succours were mere empty hopes, vanity, and vexation. It may be therefore by the will of God that a people Catholic only in name, and so irreverent towards the Church, should feel the thunderbolt of the Holy See, and draw down upon themselves the anger which is the meed of the scorner.

Since I have seen letters both from Flanders and France written after the accounts had reached them of the malignant designs and contumacy of the Council here, and in which they declare the truce with Inchiquin would be the first step to the ultimate ruin of religion, I have taken hope that much more will the Fathers approve of the mode I have adopted to withstand it, as they are ever ready benignly to defend their ministers. So much it appears to me necessary to say, remitting to your Reverence's care to add all the information which may be required, and which you so fully possess.

COMPENDIUM OF THE TREATY AND CONCLUSION OF THE TRUCE.

November 11th, 1648.

Scarcely had Baron Inchiquin retired in February after the incursions he had carried on as far as Kilkenny than events changed on a sudden to the surprise of everyone, and the Council began to negotiate a truce with him.

From the time chosen, it was evident the whole matter had been concerted previously, as it was then there arrived from France Colonel John Barry, the intimate friend of the Marquis of Ormonde; on a sudden Inchiquin declared for the King and a free Parliament, and the Council forthwith consented to a treaty and began to arrange the terms.

The Council wrote immediately to the Nuncio, to tell him of the negotiation, of the declarations of their adversary, and of the good conditions proposed, and prayed that he would come to Kilkenny. But the Nuncio, wishing to keep aloof from so suspicious a negotiation, answered that not having seen the conditions he could form no judgment of them, but as he did not think a truce necessary, and knew that it would be dangerous to religion, he could not approve of it.

They replied that he ought still to come that he might hear all the reasons for the truce, and protested they would do everything according to his pleasure, and only with his consent. On this assurance he allowed himself to be persuaded and set out, but on his way receiving another letter, he perceived plainly that he was labouring in sand since the matter was already very much advanced.

At Kilkenny, in several conferences which he held with some of the Council, he showed clearly that the truce was by no means necessary, since they could call 3,000 Ulster men into Munster, who were all prepared and to whom he would give the supplies of His Holiness, while the other forces might move towards Dublin and so destroy the heretics. And throughout this has been the true and substantial point on which the whole negotiation has hinged. But the Ulster army was not acceptable in Munster, because they never could be kept down; and, therefore, they offered to send them against Portarlington, whilst the rest of the troops under Inchiquin should make the attempt on Dublin, but with this O'Neill was never satisfied, as he knew that he should be caught between the two armies, or forced to retire into Ulster with all his forces.

Besides these strong and general reasons, the articles of the truce were examined in one congregation of four Archbishops and ten Bishops, and were condemned unanimously; in another of fifteen, authority was given to the Nuncio and four delegates to pronounce the censure, also that the Nuncio need not have the four named, but might replace them at pleasure.

In the meanwhile good hopes were entertained that at the several conferences a satisfactory adjustment might be arrived at; but all the time two Commissioners had been secretly despatched to Inchiquin to conclude the truce. The Nuncio then thought it prudent to retire to Galway as he would be better able there to leave the kingdom, but stopped on the way at Maryborough to celebrate the Feast of the Ascension with O'Neill.

This departure caused such a sensation in the Council that they sent off three Commissioners with orders to entreat of him to propose new terms and show their desire to give him satisfaction in every way. Hereupon O'Neill and the Bishops who were with the Nuncio, drew up some propositions, without however signing them, on the acceptance of which they would agree to the truce; these the Nuncio sent in a letter, urging the Council to agree to them. To the astonishment of all, no answer was returned for twelve days, and no one knew what to think of it, but it was discovered that in the meantime, not only had Commissioners been sent to put the last signature to the negotiation, but time had been thus secured for Preston to collect the army which was destined to attack O'Neill; for this they had delayed the answer which only arrived after twelve days, part of it useless, part giving no security, and an army already in front of us. It was then the Nuncio invited three of the Bishops to whom had been delegated the power to pronounce the censure; and because they all excused themselves and probably had been seduced to do so before, he with four others who were with him, and on his own and their authority pronounced sentence of excommunication.

Preston who received it with a letter sent by the Nuncio's confessor immediately betrayed for how long a time their measures had been concerted since he treated it with contempt, said that an appeal was all prepared, and that they had eight Bishops on their side, which was indeed true. Now came the appeal; but as it was not admitted, then began all those extravagant doings which followed, even to the introduction of heresy, or at least apostasy from the Holy See; much after the manner of Henry VIII.

All this time the schismatic Bishops and priests said that the appeal held good and must cause a suspension of the sentence; they preached in a horrible strain, saying that even if the Pope confirmed the sentence they would not obey it,—as if there were not some matters which admit of no appeal, and especially those of religion, and where *periculum est in mora*. 2ndly. They say too that the articles condemned in Kilkenny are not the same as those lately concluded. This is false, as anyone who reads them will observe; but those who signed them have no other means of covering their change of opinion. 3rdly. They deny the authority of the delegated Bishops; the answer is that they have authority, and that in every case the authority of the Nuncio is sufficient without any other. 4thly. They say there is no proof of the authority of the Nuncio, because he does not show it. But the Nuncio who has the privilege of exemption from any necessity to exhibit his powers, has not desired to produce them though he could do so if it pleased him, and the ecclesiastical congregation never having expressed a doubt on the subject when the peace was rejected, so the Assembly itself when they prayed him to exercise this authority against any of the laity, never cast a doubt on what they had hitherto held and acknowledged to be certain. Be it observed that in all these transactions these people, though only with a malignant intention, have professed a deep respect for the Pope, the better to give vent to their hatred against the Nuncio. That it is a hollow respect is evident from what they have done in France in mockery of His Holiness, just as the Nuncio predicted. 1st. In concluding peace with the Queen without waiting for His Holiness' opinion, and contrary to the oath of the Assembly. 2ndly. In receiving the Marquis of Ormonde as Viceroy without the Pope's approbation. 3rdly. Introducing a new peace and new measures, when they had sworn not to do so until they knew what conditions His Holiness would have determined on concerning religion. 4thly. In publicly saying that in the matter of excommunication they would not submit to His Holiness' judgment if he pronounced against them.

Whence seeing in them a clear inclination to heretical schism, the Nuncio has borne every insult rather than incur any blame, it being sufficient to him to have shown the error they have committed in making this truce, and uncovered their plots against religion.

To Cardinal Panzirolo (in Cipher).

November 29th, 1648.

By this opportunity I can only inform your Eminence that the negotiation is in the greatest confusion. This is owing not only to the state of the country, which is every day more and more distracted by faction,* but by the news that the King's party has come to a bad end, that His Majesty has submitted to the Parliament and has yielded up Ireland to them. Hence it may easily be foreseen what

---

* See Doc. XIV.

the Island will come to, and all because this party would not take my advice to make themselves masters of Dublin two years ago, and of Munster this year. Nothing has been done in the Assembly, as they say no answer has been sent by the Marquis of Ormonde to the articles sent to him; and he, with Clanricarde, is in Cork, in order it is said to quiet the fears of the English who serve under Inchiquin, and who do not wish to act against the Parliament. On the other side, O'Neill with the Marquis of Antrim is in daily treaty with Jones and the Scotch, and is sending commissioners constantly to the Assembly, so that everyone is at work but nothing decisive is done.

The disputes between us and the accusations against me have never been made public; and quite unexpectedly a fortnight ago the Dean was allowed to go freely about Kilkenny, but not to leave it; he writes that he has hopes of being sent to me to treat of a reconciliation, but I laugh at the notion that any proper satisfaction will be made to the Church, or that people such as these will ever be induced to give it except by force of arms, or by the ratification by His Holiness of all that has been done, and I see that up to the present time I have prophesied rightly. It is my duty to tell your Eminence a circumstance which seems to me of importance, that the eight Bishops who are in the Assembly, on hearing that the laity denied my authority and commanded that no one should yield obedience to me, never made the least opposition nor left the city, or made any protest, have never written to excuse themselves either to His Holiness or to me, and in fact have been willing to appear to consent to it all. The laity defend their proceedings by the example of Portugal, whence they assert Cardinal Pallotto was constrained to fly, and his auditor was imprisoned, of all which I was ignorant, and I must only be grateful that they have even thought of comparing me to so great a man.

I live, as one may say, from day to day. I keep the frigate here to be able to go off at any moment, and wait for what may happen ; and as I hear the envoys from Rome have arrived in Waterford, I think when I hear from them in person or by letter, I may be able to decide what to do. In the meantime I can scarcely resist the letters I receive from all parts of the kingdom exhorting me not to depart, and some putting it to me whether I ought not to brave imprisonment for the sake of religion.

But I know how to defend myself I hope before the tribunal which is alone superior to me ; and I may confess to your Eminence that the fear of being reduced to beggary without one farthing left, is perhaps the strongest argument for my leaving the country. It is example enough for any one to have seen as I did, the contempt with which the Earl of Glamorgan was looked upon when he was penniless. Your Eminence will have heard from me how my enemies have sequestered all my property, raised up a host of creditors true or false all at one time, constrained me to keep the frigate here at a very great expense, as I dare not send it away, nor can I find anyone to freight it, since everyone fears that he may be arrested in some port at the instance of the Spanish agent who sold the *St. Ursula,* made money by the eleven cannon which were at Wexford, is hunting out my horses and the remainder of my baggage ; and I believe it is his doing that the Dean will have difficulty in regaining his freedom. I cannot therefore refrain from reminding your Eminence how necessary it is to humble this man ; in comparison I think nothing of what the Irish have done to me, as they act only as might be expected from such a set, and like people who have falsely assumed the name of good Catholics ; but that a minister of the King of Spain should have power left to him to act in a similar manner after all my protests, my evidence of his incompetency, and my mistrust of him, and showing no respect for His Holiness nor to the dignity I hold, is not to be tolerated. And those who see how much he has done to the injury of religion, the insults offered to me, how shamefully he has joined in the Ormonde Council and abetted all their wishes, have begun to call him an agent of the Most Christian King. Soon after you receive this, my confessor Father Giuseppe will arrive with the remainder of my reports. Before his departure the Provincial of the Barefooted Carmelites of whom I hear Father Scarampi has some knowledge, had been sent with accusations against me and as it has been discovered that he was actually in the service of the Marquis of Ormonde in Dublin, it appears to me advisable that your Eminence should know the character of the man.

I can say no more until I have seen and spoken with the Envoys from Rome; their delay and having had neither letters or advices from you seem to me to fill up the full measure of my tribulations, and I can only pray the blessed God to grant me patience under them; and wishing all prosperity to your Eminence,

I am, &c., &c.

TO THE SAME (IN CIPHER).

December 23rd, 1648.

I told your Eminence three months ago of my intention to leave this kingdom and to make some stay in Flanders, and that I had at great trouble and expense brought hither the frigate *San Pietro*, which was lying at Duncannon. Nevertheless as I found that the Marquis of Ormonde had been invited to Kilkenny as Lord Paramount, put in possession of the castle, and a treaty for peace was opened by the Assembly without delay; I resolved to remain till its publication; not only from the entreaties of all the well affected, but from knowing that my presence even was a great check on the evil doers. The preliminaries of the treaty are adjusted, and I wait only for the final publication, since at this distance and entire separation from the Ormonde party, I can readily follow the instructions of His Holiness not to do any positive act or interfere in any way in a treaty entered into and concluded with heretics.

Ten weeks have elapsed since the Envoys returned from Rome and wrote some cold enough letters promising to wait upon me,—which they have never done. I hear they are the chief promoters of this most desired peace, and take so much more trouble about it than others that people say whatever in it is good or bad is all the work of the Bishop of Ferns. I am sure it will appear strange to your Eminence that this man, in order to draw other Bishops to Kilkenny besides the eight already there, sent letters telling them that in virtue of a brief from His Holiness they were called together to hear it read; but it proved to be nothing more than the answer to the letters from the Congregation, which this Monsignor brought over. Everyone was alarmed and knew not what to do; until I sent to several of them a copy of the same brief with which your Eminence had favoured me, so the fraud was discovered and in conclusion not more than three attended and even these wished to leave, but were prevented. I had given them the necessary permission to go, but left it to their own conscience to decide.

I thank God that the letter from your Eminence of 7th September reached me safely, since as His Holiness has remitted to me wholly the affair of the interdict without appeal, I have succeeded in silencing in some degree this same Bishop of Ferns, who has industriously spread the report that His Holiness, the Cardinal Protector, and all the Court of Rome disapproved of my resolution; still as I can only asseverate the truth by words, I find that many good people think I am uttering falsehoods and that the letters are forged, hence after acknowledging the humble duty I owe to the Holy Father, I pray your Eminence to send me at once, wherever I may be, the brief which His Holiness has promised me on this matter of the interdict; so that the truth may be made clear to all those who in doubting me offend in my person the beneficent Donor. Meantime, the state of affairs is this, the interdict is raised from all the cities in consequence of the supplications of the people, and with all honour to the Holy See, and that private persons are almost all absolved, or are about to be absolved; but the Council and some chiefs of the army are still contumacious, and will perhaps remain so, not only because they do not see any certainty of the coming remission, but because some few Bishops and priests with the Jesuits will not fail to make them easy in their conscience, and what is of more importance they have committed so many outrages on ecclesiastical immunities, that unless they repented of them, it would not be proper to accord them this grace. Perhaps it may be the will of God to constrain them to appear before the Supreme power, there to render an account of all their doings.

A new agent from the King of Spain has arrived who embarked with the Bishop of Down, and declared at once that the Dean of Fermo must not be detained on account of any pretensions of Don Diego to a share in the booty; on this the Dean wrote that he was free, but as he has never appeared I begin to fear some other extravagance on the part of the Council. In the meantime having nothing here to live on, I have offered the *San Pietro* for sale, and if I succeed I can depart without hurry, but if not, I must ask through necessity alone for money, as no one here will accommodate me on promise of being reimbursed in France; everyone drawing back as is usual in these cases, and those to whom the Dean in France, and I here have lent money, are not in circumstances to repay us. As affairs have turned out it seems no longer well for the Holy See to inconvenience itself to send assistance here, since the country being placed under the dominion of the Marquis of Ormonde, the Papal money could serve no other purpose than to support either his establishment or Inchiquin's. On the other hand, O'Neill from want of money has been obliged to retire, and it is doubtful whether if he persists in opposing the Marquis, he may not be forced to unite with the Parliament. If therefore assistance should be sent to him, there is the same risk of its being shared by the heretics. Already it is manifest that this miserable Confederation stands between two hosts of heretics, and with so much dissension among themselves that many believe it will soon be completely overpowered without any remedy in the future.

Since this has been written, I hear that the peace was proclaimed on the 17th instant in Kilkenny. I have not seen the articles, but will send them to your Eminence.

To the Pope.

January 24th, 1649.

The affliction which the events in this country have caused me, is not a little increased by what I hear of excesses committed in Fermo, and though I know that at this distance I cannot interpose my humble prayers to your Holiness for any of the delinquents in particular, I may hope that it is not too late to recommend the people of the city to the compassion of your Holiness. I should not think of offering any impediment to the exemplary justice of your Holiness, but I rejoice to think that the community can never have countenanced such unexampled enormities at a time when the paternal clemency invites every one to act uprightly. If my deep sense of obligation should merit this favour, it will be some consolation in this my just sorrow, since it must I fear be my defects as a Pastor which have caused in some measure the unheard of folly they have shown in these excesses. May the Lord God preserve your Holiness and sustain you in meting out justice in suppressing the crimes of the guilty.

I prostrate myself before your Holiness and reverently kiss your holy feet.

To the King of Spain.

February 6th, 1649.

The most humble may have it in their power to gratify even great Kings, by making known to them the merits of their subjects. I therefore desire to testify that Signor Francesco Frimot has always shown so much attachment to the Catholic Religion, that he has never disappointed my expectations. And as I know that the piety of your Majesty has no greater desire than to share in the views of His Holiness, I fully believe that in these matters he has well discharged the duties of his office. Deign to receive this testimony from one who feels it a duty to the Ecclesiastical dignity to make the truth known, and who is under deep obligations to your Majesty. I pray that your happiness may be in proportion to the extent of your dominion.

I make my humble reverence.

To Cardinal Panzirolo.

St. Vasto, March 14th, 1649.

More overcome by a few days of sea voyage than by a whole year of suffering in mind and body, I have been landed by contrary winds at a miserable village on the coast of Normandy. It was my intention to disembark at Havre-de-Grace, as the merchant who bought the frigate *San Pietro* was afraid to cast anchor at Ostend, for fear of some ill turn of the Spanish agent, and I was not anxious to try the Channel which is full of Parliamentary ships from which we had some narrow escapes. My life is safe however and that of my retinue, and what has ever been a subject of solicitude to me, the reports and registers. In France I find disturbances even greater than I left in Ireland and they seem to run higher in this Province of Normandy than elsewhere; for since the appointment of the Earl of Harcourt as Governor by the Queen, he has begun to quarrel with the Duc de Longueville, who is on the Parliamentary side, and everything is in confusion and danger. I intend to obtain passports from all parties and to stop at Rouen, a place which is convenient for receiving letters from France and Flanders, and where I shall be able to obey any commands sent to me by His Holiness. I did not leave Ireland as I told you and fully intended, because as soon as I was aware of the fixed determination of the factionists to bring back Ormonde at any cost, I resolved not to set off, until the final publication of the treaty; being advised that my presence was the greatest restraint on the alienated Bishops to prevent their precipitating themselves into evil, and also on the laity to prevent them from doing anything openly to endanger the revocation. But on the publication of the peace and the restoration of the Marquis they declared immediately that he could not exercise his office while a legate of the Pope remained in the kingdom, and I, that I could not remain as Nuncio to those who having been the masters, had voluntarily made themselves the slaves of a heretic—and so I gave orders for my departure.

Taking my insignificance into consideration, these events were followed by greater honour to my person and greater marks of affection from the people than could ever have been expected, for I remained where I chose, set off at will in the same vessel that had brought me in spite of the machinations and insolence of my enemies, who in the Assembly by means of Clanricarde went so far as to urge that an army might be sent to Galway to compel them to expel me; and although the frigate *San Pietro* was detained under various pretexts until the last day, so that I might be obliged according to the terms of their plot to depart when they pleased and in the first vessel that chanced to present itself. Your Eminence cannot conceive the affection of the citizens of Galway at this crisis; they ridiculed these attempts and showed such reverence for the Holy See as to be prepared to defend me by arms if necessary. The triumph of my departure when I was accompanied to the ship by the tears and lamentations of the people was greater than when I disembarked three years ago: now, a minister, beggared and persecuted, then one from whom they hoped for supplies of all kinds. Every day I bless more and more my unexpected departure from Kilkenny and the promulgation of the interdict, which put a stop to the audacious intentions of the Ormonde faction; since what they have not been able to effect in Galway, would have succeeded in Kilkenny to the great opprobrium of the Apostolic See.

The well disposed party, that is the faithful among the Bishops and clergy and those opposed to the decree who are very numerous, entreated me not to leave them, to wait at least till O'Neill had taken the field, as upon him all their hopes are founded; and as they feared after my departure some extraordinary persecution, inasmuch as it will come from the Catholics. I showed them I could not remain without danger to my person and dignity; consoling them with the promise that I would not lay down my office except at the command of His Holiness himself, and that I should ever be ready to give up all I possess in their service. As to O'Neill, his retreat from want of money and arms shows that in spite of his enmity to the Marquis little can be hoped for from him. I have always advised him not to unite with the Parliamentarians, but nevertheless I have never advised him to join Ormonde; and what this poor man will do must depend on necessity or despair. Though I do not like to prophesy, I fear everything will fall into the hands of the Parliament to the utter destruction of religion, either by force of arms or through the treachery of Ormonde and Inchiquin, who, to serve their own purposes, will abandon the Catholic Confederation and follow the fortunes of the conqueror. It is not easy to explain what part the envoys sent to Rome have taken in the conclusion of the peace, which many declare to be entirely their work;

and that the embassy thither had no object but to obtain further supplies, in order to restore the Marquis of Ormonde, and support him with the Papal subsidies. How they have conducted themselves since their return towards me, and in regard to the interdict, your Eminence will see in a separate despatch in order not to lengthen my letter; such conduct is most extraordinary in persons lately favoured by His Holiness, and with whom I have always been on terms of close friendship; but nevertheless I cannot refrain from telling your Eminence that their artifices have been the ruin of the country.

And even lately when they endeavoured to make me believe that they were coming to wait upon me with letters from the alienated Bishops, and perhaps from the Council, to obtain absolution from me; I rather rejoiced as I had no faith in them, that the master of the ship could wait no longer, so that I should not be subjected to any further mockery.

And how could I, most Eminent Lord, have believed them in this matter? Did I not see that they made no attempt to restore the intercepted letters or the money which they had first stolen and then denied the theft, and that the Assembly had committed the great and most execrable sin of proposing a decree, that for the future they would receive no minister from the Pope? This decree, however, which was passed when the Bishops were not present was revoked the next day by the efforts of the Dean of Fermo. What too is to be expected from men who, by the articles of the peace, spontaneously reinstate in their possessions all the heretics who declare for the King, and by consequence the Earl of Roscommon whose fortresses were taken three years ago at an outlay of 26,000 crowns from His Holiness' treasury, so that the Pontifical money has actually served (a thing which makes me shudder) to the exaltation of heresy!

I thank God then this negotiation is over, and that I

succeeded in getting away without having to wait for anyone's leave, and with all the honours which were paid me.

I know that if I were disposed to pride myself on vain things, I might say that the articles in this peace are all, or the greater part of them, those which were proposed in the conclave before me for the benefit of religion; and under present circumstances it is no small thing to have gained so much.

But I renounce a glory so unfortunate in its end, and will show in a separate document that matters could not have been worse, that peace could not have been concluded with less security or greater loss, and that the whole is so arranged, that finally they will yield to the Parliament as has been done in England.

I am inconsolable Most Eminent Father, that I have not been able during these three years and a half, to gain for the content of His Holiness, even the boon of a Catholic Viceroy in this island. God knows how much I have said, done, and suffered, but my sins have weighed heaviest in the balance. To read the history of the Church has been my only comfort, there I find that Cardinals eminently qualified have in less distant countries been equally unsuccessful; such as Gaetani and Campeggi in ecclesiastical matters, Cesarino and Ruteno in military affairs. I have done no other good but delayed in some degree for three years the miserable peace, and increased the desire for Divine worship; but if your Eminence will allow me to speak openly I believe I have done much to unveil the real inclinations of the English party who rule here, so that for the future, people may not be so ready to celebrate their purity and their sincerity towards His Holiness and the Court of Rome. In truth, they have neither reverence nor affection for the Church of Rome, and hold almost the same opinions as Henry VIII. and Queen Elizabeth.

In what state I left the interdict your Eminence will see

by the third document which, with the two others, I shall send by this post; and as in the letter of November 16th your Eminence favoured me by a promise that upon the arrival of the Carmelite Father, no resolutions should be taken without communicating first with me, I humbly entreat of you to adhere to this promise until I have satisfied my duty and my conscience in the narration of these matters, and till you can perfectly understand their bearing, taking into consideration with what resignation I may, that it will be well to wait to hear also what happened after my departure, which may considerably increase the knowledge of the truth. If I find the roads from this to Paris are safe, I shall resume my practice of writing by every post, interrupted, much to my disgust by my exile, the miserable state of Ireland, and the disgraceful interception of all my letters; misfortunes which will excuse me to your Eminence for this perhaps too familiar exclamation, "Blessed are the Nuncios who are on terra firma, since those on islands if not incarcerated by man, are sure to be imprisoned at all events by nature."

I am, &c.

OF THE INTERDICT.

St. Vasto, March, 1649.

On the departure from Ireland of Monsignor the Nuncio, he left in the hands of six Bishops powers to absolve all persons included in the interdict pronounced in May by him and the Bishops delegated by the congregation. In this document he protested first, that he would not lay down the title or authority of Nuncio at any time or place, until so directed by His Holiness, that the people may be consoled and convinced that it was not the labours of office from which he fled, but to provide for the security of his person and the honour of the Holy See against which plots of all kinds were laid.

It was declared in the edict, that by the said act of absolution Monsignor does not in any wise mean to imply his consent to the peace lately concluded with the Marquis of Ormonde, nor to prejudice his liberty to abstain from expressing approval or disapproval in this matter. This was said to prevent any insidious attempts on the part of the Ormondists, who both in the peace of 1646 and on many other occasions had malignantly spread abroad that he had given his consent to it, thereby inducing many persons to join their party.

It was also mentioned in the remission that His Holiness had on 7th September made over the whole matter to the arbitration of Monsignor, and that he had signified his refusal to entertain any appeal from the Council; and this is stated to contradict the reports to the contrary spread by the Roman envoys, as will be spoken of more at length in the documents concerning them.

As to the substance of the document no mention was made of the interdict, which as has been mentioned was taken off the cities at the request of the inhabitants before the end of the first six months of the league, to the great honour and glory of the Holy See, since some petitions were sent signed by the citizens with promises not to accept the truce, or to act against the wishes of the Church of Rome, as at Galway and Wexford. Others made the same supplications through the clergy, excusing themselves for not doing so directly owing to the neighbourhood of the armies or of the menaces of the Supreme Council, as at Limerick and Waterford. Finally, it was taken off Kilkenny by favour, as a reward for the long-suffering of the Dominican, Franciscan, and Capuchin Fathers, who punctually observed the interdict, while the Cathedrals, the Jesuits, and the Barefooted Carmelites are contumacious to this day. Coming now to the excommunication, not only did Monsignor leave absolution to all who had recognised, approved, or forwarded the truce, without being the principal cause of it; but before the remission arrived from His Holiness he had given it to several others who still possess it, besides having himself absolved many. During the few days that preceded his departure many came to entreat absolution, and many others wrote that they would come to obtain it at any cost, if they could believe that His Holiness had not refused the appeal, the deputies from Rome having circulated reports to this effect, whence it may be believed that all, by virtue of the powers left or through recognition of the truth with regard to the remission, will become penitent and reconciled to God.

There remain those only who, whether members of the Supreme Council or generals of armies, or in possession of any office, were the principal promoters of the truce. All these, even if the eight alienated Bishops are included (which is perhaps doubtful) are not more than twenty-four in number, as Father D. Giuseppe, confessor of the Nuncio can testify, and had they after the conclusion of the peace awaited the sentence of the Supreme Tribunal to which they had appealed, he would have offered them the absolution *ad cautelam*, as some of the Court desired and advised.

But seeing that the truce was the least of their sins, and that afterwards either, by themselves or by means of an Assembly procured by them, they had committed such excesses against the immunity and the Holy See, as only the worst heretics could conceive, and had shown in many ways that their venomous animosity was directed not only against the person of the Nuncio but against all orders of persons and things ecclesiastical, he resolved not to propose absolution until they asked for it themselves, and offered satisfaction and apologies for all they had done. He put it thus,— either they consider themselves excommunicated or not, if not, they are unworthy of absolution, as they rely upon the doctrines of those Bishops and monks by whom they have been so ill advised. If they fear the interdict, which cannot be relaxed until the excesses have been revoked, it will be much better as a Christian example to implore absolution from His Holiness, or from the Nuncio after his departure, since from His Holiness who holds the supreme power they can obtain a dispensation for many errors; and as to the Nuncio, the humility they will show in sending a messenger to France may induce him to grant somewhat more than he could in Ireland, where every act would be declared the result of fear, and the desire to escape trouble.

It is true that many persons believe that had it not been for the ill offices of the envoys to Rome the affair would have been arranged previous to the departure of the Nuncio, as not only these envoys themselves had of late appeared anxious for absolution, but what is more certain, some members of the Supreme Council then in Connaught entreated for it even when his foot was on board the frigate, showing many scruples and great fear at the thought of not obtaining it, though they might have done so if they could have brought themselves to sign a short document, but were fearful that they would be blamed by others. The same may be said of some of the eight Bishops, and others among the magistrates who may yet apply either to the Court of Rome or to the Nuncio wherever he may be.

This is the position of the few who remain unabsolved, and what may be expected to happen concerning them. The Nuncio confesses to have committed one error and entreats pardon for it: viz., that when the General of the Jesuits sent a visitor to inquire into this affair, who when thoroughly informed came to take leave of the Nuncio, and requested authority to absolve those of the company who had incurred the censure, Monsignor granted his request; he regrets having done it, because if it be true that these movers of the whole machine have some scruples, it is plain that those who are guided by them must have greater, and if the Jesuits had been left without the benefit of absolution and had to appear before some tribunal to ask for it; it would have taken from the others all excuse, all pretext for defending the deed, or power of satisfying their own conscience.

To Cardinal Panzirolo.

Caen, March 27th, 1649.

In all places through which I pass the people of France are greatly incensed against the Parliament for their excesses against the King of England. The lower orders as usual show their displeasure by annoying the English in this kingdom, injuring their vessels and commerce as they do with enemies. The officials and governors of different places have inquired curiously whether Ireland is in a condition to assist the Most Christian King or any who may desire to avenge the death of the King; it shows that the idea was not theirs alone, but comes from above, and with a desire to make Christian Princes understand what their duty is at this crisis. I uniformly replied that if Ireland had had a Catholic Viceroy (for which I had laboured during my whole embassy) I could have promised considerable assistance against the Parliament, but that as the Marquis of Ormonde a Protestant, had been reinstated and was suspected by the greater part of the island, I had left it a prey to such disunion that I was doubtful if the people could do anything of moment. It cannot be denied that this inclination of the French is worthy of approbation but without peace in the kingdom, nay, without universal peace, I do not see how it can take effect, and at present there is no hope of either the one or the other. Meanwhile Ireland is open to invasion by the Parliament, and perhaps the Queen may repent of having wished to see the Marquis reinstated in order not to injure the cause of her husband as she said; and yet, one of the charges brought against the King was that he had sent to compound with the Irish. I deem it advisable to acquaint your Eminence with this matter during my journey through Normandy.

On the Peace concluded in Ireland.

March 30th, 1649.

Some idea of this peace may be gathered from the fact, that during the Nuncio's whole residence in Ireland the articles were never seen, never printed, as is usual in such matters, nor could he obtain even a copy of them. All who had anything to do with them, wrote in general terms that it was a good peace, that under the circumstances no better one could be had, that the rights of religion were secured &c., without entering into any particulars. Some of the Bishops concerned in it assured their friends, that besides those made public, there are some secret articles still more favourable, which has caused it to be believed that their conscience accuses them for the articles which were published.

But the manner, substance, and effects of this peace must now be considered in order to judge of it correctly.

First as to the manner of conducting it, I do not believe that such a treaty was ever before made between parties formerly so hostile as the Confederation and the Marquis of Ormonde. They first sent to France, Viscount Muskerry and Geoffrey Brown to invite him to return to Ireland and renewed the proposal after making the truce with Inchiquin. On his arrival at Cork they allowed him to take up his residence in his palace at Carrick in the quarters of the Catholics. Thither they sent six ambassadors to greet him, at the head of whom was the Archbishop of Tuam. From Carrick they conducted him to Kilkenny, gave him up the castle and permitted him to garrison it, this done, they began to treat of peace and the security of religion.

As the conclusion of it was delayed, Baron Inchiquin approached Kilkenny with 400 horse declaring that if it were not expedited he would have to put his hand to it, and thus it was hurried on. The Marquis seated on a high throne in the middle of the Assembly, was entreated by the Archbishops of Tuam and Cashel in the name of all the Catholics to deign to sign the articles, to which he with the greatest condescension and many loving protestations agreed. So much for the mode of carrying it out.

As to the matter,—one might congratulate oneself on finding an express stipulation in it for the maintenance of religion; for its public celebration, for the property and revenues of the clergy, for the possession of the churches, the use of all ceremonies, processions, habits and choirs of the religious orders; and also such matters specified as that whatever is gained for the future must be given up to the Catholics, either for one church or many, according to the number of inhabitants in the places ceded to them. Thus this peace is very superior to that of '45 inasmuch as no mention was then made of any one of these things, all being left to the discretion and good feeling of the Marquis. No one can deny that the additional articles are fruits of the labour of the Conclave in the Nuncio's time in which the articles were drawn up; and to the interdict pronounced upon the truce, which by causing terror had made the Bishops and the laity use their best endeavours to prevent a revocation of this second peace as was the case with the first.

With all these improvements however, if it be not secured, the second will be no better than the first, and it seems strange that many of the Bishops who in the congregation at Waterford would not trust to the Marquis in matters of religion, have now completely changed and have given him their fullest confidence.

In effect, the Marquis has no more legitimate authority now than formerly since that given by the Queen and Prince go for nothing, and even had he that of the King it would not be legal, because extorted during his imprisonment. Besides this, between the time of the first and second peace the Marquis had incurred the gravest suspicion of perfidy, not only for having given up Dublin to the Parliament rather than to the Catholics ; but also from the strong proofs which come from France that he had secretly treated with the Parliament in England while he pretended to take refuge from his enemies in that country, and was only awaiting an opportunity of declaring himself, and deserting the Catholics entirely. How then can he be depended on, more especially when he has arms and authority in his hand ? These are the very reasons why His Holiness and the Sacred Congregation could not approve of Glamorgan's peace, to which legitimate authority was wanting and in which there was apparently no security.

The effects now remain to be considered, and on these no judgment can be passed different from that on the points already considered. Some time ago Baron Inchiquin, entirely master of Kilkenny, disposed at will of all ecclesiastical affairs ; he sold or rented the tithes, and assigned to Puritan ministers those of the Bishoprics of Cloyne and Ross ; and by virtue of the peace these two churches, the only ones which His Holiness confers without the recommendation of the Supreme Council were (horrible to relate) placed at the free disposal of Inchiquin, who bestowed them on two of his relations; and this the Bishops who were at Kilkenny after signing the articles, permitted without the slightest remonstrance. By the same articles every heretic, whether Parliamentary or not, is to be reinstated in his possessions, provided he declares for the King. The Earl of Roscommon has thus recovered all his property, and it is believed that he will obtain Thomond of Bunratty, so that the 30,000 crowns from His Holiness, which were employed in retaking these places, have assisted the heretics to recover them without any trouble, and the same may be said of all similar cases.

As to the Marquis, it was reported before the departure of the Nuncio that he had begun to use his power so despotically that even his adherents were aghast, and seemed to repent of what they had done. It is certain that when he was much entreated to admit some Bishop into the Catholic Council to assist him, and being finally satisfied with two, those of Tuam and Ferns, he nevertheless insisted on their signing simply their Christian and surnames without their titles of Bishops, and seemed to care so little about observing the conditions that Monsieur de la Monarie, the agent of the Most Christian King, who had taken a prominent part in the adjustment, sent to tell the Nuncio through Father Verdier the Jesuit visitor, that he should defer his departure if possible, since he foresaw that affairs were hurrying towards their former state. If O'Neill and the malcontents had money and courage, I am convinced this would soon be the case.

This is all that is to be said concerning this Irish peace, which, with the fate of the King of England, suggests the following reflections. That the party who, as they boasted, wished to conclude this peace and recall the Marquis solely for the benefit of His Majesty and to procure his liberation, has rather hastened than retarded his death; since one of the principal charges against His Majesty was, that he was in treaty with the Irish Catholics. The Nuncio, on the contrary, having for three years constantly declared that such a peace ought not to be made, and that the Catholics should possess themselves of all the forts, and hold them for the King till he should be at liberty, was the only one who really assisted His Majesty in the way likely to free him from his enemies and preserve his life. But this, never properly understood by the Queen, influenced her in a contrary way, so that in fear of offending the Parliament, and in order to effect the King's liberation, she never would concede a Catholic Viceroy, who would have been not only the guardian of religion, but would have been the best means of saving the life of the unhappy King, at least as far as regards that calumny.

OF THE ENVOYS SENT TO ROME.

The Nuncio was willing to excuse the envoys for having left in France the letters which were consigned to their care for him, amongst which there were some from the Palace, and some others with important domestic news, together with a Brief for which he was waiting, because, as some of their property was left in the same chest, they were only exposed to the same accidents, although now owing to his departure from Ireland, he will not be able to regain the letters, no one knowing where the chest is nor who has the key; they will therefore, be taken first to Ireland and then returned to him. It is true that as these gentlemen took care to bring over some which favoured their own designs as can be proved, the excuse is in some degree weakened, and some blame attached to their proceedings.

Monsignor is also willing to exculpate the Bishop of Ferns in the following matter:—Previous to his return, the Nuncio wrote a letter in cipher which was adroitly placed in the hands of his secretary who was then in the fort of Duncannon, with orders to decipher it on the arrival of the Bishop and present it to him. In it the Nuncio commanded him by virtue of his apostolic authority not to give the pallium to the newly elected Bishop of Tuam until he had had an interview with him. The Bishop, however, did not arrive before the departure of the secretary, but he left the letter deciphered in the hands of Father Gelasio, Chaplain of the fort, a perfectly trustworthy person, who promised to present it on the arrival of the Bishop, and as the Bishop has been twice at Duncannon since his return there is no suspicion that Gelasio failed to deliver it. Notwithstanding this, the pallium was given by him in Kilkenny to the Bishop elect. Still as there is no evidence of this but merely moral certainty, and as the Chaplain may have forgotten it, or repented of his promise, the Nuncio passes over this accusation as he does the former one.

On the arrival of the envoys at Kilkenny they took so much interest in the Ormonde peace that they actually became the two principal promoters of it, and the Bishops there have written word that the results of the peace, whether for good or evil, must be entirely ascribed to the Bishop of Ferns and Nicholas Plunket, hence those who do not look closely into the affair believe that they received instructions in Rome to conclude with the Marquis, and consequently, that everything is done with the consent of His Holiness and the Sacred Congregation.

On their arrival they whispered to the alienated Bishops and their friends that the interdict pronounced by the Nuncio and his delegates had been ill taken by the Holy Father, by some of the Cardinals, and by the whole Court, by which means they so weakened the authority of the Nuncio that when he made known that on the 7th September His Holiness had absolutely referred the whole affair to him without appeal, and had promised a Brief to confirm it, not one of the faction believed him, and some openly mocked him.

They brought with them an open letter from Cardinal Romagnese, directed to the Nuncio, informing him with the greatest condescension, that when the interdict was heard of in Rome it had been variously spoken of, and as he desired that nothing should militate against the glory the Nuncio had acquired, nor prevent the further subsidies for the aid of the Confederates, he advised him to absolve the kingdom. This letter, before it was delivered to the Nuncio, was shown and read to every one by the envoys in order to corroborate by the testimony of so high a Prelate the opinions which they were spreading, and to produce consequences which may easily be imagined.

Having with them the Brief in which His Holiness condescended to answer the Bishops of the kingdom without mentioning the Nuncio, the alienated Bishops also took upon themselves in virtue of it to summon the other Bishops who would not countenance the peace, informing them as will be seen by the enclosed, that the Pope's Briefs have the force of a monition and that they were bound to obey this rather than the Nuncio, &c. With this subtle and diabolical invention they drew three of the most timid prelates to Kilkenny, viz., the Archbishop of Cashel and the Bishops of Waterford and Emly. The third of these who was lodged in the suburbs fled suddenly as soon as the fraud was discovered; but the others who slept in the city were detained and forced to sign the peace, thus making up the number without which it would not have been binding. Thus by means of a Papal Brief a Protestant Viceroy was established in Ireland.

These same Envoys, although they had received 2,400 crowns from the Nuncio for their journey to Rome and had been the means of inducing him to pay as much more in Paris to the Marquis of Antrim, and though they knew that the Supreme Council had not only by letter entreated, but subsequently almost forced him to pay it, and that these letters had been forcibly taken from the Dean of Fermo and never restored to him; still, they neither spoke on the subject to the Assembly or to the Council, nor expressed sorrow nor excused themselves to Monsignor, treating the whole matter as though it were an affair of the Indies, and involved neither the honour of the country, nor even common justice. The Dean of Fermo adds that having been kept a prisoner in his house he had never heard a word from them, nor had they done anything towards his liberation as might have been expected from men fresh from Rome and under obligations to His Holiness.

The fact too that in nearly four months they never waited on the Nuncio at Galway, is a matter of grave moment remarked upon by everyone and demands some explanation. On their arrival they wrote twice to the Nuncio saying that as he would hear all by word of mouth in a few days they would not enlarge in a letter. They then began to write that as they saw the necessity of making peace they would wait for its conclusion and then visit him. After this they wrote that they were delayed on account of some additional matters of great importance. Meanwhile the Dean being set at liberty, came to Galway bringing letters and despatches, and saying they would arrive directly to offer submission on the part of the Council and the others who wished to be absolved. The day following letters arrived confirming this, and saying that the Envoys would set off on the 3rd of February. Two days after they wrote to the Dean that the Viceroy being at Carrick had sent for Plunket and that on his return they would come. Meanwhile, in spite of all this trifling the Nuncio was hastening the preparations for his departure so as not to lose the opportunity of a favourable wind which served on Friday. On the Tuesday before, came the last letter from the Envoys to the Provost of the Galway College saying that after they had set out on their way they had heard of Monsignor's departure, they therefore wished to know whether it was true, and if so they regretted that they had not seen him. The Provost replied that the Nuncio had not set off, but that the baggage was already embarked and that he only waited to be called on board. After this reply, he heard nothing more of them nor do I know whether they had really set off, nor whether they turned back. But the general opinion is that they had agreed together not to come and the Marquis not to urge them, or possibly to prevent their coming.

To Cardinal Panzirolo (in Cipher).

April 14th, 1649.

I arrived at this town of Pont-Audemer on the road to Rouen intending to stop there, but the Earl of Harcourt to whom I had written for a passport, replied by the enclosed, that he thought I should also require that of the Court, and that he would procure it. He has arrived here in person, and having detained me for several days I have written to the Dean of Fermo who is at Rouen with the rest of my people to go to St. Germain, and have sent him all the letters necessary, according to the advice of the Nuncio in Paris, and I hope these precautions will suffice for the present.

Concerning the journey to Flanders and the waiting there a short time, I consider this necessary for the Irish affairs, as it is most important to hear what resolution O'Neill has come to, and of what Crelly may have done in London, because if O'Neill be reconciled to Ormonde we shall have only to recommend Ireland to the mercy of God; but if he has taken the field much may yet be regained.

I did not know whether my journey to Flanders would give rise to any suspicions; I therefore only say in public that I intend going that way merely from curiosity, and in order to return by a different route to that which I travelled before, moreover, that having told His Holiness of my intention he was pleased to be satisfied; but that contrary winds had thrown me upon the coast of France. If your Eminence deems it advisable, there will be time to write to me on the subject, and if you command me to go there it will perhaps pass without exciting any doubts.

I have had two interviews with the Earl of Harcourt, and his conversation always turned on Ireland and England, manifesting the greatest desire to avenge the death of the King, which confirms what I wrote to your Eminence of the rest of France, on 27th March from Caen. I have warmly thanked Mons. dei Bagni for the pains he has taken to prevent the Provincial of the Carmelites from obtaining a censure in the Sorbonne upon my anathemas. I trust that His Holiness will make some comment on the audacity of this man, who would have brought before any other than the Supreme Tribunal of the Church an ecclesiastical cause of an Apostolic delegate; as if by extorting a favourable decree from the Sorbonne he could have forced the Holy See either to follow it up or to condemn it. I believe that other doings of his not unlike this will be speedily brought to light.

Monsignor the Nuncio of Spain, informed by me of all the circumstances of Don Diego della Torre's negotiation, writes that he had spoken of it to His Majesty, and that as nothing had been heard of it at Court, it had been determined that the King should write to him to desire him to abstain from any further attempts against me, and the letter with an ostensible copy have been placed in my hands. But it is too late, since Don Diego has already done every thing which was in his power, but the letter will serve as a proof against him that when he boasted that he had the King's orders to act, it was all false. I shall take care to inform the Nuncio of all as it happened, that His Majesty may judge of his deputy as he deserves. I expect also that the Internuncio in Flanders will not obtain much from the countenance of that Court; it was publicly said in Ireland that the whole affair had been the work of some merchants who had bribed Don Diego, and had promised him a good proportion of what might be obtained.

I have already written that the Dean of Fermo is free, and the new Spanish Deputy had much to do with this since on hearing that he had been detained at the request of Don Diego he protested that upon no account whatever would the King have desired the imprisonment of a person such as the Dean. The Supreme Council were therefore ashamed to detain him longer, as they had lost the chief pretext for this act of injustice.

I remain humbly, &c.

To the Same (in Cipher).

Rouen, April 20th, 1649.

Although the Internuncio of Flanders has forwarded me some letters from Rome he says nothing of having received any orders about the frigate, but as I signified to your Eminence, I do not think he will obtain any thing, no notice of it having been received in Spain.

I have however written to the Nuncio to say that the King's letters were too late, sending him at the same time a full account of all that occurred (which I also forward to your Eminence), that His Majesty may treat his minister as the justice which we may suppose exists at that Court must dictate. Meanwhile after sending the Dean to St. Germain with my letters, I desired him to go to La Rochelle in order to obtain whatever proceeds of the spoil are there deposited, as a favourable verdict has been given in Paris, and this would be a great satisfaction to me at this time when Don Diego thought to seize on all I possessed. I am certain therefore that His Holiness will condescend to approve my remaining here until I see how far my hopes are confirmed. Of the affairs of Ireland we hear nothing certain, all depends upon the strength of the Parliamentary troops, which it is said in the *London Gazette* threaten to attack it with 12,000 infantry, and the Catholics are between them and the Marquis of Ormonde.

To Father D. Giuseppe.

If it is approved that some displeasure shall be manifested for the excesses committed by the eight Irish Bishops and the few priests who joined them, I think the following declarations would be necessary, and may serve as an example in future times :—

1. To suspend at pleasure the Bishop of Ossory who was the first to refuse obedience to the interdict without excuse

or reserve, as though he were the supreme judge and owned no superior.

2. To summon to Rome the Archbishop of Tuam, to give an account of himself and the Bishops of Killala and Finbar who were united with him, inasmuch as he had directed some persons to force a passage through the roof of the College of Galway, and to open the Church interdicted by the Nuncio, and for having himself with the Bishop of Killala celebrated Mass there. Item—for having celebrated Mass in the church of the Barefooted Carmelites who did not observe the interdict, and therefore were excommunicated by the Nuncio in a full conclave of eight Bishops and thirty Divines in Galway.

3. To summon before the Inquisition or any other tribunal in Rome, Father Peter Welsh, a Franciscan, for having preached against the Nuncio and against the authority of His Holiness, and for having lived out of his convent without the habit of his order and other similar delinquencies.

4. Likewise, to summon the Prior of Galway and his colleague, Father Brown, both Barefooted Carmelites, who besides having refused to observe the interdict, and having celebrated Mass publicly after the excommunication by the Nuncio, incurred also the excommunication of their superior who had admonished them under pain of excommunication *ipso jure* to go to Rome. They however applied to the Supreme Council, and returned to Galway with a declaration by the said lay Council, which asserted that they had not incurred excommunication, because the commination of the visitor was founded on the sentence of the Nuncio, and therefore both one and the other were void.

5. To command the departure of Father Malone, Provincial of the Jesuits, as the General had ordered the visitor lately sent thither to do. This order he did not obey, fearing the consequences, because the Provincial had declared more than

others for the truce with Inchiquin and against the interdict, and had commanded the whole of his order not to observe it.

If they see these sentences carried out I do not doubt that the Church of Ireland, so far as regards the members of this faction, will return to that obedience towards the Apostolic See which is now nearly extinct, and the new and obedient Bishops will find themselves at ease.

To CARDINAL PANZIROLO (IN CIPHER).

Rouen, April 28th, 1649.

While detained at Pont-Audemer, expecting the passport promised by the Earl of Harcourt, I learned that my intention of travelling by way of Flanders had excited some suspicion, as Cardinal Mazarin and the Comte de Brienne forgetting that contrary winds had driven me on the coast of Flanders informed the Dean of Fermo, that by taking so long a journey I had given occasion to suspect that I had some mission from His Holiness to the Archduke, or else that I was deputed to give him at this juncture some intimation that His Holiness approved more than ever the convention against France. The Cardinal added that the object of my journey might be to hear the Archduke's approval of my having so well served the Spaniards, since he knew I had received letters of thanks from them. As to those letters however, His Eminence makes a great mistake, as of all that I received from Spain during my three years' embassy, not one touched either upon the interests of the kingdom, or on any service I had rendered. If he means that by always opposing the return of the Marquis of Ormonde I have served Spain, it is well; and I believe he has no other cause of displeasure against me. Monsignor dei Bagni assured me that the Cardinal had been the sole cause of the Marquis's return to Ireland, not only to please the Queen at so small a cost, and be quit of Her Majesty by sending her precursor, but also to have one in authority in that island who would help him with levies of soldiers whenever he desired it. May God pardon him!—a Catholic Viceroy would have done as much for him without endangering religion; and in order that it may be seen if I have served the Spaniards in this matter, it has happened that the Queen has given up her intention of going to Ireland; and that the Marquis on his arrival, at once granted two regiments to the Earl of Berehaven the new Spanish agent, in order to obtain some money which he had brought over with him : Monsignor de la Monerie disgusted with this act of partiality, returned to France declaring Ormonde to be a traitor, and bitterly complaining everywhere of his conduct. I had already given orders to the Dean that to prevent any ill-feeling on my account between His Holiness and France, he should declare that my journey in Flanders was simply from curiosity to see the world, and that if it should appear suspicious, I would immediately give it up. This he did, and the affair ended by my passport being made out for Lyons. I regret it, merely because in Flanders I could have received news from Ireland and England, now so greatly disturbed; but He who orders all things for the best, has doubtless determined on some other way to succour those poor Catholics.

The Dean will go to La Rochelle about the money resulting from the sale, and which may be of importance to me; and on the receipt of the first letters from him I shall move towards Lyons, whither your Eminence can write with His Holiness' commands, which will ever be the rule of my actions.

With humble reverence, &c.

To the Same (in Cipher).

Rouen, May 9th, 1649.

On my arrival here I visited the Duc de Longueville, who afterwards waited on me and has paid me every attention. In the course of conversation he asked me whether I should approve of the King going to Ireland. I answered, decidedly not, as his presence at the present juncture would entail an intolerable expense on a country already impoverished, and would cause the Parliament to pour out the full weight of its wrath on Ireland in order at one blow to destroy the King. I added that while the Catholics are divided on the subject of Ormonde's return, the King's presence would only increase their disunion if he attempted to retain him; as he certainly would do; or if he wished to dismiss him he could not do it, as Ormonde is just the man to turn to the Parliament as he has done before now. I concluded by saying that if the King would not become a Catholic, he at least ought to persuade and permit the Duke of York to do so, send him to represent His Majesty in Ireland while he himself should remain where he could assist his party, keep the English in check, and thus prevent their throwing all their forces into Ireland; in this case I said, he might hope for the continued assistance and favour of His Holiness. The Duke replied that he was of the same opinion and for the same reasons, but that at Court and in the Council he stood alone, since they and Cardinal Mazarin all wished the King to go to Ireland, partly as I believe that they might get rid of the Queen, and probably for other reasons too.

To the Same (in Cipher).

May 9th, 1649.

I was in some doubt whether to write to Cardinal Mazarin respecting what he had said to the Dean of Fermo, that His Holiness was more disposed to the Spaniards than ever, and that I had done them good service. However I reflected that had the Cardinal spoken or written to me on the subject I should have been obliged to answer, but as he merely gave vent to his anger to a third person I thought it unnecessary and that no good could come of it. I believe that His Eminence wishes to show that he is more powerful than ever in spite of the attacks on him, because when the Dean told him how I had been treated by the Spanish agent in Ireland (to prove the state of affairs between the Spaniards and me), he took him by the arm and said, " If it be so, it is unfortunate for the Nuncio—every one here believes to the contrary." As if my being fortunate or the contrary depends on his and the Most Christian Court's belief in a falsehood. I have therefore determined to take my leave with a simple compliment, and leave the Cardinal to believe what he will of me, trusting that God and time will show him that he should trust in the upright intentions of His Holiness.

To the Same (in Cipher).

May 13th, 1649.

The Nuncio of France told the Dean of Fermo that the Queen of England had asked for him, and that it would therefore be well to pay his respects to Her Majesty taking a letter from me. I wrote immediately and desired the Dean to take the advice of the Nuncio. But first he wished to consult with Her Majesty's confessor, who at the first meeting said that the Queen wished to take counsel with him, but at the second that Lord Jermyn and Secretary Digby had advised her not to admit him, since he was in disgrace with the Supreme Council of Ireland; adding that Her Majesty had complained of me because I had always opposed her husband, and had condemned the truce with Inchiquin after he had declared for the King and not before. The Dean merely said what was necessary, took leave and retained my letter, of which the Queen had had no notice.

I was extremely rejoiced at this because Her Majesty being completely ruled by two heretics he would only have lost his time, and it is plain that she does not recognise the real cause of her misfortunes.

To the Same.

Having seen here the articles of the Irish peace which I had never been allowed to see before I left Ireland, I have copied that alone referring to religion which I enclose to your Eminence, that His Holiness and the whole congregation may see what has been done by our good Bishops! I pass no judgment on them, leaving it wholly to the wisdom of His Holiness and their Eminences. But it grieves me to see this result of three and a half years' constant labour, and to be forced to revoke what I wrote a few days ago in some commendation at least of the peace, since I see it is in fact no other than that concluded before my arrival; and they wished that the Catholics should take through pity for the King then a prisoner and perhaps not alive, what they might not have taken for themselves. In two days I shall send a part of my retinue to Lyons, and will soon follow them myself.

To the General of the Jesuits.

Orleans, May 19th, 1649.

A month previous to my departure from Ireland, Father Verdier sent by your Reverence on a visitation, disembarked in Galway and waited upon me immediately, not only to present the letters with which he was charged, but to communicate to me the instructions received from your Reverence. To make him acquainted with all that had happened between me and the members of the society, I gave him an abstract of the enclosed document, and exhorted him not to go to Kilkenny, but to obtain information in any other place, as in that city where the Council resided, and also all who are alienated from the ecclesiastical party he would incur a risk of being baffled in every way and probably be threatened, as has been the case with many others. He did not think fit however to follow my advice, as he set off accompanied by some of the Fathers who came to Galway to invite him, and assured him he should meet with good treatment. As to the question whether the affair turned out as I expected or not, Father Verdier cannot deny that on his return he showed me the original of the enclosed letter, written by the Bishops who caused all the disturbance, in which I perceive not only the artifices which have been employed to intimidate him, but that the Fathers of the society had been the principal movers in all; as the Bishops assert that there has been an agreement between them on every point throughout.

And truly if in this business of the truce I had required anything more from the Fathers than mere neutrality or silence as to their opinions until the matter was decided by His Holiness, and that in the meantime they should give some weight to my opinion and to that of almost the whole Church of Ireland; I should have been willing to excuse what they have done, but when without writing me a line or warning me in any way, Father Malone and his followers declared themselves the heads and advisers of the opposition, subscribed books, impeded the observance of the Interdict, and other things of the same kind, your Reverence will believe me when I say that I have never seen, heard, or read of such conduct before. And to their disgrace the whole Kingdom knows that just then I had obtained for the society the Abbey Church of St. John of Kilkenny, notwithstanding all the opposition of the Regular Canons, who expected to have it, and I gave the society possession also of the Church of St. Peter in Waterford, much to the displeasure of the Bishop and the clergy.

These circumstances will convince your Reverence that

under conduct so strange there must lurk some hidden end which I am sure your wisdom will soon discover, because as those Fathers who belong to ancient Irish families, and to those provinces still strictly Irish though few in number, disagreed with the others and have been obedient to my orders in as far as they can; it will soon appear whether their conduct is to be ascribed to conscience, religious doctrine, or to some other motive, whether in short it has been a matter of feeling, or of faction. Amongst those who refused obedience to Father Malone, I must not omit to mention the Rector of Limerick, who even left the house of the Rector of Waterford, and there are others whose names I do not at this moment remember.

I hope, when I see your Reverence, to give you some particulars of Father Malone's reasons when I blamed his mode of procedure, and also of the extent to which he has carried his animosity. Meanwhile as I have no other object but to let His Holiness and your Reverence know the truth, I am satisfied with doing so, submitting myself to that wisdom which all who approach your Reverence so readily acknowledge. I have now only to lament that at this moment the Catholic Confederation is under the power of a heretic; that Munster is in possession of a Calvinist; that the Protestant Bishops and Parish Priests are already preparing to take possession of the ecclesiastical income; and that if these things continue the Kingdom will be lost; and on Father Malone and his associates will lie the greater share of the blame. May God grant your Reverence such improvement in health, and such success for the good of your people that not only elsewhere but even in Ireland the growth of Christianity may prove a rich recompense for all the evil which has been done.

To Cardinal Panzirolo (in Cipher).

22nd May, 1649.

The Archbishop of Rouen received to-day a letter from Paris, informing him of the arrival of ambassadors from the Republic of England, and that the Court was completely upset not knowing how to treat them, because if they receive them they will appear to approve of their conduct to the King, and if they refuse, the King of Spain will most certainly receive them. It was hinted that His Holiness might interpose and prohibit all Princes under pain of excommunication from receiving them; this comes from a sister-in-law of the Archbishop who is a great prelate, though in some things peculiar; he turned to me and said "You see how the King is obliged to acknowledge his dependence on the assistance of the Pope, and that Princes know that ecclesiastical authority is needful even in political affairs." I wished to write even this short notice of what has occurred, because being on my journey I may not hear anything more of it.

To the Same (in Cipher).

Sans, June 3rd, 1649.

The French Nuncio told the messenger whom I sent to him before I arrived at Rouen, that it was reported I was to remain in France as his successor; and the last few days letters from Paris to different persons here confirm the report; upon which the Archbishop of Rouen and many others congratulated me, refusing to believe all my protestations to the contrary. I determined therefore to avoid Paris, and hurry on to Lyons, so as to give no umbrage to Monsignor dei Bagni, to whom on account of the late Irish affair I am under the deepest obligations; and also not to give Cardinal Mazarin any further pretext for accusations, as he declares me to be a Spaniard at heart. At any rate, I shall be able to receive the commands of His Holiness in Lyons, and to go anywhere that the Holy Father is pleased to direct me, even to retrace my footsteps if he so wills it. These reasons determined me not to await your Eminence's letters, hoping that the honour which His Holiness has ever done me in approving of my actions may be extended to my present resolutions.

To the Same (in Cipher).

Sans, June 3rd, 1649.

Reports have reached Sans, where I now am, that Dunkirk has been besieged by land by the Archduke, and by sea by the Dutch and English. As to the English, it does not seem very probable that the new Republic could so soon be in a position to take up arms against the French. I therefore doubt the report: but I know that at Court this league is suspected, and much deliberation has taken place on the subject. Whatever may be the truth I differ in opinion from many, because it is my belief that the Flanders army may rather strengthen the peace of France; that the people will be more closely united if the enemy advance; and that peace between the Crowns, will be rendered more difficult. The inhabitants of Paris take every opportunity of vituperating openly both the Queen and the Cardinal. When the Duke of Beaufort appears in Paris he is cheered by the people, just as the Guises were at the time of Henry III.; and the Prince de Condé has quitted the Court, having taken offence because having demanded to be made Constable, the authorities took time to consider and did not yield to him at once. The King will not return to Paris, and I have heard from the Earl of Harcourt, and it has been confirmed by Mons. Tallon who was at Kilkenny, that His Majesty pretends to have made peace with the Parliament and the people, in order to deceive them and by degrees punish the guilty; which if made known to those who are inculpated, as it has been to me, will be sure to cause dissatisfaction. If however the Spaniards advance, all difficulty will be at an end, as hatred against them will prevail with the French over all their internal dissensions. If the English are really in league, please God the peace will again be set on foot and I have deceived myself—which I most earnestly desire.

To the Same (in Cipher).

June 20th, 1649.

I visited the Prince de Condé who came to Dijon to hold Council in his principality and perhaps to obtain money. This nobleman treated me in a very different manner than his Father had done, took my right hand, did not invite me to a seat, and attended me only to the door of the room: in other respects he was familiar; gave me always the title of Illustrious, and questioned me minutely upon Irish affairs for more than half an hour, particularly on the strength of O'Neill, and whether he is really a Spaniard at heart, in all of which I recognised the ideas of Cardinal Mazarin. Of their own affairs he said that he did not hope much from a universal peace, since the Spaniards were not well inclined to it, and Pequeranda had declared that he would not keep to the treaty as it stood, but that it must be begun over again; to which the Most Christian King had not as yet made any conclusive reply. The Prince added that the Duke of Orleans had gone towards Arras, and that Erlach, with the Germans, was already in the enemy's country. Then he laughed at the inconstancy of the Italian Princes; and when I began to praise the beneficence of his Father to all ecclesiastics and his ardour for the Catholic Faith, though he replied that he had in truth still a great respect for the Holy See, it appeared to me that from his manner of saying it, he considered it a thing not to be imitated and perhaps of no great weight. My opinion of him, formed during this one interview coincides with that generally held of this nobleman; and four years ago Monsignor dei Bagni gave me a similar impression of him.

To Father Giuseppe.

Bellegarde, July 9th, 1649.

From what has taken place in Irish affairs up to the present, it appears equally perilous to act or not to act. If nothing is said or done, the opposite party gain courage from this silence, the bad Bishops and Regulars triumph, while the well-affected, losing all the hope which till now has supported them, will be obliged to succumb and make peace with their enemies. On the other hand, if any resolution be taken, all the opinions and motives urged by the Sacred Council must be taken into account; and these, though they may be uncertain, are yet so powerful that it were not perhaps well to risk opposing them in such a state of uncertainty. And I am always inclined, especially in my own affairs, to defer entirely to those whom God has made my superiors, and who are consequently more enlightened than I can be.

Considering this, I now propose a measure whose effect, if I do not deceive myself, will, in some degree, aid the first of these considerations without impairing the second.

First, even during my journey to revoke all the privileges granted to the missionaries in Ireland, according to the powers vested in me. The affair should, I think, be managed thus: To print the order at the first resting place, and send sufficient copies of it to Ireland. But at the same time, in order that the kingdom be not wholly deprived of their services, to except in a separate sheet until other commands are received from His Holiness, some Bishops and Provincials, giving them power to nominate others, provided these delegates and their nominees are not among those who took part in the late disturbances. I am certain that this provision will give comfort to the good, and be some punishment to the guilty, without pledging the Holy See. To begin with the well affected, as they will see that I have issued the order so near to Rome, they will believe that it is done with the approbation of His Holiness, and that they are secure of his protection. They would see themselves completely distinguished from the evil doers, because those who are excepted will be all of their own party; and they will believe, for men easily believe what they desire, that this resolution will be succeeded by others. As to the rebellious party, without any doubt, they will be deeply mortified, and will no longer be able to boast of the excesses they committed with such impunity. To recover their former position there will be no recourse possible either to the King or the Council, or to any other than His Holiness himself; who, perfectly free to grant any favours he pleases, will show that except the authority vested in me by his Brief as to the manner, the work is all mine, and that to me they must apply. If His Holiness wishes to understand the crimes committed by them, and in some measure to proceed against them, he can take the opportunity when they come to sue for grace, demanding the reason of their sentence being different from others, and thus the accused will be forced to incriminate themselves. If they do not demand to be reinstated, it will prove that the sentence was merited. If they do demand it, their crime should be brought home to them, or they should make some atonement.

It is to be considered also that even if this should not happen, some measures must be taken on account of the abuse and contempt with which these privileges are treated at the present time, abuses so well known to Father Giuseppe that it would be superfluous to expatiate on the subject. I must add that having determined many times to make this revocation whilst in Ireland, I was on the point of doing so before my departure, but was only restrained by the fear that the Council would take revenge upon me and upon the property of His Holiness then in their possession. But these reasons no longer exist, and I shall await the approval of this proposal, with the desire of conforming myself to the opinion of those whom I am bound to obey, and content myself with these suggestions to Father Giuseppe, who will speak for me, and will add whatever he may deem necessary from his personal knowledge.

To the Same.

Lyons, July 21st, 1649.

If it be deemed advisable to grant absolution to the Irish Confederates, the following conditions should be insisted on, as much for the honour of the Holy See as to animate and encourage the good Catholics of the kingdom :—1. That they produce a lawful warrant to procure and demand absolution; because without this some of the Confederates may deny having made the request, others may boast that they did not care for the remedy; and this would be a mockery of the Holy See and of its authority.

2. That all the ecclesiastics of whatever rank or condition be excluded from absolution who, even more than others offended the Holy See and the Nuncio by insult, by preaching false doctrine &c., and who having more sacred engagements with the Holy See should be judged apart from the laity. And their guilt was all the greater inasmuch as they spread abroad and tried to make all around them believe that the excommunication was of no effect, or at least that they had not incurred it; this appears from a letter written by six Bishops to the Nuncio, but which did not arrive till after his departure. This separation of the offenders will be a great satisfaction to the well-affected, who will feel that those are in some degree kept in fear who had rashly proceeded to the last extremity.

3. As to the laity, His Holiness has decided well in making them revoke the decrees and acts passed against the Apostolic authority and the immunity of the Church; because such an act of submission and obedience will be edifying to all parties. Among the acts to be revoked, the principal are the impri-

sonment of ecclesiastics both secular and regular; the violence done to the Bishops when they came to attend the National Synod, and the oaths administered to all orders of persons binding them to fear neither the past nor the future censures of any ecclesiastical tribunal whatsoever; and other similar acts, well known to Father Giuseppe and to every one. For these, it would be sufficient to make them confess their inability to carry them into execution and promise to abstain from them in future.

4. That the absolution be formal and not solely *ad cautelam*, as this second mode would completely prejudice the sentence of the Nuncio and his delegates, since the adverse party has desired nothing more than this, and it is evident that they wished to employ it to enable them to do what they pleased without being responsible to anyone for their actions.

5. It might be taken into consideration that among the penances imposed, one should be to send some one to Rome to the feet of His Holiness, to ask pardon for their errors and render thanks for his paternal benevolence. All these conditions will not only comfort and support the well-affected, but be to the honour of the Nuncio himself, in accordance with the beneficent letters which have been at various times written to him on this subject, not only referring the whole matter to him from the beginning, but promising that he should have a voice in every resolution that should be taken. And he will be for ever grateful if the considerations now submitted to His Holiness are in part or wholly approved.

REPORT

ON THE

AFFAIRS OF IRELAND

PRESENTED

TO THE PONTIFF INNOCENT X.

BY

MONSIGNOR RINUCCINI,

AFTER HIS RETURN.

REPORT ON THE AFFAIRS OF IRELAND.

1. The Catholics of Ireland have from time immemorial been divided into two adverse factions. One under the name of the old Irish, although dispersed over all the four provinces of the Kingdom, are yet more numerous in that of Ulster, which seems to be in a manner their head-quarters, since it was there the Earl of Tyrone placed himself at their head and carried on a long war on their behalf against Queen Elizabeth. The other faction may be called the old English, a race introduced into Ireland at the time of Henry II., fifth King after William of Normandy who conquered England, and so called to distinguish them from the new English who came over with the Protestant heresy, and who having been mixed with the native Irish by means of the above mentioned colonies scattered particularly in Munster and Leinster, have also come to be called the new or modern Irish to distinguish them from the old party, and maintain a constant intercourse with the English, both in matrimonial and other relations. The discord between these two factions may be attributed to the following causes: the old party averse to heresy are also averse to the dominion of England, and refused to accept of the ecclesiastical property offered to them when the Kings of England apostatized from the Church. The modern Irish on the contrary enriched with the monastic possessions, and bound to the King no less by obligation than interest, desire nothing better than the increase of the royal prerogative; acknowledge no laws save those of that Kingdom, are completely English in their prejudices, and in consequence of their connexion with the heretics, less jealous of the difference of religion. Nature even seems to widen the breach by difference of character and qualities, the new party being for the most part of low stature, quick-witted, and of subtle

understanding, while the old are tall, simple-minded, unrefined in their manner of living, generally slow of comprehension, and quite unskilled in negotiation; they regard each other therefore with mutual distrust, and one is in constant fear of the aggrandizement of the other. Again, at the time of my arrival the greater part of the Catholic militia was under the command of the two generals, Owen O'Neill and Thomas Preston, the latter of the modern party, the former of the ancient, who were not only rivals by nature, and from party spirit, but embittered by jealousy from having both served in the Flemish wars, and having even then shown signs of mutual aversion. These introductory remarks are necessary to my report on Ireland, as it will appear that what I have related not only produced the events which preceded my arrival, but affected them during my mission, and will probably influence many for the future.

2. I must then go back to a rather earlier date, when in 1641 a glorious resolution was taken by the Irish Catholics to enter into a confederacy, in order to obtain by arms, and from the King, the free and public exercise of the Catholic Religion. Doubtless there was manifest in this determination a ray of divine wisdom, for despite the above mentioned jealousies, they at once united to oppose the English; to open the Churches; to dismiss the heretic ministers; to recall the parish priests and Bishops, and succeeded so far in establishing religious worship that the Christian world at large, and especially the English Catholics, were in the greatest hope of restoring the same public worship in England, by the example and with the assistance of the Irish. This enterprise having taken its rise in the province of Ulster was successful, and the ardour of the Confederates remained unabated exactly so long as it contained more of the divine than the human element. But religious zeal soon cooled, nature resumed her sway, suspicions returned, and dissensions arose amongst the modern party who were likewise seized with a jealous

fear that if the enterprise succeeded, all the glory and advantage would redound to the other party, who probably in that case would not hesitate to overthrow their opponents. Again, it was to be remembered that the freedom of religion demanded by the Confederates would necessarily include the restoration of at least the property originally belonging to the Churches, Cathedrals, and Curates; hence it might easily happen that the monks would demand possession of the monasteries, whereby many noble families would be despoiled of the principal and most valuable part of their income. Old jealousies naturally induced the belief that to this end all the designs of the other party had been from the first directed, and that under pretext of religion they would deprive their opponents of the abundance of fortune which they seemed to envy. To this suspicion, the power vested in me of confirming the said property to the possessors brought no antidote, for considering the large number of confiscations there were very few availed themselves of this confirmation, because the evil disposed persuaded them that if the King resumed his sway, umbrage would be taken at the reference to a foreign power, and others again with shameful malignity insinuated that the Roman concessions were not to be depended upon.

3. A council therefore was soon called, and the perils of the attempt and the state of affairs having been weighed, it was unanimously determined to oppose or overcome the other party, to advance as much as lay in their power the peace with the King and with the Protestant followers of the King, thus, leaving on their hands the war only with the Parliament, the already declared enemy of the Crown. Great facility was given to this project by the appointment of James Butler, Marquis of Ormonde, an Irishman of the modern faction, to the viceregal power, whom it was generally believed that His Majesty sent in order that through his family and adherents he might cause dissension amongst the Irish

who were at that time greatly feared, and in consequence of their late resolution, denounced as rebels to the English power. The Supreme Council almost entirely composed of the new Irish, easily obtained permission to treat of a peace with the Marquis, and under pretext of first adjusting the religious conditions to which they had bound themselves, obtained innumerable delays and procrastinations by truces, which continuing for several years entirely enervated the army and gave the Marquis certain hopes of bringing affairs to the point to which he has since finally reduced them—a point infinitely to be deplored for the gravest reasons. From these constant cessations of arms it soon appeared that the public exercise of their religion was but a pretext amongst the modern party, as they showed but little anxiety for its secure establishment, and were solely bent upon their own interests and on obtaining promises from Ormonde, proving that their object was far more to keep well with the King than to seek the glory of God. Again, the people who had at first been hardened to and anxious for war in consequence of recent victories, by tasting repose during the truces, abandoned themselves to languor and began to detest the long deferred enterprise. And finally former dissensions became more rancorous than ever, the old party protesting against any peace that did not confirm the restoration of the Churches and public worship which they had purchased with their blood; the new, deprecating any demands which it would be inconvenient to the King to grant at that juncture, upon which point the laity in private meetings, and the priests and Regulars in the pulpit, and in pamphlets, pronounced with so much violence that the dispute became almost as fierce as war itself. There was at that time in Ireland the Abate Pierfrancesco Scarampi, who had been sent thither by His Holiness Pope Urban VIII., to assist the Confederates in their so worthily commenced enterprise; but in spite of his earnest persuasions to adhere to their ,original determination, and condemn any peace that would not completely establish the Catholic Religion, he soon saw that they were rushing headlong to the precipice; he therefore wrote on the 1st September, in the year '45, to inform your Holiness that they had all but concluded the peace so deplorable in its results, so fatal to the true interests of religion.

4. It pleased your Holiness to honour the Confederates no less than myself by appointing me to the office of Nuncio Extraordinary to this kingdom, hoping that the considerable aid of money which you sent under my care, would cause my arrival to be welcomed with gratitude proportionate to the eagerness with which it had been sought. But it happened entirely otherwise; for although the modern party were prepared to receive the money with thankfulness, the advent of the Nuncio was the greatest blow they could have received. The first proof of this I had from the Queen of England, who as I then informed your Holiness refused to receive me as Minister of the Apostolic See, alleging that the laws of the kingdom and regard to the interests of her husband would not permit her to do so without scandal. Richard Belling, secretary to the Confederates, who was on his way to Rome to solicit the above mentioned money, hearing at Florence of my appointment, was so astonished that for several days it appears he could scarcely speak. The most certain proof of all was that Father Scarampi having given notice of my mission to the Supreme Council, received the following curt reply: that they had never asked for a Nuncio, nor did they wish for one, as the Father himself was all that they required; but that they had asked for assistance and money from the Pope, and that these they expected from His Holiness. In such a disposition of mind, and in such a state of affairs, I having meanwhile set sail from La Rochelle, and having had to fly for 100 miles before an English frigate which gave chase, set my foot on Irish ground in the port of Kenmare, the most barren and unfrequented spot in Munster.

5. The zeal and honour with which I was received not only by the common people, but by the nobles of both factions, from my disembarkation till my arrival in Kilkenny, were certainly highly remarkable. The only bad road in the whole kingdom is that over the Munster mountains, and as I had to cross them with a considerable suite and much baggage, I was furnished with vehicles for all and an escort to attend me, so that although I had to approach within ten miles of the enemy's quarters, I was enabled to do so without peril. At the same time I could perceive in spite of the genuflexions of the people, and the congratulations of the nobility, that the old party welcomed me as the minister of God,—the new as the treasurer of a prince. The discourse of the former was ever of an honourable peace, of the maintenance of the Churches, of the observance of their oath; that of the latter, of the King, of the royal prerogative, of the necessity for war; and if peace were spoken of at all, they disguised the spirit of it, as before they had marred the substance. On my arrival at Kilkenny also I soon found that whereas the old Irish conversed freely with me, and frequented my house, the new, except by public deputations, and these of rare occurrence, seldom came to consult with me, and paid me no attention whatsoever.

6. Nevertheless, as during the first eight months of my mission they did not fail to treat with me and testify occasionally great confidence in me, it may be advisable for the instruction of future Nuncios and for the enlightenment of the Holy See to state here their reasons, in case the Papal succours sent to the Catholic party should ever fall into the hands of this faction. It is certain that although this modern party were annoyed at the appointment of a Nuncio, because they would rather have distributed the money which I brought as they liked themselves, still they would not have wished by my non-arrival to lose it altogether. During the three months therefore that I remained in Paris, the Secretary of the Supreme Council, then

on his return from Rome, and his adherents made loud complaints of my delay, and testified the greatest anxiety to see me in Ireland, not through zeal for the honour, nor through compassion for themselves, but because they feared that owing to my delay the money would be returned to Rome or remain in France. Whence it happened that although the peace had been committed to writing many months previous, they avoided its publication until my arrival, and dissimulated the matter with infinite astuteness all the time the money was in my possession, naturally supposing that if I came to hear of so disgraceful a proceeding I should set sail again and carry back the subsidy. Finally, as I shall explain in its place, so soon as I had made a distribution of the money and emptied my purse, they, freed from all restraint, set fire to the mine and showed by the publication of the peace what they had been secretly plotting for years; for these reasons and others which I shall presently adduce, I had strong suspicions that the money entreated and prayed for with so much instance, was a large part of the price promised to the Viceroy for the said peace; as doubtless he who is a man of deep design, was anxious to make the Catholics pay dear for the free exercise of their religion; which he had indeed promised but only by word of mouth; and also for the document which was to exempt them from the pains and penalties of rebellion which they had incurred when, as the Viceroy said they had offended the Royal Majesty by taking up arms. My suspicions increased when I found that 12,000 crowns which I had at first lent to the Supreme Council for the support of a part of the Leinster army against the Scotch Puritans, had been given to the Marquis on a promise of also moving northwards, which move never took place; whereupon hearing from competent witnesses that Ormonde boasted in Dublin of having in his possession the Papal supplies, I, indignant at the trickery, and threatening to retain the rest of the money, so terrified them that my loan was **immediately repaid.** If all this proves the truth of what I have written, still less doubt will remain on the minds of those who read of all that occurred till the day of my departure, and see all that the factionists did to obtain the second remittance of money, not stopping at any means however violent, nor even at some that were almost sacrilegious. The desire to observe even in part, some secret promise evidently influenced these men, and thus would the Papal subsidy have been distributed if this party had been allowed to dispense it.

7. But to resume the thread of my subject, on my arrival I found spiritual affairs in excellent train, and the public celebration of religion splendid and well ordered. The Provincials received all due obedience from their respective orders, likewise the Bishops, although the greater number of these, avaricious in the government of their benefices and despising the constitution and usage of Rome, must be spoken of separately. I therefore hastened to supply all that was wanting, and although the doctors and lawyers, accustomed to no text-books but those of the English laws, doubted my power to erect a tribunal, I gave it as far as possible a form compatible with their principles, set on foot the custom of deciding gratis, causes which were brought before me in such great numbers, that as long as I remained at peace in the island, the Regular Clergy were allowed to remain civilly exempt from every other tribunal. But in military affairs the difficulties were almost insuperable; since the enemy having penetrated into all the four provinces of the kingdom, the Catholic union was therefore obliged to keep a standing army and a general in each of them, and alleged this expensive defence as a sufficient reason for a peace with the King, which indeed they seemed to think so necessary that according to the opinion of their theologians, they thought they ought to secure it even without insisting on the exercise of religion in proper splendour, declaring in

spite of the most binding oath, that public worship was not to be sought at such a price, and that God was sufficiently honoured in secret masses and sacrifices, when public ones would endanger the peace of the kingdom. This opinion was confirmed by the very ample authority which the Earl of Glamorgan appeared to have of treating with His Majesty's subjects, which power he so managed and increased at will that it appeared sufficient to satisfy all scruples regarding religion. But all this was utterly futile since the enemy were so weak in the provinces that had war been carried on without any truce with the Viceroy they must have been worn out in two years. The Protestants of Leinster and the Viceroy with whom only the peace was to be made, were a small and very weak party; the war with the other enemies remained on exactly the same footing; and there was sufficient defence against all, the fort of Duncannon in Munster having been lately recovered and garrisoned, as the most convenient stronghold in the province. In Ulster, General O'Neill commanded against the Scotch, and though Sligo had lately been lost, Thomas Preston was now marching into Connaught. Nor could much dependence be placed on Glamorgan's authority, which consisted of blank paper sealed with the King's private seal, by which His Majesty could not legally be bound. I was therefore occupied the whole winter in representing to the Council what infamy they would incur, and what ingratitude they would show to God and the Holy See, if at such a juncture they were to abandon the enterprise, and break their oath to establish the true religion by every means in their power in the Kingdom. Inasmuch as the Viceroy had in the meanwhile imprisoned Glamorgan in Dublin, under pretext that against the orders of the King he had bound himself by promises to the Catholics, I exerted myself so much the more to open the eyes of the Confederates; because if Ormonde so hated the very mention of the Catholic Religion as to imprison its supporter, how could they hope that he would introduce it into the conditions of the treaty ? The proof of this occurred three months after, when the King by an edict affixed on the walls of London denied having ever given any authority to Glamorgan in Irish affairs; and commanded that no faith should be given to him. But I might as well have sung to the deaf, because as I before remarked, the peace was already concluded, and all the audiences and pretended consultations were merely for the purpose of discovering whether they could obtain possession of the Papal supplies, or to what end they would be applied; since the spring was so far advanced and the need urgent.

8. During my residence in France, when yet scarcely acquainted with the state of Irish affairs, I confess I was strongly inclined to devote all your Holiness' supplies to the relief of Ulster. I thought that the situation of that province, separated from the Scotch promontories by a passage of only three hours' length, this gateway to the Kingdom, should be fortified else that it would never be safe from the Puritans. I was confirmed in my opinion, when on my arrival in the Island I heard that the Scotch were assembling from all parts in Ulster, and were about to fall upon our quarters. But the Supreme Council in conformity with their before-mentioned partiality in order that assistance might not be sent to Ulster dissimulated, if they did not even consent in this most imminent danger. I was most urgent that the supplies should be devoted to that province, but afterwards at the suggestion of a few of them I gave a part to Preston who was engaged in Connaught, as it was believed that otherwise he and O'Neill the leaders of the opposite factions, would come to blows and the Confederacy be entirely broken up. The arms were therefore divided between these two Generals, a little less than two-thirds of the whole to Preston, and the rest to O'Neill. It will not be out of place to explain the difference between the amounts of pay which the soldiers receive in these provinces

of Ireland: the inhabitants of Ulster, and in part those of Connaught, accustomed to suffering and hardened to the cold of this northern climate, have few wants and fewer wishes, not caring for bread and living on trefoil and butter, their drink is milk, and as a great treat whisky, nevertheless they have shoes, some few utensils, and a woollen mantle which covers them, but are more careful of their swords and muskets than of their own bodies. They rarely touch money and as rarely quarrel about it. Whereas the inhabitants of Leinster and those of Munster, are more civilized in their manner of life, and having been lately accustomed to wars with the English, affect for the most part their manners and insist upon having all the same comforts as the soldiers. In consequence of which Preston who had himself experienced the benefit of it, has introduced the custom of paying his troops by the Flemish tariff, so that their pay exceeds more than one-half that of the Ulster soldiers. With these preparations all at the expense of the Holy See, both the armies prepared to take the field in the summer of '46.

9. The issue was as follows. O'Neill, at the head of his army, which consisted of 5,000 infantry and eight troops of horse, advanced to meet the Scotch at the Castle of Benburb upon the borders of the County of Armagh. The enemy far more powerful than he, had resolved to make a descent upon Leinster and to open a way thither by force. There were nine regiments of infantry and fifteen companies of horse under the command of Robert Monroe a Scotchman, who boasted that he would not only fall upon, but conquer the then disunited Catholics. O'Neill delivered a grave exhortation to his soldiers, and the whole army after receiving the Sacrament, rushed to battle, in which after a doubtful conflict of five hours' duration, they obtained at last a victory. The Scotch retreated, but being followed and surprised in the mountain passes, were killed to the number of 5,000. Monroe fled in disguise; 60 officers remained prisoners, and besides

O'Neill seized all the baggage, 6 field pieces, 40 ensigns and the principal standard of the cavalry, and what was of more importance than all the rest, the enemy were so weakened that never during my time were they able to raise their heads in that province. I should expatiate upon the thanksgivings returned for the aids and benedictions of your Holiness, were it not that at the time a full account of the victory was written, and that at this day, the standards, the visible proofs of our success, are to be seen in the Roman Basilicas. I am however tempted to make one important reflection : that had that army not been ready, and had it not been favoured by God, there would not now be a spark of Catholicism left in Ireland. It appeared so easy for the Scotch to seize Kilkenny where the Supreme Council were assembled unprovided with any defence, that they actually had their quarters assigned them; and as was afterwards discovered by letters found upon the dead, the Marquis of Ormonde with his accustomed artifice had given them free passage through his territory. So signal a victory, however, sufficed only to avert the danger, since the soldiers laden with spoil dispersed in a few days, and thence arose a grave evil, with but little gain. Hence judging from the event, not indeed the highest rule of prudence, but permissible in military affairs ; seeing that the captured cities of Connaught have been restored and the Apostolic money given to the Protestants, I am sorry that I had not devoted all the Papal subsidies to the Ulster army; since if I had still had in hands the sum bestowed upon Preston, Ulster could have been completely freed from the Scotch, and those ports recovered by which they always enter the country. But let this remain for the consideration of those more far-sighted than I am. Meanwhile the Earl of Thomond having taken part with the Parliament in Munster and given up his own Castle of Bunratty ; Donald M'Carthy, Viscount Muskerry brother-in-law of Ormonde, was sent thither, who although of ancient blood was nevertheless by interest head of that which for the future in order to avoid misunderstanding I shall call the Ormonde faction. It was generally believed that the siege of this place would be protracted to the utmost length for some secret purpose of Ormonde's, and perceiving from the infinite number of delays and excuses made from day to day that such would be the case, I determined to go thither in person, just when Preston had entered Connaught and was besieging Roscommon. In the twelve days that I remained at Bunratty the siege was concluded; I provided everything that was needed, lent money to prevent any shadow of an excuse, inspected the batteries myself, and at the conclusion of the siege I had the English ensigns carried through the City of Limerick as a trophy of the Catholic Religion. Almost at the same time, Preston having reduced Roscommon and the neighbouring Castles, proposed to march against Sligo, when letters were brought from the Supreme Council with orders not to proceed further. This news which nearly overwhelmed those who were anxious to pursue the tide of victory, opened the eyes of all to the fatal cause of the dissensions in Ireland, and to the more fatal consequences that must ensue from it.

10. The Ormondists had been already considerably influenced by my repeated declarations, and by the determination of the ecclesiastics not to accept any peace, save one favourable to religion. They saw that my proceedings at Bunratty, and still more the victory gained by O'Neill, would signally increase the authority and number of adherents to the Church. The Papal supplies having been distributed they could hope for no further assistance, and old jealousies reviving, they determined to publish the long concerted peace with the Viceroy, and wrote to Preston, who was in their confidence, not to withdraw from the neighbourhood, in order to prevent any opposition which might be made. I foresaw that some great catastrophe must necessarily take place if I opposed their proceedings,

and yet, unless force was used, how futile must be all objections, nor did I fail to see that in my indecision I was accused of indifference, and blamed by those who had some authority to admonish me. Nevertheless I confess that I neither would nor could make any other determination than not to act on my own responsibility but to convoke in one congregation the whole Church of Ireland; and if there were not full agreement amongst them I resolved not to approve or disapprove of the peace, but to follow in all things the prudent instructions of your Holiness, which, commanded me to abstain from both extremes. Then the convocation in Waterford was called together, and there all the ecclesiastical orders assembled to examine the peace with no less diligence than that used by the Marquis, and his side, to publish it everywhere. Having reviewed in the first session all the articles of which many were prejudicial to religion, and none favourable to its security; all agreed unanimously that the peace was iniquitous. Having given therefore, time to the Council, the better to justify their proceedings or to find a sufficient remedy, and never having received from them, after many meetings, any satisfactory proposals, a resolution was come to that the Council were perjurers, that excommunication should be pronounced, that no one should obey them, and the peace should be totally rejected. The decree was signed by all orders of persons congregated together, even to the Provincial of the Jesuits; and I, believing this uniform agreement was the voice of God, came to the same opinion, but not without declaring before them as an act of prophecy that though I had done it in common with them all, the blame would be specially laid on me. Perhaps there never has been seen in this century a more unexpected change than this which I narrate, and if I were not writing a report to your Holiness, but a history for posterity, I should be so bold as to compare it with the most celebrated events in Europe, and would show

how true it is that every place on the earth may have a history full of interest, though all places may not have the conditions to make it appear equally remarkable. Miserable Ireland always obscured by the grandeur of England, and removed as far from the continent as from the cognizance of Europe, and lost in the rays of the overshadowing kingdom, shows no light which can be seen farther than a taper. The clergy so vilified and hated by the Ormondists, at once became masters of the kingdom. The soldiery and the officers vied in running to do battle for the clergy; some drawn by fear of the censure, some from private hatred to the Council, and some also by the common habit of joining the winning side. And finally, the Council, deprived of all authority by the above resolution, saw that by little and little they were left without supporters, and that all the real power and nominal government of the Confederates had passed to the clergy. On the other side the Marquis set out with great glee from Dublin, entered Kilkenny with much solemnity, and had the peace published by force, but did not succeed in having it done in other places. The herald was immediately commanded to leave Waterford and some other cities. In Limerick a tumult was excited against him in which he lost his life. The Marquis, however, thought to go forward into the Catholic districts to quell these disorders, but he daily saw his auxiliaries, already pledged to the clergy failing him, the friends he thought he could trust opposing him by arms, the people continually going over to the Catholic party, and fearing at last to be caught between them, he resolved to fly. He did not dare to return to Kilkenny, which only eight days before he had entered so triumphantly, and with but three horsemen, gallopping night and day, and filled with rage and confusion he returned to Dublin. Never would a negotiation so long concerted have met with so little success and so little applause had not Preston, who afterwards excused himself on the plea of being so far away that he did not know the state of affairs, on hearing the first news of the peace fired a salvo of artillery, and so caused rejoicings in the air which found no echo on the earth.

11. In the meantime the Catholic congregation had the government in its own hands and provided for everything; three considerations in particular pressed heavily on the clergy. The first was the want of money, which the people supplied with much difficulty and hesitation, and seeing that what your Holiness had given was already exhausted, they determined to supplicate anew for your blessed aid through the Dean of Fermo, who went to Rome to report of the hopes and sudden changes in the kingdom. After this, they had secondly, to discuss what enterprise should be undertaken during the remainder of the autumn; nor was it difficult for me to persuade them that it must be to attempt Dublin. This is the chief city of the kingdom, and the most secure port from which to cross to England; and if the clergy could succeed in gaining possession of it who could say their hope was a rash one, that they might carry our religion beyond the sea after having made it safe in Dublin? Ultimately the resolution was passed with applause, and orders were given to O'Neill that he should re-establish the army, and make a sudden descent into Leinster; and if he had acted with less of his accustomed caution, and pushed his troops unexpectedly against that city, or if better advised had moved across the road taken by the Marquis in his flight, one or other of two things would have followed, either of which would have ended the war; inasmuch as by this foresight the Marquis would have been secured, or by that resolution O'Neill would have entered Dublin with opened gates—so near at times in the various accidents of war does the greatest prosperity border on the most irreparable loss. But it was the third proposal which was the most difficult to decide. It was discussed whether they

ought to claim the aid of General Preston with his army, or commit the enterprise to O'Neill alone. The most sensible men urged what a direful misfortune it was for the kingdom when two of their generals could never come together without some unhappy issue, such as might be especially dreaded between these two; and in the present case Preston having already shown by his rejoicings and salvos what were his feelings towards the peace, to send him in company with O'Neill was to ruin the whole design. But the less resolute, and at their head the Bishop of Ferns, felt differently. To put they said, another general into the Province of Leinster, of which Preston had the command, would be such a flagrant indignity that he would be constrained to unite his army with that of the Marquis and the faction, and thus divide the feelings no less than the force of the kingdom. They esteemed it needful therefore to cajole him with a show of confidence, and free themselves by a little dissimulation from a manifest danger. Precisely at this moment, when Preston saw the inclination of the Provinces towards the Church, he offered himself to the clergy both by letters and messages, excusing under various pretences his proclamation of the peace, and the discharge of those salvos. The second motion then was therefore carried, and in order to unite the armies, and to be able to move them as occasion offered, they returned to Kilkenny. Here again was seen an example of human instability. Only a few days before, a thousand laudatory encomiums were showered on the Marquis in honour of the peace he had brought about; now, the same peace being rejected, the self-same composers and reciters transfer their encomiums to the ecclesiastics; these without a doubt were mockeries not praises, and so much the more to be despised that they were not gifts, but only loans.

12. To relate now the unfortunate result of the enterprise against Dublin, I find myself obliged to premise the origin

of that plot which lasted till my departure from Ireland, because its foundations were laid at this time. Already the ministers of the Queen of England, informed by the Ormondists of my opposition to the concerted peace, and persuading themselves that the clergy could not disagree with me incited Sir Kenelm Digby, her ambassador to your Holiness and at that time a Catholic, in order to make me leave the kingdom, to lay blame on all my proceedings and declare them seditious. The correspondent of Kenelm was George Digby, formerly secretary to the King, who then went to join the Queen in France. On his return to Waterford he had scarcely put his foot on land, than in order to serve his cousin and himself he began zealously to spread among the people that the Most Christian King had declared himself protector of the peace for the benefit of the Catholics; and that the Nuncio would be recalled in a few days to Rome for having transgressed the commands and instructions of your Holiness. No one can testify better than I to the effect produced on the minds of many by these false reports, for well as I knew they were contrary to the truth, and to the pure dictates of my own conscience, I nevertheless experienced those vacillations of mind which a distance of 2,000 miles suggests, when one has no power to clear up the truth by other messengers than the winds. But Digby was more confused than I, when in place of alarming me he heard that the ecclesiastics summoned by me had dismissed the Council and taken the Government upon themselves. He suddenly changed his tone, and agreed with the others outwardly to use fair words, but secretly to tighten the threads of the plot, and hinder by every means in their power the enterprise against Dublin. Preston was therefore ordered to dissemble as much as he could with the new power, but that when he approached Dublin he should see whether O'Neill might not be caught between the two armies. These were in effect the first ideas of the Ormondists, because when the Ulster men were out of the way they reckoned that my removal would necessarily follow.

13. In the interval, the Catholic congregation, before sending forward the armies, had made two important resolutions in order to diminish envy. The first was to form a new Council of three members for each county chosen from the three orders of the kingdom, as had till then been the custom, who with the ecclesiastics would have the direction of affairs. They were for the most part persons of the best intentions and friends of the clergy; and I, as head of these, was President of the whole. I know that this title has been variously spoken of in the different Courts, because the agents of those Crowns, who were then in Ireland, were all inclined to make political reflections on it. Nevertheless I feel certain that as the superior of the ecclesiastics, I could not have refused the title, nor given to another a part of that government which was entirely in their hands. On the other side, it appears to me that every shade of suspicion should have been removed when it was seen that I never acted alone, not even in the very smallest matter, nor signed any order without sufficient signatures from the others, and that in the first Assembly, before the other changes in the Council were published, I publicly renounced the charge confided to me with a solemn protest that I did not make a single claim to jurisdiction in temporal affairs. The second resolution of the ecclesiastics as it was the more difficult, so too if it had been carried out with the requisite firmness might have been the salvation both of religion and of the kingdom. The clergy saw that the sentence they had pronounced had not bowed the pride of the Council, and that they were plotting secretly in every way to produce disaffection in the provinces; hence, to guard against the obstacles which would have been raised to the enterprise, they gave orders to both the Generals to imprison in the

Castle of Kilkenny all those who had been principals in concluding or favouring the peace. They said they were guilty of high treason against God for not having promoted religion according to their oath; and they were also guilty of treason to man, because the legitimate service of the King did not appear in the articles. So, by degrees, they were committed to the castle without any one of them making the smallest resistance, then it was seen how much influence fiction and feeling may have on human actions. Preston was the chief instrument of this capture, and since, between him and Secretary Belling, there were many private grudges, he did not act in any way against his feelings in the imprisonment of the others, because in the custody of this one alone he had a private resentment to satisfy. The imprisonment had in truth more an air of enjoyment than of loss of liberty, as they were already certain that Dublin would not fall, and as every day they received letters which gave hopes of the continuance of the plot they made themselves merry, not grieving at their lot, and at every announcement of similar mischances to others, they drank toasts in glasses of beer to the downfall of religion.

14. To the Generals were assigned two different roads by which they were to meet together in the neighbourhood of Dublin, and each was to recover by himself the places in the possession of the Protestants. Hence, O'Neill beginning in the Queen's County, took Maryborough, and all the places round up to the village or country of Leixlip. But Preston passing by Gorey, having boasted to me that he would take Carlow in a few hours, quite unexpectedly and without consulting the Council, signed a truce and left that fort behind him. Everyone who heard of this act complained loudly, inasmuch as it was a clear enough indication that he was playing double and was in accord with the adversary; so when his actions were minutely observed after he had thrown out continual sneers against O'Neill, and had made

an open declaration that he would not fight against the Marquis, it became sufficiently clear what were the designs he secretly entertained. These two chiefs, so different in their aims, so opposite in their management of affairs, were still more different in their nature. The O'Neill, a man of few words, cautious and phlegmatic in his operations, a great adept in concealing his feelings; the other very subject to fits of anger in which he was so rash and outspoken that he had often to retract with apologies what he had said, so hasty in his warlike enterprises that he was sometimes called inconsiderate. And if O'Neill was held to be the imitator of Fabius, so may Preston be compared to Marcellus. Already the Council saw the effects of having sent this second General on the enterprise, and repented too late of their resolution; they met, therefore, one night in the deepest secrecy, and debated whether, in a case of such decided dereliction of duty, it did not appear necessary to imprison Preston—the votes were divided. Those few who thought of the importance of the negotiation esteemed some great demonstration absolutely necessary, because it was one of those cases which admit of no delay nor hesitation in their execution, since it had come to a point which involved the slavery or the liberation of the whole kingdom; the others laughed the proposal to scorn, and alleging that none but mild measures were customary in this Government, insisted that a measure so severe as this never could succeed. How could they hope to pacify the army, or that the provinces would not resent it? Was it not a lesser evil to tolerate this doubt, than to incur the greater of kindling a conflagration. So without going more deeply into a matter, in many respects so momentous, the Council dissolved. But there were not wanting many who prophesied with sighs that a slaughter of the Confederates was more probable than the taking of Dublin.

15. But above all I was troubled by many anxious

thoughts, because as it was certainly at my persuasion the enterprise was undertaken, so the arrangement and counsels would also be attributed to me; and if the result should be unfortunate, what blame might not fall upon me! Preston had already moved forward and had chosen his quarters five miles from Dublin. At the same place and on the same day arrived as concerted John Ulick de Burgh, Marquis of Clanricarde, President of Connaught, who hitherto holding himself neutral in act had yet always openly favoured the Marquis' party, and had now come to carry out with Preston the scheme which they had concocted together in Connaught. Later, and always doubtful of his own safety came O'Neill behind. Amid so many clouds, suspicions, and plots I determined to fear nothing, unless our two armies should come to blows. Not to gain Dublin would be a loss which might be repaired, how much greater would be the extermination of the Catholic forces. Against the opinion of many and the protest of O'Neill, I went however to Preston's quarters, and with an appearance of confidence put myself into his hands, and made the Council come there too. It might appear foolhardiness when I found myself with my single carriage on the plains of Dublin, when a few horsemen on the highway might have carried me off to the Marquis, but I weighed this danger with my wish to prevent the other and greater. It is quite certain that when Preston heard of my arrival he changed countenance, and was heard to say that I had spoilt his plans; now, since he and others tried to hinder the enterprise in every possible way, it may be safely believed that the interrupted design was that which had been concocted between him and Clanricarde against O'Neill in Connaught. And in truth I have fully proved that Preston shrank from openly breaking faith and attacking the Ulster men whilst I, the peacemaker and mediator between all was in the midst of his forces; because it was evident to me that when persons in power had proposed to him to imprison the Bishop of Clogher, and Nicholas Plunket had come to me at my quarters, Preston refused to permit it, though perhaps he was wanting in honour in not having warned me of the scheme. And I can the more readily believe this of him, if it be true as was currently said that the son of Kenelm Digby, although a Catholic like his father, had offered to take charge of my person in Dublin; of which however I have no greater proof than the prevalence of the reports and the quality of the man. Then every excuse for coming to civil war being taken from the Ormondists, the liberation of Dublin became our sole thought; to this all our strength and our efforts tended. As people every day passed to and fro between Dublin and Lucan (so this district was called), no resolution could be framed by our party without the Marquis at once hearing of it. Clanricarde did nothing but make proposals to the Council and to me of new terms and conditions. Difficulties so continually increased in our camp that already with these protracted and artful hindrances the winter was at hand. But more than all, the enterprise was ruined by a report industriously spread and made to appear probable by various circumstances. It was rumoured in both armies that some Parliamentary ships had arrived in Dublin, and that the Marquis in despair of the success of the peace, was in treaty to give up the city into their hands; and would only keep these people so long at anchor, as to see if the Catholics would come to any agreement; if this was refused, the English would disembark according to the conditions of their agreement with the Viceroy. And one day when the Council urgent to proceed were all assembled to debate on it, some one, I do not know who, knocked at the door, Preston rose quickly to open it, had a few words outside from him, returned breathless, saying that the English were already in Dublin. In a moment O'Neill and the others rose from their seats as if suddenly attacked by a serpent, and every man thinking only of himself fled from his companions. The generals by firing a cannon gave the signal that every one should return to his post, and the Council abandoning themselves to fear, early in the morning mounted their horses, set off for Kilkenny, and never drew bridle till like fugitives or as one who has an enemy at his back, they saw themselves within our quarters.

16. Thus was the enterprise overthrown, and so the Ormonde faction triumphed through these same dissensions. I could not bear to depart in the way the others had done, and determined to act with great dignity and without showing any fear. I therefore remained three days at Lucan, during which time Clanricarde never ceased to propose new terms to me. The principal one was to induce Ormonde to be satisfied with receiving Catholic garrisons as well into Dublin as into the rest of the districts which were held for the King. And in fact there was a secret compact in writing between the Viceroy and the factionists which admitted Preston's people under that compact into those places, where they could unite with the friends of the Marquis and all combine together to constrain the Council to accept the peace, at least with the additions proposed by Clanricarde. I gave my promise and remitted the determination to the Council, though Clanricarde wrote to me that they would be content with my consent only, perhaps to make Preston's action more excusable. At last, to show that I wished for some settlement I proposed that they should add to the articles one, for the exercise of religion in Dublin as in the other districts; and the Marquis not choosing to mention it, I turned my back on them and returned to Kilkenny. Then it was evident how little the satisfaction of the Nuncio imported to the Ormondists, since after my departure they pushed forward the treaty in every possible way, and Preston as it had been concerted came with his people two miles nearer to Dublin. Some differences arising afterwards

on the placing of the garrisons Preston fell into a passion; and already inclined to change owing to some letters from the Council, retired with his men beyond the river and drew near to Kilkenny. But even now he did not keep himself quiet, but even while showing that he was faithful to the Confederates, continued in every way his former practices and correspondences and involved everything in uncertainty and confusion. At last I took up the pen, and writing as to a man of a delicate conscience I touched first on some spiritual points, then begging him to confide to me the nature of his obligations with Clanricarde, I reprimanded him because by not telling the truth he kept the country in a state of fear and jealousy, where respect for religion only should reign. In his answer he declared himself vanquished; made in Kilkenny a free renunciation of all our adversaries' practices, and together with O'Neill signed a paper which was left in my keeping in which they promised amity and fidelity to each other, and that they would not attempt any affair without obtaining my consent first. Preston in order to complete this fully, wished to write to excuse himself to Clanricarde, at this moment however a letter arrived from the Marquis appointing a place of meeting with the Prestonians, and saying that he had come out with the vanguard to await him at the place. There he received and read the letter, and in it this new change of Preston's, whereupon after recovering from his astonishment, he broke out into curses against him, and returned with his troops to Dublin.

17. In the meantime at Kilkenny the Bishop of Ferns and Nicholas Plunket proposed two resolutions which, I venture to say were the cause of all the misfortunes which followed. These two gentlemen, known by your Holiness (as they have been themselves at your feet) to be men of singular ability, have always been advocates of equality for all, they appeared equally to sympathize with the old party

and the new, and though they have at times been suspected by both, they always appear to have kept a fair mean between the two; good Catholics certainly, but at the same time not bad politicians. In the first place, they recommended that a General Assembly should be called together of all the orders of the kingdom; they thought in this way to remove the odium which had been excited against the ecclesiastics, because everyone would see that they were willing to submit themselves to a higher authority. And as the Confederation were on the point of passing most important measures, it appeared to them that they would be much more successful, and would receive a more ready obedience if they were concerted in common by all, than if they proceeded from a magistrate elected exclusively by the clergy. On the contrary, many said that though it was customary to call together the Assembly every year, yet that such a step appeared by no means advisable at such a moment. Up to the present time the clergy had drawn upon themselves both calumny and envy, but had not attained sufficient power to despise them. The Ormonde party had no other object than to recover their authority, and they could not better attain it than by means of a General Assembly, in which they had always had a majority of votes. What else then could be expected but a second humiliation of the clergy, and one much greater than the first, since it is generally the second fall which is the more fatal. But Plunket and the Bishop gave still more weight to these reasons by the second measure they proposed; that those who were still in prison should be liberated, and although it was given out that this was only done in order to place them in different prisons so that they might not be able to act together, it soon appeared that this idea had no foundation either in thought or deed, since they all remained in Kilkenny where they held meetings every day, and very soon obtained permission to appear in the Assembly under pretext of desiring to clear themselves from the charges brought against them. Here they had such efficient assistance that their errors were condoned under various pretences, and their justification admitted; amongst them that of Richard Belling was the most remarkable; he deposed that he had reported to your Holiness all the conditions of the rejected peace, and that it was by the express desire of your Holiness that he had given his consent—so shameless is the audacity of an obstinate and irreverent mind. Little now was wanting to enable the clergy to foresee the fall of the ecclesiastical party. Nevertheless, as it still retained its energy, and wished to preserve its honour, it insisted in spite of prolonged opposition that the peace which it had condemned should be condemned by all the orders, and that the new governing body should be composed for the most part of persons well affected to the Church. Nevertheless, Plunket consented that Viscount Muskerry should be nominated, a brother-in-law as I have mentioned of Ormonde, and always the head of his faction. The men who had been liberated from prison triumphant by their own arts, and exultant at having defeated those of the other party, went about publicly deriding both the acts and the persons of the clergy, and secretly concocted a plot against them. Belling, unable to control his passion, said to me in a tone full of bitterness and venom, that I should soon find out on whose head the tempest would fall.

18. In the midst of these disturbances commenced the year 1647, so fatal to Ireland, as in it Dublin fell into the hands of the Parliament, and the Confederation sustained two disastrous defeats which led to the last disputed truce. The members of the Council who had been liberated from prison recovered their power, and the plot was matured against the Ulster army and the Church. I shall speak of all these events, but with greater brevity, because their bearing and details have been already given at full length

in another memoir addressed to your Holiness. I have given there details of the birth, education, and character of the Marquis of Ormonde; I mentioned that he was brought up a Catholic till the age of twelve years, that he then went to England and was placed under the care of the heretical Archbishop of Canterbury, that though a man of extraordinary sagacity and of attractive manners, he is on the other hand so proud and haughty, that though condescending to all who are beneath him he shrinks from their companionship with horror. During the parleys held at Dublin he was at first very indignant at the fickleness of Preston; and then but ill satisfied with the new Council of the Confederates, who were for the most part the friends of the clergy. In the winter he endeavoured to establish himself in the centre of the country, in order to get possession of the fortress of Athlone, which is the only pass into Connaught, and to improve his position in a thousand different ways, but as the officials throughout the country had been chosen by the clergy none of his designs succeeded. Then moved by anger and impatient of the want of money, which in the first instance had been secretly supplied by the Ormonde confederacy out of their own incomes, he began to treat with the English, and ceded Dublin to them for £13,000. Nothing in the world ever supplied matter for such a variety of opinions as this surprising intelligence. The wisest judges of public events could not sufficiently blame the treachery of this man, who whilst the King was kept a prisoner had given up the keys of Ireland to the enemies of His Majesty, and opened a path for the invasion of the Parliamentary troops. And as they could not discover any satisfactory reason to account for it they inferred rather hastily that he was in league with the Parliament, and had persuaded the Queen (who as they insisted had given her consent) to appease the English by this demonstration, and soften their feelings against the person of her husband. But it is incredible in how many ways the Ormondists excused the perfidy of this action; they believed they had made a sufficient defence when they asserted that the Catholics had driven the Marquis to desperation by refusing the peace, and that therefore he was perfectly justified in using any means in his power. As if the crime of treason could be excused by an access of passion, or as if men were bound to defend the injustice and absurdity of actions which are suggested by blind anger. However this may be, as soon as the English had entered Dublin and the Castle had been consigned to them, the Marquis embarked on board ship on 24th July and set sail for England. It is reported that when at a little distance from the port he heaved a sigh as he looked back at the city, like Hannibal when recalled to Carthage, and gave utterance to the hope that he might be destined to return to the country in such force as to efface the shame of having left it a beggar!

19. In the meantime the Council had not lost time, but had furnished three armies, one for Leinster under Preston, one for Connaught under O'Neill, and the third for Munster under Viscount Muskerry. To begin with this last, it may be observed that in the beginning of the campaign of this year, Baron Inchiquin who held in Munster the lands taken by the Parliament, sallied out unexpectedly, took without any resistance first Capoquin, then Dungarvan, a seaport near Youghal, and while all good people grieved for these losses, everyone suspected that there had been some secret intelligence in the matter. The Earl of Glamorgan already mentioned was General in Munster, and had been sent to that province by the congregation of the clergy; he daily demanded money and permission to go out into the open country, but never received any conclusive answer. Hence the Baron marched in every direction without any obstacle, and the suspicion generally entertained gradually grew stronger. Ultimately a circumstance occurred which almost

converted this suspicion into certainty. One day during the absence of the Earl the larger part of his army were seen to go over to Muskerry, and men were posted on the road to prevent the Earl from returning to resume his command. I never could discover if the Council really felt for this base action the abhorrence it deserved; or whether they wished by a double artifice to signify their secret approval; at first in a fit of indignation they declared the Viscount guilty of rebellion, and sent a messenger to him to convey their sentiments, but then at the end of two days they recalled their sentence. This is certain that when Muskerry was seen to return to political affairs, and to yield the military command to Viscount Taaffe of Connaught, it was generally believed that it had been the design of the Council to provide in Munster a colleague for Inchiquin, so as later with the assistance of both to carry to a successful termination the plot they had concocted.

20. This unfortunate affair had only just happened when Preston with a very fine army of 6,000 infantry and 1,000 horse marched against the Parliamentary forces in Leinster. He was followed in large numbers by all the Ormondists in the province, attracted by a vain boast that Dublin would be taken with the same facility with which it had been lost; they flattered themselves that they would be able to restore Dublin to the Marquis, and persuade him to return to Ireland. Preston who was already bragging of his victory, made an attempt to surprise Trim, but hearing that the enemy had shown themselves he turned back. It is the universal belief that on this occasion the General placed the cavalry in such a position that it was impossible for them to manœuvre, or that when he had submitted his fate to the arbitrament of battle, he so completely lost his head that he could not make any sudden plan or form any resolution. The enemy reinforced in the night with the greatest secrecy by more than a thousand Scots from Ulster, advanced and

began the attack. The army was led by Michael Jones an Independent, who then and during the remainder of my mission always commanded in Dublin (as I then wrote at greater length). On hearing the first shots the Catholic cavalry, composed entirely of the nobles, took to flight, but the infantry fighting bravely attacked in flank and made a great slaughter; at length seeing themselves abandoned by the cavalry, and unable to continue the defence, they were cut to pieces; 3,000 men were killed on our side; 1,500 on the heretic. All the baggage, booty, and many barrels of powder, together with Preston's portfolio, remained in the power of the Parliament. Very various were the judgments passed on this unhappy event. Many wept for the disaster of the Confederation, now so fallen from its early glory, and many recognised the justice of God, which had denied the victory to those who only desired it to call back a rebel.

21. A different but not more fortunate result attended the expedition of O'Neill into Connaught. I had in some sort the care of it, and was then in that province. I proposed that they should recover Sligo situated on the sea and on the confines, and therefore very valuable to Connaught. From this place they could pass into Ulster, and attempting the strong Castle of Enniskillen free from the hands of the heretics the so much celebrated purgatory of St. Patrick. As prayers have been offered up in this deep cave from time immemorial, so the date of their commencement is uncertain. It is known that the saint chose this place for his devotions in retirement, and the revelations which it pleased God to communicate to him have been believed, and perhaps proved by posterity. At present the Calvinists in their rage, by levelling the ground have filled up the cavity, and as one can scarce discover any vestiges of the place, so they endeavour to extinguish also the memory of the fact. It appeared to me that this equalled any of the most glorious of Apostolic missions, and that I should have in some measure fulfilled

my career, if in this place covered as much by the insults as by the earth thrown on it by the Puritans, it had been granted to me again to plant there the Cross. But I was not worthy of seeing this hope carried into execution, the want and tardy supply of money entirely ruined the design. Great dissensions arose between the General and the persons deputed to provide for the army; these complaining that O'Neill artfully delayed to advance, and he, that they never sent him succours in time. And in truth O'Neill did give cause of suspicion that he delayed, and that he did wish to remove to a distance for some purpose of his own, perhaps hoping that in Leinster the enterprise against Dublin might not succeed, and that his assistance might be necessary, since by retaining and fortifying the places he had taken the year before he showed either his ardent desire to govern in Leinster as was said to prolong his authority, or to attempt Dublin again; an enterprise the glory of which he was very unwilling to leave to Preston. Nor were we deceived in the sequel. The army wearied by the delay and with the disputes with the deputies, was on the point of disbanding, when news arrived of the rout of Preston, and by the same advices the Council called upon O'Neill to come in person to their succour. It is impossible to describe the glee of O'Neill on receiving this news; he made instantly a descent into Leinster amid the acclamations of the frightened inhabitants, placed himself not far from Trim, and there never moving for four months he hindered every attempt of the enemy to advance. This mode of acting was believed to be by those who understand warfare the saving of the Kingdom under the circumstances, because the English victorious and daring would have advanced in security to Kilkenny, if this Fabius by taking up his position amongst the bogs and dykes had not demonstrated how often patient endurance triumphs over the sword.

22. I do not know how to describe the irritation of the

adverse party at this conduct of O'Neill's. They could not endure that he should have had so much to do with the safety of the Kingdom, and that he should commonly be called the Liberator. And the Bishop of Ferns who had gone in person into Connaught to invite him, was called to account for it by the Secret Council; on which he wrote me letters full of grave complaints. On this account George Digby, who had remained in Ireland after the departure of the Marquis, went himself and sent in all directions to ask for support, and pointed out to everyone that it was necessary to humble O'Neill and to send away the Nuncio who patronized him; otherwise they never could have quiet, the Marquis would never return and peace would never be re-established. They made up a bundle of calumnies mixed with a few grains of truth, so as to produce the greater irritation. A few months before by means of an admirable stratagem, the fortress of Athlone had been taken from the Viscount Castlemaine and had come into the possession of the Clergy. In order to recover it, the Viscount declared himself a Catholic, and the Catholic congregation thought fit to order the restitution of it. But O'Neill encouraged the commander of the place to retain it for several months against the orders also of the succeeding Assembly, and had prevented him from obeying the commands of any other person; so that the key of all the four provinces might not fall into the hands of the Ormondists. It cannot be denied that during the whole war the Ulster soldiery had treated the people with such harshness, that they had excited a very bitter hatred against them, and in this matter it appeared that the General was wanting in his duty, as there was reason to suspect that he did not punish the guilty, and for no other reason than that he was in fear of losing his followers. "What then is wanting," said many, "to the absolute power of O'Neill? It is not necessary to wait for more indications of his perfidy, since he is already a tyrant of the people, disobedient to the Council, and now wishes to make himself master of this fortress." I was so well aware of the strong feeling both against O'Neill and myself, that I wrote my opinion to your Holiness that very September; and from that day to this fresh proofs of it have been constantly manifested. Baron Inchiquin already inclining to his sixth change of sides, was about to leave the Parliament and return to the Party of the King. The Ormondists considered that to gain over the Baron would materially further their designs of recalling the Marquis and humbling O'Neill, since they would have his army in addition to their own, and the ports of Munster would be at their common disposition. But to give an air of decency to this alliance, it was needful to prove to the world that it was absolutely necessary to make it. With this object in view and unable to devise a better plan, they allowed the Baron to gain the upper hand in Munster, and suffered the Catholics to sustain some defeats; then exaggerating the difficulty of resisting two enemies they alleged it was necessary to unite themselves with one. It was not long before the people had to pay with their blood for this determination of their Chiefs. The Baron having gained by treachery the fortress of Cahir, ravaged without obstacle the neighbouring counties laying the country under contribution; took Cashel by storm, and so little restrained the cruelty of his soldiery, that after they had taken the celebrated Temple of St. Patrick, where as in the highest spot the helpless had taken refuge, savagely slew with barbarous sacrilege the priests, and even the women who were embracing the statue of the Saint. And Muskerry who was in the province, though he was always going backwards and forwards and manœuvring without any effect, in the end allowed the enemy to load themselves with booty and return without any sign of fear to their quarters. This deed was so much blamed, that it seemed fitting to the Council in order to recover their credit to order the army to retire, and to give the command of it to Taaffe whom I mentioned before. But though the men were changed the designs remained the same. On 13th November followed another Battle in the County of Cork. We had 6,000 infantry and 1,200 cavalry, the Baron had 5,000 infantry and 1,300 horse, the right wing of the Catholics in front of which was placed Alexander Macdonnell the Lieutenant of Taaffe, charged so gallantly the left wing of the Baron where he had placed his bravest men, that in a very short time they put 2,000 to the sword and believing that the other wing had also been victorious, the soldiers were standing round the captured cannon and Macdonnell at a little distance from his men. But on the left wing our men fled so basely, that many of them were very soon slain; Inchiquin had time to return, and finding his enemies dispersed and secure, he cut 1,700 of them to pieces, but his own men suffered severely. Our troops lost all the cannon they had taken, and the poor Alexander when bravely defending himself against the crowd which surrounded him, even after he had spoken of surrendering and had already given up his sword, was treacherously wounded in the back, and fell dead upon the spot. Thus, with the country divided among these miserable factions, ended the year 1647, and began as usual the meeting of the General Assembly.

23. There was no one amongst the most sagacious who did not foresee in this Assembly the utter and total ruin of the Confederation. The Ormondists never made greater exertions to secure the elections both in boroughs and counties of members whose votes were wholly at their disposition; when the Assembly was full of their adherents it was easy to make it appear that the Kingdom was reduced to the utmost need through the misfortunes they had suffered, and that it was unable to sustain so many wars. They next proceeded to consider the remedies, they agreed that deputies should be sent to the Queen of England and the Prince of Wales, to arrange some method of resuscitating the peace without sacrificing the interests of Religion; and to despatch

others to your Holiness and to the two Kings, to ask for assistance. No one spoke of the return of the Viceroy, on the contrary many protested that they would never permit it. The election of the deputies was managed most ingeniously; and all suspected persons were obliged to leave the Kingdom that they might not oppose the measures which were contemplated. With the same object the Bishop of Ferns and Plunket were despatched to Rome, as they had recommended O'Neill's march into Leinster and for this reason were too much inclined to his side. Muskerry and Dr. Brown with a full knowledge of all the secrets were sent to France: and it was intended to add to them the Bishop of Clogher, a man of great capacity, the chosen friend of O'Neill and exercising as it was supposed a great influence over his actions. But the Bishop being aware of the purpose for which this honour was thrust upon him, showed such decided opposition, that in spite of their threats he was allowed to remain in the Island. Ultimately the Marquis of Antrim was sent in his place, also a native of Ulster, remarkable equally for the goodness of his intentions, and his want of firmness in action; then too he was out of heart because he saw that his vote would serve to no good purpose since according to their instructions the opinion of two was to be decisive. But Muskerry and Brown besides the published articles had secret instructions to negotiate in France for the return of the Marquis. The Marquis himself was well aware of all that had taken place, had gone from England with only two followers to the Most Christian Court, and there persuaded his Queen and possibly also the Ministers of France, that if he returned to Ireland and resumed his office and if the Nuncio of the Pope were dismissed, every obstacle to the reception of Her Majesty or the Prince in the Kingdom of Ireland would be removed. The Queen seeing every day less hope of recovering England and dreading to trust herself in Scotland where her husband had been sôld, had no stronger desire than that for repose and the refuge which was thus offered her in Ireland. So they went on by little and little to mature their designs; one of them I was fully convinced was still to keep your Holiness' money in their hands; a sight of which I had not had for fourteen months; I therefore obtained a copy of the instructions given to the Deputies to Rome, in which it was laid down that if they should obtain any sum of money they should entreat that it might be consigned to them and not to the Nuncio,—upon this I need not enlarge, because succeeding events prove it sufficiently. The Assembly then finished off with the most iniquitous resolution that had ever been heard of in my time. They proceeded to the election of the Council; the Ormondists wished for all those who had formerly been imprisoned, and as much for the exclusion of the clergy: I took a middle course, and proposed to choose some of each party; and the proposal appearing not unfair, the conspirators broached the following and most prejudicial new one. They should nominate 48 supernumeraries, all of their faction, whom they could call on to supply the place of any absent members of Council. Well knowing that if they declared their covert designs, the well intentioned would withdraw from the band, and they would thereby have a minority of votes, they found means to keep themselves in their favour. I do not know how to excuse the Bishop of Ferns in this matter, since he, against the clearest protest of the other Bishops in congregation, either in the confusion of affairs, or that he did not apprehend or would not apprehend the danger to Religion, fell into the designs of the Committee, signed the decree, and so remained guilty of the coming misfortunes. It thus often happens that in the most important affairs some blameworthy weakness leads men to take what they think is a middle course, but which almost always plunges them inevitably and to their cost into extremes.

24. But Baron Inchiquin being privy to these plots, knowing the objects they wished to accomplish, and being possibly impatient that matters were progressing so slowly, advanced in the month of February with 1,200 infantry and a mere handful of horse, and occupied once more the district held by the Confederates. His soldiers were in such a wretched plight that it was generally supposed that he had been driven to this step by the urgent want of provisions and forage. But when, after gradually approaching Kilkenny, he marched up to the walls and demanded money, to the great terror of all who were not in the secret, there were others who felt confident that the whole affair was preconcerted in order to give the Catholics a more plausible excuse for forming an alliance with him. He had previously written to warn the Parliament that, if within so many days, they did not supply him with men and money he should be constrained to make terms with the Catholics, whom, to keep up appearances, he called in the same letter rebels. What next? The Baron had scarcely exacted a contribution from the county of Kilkenny and returned to Cork when he announced in a public edict that he had gone over to the party of the King; the new Council were loud in their applause, as if their fortunes were suddenly changed; the Ormondists gave out that they had made an important acquisition, and that the war was already at an end. They pretended nevertheless that they wished to treat with him about a truce (which was all the while secretly concluded), in order that they might have his aid in the attack upon Dublin. But all these falsehoods were superfluous, as the Baron wrote letters to all his partisans, in which he announced that the whole kingdom was willing to consent to the peace about to be concluded, and that it would therefore be advisable to put down O'Neill and the Nuncio, who stood alone in persistently rejecting it. Thus the plots were dis-

covered which had previously been carried on in secret, and I learnt more from one letter of the enemy than from the endless talk and writing of those who were about me.

25. I spent nearly the whole summer in visiting the Catholic cities, celebrating services in them, and introducing reforms in conformity with the Roman ritual; and, among them all, the only two I should place in the front rank for the reverence they showed towards the Holy See, are Waterford in Leinster and Galway in Connaught. I then proceeded to Waterford in order that I might witness the embarkation of the Commissioners who were sent to Rome, and also that I might be in the neighbourhood when the Dean of Fermo should arrive. It was on the 12th of March that he landed at last at Duncannon after encountering so many obstacles, and being so many months delayed. Infinite were the discussions and designs to which his arrival gave rise. He had previously mentioned in his letters that he was bringing with him the sword of the former Earl of Tyrone, which was given to him in Rome by Luke Wadding, and that, in conformity with his directions, he intended to consign it to O'Neill, as the descendant of the said Earl. The Dean had scarcely disembarked when the certain assurance that he had actually brought this sword with him produced among the Ormondists the most extraordinary ferment. Now they cried, the secret designs of O'Neill have come at last to light; he means to seize the kingdom for himself, and he therefore desires to obtain the insignia of royalty from the Roman Pontiff. All eyes they said would now be opened, and all would resist these treacherous designs hid under the cloak of religion. But with regard to the money which your Holiness had sent, the object of these same gentlemen was nevertheless, by some means or other, to get it into their own hands. The moment, therefore, that Inchiquin's change was made public the Council began to pray that I would return to Kilkenny, in order that they

might enter into a truce with him, to which I could give my consent. I being aware that the matter was already as good as settled, and that it was intended to serve as the means of bringing back the Marquis of Ormonde and depriving O'Neill of his army, decided at first that I would not go back, but would rather remain in a place where I should have been able to deliberate on any measure the change of circumstances might suggest. But when these letters and invitations were repeated again and again, and the Council declared in one of them that nothing should be done which was not satisfactory to me, I felt unwilling to abandon in their need so large a number of my friends, or to give them any reason to complain of my timidity. I therefore returned to Kilkenny, but I immediately perceived that I had left the freedom of a harbour to enter within the narrow limits of a prison. I saw that escape was no longer possible, if the Council did not choose to permit it. Threats on every hand were not wanting, and a Carmelite came to inform me that he had heard, under the seal, there was a plot to take away my life. It now seemed to me most fitting to follow in this second controversy precisely the same course which was held in the first. Then it was intended to accept a peace to the prejudice of religion, now to accept a truce with precisely the same peril; then the Council were about to break through their oaths and abandon their cause, now they were bent on doing the same; then they were about to give up the prosecution of the war without any sufficient cause, and merely for political reasons; in the present circumstances the same objections would apply with even greater force. I summoned therefore, as I did before, all the Bishops who were able to be present, and in the first congregation fourteen assembled to meet me.

26. In this congregation we first read and examined those articles of the truce which had then been noised abroad, because the secret articles which were concerted between

the parties were not communicated to anyone. In these public articles we noted all those iniquities on which I dilated at the time, and of which I sent copies to your Holiness. We perceived that the real object in view was not so much a truce, which properly speaking is designed to let things remain *in statu quo*, as a scheme to weaken the Catholics and to give more power to the Baron. To him they gave unlimited power, they considerably increased the district under his command, and they granted to him, by an intolerable stretch of their authority, the right to exact the ecclesiastical tithes as his recompense. But besides the purpose I have mentioned it was my wish to describe to them at length the present state of the kingdom, in order that all might clearly see that so far as the Confederation were concerned there was really no need of a truce, in which case even if there were no other reasons, the conclusion of a truce with the heretics was of itself unlawful. All were perfectly convinced that the army under Jones in Dublin, which had been watching O'Neill the whole summer and had thus lost considerably in strength, could not at that moment amount to 3,000 men all told ; and that the regiments under Preston were far more than sufficient to hold them completely in check. That in Connaught and Ulster the Scotch could do nothing but make useless forays : that the Baron in Munster had only 3,000 infantry who received no pay and were all but naked, so that O'Neill's army which was possibly 6,000 strong might disperse them in a few days ; this army moreover, to remove all excuse, I offered to pay with the money of your Holiness, and promised also to take on my own shoulders the whole weight of Munster, so that it would not cost the Confederacy a farthing. The Bishops applauded this speech and when the votes were taken, all of one accord condemned the treaty as iniquitous : even the Archbishop of Tuam, who alone appeared in the first instance disposed to go against me, when he heard me offer your Holiness' money took the pen and signed with the others, declaring it was the money only which moved him to do it. All being resolved to proceed in the same manner as when the peace was rejected, delegated the authority to proceed to the censure, if, as on the first occasion, this should prove to be necessary; and in case obstacles should arise, they also granted authority to sub-delegate. What excitement was caused by the publication of this declaration, how the Ormondists were irritated, into what artifices what malignity they were hurried, it might have tasked my pen to describe, if the notoriety of the facts had not made the whole narrative familiar to everyone.

27. The Ormondists believing that they had me already in their hands endeavoured to accomplish three objects. The first was to make a written compact immediately with Inchiquin, the second to delude the clergy into the belief they were willing to come to terms which would give satisfaction to both parties, the third to get together with all possible speed the army of Preston, so that in conjunction with that under Inchiquin it might march against O'Neill. But the first and third of these resolutions were kept secret, the second only was allowed to transpire. While, however, we were in treaty I received information that Commissioners had already been sent secretly to the Baron, and that all the proposals put forward were a sham. I determined therefore to learn the whole truth from the Bishop of Limerick, one of the Council, who rather than be excluded from all participation in their power, had consented to share in their deliberations and assist in carrying out their plans. When I adjured him by the authority I held he immediately confessed to me the whole. It now seemed to me high time to consult for the safety of my own person and to determine on flight. I found myself in a city in which there were 300 cavalry armed; I had myself seen them enter with Viscount Mountgarret at their head, I knew that the men in power,

who were ill-affected towards me would in a few days be supported by the army of a heretic, who had not only assumed the command of the Confederacy, but had written circular letters in which he had declared himself against me. What security then could I hope for, what ill-treatment was there which I had not every reason to expect? On the following morning, therefore, I directed that my litter should be taken outside and within a short distance of the walls. I with only two attendants passed through the garden of the house which I occupied, mounted the ramparts, descended at a gate where there was little passing, and pushed on at a good pace to Maryborough. Here some Bishops came to visit me, and O'Neill who was on the spot, quite unconscious of the plot which was being concocted against him, remained there also, waiting like me, the issue of these new changes.

28. Those who happened to be then in Kilkenny, and are now at this Court can bear witness to the consternation into which all were thrown by my unexpected departure. Men walked about with terror in their faces, and nothing was seen or heard but small groups talking in whispers. Nor have I ever been able to believe that all this commotion was occasioned merely by the fear that I might move O'Neill to march against them, because at this time O'Neill had not collected more than 700 infantry, and if he had attempted to get the rest together the conspirators were very well aware that the forces of Preston would have been beforehand with him. I am therefore constrained to believe that all the ferment arose from the discovery that I had escaped from their hands, and that they were afraid that their designs not only on my money but on my person would be thus entirely frustrated. Nor did I change my opinion when I saw that in all the subsequent discussions my return to Kilkenny was always placed at the head of the list, as the one and only cure for all divisions; and that up to the time when I established myself in Galway, and when all hope of

a compromise was entirely at an end, the Bishop of Limerick in his letter and Father Malone the Jesuit by word of mouth, never ceased to sing me the same song, and to urge my return. It was not long before the Council were guilty of an act which sufficiently explained the object of all this importunity; when the advances I have mentioned were met by a negative they put the Dean of Fermo in prison; not being able to catch the Nuncio by fair means they determined to seize his minister by force. Thinking it was now advisable to leave Maryborough I proposed to proceed to Galway as I thought it necessary to place myself near the sea, so that in case of any disaster I might be able to set sail at once, and I knew I could depend as well on the security of the port as on the kindly feeling of the citizens. I confess that when I considered the high office which I held there was something in the very site of Galway which allured me, placed as it is on the farthest shore of Ireland, that is at the very edge of the old world, I flattered myself that while I laboured and strove there for the Catholic religion I should make it serve both as an outwork to Europe and an invitation to America. But when I was on the point of setting out, a deputation arrived from the Council; their pretext was to invite me to return, and to make new proposals with regard to the truce; but their real object was to gain more time for Preston, who was preparing to take the field. Twelve days they detained me in Maryborough with the hope of carrying through this new negotiation. I, for my part, in order to show I had every disposition to treat, and in order to save, for the sake of religion, at least the last subsidy which they held in their hands, gave my consent that O'Neill should propose such conditions as he thought necessary for his own safety and that of his followers, on the understanding that if they were granted the truce should be allowed to hold good. The answer which they sent spoke rather through the musket than the gun; for the very same evening that it reached us and was pronounced to be a mere mockery, Preston left Carlow by the Kilkenny road and marched towards Birr. The first news of this movement was brought by one of my household, who on his way from Kilkenny saw the army on its march, and with the exaggeration which is usual in such cases reported it was 10,000 strong. I observed that O'Neill first looked astonished, and then grew very pale, because as I said before he had not collected more than from seven to eight hundred of his men, though these had the name and did the duty of a much larger force. It gives me, I confess, no little pleasure when I find even in profane authors a recognition of the truth of this aphorism, that it is not possible to discover an adequate reason for the course of events in this world without a constant reference to the interposition of Providence. If this army of Preston's had but come direct to Maryborough, or had not marched on Birr, only four miles distant, they would have caught O'Neill and me unprepared, and found the place so weak that the faction might have settled all differences in their own fashion, and seen their artifice triumphant. But Preston wished first of all to put himself in a position to increase his own army with the reinforcement under Inchiquin. He supposed possibly that O'Neill was in force, misled by the same rumours which had imposed upon us. So true is it that in war it is often more important to know your enemy's strength than to defeat him, and thus that intellect does far more than force.

29. Seeing that both our forces and our prospects were reduced within such narrow limits, I confined myself in the consultation I held with O'Neill and the Bishops to discussing the best mode of escaping the danger that was imminent. When I withdrew to the centre of the island I lost the power of leaving it at pleasure, since if I had attempted to return from Maryborough to Waterford, I should have thrown myself into the very jaws of my persecutors. Nor

do I wish to deny that after the Dean arrived in Waterford I had the greatest desire to return to Italy with him. I saw even then that things were rapidly falling under the yoke of heresy; the men in power had declared against me; the patronage of the Holy See was rejected with contempt, and the rival factions were at daggers drawn, so that it is no wonder that the weakness of the flesh and those first impulses which even the weight of an Apostolic mission cannot always suppress, should have persuaded me to depart. But when my purpose was known, I have no tongue to describe the lamentations of the Catholic party, which believed I was about to abandon it. O'Neill sent a monk now in Rome to plead, as he did with the tears in his eyes, that the unvarying service which he and his forefathers had rendered to the Catholic Religion, without regard to life or fortune, deserved a better reward than to be abandoned at the very moment when he was nearly overpowered by his enemies. All his followers and the greater number of the Bishops prayed upon their knees that I would not desert so many of my children, and that if I had no regard to my own honour, I would at least consider that of the Holy See, to whose eternal reproach it would be said that after sending aids for the support of religion, it had suddenly withdrawn them alarmed by the vaguest and most shadowy of rumours. These reasons moved me to go forward with my enterprise. How then could I recur at Maryborough to the design I then rejected? The aspect of affairs was now materially changed, I was no longer able to escape, and that same O'Neill who had then appealed to me by letter now urged me in person, ready then, as ever, to risk everything he had in the world for the Catholic cause. All therefore were of opinion that I ought to make use of the authority delegated to me by the Bishops convoked at Kilkenny, and in view of the injustice of the truce, should proceed to the censure. Everyone remembered the effect it had produced in the army at the time the first peace was rejected;

and even if exactly the same result did not follow now, all hoped it would at least check, if it did not entirely put an end to the violence of the present persecution. I, for my part, though assured of the justice of the cause, could nevertheless not have felt greater apprehension of the judgment which would be passed upon me, if with languid indifference I had allowed myself, O'Neill, and the money of your Holiness to fall into the hands of the adversary, without making a single effort to prevent it. How could I stand by and see the Holy See receive a threefold injury, and not fear a deluge of reproaches for my negligence? And on the other hand how could the Holy See ever hope to obtain satisfaction for these injuries from a remote and ill affected people? I concluded therefore it was better to draw down upon my own head any possible blame for too great boldness, and to avert any injury which threatened the supreme authority, that is to say, in conformity with the duty of a minister, to prefer public interest to private. Thus on the 27th of May, I together with the sub-delegated Bishops, pronounced the excommunication against all who were accomplices in, or adherents to the truce, and the interdict on all cities which should recognise it.

30. I know of no occasion when the censure has better deserved the name of a thunderbolt. At once a great confusion arose among the people, more than 2,000 soldiers of Preston's army went over to O'Neill. The Ulster army acquired force and vigour to defend itself against every attack, while the protection extended to me enabled me to save not only myself but the greater part of my money. This great change was the salvation of the Catholic religion, and kept alive all that now remains to enable us to maintain it in this kingdom. Preston, to whom I sent my own confessor with a notice of the excommunication and such paternal monition as I judged to be fitting, was quite unable to contain himself, in fact in the two answers which he sent he

betrayed the cunning devices and designs of his faction. He said first of all, he had no fear of the censure, as he had taken the opinion of eight Bishops and of many theologians who had studied the subject before I determined to issue the interdict. He then declared he had come to that place solely to meet O'Neill, and was determined that this time one or the other of them should remain dead upon the field. And, though he spoke under the influence of the most violent passion, I believe he did not deviate one iota from the truth. From the moment the peace was rejected Digby and the Ormondists, who were bent on reversing our decision, began by means of falsehoods and promises to get up a party among the theologians (who on this occasion also were disposed to take their side), and endeavoured to remove the fears of the people, by denying on every occasion the force of the censures which they wished their dupes to believe were little better than so many blunted arrows. And as far as relates to O'Neill, Preston could not have spoken more correctly; I have already mentioned the complaints that were made against him at the time when according to agreement he marched into Munster at my expense against the Baron; the Ormondists who came from the districts he occupied, smarting from the exactions they had suffered, had but one answer to the questions I put to them—"they wanted no Ulster men in Munster." The same thing was repeated in very coarse terms to myself by a very good Catholic; when I suggested that, after all, it was better to have Catholics than heretics in the province, he replied with great effrontery, and without the least hesitation, that this was not always true. The opinions on the excommunication were therefore divided. Seventeen Bishops were in favour of the censure, eight were against it, among whom, to the general astonishment, were four of those who had signed the condemnation of the truce. The religious orders were also divided among themselves in about the same proportion, as in some the greater, in others the lesser part approved the truce. I must except the orders of St. Dominic and of the Cappuchins, in the former but one opposed, in the latter all supported me. It was a remarkable fact that among these Bishops and all the other persons, even the monks, who supported the truce there was not one who belonged to the ancient party, or who was not in league with the Ormondists. So that as far as the Bishops were concerned it was evident they had no other motive than the fear of losing their property and the desire to see the faction exalted which they favoured. This was a clear test which enables us to decide whether their opinions were suggested by true love for their country or hot zeal for their faction. In the meantime the Marquis of Clanricarde without renouncing the neutrality of which I spoke before avowed himself in favour of the truce, and desirous of reviving the peace which he had proposed under the title of President of Connaught beneath the walls of Dublin, he began to enlist men in order to defend, as he said, the province at this new crisis, but with the intention in reality of joining Inchiquin, as he very soon did. The accession of Clanricarde was made still more important by that of three Bishops of Connaught, they were the allies of the other five Bishops who opposed me, so that it almost seemed as though all had been drawn over by the power of this one man. With such divisions and such discord it was easy to foresee what was likely to be the result of the ensuing campaign, and what fruit would accrue to religion from the league entered into with a heretic.

31. I was the first to place all my property in safety. With good guides I proceeded to the house of Terence Coghlan on the borders of Connaught, this man's great prudence and his voluntary abstention from public affairs made him a favourite with all parties, and from the many signs I saw of a singular attachment to the Catholic religion, it

gave me much pleasure to converse with him. He heard one evening that Preston was expected to pass that way on the following day in order to join the troops of Viscount Dillon. He came immediately to tell me, nor was I more prompt in deciding to depart than he was intent in urging me. On the instant I mounted with my followers on horseback, and favoured by the night, in these countries very luminous, I proceeded to a very strong position on the bank of a river. The hurry of this flight and the fatigue it occasioned were not sufficient to divert some among us from contemplating with wonder the brightness of these northern nights. When we saw that the twilight was never obscured but always grazed, as it were, the horizon, we rejoiced even in our flight to see confirmed by experience the truth of those doctrines which we had learnt from the astronomic spheres in our childhood. From this place I came by water to Athlone and thence finally to Galway where I could go no further. As soon as the interdict was published some of the Council, who were well affected to the Church, retired from office; immediately an equal number of the forty-eight of whom I spoke above were appointed in their places: thus the supreme power was at last placed in the hands where the faction wished to see it. Thus every curb was removed and the Ormondists gave the rein to their inclinations. It was proclaimed that O'Neill, not having joined Inchiquin had broken his oath to the Confederacy, and was therefore denounced as a rebel and as guilty of the crime of high treason. The ecclesiastical jurisdiction fell immediately to the ground. Orders were issued that all who ever defended the censure should be put in prison without any distinction, and these orders were carried out against many. Some took to flight, among them the Visitor of the Barefoot Carmelites, who had just come from Flanders; he embarked by night in disguise. Most iniquitous oaths were imposed, so that everyone was obliged to swear that he would pay no heed to any past censures or to any more to come. In order to bring over the Bishops to their side, they threatened, in an edict, to deprive them of their churches for which the Council said they would provide successors when needful. It is true that these enormities were more or less flagrant according to the progress of O'Neill's army, which never ceased the whole summer to harass the enemy, as I shall describe in the proper place. When the Council saw there was no hope of my return they suddenly seized the Dean of Fermo, who had remained at Kilkenny; and shortly afterwards took from him all the papers I had left in his charge. They thus deprived me of the power of showing by receipts and other documents how I had administered the money intrusted to me, and what was still worse, I lost the power of recovering some thousand crowns which I had lent to them; thus it appears they were not ashamed to rob me of the very acknowledgment they themselves had given me. At the commencement of the new Assembly they had commanded me by letter to leave the kingdom, as a rebel against the crown of England, and they now wrote to Galway with instructions that no obedience should be paid to me, and that I should be treated as unworthy of the common necessaries of life. Some indeed of these last resolutions, and those the most atrocious, were issued so privately, and were then so strangely withdrawn and disclaimed as to make it evident that it had been held to be advisable not to publish them in the usual form, so that it might be equally practicable to persuade their own faction that they had been actually passed, and to those who condemned them as disgraceful, to disavow them entirely.

32. While politicians were displaying all this violence the soldiers were not idle. But I shall only touch on the campaign of this summer, so far as may be necessary for my present narrative, leaving the minute details to be woven in due time into history. There was one object on which

the Ormondists were especially bent, and this was that Preston, Inchiquin, and their followers might be able to unite on any emergency. When O'Neill heard he had been proclaimed a traitor he was full of indignation, but at the same time more resolved than ever to keep the oath he had sworn to the Confederacy, even to his latest breath. He began at once to collect an army, occupied by night the line by which Preston must have marched, if he had attempted to capture, as he had hoped, some large herds of cattle in Ulster, and pushed on rapidly to Athlone. Here he gained more exact information as to those in Munster who were ready to take up arms against the Baron, and who retained an intense hatred of the Marquis of Ormonde. He promised he would very soon make a descent into the province with a force fully adequate for his purpose. He then retired for a time to the borders of Ulster, till he had collected what he deemed a sufficient force; when his army numbered 10,000 infantry and 1,500 horse, he set out upon his march, and ravaged the country as far as the city of Kilkenny. Great was the fear which seized the Council at the approach of this army, and it was generally believed that if O'Neill had marched straight up to the walls and made an attempt on the city, the Government would have saved themselves by a precipitate flight, and the garrison surrendered without firing a shot. O'Neill excused his remissness, alleging that when he heard of the Baron's approach he was afraid of being caught between the city and the enemy; and it is true the Baron did hurry with the utmost speed to the rescue. O'Neill therefore avoided Kilkenny, and marched into the county of Tipperary. These tactics very much dissatisfied his friends; as everyone saw that if Kilkenny had been taken our troubles would have been at an end, and the republic would have been restored to the very position, with a new confederation, at which we aimed when we rejected the Ormonde peace. O'Neill was still more blamed when, instead of passing as he had promised into Munster, he turned up the course of the Shannon; here it is true he displayed great bravery in the capture of certain places, especially of the very strong pass called Buncherry. Nearly at the same time Clanricarde marched with his people into Connaught in order, as far as it was possible, to strengthen his position. He did nothing however worthy of note, except that he got possession of Athlone by means of treachery. The officer in command there had previously set at naught all the orders of the Government, under pretence that he was bound to obey O'Neill; now having bargained with Clanricarde, he gave up the town for some unknown sum of money after twenty days of siege. The Marquis, having effected his object, hastened to Fort Falkland in order to drive O'Neill from the ford which crosses the river, at this spot, most opportunely for his purpose, and so united his forces with those of Inchiquin. When these hostile armies thus met it is impossible to describe the feeling of suspense which prevailed all over the kingdom. Everyone believed that this would be the last battle fought in Ireland, and that it would determine its political state for all future time. The Ormondists having recovered in three days the castle of Buncherry seemed perfectly assured of their victory, when all of a sudden they found themselves surrounded by the Ulster army; having the river behind them, and a bog at each side, there was only a narrow tongue of land by which they could escape, and even here, as they could only march two abreast, they would have been cut to pieces by the enemy. For eight days O'Neill kept the hostile army shut up in this position, cool confidence on one side, despair upon the other, and every hour we expected the utter extermination of the forces which he thus held within his grasp. But at last the news came that the Baron had forced his way out, had offered battle, and marched off without loss, while O'Neill had decidedly declined to accept the challenge. The feelings of his followers, whose hopes had been excited to the highest pitch, are more easily imagined than described. Certain it is then his enemies were no less astonished than his friends, and Clanricarde indulging in philosophical reflections, beyond the limits which morals set to speech, declared it was easy to see that day that the Deity was not on the side of O'Neill. O'Neill's excuse was that when he saw that the whole fate of the country and all the hopes of religion turned upon the issue of that one battle, he was unwilling to risk interests, so many and so momentous, on one brief experiment. He said he had done much in keeping his army in good case and undiminished in number during the whole course of the summer, with six generals leagued against one; that any mischance on that day would have placed the Protestants upon the throne, and spread sudden dismay and destruction through all the Catholic districts; he added that his army was uninjured, more determined than ever to avenge their wrongs, and quite sufficient, if money were not wanting, to overcome the enemy. These were his excuses; soon after he withdrew again to Ulster, and left the different parties free to examine into the circumstances of the case, and according to their feelings to write and publish their opinions.

33. I remained in Galway intent on the ecclesiastical proceedings, and watching the various events which occurred in every part of the kingdom. It was indeed my intention as soon as I perceived that by the terror of the censure I had saved my own person, O'Neill's army, and a large part of the money, to call together a National Synod, in which, with general consent, I might control the course of those evils which had been clearly foreseen, or remove them if need were by a public absolution, for with the exception of Kilkenny, I was willing to remove the interdict from all who petitioned me to that effect, provided they were able to plead a valid excuse and professed unfeigned reverence for the Holy See.

But the Council together with the Assembly (which was wholly composed of the factious), conscious of their own guilt and moved by fear lest my resolutions should be confirmed by the Synod, declared they were determined to prevent it unless I returned to Kilkenny. For this purpose they posted troops of horse on all the different roads and drove back the Bishops and all the other ecclesiastics, adding another specimen of barbarity to all other sacrilegious actions I have previously mentioned. It was now for the first time that I began to think it would be well I should depart, as it seemed no longer in my power to devise any remedy. It is certainly true that if O'Neill had marched into Connaught so as even to open a communication with others of our party in Munster, I might with this army at my back, have remained somewhat longer. But he never came, even when Galway was besieged for a fortnight by Clanricarde, on account of some contribution which he pretended was due, the Ulster army to my great astonishment showed no disposition to come to its relief; it was generally believed too (whether on sufficient ground I cannot say) that Clanricarde, under the pretext of the money, wished to get possession of the person of the Nuncio. The solicitude for me grew so strong in Ulster, coupled with shame at their own supineness, that at last Colonel Roger Maguire, a soldier of the greatest courage and a most devoted Catholic, ventured to reproach O'Neill for his indifference to my sufferings, and obtained from him 2,000 infantry to open the pass into Connaught. In a few hours he took the Castle of Drumruig by storm, but while leading on his men, sword in hand, he was shot and fell dead on the spot. His death was fatal to the army, which did nothing further in this province, so that all our party lost heart, and fatal also to my mission as it compelled me to depart. Already not only in Connaught, but also in Munster, those who in any way avowed themselves the followers of O'Neill, were exposed to persecution.

The rumour of Ormonde's coming was heard like thunder in the distance, and scarcely had the thunder ceased when the thunderbolt of his arrival fell upon the coast of Cork. Those very men who had so often promised never to permit this indignity, now overpowered by numbers, either remained silent or agreed to all appearance with the others, and I found myself brought to such a pass that I might expect very soon to see both the Marquis and the Baron march exultingly before me and laugh with heretical scorn at all my exertions. Hence as it seemed the time for fortitude was passed, that neither common prudence nor the duties of my office could require my delay, I gave the order to depart. I declared however to everyone that I wished to defer my departure up to the very moment that the decisive resolutions were passed, and the re-establishment of the Marquis accomplished, so that on the one hand it might appear to be voluntary, inasmuch as it was settled by myself, and on the other to be imposed on me by force inasmuch as the Confederation was dissolved *ipso facto* by subjection to a heretic.

34. I stood in great need of a vessel, and the only one I could obtain was the frigate *S. Pietro*, purchased at Nantes, which after the arrival of the Dean had remained with the *S. Ursula* at Waterford, almost as it were, in the clutches of my persecutors, the Council. It was at this time as your Holiness is aware that the Spanish agent laid claim not only to the frigate, but also to property belonging to the Dean and some which belonged to myself under pretence of a prize that had been taken in the French seas. It is incredible how eagerly the Council took up the claims and supported the arguments of this agent, assuming the authority of judge, when they were in reality one of the parties to the suit. After certain writs had been issued against us for contempt of court, because we refused to appear before such a tribunal, they took from the Dean everything he had, they next seized my property, and proceeded to sell by auction

what little remained to me in Kilkenny; they sequestrated all that was left in different hands of the Papal subsidy, and attempted also to get possession of the frigate, *S. Pietro*, but my officers with wise foresight removed her by night and placed her under the guns of the fort at Duncannon. During all the years of my mission, no place has been more faithful to the Holy See and to the Catholic religion than this fortress. As I have mentioned already Preston had recovered it from the English two years before this date with the aid of Father Scarampi. I too have constantly supplied it with both arms and money, whenever it stood in need of either; for it seemed to me that the cause of religion could never be wholly lost in Ireland, as long as this fortress remained in our hands, standing as it does, at the mouth of the river Barrow, and in a position which guards the principal ingress to the island. With equal gratitude towards me the garrison guarded the frigate, so that no one could approach it; and at last the Council, stung by their conscience, allowed it to depart. Thus after heavy expense and incredible trouble, the frigate made the circuit of the island, for 200 miles, and arrived in the port of Galway. But the fate of the *S. Ursula* which remained in Waterford, sequestrated in the name of the agent, supplies us with a test which enables us to judge whether the Council really believed they were supporting a just claim or merely used it as a pretext; since, though all the writs had been issued in the name of the agent, the frigate eventually remained in the hands of the Marquis while the agent got nothing but words. The escape of the frigate *S. Pietro* encouraged me to hope, that other aid from Heaven would not be denied me in my need, and that, if God had decreed I should leave Ireland, he would signify his will to me by the demonstrations made to welcome Ormonde's arrival; it was these only I awaited as the final signal for my departure.

35. It was at this very time that the Marquis, after re-

maining a few days at Cork in order to confer with Inchiquin, proceeded very slowly to his own princely seat at Carrick-on-Suir, giving out as he went, that he had been sent to Ireland by the Queen in order to frame some scheme for settling affairs to the general satisfaction. In Carrick he received a solemn deputation from the Assembly sitting in Kilkenny, at the head of which was the Archbishop of Tuam. This Archbishop was the leader of all those who forgetting the reverence they owed to the Holy See had lent a hand to every kind of sacrilegious violence, yet nevertheless he is the very man who most distinctly promised me that he would never consent to the recall of this same Marquis. In a complimentary address the Marquis was publicly invited to go to Kilkenny and they assured him in private that the ecclesiastical party, to which he has always shown the greatest aversion, was so weak, and the feeling in the Assembly was so strong in his favour that he need not hesitate to set out immediately. The Marquis therefore laid aside the mask, and assuming at once the character of Viceroy, entered Kilkenny amid general acclamation. After three days he took his seat on a throne in the hall of the Assembly, and was entreated by him of Tuam, in the name of all the rest, to assume the government of the Kingdom which had fallen into such a state of misery and to comfort the people who had already experienced his watchful care. He graciously consented, assuring them it was his wish to live and die among them and began forthwith to put his authority into action. He declared the Confederation of the Catholics dissolved, and formed a new Council, comprising some members of it; after some solicitation he consented to include amongst them the Bishop of Ferns, who had just returned from Rome, but only on condition that in signing any document he should omit the title of Bishop, and restrict himself to his own name Nicholas. Great and unceasing was the marvel of all Catholics when they saw a man who so lately had been breathing the air of the Court of Rome throw himself unreservedly into the arms of the Marquis; when they saw moreover that a man who was under such a weight of obligation to your Holiness for the favours he had received in Rome, and to me for the kindness which caused him to receive them, could never contrive to find time in three months to come to Galway to greet me. The first effect of the new government was, in conformity with the articles of the truce, to replace in their old estates all the heretics who declared for the King, who thus gained possession, and without any cost, of the property which two years ago we had taken from them, with the help of your Holiness's money. To me thinking of these things it seems at times passing strange, that there are men who think it worth their while to seek for arguments to prove, that the interest of Religion has never been the end this party has in view. What clearer proof I ask could be given than the opinion held by the Ormondists, and repeatedly expressed in my presence, that no adherents of the King should be regarded as heretics, but only those who are opposed to the Crown, and consequently that war is lawful against Puritans as long as they are rebels, but unlawful the moment they return to their allegiance? As if mere regard for the King could qualify heresy, or purge the contagion which falsehood imparts to the soul, as if the aid granted by the Vicar of God could really benefit religion when it was employed in the service of Protestants.

36. When I heard of these proceedings I determined to hesitate no longer but forthwith declared that the government of a heretic was incompatible with the exercise of my mission. I announced that it was neither usual nor decorous for the Holy See to maintain a public Minister among those who spontaneously submitted themselves to one who professed any other than the Catholic religion. I invited all who had

incurred the excommunication to seek for absolution excepting only those who were the authors of the truce, from whom I required moreover their condemnation of every act which had been committed against the Holy See or the ecclesiastical immunities. A large number came to me during these last days of my stay, and for others I left sufficient authority in the hands of four Bishops. But none of the principal offenders had made application before my departure in person or even indirectly ; relying on the arguments of ecclesiastics in the opposite faction, or hoping by means of the Provincial of the barefoot Carmelites, who has just been sent to Rome, to bring about a suspension of the censure, they were far more anxious to revenge themselves on me, than to secure a reconciliation with the Church.

Having therefore discharged every duty which seemed to me important I fixed the day of my departure, and on that very day the wind took exactly the direction which the sailors desired for leaving the port. The triumph in which I was conducted to my ship amid crowds of weeping people, was even greater than that which marked my arrival three years before, in this case it was the tribute, on the completion of his mission to a poor and persecuted Minister, and could not be ascribed to the hopes of assistance which they then entertained. I know not how I can better recompense the inhabitants of Galway for the reverence they showed to your Holiness, by always presenting a bold front against every violence which threatened me than by laying their many merits at the feet of your Holiness and recording them in the Archives of Rome, so as to transmit to posterity this example of most singular loyalty. It may chance that in the adoration of the Sovereign Pontificate and the zealous defence of its Ministers this the most remote country of Christendom, may serve as a model to the corrupted nations which are nearer to Rome ; it may be necessary for people who have been nurtured in the light of truth, to journey to a distant clime where the sun is never seen, that they may fully comprehend the due subjection of the faithful to their Head.

Within the week I landed in France, so prosperous was my voyage, that it was not difficult to perceive in it new proofs of the favour of God and of the efficacy of the blessings of your Holiness.

Fragment of another Memoir.

. . . . . that my doubts may have but little foundation in matters which concern the glory of the Holy See and that of His Holiness himself. I shall advise your Eminence with all exactness and fidelity on whatever relates to religion in this kingdom, in order that I may obey the commands of His Holiness to the utmost of my power.

The good intentions of the King* of England go far beyond the limits I mentioned to your Eminence. It is certain that with the advice of the Lord Chancellor he has determined to repeal all the penal laws now in force against the Catholics. The principal among these laws are as follows: that every priest is worthy of death; that every Catholic must pay the third part of his goods; that no one can hold any office in the King's household who has not taken the oaths of fealty and supremacy, &c. If these laws were repealed it is perfectly certain that a great number of Protestants would forthwith return to the bosom of the Catholic Church. Great exertions are being made to influence the members of the Parliament about to meet; those servants of the King who are most in his confidence have shown themselves particularly zealous, and it is confidently expected that they will carry their point in an Assembly which is wholly composed of the former servants of the King and the present members of his household. Every

* Charles II.

one can easily see that if the result corresponds with our hopes it will be no small advantage to the Catholics. This I can say with confidence, that no one who has not been in that kingdom, and has not had some experience in it, can have any idea of the importance of the results which will indubitably follow. In fact we may hope for everything and more than I dare to say. Things being in this state your Eminence may wonder that I do not indulge in all the bright hopes which seem natural in such circumstances. I confess that though I am well aware of the good intentions of the English Court, I cannot help fearing that the want of common prudence in the Catholics of that country may neutralize to a great extent the success that we might hope for. The divisions among them are so great that I could not look on without shame and sore distress of mind. The heads of the Catholic clergy in London are very much incensed against the Jesuits, while the Jesuits and the Benedictines bear very little love towards each other. Charges of heresy and Jansenism are made and retorted with fury. There are some who by indiscreet zeal, by grasping prematurely at success, are risking the ruin of their party. There are some who are anxious to advance their own interests rather than the triumph of religion. There are even some among the Catholics who have been deluded by the artifices of Cromwell, and whose proceedings do little to encourage the good intentions of the King in favour of the Catholic religion. Rome may do much in this matter, and can certainly do nothing more to our advantage and honour than to check as far as possible the ill-judged proceedings of those with whom she has influence and authority. What would appear to me most necessary would be to promote as far as possible by her authority the reunion of these different parties and of all whom I have already specified. As union among them is clearly the interest of the King, so there is nothing which could have such influence on him or more effectually bind him to procure for the Catholics the advantages they desire, than such action on our part as would bring this union about. As it is necessary for this purpose that His Holiness should have some knowledge of the men who have the greatest influence over the Catholic party, I will give a short list of their names, and add a slight portrait, so to say, of each. I do not doubt that His Holiness has already received full information, but I venture notwithstanding to subjoin these my notices, which are not only perfectly honest and wholly unbiassed by any kind of interest, but derived from men of great experience, thoroughly acquainted with the condition and the feelings of the country.

The clergy of London consists almost entirely of men of singular piety, and some of them also are possessed of considerable learning, they are strongly opposed to the Jesuits and stand very well with the King. Signor Galeone, the Resident, has doubtless given to His Holiness all necessary information as to their characters and history.

The Jesuits have very many families under their control, but among the other ecclesiastics, both the Regular and Secular, the feeling is very strong against them, and the same is the case at the Court, as they have never rendered any service to the King, and always showed the greatest deference for Cromwell. The Benedictines, on the contrary, have great power among the people, and stand very high in the good graces of the King, not only on account of the efforts they made whenever it was possible to serve him, but because Father Robinson, who takes the lead among them, advanced to the King a large sum of money in the name of his order when His Majesty was an exile at the Hague, at the time of his greatest need, with fortune more adverse than ever.

There are many Catholics of high rank, but few have the merit which may be seen elsewhere. Some are merely Catholics in appearance, while others are Catholics from conviction. Among the former is the Earl of Bristol, sometime Secretary of State, who, when the cause of the King seemed lost beyond all hope, rose to great power and wealth in Spain, but abandoned his career in order to profess himself a Catholic at Brussels. He is a man of good family and some consideration at the Court, on account of the office he has held and the friends he still retains, but he is known by the King and his Prime Minister to be a man without religion, too vehement, and full of projects not only impracticable but opposed to common sense. This I write to your Eminence in confidence, because as I have always avoided any quarrel with this man I would not even give occasion for complaint. Therefore I humbly beseech you simply to act so far on this warning as to prevent them in Rome from placing too much reliance on this gentleman, who from his position has some appearance of importance, and may be inclined to certain proceedings in order to make himself remarkable, which would be viewed with little favour in England, and would by no means suit the taste of this country.

Sir Kenelm Digby, his cousin, is sufficiently well known in Rome; a restless man of scanty wisdom, who before now has taken the oath of supremacy, he is the intimate friend of Le Blanc, whose vehemence and extravagances are but too well known in Rome. Lord Brudenel is a man of great age, who has very great authority among the Catholics. Henry Howard head of the great house of Howard, has lately, through the illness of his brother who has lost his reason, been made Duke of Norfolk, that is the premier duke of England. This too is a most important step which the King has taken in favour of the Catholics. He is a man of great worth and courage, who has shown a remarkable zeal for religion, and it will be well to keep him on our side by means of all those expressions of civility and courtesy which cost us so little. There is a general expectation that he will be made Grand Marshal of England. He is the nephew of Signor d'Obigni, of whom I will speak another time. There are also Viscount Montague, Lord Arundel, Lord Andover; these are the men of most mark among the nobility. There are certainly others as I have before mentioned who stand even higher in rank, as the Marquis of Worcester of the house of Somerset, the Marquis of Winchester of the house of Paulet, the Earl of Shrewsbury of the house of Talbot, who may all possess great qualities and good intentions, but have nothing else which would tend to the advancement of religion. I reserved the Abbé Montague purposely to the last in order to give a more particular description of him than I have given of the others. He is the Grand Almoner of the Queen, the intimate friend of the Earl of St. Albans, who is the favourite of the Queen, and the confidant of Cardinal Mazarin. He was for a long time, as they say in Spanish, *Valido de Amores* of the Duke of Buckingham, he then became a Catholic when the course things were taking in England led him to believe that the Protestant religion was not likely to advance his interests

ILLUSTRATIVE DOCUMENTS.

DOCUMENTS.

No. I. (Page 3).

To Monsignor the Nuncio of France.

Rome, 10th April, 1645.

The Pontifical Rose was sent in order that your Excellency should be pleased to present it in the name of His Holiness to Her Majesty the Queen of France. Meanwhile, your letters having informed us that there are symptoms of grave displeasure at the French Court on account of the refusal to promote Father Mazarin; it is deemed advisable that you take no further steps in the matter of the presentation, unless you have since perceived that the feeling has diminished, and that you are convinced the gift would be accepted willingly. We, however, leave the matter to your Excellency's prudence to act as you think best.

To the Same.

Rome, 29th April, 1645.

With respect to the cipher annexed to your letter dated Genoa, on the subject of the Rose, you will carry out the orders lately sent to you from here touching this matter, taking no heed of the observations made upon it in Florence and Genoa, possibly in Paris likewise.

To the Same.

Rome, 1st May, 1645.

With this your Excellency will receive two copies of the note addressed by me this evening to Monsignor the Archbishop of Athens, concerning the affairs of religion in Germany; and of what has been done by His Holiness to manifest his gravest opinion of the insult offered to the Portuguese Abbé Monteros. We communicate this to you, that while not appearing to have heard of the matter from us, you may make use of it in reply to any observation you may hear on the subject, but on no account are you to begin any conversation touching upon it with any person whatsoever.

To the Same.

Rome, 8th May, 1645.

In cipher from Father Scarampi, with copy of letter from Queen of England to the Supreme Council.

"Gentlemen of the Council,—I have received great consolation from hearing by your letter of the general desire manifested to serve the King and to make peace with the Protestants who are on his side; and I assure you that you shall lose nothing nor have any reason to repent having acted in this manner. The large powers which the King has despatched to my cousin, the Marquis of Ormonde, his Viceroy, to give you every satisfaction, should be a sure pledge to you of his desire to make glad the heart of Ireland, and to leave you in peaceful enjoyment of all that is necessary to insure your tranquillity. The Rev. Mr. O'Hartigan, your agent at this court, will be able to testify to the great anxiety I feel for your welfare, and with what zeal I have embraced this opening to terminate your differences; he sees too how much the security you desire for all my said cousin the Marquis of Ormonde, will promise you, is strengthened by the guarantee of the Queen Regent, my Sovereign and Sister, which I can now offer you. Meanwhile it will be very agreeable to me to receive your letters, and to hear that your affection towards the King is maintained and increased. Also that you continue to forward the progress of the peace in his interest and your own, which are bound up together. And in conclusion, gentlemen of the Council, I pray that God may preserve you."

I send the enclosed copy for two reasons—first, to show how ready the Queen is always to treat of peace without one word concerning religion, and how she implies that the whole well-being of the Catholics depends on peace with the Protestants. I for one cannot accept this view, when these same Protestants are again to become absolute masters of everything. And this sentiment of the Queen's deserves consideration in the treaty, because she is coming immediately to Ireland, and she will probably be able to carry it into effect. The guarantee she offers of her own word and that of the Queen of France, without any idea of the unsubstantial and brittle nature of such security, shows her ardent desire for peace, and if, as your Eminence writes, that this is not pleasing to His Holiness, it may be managed easily that reasons be given to the Queen of France that she should not interfere, and to the Supreme Council of Ireland that they should not accept these proposals. Secondly, to discover in the first place the sentiments of the Supreme Council and their agents, who were invited, so at least they say, by the King to attend the treaty for peace at Oxford; now they assert that the Protestants entreat of His Majesty. to depute the Marquis of Ormonde to be Commissioner. And however true it may be that the Catholics were the first to ask for peace, and in the meantime made the truce, and that it appears from these letters that the commission has been arranged to please the Catholics and not the Protestants, still from the parsimony with which the Catholic religion is treated in the published resolutions, and even still more in the secret instructions (as I wrote in the December before last) one can see how much their minds are bent on peace, and it may be well to consider how to give succours beneficial to the Catholics without being profitable to the Protestants. On this last matter you might perhaps treat with the secretary, but I beg that your Excellency will not show the letter from Her Majesty, because it was communicated privately to me by the Supreme Council, who have not however shown me a copy of the letter which Her Majesty wrote to the King of England at the instance of Father O'Hartigan and conveyed by him, exhorting the King to give peace to the Catholics.

Perhaps your Excellency will treat also with the secretary, in order that the Supreme Council shall assign to the monks the property of the monastery of St. John in Waterford, of which I wrote at the beginning of this negotiation, &c.

No. II. (Page 7).
To the Same.

Rome, 22nd May, 1645.

When your Excellency was at Avignon we saw by your letters how fully you shared our feelings, touching the gift of the Rose, and we said in reply that in conformity with previous directions, unless you should see a very opportune moment, you should not only abstain from presenting it, but also from giving the least hint that you had it in your possession. When your Excellency is leaving Paris, if it seems advisable, and that you can with safety and without opening the box which contains it, send it to Avignon, you are at liberty to do so. But if you do not see that this plan can be carried out as you wish, then you may leave the box locked and well corded in the hands of Monsignor the Nuncio, with directions to keep it till he shall have received orders what to do with it. I must not omit to say that as your Excellency is not to communicate to anyone, the commission intrusted to you touching the Rose, so even to the Nuncio you will keep silence. Leaving all this however to your prudence, &c., &c.

No. III. (Page 23).
To the Same.

Rome, 22nd May, 1645.

From the letter in cipher written to us by your Excellency at Avignon we collect that on your way you have heard the usual complaints of the small affection, according to some ill-intentioned persons, which His Holiness entertains towards France. Now, as there is no foundation whatever for this assertion, you will be able with perfect truth to deny it altogether; His Holiness being always extremely well disposed towards His Majesty the King, the Queen, Cardinal Mazarin, and the whole Regency, your Excellency will therefore of your own motion (and not by any means as if at our suggestion) testify to them all with due earnestness the paternal feeling of His Holiness towards France, and how greatly he desires to have an opportunity to manifest it in acts. And since the foundation of these complaints lies in his having declined to promote to the Cardinalate the Reverend Chief of this Sacred Palace, you will explain that this refusal gives no reason to infer any want of good will, because His Holiness communicated with the greatest candour more than once to M. de Gramonville, and to the ministers of the French Court, the all-sufficient reasons which made it impossible for him to yield to the wishes of His Majesty, and how willingly he would otherwise have sought to meet them.

As to the assertion that of those promoted the greater number are vassals or dependents of the Crown of Spain, your Excellency knows well that the Court of Rome never regards persons in this light, but without considering whom they serve, provided they are Italians, and deserve promotion, the Popes have always advanced the Prelates; otherwise if they now pursued a contrary method, the greater number of the Prelacy of this Court, who are vassals of Spain, or of other Princes, would cease to come, and much more remain here since they would be subjected to new rules, which have always been rejected by the Roman Curia and late Pontiffs. This and other reasons which, for brevity I pass over, you can convey to anyone who seeks to impugn a truth so indubitable. You will however always speak as from yourself without showing that you have had any orders from us, not losing any opportunity however of adroitly reassuring the minds of those with whom you may happen to converse, &c., &c.

To the Same.

Rome, 29th May, 1645.

In the Consistory, held on 15th of the present month, His Holiness appointed to three of the vacant churches in Portugal, namely, Egittano, Mirando, and Viseu.

The ministers of the King of Spain, however, have endeavoured by every sort of proposal to induce His Holiness to abstain from appointing to them, asserting that their King retains a civil right in the providing for these churches, but His Holiness is determined in such a matter as this to be guided by the dictates of his own conscience, and to act according to the precept of Christ our Lord, *Pasce oves meas*, without reference to any mere human interests; he has, therefore, made the appointments of his own will and judgment. The Spanish Cardinals cleverly making themselves acquainted with this resolution, thought it better, as was then seen, not to appear in the Consistory that morning, to avoid being put to the necessity of approving a resolution, the justice of which they had previously impugned, since it is the invariable custom to laud the provision made for all the bishoprics, or, on the other hand, disapproving of this one, thereby offending against the respect and reverence due to His Holiness. I make this explanation that your Excellency may be able to give us your opinion on the matter.

To the Same.

Rome, 19th June, 1645.

If your Excellency should be in company with the Queen of France, and that she touches on His Holiness' want of affection or good will towards the affairs of that Crown, you will be able to declare with truth how greatly the Holy Father loves that kingdom, and that he entertains an indescribable esteem for Her Majesty. Should she then complain that notwithstanding her intercessions he had not promoted to the Cardinalate the Reverend Chief of the Sacred Palace, your Excellency must bring forward all the reasons before given on the subject, and assure her that His Holiness will never fail to manifest his particular regard on all occasions when no adverse reasons forbid, such as those which made it impossible for him to gratify her in this instance, though he would have extremely desired to do so. Your Excellency will take a good opportunity to impress on Her Majesty that what is said of His Holiness' partiality to the Spanish Crown is quite chimerical, as most truly there never has been any sign of partiality to the prejudice of France, because he loves both nations with true affection, much desiring to see them reunited in their former friendship and good understanding, to the great benefit of Catholic Christianity. Of all that Her Majesty may say, and that your Excellency may answer, be warned not to communicate a word to any one in the world; but write it solely for our eyes, and if Her Majesty should show a desire that you should remain longer in Paris, your Excellency will consent without making any difficulty; though you must show that you do so in obedience to her commands, assuring her that His Holiness will always meet her wishes with pleasure, however the previous negotiation may appear to her to contradict this assurance.

To the Same.

Rome, 26th June, 1645.

Sir Kenelm Digby, who has been sent here by the Queen of England, having had several audiences of His Holiness and of me, has ultimately presented the document which I now send to your Excellency, and which seeks to prove the great benefits which will result from granting her the aid she seeks. It remains however to be considered if in truth this promised benefit, if he yield to her wishes, will really serve the Catholic religion in Ireland. In the meantime your Excellency will give your best consideration to this document, and send us your opinion of it.

To the Same.

Rome, 26th June, 1645.

A letter has just arrived from Paris which tells a strange story, that some of the royal ministers have shown a strong feeling because your Excellency has been sent there by us without any letter to Monsignor dei Bagni. On its being made known to us we at once apologized for this inadvertence, and we feel assured that it must be readily excused by every one when we have shown so much candour.

Your Excellency knows that your despatches are not prepared by the Secretary of State but by the Private Secretary, to whom from the first, in the time of Urban VIII., the affairs of Ireland have always been assigned, and he having minuted all the other letters did not observe that he ought to write this one besides. Nor is it to be much wondered at that even the most able and most diligent men should inadvertently commit such a mistake without any sinister intention, as it has happened on this occasion, and your Excellency can make use of these observations to testify to the pure truth, &c., &c.

No. IV. (Page 65).
To the Same.

Rome, 3rd July, 1645.

Since your Excellency has advised us of your having been received with so much benignity by the Queen of France, His Holiness feels assured that you have not failed to discover if the gift of the Rose would be grateful to Her Majesty, inasmuch as there appears no possibility now that it would be refused. It is however quite true that the matter must be treated with all the circumspection which is to be expected from the prudence of your Excellency, &c., &c.

To the Same.

Rome, 3rd July, 1645.

A fortnight ago your Excellency was told that if by chance the Queen of France should give you any motive for remaining in that country, in order to receive answers to points which had been submitted to her, your Excellency might under some pretext prolong your stay in Paris. But since His Holiness sees that this has not happened, that Her Majesty has given you no cause to delay your journey, and that by transporting yourself to Ireland your Excellency may be of great use and give consolation to the Catholics there, he has resolved that your Excellency shall proceed on your journey in the manner first arranged, without regard to the orders last sent to you, &c., &c.

To the Same.

Rome, 3rd July, 1645.

Your Excellency is aware that the intentions of His Holiness respecting the affairs of Ireland do not go beyond the limits of pure benefit to the Catholic religion, and that your mission never had, and has no other aims than to procure its free exercise, to restore ecclesiastical discipline, and to reform the habits of the Catholics, relaxed by a long course of free living. On all that touches on the civil government, your instructions have been so framed as by no possibility to excite the jealousy of either the King or the Queen of England; nor does the Holy Father work to any other purpose in spirit, since he concerns himself solely in the propagation of the Catholic religion, without a single thought of prejudicing the temporal dominion of any one whatsoever. Nor is he too much pleased with the rumours which are spread by some Irish Catholics, that they desire to throw off their allegiance to the King because he has not chosen to grant the concessions which they demand; and His Holiness would also desire that they should speak with greater moderation of the articles of the peace. And further, he wishes them to understand that he desires to see them continue obedient to the royal power, hoping however that from the King himself, and from the protection of the Queen, that they may gain all they desire. To this end all your Excellency's persuasions and warnings must be directed; His Holiness rests securely on your prudence, whenever you can convey news to him of the Irish, whether it be of rebellion or refusal of submission to the King, and that you will warn your followers on this matter, and thus in the end all may be of one mind in the holy sentiments of the Blessed Father.

To the Same.

Rome, 3rd July, 1645.

In his last audience of the Pope, Mr. Digby made the most urgent entreaties that His Holiness should manifest his perfect goodwill towards the Queen of England, by giving her at the present time some assistance in ammunition and other munitions of war, assuring His Holiness that from the urgent necessities of the Queen in the present state of affairs in those kingdoms they would be received with the liveliest gratitude.

For this reason His Holiness was particularly disposed to accede to her request. Hence this very morning he sent for Mr. Digby, and signified to him the pleasure he feels in giving satisfaction to Her Majesty in this particular suit, but reminding him that at the present moment he is not in a position to show his good disposition towards her on as great a scale as he would otherwise desire.

I communicate this matter to your Excellency that you may make use of it as it appears best to your prudence, knowing that you will not make more display of the fact than it deserves; as the amount of assistance will be about 15,000 crowns.

But above all you will assure the Irish that the demonstration now made by the Holy Father will not diminish in the smallest degree that which he desires to do for the Catholics of Ireland; but rather is made in the hope that it must be to their great advantage, as it is impossible but that the Queen will be much more moved to benefit them by maintaining a good understanding; and your Excellency will do your utmost to confirm them in this belief.

To the Same.

Rome, 10th July, 1645.

Pay to Mr. Digby on account of the Queen of England 20,000 crowns in munitions of war, as agreed at the above date.

To the Same.

Rome, 10th July, 1645.

We observe all that your Excellency has written concerning the second conversation which the Prince de Condé held with you on the occasion of returning your visit.

In answer we repeat how greatly His Holiness is gratified by the zeal which the Prince has shown for the increase and defence of the Catholic Religion everywhere; and his particular wish to serve His Holiness, and when an occasion offers your Excellency may assure His Highness that the Holy Father will never neglect an opportunity to show his thankfulness and good disposition towards him.

And likewise he will embrace with particular pleasure all possible means to make known to France the cordiality of his wishes and the consideration with which he will treat every interest of that Crown, hoping that the Divine Goodness will make plain this indubitable truth.

In conclusion it will be necessary to avoid insisting on the Holy Father doing what has been rejected by late Popes; and which is repugnant to the dignity of the Holy See, such for example as the giving up Beauperis when he was incarcerated here at the express desire of the Minister of the French Crown, who wished the cause to be heard in Rome.

Your Excellency, who knows by what forms this Holy See regulates its affairs, will know how to reply energetically to those who may speak to you on this matter, of which we have already written at full length to Monsignor the Archbishop of Athens, &c.

To the Same.

Rome, 12th July, 1645.

As the letters and ciphers of your Excellency touching the affairs of Ireland must be placed in the hands of different secretaries it will be necessary for the future that they shall be divided into parcels of distinct letters; so that one part shall contain all political matters apart from those which belong to your mission, since in this way we can communicate or withhold here whatever we may think necessary.

To the Same.

Rome, 12th July, 1645.

When your Excellency finds a good opportunity to converse with the Queen of France, you may suggest that it would be advisable to send an Ambassador to Rome, making choice of a person of good principles, and well affected towards us, explaining to Her Majesty that observing the candour of His Holiness and his sincere affection towards France, he will be at all times able to convey from the Holy Father the highest assurances of his esteem and benevolent sentiments. He will also have an opportunity of becoming fully persuaded of the equality with which His Holiness administers the government of the Church, and of all Christianity, without the smallest thought of partiality, and of knowing that the reports on this head disseminated by persons in France ill affected to the public good, are nothing but falsehoods.

To the Same.

Rome, 12th July, 1645.

Not having had any information from your Excellency as to whether the Queen of England had admitted you to an audience, and as reports are spread that she has made some difficulty about receiving you, I take the opportunity of an express going to Paris to give you a hint to let me know at once the certainty of the matter, what is really the difficulty, what has interfered, and yet more *who* it is that has interfered. If it is owing to the Queen being displeased with your mission in Ireland, and that she does not wish to forward it by any positive act; or, if from any difference of claims, &c., or in fine if the illness of Her Majesty, which we know here to be a fact, has caused the delay of the audience, your Excellency will not fail to give us the earliest intelligence. Your Excellency's opinion on the paper presented by Sir K. Digby, of which I sent you a copy in my last, is expected here without delay.

To the Same.

Rome, 12th July, 1645.

See letter of 19th June, 1645.

*   *   *   *   *   *   *

Though I had written the above to your Excellency on 19th June, His Holiness wishes me to repeat that notwithstanding the orders you received by his command to quit the French Court, he desires you to carry these out precisely, without attending to any antecedent directions to the contrary.

To the Same.

Rome, 17th July, 1645.

Having written to your Excellency that if the Queen of France should give you any reason to remain in Paris, you need not depart for Ireland, but dexterously make some excuse, such as ill-health, &c., I repeat the same orders by this opportunity. But if Her Majesty should not show a desire for your further stay there, your Excellency must hasten your departure at once, and pass over to Ireland to apply yourself to the work of your mission.

To the Same.

Rome, 17th July, 1645.

Concerning the three heads on which the complaints are founded I answer, and can asseverate that the manner of proposing the Churches was suggested by these same Portuguese to the late Pope, and was disallowed; but now when we are inclined to it and that it has been done, they make objections, do not desire it, and are displeased.

As to the Ambassador, one has only to reflect on the regret of Pope Urban on what we have permitted.

With respect to Beaupuis, no one wished to escape from the agreement when he was retained; otherwise than as the cause being an offence against so distinguished an ecclesiastic, it could not be entertained anywhere but here. These, and other reasons have been frequently stated, and are so evident, and so true, that there is no necessity for me to reply to them at greater length. I leave it to your Excellency to represent them anew on opportune occasions in the strongest manner, and to justify to all men the principles on which we have acted, and do act, in the service of the public and for the universal good.

To the Same.

Rome, 17th July, 1645.

I have communicated to His Holiness the difficulty which your Excellency represents in your cipher of the 23rd ultimo concerning an audience with the Queen of England. His Holiness commands me to say that through Her Majesty's confessor, or any other person you consider more advisable, your Excellency should represent to her, that the sole aim of His Holiness in sending you to Paris before passing over to Ireland, was that you should see Her Majesty as head of that kingdom, and to take from her any directions she might deem it necessary to give you, for the advancement of our holy religion in that Island. It is his great desire in his character of true Pastor and Father to comfort the Catholics, and to urge them to bear every trouble for the love of the Blessed God; since in the midst of danger He has sustained and preserved them from the perfidious infection of heresy. That His Holiness has been moved by no political aim will be apparent at all times, because his sole desire is the benefit of the King; and His Holiness having heard that M. de Gramonville approved of your Excellency taking that route to see Her Majesty, the Holy Father agreed with so much the greater pleasure, because it was his own desire also, for the reasons before given; and because having been acquainted with Her Majesty when he was in Paris, he wished to assure her of the cordiality of his sentiments towards her.

However, if the Queen either for fear of injuring the King her husband, or for any private reason, does not think it well to receive you at a public or private audience, His Holiness does not wish Her Majesty to have any trouble about the matter, since he will be satisfied with any resolutions of a Queen so pious and so zealous for the Catholic faith. I am, however, to add that should your Excellency be not disposed to accept a private audience that you may not put in doubt the prerogative of the Nuncio to appear covered before all Queens (even if in France at similar audiences a Nuncio does not remain covered), still we do not see how any doubt can rest on the prerogative, whilst at all public audiences the right to be covered is established. In case you object you may send by the same person His Holiness' brief and benediction to Her Majesty, but this we leave to your own judgment if you should still consider it necessary to have the private audience, since being on the spot you can judge better than we can.

Only this you must take into consideration, that if at a private audience of the Queen of England you are uncovered, the King and Queen of France might require the same when you are taking leave of their Majesties; it will, therefore, perhaps be a good expedient for your Excellency to take leave of them first, using the prerogative of being covered, and at the last, visit the Queen of England privately. It has been deemed advisable to make these suggestions, leaving it to your Excellency to decide with your accustomed prudence.

To the Same.

24th July, 1645.

We observe all your Excellency says in your cipher of 30th ultimo, but as we have already said enough on the first head in other letters, we have nothing to add in the present.

As to the Rose, whilst you are certain that it would be accepted, yet have a doubt whether graciously or not, you must retain it. Your Excellency's prudence will suggest the best course to pursue, &c., &c.

No. V. (Page 71).
To the Same.

Rome, 31st July, 1645.

The report that your Excellency had left Rome without letters for Monsignor, the Resident Nuncio in Paris, which has been talked of by everyone, has been spread by a letter from the Abbé Bentivoglio to some persons here. As I have explained to your Excellency how the error occurred, I do not think it necessary to reply further.

To the Same.

Rome, 31st July, 1645.

The paternal and sincere affection of His Holiness towards France will always manifest itself in acts on every possible occasion, and when just and proper concessions can be made. Your Excellency can emphatically make known this assurance which comes direct from His Holiness.

To the Same.

Rome, 31st July, 1645.

Your Excellency is desired, either before or in the act of taking leave of the Queen of France and of Cardinal Mazarin, adroitly to let fall as an idea which has just occurred to you, that the best means to adjust the existing differences would be to promote a matrimonial alliance between the Prince of Spain and the daughter of the Duke of Orleans; and if you see that the idea is taken up, your Excellency might strongly urge it in conversation, and inform us here of all that is said in reply.

To the Same.

Rome, 14th August, 1645.

When your Excellency first left Italy we wrote that you should not present the Rose to the Queen of France without first knowing if Her Majesty would accept it, in any case I should have desired to know if your Excellency had done anything in the matter, and if any answer had been received. I hint this matter to your Excellency, so that if there be time you may more completely satisfy the wish of His Holiness for information.

To THE SAME.

Rome, 14th August, 1645.

The opinion of your Excellency on the document of Mr. Digby, conveyed in the paper you sent us on 21st July, is a very prudent one, and in conjunction with what is suspected here, will make us more cautious in the answers to be given to him. After the defeat of the King of England he entreated for larger succours; but His Holiness did not wish to pledge himself until he could see some certain benefit to accrue to the Catholic religion in Ireland, as well as in England. Your Excellency will however expedite your journey, because when you have once reached Ireland, you will be able to give us an account of the state of affairs there; and acting in conformity with your instructions you will find means to benefit the Catholic religion, the sole aim of your mission and of His Holiness, to whom your good offices in inducing the Queen and the nobles of her Court to give assistance proportionate to the necessities, have been very grateful. Let your Excellency go on your way rejoicing with the paternal blessing of the Holy Father upon you.

To THE SAME.

Rome, 21st August, 1645.

We were not deceived one moment respecting the treaty of peace, lately planned by the Queen of England, between the King and the Irish Catholics; we knew it must soon vanish in air, even if it did not cover, as we have always suspected, some artful design or other, because since the King and Queen will listen only to the councils of those who assist them, nothing good will ever be concluded; and if the Commissioners sent from Ireland to the Queen and the Marquis of Ormonde, although of his own faction, have not been able to agree with the Royal party in France, much less can it be believed that the King will remit the arrangement to Cardinal Mazarin, from whom nothing favourable touching the Catholic religion can be hoped.

The aid given by His Holiness to Mr. Digby is not such as to give cause of jealousy to the Irish, because the Holy Father has always made, and will make their consolation his chief aim; and every other aid which he gives will be directed to maintain the rights of the Catholic faith, a course from which he will never deviate.

Your Excellency will hasten your going to Ireland, because we see from letters received from Father Scarampi and others devoted to the common cause, every day's delay may produce the worst effects, and the season for taking the field is coming to an end.

As to the rest, be quite tranquil, no one (that I know of) has spoken of you, or of your opinions on the two points, on account of which you say some persons have taken a prejudice against your particular enterprise.

To the Same.

Rome, 23rd August, 1645.

With respect to what your Excellency mentions in a cipher of the person of Beaupuis in relation to the conversation you had lately held with the Prince de Condé, little remains for me to say in addition to what I have written over and over again to you. I therefore only add that in this affair it is not necessary for you to see what you should or should not say or adjust with M. de Gramonville, but only what was said and adjusted with His Holiness; and therefore you must be peremptory on this head, and lay down authoritatively that it is a matter already decided on principle, and not on an imaginary verisimilitude which never existed, and which is altogether foreign to the facts.

To the Same.

Rome, 28th August, 1645.

When I wrote to your Excellency that you might remain longer in Paris, it was always with the proviso that the Queen of France gave some excuse to do so for other matters than any relating to Irish affairs, but not otherwise. And therefore when you saw that no invitation was coming from her you should have continued to make preparations for your journey. Afterwards His Holiness thought it would have been much better if without further delay in Paris you had pursued your journey, and if you have not done so already you must at once set out. Neither must you on any account allow yourself to be detained by those new negotiations between the King and the Irish, lately set on foot.

To the Same.

Rome, 28th August, 1645.

Although His Holiness is persuaded that your Excellency has left Paris and are ready to embark for Ireland (stimulated by the precise orders which his Holiness sent through me in the last letter for the immediate prosecution of your journey), yet if by any accident you should still be at Court, His Holiness commands me to say that after having maturely considered all you have written in letters and ciphers touching your remaining in Paris, on account of the treaty of peace between the

King of England and the Catholics of Ireland, which the Queen of England pretends to bring before Cardinal Mazarin, or for any other reason whatsoever, His Holiness desires that you should set out at once, for Ireland, nor incur any further delay. He believes that your long stay in Paris has caused serious injury to the affairs of the Catholics, and that the longer you delay the more the mischief will increase, and though I do not believe that you will find any obstacle to your embarkation, yet if the authorities of France do not provide for you quickly and securely, it appears to His Holiness advisable that you should go on to Flanders, and taking some of the frigates lying at Dunkirk, or by some other means, transport yourself to the Island. In short, the desire and command of His Holiness is, that you delay no longer in Paris nor in France, but with the greatest possible celerity, and the easiest and shortest way, pass over into Ireland, nor allow yourself to nourish the idea that you would do greater good to the Catholics by remaining longer in Paris. His Holiness expects that you will obey these strict and precise orders without any further reply. Father Scarampi is anxious for your speedy arrival in Ireland that he may return at once to Italy; but His Holiness has desired that the Father shall not leave without further orders, and that he shall assist you for some months to come by making you acquainted with the course of affairs and by giving his help whenever you may require it.

To the Same.

Rome, 28th August, 1645.

No one can answer Cardinal Mazarin with greater force than your Excellency when he complains that His Holiness sent you to France, not merely on your way to Ireland but that you should adroitly contrive to establish yourself as Nuncio in Paris, because your Excellency knows better than any one else that before your departure the Cardinals and prelates of the Congregation of Ireland had passed a resolution that you should go direct to Ireland. But that on the arrival here of M. de Gramonville he represented to His Holiness how strange it would appear if your Excellency should not go by way of Paris, when the Queen of England had arrived there, and that it would seem as though you were sent for some other purpose than the good of the Catholics if you should travel to the place of embarkation through the states of other princes, rather than those of France. He urged that on this account, and on the Queen's also, the vicinity to Ireland, and the ready convenience of ships, your Excellency would derive greater benefit and assistance in France than you could do by embarking from any other than a French port. And since His Holiness had no other object in this mission than the service of God, and that it should be carried on with satisfaction to all princes, he yielded at once to the remonstrances of M. de Gramonville, telling him that though the Congregation had decided differently, he would permit your Excellency to go by Paris; there to take advice how his pious intentions could best be carried out. The complaint, therefore, of Cardinal Mazarin has no greater or truer foundation than that the Holy Father condescended to listen to the solicitations of M. de Gramonville, who will be a good witness to the truth; especially as in rendering many thanks to His Holiness he said that this resolution would prevent any shadow of the suspicions which persons ill inclined to the public good might have entertained. And therefore if by any chance on the arrival of this letter your Excellency has not left Paris, though you promised without fail to depart, and His Holiness believes you will have done so you will be able to explain to Cardinal Mazarin how baseless are the insinuations which he so readily believes, conveyed to him by those who regard their own interests solely, who assert as truths what His Holiness has never thought of, and with sinister intentions interpret in a wrong sense what the Holy Father, with purposes as holy as they are wise, has always done, and will do for the common good.

No. VI. (Page 115).

To the Same (in Cipher).

11th September, 1646.

After His Holiness had made known to Mr. Digby the succours which he could afford to the Catholics of Ireland and England, and to the Queen of Great Britain, and had put on paper various proposals subscribed by me, copies of which were sent to your Excellency a few weeks ago, some good English Catholics made suggestions to His Holiness, the substance of which is contained in the accompanying cipher; but on mature consideration it does not appear proper to His Holiness to recede from the treaty made with the said Digby, nor to introduce any new subjects of negotiation. I have been commanded by His Holiness to forward our conclusions to your Excellency, in order that you may be in a position to increase or diminish those conditions which you may consider profitable to the Catholic cause, and to the public service of our holy religion in Ireland; and also what may be possible to do in England. You will not cease to act according to the circumstances which may present themselves before you, His Holiness believing that nowhere better than in Ireland, and under no other Apostolic minister than your Excellency, with the assistance of Father Scarampi, can there be effected greater benefit and richer blessings for the Catholic religion than in those kingdoms. You will therefore give great attention to the arguments of Mr. Digby, and to any which may be brought forward by English or Irish Catholics, by the ministers of the Queen, or by the King himself, warning you however not to promise any larger sum of money, or of other aids than those now mentioned, as His Holiness does not intend that the power given you to diminish or increase the conditions shall extend to money, or other assistance towards continuing the war, that is, to furnish the pay, the provisions, the arms and munitions, as was asked by those who made the above propositions. We await with much anxiety news of your Excellency's arrival in Ireland, of your health, and of the state in which you find affairs there.

To the Same.

Rome, 18th September, 1645.

The displeasure of His Holiness increases at your Excellency's delay in your departure for Ireland, and he laments to see that all the negotiations, missions, and provisions which your Excellency has continued to introduce tend still more to retard it. He commands therefore again that your Excellency with all promptitude shall set out at once for that island, that you do not delay in any part of France in expectation of letters or information from Spinola whom you have sent on before, much less wait till the frigates which were to be provided by Invernizi in Flanders to accompany you shall be put in order. It would consume too much time if you were to wait for either one or the other, and it would throw great discredit on your mission if you were to remain longer in France. The campaign for this year is all but thrown away. After taking the port of Duncannon if our succours had been ready on the spot as they should have been, great progress might have been hoped for, or at least the army could have offered a gallant resistance to the Scotch, who have destroyed so many Catholics, and now becoming insolent are threatening Connaught.

The General Assembly, if they had known of your Excellency's presence, would not perhaps have dissolved without coming to some conclusion, and God knows from what they have lately done, if your Excellency be not there, whether they may not precipitately form some resolution as little beneficial to the Catholic religion as to its free exercise.

The priest sent by the Queen would not have had time to vilify our succours, and dishearten the Catholics, who will be still more desponding and full of consternation if Secretary Belling should arrive before you.

Spinola so young and inexperienced can do little in opposition to them, and in short your Excellency must feel how many disorders have been caused by your long stay in Paris, and how much better it would have been if you had carried our succours at once to Ireland. Do not then make further delay, nor more deeply afflict the soul of the Holy Father, who will not be tranquillized until he hears of your arrival in the island, and that those good Catholics are consoled by your presence and by the succours destined for them.

If however by some grave and extraordinary accident (which we do not at all expect) your Excellency has been obliged to remain some days longer in France, His Holiness wishes you to remit to Father Scarampi the money which you have with you, so that those good Catholics shall no longer be defrauded of the holy intentions of His Holiness, and the injury they have suffered be thus repaired as much as possible. The articles given to Cardinal Mazza will be considered along with your Excellency's annotations, and the answer shall be sent to Ireland.

No. VII. (Page 250).
To the Same (in Cipher).

16th October, 1645.

The letter in cipher written by your Excellency from Orleans on 10th ultimo, has been received, and His Holiness is perfectly satisfied with your proceedings touching the gift of the Pontifical Rose to the Queen; and since in two former ciphers your Excellency had only casually mentioned that it did not appear advisable to you to give it, His Holiness was desirous of hearing more exactly the reasons for your opinion; having now heard them he is content. His Holiness takes for granted that in conformity with the orders given to your Excellency you will have prosecuted your journey towards Ireland, without further delay in France, and without regulating your movements by any intelligence which you may receive from Signor Domenico Spinola sent forward before you, or from any other person whatsoever; His Holiness desiring that it should appear clearly to the whole world that the mission of your Excellency has no other object than to console and assist those good Irish Catholics. Your Excellency must therefore follow these orders punctually, consulting in the first instance with Father Scarampi from whom when on the spot, and face to face, you can better learn the wants of the people than by hearing of them at a distance.

No. VIII. (Page 258).
To the Same.

Rome, 5th November, 1645.

In a letter from Father Scarampi of the 1st of last September he advised us of the arrival in Ireland of the Earl of Glamorgan, an English Catholic, with a commission to co-operate in matters which the Marquis of Ormonde had not adjusted respecting the Catholic religion, and with some other instructions directed to the benefit of the King, and to the introduction of the public exercise of the Catholic religion in England. With these specious proposals to the Bishops of Ireland, themselves inclined to peace, he had framed some additional articles to which, as your Excellency will see, answers were given; and finally at the solicitation of the Earl in three days the negotiation was concluded. Of this agreement Father Scarampi having become aware, he remonstrated by letter not only with the Bishops, but also with the Council for the instructions, on the small foundation they had in any negotiations with the Earl, whilst the mandates which he had produced were subscribed by the King and his Secretary only, signed with the small seal, and in consequence deprived of the necessary authority, the King having no power in himself to dispose of the political affairs of these kingdoms. The whole foundation therefore of the negotiations rested on the promises of the Earl, which being made by another could not bind the King if he did not choose to be bound; moreover being a convention made with the Bishops it would scandalize the world to see that in the published articles of peace no mention was made of the Church, of ecclesiastical property, or of the authority and jurisdiction of the Bishops, which all remained at the mercy of the King, should he not wish to make peace or observe it; and inasmuch as the Catholic laity when satisfied with the articles which had reference to themselves, would not care to make a stand for others however important, in which their own interest was not involved, would have abandoned them. Although these reasons appeared very strong to the Council and to the Bishops, why they should not disgust the seculars and cause a breach between them, yet they had remitted the whole matter to the Earl, had declared themselves satisfied on their part with his proposals on ecclesiastical matters, and consented to the publication of the treaty of peace. Father Scarampi believed therefore that it would be unanimously concluded with exactly the same secret conditions, and in the manner described above. This new and unexpected event of which Father Scarampi tells us he had informed your Excellency, has been maturely considered here, and His Holiness commands me to say that if by letters from Father Scarampi or from others to be relied on, you are convinced that the peace between the Catholics of Ireland and the King of England is established with the articles and in the manner described, he will be content that you do not prosecute your journey to Ireland, and that you shall wait for further orders from His Holiness; but if the intelligence your Excellency receives does not convey the assurance that the peace is certainly concluded, then you will at once pursue your journey. When you arrive in Ireland you will conduct yourself with prudence, and according to the advice of Father Scarampi, who is so well versed and has so much experience in these affairs, and try to improve the conditions that are proposed to the Catholics, for the free exercise and maintenance of the Catholic religion. But should the peace be established with those same articles and in the manner described, then His Holiness desires that neither your Excellency nor Father Scarampi shall do anything to express approbation or disapprobation, but remain, so to say, entirely passive, regulating your stay in the Island according as the circumstances of the time may require, always keeping in view the dignity both of the Holy Apostolic See and of your mission. His Holiness commands moreover that if you remain at La Rochelle, you remit at once to Father Scarampi 3,500 crowns Roman money, in order that he may satisfy his creditors and redeem his reputation.

To the Same.

Rome, 5th November, 1645.

Before we received your Excellency's letter from La Rochelle of 5th September last, with the cipher of the same date giving an account of the time you had remained in Paris, the cipher marked No. 1 had been written; and this on advices received from Father Scarampi, that peace was all but concluded with the conditions respecting ecclesiastical affairs which had been agreed on between the Bishops of Ireland and the Earl of Glamorgan. But as the same Earl writes to your Excellency that he will not conclude anything till he can first converse with you, we have conceived some hopes that your Excellency's arrival in Ireland may improve the proposed conditions in favour of the Catholic cause, and that the immediate succour you take with you may animate the secular Catholics, so that uniting themselves with the ecclesiastical party they may make a peace, not timid nor temporary, but glorious at once for Ireland and for all Christianity. That your Excellency may be able to represent to the Supreme Council the care which His Holiness has given from the very beginning of his Pontificate to the affairs of Ireland, I send the cipher marked No. 3 in which is registered the copy of some articles adjusted here with Mr. Digby, resident minister of the Queen of England, the originals of which shall be sent to you as soon as possible, in order that should the peace be not concluded according to the treaty with the Earl of Glamorgan, you will produce this, when you see your way to do it, and endeavour to second as much as lies in your power the desires of the Holy Father who will be ready at all times to keep to his promises. All that I say now to your Excellency presupposes that you have left La Rochelle, have arrived in Ireland, been received in a befitting manner, and that you have found affairs in a proper state for negotiation in conformity with the instructions given to you here. But should you not have set out, your movements may be regulated by the tenor of cipher No. 1.

To the Same.

Rome, 5th November, 1645.

Articles sent to Monsignor Rinuccini to be treated for in Ireland, with power to add to them or to diminish according to the present state of affairs and the necessities of the time, which he will learn to know better on the spot.

1. That the King of Great Britain shall unreservedly concede to the Kingdom of Ireland, the free and public exercise of the Roman Catholic Religion, and the restoration to the Catholics of the ecclesiastical hierarchy, with all their churches and properties in conformity with the customs of the said religion. As to the monasteries which it is pretended were conceded to the present possessors by Cardinal Pole, Legate in the time of Queen Mary, the free Parliament of Ireland will consider what can and ought to be done about them. So likewise concerning the three Archbishoprics, Dublin and the two others, which are now in the hands of Protestant heretics and subject to the King.

2. That all penal laws of every kind whatsoever, enacted against the Catholics on account of their religion from the defection of Henry VIII. until now, shall be entirely revoked and annulled.

3. That for the more complete establishment of the free and public exercise of the Catholic Religion, and for the greater certainty and security of the revocation of the said laws, the King shall concede a free Parliament in Ireland independent of that of England.

4. That the command of the kingdom of Ireland, and of the principal offices shall be placed in the hands of the Catholics; that they shall be considered as capable to hold all places of honour and dignity, and be promoted to them equally with the Protestants.

5. That for the satisfaction of the Supreme Council of Ireland, the King shall put into the hands of the Irish Catholics or at the least of English Catholics, the city of Dublin, and every other held in his name in Ireland.

6. That he shall unite his forces with those of the Irish to drive the Scotch and the Parliamentarians out of Ireland.

7. That the King having done this for Ireland, and what else Monsignor Rinuccini may add to or alter in these articles, His Holiness will be willing to pay to the Queen of Great Britain 100,000 crowns of Roman money.

8. That the said King shall revoke all laws against the Catholics of England, and especially the two oaths of supremacy and fidelity, in such a manner that they may enjoy the properties, honours, liberty and prerogatives which are enjoyed by the other gentlemen of the kingdom, so that to be Catholic shall create no sort of prejudice against them. And that in the first Parliament or other settlement of the affairs of England, His Majesty shall confirm and approve the aforesaid revocation, and place the Catholics at once on a full equality with the Protestants.

9. That it shall be agreed between the King and the Supreme Council of Ireland, to send to England a force of 12,000 infantry under Irish chiefs and officers, to which shall be added 3,000 or at the least 2,500 English horse under Catholic chiefs, with the condition that these shall arrange between them the administration of the army, ports of disembarkation, and places of security as they shall judge proper and convenient.

10. That whenever these troops shall have entered England and joined forces, His Holiness shall pay the first year 100,000 crowns of Roman money in monthly instalments, to be continued a second or a third year according to his means and according to the benefit derived from the said armies.

To the Same.

Rome, 27th November, 1645.

The paternal benevolence of His Holiness has accompanied your Excellency in your journey to Ireland, and I have prayed that you may enjoy a fulness of happiness such as you could yourself desire. If the blessed God has granted my prayers, I hope a share of it has attended your arrival in Ireland, and that your presence may have brought to the Catholics there some portion of the consolation they have so long waited for. His Holiness looks eagerly for your Excellency's letters to know how you have been received in that island, and in what state you have found affairs, whether of war or of peace. Every one here however believes that peace is concluded, and the Government consequently in the hands of the Marquis of Ormonde. Should your Excellency have arrived in time His Holiness feels assured that no diligence has been omitted on your part to improve the conditions for the Catholics, and particularly for the ecclesiastics in respect to the public exercise of the Catholic Religion throughout Ireland; and that you have taken the advice of Father Scarampi who is so well informed on those affairs, and so zealous in the service of God and for the souls of the Irish.

In due time you shall be informed of the negotiation carried on here with Mr. Digby, and in the meantime I refer you to my last advices.

To the Same.

Rome, 4th December, 1645.

See original letter of 11th September, No. VII., page 250.

Document quoted in the following letter, page 462.

1. Ut rex omnes poenales leges etiam pecuniarias contra Romanos Catholicos, seminaristas, sacerdotes, et Jesuitas a tempore Henrici septimi latas revocet, et nullius posthac valoris esse declaret.

2. Ut Rex eximat omnes Catholicos a duobus illis juramentis pri-

m:tus et fidelitatis, ita ut nullo casu in posterum dicta iuramenta Catholicis praestanda ministrentur. Loco vero secundi iuramenti, si Regi ita visum fuerit, novum iuramentum concipi poterit tale, quale a Catholicis aliarum regionum praestari solet.

3. Ut Rex ipse auctoritate sua Regia mandet Exercitum Catholicum ex propriis suis subditis Hibernis compositum colligi, et in Angliam pro regia causa defendenda transferri.

4. Ut dictus Exercitus subiaceat directioni et imperio Consilii bellici, quod tribus Catholicis Anglis totidemque Hibernis constet, simul cum supremo illius Exercitus duce, et eius locum tenente generali. Huius autem Consilii directioni et potestati supremus ille dux seu generalis subdatur. Porro tres illi Hiberni Commissarii a Confoederatis Catholicis in Hibernia cum consilio Nuntii Apostolici ibi residentis nominabuntur. Tres vero Angli Commissarii nominabuntur ab illis Catholicis Anglis, quibus cum hac super re Nuntius Apostolicus in Galliis consilium inierit, quod si contingat aliquando aliquem ex tribus nominatis Commissariis Anglis vel alio quovis modo abripi, penes erit dictos Catholicos Anglos cum consilio eiusdem Nuntii Apostolici in Galliis alium in defuncti locum nominare et subrogare.

5. Ut dictus Exercitus nullos habeat duces, praefectos, vel alios quovis in imperio positos, sive equites sive pedites, nisi solos Catholicos.

6. Ut omnes Catholici Angli, qui sparsim in Regis exercitibus et castris morantur vel alibi degunt, auctoritate Regia muniantur, ut in unum conveniant, et ad exercitum Hibernum cum equitatu eorum pedestribus copiis proportionato se conferant sub conductu Ducis Catholici ab illis Catholicis eligendi, quibus cum hac super re Nuntius Apostolicus in Galliis consilium inierit.

7. Ut pecunia illa, quam Sua Sanctitas et Sedas Apostolica regiis necessitatibus contribuet, in cogendo milite et dicto exercitu Catholico tam equestri quam pedestri impendatur; et ad hunc finem, si ita Sanctitati Suae visum fuerit, tradatur in manus eorum Catholicorum Anglorum et Hibernorum, quos praedicti Catholici exercitus Commissarii elegerint, ut sic per illos cum approbatione Nuntiorum Apostolicorum in Galliis et in Hibernia commorantium, prout occasio feret, erogetur.

8. Ut Rex in manus eorum Catholicorum quos S. Sanctitas nominaverit duo vel tria loca munita tradat, ut ab iisdem custodiantur tanquam cautiones regiae sponsionis, quae quidem loca erunt illae civitates et arces, quae munitissimae sunt inter omnes quas Rex in Hibernia iam tenet, si modo praedicti Commissarii Angli in exercitu Hiberno constituti satis eas munitas et fortes esse indicaverint; vel si non habuerit Rex in possessione sua tales totidemque civitates et arces munitas, tunc tradet illis unam, duas, vel tres primas civitates et arces, quas Catholici Hiberni in Hibernia occupaverint, et quas dicti Commissarii Angli satis fortes indicaverint.

9. Ut Rex ipse hisce articulis propria manu subscribat. In qua subscriptione promittat Rex confirmaturum, et ratificaturum infea tres proximos menses duos primos articulos sub magno Regis sigillo Suae Sanctitati eiusve Ministro tradendos, et quamprimum potestas ei data fuerit curaturum insuper, ut iidem primi articuli in Comitiis Parlamentariis totius Regni ratificentur, et confirmentur, donec autem complete hoc executioni mandatum fuerit, praedictae civitates et arces a Catholicis, ut supra nominatis, cautionis loco custodiantur. Interim supplicatur Suae Sanctitati ut considerare velit auxilium illud quod Regi praestabitur non fore sufficiens, ut Rex inde reddatur potens et capax sponsionem suam exequendi, nisi tantum quantum ad integrum exercitum colligendum eidemque iam collecto annonam, arma, caeteraque necessaria suppeditandum, et ad ipsum etiam alendum sufficiat. Similiter considerabit Sanctitas Sua quod nisi subito auxilium et ante finem hyemis mittatur, frustra erit omne illud quodcumque serius venit. Quapropter humillime rogatur Sua Sanctitas quatenus dignetur quamprimum determinare quid auxilii in particulari suo et Sedis Apostolicae nomine Regi Angliae ob promissos Catholicis favores offerre dignabitur, simul etiam et determinare conditiones, quas a dicto Rege intuitu huius auxilii requirendas esse indicat, &c.

Rome, 4th December, 1645.

To the Same.

11th December, 1645.

In the despatch which I sent to your Excellency on the 5th ultimo, I sent you also a copy of the treaty which His Holiness thought it well to concede for the benefit of the Catholics of Ireland and England. We hope it has already reached your hands, and in any case we send you a duplicate, or to speak more exactly, the true copy of the document, which with my superscription has been consigned to Mr. Digby, Resident for the Queen of England at this Court.

Your Excellency will see that this copy does not differ from the other I have mentioned, except in a delay of two months added to the last article.

We had intended to send a similar one to your Excellency, superscribed and sealed, but the fear that it might fall into the hands of the Parliamentarians, determines us to send it in cipher. Mr. Digby thinks of setting out in ten days' time on his return to the Queen, and then to go on to communicate with the King, and please God the fruits of this treaty so much desired by His Holiness may follow.

ARTICLE ADDED TO THOSE SENT ON 5TH NOVEMBER, 1645.

XI. And finally that the first six articles may be at once put in force, His Holiness will wait six months from the present date for their execution. And for the eighth and ninth, which will perhaps require more time, he will wait after those six months for four more, after which time he will not be bound by his present promise.

Given in Rome on 30th November, 1645.

CAMMILLO CARDINAL PAMPHILI.
Place ✠ of the seal.

DECLARATIO FACTA PER ASSEMBLEAM GENERALEM.

Kilkenny, 22nd February, 1646.

Cum in juramento associationis haec verba quoad vires meas continentur, &c , cum in additione annexa illi juramento per hanc Assembleam Confoederator, Rom. Cath. huius Regni haec sequentia verba continentur : et pro perseveratione, maiori robore, firmitati associationis, et unionis : Nempe Regni quandocunque aliqua pax vel accomodatio ineunda vel concludenda erit cum dictis Confoederatis Catholicis, quoad posse meum insistenda promovebo sequentes propositiones. His manifestatur, declaratur et ordinatur quod Generalis Assemblea dictorum Confoederatorum Cath. tantum est non aliud Tribunal personae, vel personarum erit Judex facultatum, et iurium Confederatorum Cath. ad supportandum, et insistendum dictis propositionibus relatis in additione, aut facultatum, et virium relatarum in dicto iuramento. Ulterius ordinatur et declaratur, quod matura habita consideratione virium, facultatum, aut defectus earundem in hoc Regno per dictam generalem Assembleam non obstante ulla conditione in dicto iuramento, additione, vel propositionibus apposita, dicta generalis Assemblea tales inire poterit resolutiones et vias, quae videbuntur tali Assembleae maxime conducere ad bonum Regni.

PER GENERALEM ASSEMBLEAM CONFOED. CATH.

Kilkenny, 25th February, 1646.

Quandoquidem propositiones praesentatae per Congregationem Archiepiscoporum, Episcoporum, et Cleri Regni Hiberniae unanimi voto Assembleae admissae et scriptae fuerint sub iuramento et supplemento associationis, quibus insistendum erit non obstante hac die. Ordinatur et declaratur, quod Generalis Assemblea dictorum Catholicorum non impedietur, neque restringetur ullis propositionibus subscriptis, quominus posset procedere alia via modo vel medio viso, et consentiente Assemblea, aut dato in instructione per ipsam concernente Ecclesias et Ecclesiasticos reditus, ac decimas in quarteriis aut locis possessis per Protestantes, vel adversam partem in conclusione pacis cum eisdem Catholicis et Marchione Ormoniae et adhaerentibus ipsi, aut cum alio authoritate per Regem.

To the Same.

Rome, 27th August, 1646.

I shall continue to use my best efforts in order to induce His Holiness to remit a sum of money to Ireland, and in my next I shall advise your Excellency of it. I am very much vexed that, notwithstanding the victory gained, there is danger that no other than a political peace will be thought of, to the great damage of the Catholic religion.

The efforts you have made to keep the people back from the precipice are highly valued here, and if the Blessed God do but permit that success shall continue to follow the Confederate armies, as in the beginning, the ministers must certainly betake themselves to better counsels. In my next I will write more at length on this matter.

To the Same.

Rome, 1st October, 1646.

The sum of 15,000 crowns, destined by His Holiness for the Catholic armies in Ireland, has been already remitted to France. Father Fra Luca has also collected a sum of money to remit immediately to your Excellency, nor do we cease to think of fresh assistance, that success may happily follow, and no disgraceful peace be made now when we are at the summit of our hopes.

From the French gazettes we hear I know not what of the conclusion of peace between the Catholics and Protestants of Ireland. The conditions are not disclosed, therefore we cannot discuss them, nor give your Excellency any counsel beyond what you have in your instructions. These reports make us greatly desire to have lettters from your Excellency. Mr. Digby is expected in Rome, some indeed say he has already arrived, but at all events he has not appeared in public. We do not know what commissions he may have, or what agreement he may propose. The appointment of the Bishops will be suspended till Father Scarampi arrives (he cannot be far off now), in order that we may be perfectly assured in our choice of the persons best fitted for election.

To the Same.

Rome, 13th October, 1646.

Since the announcement of your Excellency's arrival in Ireland we have not received any letters from you or from Father Scarampi. His Holiness waits with anxiety to know if there are hopes of peace, or if the war is to be continued. The news from England becomes more and more adverse to the Royal party, while the strength and ardour of the Parliamentarians increase with victory, so that one may almost fear the extermination of the Catholic religion in that country, which God forbid. We have not been advised by Mr. Digby of his arrival in Paris, therefore we cannot conjecture what may be the nature of his negotiations with the Queen of England, or if the declarations made by His Holiness are to be accepted. Invernizzi writes from Brussels that he hopes to set off for Ireland in three days, having obtained from Duke Charles of Lorraine two bronze cannon and a quantity of ammunition, and from the Marquis of Castel Rodrigo 1,000 muskets and 1,000 bandoliers. Please God he may arrive safely. Your Excellency will please to communicate this to Father Scarampi.

To the Same (in Cipher).

Rome, 10th December, 1646.

After His Holiness and their Eminences the Cardinals had heard the Dean of Fermo several times on the state of affairs in Ireland, and had seen all the letters, ciphers, and documents which you had sent by him, and the other letters from your Excellency, of September 12th, a full congregation was held in presence of His Holiness, in which was discussed at great length the present state of Catholic affairs in Ireland. Whereupon the Holy Father in his immense piety and liberality, though pressed on all sides by the heaviest expenses, resolved to send some large assistance in money to that island, which your Excellency will expend as usefully as you have hitherto done with the sums consigned to you when you left Rome. And since the remittance must be sent to France I write to Monsignor the Nuncio to obtain permission to export it. We think there will be no difficulty in obtaining it, but if there should be, we must think of some other way of sending it to you. Meanwhile on the security of these advices you can keep those good Catholics in heart, and animate them to be faithful in the establishment and defence of the free exercise of the Catholic religion, the true goal of the Blessed Father's desires, who will be greatly encouraged when he can hear of the continued union of the two generals, O'Neill and Preston, and when the news is confirmed of the happy progress of their arms, on which His Holiness has bestowed his paternal blessing.

In the same congregation were also considered the proposals for the vacant churches in Ireland, and the larger powers asked for by your Excellency; but the two points having been remitted to a special congregation held before Cardinal Spada, I can say no more at present than that the statements made by your Excellency, and by the Dean with reference to the persons you consider suitable for the said churches, shall have every consideration, and the powers which can be properly conceded will not be denied to your Excellency. Moreover, having seen a printed paper, in which the authors and abettors of the peace between England and the Marquis of Ormonde are pronounced to be perjurers, and a protest which the Ecclesiastical Congregation has made in these precise words: Ex quibus et ex pluribus aliis causis sola nostra conscientia moti, solumque Deum prae oculis habentes, ut notum sit universis et singulis, tum Hibernis tum exteris, tali paci nosnon dedisse aut daturos *esse consensum, nisi pro Religione et pro Rege et pro patria* iuxta nostrum, iuramentum sicuti conditiones apponantur, &c., &c. And this paper is subscribed first by your Excellency, and then by the Archbishops, Bishops, and ecclesiastics of the island. It appears to His Holiness and to us, that in this your Excellency has departed from your instructions, because it never was intended to maintain the Irish when rebels against the King, but simply to assist them in obtaining the assurance of the free exercise of the Catholic religion in Ireland. Besides, even if it be true that the maintenance of the royal power may be profitable to the Catholic religion without injury to the constant, never interrupted usage of the Apostolic See, it is not considered well that Nuncios or other Apostolic ministers should make or consent to public declarations by which the Holy See appears or can appear to approve or assent to declarations made by subjects also Catholics, respecting the defence or conservation of the state and person of an heretical king. Your Excellency must therefore guard yourself against noticing such writings, declarations, or acts, so that enemies not overfull of love to the Apostolic See may not have an opportunity of calumniating it, and representing its principles to be as different as possible from those which have governed it ever since its foundation. I know that it may perhaps be difficult to separate, at least in General Assemblies and particular Congregations, the interests of religion from those of fidelity which the Catholics there profess towards the King; but it will suffice to our Holy Father that your Excellency do not show by public acts any consent or participation in the demonstrations which the Catholics are obliged or wish to make for their political interests. From the example I have drawn from this printed document, in which occur the Latin words I have mentioned, your Excellency will be able to regulate your conduct on such other occasions as may present themselves, and thus observe the tenor of your instructions. This is all which occurs to me at present.

To Monsignor the Nuncio of France.

Our Holy Father having resolved to assist the Catholics of Ireland with a considerable sum of money, in order to secure the free exercise of the Catholic religion in that island, commands me to tell your Excellency that he desires to treat with the proper person to obtain His Majesty's permission to export it to the kingdom of Ireland from France, remittances for this money, amounting to the sum of forty or fifty thousand crowns, to be sent from Rome; and you will advise us at once so that we may give immediate orders for the remittance and its exportation. His Holiness feels that it is not necessary to add any stimulus to your accustomed diligence in an affair so important, but that you will overcome every difficulty and delay if such should occur, which however he does not anticipate in so holy a cause, and one so congenial to the pastoral solicitude of His Holiness.

To Monsignor Rinuccini (in Cipher).

Rome, 16th December, 1646.

We are hastening the departure of the Dean of Fermo, and are devising whence with the greatest advantage we can remit the money which His Holiness wishes to send in aid of the Catholics of Ireland. We are also debating on the faculty which the clergy there wish us to concede to your Excellency, and on the persons to promote to the vacant bishoprics of that Kingdom. All goes on well both for the satisfaction of your Excellency, and for the benefit of the souls of that people.

There are reports current of the surrender of Dublin to the Generals O'Neill and Preston and of the imprisonment of the Marquis of Ormonde, but we cannot depend on them, as neither your Excellency nor the Nuncio of France have advised us of it: we therefore wait with anxiety to hear the certainty of the news from you. Sir K. Digby touched but little on the affairs of Ireland after hearing the resolutions of the ecclesiastics and others to adhere to their party in refusing their consent to any peace established with the Marquis of Ormonde, and of the movement of the Confederate armies towards Dublin. And as we are left in doubt as to the success of these armies we shall be much pleased to have letters from your Excellency on this matter.

To Monsignor the Nuncio of France (in Cipher).

His Holiness has commanded us to take into serious consideration the representation made to your Excellency by those English Catholics who are invited by the Independents to join their party. I will endeavour to inform your Excellency as soon as possible of the results of the consultations on Irish affairs; and advise you of anything which comes to our knowledge; but despatches from Monsignor the Archbishop of Fermo are very rare, and we shall be much relieved by any certain news sent by him.

To Father Scarampi (in Cipher).

The armies of Generals O'Neill and Preston having undertaken the enterprise against Dublin as His Excellency reports in his letters of 4th of last October, the success of affairs with you will depend on the issue of that siege. Although some of the Catholics who are inclined to the side of the Marquis of Ormonde, show themselves lukewarm in adhering to the

Catholic cause and in joining the Ecclesiastical Congregation, yet if the attack on Dublin has a happy termination, as most people expect, every one of them will turn to the victor, and free from all fear will unite themselves with real loyalty to the Ecclesiastical party. The jealousy which exists between Generals O'Neill and Preston will be suppressed by the authority of Monsignor the Nuncio and by the successful result of affairs, because neither of them will wish to lose the fruits of victories acquired with so much toil and bloodshed, and will give up dissensions so prejudicial to the secure establishment of the Catholic Religion in the Kingdom. The Holy Father will not fail on his side to send all the help in money which the press on the Ecclesiastical Treasury will permit. The bishoprics will be provided as His Excellency hopes with the most worthy and excellent persons.

No. IX. (Page 284).

To Monsignor Rinuccini.

Rome, 18th February, 1647.

So various were the reports respecting the siege of Dublin which came to us from France and Flanders that little surprise was excited by your Excellency's account of its failure. The hope of its success rested on the celerity of the movement and on the union of the two Generals, but failing in such essential conditions, besides the approach of winter, and the continued discord between the two Generals, the enterprise necessarily fell to the ground. It is of importance therefore that this rivalry and discord between them should cease, for should it continue, which God forbid, it is certain that the greater part of what has been gained will be lost. Our Holy Father is assured that your Excellency will not spare any efforts, nor lose any opportunity to accomplish this end and to unite them in heart, so that forewarned of the arts of Secretary Digby, and the deceitful conduct of the Earl of Glamorgan in following the Ormonde party, they may take the better resolution to be reunited and to obey the orders of the Council.

Of the first and second proposals made to your Excellency by Lord Clanricarde, you have not sent us copies; and though from your reflections upon them we can form some idea of his Lordship's pretensions, we cannot fully discuss them till we have had them *in extenso*. The English publication contains only the propositions from Lord Clanricarde to the Council, and the answers of the Council. They have been sent for interpretation together with the other reports and ciphers of your Excellency to their Eminences the Cardinals, to whom are deputed the affairs of Ireland, and of whose resolutions I will advise you at once. Meanwhile His Holiness is pleased with the friendly intercourse you keep up with Father Scarampi and hopes it will continue till the Father's return here.

In the Consistory to be held this morning, some of the Churches will be preconized, and successively appointed, of which your Excellency shall have a note, although I think that the Dean of Fermo will have advised you of it.

TO MONSIGNOR THE NUNCIO OF FRANCE (IN CIPHER).

I have shown His Holiness your Excellency's cipher of 18th January, in which you inform me that the Comte de Brienne has given you the regular licence to export the money from France with which His Holiness desires to succour the Catholics of Ireland. His Holiness has remitted this matter to my Lords the Cardinals of the Congregation upon the affairs of that Island. I will advise your Excellency immediately of the resolutions of their Eminences.

Ego A. B. promitto, iuro, et protestor coram Deo sanctis et angelis eius, quod durante vita mea fidelis et obediens ero suae Maiestati Domino meo Carolo Dei gratia Regi magnae Britaniae, Franciae, et Hiberniae, nec non et haeredibus et legitimis successoribus ipsius, et quoad vires meas defendere, supportare, et manutenere conabor omnia ipsius et ipsorum praerogativa haereditates et iura, potestatem et privilegia parlamenti huius Regni, leges fundamentales Hiberniae, liberum exercitium Romanae Catholicae Fidei et Religionis per totum hoc Regnum, vitas, justas libertates, possessiones, haereditates et iura omnium qui se hoc iuramento astrinxerunt vel astringent contenta iuramenti praestando, et obediendo, ratificando omnes constitutiones ordinationes et decreta facta aut facienda per supremum Consilium Confoederatorum Catholicorum huius Regni, concernentia dictam publicam causam; nec petam, nec accipiam directe vel indirecte veniam, condonationem, aut protectionem pro aliquo actu, facto vel faciendo concernente hanc generalem causam sine consensu majoris partis illius Consilii; nec directe vel indirecte faciam aliquid quod dictae causae praejudicio vel impedimento esse posset, sed cum periculo vitae et patrimonii mei perseverabo in fovendo, supportando, et manutenendo eandem. Insuper juro quod non accipiam nec submittam me alicui paci factae vel faciendae cum dictis Confoederatis Catholicis sine consensu et approbatione generalis Assembleae dictorum Confoederatorum Catholicorum; et pro praeservatione, majore robore, et firmitate associationis et unionis Regni, quandocumque aliqua pax vel accomodatio ineunda vel concludenda erit cum dictis Confoederatis Catholicis, quoad meum posse insistendo promovebo sequentes propositiones, quoadusque pax et res concludendae in articulis pacis assecurentur et effectum sortientur in parlamento. Sic me Deus adjuvet, et haec sacrosancta Evangelia.

Ego A. B. iuro et protestor quod secundum meae conscientiae et intellectus dictamen omnibus viis et modis stabilire conabor accomodationem in hac Assemblea super praesentem tractatum inter Dominum Marchionem

Ormoniae Locumtenentem Hiberniae et Confoederatos Catholicos, et hoc secundum captum meum praestantiori et excellentiori modo, redundans in bonum Romanae Catholicae Religionis, publicae causae Confoederatorum Catholicorum, et praeservationis huius Regni et Nationis. Sic me Deus adiuvet.

Propositiones a Clero formatae et oblatae Comitiis Generalibus.

1. *Ut Romani Catholici tam de Clero quam laici in suis variis capacitatibus habeant liberum et publicum exercitium Romanae Catholicae Religionis, et functionis per Regnum universum, in tam pleno splendore et magnificentia quam fuit regnante Henrico VII., aut quovis alio Catholico Rege ex praedecessoribus ipsius Regibus Angliae et Dominis Hiberniae, sive in Hibernia sive in Anglia.*

In this first article there has been no difficulty except in the words interlined, because many wished to restrict them to the districts now in the possession of the Confederates, but it has been judged that the clergy both in honour and conscience must insist that it shall extend to the whole kingdom.

2. *Ut saecularis Clerus Hiberniae videlicet Primates, Archiepiscopi, Episcopi, Ordinarii, Decani et Capitula, Archidiaconi, Praebendarii, et alii Dignitarii, Rectores, Vicarii, et omnes alii Pastores de seculari Clero, et eorum respective successores habeant et habere possint omnes et omnimodas jurisdictiones, privilegia, et immunitates in tam pleno et amplo modo ut Romanus Catholicus saecularis Clerus habuit, ac illis fruitus est intra hoc Regnum quocumque tempore durante Regno Henrici VII. aliquando Regis Angliae et Domini Hiberniae, non obstante quacumque legum declaratione, statuto, potestate, vel auctoritate quacumque in contrarium.*

In this second the Secular Clergy only are included, the Regulars are omitted because it has been resolved to speak of them apart on account of the particular difficulty of the impropriated monasteries.

3. *Ut omnes leges, et statua condita a 20 anno Henrici VIII., per quae ulla coercitio, poena, mulcta, incapacitas, aut alia quaevis restrictio imponitur aut imponi possit ulli Catholico Romano, sive dicto Clero sive Laico, ob eiusmodi dictum liberum exercitium Romanae Catholicae Religionis intra hoc Regnum, et variarum ad ipsos spectantium functionum, jurisdictionum, et privilegiorum annullent, revocent, et declarentur vacuae seu nullius roboris in proximo Parlamento per unum aut plures actus Parlamenti admittendos, sanciendos, approbandos, et firmandos in illo.*

This article is similar in every part to all those which have been drawn up more fully on this subject.

4. *Ut Primates, Archiepiscopi, Episcopi, Ordinarii, Decani et Capitula, Archidiaconi, Cancellarii, Thesaurarii, Cantores, Praepositi, Guardiani*

Collegiatarum Ecclesiarum, Praebendarii, et alii Dignitarii, Rectores, Vicarii, et alii Pastores Romani Catholici saecularis Cleri, et illorum respective successores habeant, teneant, et fruantur omnibus Ecclesiis et Ecclesiasticis Beneficiis, in tam amplo ac largo modo quam nuperus Protestans Clerus respective illis fruitus est prima die Octobris, 1641, *una cum omnibus fructibus, emolumentis, proventibus, libertatibus, et viribus partinentibus ad illorum respective sedes, et Ecclesias tam in omnibus locis, quae nunc sunt in possessione Confoederatorum Catholicorum quam in aliis omnibus quae per Confoederatos Catholicos recuperabuntur ab adversariis intra hoc Regnum, servando Romanis Catholicis Laicis sua respective jura secundum Leges Patriae.*

The last clause (with the exception of the end of the article) signifies that the Protestant Bishops having taken some lands from different laymen, under pretext of these not being included in the impropriations and investitures made by the King to those laymen, they wish to reserve the right to bring the question up for judgment according to the laws of the kingdom, in order to see to whom they will be adjudged. Time will show how this may be.

No. X. (Page 289).

To Monsignor the Nuncio of Ireland (in Cipher).

29th April, 1647.

Your Excellency will hear at full length from the Dean of Fermo with whom His Holiness has frequently conversed on the affairs of Ireland, and who has also attended the Congregations held on the same subject, so that you will perfectly understand the sentiments of the Holy Father. Hence I might be excused from explaining them in detail here, but he desires that you should receive in these few lines a new testimony and still stronger assurance of the satisfaction afforded him by your conduct in this important negotiation, and he has commanded me to say that he greatly desires the Treasury of the Holy See had been filled to abundance, so that he might have assisted with a liberal hand the wants of those good Catholics. Instead of this, he finds it (as every one knows) greatly exhausted, and he cannot undertake the weight of the expenses it would be necessary for him to incur for this purpose, therefore the Catholics themselves, both on account of their private interests and public obligations should form a holy union, with a firm resolution to save their religion and their lives; and your Excellency with your accustomed fervour and zeal will enforce the necessity of this union on the minds of the ecclesiastics and the Catholic laity, and especially on the two Generals, O'Neill and Preston, for on it will now depend the security of Catholicism in the island.

We fear that little can be hoped from the Marquis of Ormonde, for although he has heretofore shown himself favourable to the King, and an enemy of the Parliamentarians, it is perhaps because the King's affairs have never been at so low an ebb as now, and changeable as he is, God knows if for ends of his own he may not join the Parliamentarians and the Scotch, and intend with the help of his adherents in Ireland to procure the ruin of the Catholics.

Respecting the assistance to be hoped for from the two Crowns, we have no foundation for judgment, while the accounts which reach us give us reason so frequently to change the opinions we had formed some time ago. Your Excellency must shrink from giving occasion for the smallest suspicion of partiality, and by showing yourself perfectly neutral, you will not only protect yourself as you have hitherto done, but your acknowledged sincerity will enable you to make such representations as will convince the two Crowns that they are beloved equally by His Holiness. If it should happen, which however no one believes possible, that the Parliamentarians gain admission into Ireland and make progress there, it is left to your Excellency's known prudence to decide what will be most convenient and secure for the safety of your person, and to avoid every sinister attempt they may contrive to injure you.

His Holiness remits for the use of the Catholics 50,000 crowns in bills consigned to the care of the Dean of Fermo, who is charged by His Holiness if he should be obliged to carry it himself in cash from France, to endeavour to do so with very great caution, first however using every diligence possible to see if it cannot be done by remittance and bills of exchange, or if your Excellency can make the money more profitable for the Irish by making it payable in France, which would be more desirable as well as more secure. But if this cannot be done with the whole sum, it might at least be with the greater part of it, and finally His Holiness warns you that when the money or the credit arrives in Ireland, should any agreement, truce, or peace have been concluded between the parties, or is on the point of being concluded, your Excellency is not to dispose of even the smallest part of the money without new orders from His Holiness; but should the war still continue, your Excellency will endeavour to expend it in undertakings that may be of certain benefit to the Catholics. This result His Holiness thinks he may promise himself from what your Excellency has reported, and which may be of great utility for the secure maintenance of religion. Finally, His Holiness sends you his blessing and also to the Catholics around you.

To the Same (in Cipher).

His Holiness is greatly pleased with your Excellency's proceedings and the wise judgment you have exercised in the conduct of affairs in Ireland; and in truth the speech you made in the General Assembly could not have been more to the purpose or better considered. The renunciation of the office of President of the Supreme Council by you, so much desired here, will make the world sensible of the pious desire of the Holy Father, that his ministers should not meddle in political matters, but attend solely to the success of his chief object, the propagation and maintenance of the Catholic religion.

As to the Regulars who disseminate strange opinions and seek to heal the consciences of others by perilous doctrines, it will be well to turn your back on them, and your Excellency will omit no opportunity of mortifying them as you best can ; but though this may be a good expedient to preserve union among the ecclesiastics, it appears that the one thing needful is the union between the two Generals, Preston and O'Neill. It was because of their rivalry and discord that the enterprise against Dublin did not succeed, and since, if it do not cease little good can be expected, it will be a meritorious work for your Excellency's wisdom and courage to compose their dissentions, and to show these men that the service of God and of religion, which depends on them and their armies, languishes strangely while they are at variance, that their dissensions are a byword to their adversaries and an actual advantage to their cause. Your Excellency has done well in not presenting the brief to Lord Clanricarde whilst he inclines to the party of the Marquis of Ormonde and acts against the orders of your Excellency; exercise prudence however and so manage that the Archbishop of Tuam and others of his relations may induce him to follow a better path. As soon as the Congregation has discussed those affairs, you shall hear more fully of them.

To the Same (in Cipher).

Rome, 22nd July, 1647.

In the Congregation which was held on Friday last on the affairs of Ireland, the last ciphers from your Excellency were read, and particularly that of 25th of March, in which you represent the necessity the Catholics are under to seek the protection of some foreign Prince, and since you kept aloof in that discussion, having had no instructions thereon ; the matter was maturely considered here, and it was resolved (after due praise being bestowed on the sagacity and prudence of your Excellency) that it will be advisable not only that you continue to keep aloof and neutral, but that with your usual dexterity you manage that the protection of the Holy Father be not taken into consultation, because His Holiness loves those Catholics with great tenderness, and does not wish to deprive them of the protection they might receive from other Princes. You will persuade them to believe that His Holiness will never abandon them, nor deprive them of the protection they now receive from him, which not going beyond the limits of the service of God and of the Catholic religion, is so deeply implanted in the mind of His Holiness, that it cannot be rooted out by any mischance. In this security the Catholics may consider what course will be most to their advantage, and apply to the person who can in their judgment best promote their interest.

But while we cannot entertain the proposal or resolution to place these Catholics under the protection of His Holiness, you must not give any positive refusal, but by your manner leave some little hope with them of obtaining the boon they desire. We notify this holy resolution to your Excellency, because you know full well that neither to the Irish themselves, nor to His Holiness would his protection turn to good account. The jealousy of the other princes, the immense tract of sea which interposes between the Ecclesiastical States and that Island, the exhaustion of the Papal treasury and a thousand other causes, ought to restrain them from any idea of proposing it. Your Excellency will therefore maintain your position of neutrality but at the same time seek to frustrate any design they may form on this head.

The proposals made by the Clergy and presented to the General Assembly and the remarks of your Excellency upon them, have also been taken into consideration, and as they appear to be very prudent there is no occasion for further observation upon them.

The Dean of Fermo meets with some difficulty in exporting the money from France. He will spare no effort to succeed, and also to recover if it be possible the amount of the frigate which was sold.

To Monsignor the Nuncio of France (in Cipher).

If the Dean of Fermo should despair of being able to obtain leave for the exportation of the money assigned by the Holy Father in aid of the Catholics of Ireland, we think he had better go on into Flanders, and by way of Antwerp and other Catholic towns negotiate the remittance there. And should he still find it difficult or impossible in those places we think he must go into Spain, whence it is thought that it will be more easy to export or remit it, and if he has not sufficient introductions with him, for either one or the other country, they shall be sent without any delay. We believe however that with your Excellency's diligence, and the piety of the Queen and of the Ministers, he will obtain what we desire. In the meantime he does not neglect to treat about a remittance by Monsignor Rinuccini, having supposed, on his departure from Rome, that there would be some gentleman or Irish merchant who would desire to have money in France. You will please to communicate all this to the Dean.

No. XI. (Page 290.)

ACCOMODATIO INTER CONFOEDERATOS ET MARCHIONEM ORMONIAE.

1. Sit utrinque gubernium independens tam civile quam militare.

This first Article was greatly disputed, so large a number wished that the Marquis should be the Head.

2. Jurentur invicem Confoederati et Pars Regia sub Ormonio in confoederatione defensiva et offensiva.

3. Dublinium aliaque praesidia sub Ormonio assecurentur.

4. Proprii reditus Ormonio dentur in nostris quarteriis, et insuper instruatur mediis pro decentia tantae auctoritatis.

We cannot do more for the Marquis than what is contained in No. 4, and yet it appears to him as nothing.

5. Liceat Confoederatis Catholicis redire ad propria in quarteriis Ormonii, et terris ac fundis frui, et ibi tuti sint, idem fiat Protestanti parti Regiae in quarteriis Confoederatorum.

Haec reputantur substantialia.

On the 5th Article I declared myself to be in a great difficulty, because it appears to me that we cannot in conscience do any positive act to recall these Protestants; and even if it be done on the plea that the Catholics receive the like favours in their districts, it still appears to me that in any case the temporal good is a very inferior one to that spiritual good which is placed in danger.

ADDUNTUR INFRASCRIPTA A CLERO OBLATA.

1. Non tradet Ormonius gladium alicui sine consensu Confoederatorum.

2. Insuper quidquid durante confoederatione Confoederatorum armis acquiritur sit Confoederatorum, et Ecclesiae cedant Confoederatis.

3. Exercitus sub Ormonio reducatur ad tales qui Regi et Regno sint fideles, et tot qui e redditibus quarteriorum propriorum et vectigalium in eis possint sustentari.

4. Pro Ecclesiis in quarteriis Ormonii, ubi est numerus major Catholicorum, fruantur Ecclesiis et beneficiis etc.

It being certain that in all the Royal districts there are more Catholics than Protestants, it appears that this article is sufficiently favourable to religion, &c.

TO MONSIGNOR RINUCCINI (IN CIPHER).

Rome, 29th July, 1647.

The statements of Father Scarampi in Paris were simply made to show what could be done for the satisfaction of the Queen, but as the paper containing them was not signed by the said Father they were not taken into consideration between him and His Holiness, as I have mentioned with other matters to your Excellency. Little weight therefore can be attached to them, the more so as things change every day, and events in England may stimulate the Catholics to make an advantageous peace for their religion, take from the Queen and Prince the idea of regaining Ireland, and give to the Holy Father worthy cause to interest himself in a glorious manner in the service of the Catholics towards whom he never ceases to feel a paternal affection.

The Dean having started with a considerable sum of money granted by His Holiness, may make them sensible of his sentiments towards them; and though the length of the journey and the difficulty of exporting the money from France may possibly delay the speed of the succour, this affords no argument that the love of His Holiness or his zeal in their interests is in the smallest degree diminished. But it displeases him extremely that there should be any thought of truces, or of returning to the peace already rejected with such generous resolutions and execrated with so many oaths. However we may hope from the good offices of your Excellency and from hearing of the approaching arrival of the money by the Dean, that the General Assembly may change its proceedings, that the Catholic chiefs may be reanimated, the ardour of the ill-affected cooled, and finally that if by treachery they have succeeded, that the most lamentable consequences may ensue for themselves

---

No. XII. (Page 294).

Casu quo Confoederati Catholici intendant se submittae Regiae auctoritati.

1. Ad id faciendum sola via relicta est pacem jam rejectam recipere pro securitate tum vestra, tum cuiuscumque alterius qui vobiscum tractabit, praesenti Regis Statu considerato.

2. Si pro sponsionibus aut conditionibus a D. de Clanrikard oblatis, aut aliis quibusvis quae a Regina et Principe Walliae obtineri possent, talem quae rationabiliter peti et haberi possit assecurationem accipiatis, et consimiliter pro praestandis ex vestra parte dederitis.

3. Si jam penes vos non est pacem concludere, tum tempore opportuno Assembleam convocare.

4. Si in ordine ad negotium hoc promovem dum sine mora conati fueritis cessationem obtinere pro sex mensibus, a mense in mensem (et si interim per tot menses continuare non libuerit data unius mensis praemonitione) conditionibus aequalibus ex una et altera parte, quarum una (ut opinor) ex parte D. Ormonii erit talis extensio limitum suae quarteriae quae ad sustentationem suorum sufficiat, quando scilicet pactum omne cum Parlamento rescindet; quae limites restituendae erunt ut prius, si res finaliter non concordetur. Causa talis cessationis est quod ea durante poterit fieri

tractatus in Gallia cum Regina et Principe, et mutuae assecurationes concordari, et satis temporis suppetet D). Ormonio se ab obligationibus quibus Parlamento obnoxius est salvo honore subtrahere.

5. Si mihi et uni vel duobus aliis, quos idoneos iudicabitis, rem agendam commiscritis, quamdiu occultam tenere licebit: Postremo si hoc fundamento inniti volueritis, totum opus promovere conabor, et multae sunt mihi, rationes quibus suadeatur rem ad finem desideratum perventuram.

No. XIII. (Page 352).
To the Same (in Cipher).

Rome, 2nd September, 1647.

Although the Holy Father feels certain that Monsignor the Nuncio of France has advised your Excellency of the conversation between the Earl of Montrose a Scotchman, and the Dean of Fermo, he has nevertheless commanded me to send your Excellency the enclosed copy of the cipher written on this matter by Monsignor the Nuncio (signed A). He has also ordered that I shall send the annexed copy of a letter (signed B) which came from London from a person well informed on current affairs. From this you will see that all the devices of France tend to strengthen the Scotch party to maintain the war in England. While on the one hand it appears that this might be of benefit to affairs in Ireland, it is necessary to consider whether it would be wise to unite the arms of the Catholics with the Scotch who are in the Island, whilst there is the least hope or probability of being able to drive them out of the part of the country which they now occupy, and so free the whole Kingdom from the Heretics. But your Excellency who is on the spot and knows the state of affairs, will with your accustomed prudence advise what is best for the service of God and of the Catholic Religion, especially if it be true that General O'Neill has made himself master of Sligo in Connaught, and that General Preston after defeating the garrison of Dublin had returned to the siege of that city, as we are advised by the Dean of Fermo in his letter of the 9th ultimo from Paris, where he is still detained.

To the Same.

Rome, 16th September, 1647.

Affairs in England are so completely changed and are in such confusion as to the Royal authority, that nobody can judge what is on foot or on what conditions; not even whether Fairfax who has already entered London with his army, wishes to reduce the Government to a Republican form. This at least is true, that the disturbances of that Kingdom must turn the game in favour of the Confederates of Ireland, if the strife and contention between the chiefs of the Catholic army do not cause them to lose this good opportunity, the more favourable since the hostile army as your Excellency tells us, is so much reduced by sickness. The Holy Father is quite satisfied with your diligence in seeking to pacify those Generals, and desires you not to be disheartened even though you meet with great difficulties, because with the help of God they may be overcome.

The proposals of Mr. Winter Grant concerning the peace, and for permission for the Prince of Wales to take refuge in Ireland may be altogether changed by the events in England; we cannot therefore discuss them to any advantage, since at this moment the treaty may have totally vanished.

The last letters received from the Dean of Fermo are from Paris of the 22nd August; they are full of complaints of the difficulty that he has met with in his proceedings, but your Excellency's advice is so excellent that he should not set out at this moment, thus to avoid the risk of being plundered by the enemy's ships now sailing about the Island, that I have written to the same purport, so that the money from His Holiness, the arms from the Grand Duke, and the provisions collected in France may be taken over with all possible security.

He sends us an account of the negotiation he has had with the Queen of England, of which I do not remit you a copy as I feel certain that he has sent your Excellency a similar account, besides which nothing of importance has come of it, since she remains fixed in her opinion, that there are no other means to insure the tranquillity of the kingdom than to come to terms with the Marquis of Ormonde.

No. XIV. (Page 440).
To the Same.

Rome, 16th November, 1648.

We can say but little to your Excellency on the affairs of Ireland whilst the sum of our intelligence consists in the progress made by the armies of O'Neill and of the Council. We can only pray to God to unite the minds of the Catholics in order to terminate the civil war already begun, provided the public exercise of religion can be maintained in the whole island, this being the principal object, as I have often told your Excellency, of the rising and agitations in the kingdom. His Holiness compassionates all the troubles your Excellency has met with; he never could have believed that such severities would have been practised against you and the Dean; but you who are adorned with no less courage than constancy of soul will know how to control these fierce storms. We therefore have hope that the Blessed God will have preserved you safe from all the evils with which this violent tempest threatens you. The Dean of Kilkenny has sent us some papers in justification of the censure in the present state of affairs in the kingdom; but we have not answered him in the fear of our letters not being safely delivered. Solicitations have been made here by protégés of the Ambassador of France to be appointed to some of the vacant churches, but the Holy Father has excused himself on the score of the present disturbances.

Father Davit, since the fall from his carriage, has departed to Heaven.

We hear that a Carmelite father, who has arrived in Paris, is the bearer of the appeal from the Council, and also that he may come on to Rome; we await his arrival and representations, but your Excellency may rest assured we shall not come to any resolution without first communicating it to you.

To the Same.

Rome, 29th March, 1649.

Last week your Excellency's confessor, Father Gioseffo, arrived in Rome, he has not yet had audience of His Holiness owing to the many occupations of the Holy Father during these last days of Lent. He has therefore given to me and Monsignor the Assessor a full account of affairs with you, of which we much desired to have fresher intelligence, as it is now more than four months since we have had letters from you. But as we believe that this scarcity of letters arises from the few opportunities of vessels leaving Ireland for France or Flanders, we take every opportunity to write to your Excellency as frequently as we desire or is perhaps necessary; but His Holiness waits with much tranquillity for the answers, reposing in every way in your great prudence and skill. Here it is believed that the death of the King of England must constrain the Catholics of that kingdom to form a complete union among themselves; since it may be feared that if the Parliamentary Government should prevail the Catholics will be treated in all that concerns religious matters with greater harshness than when they were under the royal authority; and certainly it is easier to conquer the will of one than of many, still more than that of the people, who are moved by the lightest breath of suspicion, of self-interest or revenge. But these considerations will have already been well weighed by the wise judgment of your Excellency so as to improve this good opportunity, and to warm up General O'Neill and his followers to some great purpose, since on the progress of his army depends as you say the secure establishment of the Catholic religion in Ireland.

No audience has yet been granted to the Provincial of the Carmelites although he makes unceasing solicitations to obtain it; but until Father Gioseffo shall have been heard by His Holiness and their Eminences of the Congregation, they will not come to any resolution about the Provincial. With respect to the capture of one of the frigates which the Dean of Fermo was conducting to Ireland, your Excellency will see what has been written in the annexed cipher by the Abbot of St. Anastasia; we wait however for the answer of the Nuncio of Spain, to whom we have written on the matter, &c.

Extrait de l'Acte de Parlement d'Angleterre pour descouvrir, convaincre, et punir les Papistes qui refuseront d'abjurer.

Toute l'Europe sçait combien de Loix rigoureuses et inhumaines, qui ne sont nullement differentes de celles que les Empereurs Payens ont faites autrefois contre les Chrestiens du temps de la primitive Eglise, onte esté establies dans les Isles de la Grande-Bretagne depuis cent ans que la Divine Providence a permis qu'elles soient tombées dans les tenebres de l'Heresie. Et que par un Schisme malheureux, qui a esté l'effet d'une cause honteuse et infame, elles se soient separées du corps de l'Eglise. Et en suite combien de persecutions horribles les Catholiques y ont souffert. Cela est si notoire, que les ambassadeurs de tous les Princes Chrestiens ont esté tesmoins oculaires de ces rigueurs, et ont reconnu que la Religion seule estoit la cause de la ruine d'une infinité de familles très-considerable, et de la mort d'un grand nombre de Prestres, de Religieux, et de Laïques. A present que la mesme Providence a changé le Gouvernement de ces mesmes Isles: il semble que ceux qui y font maintenant la fonction de magistrats, veulent poursuivre ce mesme dessein touchant l'execution de ces injustes Loix: non pas tant par un esprit de fureur contre le vie de ceux qu'ils reconnoissent pour Catholiques, que par un desir insatiable qu'ils ont de s'emparer de tous les bien qu'ils possedent. L'edict, dont voicy la teneur en abregé, qui a esté publié depuis peu de jours dans la Ville de Londres, en est une prevue évidente.

Il est évident que le nombre des Papistes recusants s'accroist depuis peu grandement en la Republique, par la negligence qu'on apporte à l'execution des Loix, qui ont esté faites contre eux, et que c'est de là que viennent une infinité de dangers, qui peuvent troubler le repos public. Parce-que ces gens là sont extrêmement remuants pour toute sorte de complots, et de conspirations funestes, comme il paroist depuis peu de temps, par la revolte, et le carnage cruel, et sanglant, qu'ils ont fait en Irlande et en Angleterre. Pour obvier donc à ces maux, il a esté ordonné par l'autorité du Parlement.

1. Que les grands Jurés feront une exacte recherche de toutes les personnes soupçonnées d'estre Papistes, et aagées de seize ans, dont ils presenteront les noms, et que toutes telles personnes accusées seront obligées de comparoistre personnellement aux assises prochaines, ou pardevant la Seance generale des Juges, qui se tient par quartier en chaque Province, pour y prester et souscrire le serment d'Abjuration, en la maniere suivante.

2. J'abjure et renonce la **Primauté** du **Pape**, et toute son autorité prétenduë sur l'Eglise Catholique en general, et sur moy mesme en particulier. Et je croy que l'Eglise Romaine n'est point la veritable Eglise. Et qu'il ne se fait point de Transubstantiation dans le Sacrement de la Cene du Seigneur, ny dans les élements du pain et du vin apres leur consecration par quelque personne que se puisse estre. Je croy aussi qu'il n'y a point du tout de Purgatoire, et que ny l'Hostie consacrée, ny les Crucifix, ny les Images ne doivent point estre adorées, et que tout cela n'est digne d'aucun culte religieux. Je croy encore que notre salut ne peut estre merité par nos œuvres. Et je declare, et proteste sincerement que le Pape, ny par soy-mesme, ny par aucune autorité de l'Eglise, et du Siege de Rome, ny par quelque autre moyen que se puisse estre, avec qui que ce soit, n'a nul pouvoir de déposer le Magistrat souverain de cette Nation, ny de disposer des pays, et des terres qui luy appartiennent ; ny d'autoriser un Prince ou un Estat estranger, qui voudroit s'en rendre maistre par une usurpation violente ; ny de dispenser pas un des sujets de cette nation de l'obeïssance qu'ils doivent au souverain Magistrat ; ny de leur donner la licence de prendre les armes, d'exciter des troubles, et de faire nul outrage, ny nulle sorte de violence à la personne du dit Magistrat souverain, ou à l'Estat et au Gouvernement du pays, ou à qui que ce soit du peuple qui le compose. Outre cela je jure que j'abhorre et deteste du cœur cette damnable doctrine, et cette maudite maxime—Que les Princes, les Chefs, et les Gouverneurs des Estats qui sont excommuniez, et privez de leur puissance par le Pape, peuvent en vertu d'une telle excommunication, et privation de leurs droicts, estre tuez, assassinez et deposez de leur Souveraineté, ou Gouvernement, ou qu'ils soient justement exposez aux injures, et à la fureur de leurs peuples, ny de quelques autres sous de semblables pretextes. Je jure encore que je croy que le Pape ou l'Evesque de Rome n'a nulle autorité, ny puissance, ny jurisdiction de quelque nature que ce soit dans l'Angleterre, dans l'Escosse, et dans l'Irlande, ny sur aucune personne des dites terres. J'abjure aussi toute doctrine qui appuye les points cy-dessus exprimez, sans nulle équivoque, reserve mentale, ny autre défaite subtile, prenant les paroles que j'ay prononcées dans le sens ordinaire, où l'usage commun les employe. Et enfin je croy que nulle puissance émanée du Pape ou de l'Eglise Romaine, ou quelque autre personne que se puisse estre, n'a point le pouvoir de m'absoudre de ce serment. Et je renonce tous les pardons et toutes les Dispenses qui m'en pretendroient exempter. Ainsi Dieu me soit en aide.

3. Que tous les divers Juges de la Paix envoyeront quatre fois par an leurs mandemens aux Commissaires, et aux Marguilliers de chaque Paroisse, pour avoir une liste de toutes les personnes soupçonnées d'estre Papistes recusants de l'aage de seize ans, qui sont obligées à prester le serment. Et que sur la presentation de la liste, chaque Justice envoyera d'abord son mandement aux Commissaires des lieux, les requerant de

sommer les personnes, dont ils ont presenté les noms (soit en leur donnant en mains propres une assignation, soit en laissant en leur maison, ou dans quelque lieu qu'ils ayent pris pour leur domicile) de comparoistre personnellement pardevant les Juges du prochain quartier. Que si ces personnes là ne comparoissent pas afin de souscrire le serment; on proclamera en pleine Seance, que telles personnes comparoistront au quartier suivant. Et si elles manquent à comparoistre pour prester, et souscrire le serment, chacune d'elles sera jugée Papiste recusant, et sujette à toutes les peines qu'elle peut encourir pour ce sujet.

4. Que sur le soupçon qu'aura l'un ou l'autre Justice de la Paix, il luy sera permis de mander la personne suspecte, et de l'obliger sous peine de cent livres sterlings à comparoistre, et souscrire dans la Seance des Juges du quartier prochain. Que si la dite personne refuse de se soumettre à la peine pecuniaire, qui luy est imposée, il sera permis de la mettre en seure garde sans caution jusque à la Seance du prochain quartier. Et si cette personne ainsi condamnée à l'amande, et emprisonnée, refuse de comparoistre pour prester, et souscrire le serment, elle sera jugée Papiste recusant, comme il a esté dit cy dessus.

5. Monseigneur le Protecteur aura droit par arrest rendu en la Cour de l'Echiquier, de faire saisir et prendre pour les besoins de la Republique les deux tiers de toutes les debtes, biens, et fruits appartenants à chaque personne convaincuë comme dessus, et de confisquer les deux tiers de toutes les terres, appartenances, successions, engagements, fermes et fiefs de la mesme personne, ou qui seront en la disposition d'une autre, à qui il les aura confiez, et qui s'en trouvera saisir dans le temps de la conviction, ou apres, et tout cela sera possedé par la dite Republique, jusque à ce que la susdite personne se soit soumise au serment. A la reserve de tous les engagements, rentes, contracts, droicts, ou titres de quelque nature qu'ils puissent estre, qui sont de bonne foy avant la dite conviction, et qui seront conservez à Monseigneur le Protecteur, à ses successeurs, à toute sorte de particuliers, aux Corps de Ville, et aux autres Corps, et à leur heritiers, ou successeurs auxquels ils appartiendront. Pretendant toujours pourvoir à ce que la maison que la personne convaincuë aura choisie pour son domicile, luy sera laissée comme faisant une partie de son tiers.

6. Qu'avant la fin du terme prochain qui suit une telle conviction, elle sera signifiée à la Cour de l'Echiquier, afin que la dicte Cour puisse donner un Arrest pour la saisir des deux tiers.

7. Que depuis qu'une personne convaincuë comme dessus se presentera, soit pardevant les Juges de l'Assise, soit pardevant les Barons de l'Echiquier, pour prester et souscrire le serment en pleine Cour, elle sera exempte à l'avenir de toute sorte de peines; pourvoyant qu'une telle personne venant à mourir, et laissant un heritier, s'il est aagé de seize ans, il sera immediatement cité en jugement, et on procedera contre luy comme contre la personne defuncte.

8. Que si le dit heritier avoit atteint l'aage de seize ans, les tuteurs recevront tout le revenu de son bien, pourvoyant à ce qu'ils soient tels que les Barons de l'Echiquier les auront ordonnez pour s'en charger, et que les dits tuteurs s'obligeront de rendre compte une fois par an de tous les profits qui passeront la somme annuelle, qui aura esté accordée pour l'éducation, et l'entretenement dudit heritier suivant l'Ordonnance des seigneurs Barons, qu'ils payeront le reste au mesme heritier de seize ans, en cas qu'il preste, et souscrire le serment, ou autrement s'il ne le fait pas, à l'Echiquier qui doit aussi faire saisir le deux tiers de tout le bien à l'avenir.

9. Le mesme est ordonné à l'égard de tout l'argent, et de tout le bien qu'une telle personne laisse en mourant à sa femme, à ses enfants, ou à quelque autre personne de quelque condition qu'elle soit.

10. Que si une personne de quelque qualité qu'elle puisse estre, se marie à une autre qu'elle connoist pour convaincuë d'estre Papiste recusant, cette personne là sera elle mesme condamnée comme telle, et sujette à toutes les peines qu'elle doit pour la mesme raison encourir, jusques à ce qu'elle ait presté et souscrit les serments d'Æbjuration, et non plus longtemps.

11. Que nulle Cour sans exception ne pourra évoquer à soy l'accusation intentée contre les Papistes recusants, ny apporter aucun changement en une affaire de cette nature, pour quelque méconte que se puisse estre, mais que tout demeurera dans son entiere rigueur, jusques à ce que telles personnes ayent presté le serment.

12. Que si quelqu'un s'approprie le bien reel ou personnel d'un Papiste recusant, pour le luy conserver par une intelligence secrete, et qu'il ne la découvre pas trois mois apres qu'on l'en aura averty, il sera mis à l'amande sur son propre bien jusques à la valeur de la troisiesme partie du bien qu'il aura recelé, dont une moitié ira à Monseigneur le Protecteur, et l'autre moitié à celuy qui s'est porté pour delateur dans l'information.

13. Chaque Juge de la Paix qui ne fera pas son devoir suivant la pleine teneur de cette Ordonnance, payera vingt livres sterlings d'amande. Chaque Marguillier, et Commissaire d'une Paroisse en semblable cas en payera dix. Et le Greffier des Æssises, ou de la Paix, pour chaque cause qu'il manquera d'enregistrer, vingt. Et de toutes ces amandes, une moitié sera distribuée aux pauvres de la province, et l'autre moitié delivrée à quiconque aura voulu se rendre partie.

14. Si le bien de quelque Papiste recusant passe en propriété à quelque Protestant connu, ce Protestant apportera une attestation à la Seance du quartier, signée de la plus part des Juges que s'y rencontrent, portant qu'une tel personne de quelque sexe ou condition qu'elle soit, est véritablement telle que la profession la fait paroistre, et dehors elle jouïra de tout le bien qui luy est escheu avec exemption de toute sorte de taxes.

15. Que nulle personne convaincuë ne pourra estre en suite recevé à prester le serment, à moins qu'elle produise deux tesmoins sans reproche, qui jurent que depuis six mois elle s'est souvent trouvée le Dimanche dans quelque Assemblée Chrestienne qui soit approuvé; et qu'elle y a entendu la parole de Dieu que l'on y enseigne.

16. Que si quelqu'un apres avoir presté le serment, est relaps, il sera sujet à toutes les peines anciennes, jusque à ce qu'il se soit reconnu, et qu'il ait derechef souscrit.

17. Qu'il ne sera permis à aucun sujet de cette Republique, s'il n'est domestique d'un Ambassadeur, ou d'un Resident, d'entendre la Messe, à quelque heure que ce soit, dans leurs maisons, ou dans quelque autre lieu, que ce puisse estre, sur peine de cent livres sterlings d'amande, et d'emprisonnement pour six mois. Une moitié de l'amande ira à Monseigneur le Protecteur, et l'autre appartiendra au delateur en l'affaire.

www.ingramcontent.com/pod-product-compliance
Lightning Source LLC
Chambersburg PA
CBHW021220300426
44111CB00007B/370